W9-BYK-420

Mongolia

Michael Kohn

KHÖVSGÖL NUUR (p152)
Enormous alpine lake surrounded by
mountains and Siberian forests;
launch point for horse treks

**KHARKHIRAA UUL &
TÜRGEN UUL (p241)**
Rugged region of mountains,
glaciers and valleys that provide
a summer home for nomadic herders

DARKHAD DEPRESSION (p160)
Adventure destination
with the opportunity to trek to
reindeer herding camps

**ALTAI TAVAN BOGD
NATIONAL PARK (p229)**
Diverse park containing ancient
statues, burial mounds, alpine
lakes and glacier-wrapped
peaks, perfect for hiking

OTGON TENGER UUL (p245)
Sacred mountain with alpine
views and trekking routes

ARKHANGAI (p126)
Great area for camping,
fishing and hiking, with
the bonus of a pretty capital

TÖVKHÖN KHIID (p124)
Unique retreat temple, located
high in the hills; a former
workshop of Zanabazar

**GURVAN SAIKHAN
NATIONAL PARK (p208)**
Ice canyons, huge sand dunes
and towering peaks surrounded
by a fossil-filled desert

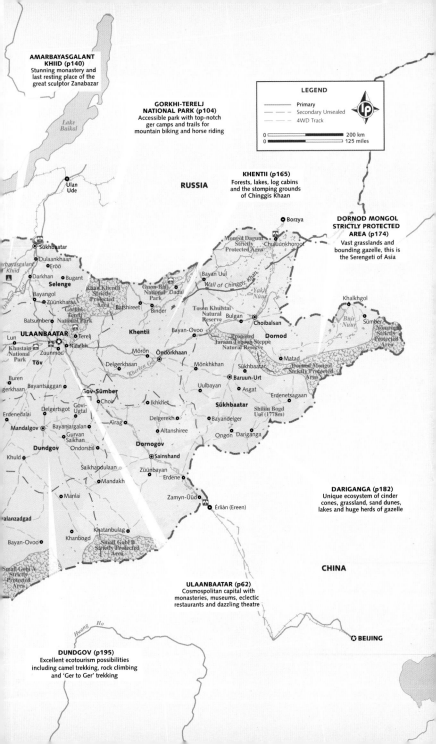

AMARBAYASGALANT KHIID (p140)
Stunning monastery and last resting place of the great sculptor Zanabazar

GORKHI-TERELJ NATIONAL PARK (p104)
Accessible park with top-notch ger camps and trails for mountain biking and horse riding

KHENTII (p165)
Forests, lakes, log cabins and the stomping grounds of Chinggis Khaan

DORNOD MONGOL STRICTLY PROTECTED AREA (p174)
Vast grasslands and bounding gazelle, this is the Serengeti of Asia

LEGEND
— Primary
--- Secondary Unsealed
--- 4WD Track

0 —————— 200 km
0 —————— 125 miles

RUSSIA

Lake Baikal

Ulan Ude

Borzya

Ulan Ude

Sükhbaatar
Dulaankhaan
Eröö
Darkhan   Bugant
Bayangol   Selenge
Züünkharaa
Batsumber   National Park
ULAANBAATAR   Terelj
Lun   Nalaikh
Khustain   Zuunmod
National Park   Töv
Buren
gerkhaan   Bayantsagaan
Delgertsgot   Govi-
Ugtal
Erdenedalai   Bayanjargalan
Mandalgov   Gurvan
Saikhan
Dundgov   Ondorshil
Khuld
Saikhandulaan
Mandakh
Manlai
alanzadgad
Bayan-Ovoo
Khatanbulag
Khanbogd   Small Gobi B
Strictly Protected
Area
Small Gobi A
Strictly
Protected
Area

Mongol Daguur
Strictly
Protected Area   Chuluunkhoroot

Bayan Uul
Wall of Chinggis

Onon-Balj
National Park   Dadal
Bayangol   Batshireet   Binder
Gorkhi-
Terelj
National Park
Toson Khulstai
Natural Reserve
Bulgan   Choibalsan
Khentii   Bayan-Ovoo   Dornod
Möron   Öndörkhaan   Proposed
Jaraan Togoon Steppe
Natural Reserve   Matad
Delgerkhaan   Mönkhkhan
Sükhbaatar   Dornod Mongol
Strictly Protected
Area
Uulbayan   Baruun-Urt
Choir   Ikhkhet   Asgat
Erdenetsagaan
Sükhbaatar
Delgerekh   Shiliin Bogd
Uul (1778m)
Airag   Altanshiree   Bayandelger
Dornogov   Ongon   Dariganga
Sainshand
Züünbayan
Erdene
Zamyn-Üüd
Erlian (Ereen)

Khalkhgol

Bair
Nuur   Sümber
Nomrog
Strictly
Protected
Area

Yakhi
Nuur

Toson Khulstai

Kh...Khentii Strictly
Protected Area

Amarbayasgalant
Khiid

Unur...

CHINA

DARIGANGA (p182)
Unique ecosystem of cinder cones, grassland, sand dunes, lakes and huge herds of gazelle

ULAANBAATAR (p62)
Cosmopolitan capital with monasteries, museums, eclectic restaurants and dazzling theatre

Hwang   Ho

BEIJING

DUNDGOV (p195)
Excellent ecotourism possibilities including camel trekking, rock climbing and 'Ger to Ger' trekking

On the Road

MICHAEL KOHN Coordinating Author

Our trekking guide to Tavan Bogd (p229) was a young Tuvan man named Ganbaatar. Despite not bringing any food, water or warm clothes, Ganbaatar led us into the mountains with storm clouds threatening overhead. When we reached the first glacier the clouds parted to reveal a spectacular amphitheatre of mountains and glaciers.

MY FAVOURITE TRIP

A man, an eagle and a horse, melded together into a medieval WMD; now that was something I had to see. This incredible hunting force, the 'eagle-hunter', could only be found in mystical Bayan-Ölgii and the hunt would only take place in winter. After a four-hour propeller-plane ride from Ulaanbaatar, I landed in Ölgii and proceeded west in -20°C temperatures to Altai Tavan Bogd National Park (p229), where I came to know half a dozen local men who proudly showed me their eagles. They invited me for the hunt and set me up with a horse to follow them as they scoured

the valleys and ravines for prey. By night we ate communal dinners of boiled sheep parts, and huddled around the stove to fend off the cold. Ten days and an equal number of numb toes later, I finally witnessed a kill – two golden eagles swooping down from the sky to converge on an unfortunate fox. I am no hunter myself but to be witness to an ancient rite that has not changed for a couple of millennia, and one even described by Marco Polo, was something truly spectacular.

ABOUT THE AUTHOR

Michael first arrived in Mongolia in late 1997, when he was hired to work at the *Mongol Messenger* in Ulaanbaatar. His three-year stint at the paper included freelance work for the Associated Press and BBC, a gig as a talk-show host on Mongol Radio, a starring role in a Mongolian film and a short run as a local TV news broadcaster. His travels have led him through all 21 aimags, occasionally by bicycle or in the back of a truck with sheep, and other times in helicopters or Humvees with politicians and diplomats. Michael's articles on Mongolian culture, politics and history have appeared in the *New York Times, Wall Street Journal* and *San Francisco Chronicle*. He is also the author of two books, *Dateline Mongolia* and *Lama of the Gobi*. Find him on the web at www.michaelkohn.us.

Mongolia Highlights

The highlights of Mongolia are not usually found in museums or galleries. They are found in the smiles of a nomad family, the blaze of a Gobi sunset or the warmth of a campfire after a long day in the saddle. Memories that seem to linger longest are of the Mongolian people, whose kindness and generosity seem at odds with the harshness of this unforgiving landscape.

NIGEL NEAL

1 **STEPPE BACK IN TIME**

The 'road' to our ger camp (p249) was only identifiable by the potholes; though not more than 100km, the trip took about three hours. We arrived to find openness in all directions and a dozen round felt gers set in the brown dirt, which was dotted with small patches of snow and ice. All the gers were the same: about seven or eight metres in diameter, with a thin stovepipe poking out of the narrow cone top. On entering we were hit by three surprises: the bright and colourful interiors; the difference in temperature (from around -10°C outside to 30°C inside); and that the couple we were to share with were also New Zealanders. The cosiness inside made the inevitable early morning 'call of nature' (in -20°C) all the more speedy.

Nigel Neal, Lonely Planet staff member

CHRISTOPH & FRIENDS / DAS FOTOARCHIV / ALAMY

PLENITUDE IN SOLITUDE

In the Gobi, Ömnögov (p204) is home to one person per 3 sq km. Standing there you'll be the only high point as far as the eye can see. Pricking up your ears, you'll hear only your breath. Digging yourself in, you'll feel only quietness.

miss_laurence, Bluelist contributor

2

SHAMAN DANCES

I was in a little village in eastern Mongolian when a woman asked me if I'd seen the fat shaman, Tsereng. When I said I had not she waved towards some distant hills – indicating that I should go pay the shaman a visit. Of course, I decided to go. I hitch-hiked, walked, got lost, camped for the night and eventually found Tsereng's lodge the following day. A group of shamans had convened to study under Tsereng and during my brief stay I watched two bona fide shaman dances – simply fascinating. For me it was further proof that the best travel adventures are the ones that are not planned.

Michael Kohn, Lonely Planet author

3

BRADLEY M

4

ANDRE

HOW DO YOU SAY 'TIGER WOODS' IN MONGOLIAN?

Of all the unique personality characteristics of Mongolians, perhaps the most consistent is their unrestrained confidence. Most Mongolians never fear to jump right into any activity, no matter if it's related to automotive mechanics, animal husbandry, or golf. Yes, even golf (p251). It only took a few demonstration swings of my three iron for a line of locals to form, young and old alike, waiting for a chance to take their own swings. Although my golf club suffered its share of shocking strikes in the rock-covered terrain, it never took long for one or two individuals to produce some impressive shots. With a country that resembles an enormous golf course and a population that is brimming with self-confidence, don't be surprised if the next great golfer hails from the steppe.

Andre Tolmé, author of *I Golfed Across Mongolia*, **www.golfmongolia.com**

OVOO OFFERING

Pause at an *ovoo*, one of Mongolia's stone cairns. While there, perform a ritual (p38) that predates both Buddhism and shamanism. Circling three times around these piles of stones found atop hills pays gratitude to the spirits and ancestors protecting the surrounding land. It will also bring you luck. Do like Chinggis Khaan and make an offering.

luppy2, Bluelist contributor

5

BRADLEY MAYHEW

DINOSAUR DESERT

In the bleak western stretches of the Gobi Desert, the crumbling gorges and plateaus of Nemegt are dinosaur country (p206). Just getting there is difficult: it's a long drive if you don't have the luxury of arriving, as we did in August 2007, on a Mikoyan MI8 helicopter, an old Russian troop carrier. The trek was worthwhile, though – close to our campsite a Mongolian-Canadian team of palaeontologists had just unearthed the skeleton of a small dinosaur, hunched protectively over a nest of 'recently' laid eggs. Their excitement was evident: 'Only a few times has a dinosaur ever been discovered actually with the eggs it laid,' one of the team explained.

Tony Wheeler, Lonely Planet founder

6

CATHLEEN NAUNDORF

7

JERRY GALEA

SUNSET ON THE STEPPES

Known for its open dry spaces, Mongolia is the place to go for idyllic and stunning views. Such as the town of Renchinlkhumbe (p161) in northern Mongolia. Sitting on the veranda of the Saridag Inn, I watched the sun set behind ice-topped mountains in the distance.

sjeffs, Bluelist contributor

TERELJ TRADITION

After a night spent in a ger in the snow-covered Terelj area (p110) we walked to a nearby small village with its two or three shops. Out of the forest came a Mongolian horseman clothed in beautiful traditional dress. When asked, through sign language, he proudly posed with his horse to be photographed by a couple of foreigners.

Warren and Diana Garrett, travellers, Australia

8

JAMMED IN A VAN

Hitching in Mongolia (p278) is never fast but always amazing. There are countless social stops, party stops, possibility-of-a-party stops, and the obligatory *airag* (fermented mare milk) stops. But when our worse-for-wear driver stopped our crowded Lada on a hill in a forest we weren't sure what the occasion was. The others gestured to their mouths and headed for the trees. Turns out we were hunting for wild strawberries – the kids showed us where to find them. Smaller and sweeter strawberries I have never tasted.

Steve Waters, Lonely Planet staff member

9

10

ONE MORE FOR THE ROAD

Mongolian hospitality (p33) can be a dangerous thing. I had been invited to the horse race at Naadam Festival. At the ger (which the family had pitched for the occasion) I met a cousin who greeted me with two shots of vodka. He told me he was an executive in a gold-mining venture with the Russians and I noticed the vodka rather appropriately had tiny gold flecks in it. I downed the shot in one go as I had learnt custom dictates. My host was so pleased with my efforts he poured me another. I soon found myself in a drinking competition with a man twice my size who clearly knew how to drink. I was not optimistic about my prospects of surviving this but politeness left me with no avenue of escape. We went through several rounds (I have no idea how many). By sheer miracle my host lost his head first and ran like a crazy man out of the ger and up the nearby mountain. I couldn't believe my luck, made my excuses and stumbled back to my flat, relieved that I was still alive.

Daniel McGlone, traveller, Australia

Contents

9

Regional Map Contents

WESTERN
MONGOLIA
pp220-1

NORTHERN MONGOLIA
pp134-5

ULAANBAATAR
p64

EASTERN
MONGOLIA
pp166-7

CENTRAL
MONGOLIA
pp102-3

THE GOBI
(WESTERN)
p210

THE GOBI
(EASTERN & CENTRAL)
p194

Destination Mongolia

Mix up vast landscapes of empty deserts, snowcapped mountains, dramatic gorges and sparkling lakes. Sprinkle in the felt homes of the nomad and the cry of an eagle. Add Buddhist temples, mysterious ruins, abundant wildlife and legendary hospitality. Then top it all off with a conqueror who started with nothing and ended up changing history.

If this description perpetuates your belief in an untouched country, then you also need the scoop on the new Mongolia. Add to the above internet cafés, herders chatting on mobile phones, Manhattan-style cocktail bars, eco-yurts and vegetarian cafés. The Humvees plying Peace Ave would probably have Chinggis Khaan turning green with envy.

Since the fall of communism, Mongolia has done just about everything in its power to open itself up to the world. While the old traditions survive and the wild nature is still mostly intact, Mongolia has also reached out to the West for economic and cultural ties. It's not uncommon to meet Mongolians with degrees from universities in the USA, Europe or Australia.

Along with Japan and South Korea, Mongolia is one of the only legitimate democracies in the whole of Asia. Elections have proven to be free and fair. A constant parade of street protests have forced policy change on everything from mining laws to bus fares.

Democracy has given foreign investors enough confidence to stick with Mongolia during hard times. Attractive investment laws have lured some of the big boys of the mining world – the major target of Mongolia's economic reformers. Despite their progression, Mongolia still faces enormous economic and social challenges; it remains one of the poorest countries in Asia, with typical salaries at less than US$100 a month.

Tourism, along with mining and cashmere, has become a key feature of the economy. The poor infrastructure and short travel season have kept receipts small, but a growing network of ger camps cater to travellers seeking ecotourism adventures. Without fences or private property to restrict a traveller's movement, Mongolia is a perfect destination for horse trekking, long-distance cycling or hiking, or more leisurely activities such as fly-fishing, yak carting or camping out under a sprawling mass of stars.

Most travellers come for Naadam, the two-day summer sports festival that brings Ulaanbaatar to a standstill. But Mongolia's unique charm will always lie in the countryside where, rather than being a spectator to the wrestling, you may find yourself making up the numbers! Outside the villages it's easy to meet nomad families whose relentless sense of hospitality can at times be nothing short of overwhelming.

Mongolia is an up-and-coming Asian country with a young, well-educated population. The economy grows at a robust 7.5% per year – thanks mainly to China's insatiable appetite for Mongolia's raw materials. But Mongolia sits at a crucial crossroads: if the booming economy continues down the road of corruption, with a few getting rich and everyone else left behind, the country may never develop to its full potential.

As a travel destination, Mongolia is a special place for people who enjoy the outdoors and adventure. Heading out on the vast plains, riding horses and camping with nomad families, it offers the chance to step back in time to a simpler age and way of life. It is an invigorating and exhilarating place to visit, and remains one of the last unspoiled travel destinations in Asia.

FAST FACTS

Population: 2,576,000 (2007)

GDP: US$2100 per capita, ranking Mongolia 125 out of 182 listed countries

Leading 2007 exports: copper, wool, gold, cashmere, leather

Literacy rate: 98%

Voter turnout: often over 80%

Horse-to-human ratio: 13 to 1

Average life expectancy: 64 years

Annual economic aid received: approximately US$203 million

Telephone usage: 156,000 landlines; over 800,000 mobile phones

Proportion of people living below the poverty line: 36%

Head of livestock: 34 million

Getting Started

Mongolia offers plenty of scope for offbeat, adventurous and simply fascinating travels. While there are plenty of tourist attractions that are worth visiting, Mongolia is not the sort of place where travellers need a rigid sightseeing schedule.

An eight-day horseback trip through the mountains outside of Ulaanbaatar, done independently or with a group, can be just as rewarding as a driving tour to the country's best-known attractions, if not more so. What makes the journey unique is Mongolia's unbounded hospitality and nomadic culture; a visit to a herder's ger is often the best part of any trip to Mongolia and something that can be done without mounting a major expedition.

Organising a trip is surprisingly easy, and you'll make some headway by connecting with tour operators and hotel owners ahead of time. Russian Cyrillic is widely used and not too difficult to pick up, making street signs relatively easy to read. In Ulaanbaatar, an English speaker is never too far away. Trips can be made to suit all budgets, though backpackers should expect to pay slightly more than they would in south Asia; jeep-hire costs can add up. Vehicle breakdowns, petrol shortages, extreme weather and shocking roads present their own challenges. But the country is also stunning, safe and relatively healthy; with a bit of resolve and patience, any amount of travel is possible.

WHEN TO GO

Mongolia has an extreme continental clime; it is so far inland that no sea moderates its climate. Only in summer does cloud-cover shield the sky. Humidity is usually zilch and sunshine is intense. With more than 260 sunny days a year, Mongolia is justifiably known as the 'Land of Blue Sky'.

See Climate Charts (p252) for more information.

The travel season begins in mid-May. Ger camps start opening their doors and more travellers are around to share vehicles. The weather is generally fair although early May can still see snowfall, especially in the north.

June weather is fine and generally dry throughout the central and southern regions. The mountains and northern areas can still be cold.

July is the time to see the Naadam Festival (p96). Unfortunately, this is also the peak tourist season when Ulaanbaatar's inadequate accommodation and creaky transport is stretched to breaking point. It's a good time to look for travel partners and get out of the city. Gobi temperatures this month can hit 40°C.

DON'T LEAVE HOME WITHOUT...

- A good pair of binoculars and a high powered lens for your SLR camera. Distances are vast in Mongolia and both of these will help when spotting wildlife.

- Camping gear. Tents, sleeping bags and other equipment are available in Mongolia, but you'll save money by bringing your own.

- Chapstick, sun block, sunglasses and anything else that protects you from Mongolia's relentless sun, dust and wind.

- English-language travel literature and books.

- New US dollars; it's difficult to change bills that pre-date 2000.

- A1 steak sauce, spice packets or jar of mustard to flavour up your boiled mutton.

- Studying your phrasebook. You'll find that LP's *Mongolian Phrasebook* is worth its weight in gold.

MONGOLIA IN WINTER

Visiting Mongolia in winter is not as crazy as it sounds. While you may imagine everything is buried under snow, the country does still function; museums will be open, transportation runs unabated and other facilities like shops and restaurants will still be up and running.

One advantage is a big reduction in Ulaanbaatar hotel prices – over 30% for most top-end hotels. Another benefit of winter travel is that vehicles in northern areas can reach places that are otherwise difficult to access. For example, thanks to the frozen ground, lakes and rivers, cars can drive from Khatgal over Jigleg Pass and onto to Renchinlkhumbe; in summer this area is just boggy marsh, only accessible by horse.

In winter, ger camps will be closed (except for a few in Terelj). Other disadvantages include thick air pollution in Ulaanbaatar and shorter daylight hours (it will be dark by 4pm or 5pm).

In the countryside, activities such as hiking and horse riding won't really be feasible because of the cold. However, you could try ice fishing, cross-country skiing or even offbeat adventures like dog sledding.

Wind of Mongolia (p82) runs dog-sledding trips in Terelj from December to February and then on Khövsgöl Nuur in March and April.

In Ulaanbaatar, LG Guesthouse (p83) runs winter star-gazing tours. Winter is also the time to watch the Kazakh eagle-hunters in action; contact Blue Wolf Travel (p224). Hard-core ice-skaters can join a long-distance ice-skating trip on Khövsgöl Nuur, organised by Nomadic Journeys (p81).

August can see lots of rain in the northern and central areas. This weather fills up rivers and brings fresh grass to the steppes, but it can also bog the roads with mud and attract mosquitoes. Still, it's a great time to travel in Mongolia.

September is another fine month. Cooler weather brings relief to the Gobi and the changing colours in the northern forests make for spectacular scenery. Flies and mosquitoes start to disappear.

October is cool and sees the occasional snow flurry up north but is still fine for travel, especially in the Gobi. Weather patterns at this time are particularly vulnerable to change. One minute you're walking around in a T-shirt, the next you need an overcoat and boots, then it's back to T-shirts.

The cold season runs from November to February. Read the boxed text (above) for details.

Mongolians, especially nomads, consider March and April the worst months. After the long winter, livestock will already be thin and a lack of rain means many will die, causing financial and psychological hardship. If the spring is a harsh one, staying with a nomad family at this time is not recommended.

Ulaanbaatar is possibly the coldest capital city in the world. Temperatures generally start to drop below 0°C in late October, sink to -30°C in January and February and remain below freezing until April. July through September is pleasant, but it can still turn suddenly cold and, unfortunately, most of the city's rain falls in this period. Summer daylight lasts until 10pm.

HOW MUCH?

Local newspaper T500

Can of Chinggis beer T1000

Guanz (canteen) lunch T2000

Internet per hour T700

Taxi from the airport to Sükhbaatar Sq T6000

Souvenir T-shirt T12,000

Best seat at the Naadam opening US$25

COSTS & MONEY

Within Mongolia, travellers on organised tours spend around US$100 per day (more for extra luxuries). Independent travellers can see the same sights and stay in midrange accommodation for around US$80 per day. Sharing the cost of a private jeep or minivan and camping rather than staying in more-expensive ger camps can bring this down to about US$25 to US$40 per day. (For more information on tourist ger camps see p249.) If you are hitching and using public transport around the countryside, allow about US$10 to US$15 per day for this.

TOP **10**

Ulaanbaatar •
MONGOLIA

ROAD-TRIP DELIGHTS

There are certain essential factors that make every road trip complete:

1 Hot-water bathhouses

2 Paved roads

3 Drivers named Bold or Dorj

4 Spare parts found by the roadside

5 Yak cream with fresh blueberries on Russian bread

6 Yogurt delivered by passing nomads

7 Getting a lift

8 Ability to sing at least one song in English and Mongolian

9 Stomach for blowtorched marmot

10 Mars Bars

SURVIVAL PHRASES

While bouncing around in your jeep or entering a nomad's ger, bear in mind these key phrases:

1 Hold the dog! *Nokhoi khorio!*

2 When will you move your ger next? *Tanakh khetzee nukh ve?*

3 *Exactly* what time are we going to leave? (ask while jabbing at your watch, and emphasise the word *'Yag'*, or the answer will invariably be 'now') *Yag, kheden tsagt yavakh ve?*

4 May we camp near your ger? *Tanaa khajuud maihantaigaa honogloj boloh uu?*

5 Are your sheep fattening up nicely? *Mal sureg targan tavtai uu?*

6 Not too much, please (food, tea, vodka). *Dunduur*. Or, *jaakhan, jaakhan.*

7 Where is a good spot for fishing? *Yamar gazar zagas ikhtei ve?*

8 I would like to ride a calm (nonagressive) horse. *Bi nomkhon mori unmaar baina.*

9 In which direction is ___ town? ___ *sum ail zugt baina ve?*

10 Please write down your address and I will send your photo later. *Ta nadad hayagaa bichij ogno uu. Bi tand zurag ilgeene.*

BEST FESTS

Festivals offer a great chance to meet locals and enjoy local customs. Try to make it to one of the following:

1 Tsagaan Sar in Bulgan *sum* (village), Ömnögov (January or February)

2 Khatgal Ice Festival (28 February)

3 Camel Polo Festival in Ulaanbaatar (mid-March)

4 Navrus in Bayan Ölgii (21 March)

5 Roaring Hooves Music Festival (late June)

6 Naadam in any *sum*, better than a big city (mid-July)

7 Yak Festival in Tariat (early August)

8 Gongoriin Bombani Hural at Amarbayas-galant Khiid (9 to 11 August)

9 Airag Festival in Dundgov (late August)

10 Eagle Festival in Ölgii or Sagsai (first Sunday in October)

Accommodation and food will cost at least US$10 per day in Ulaanbaatar, but allow up to US$20 per day for half-decent accommodation, some tastier, Western-style meals and trips to the theatre and museums.

TRAVEL LITERATURE

Dateline Mongolia: An American Journalist in Nomads Land, by Michael Kohn, is a memoir and travelogue written by the author of this guidebook. It recounts his memorable three years working as a reporter for the *Mongol Messenger.*

Lost Country: Mongolia Revealed, by Jasper Becker, describes the author's travels in Mongolia in the early 1990s and his attempts to uncover the secrets of the purge years that plagued Mongolia in the 1930s.

Wild East, by Jill Lawless, is a tightly written, very funny account of the author's experience in Mongolia, during which she spent two years editing the *UB Post.* This lightning-fast book serves as a good armchair read before visiting Mongolia.

Hearing Birds Fly, by Louisa Waugh, describes the year the author spent living in Tsengel, a Kazakh village in western Mongolia. Waugh does an outstanding job of describing the stark landscapes, personal stories and ironies in one of Mongolia's most remote areas.

Eagle Dreams: Searching for Legends in Wild Mongolia, by Stephen J Bodio, describes the remote and enchanting Bayan-Ölgii aimag. It gives a good account of Kazakh contemporary life and the 'eagle-hunters'.

Among the Mongols, by James Gilmour, was written by a Scottish missionary who travelled to Mongolia in the late 19th century. Some of his observations of life at the time are remarkably compatible with modern Mongolia.

For more book ideas see www.mongoliacenter.org/bookstore.

INTERNET RESOURCES

Living in Mongolia (www.living-in-mongolia.com) News and information site geared towards expats living in Mongolia.

Lonely Planet (www.lonelyplanet.com) Includes info on Mongolia with links to other websites, and the Thorn Tree travellers' forum.

Mongol Uls (www.mongoluls.net) Cultural articles, links and handy language tutorial.

Mongolia Expat (www.mongoliaexpat.com) Up-to-date website with sights and activities in contemporary Mongolia.

Mongolia National Tourism Centre (www.mongoliatourism.gov.mn) Includes lists of hotels, ger camps and travel agencies.

The Mongolia Society (www.mongoliasociety.org) An excellent resource with lots of links.

Mongolia Today (www.mongoliatoday.com) A colourful online magazine covering all aspects of Mongolian culture.

Mongolian Matters (www.mongolianmatters.com) Blog by a UB expat, commenting on important news stories in Mongolia.

Shaggy Yak (www.shaggyyak.com) A great starting point, with handy tips on visas, planning and logistics for a trip to Mongolia.

UN in Mongolia (www.un-mongolia.mn) Development news and links to UN agencies.

Itineraries
CLASSIC ROUTE

THE BIG LOOP   Three Weeks / Ulaanbaatar to the Gobi & the North
From Ulaanbaatar, head south to the eerie rock formations of **Baga Gazryn Chuluu** (p197) and the ruined castle at **Süm Khökh Burd** (p197), stopping at **Eej Khad** (Mother Rock; p109) en route. From Süm Khökh Burd, stop by **Ulaan Suvraga** (p198) on your way south.

At least three days are needed to explore Ömnögov: the spectacular ice canyon at **Yolyn Am** (p208), the massive sand dunes at **Khongoryn Els** (p209) and the dinosaur quarry at **Bayanzag** (p208).

From Bayanzag go north to the ruins of **Ongiin Khiid desert monastery** (p197), a perfect place to organise a camel trek.

Leaving the Gobi, your first stop is **Erdene Zuu Khiid** (p120), the country's oldest monastery. Head west to **Tsetserleg** (p126), a good place to break the journey, before proceeding to **Terkhiin Tsagaan Nuur** (p130) for fishing, swimming, hiking or horse riding.

An additional five to seven days are needed for a trip north to spectacular **Khövsgöl Nuur** (p152). On the route back to Ulaanbaatar don't miss **Amarbayasgalant Khiid** (p140), an architectural gem.

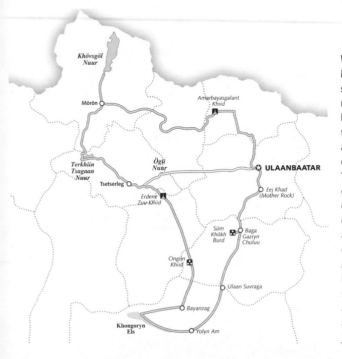

Welcome to Mongolia 101, the starter route for most first-timers keen to see the top attractions and a wide range of landscapes. This 2600km route gives you the best of the best: sand dunes, alpine lakes and the ancient capital Karakorum. Although seemingly on 'main routes', this is still a rough, remote and unpredictable journey.

ROADS LESS TRAVELLED

WESTERN MONGOLIA   One Month / Khovd to Uliastai

The western aimags offer adventurous travel and exploration. Adrenaline junkies can break out the mountain bike, kayak or mountaineering gear.

Start with a flight to **Khovd** (p232), from where you can hire a jeep and driver for a bird-watching and wildlife expedition at **Khar Us Nuur National Park** (p235). At nearby **Chandmani** (p236) visit the renowned throat singers. Looping back through Khovd, continue northwest to the beautiful pastures and valley around **Tsambagarav Uul** (p228). You could easily spend a couple of days here before moving on to **Ölgii** (p223), a great place to recharge your batteries.

Heading west from Ölgii, spend at least five days getting to, from and around **Altai Tavan Bogd National Park** (p229). With more time, consider doing a horse trek around **Khoton Nuur** (p230). With proper equipment, permits and some logistic support, it's even possible to scale Mongolia's highest peak, the 4374m **Tavan Bogd** (p231), though a visit to the base camp and glacier is more feasible.

On the way to Tavan Bogd, stop in at **Sogoog** (p229), the only village in Mongolia with an espresso machine!

From Ölgii, the main road winds northeast, passing **Üüreg Nuur** (p240) en route to **Ulaangom** (p237). Allow a week for trekking around **Kharkhiraa Valley** (p241). An experienced driver can get you from Ulaangom to **Uliastai** (p243), visiting **Khyargas Nuur** (p242) and **Ikh Agui** (p246) en route. From pretty Uliastai you can get a flight to Ulaanbaatar, but not before mounting a horse or hiking to **Otgon Tenger Uul** (p245).

This 1500km journey takes you to the 'wild west', a dreamy landscape of mountains, glaciers, lakes and rushing rivers. Your inner adventurer will be satiated with the remoteness of the landscape and its unique inhabitants: throat singers, eagle-hunters and the odd cattle rustler. You'll need at least 10 days in the area; more for trekking in the Altai Mountains.

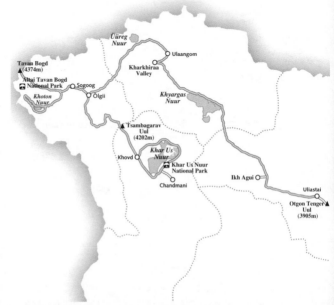

EASTERN MONGOLIA

12 Days / Ulaanbaatar to Khentii, Dornod & Sükhbaatar

Eastern Mongolia offers a delightful romp through grasslands, forest and some unique historical sights. Best of all, it's almost completely devoid of tourists.

Heading east from UB, you'll pass the new **Chinggis Khaan statue** (p110) on the way to **Khökh Nuur** (p171), a pretty alpine lake that saw the coronation of the great khaan. Continue northeast, visiting **Baldan Baraivan Khiid** (p171), **Öglögchiin Kherem** (p171), **Batshireet** and **Binder** (p171) as you travel through Khentii's scenic countryside. **Dadal** (p173) is a good place for horse trekking or just kicking back with some locals, and is an excellent destination for Naadam.

Following the Ulz Gol further east you'll pass pretty Buriat villages, such as Bayan-Uul and Bayandun, and nature reserves including **Ugtam Uul** (p178) before turning south to **Choibalsan** (p175).

An alternative route to Choibalsan goes via the nature reserve **Toson Khulstai** (p175) and ancient ruins at **Kherlen Bar Khot** (p177).

From Choibalsan take the train to **Chuluunkhoroot** (p178) to visit **Mongol Daguur B** (p178), a protected area for wader birds, or travel across the empty steppes to **Khalkhiin Gol** (p179), a remote landscape of lakes, rivers, wildlife and historical sights. Highlights include giant Buddha statues carved into a hillside and monuments dedicated to soldiers who died here during WWII.

You'll need another couple of days to visit the lush **Nömrög Strictly Protected Area** (p174) and **Sangiin Dalai Nuur** (p179).

The **Dariganga region** (p182), with its sand dunes, cinder cones and scattered stone statues, requires two or three days. Horse trekking is also possible here. Return to UB via **Baruun-Urt** (p180) and **Öndörkhaan** (p168), or travel to **Sainshand** (p199) for a taste of the Gobi and a visit to **Khamaryn Khiid** (p202).

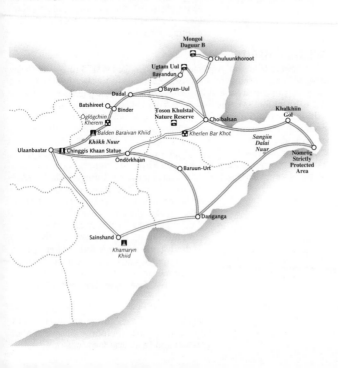

Eastern Mongolia is a perfect place for trailblazers. Very few tourists take this 2300km loop so you'll have the enormous steppes, fish-filled lakes and forests to yourself. The region is rich in wildlife and with a serious zoom camera you can photograph some fleet-footed gazelle.

TAILORED TRIPS

EAGLES, WOLVES AND GAZELLE, OH MY!

Patience, luck and a pair of binoculars are essential items for wildlife spotting in Mongolia. You're unlikely to see much on a quick tour but head out to the furthest reaches of the country and you'll be in for some surprises.

The plains of **Dornod** (p174) and **Sükhbaatar** (p180) aimags are home to hundreds of thousands of gazelle – their migrations can rival those on the Serengeti. A tripod and a lens of at least 600mm will come in handy if you're hoping to photograph them.

Khustain National Park (p115), 100km west of Ulaanbaatar, is home to dozens of *takhi* horses (Przewalski's horse – the world's only purely wild horse).

Southeast of here, at **Ikh Nart** (p198), you stand a good chance of spotting argali sheep. While in remote Gov-Altai aimag the **Great Gobi Strictly Protected Area** (p218) is home to wild asses, wild camels and Gobi bears.

Travel in northern **Khövsgöl** (p148) aimag and you will eventually spot wolf, fox and, with luck, the odd deer or moose.

Bird-watchers shouldn't miss Khetsuu Khad, an enormous rock on the southern shore of **Khyargas Nuur** (p242), where hundreds of cormorant birds roost in summer. Other great places to see birds include **Khar Us Nuur** (p235) in Khovd and in **Bayan-Ölgii** (p222) where Kazakhs keep eagles for hunting purposes.

BUDDHIST HERITAGE

After viewing UB's two exquisite monasteries, **Gandan Khiid** (p73) and **Choijin Lama** (p75), take a short trip south near Zuunmod to see **Mandshir Khiid** (p106), located on a forested flank of Bogdkhan Uul. Add to the pilgrimage by travelling there on foot over the mountain from UB, a seven-hour hike.

In the east of the country, the legacy of Buddhism is not a monastery at all but an enormous statue of **Janraisag** (p179) carved into the hillside in Dornod.

Heading west from UB, travel on a decent road to **Övgön Khiid** (p125), located at the foot of the pretty Khogno Khan Uul. From here you are just a couple of hours from Mongolia's oldest monastery, **Erdene Zuu Khiid** (p120).

From Erdene Zuu Khiid swing southwest to the lovely mountainside hermitage of **Tövkhön Khiid** (p124), where the famed Buddhist artist Zanabazar had a workshop and retreat.

Returning on the same road, proceed to Tsetserleg and the **Zayain Gegeenii Süm** (p127), now converted into one of the country's nicest museums. Heading back east, visit the jewel in this class, **Amarbayasgalant Khiid** (p140).

With more time and a sturdy jeep, head into the Gobi for a special pilgrimage to the sights associated with the famed mystic monk Danzan Ravjaa, including **Khamaryn Khiid** (p202) and **Demchigiin Khiid** (p207).

History By Jack Weatherford & Dulmaa Enkhchuluun

Over the past 2000 years, possibly no other place on the planet has exported as much history as Mongolia. In three dramatic waves – Hun, Turk and, finally, Mongol – hordes of warriors rode their small but powerful horses down from the Mongolian Plateau to challenge and transform the world. The steppe warriors not only conquered nations, they swept up whole civilisations and reassembled them into intercontinental empires of a scale never before reached by any other people.

Although each of the three waves produced its distinctive influence, the name of Chinggis Khaan achieved a unique spot in the world's imagination. He created the nation in 1206 and named it after his Mongol lineage. Mongols still maintain an intimate tie to him, but beyond the use of his iconic image and name, there seems to be surprisingly little in the nation connected directly to him. Chinggis Khaan left behind a nation, but he did not leave a monument to himself, a temple, pyramid, palace, castle or canal, and even his grave was left unmarked in the remote area where he grew up and hunted as a boy. As he himself wished, his body could wither away so long as his great Mongol nation lived, and today that nation is his monument.

The lack of tangible ties to Chinggis Khaan presents both a challenge and an opportunity to visitors; Mongolia does not yield its history promiscuously to every passer-by. Its story is not told in great books, large stone monuments or bronze statues. A hiker crossing a hilltop can easily find etchings of deer with baroque configurations of antlers, soaring falcons or shamans without faces, but was the image etched last year by a bored herder, a century ago by a pious lama or 25,000 years ago by a passing hunter? A small stone implement could have been abandoned there centuries ago by a Hun mother preparing a family meal or by a Turk warrior on a raid; the modern visitor might easily be the first human to clutch it in 3000 years. The artefact does not come labelled, classified and explained. The stories of the steppe are incomplete, and history emerges slowly from the objects, the soil and the landscape.

HUNS: CHILDREN OF THE SUN

The first of the steppe nomads to make an impact beyond Mongolia were the tribe whom the Mongols now call the 'People of the Sun', the Hunnu, better known as the Huns. They created the first steppe empire in 209 BC under Modun, a charismatic leader who took the title *shanyu* (king) and ruled until his death in 174 BC. Modun created a disciplined and strong cavalry corps personally devoted to him, and used the corps to overthrow and kill his father.

Anthropologist Jack Weatherford wrote *Genghis Khan and the Making of the Modern World*, for which he received the Order of the Polar Star, Mongolia's highest state honour.

Dulmaa Enkhchuluun graduated from Augsburg College in Minnesota and now owns Borijin Travel, a company devoted to culturally and environmentally responsible tourism and commercial development in Mongolia.

Khan means *Chief* or *King*; Khaan means *Emperor* or *Great Khan*.

TIMELINE

209 BC–174 BC	AD 552–744	744–840
Reign of Modun, as *shanyu* of the Huns; the first great steppe empire of Mongolia stretches from Korea to Lake Baikal in Siberia and south into northern China.	Succession of two Turkic empires; greatest ruler is Bilge Khan. Following his death in 734 a monument is erected near Lake Ögii.	The Uighur empire occupies central Mongolia until expelled by the Kyrgyz tribe; the Uighur move south into western China and control the Silk Route for nearly 1000 years.

Between the creation of the Qing dynasty in China in 221 BC and the collapse of the Han dynasty in AD 220, the Chinese became the dominant economic power in East Asia, but the steppe tribes under the Huns grew into a great military power. The Chinese and the Huns vied for dominance through protracted wars with intermittent truces, during which the Chinese bribed the steppe warriors with tributes of goods and women, including imperial princesses. Using the merchandise extracted from the Chinese, the Huns extended the trade routes connecting the civilisations around them.

Following the collapse of the Hun empire in the 4th century AD, various newly independent tribes left the Mongolian homeland, wandering from India to Europe in search of new pastures and new conquests. By the 5th century, one of these branches reached Europe and created a new Hun empire that stretched from the Ural Mountains to Germany. Under their most famous leader, Attila the Hun, they threatened Rome and ravaged much of Western Europe, and for the first time in history mounted archers from the Mongolian steppe created an intercontinental reputation for their fierceness and tenacity in battle.

TURKS: CHILDREN OF THE WOLF MOTHER

In the 6th century a new sense of order returned to the Mongolian Plateau with the rise of a series of tribes speaking Turkic languages. These tribes claimed descent from a boy who was left for dead but saved and adopted by a mother wolf who raised him and then mated with him, creating from their offspring the ancestors of the various steppe clans. Compared with both the Huns before them and the Mongols after them, the literate Turks sought to blend the traditional nomadic herding life with a sedentary life of agriculture, urbanisation and commerce; consequently, they left more physical remains than the others in the ruins of Turkic cities and ceremonial centres. Along the Orkhon Gol in central Mongolia they built their small cities of mud, the most famous of which were erected during the time of the Uighurs, the last of the great Turkic empires of Mongolia. The Turkic era reached its zenith in the early 8th century under Bilge Khan and his brother Kultegen, the military general. Their monuments near the Orkhon Gol are probably the oldest known examples of writing in a Turkic language.

Like the Huns before them the Turks moved down off the Mongolian Plateau, spreading from what is today China to the shores of the Mediterranean. Another invading Turkic tribe, the Kyrgyz, overthrew the Uighur empire in AD 840, destroying its cities and driving the Uighur people south into the oases of western China. But the Kyrgyz showed no inclination to maintain the cities or the empire they had conquered. With the expulsion of the Uighurs came another period of decentralised feuding and strife, before the greatest of all Mongolian empires arose at the beginning of the 13th century: the rise to power of Chinggis Khaan.

The *Encyclopedia of Mongolia and the Mongol Empire*, by Christopher P Atwood, is an authoritative history reference book with special emphasis on Buddhism.

Anthropologist Chris Kaplonski maintains an excellent site devoted to Mongolian culture and history at www .chriskaplonski.com

Chinggis Khaan never erected any statues or grand monuments to himself, but recent years have seen modern Mongolians trying to catch up in this area. Statues of Chinggis can be seen at Sükhbaatar Sq in UB, on the Ulaanbaatar–Khentii road, in Öndörkhaan and in Dadal.

1162	1204	1206
Birth of Temujin, the child destined to become Chinggis Khaan, near the Onon River. According to legend, Temujin emerges with a blood clot clutched in his fist.	Chinggis Khaan establishes the Mongolian state script based on the Uighur alphabet, which had Semitic origins but was written vertically from top to bottom.	Chinggis Khaan calls a massive conclave at Kherlen Gol and creates his empire to which he gives the name Great Mongol Nation.

THE FIRE CULT OF THE JESUS BUDDHA

During the Turkic empires from the 6th century through 9th century, the steppe nomads refused to convert to any of the major world religions, such as Islam, Buddhism or Christianity. They chose to follow the teachings of 3rd-century Persian prophet Mani, who was martyred for preaching a doctrine of dualism: good and evil represented through light and dark.

Manicheans accepted the teachings of Jesus, Hermes, Buddha and Zoroaster as well as those of philosophers such as Plato and Socrates. They sang hymns to 'Jesus Buddha' as well as to light, for which Christians dismissed them as idolatrous fire worshippers.

Manicheism spread as an underground religious movement from India to Egypt, but Christian and Muslim authorities persecuted followers and chased them to ever more remote areas until the religion made its last and most important refuge in Mongolia. When the Uighur king in central Mongolia converted in AD 763, the Uighur empire became the only nation in history to accept Manicheism as the state religion.

Manicheans compared their religion to a great world ocean, into which all rivers of knowledge flow, and this imagery persisted in Mongolian culture, as shown in the title 'Chinggis Khaan' (Ocean King). Similarly, son Ögedei and grandson Guyuk used the title 'Dalai Khaan' from the Mongolian *dalai* meaning *sea*. In the 16th century, Altan Khaan bestowed this ancient title on a new line of Buddhist monks from Tibet, allowing them to call their leader Dalai Lama, meaning 'Sea of Wisdom'.

MONGOLS: CHILDREN OF THE GOLDEN LIGHT

The decline of the Turkic tribes gave the opening for a new tribe to emerge. Scholars offer varying explanations for when and where these new people arrived, but the Mongols ascribe their origins to the mating of a blue wolf and a tawny doe beside a great sea, often identified as Lake Baikal (in Russia). They further credit the origin of Chinggis Khaan's own clan to a mysterious and sacred woman called Alan Goa, who gave birth to two sons during her marriage, and had an additional three sons after her husband died. The elder sons suspected that their younger brothers had been fathered by an adopted boy (now a man) whom their mother had also raised and who lived with her.

Upon hearing of their suspicions and complaints, Alan Goa sat her five sons around the hearth in her ger and told them that the three younger sons were fathered by a 'Golden Light'. She then handed each an arrow with the command to break it. When they had done this, she handed each a bundle of five arrows with the command to break them all together. When the boys could not do so, she told them that it mattered not where the brothers came from so long as they remained united.

No matter what the Mongol origin, the story of Alan Goa had a persistent and profound influence on the development of Mongolian culture, on everything from the role of women and attitudes towards sexuality to

A Mongol is a member of the Mongol ethnic group; a Mongolian is a citizen of Mongolia. Kazakhs of Bayan-Ölgii are Mongolians but not Mongols; the Kalmyks of New Jersey are Mongols but not Mongolians.

1235	1260	1271
Ögedei Khaan completes the imperial capital at Karakorum. In addition to a great palace, the city has Muslim mosques, Christian churches and Buddhist temples.	The end of Mongol expansion with their defeat by the Mamluk army of Egypt at the Battle of Ayn Al-Jalut near the Sea of Galilee.	Kublai Khaan claims the office of Great Khan and also makes himself Emperor of China by founding the Yuan dynasty.

the political quest for unity and the herder's value of practical action over ideology or religion.

THE MONGOL EMPIRE

The Mongols were little more than a loose confederation of rival clans until the birth of Temujin in 1162. Overcoming conditions that would have crushed lesser men, Temujin rose to become the strongest ruler on the steppe, and in AD 1206 founded the Mongol empire and took the title 'Chinggis Khaan'. He was already 44 years old and since the age of 16, when his bride was kidnapped, he had been fighting one clan feud and tribal war after another. Frustrated with the incessant chaos, he began killing off the leaders of each clan as he defeated them and incorporating the survivors into his own following. Through this harsh but effective way, Chinggis Khaan forced peace onto the clans around him.

He named the new state Yeke Mongol Ulus (Great Mongol Nation). His followers totalled probably under a million people, and from this he created an army of nine units of 10,000 and a personal guard of another 10,000. With a nation smaller than the workforce of a modern corporation such as Wal-mart, and an army that could fit inside a modern stadium, the Mongols conquered the greatest armies of the era and subdued hundreds of millions of people.

In battle Chinggis Khaan was merciless, but to those who surrendered without fighting he promised protection, religious freedom, lower taxes and a heightened level of commerce and prosperity. His law and incorruptible officials did more to attract people into his empire than his military power. Based on military success and good laws, his empire continued to expand after his death until it stretched from Korea to Hungary and from India to Russia.

THE DECLINE

After Chinggis Khaan's death, his second son Ögedei ruled from 1229 to 1241, followed by Ögedei's widow Töregene Khatun and the brief 18-month reign of Ögedei's son Guyuk from 1246 through 1248. Tensions began to develop among the branches of his descendants, and broke into open civil war when Arik Boke and Kublai each claimed the office of Great Khan after the death of their brother Möngke in 1259. Arik Boke controlled all of Mongolia, including the capital Karakorum, and enjoyed widespread support from the ruling Borijin clan. Yet Kublai controlled the vast riches of northern China, and these proved far more powerful. Kublai defeated his brother who then perished under suspicious circumstances in captivity.

Kublai won the civil war and solidified his hold over China, but it cost him his empire. Although they still claimed to be a single empire, the nation of Chinggis Khaan had been reduced to a set of oft-warring sub-empires.

Rivers in Mongolia are female and may be called *ej* (mother). A river, spring or lake that never runs dry is called a *khatun* (queen).

Geoffrey Chaucer's *The Canterbury Tales* (1395), recognised as the first book of poetry written in English, includes an early account of Chinggis Khaan in the 'Squire's Tale'.

1368	1448	1449
Yuan dynasty collapses in China but the Mongol government return to Mongolia refusing to submit to the newly created Ming dynasty. They continue ruling as the 'Northern Yuan'.	Birth of Mongolia's greatest queen, Manduhai the Wise, who reunites Mongolia by the end of the century.	Esen Taishi defeats the Chinese and captures the Ming emperor. His reign marks the rise of western Mongolia and the Oirat people as major powers of Inner Asia.

CHINGGIS KHAAN: MAN OF THE MILLENNIUM

Known to the world as a conqueror, Mongolians remember Chinggis Khaan as the great lawgiver and proudly refer to him as the Man of the Millennium (a title bestowed on him by the *Washington Post* in 1995). His laws derived from practical considerations more than ideology or religion.

After the abduction of his wife Borte, Chinggis recognised the role of kidnapping in perpetuating feuds among clans and outlawed it. Similarly, he perceived religious intolerance as being a source of violence in sedentary society and so decreed religious freedom for everyone and exempted religious scholars and priests from taxes.

To promote trade and communications, Chinggis built an international network of postal stations that also served as hostels for merchants. He decreased and standardised the taxes on goods so that they would not be repeatedly taxed. Under these laws the Mongol empire formed the first intercontinental free-trade zone.

In an era when ambassadors served as hostages to be publicly tortured or killed during times of hostilities, Chinggis Khaan ordered that every ambassador be considered as an envoy of peace. This law marked the beginning of diplomatic immunity and international law. Today nearly every country accepts and promotes, at least in theory, the ideas and policies behind the 'Great Law of Chinggis Khaan'.

The Mongols of Russia became in effect independent, known later as the Golden Horde, under the lineage of Chinggis Khaan's eldest son Jochi. Persia and Mesopotamia drifted off to become the Ilkhanate under descendents of Kublai's only surviving brother Hulegu, the conqueror of Baghdad.

Kublai created a Chinese dynasty named Yuan, took Chinese titles and, while still claiming to be the Great Khan of the Mongols, looked southward to the remaining lands of the Sung dynasty, which he soon conquered.

Much of Central Asia, including Mongolia, pursued an independent course and acknowledged the Yuan dynasty only when forced with a military invasion or enticed with extravagant bribes of silk, silver and other luxuries. By 1368 the subjects had mostly overthrown their Mongol overlords, and the empire withdrew back to the Mongolian steppe where it began. Although most Mongols melted into the societies that they conquered, in some distant corners of the empire, from Afghanistan to Poland, small vestiges of the Mongols still survive to the present.

In 1368 the Ming army captured Beijing, but the Mongol royal family refused to surrender and fled back to Mongolia with the imperial seals and their bodyguards. Much to the frustration of the Ming emperors in China, the Mongols continued to claim to be the legitimate rulers of China and still styled themselves as the Yuan dynasty, also known as the Northern Yuan. Even within Mongolia, the Imperial Court exerted little power. Unaccustomed to the hardships of the herding life and demanding vast amounts of food, fuel and other precious resources for their large court

The English word 'horde' derives from the Mongol *ordu*, meaning 'royal court'.

The best source for information on the life of Chinggis Khaan can be found in *The Secret History of the Mongols*, which was written in the 13th or 14th century and was not made public until the 20th century.

1585	**1603**	**1634**
Founding of Erdene Zuu, first Buddhist monastery in Mongolia, at the site of the Mongol capital, Karakorum (modern Kharkhorin).	A descendant of Chinggis Khaan and great-great grandson of Queen Manduhai is enthroned in Lhasa Tibet as the fourth Dalai Lama, the only Mongolian Dalai Lama.	Death of Ligden Khaan, the last of Chinggis Khaan's descendants to rule as Great Khan. Eastern Mongolia becomes part of the Manchu empire, but western Mongolia holds out.

CAPITALS OF THE MONGOLS

■ **Avarga** – the first capital of the Mongols consisted of a nomadic camp with a few storage buildings where the Avarga stream joins the Kherlen Gol in Khentii aimag. Originally known as Khödöö Aral, Avarga later became a shrine for the cult of Chinggis Khaan.

■ **Karakorum** Needing a larger, more permanent centre, Chinggis Khaan's son Ögedei Khaan built Karakorum (modern Kharkhorin), the place of black walls, and used it as his capital until his death in 1241. The city had temples of all the major religions and included workmen from around the empire, the most famous of whom was the French goldsmith who sculpted a large silver tree with four fountains. Little of ancient Karakorum remains above the ground other than one large stone tortoise.

■ **Khanbalik and Shangdu** By 1266 Kublai Khaan located his base of operations in northern China, as close to Mongolia as possible yet connected by canal to the Yellow River in order to obtain goods from throughout China. Over the next decade he created his winter capital Khanbalik (modern Beijing). In the summer the court moved out on the steppes to Shangdu, also called Xanadu.

■ **Uliastai and Ulaanbaatar** In 1733 the Manchus founded Uliastai in modern Zavkhan aimag, and it served as the capital of Outer Mongolia until 1911. When Mongolia broke from the Manchus, Mongolia's religious leader, the Bogd Khan, moved the capital to its present location, then called Urga or Ikh Khuree. In 1924 the communists changed the name to Ulaanbaatar Hot, meaning 'Red Hero City'.

---

and retainers, the Mongol rulers devastated their own country, alienated the increasingly impoverished herders and eventually became the captive pawns of the imperial guards.

In the 15th century, the Mongols united with the Manchus for the new conquest of China and the creation of the Qing dynasty (1644–1911). Initially, the ruling Manchus treated the Mongols with favour, gave them an exalted place in their empire and intermarried with them. Gradually, however, the Manchus became ever more Sinicised by their Chinese subjects and less like their Mongol cousins. The Mongols were reduced to little more than a colonised people under the increasingly oppressive and exploitative rule of the Manchus.

Voltaire's The Orphan of China, the first European play on the life of Chinggis Khaan, debuted in Paris in 1755.

REVOLUTIONS

In 1911 the Qing dynasty crumbled. The Mongols broke away and created their own independent country under their highest Buddhist leader, the Jebtzun Damba (Living Buddha), who became both spiritual and temporal head of the nation as the Bogd Khan (Holy King). When the Chinese also broke free of the Manchus and created the Republic of China, the new nation claimed portions of the Manchu empire, including Tibet and Mongolia.

1639	**1644**	**1696**
Zanabazar, a direct descendent of Chinggis Khaan and the greatest artist in Mongolian history, is recognised as the first Jebtzun Damba, the supreme religious leader of Mongolia.	The Manchus expel the Ming dynasty and with the support of their Mongolian allies create the Qing dynasty over China.	The Manchus defeat Galdan Khaan of Zungaria and claim western Mongolia for the Qing Dynasty, but some western Mongolians continue to resist foreign rule for several generations.

WARRIOR QUEENS OF MONGOLIA

Chinggis Khaan's greatest disappointment in life was the quality of his sons, but his greatest pride was in the daughters. He left large sections of his empire under the control of his daughters, although they gradually lost power to his sons.

The Mongol women presented a strange sight to the civilisations they helped conquer. They rode horses, shot arrows from their bows and commanded the men and women around them. In China, the Mongol women rejected foot-binding; in the Muslim world, they refused to wear the veil.

At Ögedei's death, probably in an alcoholic stupor, in 1241 his widow Töregene assumed complete power. She replaced the ministers with her own, the most important of whom was another woman, Fatima, a Tajik or Persian captive from the Middle Eastern campaign. In addition to the rule of Töregene and Fatima from Karakorum in Mongolia, two of the other three divisions of the empire also had female governors. Only the Golden Horde of Russia remained under male rule. Never before had such a large empire been ruled by women.

Töregene passed power on to her inept son Guyuk in 1246, but he died mysteriously within 18 months and was replaced by his widow Oghul Ghamish, who had to face Sorkhokhtani, the most capable woman in the empire. With the full support of her four sons, whom she trained for this moment, Sorkhokhtani organised the election of her eldest son Möngke on 1 July 1251. So great was her achievement that a Persian chronicler wrote that if history produced only one more woman equal to Sorkhokhtani then surely women would have to be judged as the superior sex.

While Kublai Khaan ruled China, his cousin Khaidu continued to fight against him from Central Asia and, true to the Mongol tradition, Khaidu's daughter Khutlun fought with him. According to Marco Polo, who called her Aiyaruk, she was both beautiful and powerful. She defeated so many men in wrestling that today Mongolian wrestlers wear an open vest in order to visibly distinguish male from female wrestlers.

After the fall of the Mongol empire, the men returned to squabbling over sheep and stealing horses, but the women kept the imperial spirit alive. In the late 15th century, a new conqueror arose determined to restore the empire. Known to the grateful Mongols as Manduhai the Wise Queen, she took to the battlefield and united the scattered tribes into a single nation. She fought even while pregnant and was once injured while carrying twins. She and the twins survived, and her army won the battle.

Faced with Manduhai's tenacity and skill, the Chinese frantically expanded the Great Wall. Although she left seven sons and three daughters, the era of the great warrior queens of Mongolia had passed, but Mongolians still watch and wait for a new Manduhai.

In May 1915 the Treaty of Khyakhta, which granted Mongolia limited autonomy, was signed by Mongolia, China and Russia.

The Russian Revolution of October 1917 came as a great shock to Mongolia's aristocracy. Taking advantage of Russia's weakness, a Chinese warlord sent his troops into Mongolia in 1919 and occupied the capital. In February 1921, retreating White Russian (anticommunist) troops entered

1911	1915	1921
Mongolia declares independence from the dying Manchu empire and sets up religious leader Bogd Khan as the head of state.	Treaty of Khyakhta is signed by Mongolia, China and Russia, granting Mongolia limited autonomy.	The mad Russian baron, Ungern von Sternberg, briefly conquers Mongolia but the Red Army and Mongolian forces under D Sükhbaatar defeat him.

THE MAD BARON

An unusual character in Mongolia's history was Baron Roman Nikolaus Fyodirovich von Ungern-Sternberg, a renegade White Russian officer who believed he was the reincarnation of Chinggis Khaan, destined to restore the Mongol warlord's previous empire. Contemporaries paint a fine picture of Baron von Ungern-Sternberg, later known as the Mad Baron, describing him as haunted-looking, with a psychotic stare that fixed on people 'like those of an animal in a cave'. He spoke with a high-pitched voice and his bulging forehead bore a huge sword scar, which pulsed with red veins whenever he grew agitated. As a finishing touch, one of his eyes was slightly higher than the other.

The Bolshevik victory in Russia forced the Baron east, and he slowly accumulated a desperate army of renegade mercenaries. He enforced discipline with a reign of terror, roasting deserters alive, baking defiant prisoners in ovens and throwing his rivals in locomotive boilers. He was also a fervent Buddhist, convinced that he was doing his victims a favour by packing them off to the next life sooner rather than later.

With an army of 6000 troops (and tacit backing of the Japanese), the Baron crossed the Mongolian border in the summer of 1920 with the aim of establishing a Pan-Mongol empire. By October his forces attacked Urga, but were driven back four times before finally taking the city. He freed the Bogd Khan (who had been imprisoned by the Chinese), but Mongol joy turned to horror as the next three days saw an orgy of looting, burning and killing. In May 1921 the Baron declared himself the Emperor of Russia.

After only a few months, the Bolshevik advance forced the Baron to abandon Urga. Out on the steppes, his own followers tried to kill him, shooting him in his tent, but he managed to escape. A group of Mongolian herders later found him dying in the grass, tortured by biting ants. He was eventually taken by the Bolsheviks, deported to Novosibirsk and shot on 15 September 1921, presumed mad. Dr Ferdinand Ossendowski, a Polish refugee living in Mongolia in the early 1920s, offers an excellent account of the Mad Baron in his book *Beasts, Men and Gods*.

Modern composer N Jantsannarov created a series of symphonies and other musical works covering Mongolian history including Chinggis Khaan and Queen Manduhai.

Russian Cossacks adopted the Mongol battle cry of 'hurray!' and spread it to the rest of the world.

Mongolia and expelled the Chinese. At first the Bogd Khan seemed to welcome the White Russians as saviours of his regime, but it soon became apparent that they were just another ruthless army of occupation.

Mongolian nationalists believed their best hope for military assistance was to ask the Bolsheviks for help. The White Russians disappeared from the scene when their leader, Baron von Ungern-Sternberg, was captured, tried and shot. In July 1921 Damdin Sükhbaatar, the leader of the Mongolian army, marched uncontested into Urga (modern-day Ulaanbaatar) alongside Bolshevik supporters. The People's Government of Mongolia was declared and the Bogd Khan was retained as a ceremonial figurehead with no real power. Led by a diverse coalition of seven revolutionaries, including Sükhbaatar, the newly formed Mongolian People's Revolutionary Party (MPRP), the first political party in the country's history (and the only one for the next 69 years), took the reins of power.

1924	1939	1944
The Bogd Khan, the eighth reincarnation of the Jebtzun Damba, dies; the People's Republic of Mongolia is created on 26 November.	Japan invades Mongolia from Manchuria in May. With help from the Soviet Union, and after heavy fighting along the Khalkh Gol, the Mongols defeat Japan by September.	The Soviet Union annexes Tuva from Mongolia; many Tuvans flee to Mongolia (and remain a minority ethnic group in Mongolia to this day).

SOVIET CONTROL

After Lenin's death in Russia in 1924, Mongolian communism remained independent of Moscow until Stalin gained absolute power in the late 1920s. Then the purges began in Mongolia. MPRP leaders were disposed of until Stalin finally found his henchman in one Khorloogiin Choibalsan.

Following Stalin's lead, Choibalsan seized from aristocrats their land and herds, which were redistributed to nomads. Herders were forced to join cooperatives and private business was banned. The destruction of private enterprise without time to build up a working state sector had the same result in Mongolia as in the Soviet Union: famine. Choibalsan's policy against religion was just as ruthless – in 1937 some 27,000 people were executed or never seen again (3% of Mongolia's population at that time), of whom 17,000 were monks.

Choibalsan died in January 1952 and was replaced by Yumjaagiin Tsedenbal – no liberal, but not a mass murderer – and Mongolia enjoyed a period of relative peace. With the Sino–Soviet split in the early 1960s, the Mongolians sided with the Soviet Union. The Mongolian government expelled thousands of ethnic Chinese and all trade with China came to a halt.

Throughout the 1970s, Soviet influence gathered strength. Young Mongolians were sent to the USSR for technical training, and Tsedenbal's wife, a Russian woman of modest background named Filatova, attempted to impose Russian culture – including food, music, dance, fashion and even language – on the Mongolians.

VI Pudovkin's Soviet masterpiece *Storm over Asia* was the first Mongolian film and contains the best extant images of herders and monasteries in the early 20th century.

THE GREAT TRANSITION

The unravelling of the Soviet Union resulted in decolonisation by default. In March 1990, in sub-zero temperatures, large pro-democracy protests erupted in the square in front of the parliament building in Ulaanbaatar. Hunger strikes were held and in May 1990 the constitution was amended to permit multiparty elections in July of the same year.

The political liberation of Mongolia from the Soviets came as an economic disaster for Mongolia because of the heavy subsidies that the Soviets had paid to keep Mongolia as a buffer state between itself and China. The Mongols lost much of their food supply and, unable to pay their electrical bills to the Russian suppliers, the western districts were plunged into a blackout that lasted for several years. The economy of Mongolia withered and collapsed.

The harsh conditions called for stringent measures and Mongolians created a unique approach to the new challenges. They began a radical privatisation of animals and large state-owned corporations. Unlike the other Soviet satellites in Eastern Europe and Central Asia that expelled the communist party, the Mongolians created a new democratic synthesis that included both the old communists of the MPRP and a coalition that became known as the Democrats. Freedom of speech, religion and assembly were all granted. The era of totalitarianism had ended.

During WWII, Mongolia donated 300kg of gold and more than six million animals to supply Soviet and Allied forces. More than 2000 Mongolians died fighting Japan.

The Blue Sky, by Galsan Tschinag, presents a beautifully written story about a remote Tuvan herding family in Mongolia during socialist times.

1945	**1956**	**1961**
In a UN-sponsored plebiscite, Mongolians vote overwhelmingly to confirm their independence but the USA and China refuse to admit Mongolia to the UN.	The Trans-Siberian railroad through Mongolia is completed, connecting Beijing with Moscow; the Chinese and Russian trains still operate on different gauges, requiring a long delay to change the wheels at the Chinese–Mongolian border.	Mongolia admitted to the UN as an independent country, but the Soviet Union continues to occupy Mongolia with troops and run the country as a satellite state.

THE MONGOL WHO SLAPPED STALIN

In 1932 P Genden became the ninth prime minister of Mongolia, and he used the slogan 'Let's Get Rich!' to inspire Mongolians to overcome the troubled fighting since the break up of the Manchu Empire and the establishment of an independent country. Mongolia was the second communist state, after the Soviet Union, but at this time Genden was trying to keep Mongolia as an ally of the Soviets rather than a colony or satellite.

Genden resisted Stalin's demands that Mongolia purge the Buddhist monks and charged the Russians with 'Red Imperialism' for seeking to send Soviet troops into Mongolia. Amidst much drinking at a reception in the Mongolian embassy in Moscow in 1935, the two men clashed, literally. Stalin kicked Genden's walking stick; Genden slapped Stalin and broke Stalin's trademark pipe that always accompanied him.

Stalin held Genden under house arrest until he was convicted as a Japanese spy and executed by firing squad on 26 November 1937 – a day of great symbolic importance to the Mongols because it was the date of their declaration of independence and creation of the Mongolian People's Republic.

In 1996 Genden's daughter G Tserendulam opened the Victims of Political Persecution Memorial Museum (p73) in Ulaanbaatar in memory of her father and all those who died in defence of Mongolian independence.

The Mongolians gradually found their way towards the modern global economy and embraced their own brand of capitalism and democracy that drew heavily on their ancient history while adjusting to the modern realities of the world around them. Despite difficult episodes, such as the unsolved murder of the Democratic leader S Zorig in 1998 and some heated demonstrations between government and citizens, Mongolia managed to move forwards with tremendous cultural vigour. While maintaining staunch friendships with old allies such as North Korea, Cuba and India, Mongolia reached out to Europe, South Korea, Japan and, most particularly, to the USA, which they dubbed their 'Third Neighbour' in an effort to create a counterpoint to China and Russia.

In the mid-1950s Howard Hughes cast John Wayne as Chinggis Khaan in *The Conqueror*, one of the worst films ever made by Hollywood.

The traveller in Mongolia today sees a country that plays an increasingly important role in world affairs, yet it is a country where any one of the earlier rulers such as Modun, Bilge, or Chinggis could return today and feel completely at home in a ger with a herding family. They would know what tasks needed to be done and they would easily recognise the food, language, music and dress because with only slight modifications the Mongolians have maintained their traditional ways while slowly moving into the modern world. Probably no country today preserves as much of its ancient way of life as Mongolia, but that past is so alive that for many of us it is difficult to see it. Perhaps this is the true gift of Chinggis Khaan to Mongolia and the world: that, as he so ardently prayed, his body died but his nation survived.

1990	1996	2005
Democracy demonstrations break out in Ulaanbaatar. The Soviets begin withdrawal in March, and in June the first free, multiparty elections are held, with the Mongolian People's Revolutionary Party (MPRP) winning 85% of the vote.	First noncommunist government is elected in Mongolia (although the 'ex-communist' MPRP is returned to office in 2000).	N Enkhbayar of the MPRP becomes Mongolian president; George W Bush becomes the first US president to visit Mongolia.

The Culture

THE NATIONAL PSYCHE

Mongolians call themselves Asian by ethnicity but Western by culture. As abstract as that might sound, your first encounters with Mongolians might knock back a few preconceptions. It could be the European influence in which their Russian masters immersed them throughout the 20th century, or perhaps the long hours they now spend glued to CNN and MTV. But the Mongolian likeness to Western thinking – and the distance the country has put between itself and the rest of Asia – probably owes more to its nomadic past and its environment than it does to any external influences.

The freedom to move about with their herds, the timelessness of the land and the delicate relationship with the earth and its resources have all had a profound effect on the Mongolian character. These persuasions have made Mongolians humble, adaptable, good-humoured, uncannily stoic and unfettered by stringent protocol; this causes visitors to wonder if these are the same people who for centuries were vilified in the West as the 'scourge of God'.

The great emptiness of their landscape and the vast distances gave birth to a horse culture that is inseparable from Mongolian life. Reverence towards the land, a product of shamanic beliefs, has attuned them to nature; the thought of degrading the land or altering nature strikes many locals as profane.

The *soyombo* is the national symbol of Mongolia and signifies freedom and independence. Its components symbolise many other characteristics. Legend attributes the *soyombo* to Zanabazar, the Living Buddha.

The empty steppes have also made hospitality a matter of sheer necessity rather than a social obligation. It would be difficult for anyone to travel across the steppes without the hospitality that has developed, as each ger is able to serve travellers as a hotel, restaurant, pub and repair shop. As a result, Mongolians are able to travel rapidly over long distances without the weight of provisions. This hospitality is readily extended to strangers and usually given without fanfare or expectation of payment; foreigners are often perplexed by the casual welcoming they receive at even the most remote of gers.

The Mongolian ger plays a vital role in shaping both the Mongolian character and family life. The small confines compel families to interact with one another, to share everything and work together, tightening relationships between relatives. It prevents privacy but promotes patience and makes inhibitions fade away. It also creates self-sufficiency; ger dwellers must fetch their own water and fuel, and subsist on the food they themselves produce.

The weather and the seasons also play a significant role in shaping the Mongolian character. Spring in particular is a crucial time for Mongolians. Because the country's rainy season comes towards the end of summer, spring is dry, dusty, windy and unforgiving. This is the time when the weaker animals die and, it is said, when people die. Despite the severe temperatures, it is during winter that Mongolians feel most comfortable. After a difficult summer filled with chores and tending to livestock, winter is a time of relaxation.

Modern politics, economics and external forces further combine to complete the Mongolian psyche. As an outward-looking people, Mongolian culture was greatly affected by Russian influences during the communist period. The USSR's implementation of universal education brought literacy to every man, woman and child. In recent years, the age of democracy has led to globalisation, and a Brave New World of mobile phones, the internet and material excess. Having been isolated for millennia, Mongolians are hungry for all that the world offers and many dream of living and studying overseas.

As a small country, Mongolia is eager to show itself on the world stage and has sent peacekeeping forces to conflict zones worldwide. It was one of the first countries to join the 'coalition of the willing' when the US invaded Iraq in 2003. A surprising number of people still support that decision and Mongolia may be the only country on earth that did not vehemently protest a visit by George W Bush (in January 2006). There is a less-favourable attitude towards the war in the predominantly Muslim Bayan-Ölgii.

More than anything, an open Mongolia has brought a rekindled interest in Mongolian culture, national pride and most of all, Chinggis Khaan. In Ulaanbaatar, and even in many parts of the countryside, the modern world has found a place alongside the traditional.

LIFESTYLE

About half of all Mongolians live in a ger, the one-room round felt tent traditionally used by nomads. The other half live in Russian-style apartment blocks. Only since the late 1990s have Mongolians started constructing more elaborate Western-style homes; most of these are upgraded dachas found outside of Ulaanbaatar.

Apartments are rabbit-hole affairs, usually two or three rooms with Russian furnishings and large carpets hanging from the walls. Gers are often equipped with traditional furnishings painted bright orange with fanciful designs. Set out in like manner, gers have three beds around the perimeter, a chest covered with Buddhist iconography at the back wall and a low table upon which food is set. Everything revolves around a central hearth, with the women's side to the right and the men's to the left. The head of the household sits at the northern end of the ger with his most honoured guest to his right. The area near the door is the place of lowest rank and the domain of children.

In ger districts, people get their water from a central pump house and cart it home in metal jugs. Each *hashaa* (fenced area) has a pit toilet. Those in need of a shower may visit the apartment of a friend or relative, or stop by a public bathhouse. Given the lack of water in most areas, regular bathing is impossible for most nomads.

Nomads tend to move two to four times a year, although in areas where grass is thin they move more often. One nuclear family may live alone or with an extended-family camp of three or four gers (known as an *ail*); any more than that would be a burden on the grassland.

A livestock herd should contain around 300 animals to be self-sustaining, although some wealthy herders may have 1000 head of livestock. Nearly all families have a short-wave radio to get national and world news, and these days many families also have satellite TV, DVD players and mobile phones. In winter the children of the ger go to school in the nearest town (where they live in dorms), visiting their parents during holidays and summer.

Regular schooling has brought near-universal literacy – you'll frequently see nomads reading out-of-date newspapers. Despite the distances, people remain connected to markets, selling their goods in towns or to traders who drive around the countryside, swapping sacks of flour or other goods for skins, meat and wool. Doctors also make house calls, driving ger to ger to give check-ups. Traditional medicine is not widely practised, except for centuries-old home remedies and some specialised clinics in the capital.

ECONOMY

Mongolia has done much to erase the legacy of its Soviet-era command economy. Around 80% of the GDP is now produced by private companies, and foreign investment is on the rise, with 40% of investments coming from China.

As it has for centuries, livestock herding remains the backbone of the economy. Around 40% of the population manages to herd the nation's

Modern Mongolia, Reclaiming Ghengis Khan, edited by Paula Sabloff, is a pictorial account of recent developments in Mongolia. Written with a sometimes controversial edge, it discusses the economy, ger etiquette, social issues and Chinggis Khaan's principles, and suggests these are the foundations of modern Mongolia.

Women of Mongolia, by Martha Avery, contains a string of interviews in which local women speak about the changes and challenges affecting both nomadic and urban women.

More Mongols live outside Mongolia than in it. Around 3.5 million ethnic Mongols are citizens of China and nearly a million are citizens of Russia. Descendants of Mongolian armies can still be found in Afghanistan and on the shores of the Caspian Sea.

RESPONSIBLE CULTURAL TOURISM

The chief attraction of Mongolia is not its historic places of interest but rather the nomadic culture and its people. Keep in mind the following tips for acting responsibly when visiting a ger and interacting with locals.

- Hospitality is an old custom on the steppes; visitors are invited in without question on arrival at a distant ger. While you should enjoy Mongolia's unique hospitality, please do not take advantage of it. If you spend a night and have a meal leave a minimum of T5000 or a useful gift such as rice, children's books in Mongolian or AA- or D-size batteries.
- Mongolians are not keen on bargaining and don't play the bargaining game. When haggling for a hotel room or jeep, never expect to get the price you demand. If you're lucky you may be able to knock down a price by 10% but not more.
- Don't pay to take a photo of someone, or photograph someone if they don't want you to. If you agree to send someone a photograph, please follow through on this.

When visiting a ger, note the following customs and habits. See also p46 for some hints about eating etiquette.

- Say hello (sain bai-na uu) when you arrive (but repeating it again when you see the same person later that day or even the next day is considered strange to Mongolians).
- Avoid walking in front of an older person or turning your back to the altar or to religious objects (except when leaving).
- If someone offers you their snuff bottle, accept it with your right hand (as if you were shaking hands). If you don't take the snuff, at least sniff the top part of the bottle. But don't grab the bottle from the top.
- Try to keep ger visits to less than two hours to avoid interrupting the family's work.

Bear in mind the following superstitions and religious habits:

- When offered some vodka, dip your ring finger of your right hand into the glass, and lightly flick a drop (not too much – vodka is also sacred!) once towards the sky, once in the air 'to the wind' and once to the ground. If you don't want any vodka, go through the customs anyway. Then put the same finger to your forehead, say thanks and return the glass to the table.
- Don't point a knife in any way at anyone; when passing a knife pass it handle first; when cutting (eg from a chunk of meat held in one hand) use the knife to cut towards you, not away.
- Don't point your feet at the hearth, at the altar or at another person. Sleep with your feet pointing towards the door.
- If you have stepped on anyone, or kicked their feet, immediately shake their hand.
- Don't stand on or lean over the threshold.
- Don't lean against a support column.
- Don't touch another person's hat.

34 million head of livestock (which accounts for 20% of the GDP). Most of the meat is used for domestic purposes while the bulk of the skins, wool, cashmere and leather are exported to Russia and China. Cashmere is the country's biggest moneymaker – Mongolia exports 3000 tonnes of the stuff per year, which is 21% of the world market. Other sectors are catching up, notably mining, and many herders have swapped their horse whips for gold pans. In some cases Mongolia's fierce climate has dictated where people work – when storms decimate livestock, as they did in 1999–2002, herders are forced to seek alternative employment, often in illegal mining camps.

The 2006 film *Tuya de hun shi* (Tuya's Marriage) describes the troubled life of shepherdess Tuya, an Inner Mongolian woman forced to find a new provider after her husband is crippled by an explosion. It's an Inner Mongolian film directed by Quanan Wang and winner of the prestigious Golden Bear at the Berlin International Film Festival.

More organised and legal forms of mining are also taking shape. It's predicted that within the next two decades the Mongolian economy will grow 10 times on the back of its mineral resources, heavily sought after by China. GDP is only US$2100 per person but that could be up to US$15,000 by 2021. While these may seem like pie in the sky figures, the projections are mainly based on the expected output of Oyu Tolgoi, which could spit out 450,000 tons of copper annually (4% of global output).

Of course, these riches may end up in the pockets of a few robber barons and government insiders. Corruption is rife in Mongolia and there seems to be no limit to its extent. Democracy, which has allowed the media and civil society to act as watchdogs, has at least prevented the formation of a total kleptocracy.

While Mongolians watch and wait for some of the biggest mines to provide returns, the country remains mired in poverty. Unemployment hovers at 30% to 40% although precise figures are difficult to determine as so many Mongolians work as unregistered drivers or traders. Tourism is another important sector and now accounts for 18% of the economy – not bad since it really only functions for three months a year.

Despite the unemployment rate, money still flows around the country and few people go hungry. You'll find most Mongolians live in a healthy, robust state even if they have been out of work for months or even years, supported by strong family networks. One family member with a decent job has the responsibility to distribute his wealth among siblings.

Relatives working abroad also send remittances – approximately 100,000 Mongolians work overseas, about 8% of the workforce. In Ulaanbaatar, government salaries are less than US$100 per month while salaries in the private sector can be two or three times higher (sometimes much more).

THE CULT OF THE GREAT KHAAN

In early 2006 Ulaanbaatar unveiled a daring piece of modern architecture – the US$10 million frontal portage to Government House, an enormous wing of marble columns, arching glass and the *pièce de résistance,* a glowering bronze statue of Chinggis Khaan.

The grandiose monument is only the latest chapter in a long and storied obsession with the khaan we know as Ghengis. Worship of Chinggis began under the reign of his grandson Kublai Khaan, who established a sort of Chinggis travelling museum in the Ordos Desert (now Inner Mongolia). Spirit worship of the great khaan has taken place in other parts of Mongolia including Shankh Khiid (Övörkhangai; p119) and Burkhan Khalduun (Khentii; p172).

Chinggis Khaan had been outlawed during communism, a time when the Soviets thought Mongolians needed to move forward into a great Socialist future. But since the early 1990s the Mongolians have brought Chinggis back, often into pop culture – a rock band and brewery have been named in his honour and you'll spot Chinggis Khaan T-shirts, coffee mugs and key-chains in souvenir shops. As evidence of his godlike status, one can commonly see pictures of Chinggis on the family altar, flanking those of Buddhist deities.

Why all the hype? Chinggis has suffered from 800 years of bad press in the West but to Mongolians he embodies strength, unity and law and order. He introduced a written script in the Mongolian language and preached religious tolerance. Chinggis is the young king who united the warring clans and gave Mongolians a sense of direction, not to mention more wealth than the country had seen before or since. This is what postcommunist Mongolia looks for today – a leader in the mould of Chinggis who can rise above confusion and uncertainty.

None of Mongolia's current crop of politicos has galvanised the nation as Chinggis once did, but there remains hope for the future; according to a prediction by Nostradamus (in the 16th century), an incarnation of Chinggis Khaan was born in September 1999. While that may sound like bad news for the rest of us, the Mongolians, an optimistic lot, look ahead with great expectations.

POPULATION

Of Mongolia's population (around 2.6 million people), 50% live permanently in urban areas and around 25% are truly nomadic. Another 25% are seminomadic, living in villages in winter and grazing their animals on the steppes during the rest of the year. With population growth at an all-time low (having fallen from 2.4% to 1.4% over the past 15 years), the government offers economic benefits for newborns and newlywed couples.

In recent years the population has shifted from the countryside to Ulaanbaatar, as Mongolians search for work opportunities not available in rural areas. Since 1999, internal migration to the capital has increased by around 13% per year – the city hit the one million mark in 2007.

The majority (about 86%) of Mongolians are Khalkh Mongolians (*khalkh* means 'shield'). Clan or tribal divisions are not significant social or political issues in modern Mongolia. The other sizable ethnic group, the Kazakhs, make up about 6% (110,000) of the population and live in western Mongolia, mainly in Bayan-Ölgii aimag.

The remaining 8% of the population are ethnic minority groups. These groups are located along the border areas and in the far west, and their numbers range from some 47,500 ethnic Buriats who live along the northern border to just 300 Tsaatan, the reindeer people of northern Khövsgöl aimag.

SPORT

Mongolian sports – wrestling, horse racing and archery – are an extension of the military training used for centuries by Mongolian clans.

Wrestling is still the national pastime. The Mongolian version is similar to wrestling found elsewhere, except there are no weight divisions, so the biggest wrestlers (and they are big!) are often the best. Out on the steppes matches can go on for hours, but matches for the national Naadam have a time limit – after 30 minutes a referee moves the match into something akin to 'penalty kicks' (the leading wrestler gets better position from the get go). The match ends only when the first wrestler falls, or when anything other than the soles of the feet or open palms touches the ground.

The biggest wrestling tournament is the national Naadam Festival (p96), which has 512 contestants and is held in Ulaanbaatar on 11 and 12 July. Other tournaments are held throughout the year at the **Wrestling Palace** (Map p64; ☎ 456 443; Peace Ave; admission T1000-5000). Wrestling events are the same elsewhere – small matches held during the year and a big one for Naadam.

Mongolia's second-biggest sport is horse racing. Jockeys – traditionally children between the ages of five and 12 years – race their horses over open countryside rather than around a track. Courses can be either 15km or 30km and are both exhausting and dangerous – every year jockeys tumble from their mounts and horses collapse and die from exhaustion at the finish line.

Winning horses are called *tümnii ekh*, or 'leader of 10,000'. Riders and spectators rush to comb the sweat off these best horses with a scraper traditionally made from a pelican's beak. The five winning riders must drink some special *airag* (fermented mare milk), which is then often sprinkled on the riders' heads and the horses' backsides. During the Naadam Festival, a song of empathy is also sung to the two-year-old horse that comes in last.

The third sport of Eriin Gurvan Naadam (Three Manly Sports) is archery, which is actually performed by men and women alike. Archers use a bent composite bow made of layered horn, bark and wood. Usually arrows are made from willow and the feathers are from vultures and other birds of prey. After each shot, judges who stand near the target emit a short cry called *uukhai*, and raise their hands in the air to indicate the quality of the shot. See www.atarn.org for articles on Mongolian archery.

Mongolia has the world's lowest population density at just 1.4 persons per sq km.

Mongolians tend to use just one name but, to differentiate themselves from people with the same name, they sometimes add their father's name. A recent government registration system has encouraged the use of clan names as surnames – the most popular is Borjigan, the clan of Chinggis Khaan.

A Mongolian legend recounts that one Amazonian-type female entered a wrestling competition and thrashed her male competitors. In order to prevent such an embarrassing episode from happening again, the wrestling jacket was redesigned with an open chest, forcing women to sit on the sidelines.

Sumo wrestling has grown as a spectator sport as Mongolian athletes dominate the Japanese circuit – all tournaments in Japan are broadcast on Mongolian TV. The best-known Mongolian wrestler is Dolgersuren Dagvadorj. His nickname, the 'Bathtub Brawler', was bestowed after a punch-up with another wrestler while the two bathed after a match.

According to legend, the sport of polo began when Chinggis Khaan's troops batted the severed heads of their enemies across the steppes. Whether true or not, polo has recently been revived in Mongolia with the help of foreign players. It hasn't quite caught fire yet, but there may be an exhibition in summer. Likewise, matches of polo on camelback are organised for some Gobi naadams (games).

Basketball and other Western-style sports are increasing in popularity. There is now a professional basketball league in Ulaanbaatar, and even at the most remote gers you'll find a backboard and hoop propped up on the steppe.

RELIGION
Buddhism

The Mongols had limited contact with organised religion before their great empire of the 13th century. It was Kublai Khaan who first found himself with a court in which all philosophies of his empire were represented, but it was a Tibetan Buddhist, Phagpa, who wielded the greatest influence on the khaan.

In 1578 Altan Khaan, a descendant of Chinggis Khaan, met the Tibetan leader Sonam Gyatso, was converted, and subsequently bestowed on Sonam Gyatso the title Dalai Lama (*dalai* means 'ocean' in Mongolian). Sonam Gyatso was named as the third Dalai Lama and his two predecessors were named posthumously.

Mass conversions occurred under Altan Khaan. As Mongolian males were conscripted to monasteries, rather than the army, the centuries of constant fighting seemed to wane (much to the relief of China, which subsequently funded more monasteries in Mongolia). This change in national philosophy continues today – Mongolia is the world's only UN-sanctioned 'nuclear-free nation'.

Buddhist opposition to needless killing reinforced strict hunting laws already set in place by shamanism. Today, Buddhist monks are still influential in convincing local populations to protect their environment and wildlife.

In 1903, when the British invaded Tibet, the 13th Dalai Lama fled to Mongolia and spent three years living in Gandan Khiid in Urga (modern-day Ulaanbaatar).

Buddhism in Mongolia was nearly destroyed in 1937 when the young communist government, fearing competition, launched a purge that wiped out nearly all of the country's 700 monasteries. Up to 30,000 monks were massacred and thousands more sent to Siberian labour camps. Freedom of religion was only restored in 1990 with the dawn of democracy.

Restoring Buddhism has been no easy task as two generations had been essentially raised atheist. Most people no longer understand the Buddhist rituals or their meanings but a few still make the effort to visit the monasteries during prayer sessions. Numbers swell when well-known Buddhist monks from Tibet or India (or even Western countries) visit Mongolia.

As they have for centuries, Mongolians believe that monks have the powers to heal or altar the course of future events; they will often pay hard-earned money for the reading of appropriate prayers to secure better test scores, improved business or marital security.

Religions of Mongolia, by Walther Heissig, provides an in-depth look at the Buddhist and shamanist faiths as they developed in Mongolia.

Islam

In Mongolia today, there is a significant minority of Sunni Muslims, most of them ethnic Kazakhs, who live primarily in Bayan-Ölgii. These Kazakhs have connections with Islamic groups in Turkey and several have been on a hajj to Mecca.

Christianity

Nestorian Christianity was part of the Mongol empire long before the Western missionaries arrived. The Nestorians followed the doctrine of Nestorious (358–451), patriarch of Constantinople (428–31), who proclaimed

IMPORTANT FIGURES & SYMBOLS OF TIBETAN BUDDHISM

This brief guide to some of the deities of the Tibetan Buddhist pantheon will allow you to recognise a few of the statues you'll encounter in Mongolia, usually on temple altars. Sanskrit names are provided as these are most recognisable in the West; Mongolian names are in brackets.

The Characters
Sakyamuni The Historical Buddha was born in Lumbini in the 5th century BC in what is now southern Nepal. He attained enlightenment under a *bo* (peepul) tree and his teachings set in motion the Buddhist faith. Statues of the Buddha include 32 distinctive body marks, including a dot between the eyes and a bump on the top of his blue hair. His right hand touches the earth in the Bhumisparsa Mudra hand gesture, and the left hand holds a begging bowl.

Maitreya (Maidar) The Future Buddha, Maitreya is passing the life of a bodhisattva (a divine being worthy of Nirvana who remains on the human plane to help others achieve enlightenment) and will return to earth in human form 4000 years after the disappearance of Sakyamuni to take his place as the next earthly Buddha. He is normally seated with his hands by his chest in the *mudra* of 'turning the Wheel of Law'.

Avalokitesvara (Janraisig) The Bodhisattva of Compassion is either pictured with 11 heads and 1000 pairs of arms *(chogdanjandan janraisig)*, or in a white, four-armed manifestation *(chagsh janraisig)*. The Dalai Lama is considered an incarnation of Avalokitesvara.

Tara The Saviour, Tara has 21 different manifestations. She symbolises purity and fertility and is believed to be able to fulfil wishes. Statues of Tara usually represent Green Tara (Nogoon Dar Ekh), who is associated with night, or White Tara (Tsagaan Dar Ekh), who is associated with day. White Tara is the female companion of Avalokitesvara.

Four Guardian Kings Comprising Virupaksa (red; holding a snake), Dhitarastra (white; holding a lute), Virudhaka (blue; holding a sword) and Vaishrovana (yellow; sitting on a snow lion), the kings are mostly seen guarding monastery entrances.

The Symbols & Objects
Prayer Wheel These are filled with up to a mile of prayers and are turned manually by pilgrims to gain merit.

Wheel of Life Drawings of this wheel symbolise the cycle of death and rebirth, held by Yama, the god of the dead. The six sections of the circle are the six realms of rebirth ruled over by gods, titans, hungry ghosts, hell, animals and humans.

Stupas (suvrag) Originally built to house the cremated relics of the Historical Buddha, they have become a powerful symbol of Buddhism. Later stupas also became reliquaries for lamas and holy men.

---

that Jesus exists as two separate persons – the man Jesus and the divine son of God. Historically the religion never caught hold in the Mongol heartland, but that has changed in recent years with an influx of Christian missionaries, often from obscure fundamentalist sects.

Mongolian authorities are wary of these missionaries, who sometimes come to the country under the pretext of teaching English. In Ulaanbaatar, there are now more than 50 non-Buddhist places of worship. Mormons, the most recognisable, have built modern churches in Ulaanbaatar, Nalaikh, Choibalsan, Erdenet and other cities. The Catholics, also here in large numbers, have constructed an enormous church on the eastern side of Ulaanbaatar.

The online magazine www.mongoliatoday.com has several interesting articles on Mongolian culture, religion, society and ethnography.

Shamanism

Ovoos, the large piles of rocks found on mountain passes, are repositories of offerings for local spirits. Upon arriving at an *ovoo,* walk around it clockwise three times, toss an offering onto the pile (another rock should suffice) and make a wish.

Whether shamanism is a religion is open to debate (there is no divine being or book of teachings), but it is a form of mysticism practised by some Mongolians in the north, including the Tsaatan, Darkhad, Uriankhai and Buriats. It was the dominant belief system of Chinggis Khaan and the Mongol hordes but has now been pushed to the cultural fringes.

Shamanism is based around the shaman – called a *bo* if a man or *udgan* if a woman – who has special medical and religious powers. If a shaman's powers are inherited, it is known as *udmyn;* if the powers become apparent after a sudden period of sickness and apparitions it is known as *zlain.*

One of a shaman's main functions is to cure any sickness caused by the soul straying, and to accompany the soul of a dead person to the other world. Shamans act as intermediaries between the human and spirit worlds, and communicate with spirits during trances, which can last up to six hours.

Shamanist beliefs have done much to shape Mongolian culture and social practices. The lack of infrastructure during the course of Mongolia's history can be traced to shamanic rules on maintaining a balance with nature, ie not digging holes or tearing the land. Even today when nomads move their camps they fill in any holes created by horse posts.

Around 80% of Mongolians claim to be Buddhist of the Mahayana variety, as practised in Tibet. Some 5% follow Islam (mainly Kazakhs living in Bayan-Ölgii aimag). Approximately 5% of Mongolians claim to be Christians, Mongolia's fastest-growing religion, and around 10% are atheist (the creed of the former communist state).

Sky worship is another integral part of shamanism and you'll see Mongolians leaving blue scarves (representing the sky) on *ovoos.* Sky gods are likewise honoured by flicking droplets of vodka in the air before drinking.

ARTS

From prehistoric oral epics to the latest movie from MongolKino film studios in Ulaanbaatar, the many arts of Mongolia convey the flavour of nomadic life and the spirit of the land. Influenced by Tibet, China and Russia, Mongolia has nonetheless developed unique forms of music, dance, costume, painting, sculpture, drama, film, handicrafts, carpets and textiles.

There are several art and music festivals every year, one of the biggest being the **Roaring Hooves Music Festival** (www.roaringhooves.com). In late October you could check out the Altan Namar (Golden Autumn) festival, usually held at the circus.

For more information on the arts in Mongolia, contact the **Arts Council** (☎ 011-319 015; www.artscouncil.mn) in Ulaanbaatar.

Literature & Poetry

The heroic epics of the Mongols were all first committed to writing more than 750 years ago. Later, Mongolia developed an enormous amount of Buddhist literature. Surprisingly, the National Library of Mongolia in Ulaanbaatar holds the world's largest single collection of Buddhist sutras (almost all of it confiscated during the 1937 purges).

The website www.ulaanbaatar.net has links to the Mongolian National Modern Art Gallery (p76); click on Mongol Arts and then Museums.

Only recently have scholars translated into English the most important text of all – *Mongol-un niguca tobchiyan* (The Secret History of the Mongols). The text was lost for centuries until a Chinese copy was discovered in 1866 by the implausibly named Archimandrite Palladius, a Russian scholar and diplomat then resident in Beijing. Intriguing structural comparisons have been made between *The Secret History of the Mongols* and the Bible, prompting theories that the Mongolian author was strongly influenced by the teachings of Nestorian Christianity.

While fiction has never enjoyed much popularity, Mongolians have always been fond of poetry. Dashdorjiin Natsagdorj (1906–37), Mongolia's best-known modern poet and playwright, is regarded as the founder of Mongolian literature. His works include the dramatic nationalist poems *My Native Land*

and *Star* and his famous story, *Three Fateful Hills*, which was adapted into an opera that is still performed in Ulaanbaatar.

The most prolific poet to look out for is Danzan Ravjaa (1803–56), a monk from the Gobi Desert known for his poems of wine and love. A collection of his poems, *Perfect Qualities*, translated by Simon Wickham-Smith can be found in Ulaanbaatar.

The best-known contemporary writer is Ochirbatyn Dashbalbar, a nationalist, politician and xenophobe who died under mysterious circumstances in 2000.

Cinema

During communism, Mongolia had a vibrant film industry led by Moscow-trained directors who excelled at socialist realism. MongolKino's most famed directors, L Vangad and D Jigjid, directed many communist-era films, including *Serelt* (Awakening), one of the all-time classics. This anti-Buddhist film describes the life and times of a young Russian nurse sent to Mongolia to set up a hospital in a rural area. It starred Dorjpalam, the mother of Democratic leader Sanjaasurengiin Zorig (p74). Other classic films that still bring a tear to the Mongolian eye are *Tungalag Tamir* (directed by Ravjagiin Dorjpalam) and *Sükhbaatar* (directed by IE Heifits).

The biggest star of the new generation is Byambasuren Davaa, whose touching tale *The Weeping Camel* went from obscurity to award winner in 2004. Her second effort, *Cave of the Yellow Dog*, describes the life of a nomad family and the changing life on the steppes.

Mongolians are avid movie watchers. The best place to catch a film is the three-screen multiplex Tengis (p93), which is next to Liberty Sq in Ulaanbaatar.

Music
MODERN

Western music, mainly alternative rock and hip-hop, is popular with young Mongolians in Ulaanbaatar, but they also enjoy listening to local groups, who sing in the Mongolian language but have definite Western influences. These include alterative rockers The Lemons and Nisvanis, and old-school pop bands Hurd and Haranga. Ballad singers are also popular, including female vocalists Otgoo, Ariunaa and Saraa. Recent years have seen a profusion of one-hit-wonder boy bands and hip-hop acts; the latest big acts are Lumino and Tatar. Some bands have taken to incorporating traditional instruments in their music; one such band, Legend, performs frequently at Ulaanbaatar's History Club (p93).

TRADITIONAL

Get an urbanised Mongolian into the countryside, and they will probably sing and tell you it is the beauty of the countryside that created the song on their lips. Mongolians sing to their animals: there are lullabies to coax sheep to suckle their lambs; songs to order a horse forward, make it stop or come closer; and croons to control a goat, milk a cow or imitate a camel's cry.

Traditional music involves a wide range of instruments and uses for the human voice found almost nowhere else. *Khöömii* (throat singing) found in Mongolia and neighbouring Tuva, is an eerie sound that involves the simultaneous production of multiple notes. See the boxed text (p236) for more details.

Another unique traditional singing style is *urtyn duu*. Sometimes referred to as 'long songs' because of the long trills, not because they are long

The US$30 million Japanese blockbuster *Aoki Okami: chi hate umi tsukiru made* (Genghis Khan: To the Ends of Earth and Sea), was filmed on location in Mongolia and released in 2007. The making of the film required some 30,000 local extras to don Mongol warrior garb for the battle scenes.

The Weeping Camel (2004), directed by Byambasuren Davaa and Luigi Falomi, is a moving documentary about a camel that has rejected its offspring and how the family that owns the camels attempts to reconcile their differences.

Chinggis Blues (1999), directed by Roko and Adrian Belic, traces the inspirational journey of a blind American blues singer from San Francisco to Tuva to learn the secrets of *khöömii* (throat singing).

songs (though some epics are up to 20,000 verses long), *urtyn duu* involves extraordinarily complicated, drawn-out vocal sounds, which relate traditional stories about love and the countryside. The late Norovbanzad is Mongolia's most famous long-song diva.

Several souvenir shops in Ulaanbaatar, including the State Department Store, sell recordings of traditional music. Anyone who takes a long-distance trip on public transport will hear impromptu Mongolian folk songs – normally when the transport breaks down.

Architecture

Constructing permanent buildings is contradictory to a nomadic society. Ulaanbaatar, largely a Soviet creation, is filled with Brezhnev-era apartment blocks and Stalinist government buildings. The only constructions that can be considered old are Buddhist temples, which were largely designed by Chinese and Tibetan architects between the 17th and 20th centuries. Traditional Mongolian architecture consists solely of the ger, a well-designed home for nomadic use.

Gers can be erected in about an hour and are easily packed up and moved. The circular shape and low roof are well suited to deflect wind. The door always faces south, providing protection against the predominantly northern winds. The felt used to make the ger is traditionally made by the herders themselves, often in late summer, from the wool from their own flocks. At some ger camps, tourists sites and even the back of bank notes you might find gers set on giant wooden carts. Your guide may proudly explain that this was how the khaans moved around during the imperial age, but recent findings have proven this to be a historical myth. Despite the great desire for more modern apartments, demand for new gers also remains high (thanks to expanding ger suburbs in Ulaanbaatar) and the average price for a ger has doubled in recent years from US$300 to US$600 or more.

Painting & Sculpture

TRADITIONAL PAINTING & SCULPTURE

Much of Mongolian traditional art is religious in nature and closely linked to Tibetan art. Traditional sculpture and scroll painting follows strict rules of subject, colour and proportion, leaving little room for personal expression. Tragically, most early examples of Mongolian art were destroyed during the communist regime.

One of the most enduring images of communism was a socialist-realism painting of a young, wide-eyed Sükhbaatar meeting a lecturing Lenin. You may even see a copy of it in some offices. While many still assume the incident occurred, contemporary historians now disregard the story as mythical propaganda.

Mongolia's best-known painter is Balduugiyn Sharav (1869–1939). He spent his childhood in a monastery and later travelled all around the country. His most famous painting is *One Day in Mongolia,* which you can see in the Zanabazar Museum of Fine Arts (p69). It is a *zurag* (painting), a classic work of Mongolian landscape storytelling, crowded with intricate sketches depicting just about every aspect of the Mongolian life, from felt-making to dung-collecting.

Zanabazar was a revered sculptor, politician, religious teacher, diplomat and Living Buddha. Many Mongolians refer to the time of Zanabazar's life as Mongolia's Renaissance period. His most enduring legacy is the sensuous statues of the incarnation of compassion, the deity Tara. Some of Zanabazar's bronze sculptures and paintings can be seen today in Ulaanbaatar's Gandan Khiid (p73), the Zanabazar Museum of Fine Arts (p69) and the Winter Palace of Bogd Khaan (p75). For more on the man, see p142.

Religious scroll paintings *(thangka)* grace the walls of monasteries all over the country. They are tools of meditation, used by practitioners to visualise themselves developing the enlightened qualities of the deities depicted.

Mongolian scroll paintings generally mirror the Tibetan variety, but you can notice distinctive regional features such as the introduction of camels, sheep and yaks in the background.

Appliqué scroll paintings, made from Chinese silks, were popular at the turn of the 20th century. There are some fine examples in the Zanabazar Museum of Fine Arts (p69).

Gandan Khiid's master artist, Purevbat, has revived Buddhist art since the late 1990s, after receiving training from masters in India and Nepal. Purevbat has displayed his art at exhibitions overseas but is currently concentrating his efforts on Mongolia, in particular the reconstruction of Demchigiin Khiid (p207) in Ömnögov.

The website www.mon golart.mn explores the culture of Mongolia, with pages on music, art, theatre, dance, film and religion.

MODERN ART

Mongolian painting in the 20th century was dominated by socialist realism but has recently spread to embrace abstract styles. There is a vibrant modern-art scene in Ulaanbaatar. A couple of artists to look out for are M Erdenebayar and his wife S Munkhjin; he paints abstract scenes of horses and she paints the female figure. In galleries you'll also spot work by S Saransatsralt whose conceptual paintings are occasionally provocative. Ancient beliefs and customs are often incorporated in the work of S Tugs-Oyun. More pieces can be found by following the links to Mongolian Masterpieces at www.khanbank.com and clicking on Community Collections. In Ulaanbaatar you can see contemporary pieces at the Mongolian Artists' Exhibition Hall (p76) diagonally opposite the post office.

Theatre & Dance

The extraordinarily talented Danzan Ravjaa (see p201) is the patron saint of modern Mongolian theatre.

In the 1820s Ravjaa organised a theatre group at Khamaryn Khiid (see p202), based on the Chinese-style operas and Tibetan dramas he had witnessed while studying in Inner Mongolia. His major achievement was the production of *Saran Khöökhöö Namtar* (Story of the Moon Cuckoo), an old Tibetan play that describes the troubled life of a prince betrayed by his best friend. The theatre group performed the play at various monasteries in the Gobi and it continued to be performed after the death of Danzan Ravjaa until the 1920s.

The Russians brought European theatre and ballet to Mongolia in the 1920s, and every village built during the Soviet period included a requisite drama theatre. Ballet became a popular form of dance, as did the waltz, although Mongolia does have a traditional form of dance (*bujig*) that involves much leaping and bounding by the performers. Performances of theatre, opera and ballet are frequently held at Ulaanbaatar's Opera House (p92) and Drama Theatre (p92) but very rarely at theatres outside the capital. You'll need to personally visit the theatres in aimag capitals and ask around for what's on, as advertising is almost nonexistent.

The website www.uma .mn has links to virtually every member of Ulaanbaatar's artistic community.

Food & Drink

The culinary masters of Mongolia's barren steppes have always put more stock in survival than taste. Mongolian food is therefore a hearty, if somewhat bland, array of meat and dairy products. Out in the countryside, green vegetables are often equated with animal fodder and spices may be an alien concept.

The reasons for this stem from the constraints of a nomadic lifestyle. Nomads cannot reasonably transport an oven, and so are prevented from producing baked goods such as bread. Nor can nomads plant, tend to or harvest fruits, vegetables, spices or grains. They can, however, eat the food that their livestock produces.

Mongolian food is seasonal. In the summer months, when animals provide milk, dairy products become the staple food. Meat (and copious amounts of fat) takes over in winter, supplemented with flour (in some form) and potatoes or rice if these are available.

Imperial Mongolian Cooking: Recipes from the Kingdoms of Ghengis Khan (2001), by Marc Cramer, describes a variety of recipes from Mongolia, China, Central Asia and other lands that were once part of the Mongol empire. Many recipes are from the author's grandfather, who worked as a chef in Siberia.

Flour and tea were only introduced into the Mongolian staples after the Mongols established trade links with China. The Chinese have been particularly influential in Inner Mongolia (now in China), where the mixing of cuisines resulted in 'Mongolian barbecue', or 'Mongolian hotpot'. Although unheard of in most of Mongolia, the dish has recently found its way into a few restaurants geared towards tourists.

Menus have been expanding over the past decade thanks to the government-sponsored 'Green Revolution', which allows urbanites to grow vegetables in small, private garden plots. (Most vegetables sold in markets come from China.) Increased trade has brought in packaged and processed food products, as well as international restaurants; the vast array of high quality, foreign-owned restaurants in Ulaanbaatar comes as a pleasant surprise to visitors expecting a mostly muttonish diet.

STAPLES & SPECIALTIES

Almost any Mongolian dish can be created with meat, rice, flour and potatoes. Most meals consist of *talkh* (bread) in the towns and cities and *bortzig* (fried unleavened bread) in the gers, and the uncomplicated *shölte khool* (literally, soup with food) – a meal involving hot broth, pasta slivers, boiled mutton and a few potato chunks.

Buuz (steamed mutton dumplings) and *khuushuur* (fried mutton pancakes) are two of the most popular menu options you'll find in restaurants. *Buuz*, similar to Chinese *baoza* or Tibetan *momo*, are steamed pasta shells filled with mutton and sometimes slivers of onion or garlic. Miniature *buuz*, known as *bansh*, are usually dunked in milk tea. *Khuushuur* are best if prepared in the form of small meat envelopes, but are less tasty if squashed into a pancake.

The well-researched www.mongolfood.info includes notes on Mongolian cuisine, plus cooking techniques and recipes to dispel the myth that Mongolian menus stop at 'boiled mutton'.

Other dishes include *tsuivan*, lightly steamed flour slices with meat, and *khuurag* (fried food), which can be prepared with *buudatei khuurag* (rice) or *nogotei khuurag* (vegetables).

The classic Mongolian dinner staple, and the one most dreaded by foreigners, is referred to simply as '*makh*' (meat) and consists of boiled sheep bits (bones, fat, indiscernible organs and the head) with some sliced potato, served in a plastic bucket. Utensils include a buck knife and your fingers. The head is considered a delicacy. If you're having trouble identifying what part of the sheep you're munching on, just ask your host. This is still the most common food in rural areas, but rarely served in an urban household.

The other main highlight of Mongolian cuisine is *khorkhog*, made by placing hot stones from an open fire into a pot or urn with chopped mutton, some water and sometimes vodka. The container is then sealed and left on the fire. When eating this meal, it is customary to pass the hot, greasy rocks from hand to hand, as this is thought to be good for your health.

Borts (dried meat) is very popular among Mongolians, and many jeep drivers like to take it on long-distance trips to add to soups.

Mongolians don't concern themselves much with breakfast; a bowl of hot *süütei tsai* (milk tea) and some pieces of *bortzig* (fried unleavened bread) will usually suffice. Desserts are equally uncommon, although *süütei budaa*, made from rice, sugar and milk, is an occasional treat.

In summer, you can subsist as the Mongols do on *tsagaan idee* (dairy products; literally 'white foods'): yogurt, milk, fresh cream, cheese and fermented milk drinks.

Süü (milk) may be cow, sheep or goat milk and the *tarag* (yogurt) is always delicious. *Khoormog* is yogurt made from camel milk. When you visit a ger you will be offered dairy snacks such as *aaruul* (dried milk curds), which are as hard as a rock and often about as tasty. You may also be served a very sharp, soft, fermented cheese called *aarts*.

> Traveller Dan Bennett describes his adventures dining with a Mongolian family, and the challenges of eating sheep head, at www.fotuva .org/travel/potato.html.

DRINKS
Nonalcoholic Drinks

Mongolians are big tea drinkers and will almost never start a meal until they've had a cup of tea first, as it aids digestion. However, Mongolian tea *(tsai* in Mongolian; *shay* in Kazakh) tends to be of the lowest quality. In fact, it's mostly 'tea waste': stems and rejected leaves that are processed into a 'brick'.

Süütei tsai, a classic Mongolian drink, is milk tea with salt. The taste varies by region; in Bayan-Ölgii you may even get a dollop of butter in your tea. If you can't get used to the salty brew, try asking for *khar tsai* (black tea), which is like European tea, with sugar and no milk. (The word 'Lipton' is often understood and used in restaurants as an alternative to black tea.)

> It is customary to flick spoonfuls of milk in the direction of departing travellers. This goes for people travelling by horse, car, train or plane.

TASTY TRAVEL

One taste of fresh *öröm* (sometimes called *üürag*) and you'll soon find yourself scraping away at the bottom of the bowl. This rich, sweet-tasting cream is made by warming fresh cow milk in a pot and then letting it sit under a cover for one day. Yak milk (which contains twice as much fat as cow milk) will make an even sweeter cream. Another excellent treat, available in summer, is Mongolian blueberry jam. Most regions produce a sour version but the blueberries from around Khövsgöl Nuur are as sweet and tasty as you'll find anywhere.

We Dare You

Got a hankerin' for blowtorched rodent? Pop into a ger and ask around for some *boodog,* the authentic Mongolian barbeque. This summer delight first involves pulling the innards out of the neck of a goat or marmot. The carcass is then stuffed full of scalding rocks and the neck cinched up with wire. The bloated animal is then thrown upon a fire (or blowtorched) to burn the fur off the outside while the meat is cooked from within. The finished product vaguely resembles a balloon with paws.

Like most things involving a blowtorch, preparing *boodog* is true men's work. Furthering the adventure, it's worth noting that the bubonic plague, or Black Death as it was known to medieval Europe, can be passed by handling marmot skins. Most cases occur in August and September.

Other regional delicacies include *kazy* (salted horse-meat sausages), prepared by Kazakhs in Bayan-Ölgii aimag. Gobi people occasionally eat camel meat; the cut might be a bit gamey as it is the older camels that are usually killed for their meat.

Alcoholic Drinks

Mongolians can drink you under the table if you challenge them. There is much social pressure to drink, especially on males – those who refuse to drink *arkhi* (vodka) are considered wimps. The Russians can be thanked for this attitude, which started in the 1970s. Mongolian women prefer to drink beer more than vodka. Western women will be gently encouraged to drink but it's unlikely to be forced on them.

Locally produced beer labels such as Mongol, Chinggis and Khan Brau are growing in popularity as most young people consider it trendier to drink beer rather than go blind on the hard stuff preferred by their parents. Popular vodkas include the very smooth Chinggis black label which costs just US$8 a bottle.

While it may not seem obvious at first, every countryside ger doubles as a tiny brewery or distillery. One corner of the ger usually contains a tall, thin jug with a plunger that is used for fermenting mare milk. The drink, known as *airag* or *koumiss,* has an alcohol content of about 3%.

Although you aren't likely to get drunk from *airag* alone, many Mongolians distil it further to produce *shimiin arkhi,* which boosts the alcohol content to around 12%. Go easy on the *airag* from the start or your guts will pay for it later.

Mongolia's major brewing labels include APU (which produces Mongol-brand beer), Chinggis Beer and Khan Brau. In 2007 Tiger Beer opened a US$20 million brewery in east Ulaanbaatar.

CELEBRATIONS

Tsagaan Sar, the Mongolian New Year, is a festival for a new beginning. Everything about the holiday is symbolic of happiness, joy and prosperity in the coming year, and it is food that represents many of these rites.

Mongolians are an optimistic lot – a full belly during Tsagaan Sar is said to represent prosperity in the year ahead; *buuz* (steamed mutton dumplings) in their thousands are therefore prepared and consumed during the holiday. Likewise, the central meal of the holiday must be the biggest sheep a family can afford to buy; pride is at stake over how much fat will appear on the table.

The *buuz* itself carries one of the most important symbols of the holiday – one dumpling will hide a special silver coin that represents wealth to the lucky individual who finds it (watch your teeth!).

During Tsagaan Sar, food even plays a role in the decoration, as the centrepiece is made from layers of large biscuits called *ul boov.* Young people stack three layers of biscuits, middle-aged folk five layers and grandparents seven layers. Littering the table are chocolates and boiled sweets, decorations and the sheep itself, representing wealth in the year ahead.

Mongolians rarely need encouragement to drink or eat but birthdays are another time to celebrate. In cities these are usually held at restaurants. Mongolians also have a special party for three-year-olds, whose heads are shorn as part of the festivities.

Mongolia Expat magazine has an article describing the different types of Mongolian vodka. Go to www.mongoliaexpat .com and download the Naadam Festival issue from the archives.

Each year Mongolians consume 26L of alcohol per person. Of that, just 0.9L is beer.

WHERE TO EAT & DRINK

The most basic Mongolian eatery is the ubiquitous *guanz* (Гуанз), or canteen. *Guanz* are usually found in buildings, gers or even in train wagons, in aimag capitals, a few *sums,* all over Ulaanbaatar and along major roads where there is some traffic. They usually offer soup, *süütei tsai* and either *buuz* or *khuushuur.*

In the countryside, the ger *guanz* is a great way to see the interior of a ger and meet a family, without the lengthy stops and traditions expected with normal visits. These are scattered along main roads.

In the countryside most *guanz* seem to close for dinner (and often lunch as well). In reality, opening hours are often at the whim of staff. The city *guanz,* a good option for budget travellers or people in a hurry, will sometimes masquerade under more alluring names, including *tsainii gazar* (tea house). Some of the ones on main streets now stay open 24 hours, but the usual hours are 10am to 7pm.

Restaurants, usually open 10am to 10pm daily, are nearly always more hygienic than *guanz* and therefore a good choice for children and families. Some stay open to midnight but the kitchen will close by 10pm.

You will probably be assigned an overly attentive waiter or waitress who will polish your silverware to perfection and pour your drinks. In Ulaanbaatar, many restaurants – especially the good ones – will be busy and often full between about 1pm and 2pm. It pays to get a table before 12.30pm to beat the rush.

Menus are usually in Cyrillic but use the decoder on p46 and point to what you want. Listed menu items are often not available *(baikhgui* means 'we don't have any') so you may need to make a few attempts.

Meals prices range from US$1 to US$3 for a basic meal to US$5 to US$8 for something at a Western-style restaurant. At some of the best places you may end up spending US$15 to US$20 or more, but this is rare. A value-added tax (VAT) will be added to your bill. Tipping is not required but is appreciated.

Quick Eats

The concept of the street café is new in Mongolia and many Mongolians feel awkward about eating on the pavement where, they claim, car exhaust and dust can pollute their meal. Likewise, Mongolians don't eat while on the go, with the exception of ice cream.

Some Mongolians, however, have warmed to the idea of shashlik (grilled meat kebabs). This delicious snack, served with bread and slices of onion and cucumber, is usually prepared by expat Uzbeks, but only in summer. While they may look very tempting, avoid the more itinerant-looking shashlik sellers as their meat is often low grade or old.

VEGETARIANS & VEGANS

Mongolia is a difficult, but not impossible, place for vegetarians. If you don't eat meat, you can get by in Ulaanbaatar, but in the countryside you will need to take your own supplements and preferably a petrol stove. Vegetables other than potatoes, carrots and onions are rare, relatively expensive and usually pickled in jars, so the best way for vegetarians to get protein is from the wide range of dairy products. In aimag capitals you can patch together a meal by poking around the shops. In villages you should be able to track down instant noodles and hot water. Hygiene can be an issue so it's best to boil or fry your vegetables.

Vegans will either have to be completely self-sufficient, or be prepared to modify their lifestyle for a while.

HABITS & CUSTOMS

While traditions and customs do surround the dinner table, Mongolian meals are generally casual affairs and there is little need to be overly concerned about offending your hosts.

In a ger in the countryside, traditional meals such as boiled mutton do not require silverware or even plates; just trawl around the bucket of bones until a slab catches your fancy. Eat with your fingers and try to nibble off as much meat and fat as possible; Mongolians can pick a bone clean and consider leftovers to be wasteful. There'll be a buck knife to slice off larger chunks. A common rag will appear at the end of the meal for

Scientists claim that drinking a few cups of *airag* (fermented mare milk) on a consistent basis can improve health, clear the skin and sharpen the eyesight.

A chunk of salt inside your *buuz* during Tsagaan Sar means safety and protection. If too much flour is used when preparing the dumplings and there are meat leftovers, it's a sign that the family will have enough clothing in the year ahead.

William of Rubruck's description of 13th-century Mongolian cuisine is at http://depts .washington.edu/silkroad (search for 'Rubruck Mongolia'). Based on his writings, it would seem the Mongols have been partial to a drink for the last 750 years.

DOS AND DON'TS AT THE TABLE

Do

- Cut food towards your body, not away.
- Accept food and drink with your right hand; use the left *only* to support your right elbow if the food is heavy.
- Drink tea immediately after receiving it; don't put it on the table until you have tried some.
- Take at least a sip, or a nibble, of the delicacies offered even if they don't please you.
- Hold a cup by the bottom, and not by the top rim.
- Cover your mouth when you are using a toothpick.

Don't

- Point a knife at anyone; when passing the knife, offer the handle.
- Get up in the middle of a meal and walk outside; wait until everyone is finished.
- Cross your legs or stick your feet out in front of you when eating; keep your legs together if seated or folded under you if on the floor.

Because of his failing health, the advisors of Ögedei Khaan (a son of Chinggis) suggested that he halve the number of cups of alcohol he drank per day. Ögedei readily agreed, then promptly ordered that his cups be doubled in size.

you to wipe off the grease (have a bandana ready if you are fussy about hygiene).

Most other meals in the rest of Mongolia are eaten with bowls, knives, forks and spoons. Chopsticks are only used at Chinese restaurants in Ulaanbaatar.

It is always polite to bring something to contribute to the meal; drinks are easiest, or in the countryside you could offer a bag of rice or sweets for desert. 'Bon appétit' in Mongolian is *saikhan khool loorai*.

Meals are occasionally interrupted for a round of vodka. Before taking a swig, a short ritual is employed to honour the sky gods and the four cardinal directions. There is no one way of doing this, but it usually involves dipping the left ring finger into the vodka and flicking into the air four times before wiping your finger across your forehead.

The woman of the household may offer you a variety of small food items. Try to taste everything you have been offered. An empty bowl is a sign to the host that you want more food. If you are full, just leave a little bit at the bottom of the bowl. If you are eating with Kazakhs, covering the bowl with your right hand means you are done.

EAT YOUR WORDS

Mongolian language is a scrambled-up soup of lispy vowels and throaty consonants. Get behind the cuisine scene by getting to know the language. For pronunciation guidelines, see p293.

The tradition of dipping the ring finger into vodka began centuries ago; if the silver ring on the finger changed colour after being submerged it meant that the vodka was poisoned.

Useful Phrases in Mongolian

I don't eat meat.	bi makh id-deggui	Би мах иддэггүй
Can I have a menu please?	bi khool·nii tses avch bo·lokh uu	Би хоолны цэс авч болох уу?
How much is it?	e·ne ya·mar ü·ne·tei ve	Энэ ямар үнэтэй вэ?
What food do you have today?	ö·nöö·dör ya·mar khool baina ve	Өнөөдөр ямар хоол байна вэ?
When will the food be ready?	khool khe·zee be·len bo·lokh ve	Хоол хэзээ бэлэн болох вэ?

Food Glossary

airag	айраг	fermented mare milk
aaruul	ааруул	dried curds
baitsaani zuush	байцааны зууш	cabbage salad
banshtai shöl	банштай шөл	dumpling soup
banshtai tsai	банштай цай	dumplings in tea
bifshteks	бифштекс	patty
boodog	боодог	meat roasted from the inside with hot stones
budaatai	будаатай	with rice
budaatai khuurag	будаатай хрраг	meat with rice
buuz	бууз	steamed mutton dumplings
guriltai shöl	гурилтай шөл	handmade noodle soup
goimontoi shöl	гоймонтой шөл	noodle soup
khoniny makh	хонины мах	mutton
khool	хоол	food
khoormog	хоормог	camel yogurt
khorkhog	хорхог	mutton, water and hot stones cooked in a pot
khuurag	хрраг	fried food
khuushuur	хуушуур	fried meat pancake
luuvangiin zuush	луувангийн зууш	carrot salad
makh	мах	meat
niislel salad	нийслэл салат	potato salad
nogoon salad	ногоон салат	vegetable salad
nogootoi	ногоотой	with vegetables
öröm	өрөм	cream
rashaan us	рашаан ус	mineral water
shar airag	шар айраг	beer
sharsan öndög	шарсан өндөг	fried egg
sharsan takhia	шарсан тахиа	fried chicken
shnitsel	шницель	schnitzel
shöl	шөл	soup
süü	сүү	milk
süütei budaa	сүүтэй будаа	milk with rice
süütei tsai	сүүтэй цай	Mongolian milk tea
talkh	талх	bread
tömstei	төмстэй	with potato
tsai	цай	tea
tsagaanidee	цагаан-идээ	white food (dairy)
tsötsgii	цөцгий	sour cream
tsuivan	цуйван	fried slices of dough with meat
zagas	загас	fish
zaidas/sosisk	зайдас/сосик	sausage

Environment

Mongolia is the sort of country that naturalists dream about. With the world's lowest population density, huge tracts of virgin landscape, minimal infrastructure, varied ecosystems and abundant wildlife, Mongolia is rightfully considered to hold the last bastion of unspoiled land in Asia. Mongolia's nomadic past, which did not require cities or infrastructure, along with Shamanic prohibitions against defiling the earth, have for centuries protected the country from overdevelopment.

Traditional beliefs, however, are always at odds with modern economics. The environmental situation started going downhill when the Soviets introduced mining, railways, factories and power plants, but compared with the disastrous environmental record evoked in China or neighbouring Central Asian countries such as Kazakhstan and Uzbekistan, Mongolia emerged from this period relatively unscathed. The new threat is capitalism. With no more subsidies coming from the USSR, Mongolia has spent nearly two decades looking for ways to earn revenue, and the easiest solution has been the sale of its resources. Consequently, the wildlife and landscape are now being degraded at an alarming rate, but there is hope among conservationists that ecotourism will provide a new direction for government fiscal policy.

THE LAND

Conservation Ink (www .conservationink.org) produces maps and postcards dedicated to Mongolia's national parks. The website contains links, information and beautiful photography.

Mongolia is a huge landlocked country. At 1,566,500 sq km in area, it's about three times the size of France, over twice the size of Texas and almost as large as Queensland in Australia. Apart from the period of Mongol conquest under Chinggis Khaan and Kublai Khaan, Mongolia was until the 20th century about twice its present size. A large chunk of Siberia was once part of Mongolia but is now securely controlled by Russia, and Inner Mongolia is now firmly part of China.

The southern third of Mongolia is dominated by the Gobi Desert, which stretches into China. Only the southern sliver of the Gobi is 'Lawrence of Arabia–type desert' with cliffs and sand dunes. The rest is desert steppe and has sufficient grass to support scattered herds of sheep, goats and camels. There are also areas of desert steppe in low-lying parts of western Mongolia.

Much of the rest of Mongolia is covered by grasslands. Stretching over about 20% of the country, these steppes are home to vast numbers of gazelle, birdlife and livestock. The central, northern and western aimags (provinces), amounting to about 25% of Mongolia, are classed as mountain forest steppe. Home to gazelle and saiga antelope, they have relatively large numbers of people and livestock.

Mongolia's Wild Heritage (1999), by Christopher Finch, was written in collaboration with the Mongolian Ministry of Nature & Environment. This outstanding book contains excellent photos and brief but relevant information on Mongolia's fragile ecology.

Mongolia is also one of the highest countries in the world, with an average elevation of 1580m. In the far west are Mongolia's highest mountains, the Mongol Altai Nuruu, which are permanently snowcapped. The highest peak, glaciated Tavan Bogd Uul (4374m), towers over Mongolia, Russia and China. Between the peaks are stark but beautiful deserts where rain almost never falls.

The far northern areas of Khövsgöl and Khentii aimags are essentially the southern reaches of Siberia and are covered by larch and pine forests known by the Russian word 'taiga'.

Near the centre of Mongolia is the Khangai Nuruu range, with its highest peak, Otgon Tenger Uul, reaching 3905m. On the northern slope of these mountains is the source of the Selenge Gol, Mongolia's largest river, which flows northward into Lake Baikal in Siberia. While the Selenge Gol is the largest in terms of water volume, the longest river is the Kherlen Gol in eastern Mongolia.

Just to the northeast of Ulaanbaatar is the Khentii Nuruu, the highest mountain range in eastern Mongolia and by far the most accessible to hikers. It's a heavily forested region with meandering rivers and impressive peaks, the highest being Asralt Khairkhan Uul (2800m). The range provides a major watershed between the Arctic and Pacific oceans.

Mongolia has numerous saltwater and freshwater lakes, which are great for camping, bird-watching, hiking, swimming and fishing. The largest is the low-lying, saltwater Uvs Nuur, but the most popular is the magnificent Khövsgöl Nuur, the second-oldest lake in the world, which contains 65% of Mongolia's (and 2% of the world's) fresh water.

Other geological and geographical features include caves (some with ancient rock paintings), dormant volcanoes, hot and cold mineral springs, the Orkhon Khürkhree (Orkhon Waterfall), Great Lakes Depression in western Mongolia and Darkhad Depression west of Khövsgöl Nuur.

WILDLIFE

In Mongolia, the distinction between domestic and wild (or untamed) animals is often blurry. Wild and domesticated horses and camels mingle on the steppes with wild asses and herds of wild gazelle. In the mountains there are enormous (and horned) wild argali sheep and domesticated yaks along with wild moose, musk deer and roe deer. Reindeer herds are basically untamed, but strangely enough they can be ridden and are known to return to the same tent each night for a salt-lick.

Animals

Wildlife flourishes in Mongolia despite a number of impediments: an extreme climate, the nomadic fondness for hunting, the communist persecution of Buddhists who had set aside areas as animal sanctuaries and a penniless government that lacks the political will to police nature-protection laws. Your chances of seeing some form of wildlife are good, though the closest

Roy Chapman Andrews wrote several excellent books on Mongolia's flora and fauna following his research expeditions across the country in the early 1920s. Look out for his classic titles *Across Mongolian Plains* and *On the Trail of Ancient Man*.

THE GREAT ZUD

The winters of 1999–2000 to 2001–02 were the coldest and longest in living memory. They were classed as *zud*, a Mongolian word that can mean any condition that stops livestock getting to grass; in this case heavy snowfall and an impenetrable ice cover. Unusually early snowfalls compounded an earlier summer drought and rodent infestation, which left animals emaciated and pastures degraded before winter even hit. Other causes for the *zud* trace back 10 years; the move towards capitalism promoted the boom in livestock that caused overgrazing, leaving pastures tired and depleted. After three bad winters the livestock population plummeted from 33 million to 24 million.

In the worst-hit areas of Dundgov, Bayankhongor, Arkhangai and Övörkhangai, herders lost a quarter to half of their livestock (their only form of income, food, fuel, security – almost everything, in fact). The disaster was equal to the great *zud* of 1944, when 7.5 million livestock were lost, but at that time herders had the safety net of the communist collective. During the recent freeze, only a handful of international agencies came to the aid of the herders.

Some analysts have suggested that the disaster was exacerbated by the inexperience of numerous new herders, who chose not to embark on the traditional month-long trek *(otor)*, which takes herders to other pastures in autumn. Tragically, the poorest herders were the most affected, just when they least needed it. In the years since the *zud*, many of the affected herders migrated to Ulaanbaatar to seek work (see the boxed text, p77) or entered the field of illegal gold prospecting (p147).

you will realistically get to a snow leopard *(irbis)*, argali sheep *(argal)* or moose *(khandgai)* is in a museum.

Despite the lack of water in the Gobi, numerous species (many of which are endangered) somehow survive. These include the Gobi argali sheep, wild camel *(khavtgai)*, Asiatic wild ass *(khulan)*, Gobi bear *(mazaalai)*, ibex *(yangir)* and black-tailed gazelle *(khar suult zeer)*. In the wide open steppe you may see the rare saiga antelope, Mongolian gazelle *(tsagaan zeer)*, several species of jerboa *(alag daaga)*, which is a rodent endemic to Central Asia, and millions of furry marmots *(tarvaga)*, waking up after their last hibernation or preparing for the next.

Further north in the forests live the wild boar *(zerleg gakhai)*, brown bear *(khuren baavgai)*, roe deer *(bor görös)*, wolf *(chono)*, reindeer *(tsaa buga)*, elk *(khaliun buga)*, musk deer *(khuder)* and moose, as well as plenty of sable *(bulga)* and lynx *(shiluus)*, whose furs, unfortunately, are in high demand. Most of the mountains are extremely remote, thus providing an ideal habitat for argali sheep, ibex, the very rare snow leopard and smaller mammals such as the fox, ermine and hare.

BIRDS

Mongolia is home to 469 recorded species of bird. In the desert you may see the desert warbler, saxaul sparrow *(boljmor)* and McQueen's bustard *(toodog)*, as well as sandgrouse, finch *(byalzuuhai)* and the cinereous vulture *(tas)*.

On the steppes, you will certainly see the most charismatic bird in Mongolia – the demoiselle crane *(övögt togoruu)* – as well as the hoopoe *(övöölj)*, the odd falcon *(shonkhor)*, vulture *(yol)*, and golden and steppe eagle *(bürged)*. Other steppe species include the upland buzzard *(sar)*, black kite *(sokhor elee)* and some varieties of owl *(shar shuvuu)* and hawk *(khartsaga)*. Some black kites will even swoop down and catch pieces of bread in midair if you throw the pieces high enough. These magnificent raptors, perched majestically on a rock by the side of the road, will rarely be disturbed by your jeep or the screams of your guide ('Look. Eagle!! Bird!! We stop?') but following the almost inaudible click of your lens cap, these birds will move and almost be in China before you have even thought about apertures.

In the mountains, you may be lucky to spot species of ptarmigan *(tsagaan yatuu)*, bunting *(khömrög byalzuuhai)*, woodpecker *(tonshuul)*, owl and the endemic Altai snowcock *(khoilog)*. The lakes of the west and north are visited by Dalmatian pelican *(khoton)*, hooded crane *(khar togoruu)*, relict gull *(tsakhlai)* and bar-headed goose.

Eastern Mongolia has the largest breeding population of cranes, including the hooded and Siberian varieties and the critically endangered white-naped crane *(tsen togoruu)*, of which only 4500 remain in the wild.

FISH

Rivers such as the Selenge, Orkhon, Zavkhan, Balj, Onon and Egiin, as well as dozens of lakes, including Khövsgöl Nuur, hold 76 species of fish. They include trout, grayling *(khadran)*, roach, lenok *(zebge)*, Siberian sturgeon *(khilem)*, pike *(tsurkhai)*, perch *(algana)*, the endemic Altai osman and the enormous taimen, a Siberian relative of the salmon, which can grow up to 1.5m in length and weigh up to 50kg.

ENDANGERED SPECIES

According to conservationists, 28 species of mammals are endangered in Mongolia. The more commonly known species are the wild ass, wild camel, argali sheep, Gobi bear and ibex; others include otter, wolf, saiga antelope and some species of jerboa. The red deer is also in dire straits; over the past

---

The Wildlife Conservation Society's Mongolia programme strives to address wildlife conservation issues through various approaches that reach local communities, wildlife biologists, provincial governments and national ministries. Read more at www.wcs.org/Mongolia.

Mongolians consider wolf parts and organs to contain curative properties. The meat and lungs are good for respiratory ailments, the intestines aid in digestion, powdered wolf rectum can soothe the pain of haemorrhoids and hanging a wolf tongue around ones neck will cure gland and thyroid ailments.

Mongolia's river monsters, known as taimen, are the ultimate strike for some anglers. Taimen Conservation Fund has created an enlightening video on YouTube (www.youtube.com and search for 'Mongolia taimen').

two decades its numbers have dropped from 130,000 to just 8000 (and falling). Brown bears have also been hit hard by poachers – in October 2000, Vietnamese smugglers were caught trying to leave Mongolia with 80 brown-bear gall bladders (each worth up to US$200).

There are 22 species of endangered birds, including many species of hawk, falcon, buzzard, crane and owl. Despite Mongolian belief that it's bad luck to kill a crane, the elegant white-naped crane is threatened with extinction due to habitat loss. German ornithologists have recently conducted surveys on the crane and estimate there are just 5000 breeding pairs left in the wild. The best place to see them is in Dornod's Mongol Daguur Strictly Protected Area (p174).

Every year the government allows up to 300 falcons to be captured and sold abroad; the major buyers are the royal families of Kuwait and the United Arab Emirates. A licence for each bird costs US$4600. On top of this, unknown numbers of other falcons (possibly in their hundreds) are illegally smuggled out of the country. As a direct result, breeding pairs dropped from 3000 to 2200 over the past five years.

One positive news story is the resurrection of the *takhi* wild horse. The *takhi* was actually extinct in the wild in the 1960s. It has been successfully reintroduced into three special protected areas after an extensive breeding program overseas. For more on the *takhi* see p116.

In preserved areas of the mountains, about 1000 snow leopards remain. They are hunted for their pelts (which are also part of some shamanist and Buddhist traditional practices), as are the leopards' major source of food, the marmot. For details on the attempt to save the snow leopard see p216.

Each year the government sells licences to hunt 300 ibex and 40 argali sheep, both endangered species, netting the government more than US$500,000.

Plants

Mongolia can be roughly divided into three zones: grassland and shrubland (55% of the country); forests, which only cover parts of the mountain steppe (8%); and desert (36%). Less than 1% of the country is used for human settlements and crop cultivation. Grasslands are used extensively for grazing and, despite the vast expanses, overgrazing is not uncommon.

Forests of Siberian larch (sometimes up to 45m in height), Siberian and Scotch pine, and white and ground birch cover parts of northern Mongolia.

In the Gobi the saxaul shrub covers millions of hectares and is essential in anchoring the desert sands and preventing degradation and erosion. Saxaul takes a century to grow to around 4m in height, creating wood so dense that it sinks in water.

Khentii aimag and some other parts of central Mongolia are famous for the effusion of red, yellow and purple wildflowers, mainly rhododendrons and edelweiss. Extensive grazing is the major threat to Mongolia's flowers, trees and shrubs; more than 200 species are endangered.

PROTECTED AREAS

The Ministry of Nature & Environment (MNE) and its **Special Protected Areas Administration** (SPAA; ☎ 011-326 617; fax 328 620; Baga Toiruu 44, Ulaanbaatar) control the national park system with a tiny annual budget of around US$650,000. With this budget and substantial financial assistance and guidance from international governments and nongovernmental organisations, the animals, flora and environment in some parts of the country are being preserved. Unfortunately, in many protected areas the implementation of park regulations is weak, if not nonexistent.

Silent Steppe: The Illegal Wildlife Trade Crisis (July 2006), published by the Netherlands-Mongolia Trust Fund for Environmental Reform (NEMO), is an important publication that highlights the decimation of wildlife in Mongolia. You can download the document by going to the World Bank website (www.worldbank.org/nemo).

The *takhi* horse also goes by the name Przewalski's horse. It was named after Colonel Nikolai Przewalski, an officer in the Russian Imperial Army who made the horse's existence known to Europe after an exploratory expedition to Central Asia in 1878.

American actress Julia Roberts stepped out of her usual star-studded element in 2000 to host a documentary on the horses and nomad culture of Mongolia. The programme was filmed by Tigress Productions (UK) and can be viewed at the Khustain Nuruu information centre (p115).

THE FIVE SNOUTS

Mongolians define themselves as the 'people of five animals' *(tavan kosighu mal):* horses, cattle (including yaks), sheep, goats and Bactrian camels. The odd one out is the reindeer, which is herded in small numbers by the Tsaatan people *(tsaa* means 'reindeer') near the Siberian border. Chickens and pigs are rare in Mongolia. A rough ratio exists for the relative values of the five animals: a horse is worth five to seven sheep or seven to 10 goats. A camel is worth 1½ horses.

The horse *(mor)* is the pride of Mongolia and there are few, if any, nomads who haven't learned to ride as soon as they can walk. Mongolian horses are shorter than those in other countries (don't call them ponies – Mongolians will be offended). They provide perfect transport, can endure harsh winters and, importantly, produce that much-loved Mongolian beverage: fermented mare milk, or *airag.* Mongolians have more than 300 different words to describe the country's two million horses, mostly relating to colouring.

Together, cows *(ükher)* and yaks *(sarlag)* number around two million, and are used for milk, meat (especially *borts,* which is dried and salted meat) and for their hides. Most yaks are actually a cross between a yak and a cow (known as a *hainag* in Mongolian), as *hainags* supply more milk than thoroughbred yaks.

Fat-tailed sheep *(khon)* are easy to herd and provide wool for clothes, carpets and ger insulation, as well as meat (the ubiquitous mutton) – every nomadic family wants to own at least a few sheep. Goats *(yamaa)* are popular for their meat and, especially, for cashmere wool. There are around 11.5 million sheep and 11 million goats in Mongolia.

Camels *(temee)* are used for long-distance (though slow) transport, and once crossed Mongolia in large caravans. Considered valuable for their adaptability and their wool, they number about 260,000. They're considered proud, intelligent creatures and actually quite athletic – Mongolians have recently put them to use as charges in a new camel-polo club.

The MNE classifies protected areas into four categories (from most protected to least):

Strictly Protected Areas Very fragile areas of great importance; hunting, logging and development is strictly prohibited and there is no established human influence.

National Parks Places of historical and educational interest; fishing and grazing by nomadic people is allowed and parts of the park are developed for ecotourism.

Natural & Historical Monuments Important places of historical and cultural interest; development is allowed within guidelines.

Nature Reserves Less important regions protecting rare species of flora and fauna, and archaeological sites; some development is allowed within certain guidelines.

The 60 protected areas in Mongolia now constitute an impressive 13.8% of the country (21.52 million hectares). The strictly protected areas of Bogdkhan Uul, Great Gobi, Uvs Nuur Basin, Dornod Mongol and Khustain Nuruu are biosphere reserves included in Unesco's Man and Biosphere Project.

At the time of independence in 1990, some proposed that the *entire country* be turned into a national park, but the government settled on 30% (potentially creating the world's largest park system). This goal, however, has stalled in recent years as the government has given favour to expanding mining operations and the sale of mining rights.

Permits

To visit Mongolia's parks – especially strictly protected areas, national parks and some monuments – you will need a permit, either from the local SPAA office or from rangers at the entrances to the parks. The permits are little more than an entrance fee, but they are an important source of revenue for the maintenance of the parks.

Mongolians collect various wild herbs and flowers for their medicinal properties: yellow poppies to heal wounds, edelweiss to add vitamins to the blood, and feather grass to cure an upset stomach.

The area around Bogdkhan Uul, near Ulaanbaatar, was protected from hunting and logging as early as the 12th century, and was officially designated as a national park in 1778.

National Parks	Features	Activities	Time to visit
Altai Tavan Bogd National Park (p229)	mountains, glaciers, lakes: argali sheep, ibex, snow leopard, eagle, falcon	mountaineering, horse trekking, backpacking, fishing, eaglehunting (in winter)	Jun–Sep
Gorkhi-Terelj National Park (p104)	rugged hills, boulders, streams	river rafting, hiking, mountain biking, rock climbing, camping, cross-country skiing, horse riding	year-round
Gurvan Saikhan National Park (p208)	desert mountains, canyons, sand dunes: Gobi argali sheep, ibex, black-tailed gazelle	hiking, sand-dune sliding, camel trekking, bird-watching	May–Oct
Khorgo-Terkhiin Tsagaan Nuur National Park (p130)	lake and mountains: wolf, deer, fox	fishing, hiking, horse trekking, bird-watching	May–Sep
Khövsgöl Nuur National Park (p152)	lake, mountains, rivers: fish, moose, wolverine, bear, sable, elk, roe deer	mountain biking, kayaking, fishing, hiking, horse trekking, bird-watching	Jun–Sep
Khustain National Park (p115)	rugged hills and the Tuul river: *takhi* horse, gazelle, deer, wolf, lynx, manul wild cat	trekking, wildlife spotting	Apr–Oct
Otgon Tenger Uul Strictly Protected Area (p245)	mountains, rivers, lakes: argali sheep, roe deer, wolf	horse trekking, hiking, swimming	May–Sep

Entrance fees are set at T3000 per foreigner and T300 per Mongolian (although guides and drivers are often excluded).

If you are not able to get a permit and are found in a park without one, the worst penalty you're likely to suffer is being asked to leave or pay a fine to the park ranger.

If you think you might need permits for conducting research in a park, it's best to contact the MNE's SPAA department directly. The ministry is located just behind the Ulaanbaatar Hotel (Map pp70–1) in UB.

ENVIRONMENTAL ISSUES

Mongolia's natural environment remains in good shape compared with that of many Western countries. The country's small population and no-madic subsistence economy have been its environmental salvation.

However, Mongolia does have its share of problems. Communist production quotas in the past put pressure on grasslands to yield more crops and support more livestock than was sustainable. The rise in the number of herders and livestock has wreaked havoc on the grasslands; some 70% of pastureland is degraded and near village centres around 80% of plant species have disappeared.

Forest fires, nearly all of which are caused by careless human activity, are common during the windy spring season. The fires destroy huge tracts of forest and grassland, mainly in Khentii and Dornod aimags. In 1996 alone around 80,000 sq km of land was scorched, causing up to US$1.9 billion of damage.

Other threats to the land include mining, which has polluted 28 river basins in eight aimags (there are more than 300 mines in Mongolia). The huge Oyu Tolgoi mine in Ömnögov will require the use of 360L of water *per second*, which environmentalists say might not be sustainable. China's insatiable appetite for minerals and gas is opening up new mines, but the bigger threat is China's hunt for the furs, meat and body parts of endangered animals. Chinese demand has resulted in a 75% decline in the number of marmots and an 85% drop in the number of saiga antelope.

The World Wide Fund for Nature website at www .wwf.mn has relevant news on Mongolia's environment and topical information that affects the country. It also includes statistics, data and conservation threats.

In 2007 Tsetsegee Munkhbayar, a herder from central Mongolia, was awarded the prestigious Goldman Environmental Prize for his efforts to block aggressive mining on the Ongii River. You can watch a short video on his heroic story at www.goldmanprize .org/node/606.

RESPONSIBLE ECOTOURISM

Mongolia's environment, flora and fauna are precious. Decades of Soviet exploitation, urban sprawl and development have greatly affected the ecology; Mongolia does not need tourism to exacerbate the problems. Please bear the following pointers in mind as you travel around the country. If camping or hiking, please note the boxed text on p60. In protected areas or areas of natural beauty try to keep to existing jeep tracks rather than pioneering new trails, which quickly degenerate into an eroded mess.

■ Patronise travel companies and ger camps that you feel advance sustainable development, safe waste management, water conservation and fair employment practices.

■ When on a jeep trip have a designated rubbish bag. Make an effort to carry out rubbish left by others.

■ Don't buy goods made from endangered species.

■ Don't engage in or encourage hunting. It is illegal in all parks and reserves.

■ Don't spend all your money with one company (easily done on a tour) but spread your money through the economy. Support local services, guides and initiatives.

■ When fishing, buy a permit and practise standard 'catch and release' policy. Use barbless hooks.

While browsing through Ulaanbaatar souvenir shops keep an eye out for two great ecology books: *Lake Khövsgöl National Park – A Visitor's Guide* (1997), published by Discovery Initiatives, and *The Gobi Gurvansaikhan National Park*, written by Bernd Steinhauer-Burkart.

Urban sprawl, coupled with a demand for wood to build homes and for heating and cooking, is slowly reducing the forests. This destruction of the forests has also lowered river levels, especially the Tuul Gol near Ulaanbaatar. In recent years the Tuul has actually gone dry in the spring months due to land mismanagement and improper water use.

Large-scale infrastructure projects are further cause for concern. The 18m-tall Dörgön hydropower station, currently being built on the Chon Khairkh Gol in Khovd, will submerge canyons and pastures. The dam threatens fish and will only run in summer when electricity is in lower demand compared with winter.

Conservationists are also concerned about the 'Millennium Rd' which will likely cut through important gazelle migration routes in eastern Mongolia. Its completion is sure to increase mining and commerce inside fragile ecosystems.

Air pollution is becoming a serious problem, especially in Ulaanbaatar. At the top of Zaisan Memorial in the capital, a depressing layer of dust and smoke from the city's three thermal power stations can be seen hovering over the city. This layer is often appalling in winter, when all homes are continuously burning fuel and the power stations are working overtime. Ulaanbaatar has also suffered from acid rain, and pollution is killing fish in nearby Tuul Gol in central Mongolia.

Mongolia Outdoors

Mongolia is a giant outdoor park. With scattered settlements, few roads and immense areas of steppe, mountain and forest, the entire country beckons the outdoor enthusiast. But the lack of infrastructure is a double-edged sword: while there are many areas that have potential for eco-tourism, only a few (ie Khövsgöl Nuur, Terkhiin Tsagaan Nuur and Terelj National Park) can really handle independent travellers. Signing up with a tour group, on the other hand, gives you instant logistical help. Tour agencies can act like mobile support centres, using vans, trucks and helicopters to shuttle clients and their gear around. Independent travellers hoping to explore remote areas of the country will need to be completely self-sufficient. This chapter provides tips on how to deal with these logistical hurdles.

CYCLE TOURING

Mongolia is an adventure cyclist's dream. There are few fences, lots of open spaces and very little traffic. Roads are mainly dirt but the jeep trails are usually hard-packed earth, allowing you to cover 40km to 50km per day. Overlanding by bike does require careful planning and thought; you'll need to be totally self-sufficient in terms of tools and spare parts. Other factors include washed-out bridges, trails that disappear into rivers or marshland and, in late summer, heavy rain and mud. On the plus side, locals will be pleasantly intrigued by your bike. You'll have lots of chances to swap your bike for a horse and go for a short canter, but don't forget to show your Mongolian counterpart the brakes! A few more tips to keep in mind:

- Dogs can be ferocious and will chase you away from gers. If you stop and hold your ground they will back off; it helps to pick up a rock. The faster you cycle away the more they want to chase you.
- Cyclists usually follow river valleys. However, in Mongolia it's often better to go over the mountains. Roads along rivers are usually sandy or consist of loose stones that make riding difficult.
- Most cyclists consider the best trip to be a cross-country adventure but in Mongolia (where there are vast areas of nothingness) consider focussing on one small area and doing a loop. There are great routes to explore in Khövsgöl and Bayan-Ölgii aimags.
- Bring all the spare parts you may need, including brake pads, cables and inner tubes. Spare parts are hard to find in Mongolia, but you could try the Seven Summits (p93) in Ulaanbaatar.

Planning a cycle tour of Mongolia? Have a look at Freewheelers Mongolia Route website (www .geocities.com/aliingi /mongolia/mongoliaroute .html), which has day-by-day details of usual bike routes in Mongolia.

Gear, Bike Hire & Tours

Mountain bikes are most suitable for Mongolia's rough terrain. But if you are planning on doing a long-distance trip, a touring bike with wide wheels will also suffice. Bring all your equipment from home as the stuff on offer in Mongolia is often unreliable, poor quality or may not be available. Otherwise, you could try renting a bike from the Seven Summits, Mongolia Expeditions (p81) or Karakorum Expeditions (p81) in Ulaanbaatar. Guided tours are led by **Bike Mongolia** (www.bikemongolia.com). In summer, Korean-made bikes are sold in the plaza opposite the State Department Store.

Routes

The following trips require several days. They can be made solo provided you are equipped with a tent, sleeping bag, food, tools and spare parts. Another option is to use vehicle support; hire a jeep and driver to take you

---

ABANDON JEEP

In the past, most travellers rocked up to Mongolia with one plan in mind: hop into a jeep, set off across the steppes and tour the major sights, stopping to stay in ger camps, ride horses and meet nomad families. While the jeep is still a valid travel option, there are many alternatives, including the following:

▪ Volunteering – Join a volunteer project in Ulaanbaatar's ger districts with Rinky Dink Travel Mongolia (p81)

▪ Ger to Ger programme – Walk, horse trek and raft between nomadic families (p59)

▪ Dog sledding – Join guide Joel Rauzy on a winter dog-sled trip in Terelj or Khövsgöl (p82)

▪ Rock climbing – Grab some granite in Terelj (p112) or Dundgov (p198)

▪ Ranch work – Bust some broncos at the Anak Ranch (p144)

▪ Yak carting – Available in Terelj through Nomadic Journeys (p81)

▪ Backcountry walking – Trek near Kharkhiraa Uul (p241) in Uvs aimag or do the Khövsgöl Lake-to-Renchinlkhumbe route (p156)

▪ Cycle touring – Pedal your way across the country (p55)

▪ Dune-buggy tour – Kick up some dirt with a buggy; contact Vast Gobi (p251)

---

out to the best biking areas and keep all your gear in the vehicle while you ride unhindered. For this type of trip, a vehicle will cost around US$35 to US$40 per day, plus petrol costs. This small investment will definitely make life easier and will also provide security; it makes a lot of sense if you are travelling in a group.

Note that these routes are only starter suggestions. You could cycle around many areas of northern, eastern and western Mongolia; consult with travel experts in Ulaanbaatar about the possibilities (p80). Mongolia Expeditions, Seven Summits and Tseren Tours are places to start. Gobi areas, due to their lack of water and facilities, are places to avoid.

OUT OF ULAANBAATAR

The roads out of Ulaanbaatar are busy with cars and trucks so try getting a lift 100km out of town until the traffic thins out. Remember that you can also ride on the dirt tracks to the side of the modern highways. Heading west, if you are travelling to Tsetserleg, take the route that goes to Ögii Nuur and Tsetserleg (the direct route from Dahinchinlen to Kharkhorin is an awful mess of sand and mud).

ERDENET TO TERKHIIN TSAGAAN NUUR

This multi-day adventure takes you from the rolling, forested hills of Bulgan to the more rugged Arkhangai. Start by taking the train or bus from Ulaanbaatar to Erdenet. If you ride to Erdenet don't miss a side trip to Amarbayasgalant Khiid.

From Erdenet, travel due west of the town to Bugat, a 27km ride, then continue west on what is essentially the road to Khövsgöl. It will take about three days to cover the 160km of trails that connect Bugat to Khairkhan, just inside Arkhangai aimag. You'll find rolling steppe and hard roads the whole way.

From Khairkhan it's another two days to Ikh Tamir (approx 140km). From Ikh Tamir you can follow the Tamir River west, then follow the road when it splits from the river and continue to the town of Chuluut. From here you continue down the Chuluut River to Tariat and Terkhiin Tsagaan Nuur.

CHINGGIS KHAAN TRAIL

This trail in northern Khentii offers plenty of cultural heritage and nice riding terrain. Get a ride from Ulaanbaatar to Tsenkhermandal in Khentii aimag, then cycle north to Khökh Nuur, buried deep in the Khentii Mountains. Continue northwest to Khangal Nuur and the very bumpy road to Balden Bereeven Khiid; another 17km brings you to the deer stones and then Öglögchiin Kherem. Continue to Batshireet, Binder and finally, Dadal. This trip takes four to six days. From here, either return to Ulaanbaatar or continue your trip into northern Dornod and the towns of Bayan-Uul, Bayandun and Dashbalbar.

ULAANGOM TO ÖLGII

It's difficult to get lost on this route in northwestern Mongolia, which follows the main jeep trail from Ulaangom to Ölgii city. You'll pass by lakes, over mountain passes and through dramatic canyons. From Ulaangom, travel northwest over Üüreg Nuur. Veer south over Bairam Pass and then onto the coal mining town of Khotgor. Cycle to the southeast corner of Achit Nuur (where there is a bridge over the river) and follow the road to the Khovd Gol canyon. The section from Achit Nuur to the canyon is hot, dry and buggy so you'll want to move quickly through this area. The 18km stretch through the canyon is the most scenic part of the trip. It's another 17km from the end of the canyon to Ölgii. From Ölgii you could continue on to Altai Tavan Bogd National Park. Get a ride into the park from a local driver, explore the area with your bike and then cycle back to Ölgii.

KHÖVSGÖL AIMAG

Khövsgöl is a great area for cycling; there are numerous attractions and various route options. A nice route leads south from Mörön to Tariat in Arkhangai, via the towns of Shine-Ider, Galt and Jargalant. The more popular route is from Mörön up to Khatgal and then along either side of Khövsgöl Nuur. The slightly more adventurous could cycle in the spectacular Chandman-Öndör area.

TSETSERLEG TO BAYANKHONGOR

This 200km route, from Tsetserleg in Arkhangai to Bayankhongor city, takes four days and involves lots of river crossings and loose stones. This is a difficult and challenging trip with rugged terrain, travelling over alpine passes in Khangai Nuruu National Park. On the first day it's 32km from Tsetserleg to Bulgan *sum* centre; camp near the town or just past it. On the second night plan on camping around 10km south of the last pass. On the third day it's downhill but you'll need to cross the Tüin Gol a few times. There are plenty of camping spots near the river as you head south towards Erdenetsogt. On the fourth day you pass through Erdenetsogt before reaching Bayankhongor; this is the most difficult day with lots of rocks before Erdenetsogt.

ÖLGII TO ULAANBAATAR

This mammoth 1450km expedition will take three or four weeks. In summer, the prevailing winds in Mongolia travel from west to east, which means that you'll enjoy tailwinds if you start in Ölgii and end in Ulaanbaatar. Ending in UB also gives you something to look forward to – a cold beer at Dave's Place (p91)! The northern route, via either Mörön or Tosontsengel, is more interesting than the southern Gobi route.

Cyclists should pick up a copy of *Where the Pavement Ends*, by Erika Warmbrunn, which describes the author's sometimes harrowing account of biking through Mongolia, China and Vietnam. It's well written and provides useful cultural insight for cyclists travelling across the steppes.

FISHING

With Mongolia's large number of lakes *(nuur)* and rivers *(gol)*, and a sparse population that generally prefers red meat, the fish are just waiting to be caught. The best places to dangle your lines are at Khövsgöl Nuur (p155), for grayling and lenok, and Terkhiin Tsagaan Nuur (p130), which has a lot of pike. The season is mid-June to late September. You can get a fishing permit from the national park office. Permits are valid for two days or 10 fish, whichever comes first. For the truly intrepid, visit either lake in winter for some hard-core ice fishing.

Outside magazine carries a touching article on its website about fly-fishing in northern Mongolia. Go to http://outside.away .com and enter 'fly-fishing Mongolia' in the site's search engine.

Serious anglers will want to try out Mongolia's rivers – the fly-fishing is some of the best anywhere. The major target is taimen, an enormous salmonoid that spends its leisure time hunting down unfortunate marmots attempting to cross the river. These monsters can reach 1.5m in length and weigh 50kg. Unfortunately they are also prized by poachers and are thus carefully guarded by locals along the river. To avoid any problems, you must fish for taimen with a reputable outfitter. Catch and release is standard practice. Outfitters run fishing trips on the Ider, Chuluut, Selenge, Orkhon, Eg, Onon and Delgermörön Gols.

While it's relatively easy to get a fishing permit in a national park, buying one for other areas is much more difficult. Anglers must have a special permit authorised by the **Ministry of Nature & Environment** (☎ 011-326 617, fax 011-328 620; Baga Toiruu 44, Ulaanbaatar), which costs US$50 a week. But to get the permit you need a contract with the *sum* where you plan to fish and approval by the aimag. Obviously this is not possible for casual tourists – the whole system has been set up so that it can be effectively managed by tour operators. Before signing up, make sure your outfitter has the necessary agreements and permits; some take the risk of fishing illegally which can get you in big trouble if you're caught.

Responsible outfitters concerned with poaching have started the Taimen Conservation Fund (www .taimen.org), which works with local communities to protect the rivers. Efforts are being made to ensure that locals benefit from tourism (some are hired as guides and wranglers).

If you fish without a permit you will be fined and have your equipment confiscated. Killing a taimen brings more problems than you want to deal with – locals believe such an offence brings misery to 999 human souls.

Four responsible fly-fishing tour operators are **Mongolia River Outfitters** (www.mongoliarivers.com), **Fish Mongolia** (www.fishmongolia.co.uk), **Sweetwater Travel** (www .sweetwatertravel.com/mongolia.htm) and **Nemekh Tour** (www.nemekh.com). The cost for two people on an 11-day package trip will be in the neighbourhood of US$3500 all-inclusive, more if you take a Cessna flight direct to the camps from UB.

It's possible to buy equipment in Mongolia but, to ensure you have the best quality stuff, bring it from home (use barbless hooks to protect the fish). In many places, all you need is a strong handline and a lure.

HIKING

Anglers heading out to the rivers and lakes should pack a copy of Fishing in Mongolia, published by the US-based Avery Press.

As a country with few cars or paved roads, hiking opportunities abound. The biggest obstacle faced by hikers is finding transport to the mountains once they get far afield from Ulaanbaatar. However, in the regions around Bogdkhan Uul (p107) and Terelj (p111), which are not far from Ulaanbaatar, there are enough mountains to keep hikers busy for a few days.

Pay any fees and procure any permits required by local authorities. Be aware of local laws, regulations and etiquette about wildlife and the environment. Decent maps are hard to come by. The 1:1,000,000 topographic maps available in Ulaanbaatar are your best bet.

Mosquitoes and midges are a curse. The situation is at its worst during spring and early summer, with the marshy lakes and canyons in the western deserts the most troublesome areas.

In western Mongolia, prime hiking areas include the Altai Tavan Bogd National Park (p229) around Khoton Nuur or between the lakes and Tavan

---

GER TO GER

As the most innovative tourism concept in Mongolia, the **Ger to Ger programme** (Map pp70-1; ☎ 313 336; www.gertoger.org; Arizona Plaza, Suite 11, Baruun Selbe 5/3, Ulaanbaatar) should be near the top of every traveller's wish list. By combining hiking, sports, Mongolian language and visits with local families, the experience promises total cultural immersion.

The concept is simple. Travellers can choose one of several routes in Dundgov, Arkhangai, Bulgan or Terelj, or do a combination of routes if they have more time. Prior to departure they are educated in local social graces, culture and appropriate Mongolian phrases. Transport is organised to the starting point and then the trekkers begin walking from ger to ger, which can be anywhere from 5km to 20km apart. Once the trekkers have reached the appointed ger, the local family prepares a meal and helps them set up camp (tents and gear are carried by pack animals).

Activities are available at each ger. The Arkhangai route, for example, carries the theme 'three manly sports'; participants learn archery, wrestling and horse training at one or another ger.

Because distances vary between gers, there may be different modes of transport between them – you may take a yak cart for one stretch or go by horse on another. The programme is not forced on the host families; they are still nomadic and may move their ger if they have to (gers along the route keep in regular contact and will know the location of other families). Participant families are also paid fairly (many have tripled their incomes) and a portion of the proceeds goes to community development.

You pay for your entire trip in Ulaanbaatar, which means you won't have to pull out your wallet each hour to pay for goods and services. But you may want to bring along some extra cash because part of the trip includes a visit to a local cooperative where you can buy products made by herders (you can get some great bargains on handmade cashmere sweaters and the like).

Bogd. In Uvs aimag try the Kharkhiraa and Türgen uuls (p241), which have hiking trails of three to seven days.

In northern Mongolia there is great hiking in the Khövsgöl Nuur area (p155). Down in the Gobi, it's possible to hike in Gurvan Saikhan National Park (p208), especially around Yolyn Am.

HORSE & CAMEL TREKKING

Horse treks in Mongolia range from easy day trips with guides, to multi-week solo adventures deep in the mountains. Inexperienced riders should begin with the former, organising their first ride through a ger camp or tour operator. The prettiest, most accessible places to try are the camps at Terelj and Khövsgöl Nuur, where you can normally hire a horse and guide for less than US$20 a day.

Even the most experienced riders will benefit from a lesson in how to deal with a Mongolian horse. The local breed is short, stocky and half-wild; Mongolian horsemen can provide instruction on saddling, hobbling and caring for a horse. You'll also get tips on the best places to ride and on purchasing saddles and other equipment. Try Stepperiders (p108) in Töv aimag. For further tips see the boxed text, p281.

Of the dozens of possible horse treks, several are popular and not difficult to arrange. Tsetserleg to Bayankhongor (p57) is a rugged wilderness trip that crosses a series of alpine passes. In the east, try the Binder area (p171) of Khentii aimag, which can include a ride to Dadal near the Siberian border.

The most popular horse-trekking area is Khövsgöl Nuur (p152), largely because there is such a good network of guides and available horses. Some travellers have horse-trekked from Terkhiin Tsagaan Nuur to Khövsgöl Nuur. By land (following the twisting river valleys) it's around 295km and takes at least two weeks by horse. Closer to Ulaanbaatar, the areas of Terelj and Bogdkhan are both excellent if you don't have a lot of time.

While hiking, it will also be handy to have a working knowledge of appropriate phrases, such as 'Can I cross the next river?' *(Ter goliig gatlaj bolohuu?)*, 'Where am I?' *('En yamar nertei gazar ve?')* and 'Is that dog dangerous?' *('En nokhoi ayultai uu?')*

Travelling by Mongolian Horse, by Bekhjargal Bayarsaikhan, is required reading for anyone planning their own expedition. The book gives invaluable tips on horse care and riding.

RESPONSIBLE CAMPING & HIKING

To help preserve the fragile ecology and beauty of Mongolia, consider the following tips when camping and hiking.

Rubbish

- Carry out all nonbiodegradable items and deposit them in rubbish bins in Ulaanbaatar (other villages and towns won't have proper methods of disposal). Don't overlook easily forgotten items, such as silver paper, orange peel and cigarette butts. Make an effort to carry out rubbish left by others.

- Never bury your rubbish: digging disturbs soil and ground cover, and encourages erosion. Buried rubbish will likely be dug up by animals, who may be injured or poisoned by it. It may also take years to decompose.

- Minimise waste by taking minimal packaging and no more food than you will need. Take reusable containers or stuff sacks.

- Sanitary napkins, tampons and condoms should be carried out despite the inconvenience. They burn and decompose poorly.

- Don't rely on bottled water. Disposal of plastic bottles can be a major problem. Use iodine drops or purification tablets instead.

Human-Waste Disposal

- Contamination of water sources by human faeces can lead to the transmission of all sorts of nasties. Where there is no toilet, choose a spot at least 100m from any water source, bury your waste at least 15cm deep, and bury or burn toilet paper, if possible. Cover the waste with soil and a rock. In snow, dig down to the soil.

Washing

- For personal washing and teeth cleaning, use biodegradable soap and toothpaste and a water container. Perform your ablutions at least 50m away from the watercourse. Disperse the waste water widely to allow the soil to filter it fully before it seeps back to the watercourse.

- Don't use detergents within 50m of watercourses, even if they are biodegradable. Try to wash cooking utensils 50m from watercourses and use a scourer, sand or snow instead of detergent.

Erosion

- Hillsides and mountain slopes, especially at high altitudes, are prone to erosion. Stick to existing trails and avoid short cuts.

- If a well-used trail passes through a mud patch, walk through the mud so as not to increase the size of the patch.

- Avoid disturbing the plant life that keeps topsoil in place.

Fires & Low-Impact Cooking

- Don't rely on open fires for cooking and use a petrol stove whenever possible. Avoid stoves powered by disposable butane-gas canisters. If you *have* to make an open fire, use existing fire rings wherever possible; only use dead, fallen wood and remember that fire is sacred to Mongolians (so don't pee on it). Use minimal wood – just enough for cooking purposes. Dried dung burns with great efficiency.

- Ensure that you fully extinguish a fire after use. Spread the embers and douse them with water.

- If you are hiking with a guide and porters, supply stoves for the whole team. In alpine areas, ensure that all members are outfitted with enough clothing so that fires are not a necessity for warmth.

SAFETY GUIDELINES FOR HIKING

Before embarking on a walking trip, consider the following points to ensure a safe and enjoyable experience:

- Be aware that weather conditions and terrain vary significantly from one region (or even one trail) to another. Seasonal changes can significantly alter any trail. These differences influence the way hikers dress and the equipment they carry.

- Don't forget about Mongolia's notoriously changeable weather – a sudden wind from the north will make you think you're in the Arctic rather than the Gobi. Only from June to August can you expect balmy temperatures, but this is also when it rains the most.

- Essential survival gear includes emergency food rations and a leak-proof water bottle (take a minimum of 2L of water a day, and more during summer).

- It's best to hike with at least one companion and always tell someone where you're going. Refer to your compass frequently so you can find the way back. A GPS is also a handy tool.

- Unless you're planning a camping trip, start out early in the day so that you can easily make it back before dark.

In Western Mongolia there is great horse trekking around Otgon Tenger Uul (p245); it can take six days to circle the mountain. In Altai Tavan Bogd National Park (p229), try a horse trek around Khoton Nuur. There is also horse trekking around Tsast Uul and Tsambagarav Uul. Tour operators in Ölgii can help set something up, or just turn up in any nearby village and ask around for horses.

At touristy places such as the ger camps at Terelj and in the south Gobi you can ride a camel, though these are more like photo sessions than serious sport. Some of the ger camps at Ongiin Khiid (p197) can arrange a multiday camel trek.

In the Empire of Ghengis Khan, by Stanley Stewart, is an account of the author's travels across Mongolia by horse. Despite its persistent sarcasm, the book does present a vivid picture of Mongolia and what it's like to travel by horse.

KAYAKING, CANOEING & RAFTING

Mongolia's numerous lakes and rivers are often ideal for kayaking and rafting. There is little white water but, during the summer rains, rivers can flow at up to 9km/h.

One of the most popular river trips is down the Tuul Gol, from the bridge at the entrance to Terelj and back to Ulaanbaatar.

There are more adventurous options that begin in Khövsgöl aimag. It's possible to put a boat or kayak in the Eg or Delgermörön Gols (on the Eg you could start at Khatgal; on the Delgermörön, Bayanzürkh) and continue downstream to Sükhbaatar city in Selenge aimag. From Mörön it's a 14-day trip and towns along the way are two to four days apart. From Sükhbaatar you can take the train back to Ulaanbaatar.

In Bayan-Ölgii it's possible to raft down the Khovd Gol from Khurgan Nuur, past Ölgii city and onto Myangad in Khovd aimag.

Rafting is organised along the Tuul and Khovd rivers by agencies based in Ulaanbaatar (p80), including Juulchin, Khövsgöl Lodge Company and Nomadic Journeys. Another good contact is a small outfit called Mongolia Canoeing (www.mongoliacanoeing.com), which offers multiday trips on the Orkhon and Tuul rivers.

There is nothing stopping you from heading out on your own. The Seven Summits (p93) rents inflatable kayaks for about US$25 a day. If you're serious, bring your own gear.

The best time for kayaking is in summer (June to September); the best time for rafting is July and August, after some decent rain.

Lost In Mongolia, by Colin Angus, describes the first descent of the Russian river the Yenisey, completed by the author and three friends in 2001. While only half of the book actually takes place in Mongolia (the other half is in Russia), it stands as a thrilling account of exploration in one of the more remote parts of the country.

Ulaanbaatar
Улаанбаатар

If Mongolia's yin is its pristine countryside, then Ulaanbaatar (UB) conforms nicely to its yang. An enormous city of pulsating commerce, heavy traffic, sinful nightlife and bohemian counter-culture, the Mongolian capital stirs as much shock as it does excitement.

UB is a cauldron of concrete and dirt. New buildings are thrown up on any available patch of ground, while Humvees battle Landcruisers and yellow taxis for right of way on pot-holed boulevards. On the high street, tourists and new-moneyed Mongols look for bargains in European fashion shops and Mongolian cashmere boutiques.

Between these chaotic scenes are islands of serenity – quiet monastery courtyards, public squares and the odd beer patio. The river, the Tuul Gol, offers a cool respite to the south while the four holy mountains surrounding the city provide its backdrop. Ever-expanding ger (yurt) suburbs still surround the city, offering a glimpse back to before Soviet urban planning.

As Mongolia's cultural, political, economic and social hub, Ulaanbaatar is the logical base for excursions into the countryside. As you're planning your plunge take the time to explore its excellent sights and museums, fill up at some great restaurants and soak in the eclectic vibe. This ever-changing city may be the biggest surprise of your Mongolian adventure.

HIGHLIGHTS

- Walk the prayer circuit around **Gandan Khiid** (p73), the country's largest monastery

- Wonder at the eccentric collection of animals, curios and artefacts at the **Winter Palace of the Bogd Khan** (p75)

- Take in a performance of traditional dance, song, horse-head fiddles and contortionists at the **National Academic Drama Theatre** (p92)

- Get lost in the rambling hallways of the **Museum of Natural History** (p69) until you at last come face to face with the extraordinary dinosaur collection

- Enjoy a bottle of wine at **Veranda** (p88) while overlooking the Choijin Lama Temple Museum

- Weave through Mongolia's ancient past at the **National Museum of Mongolian History** (p69)

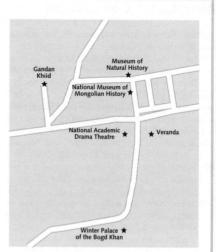

Gandan Khiid ★

Museum of Natural History ★

National Museum of Mongolian History ★

National Academic Drama Theatre ★

★ Veranda

Winter Palace ★ of the Bogd Khan

▪ TELEPHONE CODE: 011	▪ POPULATION: ONE MILLION	▪ AREA: 1368 SQ KM

HISTORY

The first recorded capital city of the recent Mongolian empire was created in 1639. It was called Örgöö and was originally located at the monastery of Da Khuree, some 420km from Ulaanbaatar in Arkhangai aimag (province). The monastery was the residence of five-year-old Zanabazar who, at the time, had been proclaimed the head of Buddhism in Mongolia. Because it consisted of felt tents, the 'city' was easily transported when the grass went dry. Some 25 movements were recorded along the Orkhon, Selenge and Tuul Gols (rivers). Throughout such movement, the city was given some fairly unexciting official and unofficial names, including Khuree (Camp) in 1706.

In 1778 Khuree was erected at its present location (GPS: N47° 55.056', E106° 55.007') and called the City of Felt. Later, the city became known as Ikh Khuree (Great Camp), and was under the rule of the Bogd Gegeen, or Living Buddha. The Manchus, however, used Uliastai as the administrative capital of Outer Mongolia.

In 1911 when Mongolia first proclaimed its independence from China, the city became the capital of Outer Mongolia and was renamed Niislel Khuree (Capital Camp). In 1918 it was invaded by the Chinese and three years later by the Russians.

Finally, in 1924 the city was renamed Ulaanbaatar (Red Hero), in honour of the communist triumph, and declared the official capital of an 'independent' Mongolia (independent from China, not from the Soviet Union). The *khangard* (garuda), symbolising courage and honesty, was declared the city's official symbol. In 1933 Ulaanbaatar gained autonomy and separated from the surrounding Töv aimag.

From the 1930s, the Soviets built the city in typical Russian style: lots of ugly apartment blocks, large brightly coloured theatres and cavernous government buildings. Tragically, the Soviets also destroyed many old Russian buildings as well as Mongolian monasteries and temples. Today the city booms with new private construction projects although a comprehensive infrastructure plan has been slow to implement. It has also enjoyed cultural resurgence with lots of museums, galleries, theatre performances and clubs bringing out the best in traditional Mongolian culture.

ORIENTATION

Most of the city spreads from east to west along the main road, Enkh Taivny Örgön Chölöö, also known as Peace Ave. At the centre is Sükhbaatar Sq, often simply known as 'the Square' *(talbai)*, which is just north of Peace Ave. Sprawling suburbia is limited by the four majestic mountains that surround the city: Bayanzürkh, Chingeltei, Songino Khairkhan and Bogdkhan. The river to the south, the Tuul Gol, also somewhat limits the growth of suburban expansion.

Around the Square are the Central Post Office (CPO) and the Palace of Culture, and a couple of blocks west of the Square is the State Department Store.

The city is divided into six major districts, but there's a multitude of subdistricts and microdistricts. Mongolians rarely use street names and numbers, so tracking down an address can be difficult. A typical address might be something like: Microdistrict 14, Building 3, Flat 27. The problems with this are numerous – you are unlikely to know which microdistrict it refers to, many buildings are not numbered or signed, and most street signs are in Mongolian Cyrillic. This is why most locals will give you an unofficial description, such as 'Door 67, building 33, last door of a white-and-red building, behind the Drama Theatre'. To find your way around Ulaanbaatar, a good map, phrasebook and sense of direction are vital. Because of the confusing state of affairs, small maps are usually on the back of business cards.

Ulaanbaatar is another reason to get a local SIM card for your phone; you'll use it frequently to call places for directions when you get lost. (While it helps to speak basic Mongolian, many places that travellers are likely to call will have an English speaker.) As street addresses are not always obvious, it's best to navigate using the map in this book.

The train station is southwest of the centre. Bus 4 runs from here to Sükhbaatar Sq. The airport is 18km southwest of the city; to get to Sükhbaatar Sq take bus 11 or 22.

Maps

There are several maps available of Ulaanbaatar; the best is the 1:10,000 *Ulaanbaatar City Map* (T5500), updated annually. On the back is a 1:200,000 map of the area around Ulaanbaatar. Maps can be found in bookshops and hotels.

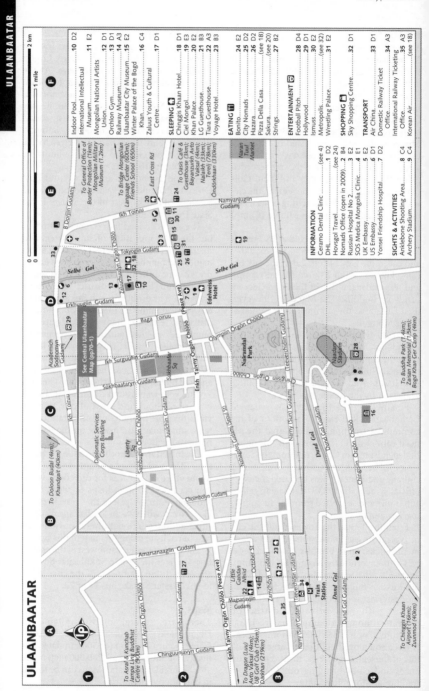

ULAANBAATAR

Indoor Pool	.10 D2
International Intellectual Museum	.11 E2
Mongolian National Artists Union	.12 D1
Orchlon Gym	.13 D1
Railway Museum	.14 A3
Ulaanbaatar City Museum	.15 E2
Winter Palace of the Bogd Khan	.16 C4
Zaluus Youth & Cultural Centre	.17 D1

SLEEPING

Chinggis Khaan Hotel	.18 D2
Ciel Mongol	.19 E3
Khan Palace	.20 E2
LG Guesthouse	.21 B3
Tiara Guesthouse	.22 A3
Voyage Hotel	.23 B3

EATING

Bonito	.24 E2
City Nomads	.25 D2
Hazara	.26 D2
Pizza Della Casa	.(see 20)
Sakura	.(see 20)
Strings	.27 B2

ENTERTAINMENT

Football Pitch	.28 D4
Hollywood	.29 D1
Ismuss	.30 E2
Metropolis	.(see 32)
Wrestling Palace	.31 E2

SHOPPING

Sky Shopping Centre	.32 D1

TRANSPORT

Air China	.33 D1
Domestic Railway Ticket Office	.34 A3
International Railway Ticketing Office	.35 A3
Korean Air	.(see 18)

INFORMATION

Ceramo Dental Clinic	(see 4)
DHL	1 D2
Hovsgol Travel	(see 24)
Nomads Office (open in 2009)	2 B4
Russian Hospital No 2	3 E2
SOS Medica Mongolia Clinic	4 E1
UK Embassy	5 E2
US Embassy	6 D1
Yonsel Friendship Hospital	7 D2

SIGHTS & ACTIVITIES

Anklebone Shooting Area	8 C4
Archery Stadium	9 C4

The best place to obtain maps is the **Cartography Co Map Shop** (Map pp70-1; ☎ 9115 6023; Ikh Toiruu; ☼ 9am-1pm & 2-6pm Mon-Fri, 10am-4pm Sat year-round, 10am-4pm Sun May-Sep) on Ikh Toiruu, near the Elba Electronics shop. You can also buy good topographic maps of Mongolia here.

A more central map shop is the **Gazaryn Zurag Map Shop** (Map pp70-1; ☎ 328 147, 9918 9182; Cho-Burt Bldg, Seoul St; ☼ 10am-6pm Mon-Sat). It produces its own maps, some of which are cheaper than those of Cartography Co, but the selection is much smaller and it doesn't have topo maps.

INFORMATION
Bookshops
English-language bookshops in Mongolia are small and limited. Besides the following shops, you could try poking around the newspaper kiosk in the CPO or the State Department Store (3rd and 5th floors).

Books in English (Map pp70-1; ☎ 9920 3360; Peace Ave; ☼ 11am-7pm Mon-Fri, noon-6pm Sat & Sun) Small bookshop, located next to the Za Internet Café.

Librairie Papillon (Map pp70-1; ☎ 331 859; Ikh Surguuliin Gudamj; ☼ 11am-8pm) Ulaanbaatar's finest bookshop, although almost everything is in French.

Nomin Ikh Delgur (Map pp70-1; ☎ 330 900; Baga Toiruu east; ☼ 10am-8pm) This place is well-stocked in Mongolian-language books and has a few English titles on the 2nd floor.

Xanadu (Map pp70-1; ☎ 319 748, 311 045; Marco Polo Bldg; ☼ 10am-7pm Mon-Sat) Offers the best selection of fiction and nonfiction books in English, plus titles about Mongolia. It also carries a selection of Lonely Planet titles.

Emergency
It might take a few minutes to get hold of an English speaker for these numbers.

Emergency aid/ambulance (☎ 103)
Fire (☎ 101)
Police emergency (☎ 102)
Robbery Unit (☎ 318 783)

Internet Access
In Ulaanbaatar an internet café (Интэрнэт Кафэ) is never more than a block or two away, just look for the signs, which are usually in English. Hourly rates are reasonable at about T400 to T800; but double that price at hotel business centres. Connections are generally good. You can scan photos in many places for around T200.

Internet café (Map pp70-1; ☎ 7010 2486; Peace Ave; per hr T600; ☼ 24hr) Located inside the CPO.

> **WI-FI ACCESS**
>
> There are a growing number of wireless hotspots in Ulaanbaatar. Cafés and restaurants that offer free (sometimes unstable) wi-fi include the Grand Khaan Irish Pub (p89), Silk Road (p88), City Café (p87) and Narya Café (p89). The best connection is at Michele's French Bakery (p89).

Internet Center (Map pp70-1; ☎ 327 438; Negdsen Undestnii Gudamj) Next to the Orange coffee shop.

Internet Centre (Map pp70-1; ☎ 312 512; Tserendorjiin Gudamj 65; per hr T800; ☼ 9am-2am) One of the largest internet cafés with at least 35 computers.

Orchuulin Tovchuu (Map pp70-1; ☎ 310 902; Baga Toiruu north; per hr T400; ☼ 9am-11pm) On the northeast bend of Baga Toiruu.

Za Internet Café (Map pp70-1; ☎ 320 801; Peace Ave 62; per hr T600; ☼ 24hr) Located 100m west of the State Department Store.

Laundry
Almost all of the hotels in Ulaanbaatar offer a laundry service for between T500 and T1500 per kilogram, but they may not advertise it – so just ask. If you can be bothered, it's not difficult to do some laundry yourself – the markets and shops sell small packets of detergent and bleach.

Metro Express (☎ 470 789, 9919 4234) has 10 branches scattered across the city, including one next to the Dalai Eej supermarket (Map pp70–1). A load of laundry costs T5500 and turn-around time is about four hours.

Left Luggage
Most hotels and guesthouses can store luggage while you are off getting lost in the Gobi. There is usually no fee if you've stayed a few nights.

Libraries
The **National Library of Mongolia** (Map pp70-1; ☎ 322 396; Chingisiin Örgön Chölöö; ☼ 9am-8pm) has a vast number of English-language books and documents; the trouble is accessing it. Texts are kept in storage and you need to fill out a small slip of paper (*shefer*) to request the book you want. If you don't have a library card (T4000) you'll need to leave some ID for a deposit. Nearly all texts in English are of the Mongolia genre.

The **American Center for Mongolian Studies** (Америкийн Монгол Судлалын Төв; Map pp70-1; ☎ 350 486; www.mongoliacenter.org; Mongolian National University, Bldg 5, Room 304, Baga Toiruu; ⏱ 10am-5pm Mon-Fri) has a small library of books on Mongolia. In summer, the centre also hosts weekly lectures by Western academics, authors and other people of interest (check the *UB Post* for events).

Media

Democracy has brought an explosion of Mongolian-language newspapers, with controversies and scandals forming popular topics. Ulaanbaatar's two English-language weekly newspapers, *Mongol Messenger* and (the better) *UB Post*, are well worth picking up for local news and entertainment information.

Medical Services

While Ulaanbaatar may be a fairly healthy city, its hospitals are abysmal and best avoided. The only really reliable place is SOS (listed following) but full-blown emergencies are sent to Seoul or Beijing. Pharmacies (*aptek*; Аптек) are common in Ulaanbaatar, stocking Mongolian, Russian, Chinese and Korean medicine. Check expiry dates carefully.

Russian Hospital No 2 (Map p64; ☎ 450 129, 450 230; cnr Peace Ave & Tokyogiin Gudamj) This is the best Mongolian hospital in town, though it's hardly the place you'd want to visit for a critical ailment. It's 200m west of the British embassy. Consultations cost US$10 to US$20.

SOS Medica Mongolia Clinic (Map p64; ☎ 464 325; 4a Bldg, Big Ring Rd; ⏱ 9am-6pm Mon-Fri) This clinic has a staff of Western doctors on call 24 hours (after hours call ☎ 9911 0335). Its services don't come cheap (examinations start from around US$195), but it's the best place to go in an emergency.

Yonsei Friendship Hospital (Map p64; ☎ 310 945; Peace Ave; ⏱ 9am-4.30pm Mon-Fri) This South Korean–sponsored clinic is fairly reliable and reasonably priced. English-speaking doctors are sometimes on hand and the prices are very reasonable (less than T5000 for a consultation). The hospital is located close to the Selbe Gol bridge.

The best place for dental work is at **Ceramo Dental Clinic** (Map p64; ☎ 464 330, 9666 0670) in the same building as SOS Medica Mongolia Clinic. An optometrist is located on the 1st floor of the State Department Store.

Money

You won't have to go far to change cash or travellers cheques, or get a cash advance on your credit card. Many banks in central Ulaanbaatar even offer 24-hour services. The bigger hotels also offer exchange services for their guests. Avoid changing money with street dealers at the markets: the rate is only slightly better than at official moneychangers and you run the risk of being cheated.

ATMs are popping up in many places including the lobbies of the Ulaanbaatar, Bayangol and Chinggis Khaan hotels, as well as department stores and supermarkets.

Both Golomt and Trade & Development Bank (T&D Bank) will allow you to receive money wired from abroad. It will cost the sender US$50 to wire any amount of money; there is no charge for receiving cash. For general information on money, see p257.

Golomt Bank (Map pp70-1; ☎ 330 436; ⏱ 24hr) Around-the-clock banking services. Changing travellers cheques into tögrög carries a fee of 1.5%. You can get a cash advance with no commission on Visa or MasterCard. There are six branches around town, including Seoul St and just south of the corner of Juulchin Gudamj on Baga Toiruu.

Khan Bank (Map pp70-1; ☎ 456 154; cnr Sambugiin Örgön Chölöö & Baga Toiruu; ⏱ 24hr)

Mongol Shuudan Bank (Map pp70-1; ☎ 310 103; Kholboochdiin Gudamj 4; ⏱ 9am-1pm & 2-4pm Mon-Fri)

State Department Store (Map pp70-1; Peace Ave 44) Also has exchange booths.

Trade & Development Bank (T&D Bank; Map pp70-1; ☎ 327 095; ⏱ 9am-4pm Mon-Fri) Travellers cheques are changed into tögrög with a 1% fee or into US dollars with a 2% fee. For foreigners, the place to do business is on the 2nd floor of the main branch on the corner of Juulchin Gudamj and Baga Toiruu. Here you also get a cash advance on your credit card; MasterCard carries a 4% commission, Amex and Visa are both commission-free. The bank will also replace lost Amex travellers cheques. A second branch is located on Peace Ave, opposite the Ulaanbaatar Hotel.

Valiut Ariljaa (Map pp70-1; Baga Toiruu west ⏱ 8.30am-9pm) There are several exchange offices on this square, known by locals as Ard Kino. The exchange offices here have some of the best rates in town.

Permits

If you are travelling to border areas such as Altai Tavan Bogd National Park in Bayan-Ölgii, the **General Office of Border Protection** (off Map p64; ☎ 286 788, 454 142; Border Defence Bldg; ⏱ 10am-12.30pm & 2-5pm Mon-Fri), in the east of the city, is the place to come for permits. Permits are free but you must send a Mongolian on your behalf to apply. The office requires a passport photocopy and a map showing your route. The office is in a grey building just west of the Mongolian Military Museum.

Police

The police can be found on Sambugiin Örgön Chölöö or on Negdsen Undestnii Gudamj but, as in the rest of the country, don't expect much assistance.

Post

Central Post Office (CPO, Töv Shuudangiin Salbar; Map pp70-1; ☎ 313 421; cnr Peace Ave & Sükhbaataryn Gudamj; ☺ 7.30am-9pm Mon-Fri, 9am-8pm Sat & Sun) Located near the southwest corner of Sükhbaatar Sq. As you enter the main hall, the oversize-package desk is on the left and the Telecom office is to the right. The Postal Counter Hall is the place to post mail and check poste restante (counter No 1; letters are free but there's a T300 charge to pick up a package, and you'll need to show your passport). EMS express (priority) mail can also be sent from here. There is also a good range of postcards, small booklets about Mongolia in English and local newspapers for sale. Note that while open, most services are nonexistent on Sunday. DHL and FedEx are more reliable than anything the CPO can offer.

DHL (Map p64; ☎ 310 919; www.dhl.mn; Peace Ave 15a; ☺ 9am-6pm Mon-Fri, 9am-noon Sat) Near the Edelweiss Hotel.

FedEx (Map pp70-1; ☎ 312 092; fedex@tuushin.mn; Amaryn Gudamj 2; ☺ 9am-6pm Mon-Fri) In front of the Tuushin Hotel. A 500g letter to Australia is US$36; to the UK and USA it is US$45.

Telephone & Fax

For local calls, you can use the phone at your hotel, often for free. Other hotels, including those with business centres, and some of the street stalls with telephones charge T100 for a call to a landline (six digits) or a mobile number (eight digits). You can also make local calls from the CPO or at any number of street-side peddlers whose entire business is selling phone calls on ubiquitous portable white phones.

Private, inexpensive international phone offices *(Olon Ulsiin Yariin)* are sometimes tucked into corners of shops, restaurants or computer-game centres. One is located at Peace Ave 62, below the Za Internet Café (Map pp70-1). Calls are dirt cheap (ie T50 per minute to the US or T100 per minute to Europe). Many internet cafés are equipped with headsets and webcams for easy Skype calls.

International phone calls from the CPO are more laborious and more expensive, but it's open all night.

Most mid- to top-range hotels have a fax that can be used by guests for about T1500 to T2000 per page. The CPO offers a less user-friendly service, with cheaper rates. Hotels charge around T500 to receive a fax on your behalf.

Toilets

Public toilets can be found on Seoul St by the Natsagdorj Library and opposite California restaurant.

Tourist Information

Discovery Mongolia Information Centre (Map pp70-1; ☎ 319 371; Narny Gudamj; ☺ 10am-7pm) Sells maps and books and provides general tourist info.

Tourist Information Centre (Map pp70-1; ☎ 311 423, 311 409; cnr Peace Ave & Sükhbaataryn Gudamj; ☺ 9am-8pm) Located in the back hall of the CPO, this info desk has an English-speaking staff that can give general info on city tours and nationwide travel. The desk also sells books and maps about Mongolia. It has branches at the airport and the train station.

Travel Agencies

Staff at backpacker guesthouses can help with visa registration and train tickets. All the guesthouses mentioned in this book offer reliable help. For a small fee, some guesthouses even help visitors staying at other hotels.

The Russian embassy usually refers travellers to **Legend Tour** (Map pp70-1; ☎ 315 158, 9984 2999; www.legendtour.ru; Seoul St, Sant Asar Trading Centre; ☺ 9am-1pm & 2-6pm Mon-Fri) for visa help. Some travellers have given some negative feedback about this operation, but it may be your only choice if you want that elusive Russian visa. Make sure you are clear on the full itinerary and any additional costs.

The following agencies are good for organising air tickets. For details of local agencies offering tours either within or outside of Ulaanbaatar, see p80.

Air Market (Map pp70-1; ☎ 366 060, 9927 9114; www.air-market.net; cnr Peace Ave & Chingisiin Örgön Chölöö; ☺ 9am-8pm)

Air Network (Map pp70-1; ☎ 322 222; airnetwork@ magicnet.mn; Baga Toiruu west; ☺ 9am-7pm Mon-Fri, 10am-3pm Sat & Sun)

Air Trans (Map pp70-1; ☎ 310 061, 313 131; airtrans@ magicnet.mn; cnr Sükhbaataryn Gudamj & Sambugiin Örgön Chölöö; ☺ 9am-7pm Mon-Fri, 10am-3pm Sat) Very reliable air-ticketing agency.

Silk Road Network (Map pp70-1; ☎ 320 405; silkroad@mongolnet.mn; Peace Ave, east side of State Department Store; ☺ 10am-8pm)

DANGERS & ANNOYANCES

Ulaanbaatar is a fairly carefree and easygoing city and it's unlikely you'll experience any problems but there are a few concerns to keep in mind, chief among them are pickpockets and dangerous traffic.

Theft

Pickpockets and bag slashers are a recent and growing problem, although theft is seldom violent against foreigners, just opportunistic. One guesthouse owner reported that 5% of his guests are 'picked' while in Ulaanbaatar.

Crowded places are the trouble spots: getting onto a bus or getting held up in human traffic at the Naran Tuul market. The worst time is around Naadam Festival when pickpockets lurk around the Square and stadium – keep close watch on your camera. Beware of pickpockets who masquerade as coin sellers.

Pickpockets often work in teams; two or three will block your path and push from the front while another dives a hand into your pockets. During winter, the pockets of bulging coats are popular targets.

At Gandan Khiid, unsuspecting tourists, mesmerised by enchanting ceremonies, have been relieved of their money and passports. The same goes for foreigners engrossed in computer screens at internet cafés. When possible, leave valuables in the safe in your hotel. If you must take valuables on the street, use a money belt, and on public transport carry your bag in front of you. You can even get a temporary safe-deposit box at one of the 24-hour Golomt Banks.

Violent Crime

Violent crime and muggings most often occur in the darkened alleys, courtyards and ger districts that lie off the well-lit boulevards. Avoid these areas after dark. Foreigners should use an official taxi – as opposed to a private vehicle – for lifts around town late at night.

Be careful when leaving nightclubs in Ulaanbaatar, where alcohol and comparatively rich foreigners are a potentially vulnerable mixture. Try to leave in a group rather than alone.

Alcoholism

Alcoholism is becoming less of a problem these days as beer rapidly replaces vodka as the local beverage of choice. You'll still encounter drunks in and around Ulaanbaatar, especially around Naadam time, but they are usually more annoying than dangerous. Be sensible in bars and nightclubs; you're only asking for trouble if you flash around a lot of money or get into arguments about the virtues or otherwise of Chinggis Khaan or other issues of sensitivity.

Queues

It could be the warrior-like bloodlines from Chinggis Khaan, a penchant for wrestling or habits from the communist days where demand always exceeded supply, but Mongolians rarely queue – they bustle, huddle and scramble. You will often need to sharpen your elbows, learn some appropriately argumentative phrases in Mongolian, and plough headfirst through the throng. Being polite won't really help, nor will getting angry.

Traffic

Probably the most dangerous thing you can do in Ulaanbaatar is cross the street. Pedestrian rights are zilch so be careful when stepping off the curb. Drivers have a habit of speeding up when pedestrians are in the street – they are not really trying to kill you, it's their way of warning you to look out. Be careful even when the traffic lights are in your favour. A particularly dangerous crossing is right in front of the State Department Store.

Other Annoyances

Virtually no stairways in the whole country have lights, so carrying a torch (flashlight) is a good idea, even during the day. Hot-water shortages and blackouts are common throughout the year.

Most offices have security guards in the lobby checking the ID cards of everyone who enters and leaves the buildings – it can sometimes be a nightmare getting past them. Police can also be unhelpful, see p254.

The number of street children and beggars in Ulaanbaatar has noticeably decreased in recent years but there are still a few around. While it is better not to give anything as this just encourages them to stay on the street, handing out food and drinks is better than money.

SIGHTS

Most sights are located within a 15-minute walk from Sükhbaatar Sq. The Winter Palace of the Bogd Khan and the Zaisan Memorial are a short bus ride south of the city. Gandan Khiid is about 2km to the northwest.

Museums

NATIONAL MUSEUM OF MONGOLIAN HISTORY МОНГОЛЫН ТҮҮХИЙН УНДЭСНИЙ МУЗЕЙ

Still sometimes referred to by its previous name, the Revolutionary Museum, this **Mongolian history museum** (Map pp70-1; ☎ 325 656; cnr Juulchin Gudamj & Sükhbaataryn Gudamj; admission T2500, photos T5000; ⏱ 10am-4.30pm Tue-Sat) is an Ulaanbaatar highlight.

The recently renovated 1st floor has some interesting exhibits on Stone Age sites in Mongolia, as well as petroglyphs, deer stones (stone sculptures of reindeer and other animals) and burial sites from the Hun and Uighur eras.

The 2nd floor houses an outstanding collection of costumes, hats and jewellery, representing most of Mongolia's ethnic groups. Take a gander as some of the elaborate silverwork of the Dariganga minority or the outrageous headgear worn by Khalkh Mongols. Some of the outfits contain 20kg to 25kg of silver ornamentation!

The 3rd floor is a must-see for fans of the Mongol horde. The collection includes real examples of 12th-century Mongol armour, and correspondence between Pope Innocent IV and Guyuk Khaan. Written in Latin and Persian and dated 13 November 1246, it bears the khaan's seal. The centrepiece is an enormous model of ancient Karakorum, which is quite astonishing to see if you've already been to the site of Karakorum, of which almost nothing remains. There is also a display of traditional Mongolian culture with, among other things, a furnished ger, traditional farming and domestic implements, saddles and musical instruments. One hall features early-20th-century history; look out for the very colourful Mongolian dollars, the first currency of the modern republic.

ZANABAZAR MUSEUM OF FINE ARTS ЗАНАБАЗАРЫН УРАН ЗУРГИЙН МУЗЕЙ

This **fine arts museum** (Map pp70-1; ☎ 326 060; Juulchin Gudamj; adult/student T2500/1000; ⏱ 10am-6pm May-Sep, 10am-5pm Oct-Apr) has a superb collection of paintings, carvings and sculptures, including many by the revered sculptor and artist Zanabazar. It also contains other rare, and sometimes old, religious exhibits such as scroll *thangka* (paintings) and Buddhist statues, representing the best display of its kind in Mongolia. A bonus is that most

of the exhibit captions in the museum are in English.

The second room contains some fine examples of the sculptor's work including five Dhyani, or Contemplation, Buddhas (cast in 1683) and Tara in her 21 manifestations.

Also worth checking out are the wonderful *tsam* masks (worn by monks during religious ceremonies) and the intricate paintings, *One Day in Mongolia* and the *Airag Feast*, by renowned artist B Sharav. These depict almost every aspect of nomadic life.

Worthy of a visit in itself, the **Red Ger Art Gallery** (☎ 323 986) on the 1st floor showcases modern artwork by Mongolia's top contemporary painters. English-speaking guides are available. From the gallery, continue towards to the back of the building to find two more halls, one featuring prints and the second containing folk art.

The building itself carries some historical value. It was built in 1906 and for many years served as Ulaanbaatar's biggest department store. Shortly after the 1921 Communist Revolution, Soviet Red Army troops were stationed here.

MUSEUM OF NATURAL HISTORY БАЙГАЛИЙН ТҮҮХИЙН МУЗЕЙ

This **natural history museum** (Map pp70-1; ☎ 321 716; cnr Sükhbaataryn Gudamj & Sambugiin Örgön Chölöö; adult/student T2500/1000, photos T5000, video T10,000, photos of dinosaur skeletons extra T5000; ⏱ 10am-5.30pm, closed Mon & Tue mid-Sep–mid-May) is a serious throwback to the Soviet era. It has exhibits featuring Mongolia's geography, flora and fauna, including the requisite section with stuffed and embalmed animals, birds and even fish. The general impression, however, is that you've stumbled into the warehouse of a long-deceased taxidermist, rather than into a serious scientific exhibition. Some of the animals have been fixed with puzzling expressions, as if they remain perplexed as to how they ended up in such an unfortunate state. In any case, budding geologists may appreciate the generally stoic **meteorites**.

The most impressive section is the Palaeontology Hall and its array of complete **dinosaur skeletons**, including a 3m-tall, 5-tonne, flesh-eating tarbosaurus. For a bird's-eye view, clamber up the stairs outside the hall to a gallery on the 3rd floor.

The gallery that is next door to the hall is full of interesting knick-knacks, such as

ULAANBAATAR

CENTRAL ULAANBAATAR

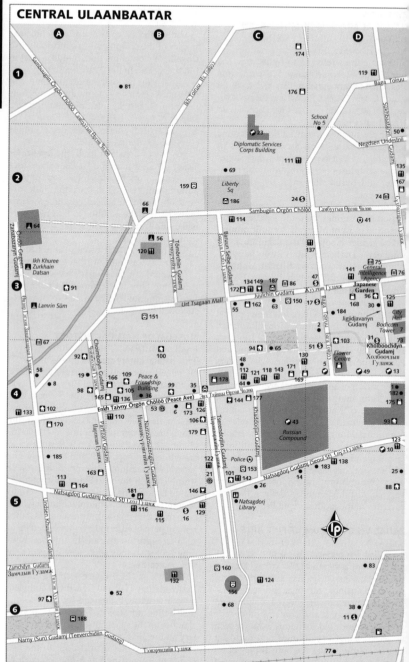

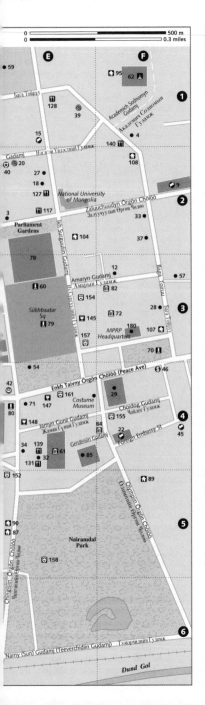

INFORMATION

Continued on p72

ULAANBAATAR

petrified wood, dinosaur eggs and some huge leg bones, which look like something out of the Flintstones. Look out for the world-famous 'fighting dinosaurs', a velociraptor and protoceratops that were buried alive (probably when a sand dune collapsed on top of them) in the midst of mortal combat, some 80 million years ago. For more on Mongolia's remarkable dinosaurs see the boxed text, p206.

VICTIMS OF POLITICAL PERSECUTION MEMORIAL MUSEUM

This little-known **museum** (Map pp70–1; ☎ 320 592; cnr Gendeniin Gudamj & Olympiin Örgön Chölöö; admission US$2, photos US$5, video US$10; ⏰ 9am-5pm) consists of a series of haunting displays that chronicle the bloody communist purges of the 1930s – an aggressive campaign to eliminate 'counter-revolutionaries'. During the campaign, intellectuals were arrested and put on trial, sent to Siberian labour camps or shot. Mongolia lost its top writers, scientists and thinkers. One hall reveals this tragedy most vividly with a display of human skulls pierced with bullet holes.

The museum was inspired by the deeds of former prime minister P Genden, who was executed in Moscow by the Komitet Gosudarstvennoy Bezopasnosti (KGB; Committee for State Security) in 1937 for refusing Stalin's orders to carry out the purge. Stalin found a more willing puppet in Marshall Choibalsan, whose purge ended in the deaths of more than 28,000 Mongolians, mostly lamas. The house containing the museum once belonged to Genden and it was his daughter, Tserendulam, who converted it into a museum in 1996.

The large, white square building located just southwest of the museum, is called the **Wedding Palace** (Map pp70–1; Khurimiin Ordon). Built in 1976 by the Russians, it has since been used for tens of thousands of wedding ceremonies, including the marital vows of a few foreigners.

OTHER MUSEUMS

The **Ulaanbaatar City Museum** (Map p64; ☎ 450 960; Peace Ave; admission T1500; ⏰ 9am-6pm Mon-Fri) offers a brief but insightful view of Ulaanbaatar's history through old maps and photos. The most interesting item is a huge painting of the capital as it looked in 1912, in which you can clearly make out major landmarks such as Gandan Khiid and the Winter Palace of Bogd Khan.

The **Museum of the General Intelligence Agency** (Map pp70–1; ☎ 264 281, 5126 4281; admission T1000; ⏰ 10am-4pm Mon-Fri) is dedicated to the Mongolian version of the KGB and the spy game dating back to the Chinggis Khaan era. The curators are retired secret service agents and will provide colourful insight on some of the photographs (all captions are in Mongolian). To get there, walk behind the National Museum and down a narrow alley heading west. It's on the left side of the alley. If the museum is locked, try ringing or ask at the front desk of the General Intelligence Agency (GIA) headquarters on Juulchin Gudamj.

The **International Intellectual Museum** (Map p64; ☎ 461 470; www.iqmuseum.mn; Peace Ave 10; admission T3000; ⏰ 10am-6pm Mon-Sat), also known as the Mongolian Toy Museum, is in a pink building behind the round 'East Centre'. It has a collection of puzzles and games made by local artists. One puzzle requires 56,831 movements to complete, says curator Zandraa Tumen-Ulzii.

The **Railway Museum** (Map p64; ☎ 944 493; Octoberyn Gudamj; admission free; ⏰ 9am-noon & 1-4pm Mon-Fri) is great for kids and railway buffs. It is about 400m northeast of the station. Other train-spotting options include the **old train engines** (Map pp70–1) parked in front of the Jiguur Grand hotel.

The **Theatre Museum** (Map pp70–1; ☎ 311 320; Amaryn Gudamj; admission T1000; ⏰ 10am-4pm Mon-Fri) is worthwhile if you're interested in the dramatic arts – the collection of puppets is wonderful. The museum is on the 3rd floor of the Palace of Culture (its entrance is on the northern side of building).

The **Hunting Museum** (Map pp70–1; Öndör Gegeen Zanabazaryn Gudamj; admission T1000; ⏰ 10am-5pm Mon-Fri, 10am-2pm Sat), on the 2nd floor of the Baigal Ordon (Nature Palace) on the street leading to Gandan Khiid, shows off centuries-old trapping and hunting techniques that are used by both nomads and urban cowboys. It's usually locked so ask for the key from the ladies running the hotel downstairs.

Monasteries & Temples

Around the start of the 19th century, more than 100 *süm* (temples) and *khiid* (monasteries) served a population of only about 50,000 in Ulaanbaatar. Only a handful survived the religious purges of 1937. Only since the early 1990s have the people of Mongolia started to openly practise Buddhism again.

GANDAN KHIID ГАНДАН ХИЙД

This **monastery** (Gandantegchinlen Khiid; Map pp70–1; Öndör Gegeen Zanabazaryn Gudamj; admission free; ⏰ 9am-9pm) is one of Mongolia's most important, and also one of its biggest tourist attractions. The full name, Gandantegchinlen, translates roughly as 'the great place of complete joy'.

Building was started in 1838 by the fourth Bogd Gegeen, but like most monasteries in

ULAANBAATAR

ZORIG – THE FATHER OF MONGOLIAN DEMOCRACY

While Mongolia's 1990 pro-democracy demonstrations were gathering steam, a mob appeared on Sükhbaatar Sq, poised to lay siege to the Parliament House and the meagre police force protecting it. Foreseeing a bloodbath, activist leader Sanjaasurengiin Zorig clambered onto the shoulders of his comrades and ordered the demonstrators to sit, and they listened.

The image of Zorig pacifying the crowd from the steps of the Parliament House became iconic of the 1990 Revolution, and said much about the man's persona. A pragmatist and a negotiator, Zorig was known for his ability to find common ground between party officials and the agitators on the street.

Like other young reformers of his generation, Zorig was Moscow-educated and the son of a prominent Mongolian People's Revolutionary Party (MPRP) member; he was well placed to lead Mongolia through of confusion of its transformation from a communist state to a democracy and market economy. For his efforts he was known as the 'Golden Magpie of Democracy.'

On 2 October 1998, the 36-year-old Zorig, was stabbed 18 times by masked assailants in his apartment. The incident occurred during a period of political instability, and he was the likely candidate for the vacant position of prime minister.

The killers have never been brought to justice, though his death is linked to a corrupt casino deal, which he helped to block. A decade on, the government and police have revealed few clues as to their findings.

The murder came as a great shock to the Mongolian people, who lined the streets in their tens of thousands for the burial procession. A statue of Zorig was unveiled on his birthday, 20 April, in 1999 opposite the Central Post Office, to honour his legacy.

Zorig's efforts to fight corruption have been carried on by his sister Oyun, who left her job as a geologist to win Zorig's seat in parliament. She now heads her own political party, as well as the **Zorig Foundation** (www.zorigfoundation.org.mn), which promotes democracy, transparency and good governance in Mongolia.

Mongolia the purges of 1937 fell heavily on Gandan. When the US Vice President Henry Wallace asked to see a monastery during his visit to Mongolia in 1944, then prime minister Choibalsan guiltily scrambled to open this one to cover up the fact that he had recently laid waste to Mongolia's religious heritage. The *khiid* remained a 'show monastery' for other foreign visitors until 1990 when full religious ceremonies commenced. Today, more than 600 monks belong to the monastery.

As you enter the main entrance from the south, a path leads towards the right to a courtyard containing two temples. The northeast building is **Ochidara Temple** (sometimes called Gandan Süm) where the most significant ceremonies are held. Following the *kora* (pilgrim) path clockwise around this building, the large statue behind glass is **Tsongkhapa**, the founder of the Gelugpa sect. The two-storey **Didan-Lavran temple** in the courtyard was home to the 13th Dalai Lama during his stay here in 1904.

At the end of the main path as you enter is the magnificent white **Migjid Janraisig Süm** (admission T2500, photos T5000, video T10,000; ⏲ 9am-6pm May-Oct, 10am-4pm Nov-Apr), the monastery's main attraction. Lining the walls of the temple are hundreds of images of Ayush, the Buddha of longevity, which stare through the gloom to the magnificent Migjid Janraisig statue.

The original statue was commissioned by the eighth Bogd Khan in 1911, in hopes that it might restore his eyesight – syphilis had blinded him; however it was carted away by Russia in 1937 (it was allegedly melted down to make bullets). The new statue was dedicated in 1996 and built with donations from Japan and Nepal. It is 26m high and made of copper with a gilt gold covering. The hollow statue contains 27 tonnes of medicinal herbs, 334 sutras, two million bundles of mantras, plus an entire ger with furniture!

To the east of the temple are four colleges of Buddhist philosophy, including the yellow building dedicated to Kalachakra, a wrathful Buddhist deity.

To the west of the temple is the **Öndör Gegeen Zanabazar Buddhist University**, established in 1970. It is usually closed to foreigners.

You can take photos around the monastery and in Migjid Janraisig Süm, but not inside the other temples. Try to be there for the captivating ceremonies – they usually start at around 10am, though you may be lucky and see one at another time. Most chapels are closed in the afternoon.

Pickpockets sometimes target the monastery, so take care, especially when among crowds.

WINTER PALACE OF BOGD KHAN
БОГД ХААНЫ ӨВЛИЙН ОРДОН
Built between 1893 and 1903, this **palace** (Map p64; ☎ 342 195; Chingisiin Örgön Chölöö; admission T2500, photos US$10, video US$15; 🕙 9am-5.30pm summer, 9.30am-4.30pm Fri-Tue winter) is the place where Mongolia's eighth Living Buddha, and last king, Jebtzun Damba Hutagt VIII (often called the Bogd Khan), lived for 20 years. For reasons that are unclear, the palace was spared destruction by the Russians and turned into a museum. The summer palace, on the banks of Tuul Gol, was completely destroyed.

There are six temples in the grounds. The white building to the right as you enter is the Winter Palace itself. It contains a collection of gifts received from foreign dignitaries, such as a pair of golden boots from a Russian tsar, a robe made from 80 unfortunate foxes and a ger lined with the skins of 150 snow leopards. Mongolia's Declaration of Independence (from China) is among the exhibits.

The Bogd Khan's penchant for unusual wildlife explains the extraordinary array of stuffed animals in the palace. Some of it had been part of his personal zoo – look out for the photo of the Bogd's elephant, purchased from Russia for 22,000 roubles.

The Winter Palace is a few kilometres south of the Square. It is a bit too far to walk, so take a taxi or catch bus 7 or 19. A **booklet** (T2200), available at the entrance, gives a very brief explanation of the temples in English, and includes a handy map showing the temple locations.

CHOIJIN LAMA TEMPLE MUSEUM
ЧОЙЖИН ЛАМЫН ХИЙД-МУЗЕЙ
This **temple museum** (Map pp70-1; ☎ 324 788; http://choijin.on.mn; admission T2500, photos T5500, video T12,000; 🕙 9am-6.30pm mid-May–Sep, 10am-4pm Oct–mid-May) is a hidden gem of architecture and history, smack in the middle of downtown Ulaanbaatar. Sadly, it's under threat of losing its quaint character, as shoddily constructed buildings are thrown up all around it. Already

the view of the complex is hindered by ugly buildings that now form its backdrop.

Still, Choijin Lama is well worth a visit. It was the home of Luvsan Haidav Choijin Lama ('Choijin' is an honorary title given to some monks), the state oracle and brother of the Bogd Khan. The construction of the monastery commenced in 1904 and was completed four years later. It was closed in 1938 and probably would have been demolished but it was saved as a museum in 1942 to demonstrate the 'feudal' ways of the past. Although religious freedom in Mongolia recommenced in 1990, this monastery is no longer an active place of worship.

There are five temples within the grounds. As you enter, the first temple you see is the **Maharaja Süm**. The **main temple** features statues of Sakyamuni (the historical Buddha), Choijin Lama and Baltung Choimba (the teacher of the Bogd Khan), whose mummified remains are inside the statue. There are also some fine *thangka* and some of the best *tsam* masks in the country. The *gongkhang* (protector chapel) behind the main hall contains the oracle's throne and a magnificent statue of *yab-yum* (mystic sexual union).

The other temples are **Zuu Süm**, dedicated to Sakyamuni; **Yadam Süm**, which contains wooden and bronze statues of various gods, some created by the famous Mongolian sculptor Zanabazar; and **Amgalan Süm**, containing a self-portrait of Zanabazar himself and a small stupa apparently brought to Ulaanbaatar by Zanabazar from Tibet.

Free cultural performances are held here in summer at 5pm; this is a great chance to see *tsam*-mask dancing and listen to *khöömii* (throat singing). The complex is located off Jamyn Gunii Gudamj, with the entrance on the south side.

CENTRE OF SHAMAN ETERNAL HEAVENLY SOPHISTICATION МӨНХ ТЭНГЭРИЙН ШИД БӨӨ ШҮТЭЭНИЙ ТӨВ
Ulaanbaatar's official **Shaman Centre** (Map pp70-1; ☎ 9994 3609; Öndör Gegeen Zanabazaryn Gudamj; admission free; 🕙 10am-6pm Sun-Fri May-Sep) is a ramshackle collection of squalid gers teetering on the slope that leads to Gandan Monastery. While not particularly mystifying at first sight, this is the real deal, with a bona fide shaman at its helm, holding daily court. The resident shaman, Zorigtbaatar, is known for his fiery orations that rile up the faithful into a frenzy. There are two gers: one that honours

the shamanic spirits and another that replicates nature, complete with a small lake, trees and stuffed animals. It is in the nature ger where the shaman performs his dance. If there is a ceremony going on, and you want your fortune told, you'll need to make a small donation.

OTHER MONASTERIES & TEMPLES

Belonging to Gandan Khiid, **Gesar Süm** (Map pp70-1; ☎ 313 148; cnr Sambugiin Örgön Chölöö & Ikh Toiruu west; admission free; ⏰ 9am-8pm) is named after the mythical Tibetan king. The lovely temple is a fine example of Chinese-influenced architecture. It is a popular place for locals to request, and pay for, *puja* (a blessing ceremony). Allegedly, the temple was placed here to stop the movement of the hill behind it, which was slowly creeping towards the centre of the city. It's easy to visit the temple as it lies between Gandan and the city centre.

Tasgany Ovoo (Map pp70–1), about 300m north of Gesar Süm, is worth a look if you haven't yet seen an *ovoo*, a sacred pyramid-shaped collection of stones.

The **Bakula Rinpoche Süm** (Map pp70-1; ☎ 322 366; admission free; ⏰ 9am-6pm), also known as the Pethub Stangey Choskhor Ling Khiid, was founded in 1999 by the late Indian ambassador, himself a reincarnate lama from Ladakh. The Rinpoche's ashes were interred inside a golden stupa inside the temple in July 2004. The monastery, used mainly as a centre for Buddhist teaching, also has a **Centre for Buddhist Medicine** (☎ 9199 7894; ⏰ 9am-5pm Mon-Fri, 9am-noon Sat). The monastery is not a must-see unless you are interested in learning about traditional medicine. The complex is located where Ikh Toiruu meets Sambugiin Örgön Chölöö, behind the Container Market.

Dashchoilon Khiid (Map pp70-1; ☎ 350 047; Academich Sodnomyn Gudamj; admission free) was originally built in 1890, but was destroyed in the late 1930s. The monastery was partially rebuilt and is now located in three huge concrete gers that once formed part of the State Circus. There are plans afoot to expand the monastery to include a six-storey building which will house a 17m-high statue of Maidar. So far, the only part of the statue to exist is the 108-bead rosary, donated by monks from Japan (each bead weighs 45.5kg, making it the largest in the world). You can get to Dashchoilon from a lane running off Baga Toiruu – look out for the orange-and-brown roof.

Art Galleries

As well as music, Mongolians love the visual arts, and there are a number of galleries in Ulaanbaatar worth visiting.

MONGOLIAN NATIONAL MODERN ART GALLERY МОНГОЛЫН УРАН ЗУРГИЙН ҮЗЭСГЭЛЭН

Sometimes called the **Fine Art Gallery** (Map pp70-1; ☎ 331 687; admission T2000, photos T5000, video T10,000; ⏰ 10am-6pm May-Sep, 9am-5pm Oct-Apr), it contains a large and impressive display of modern and uniquely Mongolian paintings and sculptures. It has a mixture of depictions of nomadic life, people and landscapes, ranging from impressionistic to nationalistic. The Soviet romantic paintings depicted in *thangka* style are especially interesting, but the most famous work is Tsevegjav Ochir's 1958 *The Fight of the Stallions*.

The entrance is in the courtyard of the Palace of Culture. The main gallery is on the 3rd floor, there are temporary exhibits on the 2nd floor and a shop on the 1st floor.

OTHER ART GALLERIES

A unique cultural experience in Ulaanbaatar is a visit to the studios of the **Mongolian National Artists Union** (Уран Бүтээлчдийн Урлан; Map p64; ☎ 325 849; www.uma.mn; cnr Erkhuugiin Gudamj & Ikh Toiruu; ⏰ 9am-1pm & 2-6pm). The artists are welcoming and you can offer to buy their work on the spot. It's in a blue building with a bronze statue of a seated monk above the door. The **Arts Council of Mongolia** (Map pp70-1; ☎ reservations 319 015; www.artscouncil.mn; cnr Juulchin Gudamj & Baruun Selbe Gudamj) conducts tours here for US$25 per group of five.

If you want to see more Mongolian art, and maybe buy some, head into the **Mongolian Artists' Exhibition Hall** (Монголын Зураачдын Үзэсгэлэн Танхим; Map pp70-1; ☎ 327 474; cnr Peace Ave & Chingisiin Örgön Chölöö; admission free; ⏰ 9am-6pm), on the 2nd floor of the white marble building diagonally opposite the CPO. This is a rotating collection of modern and often dramatic paintings, carvings, tapestries and sculptures. The displays often change and there's a good souvenir shop.

The **Children's Art & Creation Centre** (Map pp70-1; ☎ 329 426; Baga Toiruu north; admission T3000; ⏰ 10am-5pm Mon-Fri) shows off the extraordinary art of young Mongolians. Themes are mainly traditional scenes of hunting and pastoralism.

ULAANBAATAR'S ONE MILLIONTH CITIZEN: NO CAUSE FOR CELEBRATION

When Ulaanbaatar's official population hit one million people in 2007, the city authorities decided this milestone was cause for celebration. Three newborns were credited as the city's official millionth citizens, an honour that earned each a set of keys to brand new apartments.

But who really deserved such a title? Quaint as it may be to honour the newborns, Ulaanbaatar's one millionth citizen was more likely an internal migrant from the countryside, arriving in the capital without money or prospects for work.

The statistics tell the truth behind the city smokescreen – from 2004 to 2007 Ulaanbaatar's population has increased by 12% while the population of rural aimags decreased on average by 1% to 3%. Töv aimag has been hardest hit by the problem, losing more than 20% of its population.

While a better life in the city may seem attractive to Mongolia's rural poor, the rapid urbanisation of the country is having a critical impact on several fronts. Ulaanbaatar's infrastructure is unable to cope with the influx of cars and people. Traffic jams wreak havoc while expanding ger (yurt) districts crawl up once-virgin hillsides. Air pollution in winter is 10 times higher than healthy levels.

Meanwhile, the newly arrived migrants are not finding life in Ulaanbaatar to be much easier than the countryside. In 2006, only 2.5% of the internal migrants to Ulaanbaatar found permanent housing. The highly touted 40,000 homes project, which seeks to build apartments for low-income families, proceeds at a pace too slow to keep up with demand. If current trends continue, half of the national population will live in Ulaanbaatar within 10 years.

Leaders do recognise this growing problem although little has been done to stem the tide of internal migrants. Current business policies and infrastructure make it almost impossible to do serious business anywhere but Ulaanbaatar and the national road-development scheme is basically designed to funnel traffic, and people, into the capital. Unless serious regional development plans are worked out the situation seems destined to only grow worse.

Other Sights

SÜKHBAATAR SQUARE
СУХБААТАРЫН ТАЛБАЙ

In July 1921 in the centre of Ulaanbaatar, the 'hero of the revolution', Damdin Sükhbaatar, declared Mongolia's final independence from the Chinese. The Square (Map pp70–1) now bears his name and features a **statue** of him astride his horse. The words he apparently proclaimed at the time are engraved on the bottom of the statue: 'If we, the whole people, unite in our common effort and common will, there will be nothing in the world that we cannot achieve, that we will not have learnt or failed to do.'

Sükhbaatar would have been very disappointed to learn that the Square was also where the first protests were held in 1990, which eventually led to the fall of communism in Mongolia. Today, the Square is occasionally used for rallies, ceremonies and even rock concerts, but is generally a serene place where only the photographers are doing anything. Near the centre of the Square, look for the large plaque that lists the former names of the city – Örgöö, Nomiin Khuree, Ikh Khuree and Niislel Khuree.

The enormous marble construction on the north end was completed in 2006 in time for the 800-year anniversary of Chinggis Khaan's coronation. At its centre is a seated bronze **Chinggis Khaan statue** lording over his nation. He is flanked by Ögedei (on the west) and Kublai (east). Two famed Mongol soldiers (Boruchu and Mukhlai) guard the entrance to the monument.

Behind the Ghengis monument stands **Parliament House**, which is commonly known as Government House. An inner courtyard of the building actually holds a large ceremonial ger for hosting visiting dignitaries.

To the northeast of the Square is the tall, modern **Palace of Culture**, a useful landmark containing the Mongolian National Modern Art Gallery and several other cultural institutions. At the southeast corner of the Square, the salmon-pinkish building is the **State Opera & Ballet Theatre**.

The clay-red building to the southwest is the **Mongolian Stock Exchange**, which was opened in 1992 in the former Children's Cinema. The small park opposite the Stock Exchange contains a **0-kilometer marker**, the point from which all distances in Mongolia are measured. For a blast from the past, walk east from the southeast corner of the Square to the **Lenin statue**. (For an even more dramatic bust of Lenin walk into the former **Lenin Museum**, on the north side of Liberty Sq.)

ZAISAN MEMORIAL & BUDDHA PARK

The tall, thin landmark on top of the hill south of the city is the **Zaisan Memorial** (Зайсан Толгой; off Map p64). Built by the Russians to commemorate 'unknown soldiers and heroes' from various wars, it offers the best views of Ulaanbaatar and the surrounding hills. The enormous tank at the bottom of the hill – part of the Mongolia People's Tank Brigade – saw action against the Nazis during WWII.

West of the memorial is the **Buddha Park**, featuring a 16m-tall standing Sakyamuni image. The funds to build the park were donated by a 99-year-old Mongolian monk named Guru Dev. Below the statue is a small room containing *thangkas*, sutras and images of the Buddha and his disciples.

To get there, catch bus 7 to the memorial. This bus departs from the Bayangol Hotel or Baga Toiruu near Anod Bank.

NAIRAMDAL PARK НАЙРАМДАЛ ПАРК

Also called the Children's Park, **Nairamdal Park** (Friendship Park; Map pp70-1), which includes a small amusement park, is being renovated by a Japanese company and will hopefully be operational by 2008. You can enter the park from south of the of Choijin Lama Temple Museum, or opposite the Bayangol Hotel.

ACTIVITIES

For a swim, try the heated **indoor pool** (Map p64; ☎ 318 180; Zaluuchuudyn Örgön Chölöö; per hr T4500; ☻ 8am-8pm Wed-Sun, closed 15 Jul-1 Aug) at the Zaluus Youth & Cultural Centre. When it's closed in summer you can join the locals and jump in the Tuul near the bridge by Zaisan Memorial. Across the street from the pool, the **Orchlon Gym** (Map p64; ☎ 354 326; Zaluuchuudyn Örgön Chölöö; per day/month T20,000/US$120; ☻ 7am-10pm Mon-Thu, 7am-7pm Fri, 10am-8pm Sat & Sun) has modern exercise facilities. **Titan Fitness** (Map pp70-1; ☎ 9905 2427; Chingisiin Örgön Chölöö; per day/month T6000/60,000; ☻ 6am-9pm) is another good option.

The **UB Golf Club** (off Map p64; ☎ 9979 9945, 9976 3377; 1 round US$20, caddy US$5, ball boy US$1) is a wild place where balls tend to get swallowed up even on the fairways – down marmot holes or

in the high grass. It's located 20km west of the city, about 3km before the Nairamdal Zulsan International Children's Centre. Additionally, there are two golf courses in Terelj National Park (p111).

If you are interested in paragliding lessons, contact Fly Mongolia (p114).

WALKING TOUR

Start/Finish Sükhbaatar Sq
Distance 5km
Duration 2½ hours

This walking tour will take you between some of the main downtown historical sites. Some parts are fairly exposed to the summer sun so bring a hat and sunblock.

Begin in **Sükhbaatar Sq** (1; p77) and head to the northwest corner where you'll spot the square-shaped **National Museum of Mongolian History** (2; p69). This offers a worthwhile introduction to Mongolian culture and will give you some idea of things you can expect to see in the countryside. Across the street is a Japanese garden donated by a Mongolian sumo wrestler.

Continue walking west on the newly named 'Tourist St'; the grey building on your right is the headquarters of the **General Intelligence Agency** (3, the Mongolian KGB), which has an excellent museum around the back. At the end of this building is **Taliin Mongol** (4; p86) our favourite restaurant in the city for Mongolian food (come back here later for dinner). On the next block you'll spot the **Zanabazar Museum of Fine Arts** (5; p69) which faces something called Builder's Sq. Across the street from the square is the **Federation for the Preservation of Mahayana Tradition** (6; opposite) Buddhist centre and its excellent Stupa Café – definitely worth popping in for a drink or snack. Between FPMT and the next street there are several excellent antique shops that are worth browsing.

The next block is **Urt Tsagaan (7)** pedestrian mall. There is nothing terribly exciting about the place, although it does have plenty of small shops, cafés, barbers and little stalls selling clothing and knick-knacks.

Continue towards Gandan Khiid, passing **Bakula Rinpoche Süm** (8; p76) and **Gesar Süm** (9; p76). The lane uphill towards Gandan Khiid leads into the original ger district that has circled the monastery for 170 years. Near

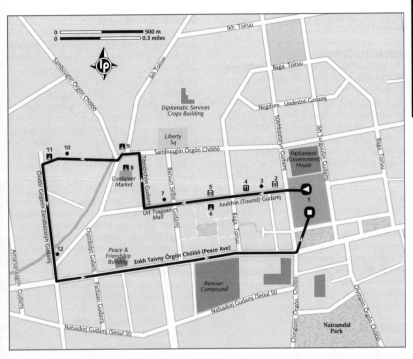

the eastern gate you might see **fortune tellers (10)** who make divinations using coins, sheep ankle bones and tarot cards. From **Gandan Khiid (11**; p73), walk down Öndör Gegeen Zanabazaryn Gudamj, passing the **Centre of Shaman Eternal Heavenly Sophistication (12**; p75) on your left. End this tour with a stroll down Peace Ave and back to the Square.

COURSES
Language

It's possible to ask around for 'exchange lessons' at the National University of Mongolia and the Institute of Foreign Languages (p80) in Ulaanbaatar. A better idea is to attend one of the language schools in Ulaanbaatar, which can organise long- and short-term courses. Recommended schools in Ulaanbaatar include the following:

Bridge Mongolian Language Center (off Map p64; ☎ 367 149; www.bridge.url.mn/english; PO Box 955, Ulaanbaatar-13) Receiving consistently positive reviews, this language centre offers an intensive two-week survival course, as well as longer courses and individual tuition. Costs are US$5 to US$7 per hour for a private lesson or US$4 per person for a group lesson. Note that the direc-

tions it gives on its website are obsolete; it's on the eastern side of the city past the Khan Palace hotel.

Friends School (off Map p64; ☎ 454 513; www.friendscompany.mn; Apt 64/2 Bayanzürkh District, 5th Microdistrict) Short-term survival Mongolian classes are available. Located just northeast of the Bridge School.

International Language Center (Map pp70-1; ☎ 313 727; www.ilcschool.com; Choimbolyn 6) Language courses for a reasonable T40,000 per month or T5000 per hour. Convenient central location.

Buddhism

The **Federation for the Preservation of Mahayana Tradition** (FPMT; Map pp70-1; ☎ 321 580, 9987 9535; www.fpmtmongolia.mn; Builder's Sq, Juulchin Gudamj) is involved in the regeneration of Buddhist culture in Mongolia. The centre offers free lectures and courses on various aspects of Buddhist tradition and meditation. Lectures are given in English (at the time of writing, Monday to Thursday at 6.30pm); look for the pink-tiled building west of the Mormon Church.

Yoga

The Ananda Café & Meditation Centre (p90) offers yoga courses nightly at 6.30pm. (Hatha yoga with chanting and meditation.) Contact ☎ 9913 2100 for details.

University Courses

The **National University of Mongolia** (NUM; Map pp70–1; ☎ 320 159; www.num.edu.mn; Ikh Surguuliin Gudamj 1, PO Box 46a/523, 210646) is northeast of Sükhbaatar Sq. The school offers specialised classes on Mongolian culture and language, and has a foreign-student department. The office is in the main building, room 213. Response to these programmes by students is quite mixed particularly when it comes to teaching Mongolian (the general consensus is that the language schools do a much better job at this).

Flexible group and private Mongolian-language lessons are available at the **Institute of International Studies** (Map pp70–1; ☎ 329 860; dash purev@magicnet.mn), opposite the university.

The **American Center for Mongolian Studies** (Map pp70–1; ☎ 350 486; www.mongoliacenter.org; National University of Mongolia, Bldg 5, Room 304) has a good website listing courses and can recommend study possibilities.

TOURS
Ulaanbaatar

It is not particularly easy to join an organised tour of Ulaanbaatar if you have arrived as an independent traveller. You can try to contact one of the companies offering tours under Outside Ulaanbaatar (right) and see what they have available.

Ulaanbaatar is a walkable city so it's easy enough see it on your own using this guide and a map. Alternatively, leave this book in your hotel and go and wander off on your own for a while. Although not really necessary, if you do hire a taxi to drive you around, a guide-cum-interpreter could be handy.

The **Arts Council of Mongolia** (Map pp70–1; ☎ 319 015; www.artscouncil.mn; cnr Juulchin Gudamj & Baruun Selbe Gudamj) sponsors two excellent specialised city tours twice a month or by appointment. 'Myths and Truths: the Socialist Legacy in Mongolia Tour' visits places associated with the communist era, and the 'Mongolian Buddhism Tour' explores Ulaanbaatar's Buddhist legacy beyond the main tourist attractions. Both tours, which last from 10am to 4pm, provide excellent commentary and lunch at a nice restaurant. Prices vary depending on the size of your group, but count on paying about US$70 per person.

Outside Ulaanbaatar

Of the hundred or more travel agencies offering tours that have sprung up around Ulaanbaatar in the past few years, the dozen or so listed following are recommended as being generally reliable. You can expect to pay around US$30 to US$50 including food, accommodation, tickets to sights and guide (who will double as a cook). The price of a vehicle is an extra US$60 per day including driver and petrol, so you can lower your costs if you have more people to split this cost.

Budget travellers often organise ad-hoc tours via their guesthouse or Chez Bernard Café (p90). If you do this try to meet the driver and guide before the trip and ensure that everyone knows the itinerary and exactly what is included. Khongor, Idre's, Golden Gobi and UB guesthouses (see p82) all run fairly standard trips that get consistently good reviews. Shop around and see who can offer the most creative schedule at the best price. You can expect to pay around US$50 to US$60 for a vehicle and another US$15 per day for a guide (optional). Budget tours don't include food or accommodation; however, they usually include stoves for cooking your own food and tents for camping out.

The main difference between the tour operators and the guesthouses is the quality of the guides. Guides from guesthouses are usually inexperienced in the field and not particularly knowledgeable when it comes to history or culture. Oftentimes they are students and their main qualification is that they can speak English (which at least allows you to communicate with locals and the driver). Tour operators, on the other hand, hire specialists in history and culture or they may be particularly skilled trekking or horse guides. This can be a huge help in the backcountry as rural guides and horse boys won't speak English.

In summer you may be approached by students or other young Mongols who organise their own tours, charging around US$90 per day for up to six people. One such person is the delightfully energetic **Meg Erdenekhuu** (☎ 9964 3242; travelwith_meg@hotmail.com) who specialises in trips to the Gobi (her area of expertise is geology and palaeontology) but can take you to virtually any corner of the country.

Active Mongolia (Map pp70–1; ☎ 329 456; www .activemongolia.com) This reliable Scottish-German operation specialises in rugged hiking, rafting and horseback trips, plus mountain biking. Most of the trips are to the

ASRAL & KUNCHAB JAMPA LING BUDDHIST CENTRE

Located in the northwest corner of the city, **Asral** (Map p64; ☎ 304 838; www.asralmongolia.org) is a new NGO and Buddhist social centre that supports impoverished families. Its main aim is to stop disadvantaged youths from becoming street children. It also provides skills and jobs for unemployed women; an on-site felt-making cooperative turns out some lovely products.

The Buddhist arm of the organisation has classes on Buddhism and meditation although for now these are only offered in Mongolian. In summer, a high Tibetan Lama, Panchen Otrul Rinpoche, visits the centre and provides religious teachings.

Asral encourages travellers to visit the centre. You can meet the felt-makers and buy their products or even volunteer your time. The centre is always looking for English teachers or gardeners to work on a small farm in Gachuurt. The centre is in the 3/4 district opposite the Gobi Sauna, slightly off the main road. It's best to call before you visit. Take bus 21, 29 or 13 to the last stop and continue walking for 300m. Asral is a two-storey cream-coloured building on your right.

---

aimags Khövsgöl, Arkhangai and Khentii. It's based at Seven Summits, opposite the CPO. Contact Sylvia Hay.

Happy Camel (Map pp70-1; ☎ 8810 0133; www .happycamel.com; Peace Ave 27) It operates out of Chez Bernard; see p90.

Hovsgol Travel Company (Map pp70-1; ☎ 460 368; www.hovsgoltravel.com; PO Box 2003; Namyanjugiin Gudamj) Specialises in boat and horse trips around Khövs-göl. Runs the popular Camp Toilogt.

Juulchin (Map pp70-1; ☎ 328 428; www.juulchin .com; Bayangol Hotel, 5b Chingisiin Örgön Chölöö) Its office is at the back of Bayangol Hotel.

Karakorum Expeditions (Map pp70-1; ☎ 320 182, 9911 6729; www.gomongolia.com; PO Box 542) The leader in bike and hiking tours in western Mongolia, it also offers trips to China. The company has a good philosophy: a big plus is that it runs snow-leopard research trips and wildlife tours. The office is behind the State Circus in the Gangaryn Gurav building. Contact Graham Taylor.

Khövsgöl Lodge Company (Map pp70-1; ☎ 9911 5929; www.boojum.com; Sükhbaatar District, Bldg 33, Room 16) This experienced outfitter is part of the US-based Boojum Expeditions. It is in an apartment block behind the Drama Theatre, but you are better off calling first to get someone to meet you. Contact Bobo or Anya.

Mongolia Expeditions (Map pp70-1; ☎ 329 279, 9909 6911; info@mongolia-expeditions.com; Jamyn Gunii Gudamj 5-2) Specialises in adventure travel, including cycle touring, mountaineering, caving and rafting trips, as well as more sedentary options such as flower-watching tours. It is particularly experienced in tours to western Mongolia. It's located on the west side of the Choijin Lama Temple Museum.

Nomadic Expeditions (Map pp70-1; ☎ 313 396, 325 786; www.threecamellodge.com; Peace Ave 76) This is the Mongolian office of the US-based travel company (see the boxed text, p270).

Nomadic Journeys (Map pp70-1; ☎ 328 737; www .nomadicjourneys.com; Sükhbaataryn Gudamj 1) This Swedish-Mongolian joint venture, concentrating on low-impact tourism, runs fixed-departure yak, camel and horse treks and can also arrange rafting trips on the Tuul Gol. Its trip in Terelj is unique – you walk while yaks haul your own portable ger on a cart. This is a great outfit for the eco-conscious traveller. Contact Jan Wigsten or Manduhai.

Nomads (Map pp70-1; ☎ /fax 328 146; www .nomadstours.com; Suite 8-9, 3rd fl, Peace & Friendship Bldg, Peace Ave, PO Box 1008) Offers a wide range of fixed-departure tours, including popular horse treks in Khentii and through Terelj, visiting Günjiin Süm. Nomads also offers fabulous jeep trips to more remote areas in the far west and camel treks in the Gobi. Its office location will change in 2009; check the website.

Radiant Sky (Map pp70–1; ☎ 9192 9366; www .radiant-sky.com; Peace Ave 15, Apt 6) Mongolian-run outfit that does reasonably priced tours across the country. It specialises in small-group horseback and jeep adventures in western and northern Mongolia.

Rinky Dink Travel Mongolia (☎ 9974 4162; www .rinkydinktravel.com, susanmongolia@yahoo.com; PO Box 1927) As the name indicates, this is a small tour company that keeps its trips simple, safe and fun. It has homestays in ger districts and takes you out of Ulaanbaatar to meet nomad families. It is involved in social development programmes in poor neighbourhoods and invites tourists to volunteer for its projects. There is no actual 'office' to drop into – you just contact them and they will pick you up.

Samar Magic Tours (Map pp70-1; ☎ 311 051, 9928 2459; www.samarmagictours.com; PO Box 329) Based at El Latino restaurant, this company runs fishing expeditions and a ger camp near Terelj. Contact Spanish- and English-speaking Christo Camilo Gavilla Gomez.

Tseren Tours (Map pp70-1; ☎ 9974 0832, 327 083; www.tserentours.com; Baruun Selbe Gudamj 14/1) Dutch-and Mongolian-run outfit that does countrywide tours, biking trips and stays with nomad families.

Tsolmon Travel (Map pp70-1; ☎ 322 870; www .tsolmontravel.com; Chinggis Örgön Chölöö 61/19) Country-wide tours and the operator of Buveit ger camp in Terelj.

Wind of Mongolia (Map pp70-1; ☎ 328 754, 9909 0593; www.windofmongolia.mn; Sükhbaatar District, 5th Microdistrict, Bldg 17, Apt 15) This French-run tour operator offers creative and offbeat trips, including rock climbing, dog sledding (in winter) and tours that focus on Buddhism. Contact Joel Rauzy.

FESTIVALS & EVENTS

The biggest event in Ulaanbaatar is undoubtedly the **Naadam** (Festival), held on 11 and 12 July. Some visitors may not find the festival itself terribly exciting, but the associated activities during the Naadam week and the general festive mood make it a great time to visit. For more information, see the boxed text, p96.

Around Naadam and other public holidays, special cultural events and shows are organised. It is worth reading the local English-language newspapers and asking a Mongolian friend, guide or hotel staff member to find out what may be on.

At the end of July, on a date set by the lunar calendar, you can see **tsam-mask dancing** at Dashchoilon Khiid.

The last week in October sees the **city's birthday** – it was founded in 1639. Events and concerts are usually put on at this time at the Palace of Culture or State Opera & Ballet Theatre. See www.artscouncil.mn for details.

In the middle of March, it's definitely worth checking out the **Camel Polo Winter Festival**, featuring camel polo and racing. This is a nontouristy event and you'll be able to mix and mingle with spectators dressed in traditional attire (big *dels* – traditional coats – and boots). Participating teams come mainly from the Gobi and even Inner Mongolia. A camel parade in Sükhbaatar Sq is part of the festivities.

For more info see p255.

SLEEPING

There is a wide range of places to stay in the capital city, with some of the best deals at the bottom and top ends. During the week surrounding Naadam, accommodation may be in short supply and prices are often higher.

Budget

APARTMENTS

If you are planning to stay in Ulaanbaatar for a while or you are travelling in a small group, it's worth looking around for an apartment to rent. A reasonable, furnished, two-bedroom apartment with a kitchen in an old Russian

building costs from US$200 to US$300 per month. Check the classified sections of the local English-language newspapers. **Mongolian Properties** (Map pp70-1; ☎ 324 545; www.mongolia -properties.com; Seoul St 48/13) has apartments for rent on a long-term basis. Another recommended agent is **Mongolian Real Estate** (☎ 9918 1786; www.mongolianrealestate.com). You could also ask at the guesthouses, which sometimes rent out apartments for around US$20 to US$30 per night for short-term stays.

GUESTHOUSES

Most city guesthouses have been carved out of the old Russian apartments; this sometimes makes them hard to find as you need to weave through courtyards and find the correct door out of many anonymous steel doors. Most guesthouses offer a hot shower and a kitchen. Almost all offer trips to nearby attractions, as well as visa extension and registration, laundry and the booking of train tickets. If overbooked you may be shoved into an apartment with the owner's grandmother – there's always room for one more.

Gana's Guest House (Map pp70-1; ☎/fax 367 343; www.ganasger.mn; Gandan Khiid ger district, House No 22; dm/ger US$3/5, d US$15; 💻) If you fancy staying in a ger district, drop by this longtime backpacker hangout. Owner Gana has accommodation in private rooms inside a main block, or you could stay in a ger on the roof. Facilities include free internet, breakfast and 24-hour security. To find it, head up Öndör Gegeen Zanabazaryn Gudamj on the way to Gandan Khiid and look for the small sign that points right down a narrow alley.

ourpick Khongor Guest House (Map pp70-1; ☎ 316 415, 9925 2599; http://get.to/khongor; Peace Ave 15, Apt 6; dm/s/d US$4/10/12; 💻) The experienced, English-speaking manager Toroo offers well-appointed accommodation in three separate buildings, each convenient and central. Amenities include free airport/train station pick up, breakfast, free email checks and safety lock-up box – check out the glowing reports on the website. Among the guesthouses, Khongor's trips get some of the best reviews and the management bends over backwards in handling logistics, ticketing and visa matters. The entrance of the guesthouse is around the back of the third building west of the State Department Store.

Idre's Guest House (Map pp70-1; ☎ 316 749, 9916 6049; www.idretour.com; Undsen Khuulin Gudamj; dm

---

GOING UNDERGROUND

While the streets of Ulaanbaatar heave with traffic and congestion, a group of people have found quiet and warm refuge beneath the pavement. Since the early 1990s, homeless people (both adults and children) have made homes in the sewer systems of Ulaanbaatar. The sewers are particularly useful in winter when the hot water pipes keep them warm.

In the mid-1990s up to 6000 people lived in the sewers, most of them children. An increase in the number of orphanages has since brought the number down into the hundreds. Many of the kids (especially boys) prefer the freedom of the streets in summer rather than the strict rules and classes of homeless shelters, but winters are brutal. Girls often end up in prostitution. Both sexes suffer from high rates of malnutrition, syphilis, scabies and body lice.

Some kids who grew up on the streets in the 1990s are now part of a growing criminal element, although many are now in jail (if they haven't already died). There have been a few turnaround stories, however, including one former street girl who was taken in by the Lotus Children Centre, learned English and now makes US$300 a month as a translator at a mining company.

Ulaanbaatar has around 20 shelters, many run by foreign NGOs, with beds for around 500 children. Several aid agencies work with the children, including **Save the Children** (www.savethechildren .org), the National Centre for Children and the **Lotus Children's Centre** (www.lotuschild.org).

The **Christina Noble Foundation** (☎ 9909 8377; www.cncf.org) operates a shelter on the edge of town and runs several education and health programmes. If you ring ahead you might be able to visit the facilities. The Lotus Children's Centre is also happy to meet visitors – visits are usually handled by Tseren Tours (p81). Money is not usually requested, but the centres are happy to accept donations.

US$4, s/d US$14/16, s/d without bathroom US$12/14; 🖳) Amiable host Idre has constructed a single-floor guesthouse with several dorms and private rooms. There is a central lounge, small kitchen and a book exchange. It's located near the old long-distance bus station (Teeveriin Tovchoo) in a dusty corner of town. Idre also runs ger accommodation in Töv Aimag, near Mandshir Khiid.

UB Guesthouse (Map pp70-1; ☎ 311 037, 9119 9859; www.ubguest.com; Tserendorjiin Gudamj; dm/s/d US$5/10/16; 🖳) At the time of writing this popular guesthouse was planning to move to a six-storey building opposite the State Department Store. The new guesthouse will have more than 100 beds, making it easily the biggest in this category. The management here gets very mixed reviews.

Golden Gobi (Map pp70-1; ☎ 322 632, 9665 4496; www .goldengobi.com; dm/d US$5/16, d without bathroom US$14; 🖳) With its colourful walls, funky décor and friendly vibe, this has become one of the most popular backpacker places in town. It has two lounges and some rooms with private bathroom. A young, friendly and totally laid-back management is another bonus. Price includes breakfast. It's off the corner of Baruun Selbe Gudamj and Peace Ave.

LG Guesthouse (Map p64; ☎ 328 243, 9989 4672; www .lg.url.mn; Narny Gudamj; dm US$5-7, s/d US$12/16; 🖳)

With 12 rooms this is one of the largest guesthouses in the city. It has dorms and private rooms with attached bathroom, a common area, kitchen where you can cook your own meals and a restaurant on the ground floor. Bathrooms are clean and have hot-water boilers – important in summer when other places only have cold water. It's a little out of the centre, on the road towards the train station.

Tiara Guesthouse (Map p64; ☎ 2125 2319, 9905 4244; www.tiaraguesthouse.com; October St 28-35, Bogd Ar Subdistrict No 5A; dm US$7; 🖳) Likable Dutch- and Mongolian-run guesthouse with smart dorms and a brightly-lit lounge. It's one of the best backpacker setups in town, although a little outside the centre. It's hard to spot: with your back to the XAAH Bank, walk through the gap to the right of the Fresco Market (the red-roofed temple is to your right). After 50m turn left up the ramp and look for the sign.

Zaya Backpacker Hostel (Map pp70-1; ☎ 316 696, 9918 5013; www.zayahostel.com; Peace Ave; dm US$10, s/d US$24/28, s/d with shared bathroom US$22/24; 🖳) Unlike most other guesthouses, this one is in a new building with hardwood floors, modern bathrooms, a comfortable lounge and new furnishings. Value for money, it's even better than most midrange hotels in the city. It's on the 3rd floor of an orange building behind the Peace & Friendship Building; when it's full, guests are moved to less desirable apartments across the road (but pay the same rates).

Oasis Café & Guesthouse (off Map p64; ☎ 463 393, 9909 3696; www.intergam-oasis.com; Nalaikh Gudamj; dm US$12; **P** 🖳) Austrian-German-run place with beautiful accommodation in dorms, gers and private rooms with attached bathroom. It has a large yard and a brightly-painted café, which serves excellent Austrian meals and pastries. Located 5km east of Sükhbaatar Sq (in the Amgalan district; GPS: N47° 54.706', E106° 58.857'). Prices include breakfast.

More recommended guesthouses include the following:

Chinggis Guesthouse (Map pp70-1; ☎ 325 941, 9927 1843; www.chingisguest.mn; dm US$6; 🖳) Clean and friendly four-room apartment guesthouse. It's back behind the National Academic Drama Theatre and Bayangol Hotel.

GobiTours & Guesthouse (Map pp70-1; ☎ 322 339, 9982 1598; www.gobitours.com; Peace Ave 61, Door 20, Room 25; dm US$6; 🖳) Welcoming and friendly guesthouse but it's a bit small and does get crowded. Very central, it's in the U-shaped white apartment block opposite the post office.

Nassan's Guest House (Map pp70-1; ☎ 321 078, 9919 7466; www.nassantour.com; Baga Toiruu west; dm US$6, s/d/tr US$16/18/20; 🖳) In the heart of the city, Nassan offers accommodation in one of six apartments spread over one apartment block. Each apartment has kitchen facilities.

Ciel Mongol (Map p64; ☎ 9977 2960; www.cielmongol .com; Khoroolol 13, Bldg 22-6, Door 5-p; dm US$7, d without bathroom US$17; 🖳) French-owned guesthouse with clean, nicely decorated rooms. It's hidden among apartment blocks so call ahead for a pick-up.

HOTELS

There are few hotels to recommend in the budget category and most backpackers wind up at a guesthouse. But if you're set on staying at a proper hotel the following options are doable.

Mandukhai Hotel (Map pp70-1; ☎ 322 204; s/d/tr T12,000/18,000/23,000, lux s/d T25,000/40,000) Rooms in the Soviet-era Mandukhai have been renovated with new carpets, drapes and bathrooms but the rambling hallways are still very rundown. Located in the second building west of the Wrestling Palace.

Hotel Örgöö (Map pp70-1; ☎ 313 772; cnr Juulchin Gudamj & Jigjidjavanyn Gudamj; s/d US$25/40, ste s/d US$45/60) Although it's in dire need of renovation, this old dinosaur is still worth mentioning for its central and quiet location. Fine for a night or two at this price.

Guide House Hotel (Map pp70-1; ☎ 353 582, 353 887; guidehouse@mobinet.mn; Baga Toiruu north; r US$30, half-lux US$45, lux US$60) Between Dashchoilon Khiid and Baga Toiruu, this hidden hotel offers clean and comfortable rooms. Its best feature is its large and modern bathroom, plus the free Swedish breakfast. It's the best pick in this range.

CAMPING & GER CAMPS

There are no official camping grounds in Ulaanbaatar but you'll find endless patches of grass to pitch a tent on Bogd Khan Uul to the south of the city. Try the valley behind the Zaisan Memorial. The main problem, of course, is what to do with all your stuff during the day; theft is a problem, so you're probably better off going to Gachuurt (p114) or Mandshir Khiid (p109).

Bogd Khan Ger Camp (off Map p64; ☎ 9191 9129, 9666 0229, 8811 1292; ger T35,000-45,000, ger without bathroom T12,000-20,000) Sports around 100 gers, some basic with shared bathroom and others decked out with furniture and modern attached bathroom. It's 3km south of the Tuul Gol (behind Zaisan) although there is no regular transport.

Midrange

Ulaanbaatar is definitely short on decent midrange hotels but the following are a few reasonable options. Places in this range normally include breakfast.

Seoul Hotel (Map pp70-1; ☎ 314 507; Peace Ave; s/d US$30/40, lux s/d US$50/60; 🖳) Although not a family-oriented hotel (it has a striptease bar on the 2nd floor and condom bowls scattered throughout), it's reasonably priced and clean.

Voyage Hotel (Map p64; ☎ 327 213; Narny Gudamj; s/d/half-lux/lux US$30/50/65/90; 🖳) Representing good value, the 30-room Voyage has attentive staff and pleasant rooms. Facilities include two restaurants (European and Korean), free internet and sauna. The low price is a reflection of its less than perfect location, on the busy road to the train station.

Kharaa Hotel (Map pp70-1; ☎ 313 733; Choimbolyn Gudamj 6; d/half-lux/lux US$35/45/60; 🖳) One of the few hotels in this range to have been renovated with a tasteful, retrained style. Each of the 29 rooms contains a fridge, TV and desk. Views are best from the street side of the building.

Genex Hotel (Map pp70-1; ☎ 319 326; www .generalimpex.mn; Choimbolyn Gudamj 10; s/d US$35/56,

---

GER DISTRICT DIGS

As Ulaanbaatar's centre booms with high-rise construction sites and multimillion dollar property developments, its ger (yurt) districts remain trapped in time. By staying in one you'll get a real sense of traditional Mongolian family life, at the same time gaining an appreciation for the difficulties that ger residents must endure. Several tour companies offer walks through ger districts but to achieve the full living experience contact **Rinky Dink Travel Mongolia** (see p81) which can set you up with a homestay in a ger district and place you as a volunteer in its social development projects. A typical stay might include digging a pit toilet, repairing a fence, doing art projects with street kids or teaching English. You'll live like the locals (pit toilets, no running water, difficult transport) but you'll also encounter some of the friendliest people anywhere and gain a perspective on the city that few people encounter. Visits can last between three days to several weeks.

---

half-lux US$48/80, lux US$75/120) Bland but clean rooms overlook a quiet street near Gandan Monastery and Peace Ave. Tacky, pseudo-European atmosphere prevails. The lux rooms are a little odd-looking, with two queen-size beds pushed into a triangular-shaped alcove.

Zaluuchuud Hotel (Map pp70-1; ☎ 324 594; www .zh.mn; Baga Toiruu 43; s/d/ste incl breakfast US$35/65/90; ▣) One of Ulaanbaatar's oldest hotels, the Zaluuchuud (Young People) has seen renovations that have raised it to the midrange category. Not all the rooms are the same size so you might try asking for an en suite standard, which includes a bedroom and a sitting room with TV. Room 300 is a good choice.

Top End

All top-end places include breakfast, but often they also include service and government charges of between 10% and 20%. Major credit cards are accepted and reservations are advisable in the peak season, especially around Naadam time. In addition to the following, a Hilton is expected to open its doors in 2008.

Ulaanbaatar Hotel (Map pp70-1; ☎ 320 620; http:// welcome.to/ubhotel; Baga Toiruu; s US$60-70, d US$90, s/d ste US$90/120, s/d lux US$120/160; ▣) The Ulaanbaatar Hotel is the grand old dame of Mongolia. Built back in the 1950s, this was where Soviet dignitaries stayed during their visits to UB. It still carries an air of the Khrushchev era with its high ceilings, chandeliers, a marble staircase and a lavish ballroom. The hotel also contains two restaurants, a bar, a travel agency, business centre, sauna and beauty parlour. Amazingly, it also contains a golf practice range.

Bayangol Hotel (Map pp70-1; ☎ 312 255; www .bayangolhotel.mn; Chingisiin Örgön Chölöö 5; s/d US$76/97, lux US$142/174, ste US$252/295; ▣ ☒ ▣) One of Ulaanbaatar's biggest and most reliable ho-

tels, the Bayangol consists of two 12-storey towers that dominate the skyline south of the Square. Rooms have been renovated and even come with a personal computer, which you can use for work or internet. There is an imported-goods shop here and two excellent restaurants, the Casablanca (for Singaporean food) and the Taj Mahal (for Indian).

Chinggis Khaan Hotel (Map pp70-1; ☎ 313 380; www .chinggis-hotel.com; Tokyogiin Gudamj 10; s US$84, d US$107- 119, s/d half-lux US$119/144, s/d lux US$179, ste US$333; ▣ ▣ ☎) The Chinggis Khaan is Mongolia's biggest, brashest hotel. It has all the facilities you could dream of, including indoor pool, travel agent and an attached shopping mall. Rooms are well-appointed and of international four-star standard; choose one that faces west for a view of the Bogd Khan mountain and downtown Ulaanbaatar.

Khan Palace (Map p64; ☎ 463 463; www.khanpalace .com; East Cross Rd; s/d US$98/121, half-lux US$115/144, lux US$173/219, ste US$345-518; ▣ ☒ ▣) Ulaanbaatar's newest luxury hotel is a Kempinski-managed Japanese-invested venture on the east end of Peace Ave. Rooms are plush, with a tasteful design and little niceties such as humidifier, robes and slippers. The hotel also has free internet, a fitness centre and sauna, but no swimming pool. Expats say the breakfast is the best in town.

our pick Corporate Hotel (Map pp70-1; ☎ 334 411; www.corporatehotel.mn; Chingisiin Örgön Chölöö 9- 2; s/d US$140/185, half-lux US$160/220, lux US$180/240, ste US$350/460; ☒ ▣) With its slender tower and minimalist design, the Corporate looks like a slice of Tokyo lost in the tangle of Ulaanbaatar's ungainly Soviet architecture. Thanks to the unique design of the building, most rooms are on corners, with windows facing in two directions. It has a restaurant, sauna, Jacuzzi, fitness room and a spectacular roof-top bar on the 11th floor. This is a great place to come for a drink even if you're not staying here.

Also recommended:

Puma Imperial (Map pp70-1; ☎ 313 043; www .mongolianpumahotel.com; Ikh Surguuliin Gudamj; s/tw/d US$63/100/105; **P** **Ⓛ**) Popular with visiting journalists and diplomats wanting to be close to the Square. None of the rooms have a particularly good view.

Continental Hotel (Map pp70-1; ☎ 323 829; www .continentalhotel.ulaanbaatar.net; Olympiin Örgön Chölöö; s/d US$79/107, half-lux US$105/132, lux US$130/168; **P** **Ⓛ**) This rather incongruous hotel bears a striking resemblance to the White House. Facilities include a small fitness centre, with a charge of US$9 per hour.

Narantuul Hotel (Map pp70-1; ☎ 330 565; www .narantuulhotel.com; Peace Ave; s/d/tr US$79/89/99, half-lux s/d/tr US$109/119/129, lux s/d US$149/159; **Ⓛ**) Eye-pleasing rooms have modern but subtle décor, with a few nice touches, such as flat-panel TVs. It has two restaurants, a business centre, sauna and beauty salon.

EATING

The two best roads for all kinds of restaurants and cafés are Baga Toiruu west and Peace Ave, near the State Department Store.

Restaurants

Forget everything you've heard about the food in Mongolia, Ulaanbaatar is blanketed with marvellous locally owned bistros and restaurants, and a few top-end places run by Western and Asian expats.

MONGOLIAN

There has been a small explosion of restaurants serving gourmet Mongolian cuisine, as unlikely as that may sound. Some are the genuine article, serving Mongolian delicacies (various forms of meat and milk combinations) in a pleasant atmosphere. Other places are geared towards the tourist crowd, usually dealing in Mongolian barbecue (the Americanised version of Mongolian food).

Taliin Mongol (Map pp70-1; ☎ 319 451; Juulchin Gudamj; meals T4000-6000; ☯ 9am-midnight) Once you've eaten at this delicious restaurant Mongolian food will never taste the same again. Walk inside to find walls covered with tasteful art and *tamga* (traditional livestock brands used by herders), as well as a miniature felt ger with faux fire and furniture. Start your meal with a 'soup of power' (flavoured with *aarts*, a type of sour whey), and then try any

number of Mongol treats, including grilled yak cheese with yogurt, Buriat pancakes, lamb *khorkhog* (steamed meat), traditional Kazakh horse sausage and even boiled lamb's head! Wash these gourmet delights down with a glass of camel milk or sea buckthorn wine. It's located on the east side of the Mongolian GIA building.

City Nomads (Map p64; ☎ 454 484; Peace Ave 16; dishes T4000-8000; ☯ noon-11pm) Upscale Mongolian atmosphere although most of the steak, chicken and fish menu is Western in style and taste. It's attached to the Negdelchin Hotel.

Nomad Legends Mongols Club (Map pp70-1; ☎ 326 631; Sükhbaataryn Gudamj 1; meals T6000-8000; ☯ noon-midnight) A branch of City Nomads, this smaller restaurant-café is a great place to stop for a Mongolian milk tea or plate of not-so-greasy *khuushuur* (fried meat pancake). The décor of contemporary Mongol art looks touristy, but it's quite popular with locals. Both this place and City Nomads are related to the inferior Modern Nomads.

BD's Mongolian Barbeque (Map pp70-1; ☎ 311 191; Seoul St; all-you-can-eat BBQ T7700; ☯ noon-midnight) This is the first American chain restaurant to open a franchise in Mongolia – ironically, it's not American cuisine but Mongolian barbecue. Despite the staged atmosphere, Mongolians seem to like it and it's certainly a filling option if you're half-starved after a countryside trip. Profits from the restaurant go to the Mongolian Youth Development Federation (MYDF).

There are dozens of **Mongolian fast-food restaurants** (*guanz*) and they can be found on every block in the city. Some are chain restaurants and you'll start to recognise prominent eateries, including Zochin Buuz (Зочин Бууз), Khaan Buuz (Хаан Бууз) and Mongol Khuushuur (Монгол Хуушуур). They serve up industrial-sized *buuz* (steamed mutton dumplings), plus soups and *bifshteks ondogtei* (beefsteak with egg); many of these places operate 24 hours. Meals cost T900 to T1500. There is a popular Zochin Buuz (Map pp70–1) on Peace Ave, opposite the Russian embassy, and a nice Khaan Buuz (Map pp70–1) west from the Flower Center on Baga Toiruu west.

ASIAN

Just about every block in downtown Ulaanbaatar has a Korean barbecue restaurant. And if you don't spot one of those, a Chinese, Japanese or Indian restaurant won't be far

---

HOTEL BARS & RESTAURANTS

In most cities, travellers tend to overlook the restaurants and bars set inside hotels, or only eat at the hotel in which they are staying. Ulaanbaatar, however, has a number of excellent restaurants and bars, privately owned and managed, inside the city's top end hotels. The best include:

- Khan Palace: Sakura (below) is an excellent Japanese restaurant. The hotel also offers a quality breakfast buffet complete with omelette chef!
- Chinggis Khaan Hotel (p85): Mr Wang is a good Chinese restaurant.
- Bayangol Hotel (p85): There are two great restaurants in the Casablanca and Taj Mahal (below).
- Puma Imperial (opposite): Delhi Darbar is an Indian restaurant.
- White House Hotel: Strings (p88) is the closest thing Mongolia has to a Hard Rock Café.
- Corporate Hotel (p85): Home to View Lounge, a spectacular roof-top bar.

---

away. The Korean, Chinese and Japanese script on the signboard is usually covered (an edict issued by a Mongolian nationalist gang called Dayan Mongol), so the signs will be in Cyrillic or English.

Taj Mahal (Map pp70-1; ☎ 311 009; Bayangol Hotel, Tower B, Chingisiin Örgön Chölöö 5; dishes T4000-5000, thalli T6000; ◷ noon-midnight) Amiable owner Babu prepares a range of tandoori and North Indian dishes such as *murgh makhni* (butter chicken). The lunchtime *thalli* (set menu) gives you three curries, dhal, salad, rice, bread and dessert. We liked the interior too – the papier-mâché elephant and reconstruction of the Taj Mahal façade adds a nice touch.

Mokran Pyongyang Restaurant (Map pp70-1; ☎ 9986 9305; cnr Peace Ave & Öndör Gegeen Zanabazaryn Gudamj; meals T5000, sushi platter T10,000; ◷ noon-10.30pm) Offers a mix of Japanese and Korean dishes. Sushi is half-price here on weekends but the real reason to come here is to experience the 'Friendship Cultural Centre of North Korea'. There are paintings of North Korea on the walls and you can watch North Korean DVDs while you eat (ask to see the Mass Games DVD). It's a unique chance to speak with the North Koreans who run the place and well-worth visiting if you have an interest in the hermit kingdom.

Hazara (Map p64; ☎ 480 214, 9919 5007; Peace Ave 16; dishes T6000-8000; ◷ noon-2.30pm & 6-10pm) This North Indian restaurant has been serving up delectable dishes for more than a decade, always with the same winning menu and colourful décor. Each table is covered by a colourful *samiyan* (Rajasthani tent), so it's easy to escape to India for an hour or two while you dine on excellent *murgh makhni*, naan basket and saffron rice. In terms of pure

taste, quality of service, freshness of food and consistency, this is arguably the best restaurant in town. Hazara is located behind the Wrestling Palace.

Other recommendations:

Ba Shu Restaurant (Map pp70-1; ☎ 321 767; cnr Peace Ave & Baruun Selbe Gudamj; dishes T2500) Reasonably priced and central Chinese restaurant.

City Café (Map pp70-1; ☎ 328 077; cnr Peace Ave & Chingisiin Örgön Chölöö; dishes T3800-6000; ◷ 10am-11pm; wi-fi) On the 1st floor of the Mongolian Artists' Exhibition Hall, it has some surprisingly good Chinese and Korean dishes.

Shilla (Map pp70-1; ☎ 9119 2231; Od Plaza, Seoul St; meals T6000-8000) Slick and professional Korean barbecue.

A great place for Japanese is the restaurant **Sakura** (Map p64; Khan Palace Hotel; East Cross Rd; meals T4500-9000). There are a few other hotels with decent Asian restaurants, including a Chinese place at the Chinggis Khaan (p85), another Chinese restaurant in the Ulaanbaatar Hotel (p85) and the Singaporean-styled Casablanca restaurant at the Bayangol Hotel (p85).

WESTERN

CCCP (Map pp70-1; ☎ 9927 4740; cnr Ikh Surguuliin Gudamj & Zaluuchuudyn Örgön Chölöö; dishes T2500-4000; ◷ 11am-midnight) The Beatles song 'Back in the USSR' will spring to mind when you enter this kitsch Soviet time warp. Meals include old Russian favourites such as *pelmeni* (dumpling soup) and borsch, plus other treats from the former Soviet world, such as Georgian stewed meat, Uzbek *manti* (lamb dumplings) and Kyrgyz pancakes. It has a great atmosphere, with pictures of the old Soviet republic capitals, statues of Lenin and covers of old Russian magazines.

Los Bandidos (Map pp70-1; ☎ 314 167, 9919 4618; Baga Toiruu north; dishes T4000-5000; 11.30am-midnight) This place is advertised as 'the only Mexican and Indian restaurant in Mongolia', a claim that we won't try to argue with. It serves nachos, fajitas, enchiladas and burritos, as well as meals hot from the tandoori oven.

Pizza Della Casa (Map pp70-1; ☎ 324 114; Peace Ave; pizzas T4000-6000; noon-11pm) This longtime favourite dishes up some of Mongolia's best pizzas, pastas and calzone at reasonable prices. The *toon* (tuna) is highly recommended. There are two locations, the Peace Ave one is near the Peace & Friendship Building, and the second is in the Sky Shopping Mall. It has free delivery for orders over T7500.

Marco Polo (Map pp70-1; ☎ 318 433; Seoul St 27; pizzas T4500-6500; 11am-midnight) The place has brick-oven pizza that is considered by many to be the best in town. The décor is a bit odd – a mix of European ambience plus Mongolian antiques, *tsam* masks and the odd mastodon tusk thrown in for good measure. Try not to let the kiddies wander off unaccompanied, Ulaanbaatar's most notorious strip club is right upstairs!

Millie's Café (Map pp70-1; ☎ 330 338; Marco Polo Bldg; lunch mains T5000, dinner mains T12,000; 9am-4pm & 6-9pm Mon-Sat) Drop by Millie's at noon any day of the week and you'll find the place packed with consultants, aid workers and journalists sipping excellent shakes and gobbling steak sandwiches and lemon pie. The restaurant completely changes for dinner time; tablecloths are spread out, candles are lit and a gourmet menu appears. Dinner is a fusion of Mediterranean, Cuban and South African cuisines; presentation is perfect and taste impeccable.

Le Bistro Français (Map pp70-1; ☎ 320 022; Ikh Surguuliin Gudamj 2; pasta T5000, meat dishes T9000-15,000; 9am-midnight Mon-Fri, 10am-midnight Sat & Sun) The soft lighting, cream-coloured walls and French art give this bistro a peaceful, romantic ambience. Having settled in, enjoy a starter of Burgundy snails followed by a Chateaubriand flambé with cognac, washed down with a French red wine. We were a bit disappointed with the pastas, but the meat dishes are highly recommended. Ice cream and crepe desserts are excellent.

our pick **Veranda** (Map pp70-1; ☎ 330 818; Jamyn Gunii Gudamj 5/1; mains T6000-8000; noon-midnight) One of the most popular places in town, this Italian restaurant excels at meat dishes, such as a nice lamb roll with blackcurrant sauce on a bed of greens. The house speciality is the Veranda, a tender, flavourful grilled beef tenderloin that goes well with one of the Italian wines on offer. The atmosphere is very comfortable; rather than chairs you sit on couches, and there are fine views of the Choijin Lama Temple Museum.

Strings (Map p64; ☎ 365 158; Damdinbazaryn Gudamj; dishes T6500-10,500; noon-midnight) One of the most popular places in town, thanks largely to the in-house rock band from the Philippines. Moneyed expatriates from the US favour the place – the Hard Rock Café atmosphere provides a taste of home. For a filling meal try the fajitas, the Hawaiian pork stir-fry or a teriyaki chicken sandwich.

Silk Road Bar & Grill (Map pp70-1; ☎ 318 864, 9191 0211; Jamyn Gunii Gudamj 5/1; meal with drink T7500; 12.30-11pm) Owner and chef Enkhee (aka Eddie) is Mongolia's original restaurateur. Silk Road, his third restaurant, features lots of cosy couches and bas-relief scenes of the ancient Silk Road from China to Europe. The menu reflects the name of the place, and you'll find sprinklings of Indian, Central Asian and Mediterranean treats, including shish kebabs, chicken tikka and pork *gyros* (pitta with meat and vegetables). You can try a sampling of these at the Sunday smorgasbord (between 12.30pm and 3pm).

California (Map pp70-1; ☎ 319 031; Seoul St; meal with drink T9000; 8am-midnight) One of Ulaanbaatar's most popular restaurants, this place has an array of eclectic menu items, including a Thai steak salad with Caesar dressing, authentic chicken tacos and *shorlog* (shish kebab with cream sauce). All of these are recommended. There is a huge variety of food to choose from and the portions are generous and heavy on the calories (this place is a real diet killer). It's also one of the few places in town that is open for breakfast.

Other recommendations:

Ala Turka (Map pp70-1; ☎ 9900 5341; Peace Ave; dishes T2000-4500; 10am-midnight) Filling platters of Turkish food. If you want doner kebab, arrive before 7pm because they usually run out.

El Latino (Map pp70-1; ☎ 311 051; Peace Ave 3; dishes T2500-4000; 11am-10pm) Cuban restaurant with colourful décor. However, the chef is from Belarus so there are also some tasty Russian dishes.

UB Deli (Map pp70-1; ☎ 325 240; Seoul St 48; mains T3500-5000; 10am-9pm) American-owned restaurant that specialises in big sandwiches, including Philly cheese and grilled reuben. It delivers for a small fee.

Emerald Bay (Map pp70–1; ☎ 320 120; Tserendorjiin Gudamj; mains T6000-10,000) Excellent Mediterranean menu includes pork *gyros* (T6500) and grilled salmon (T10,000). Vegetarians should be able to find a salad or soup to their liking.

Bonito (Map p64; ☎ 9909 1421; Namyanjugiin Gudamj; ⏰ noon-3pm & 5-10pm Mon-Fri, noon-10pm Sat & Sun) For T12,000 you get an all-you-can-eat feed of Brazilian meats, soups and salads. It also serves wine and excellent cocktails.

Brew Pubs

The following establishments fall under the categories of restaurant and bar. You can enjoy excellent food (and they are kid-friendly too), but by late evening they cater mainly towards a drinking crowd.

Ikh Mongol (Map pp70–1; ☎ 305 014; Seoul St; meal with beer T6000-8000; ⏰ noon-midnight) The flagship restaurant for APU, one of Mongolia's largest food and alcohol producers, Ikh Mongol doles out huge platters of grilled meat and jugs of beer. Needless to say, it's not a great place for calorie-watchers. There is daily live music (10pm) and a large beer patio built on two levels. It's on the east side of the State Circus.

Chinggis Club (Map pp70–1; ☎ 325 820; Sükhbaataryn Gudamj 10; large beer T1800, meal with beer T6000-8000; ⏰ 10am-midnight) Microbrewery serving some of the best beer in the country. There's also a filling meat-and-potatoes menu designed by a German chef.

Khan Brau (Map pp70–1; ☎ 324 067; Chingisiin Örgön Chölöö; meal with beer T6000-8000; ⏰ 11am-midnight) Popular European-run place in the city centre, the porch attracts a good crowd in summer. There is live music from Tuesday to Saturday.

Grand Khaan Irish Pub (Map pp70–1; ☎ 336 666; Seoul St; meal with beer T7000; ⏰ 11am-midnight; wi-fi) Big crowds, lots of smoke, free-flowing beer and loud music set the scene for Ulaanbaatar's most popular night spot. The pub-grub menu includes an array of salads. An attached café (open 8am to 10pm) serves espressos, cappuccinos and croissants, plus English and German breakfasts.

Brau Haus (Map pp70–1; ☎ 490 071; Seoul St; meal with beer T8000; ⏰ 11am-midnight) 'Two slices of crusty pork roast' and 'one whole pork knuckle' may not sound like the most appetizing menu items, but rest assured this brew pub can serve up some tasty dishes to go with tall glasses of beer. The bar has an attractive, airy layout, made more interesting with some B&W photos of old Ulaanbaatar. It has live music on Friday.

Cafés

In summer, most restaurants disgorge deck chairs and tables to the pavements, forming an excellent café culture where you can sip a coffee or Coke and watch Ulaanbaatar go about its business.

Sacher's Café (Map pp70–1; ☎ 324 734; Baga Toiruu west; snacks T500-2000, light meals T3000; ⏰ 9am-9pm) Mongolia's first genuine bakery, this German-owned operation doles out filter coffee, pretzels, pastries and excellent fresh bread. It has a nice outdoor patio, where you can enjoy reading the local English newspapers or imported German magazines. The menu includes hot soups and sandwiches.

ourpick Michele's French Bakery (Map pp70–1; ☎ 9916 9970; items T750-4100; ⏰ 8am-8pm; wi-fi) A popular haunt among savvy Ulaanbaatar expatriates, this bakery and coffee shop serves an array of reasonably priced treats, including apple strudel (T750) and chocolate croissants (T800). You can also enjoy panini sandwiches (T2200) and crepes (T2200 to T4100) while listening to a great music playlist. Coffee and other hot drinks are available; no alcohol is served but the owner Alex allows you to bring in a bottle of wine or beer to round off your meal.

Stupa Café (Map pp70–1; ☎ 319 953; Builder's Sq, Juulchin Gudamj; snacks T1500-2000; ⏰ 10am-8pm Mon-Fri, 10am-7pm Sat & Sun) This very charming café is decked out with orange ger furniture and photos of camel trains. It also has a shelf full of English-language books and magazines, which you can read while enjoying a sandwich, coffee or tea (you can also check the books out against a deposit). It's also a great place if you have kids as there are toys to keep tots occupied. Ask about seasonal treats; in late summer you can buy Khövsgöl berries mixed with *tarag* (yogurt). It's part of the FPMT Buddhist centre and profits go towards supporting the restoration of Buddhism in Mongolia.

Café Amsterdam (Map pp70–1; ☎ 321 979; cnr Peace Ave & Baruun Selbe Gudamj; items T1500-3000; ⏰ 7am-midnight; wi-fi) At the time of writing this place was set to open as Mongolia's first literary café. The Dutch owners have promised café au lait, pannekoeken (crepes) and homemade cheese (in season), as well as shelves of books that you can borrow, trade or buy. Poetry readings and guest speakers are expected so check the chalkboard for upcoming events.

Narya Café (Map pp70–1; ☎ 317 098, 9911 1361; Builder's Sq, Juulchin Gudamj; sandwiches T2500-3500;

⏰ 8.30am-9pm Mon-Fri, 10am-8pm Sat & Sun; wi-fi) The Latin music playing in the background, ochre-painted walls and contemporary artwork make for a pleasant sight when entering this laid-back café. The menu offers reasonably priced sandwiches, soups and home-baked muffins, plus hot dishes such as a 'sloppy dorj' (the Mongolian version of a sloppy joe). Food quality can be inconsistent.

Ananda Café & Meditation Centre (Map pp70-1; ☎ 316 986; Baga Toiruu west; meals T3000; ⏰ 10am-8pm Mon-Sat) Enjoy herbal teas and some excellent vegetarian dishes made from rice, buckwheat, tofu, lentils and other natural products. Vegetarian *buuz* and *khuushuur* are also available. Profits from the café go to supporting a local orphanage, the Lotus Children's Centre, and as the name suggests, yoga classes are available, as are vegetarian cooking classes.

Chez Bernard (Map pp70-1; ☎ 8810 0135; Peace Ave 27; dishes T4000-6000; ⏰ 9am-8pm) The most popular backpacker hangout in Ulaanbaatar, this Belgian-owned café has European breakfast platters crammed with fruit, cheese, yogurt, eggs, bacon and toast. Food quality is somewhat hit-and-miss and the bakery items are overpriced (T1500 to T2500), but the place does have atmosphere, especially in summer when you can sit on the deck. There's a noticeboard for organising trips to the countryside or swapping used books. It also sells new and used camping gear.

Quick Eats

For something really quick and filling, order some shashlik (meat kebabs), usually served with onions and cucumber, from any number of street Uzbek vendors (June to August only). The best ones are next to the State Department Store or at City Café (p87). For *buuz*, *khuushuur* or other cheap Mongolian favourites try a *guanz* (canteen or fast-food restaurant; see p86); the Khaan Buuz opposite the State Department Store is one example. There are also a few *guanz* on Baga Toiruu west opposite MIAT.

Soyolj (Map pp70-1; ☎ 5015 1060; Baga Toiruu; dishes T200-500; ⏰ 8am-10pm Mon-Fri) Serves warm tofu, freshly pressed soy milk, soups and an array of pint-sized salads. It's a great place for vegetarians tired of trying to de-mutton their *buuz*. It's one building past the Zaluuchuud Hotel, heading northwest.

Berlin (Map pp70-1; ☎ 328 505; cnr Baruun Selbe Gudamj & Sambugiin Örgön Chölöö; meals T1500; ⏰ 9am-9pm Mon-Fri, 10am-10pm Sat & Sun) An old stand-by, this cafeteria-style place has good-value burgers and spaghetti. Long lines form during lunch hour.

Indra (Map pp70-1; ☎ 323 769; Jigjidjavanyn Gudamj 9; meals T1500-2000; ⏰ 9am-9pm) Located just off the Square, this popular eatery, housed in a converted basketball court, serves decent pasta, *ramen* (Japanese egg noodles), salad and pizzas.

Self-Catering

These days there are very few things you can't get in the city if you look hard enough, though you may have to visit several markets to track them down. Most markets are open from about 10am to 8pm daily. There are also several shops that specialise in items imported from the US; try the 1st floor of the Nayra Café (p89) or the 2nd floor of Ayanchin Outfitters (p94), both of which stock rare treats such as Snapple and Arizona Iced Tea.

Container Market (Map pp70-1; Bömbögör market; Ikh Toiruu west; ⏰ 10am-8pm Tue-Sun) This is the cheapest place for everyday food purchases. Half the market burned down in 2006 but there are plans to rebuild and expand. It's just south of Bakula Rinpoche Süm.

Minii Delguur & Merkuri Markets (Map pp70-1; ⏰ 10am-7pm Mon-Sat, 10am-6pm Sun) Merkuri (Мэркури) is sort of a flea market for food where you can bargain with individual vendors for all manner of imported goods, meat, cheese and vegetables, as well as luxuries such as caviar and crab sticks. It's around the back of Minii Delguur (also known as Dalai Eej), a more standard form of supermarket off Tserendorjiin Gudamj.

Werner's Deli (Map pp70-1; ☎ 5515 1419; Passage Market; ⏰ 10am-7pm Sun-Fri, 11am-5pm Sat) Genuine German deli serving all cold cuts and sandwiches, Werner's is located at the back of the Passage Market (the same complex as Minii Delguur and Merkuri Market).

State Department Store (Map pp70-1; Peace Ave 44) The 1st floor towards the back has a very good selection of fruit, deli and imported goods, though at slightly higher prices than elsewhere.

DRINKING

Although vodka remains the drink of choice in the countryside, most Ulaanbaatarites prefer beer these days. There are many good, clean and safe watering holes in the downtown area and while there is no bar district, they are still close enough to put together some semblance of a pub crawl. Many imported beers are available, but the brand of choice is the locally brewed Chinggis, which comes in green cans or on tap. City regulations require that bars close at midnight, after which time you can continue drinking at a nightclub. *Airag* (*koumiss*; fermented mare milk) is available on sidewalk gers in summer, usually after Naadam. Besides the places following, try the brew pubs (p89) or enjoy a drink at one of the open-air beer and shashlik stands that open in summer near the State Department store.

Dave's Place (Map pp70-1; ☎ 9979 8185; mongoliadave @yahoo.com; wi-fi) This bar on the patio of the Palace of Culture near the Square offers the popular Thursday 'Quiz Night', starting at 8.30pm. Winners receive a jar of cash and free beer. In cool weather the whole operation retreats to a speakeasy-style bar in the basement. It was closed at the time of research but will hopefully be re-opened.

Dublin (Map pp70-1; ☎ 328 626; Seoul St) With a cosy atmosphere, cream-coloured walls and dark wood finish, Dublin does a fine job of transplanting a bit of Ireland to the steppes. It's a popular expat hangout (especially for miners), but also frequented by young Mongolians. There is plenty of alcohol on tap, as well as Irish coffee and tasty pub grub. With one day's advance notice you can order the leg of lamb, pan-fried in whiskey sauce (for four to six people, T56,000).

Level (Map pp70-1; ☎ 334 444; Peace Ave; cocktails T2500-5000) Chic bar and restaurant that fuses nouveau Japanese décor with bits of England (telephone box) and Mongolia (ancient Buddhist block prints behind glass). All manner of drinks are served, plus a selection of appetizers and main items, including a mixed meat platter for four people. It's in the 1st floor of an orange apartment, behind the Peace & Friendship Building.

Detroit (Map pp70-1; ☎ 320 033; Seoul St; ☽ 6pm-2am) This US-inspired bar takes its theme from the Motor City, with photos on the walls of professional sports teams from Detroit. It has a foosball table and sports teams from Detroit on the TV for homesick Americans. Besides alcohol, you can order burgers, fries and sandwiches. Live music is staged on Friday at 10pm. It's under BD's Mongolian Barbeque.

Other recommendations:

Crystal Lounge (Map pp70-1; Peace Ave; cocktails T3500-6000; ☽ 6pm-midnight) The stunning white-on-white décor and bubbling water in the walls makes for a mystifying experience, like stepping into a scene from *2001: A Space Odyssey*. It serves cocktails only.

Greenland (Map pp70-1; Peace Ave; beer T1000-1800; ☽ noon-midnight Jun-Aug) Oktoberfest-style tent, opposite Sükhbaatar Sq. It's open in summer only.

UB Club (Map pp70-1; ☎ 8800 3639; Juulchin Gudamj) Grungy student club with mismatched furniture, foosball, billiards and darts.

ENTERTAINMENT

Culture vultures will want to check the weekly English-language *UB Post* or *Mongol Messenger* for events. The **Arts Council of Mongolia** (Map pp70-1; ☎ 319 015; www.artscouncil .mn) produces a monthly cultural events calendar, which covers most theatres, galleries and museums. You can pick up a brochure at hotel lobbies or the MIAT office. Theatres and galleries sometimes post English ads outside or you could just buy a ticket and hope for the best.

Theatre
TRADITIONAL MUSIC & DANCE

A performance of traditional music and dance will be one of the highlights of your visit to Mongolia and should not be missed. You'll see outstanding examples of the unique Mongolian throat-singing, known as *khöömii*; full-scale orchestral renditions of new and old Mongolian music; contortionists guaranteed to make your eyes water; traditional and modern dancing; and recitals featuring the unique horse-head violin, the *morin khuur*.

The Tumen Ekh Song & Dance Ensemble at the **State Youth & Children's Theatre** (Map pp70-1; ☎ 9666 4374, 9665 0711; Nairamdal Park; admission T6000, photos T3000, video T10,000; ☽ 6pm May-Oct) is the most popular cultural show in town, featuring traditional singers, dancers and contortionists. It's a great chance to hear *khöömii* and see some fabulous costumes. You can buy CDs (T20,000) of the performance after the show. There is a café and gallery in the traditional-style hall. The Khatan Ekh National Song & Dance Group at **Discovery Mongolia Information Centre** (Map pp70-1; ☎ 330 778, 9929 9918; Narny Gudamj; admission US$6; ☽ 6pm May-Oct) is similar.

The Moonstone Song & Dance Ensemble at **Tsuki House** (Map pp70-1; ☎ 318 802; admission T7000, photos US$5, video US$10; ☽ 2pm, 4pm, 6pm & 8pm May-Oct) puts on a Mongolian cabaret. You get the lot: contortionists, throat singers, musicians, *tsam* mask dancers and an electrifying shaman dance done in contemporary fashion. One drink is included in the price of the ticket and food is available. Tsuki House is the modern glass building next to the Circus (on the north side).

The **Mongolian National Song & Dance Ensemble** (www.mon-ensemble.mn) puts on performances for tourists throughout the summer in the **National Academic Drama Theatre** (Map pp70-1; ☎ 324 621; cnr Seoul St & Chingisiin Örgön Chölöö; admission T7000; ☻ 6pm). Shows are less frequently staged at the **Palace of Culture** (Map pp70-1; ☎ 321 444) on the northeast corner of Sükhbaatar Sq.

You can also see traditional song and dance at the Choijin Lama Temple Museum (see p75) in summer at 5pm.

OPERA & BALLET

Built by the Russians in 1932, the **State Opera & Ballet Theatre** (Map pp70-1; ☎ 322 854, 9919 4570; admission T5000-8000; ☻ closed August) is the salmon-pinkish building on the southeast corner of Sükhbaatar Sq. On Saturday and Sunday evenings throughout the year, and sometimes also on weekend afternoons in the summer, the theatre holds stirring opera (in Mongolian) and ballet shows.

One of the best local operas is *Three Fateful Hills* – sometimes known as the *Story of Three Lives* – by Mongolia's most famous poet and playwright, D Natsagdorj. The debut performance of *Chinggis Khaan*, by B Sharav, was shown in 2003. Another recommended opera is *Uran Khas*, written by J Chuluun. Other productions include an exhilarating (but long) rendition of *Carmen*, plus plenty of Puccini and Tchaikovsky.

A board outside the theatre lists the shows for the current month in English. Advance purchase is worthwhile for popular shows because tickets are numbered, so it's possible to score a good seat if you book early. The box office is open 10am to 1pm and 2pm to 5pm Wednesday to Sunday.

DRAMA

National Academic Drama Theatre (Map pp70-1; ☎ 324 621, 9908 1178; cnr Seoul St & Chingisiin Örgön Chölöö; admission T7000; ☻ ticket sales 10am-7pm) During most of the year, this large, fire-engine-red theatre shows one of a dozen or so Mongolian-language productions which are penned by, among others, William Shakespeare and Jean-

Paul Sartre, as well as various Mongolian playwrights. There are only between six and 10 performances every month, and schedules are sporadic. Check show listings in the *UB Post*. You can buy tickets in advance at the booking office, which is on the right-hand side of the theatre.

On the left-hand side of the theatre, as you approach it from the road, is a door that leads to a **puppet theatre** (☎ 323 959; adult/chid T1000/500; ☻ 2.30pm Sat & Sun), which is great if you are travelling with children.

Nightclubs

Ulaanbaatar has a lively nightlife that has matured in recent years – you can experience everything from small jazz bars and cocktail lounges to gargantuan dance halls and the odd strip club. Places go out of fashion pretty quickly, so you'll need to ask the locals about what is popular.

Metropolis (Map p64; ☎ 9973 0569; Sky Shopping Centre; admission T5000; ☻ 8pm-4am) The most stylish place in Ulaanbaatar, Metropolis has a large dance floor and a VIP voyeur terrace. The French-Cambodian DJ plays an eclectic mix of disco, salsa, pop, rock and techno. Monday and Tuesday are reserved for electronica. Drinks go for T4000 to T6000. It's set inside a large vault next to the entrance to the Sky Shopping Mall.

Oasis (Map pp70-1; ☎ 311 719, 9973 31222; Seoul St; admission T4000; ☻ 6pm-late) Oasis attracts a mixed crowd of expats, travellers and Mongolians. There is an outdoor patio area where you can order food off the grill. It's tucked off Seoul St behind a supermarket.

Face Club (Map pp70-1; ☎ 313 961; Juulchin Gudamj; men/women Sat-Thu T3000/1000, Fri T5000/3000; ☻ 7pm-3am) The Face Club is a lively little place with a Tahitian theme. It has live bands and DJs.

Hollywood (Map p64; ☎ 9927 7370; Academich Sodnomyn Gudamj; admission free; ☻ 8pm-late) This throbbing nightclub, with DJ and elevated dance floor, is just past Dashchoilon Khiid. Friday carries a T1000 cover charge.

Muse (Map pp70-1; ☎ 312 601; Maral Tavern Bldg, Baga Toiruu; admission free; ☻ 8pm-late) One of the top nightclubs for the yuppie crowd, it's located just north of the Zaluuchuud Hotel.

Zouq (Map pp70-1; ☎ 8811 9687; Peace Ave; admission T3000; ☻ 9pm-late Mon-Sat) Egyptian-themed disco with a catwalk dance floor, voyeur terrace and lots of bizarrely-shaped furniture. It's opposite the Square, next to the Greenland tent.

Silence (Map pp70-1; ☎ 7011 0020; Sambugiin Örgön Chölöö; admission T5000; ☟ 10pm-4am Mon-Sat) Multilevel dance club with blood-red lights igniting the bar and waiters that can't keep track of your tab. The place gets going after 1am and the DJ plays mainly trance music.

Ismuss (Map p64; ☎ 9981 8181; Peace Ave; ☟ 2pm-2am) The centrepiece of this multilevel club is a 7m-tall statue of Joseph Stalin, which once stood in front of the National Library. Even if you are not into nightclubs this slice of retro Soviet chic is a must-see.

Live Music

History Club (Map pp70-1; ☎ 311 732; www.mongolia historytravel.com; Juulchin Gudamj; ☟ noon-midnight) This restaurant and bar is popular with the locals and hosts traditional Mongolian music acts. The band that usually performs here is Legend, a five-piece group that plays contemporary music with traditional instruments. The band usually performs Monday to Friday at 8pm but its schedule changes frequently so you'll need to call ahead to find out when it's on. There is also karaoke, dancing and skilfully prepared Mongolian cuisine. Look for the ger sticking out of the side of the building.

River Sounds (Map pp70-1; ☎ 320 497; Olympiin Örgön Chölöö; admission T5000; ☟ 8pm-3am) This is one of the best places to hear music as it's a dedicated live-music venue with jazz bands and the occasional indie rock band.

Another popular place is Strings (p88), which has a house band playing classic rock covers. A few brew houses and bars also have live music, including the Brau Haus (p89) Detroit (p91) and Grand Khaan (p89) on Fridays, and Khan Brau (p89), from Tuesday to Saturday.

Cinema

Tengis (Map pp70-1; ☎ 326 575; www.tengis.mn; Liberty Sq; regular show T2500, matinee T1500) Air-conditioned halls, comfortable seats (with cup holders!) and a modern projection system make this theatre a very worthwhile experience. It usually has one or two Hollywood blockbusters (in English, subtitled with Mongolian) and a Korean or Mongolian film.

Gay & Lesbian Venues

There are no dedicated gay bars as such but some members of the gay community will meet at one place or another for a few weeks and then move on. Attitudes towards gays are loosening up a little but it's better to err on the side of discretion when asking about meeting places.

Circus

State Circus (Map pp70-1; ☎ 320 795) In the recognisable round building with the blue roof at the end of Tserendorjiin Gudamj. There are usually a variety of acts including acrobatics and juggling, and extraordinary contortionists, but it was closed for renovations at the time of research.

Sport

The annual Naadam features wrestling, horse racing and archery; see boxed text, p96, for more details. In the lead-up to Naadam, you should be able to catch some informal, but still competitive, wrestling at the Naadam Stadium. For wrestling at other times of the year check out the schedule at the **Wrestling Palace** (Map p64; ☎ 456 443; Peace Ave; admission T1000-5000), which is the ger-shaped building south of the Chinggis Khaan Hotel. Wrestling and basketball are also held at the **Central Sports Palace** (Map pp70-1; Baga Toiruu) during the year.

On weekends during the short summer (but not around the time of the Naadam), the Mongolian Football League plays football (soccer) matches at a **football pitch** (Map p64) just south of the Naadam Stadium.

SHOPPING

After decades of dollar shops, ration tickets and a general milieu of nonproductivity, capitalism has come to Ulaanbaatar with a vengeance. Some higher-end places accept credit cards but cash is still king in most places of business.

Camping Gear & Tools

Besides the following, there is a decent camping section on the 3rd floor of the State Department Store. Be well aware that Western-quality camping gear is not cheap in Mongolia so you may want to bring stuff from home. Cheap Chinese-made products are available if you're desperate, though most of it breaks down before you even leave the city.

Seven Summits (Map pp70-1; ☎ 329 456; www .activemongolia.com/7summits; btwn Peace Ave & Seoul St; ☟ 10am-7pm) Stocks German-made Vaude gear, GPS units, maps, travel books and accessories. It also hires out gear, including tents, sleeping bags, gas stoves, mountain bikes (US$16 per day) and inflatable kayaks (US$25 for one day, US$45 for two days). It's opposite the CPO.

Ayanchin Outfitters (Map pp70-1; ☎ 319 211; www .ayanchin.com; Seoul St 21) This place sells Western camping, fishing and hunting equipment, plus GPS units, mainly imported from the US.

Pro Shack (Map pp70-1; ☎ 318 138, 9911 4438; Ikh Toiruu 6) If you need tools for a self-organised jeep/motorcycle trip or a generator big enough to power a Mongolian village, drop by this German-owned hardware outlet. The shop will move in 2009 so call for its new location.

Northland (Map pp70-1; ☎ 9918 0001; Peace Ave 62; ☺ 10am-7pm Wed-Mon) Sells fishing tackle and Chinese-brand (but acceptable quality) camping gear at reasonable prices.

Shonkhor Saddles (Map pp70-1; ☎ 311 218, 9191 1190; jturuu@yahoo.com) Produces and sells saddles and other horse paraphernalia. The workshop is behind School No 5 on Baga Toiruu but is difficult to find on your own – contact the owners at the internet centre opposite the German embassy. Ask for Tomor or Nara.

Antiques

The antique trade is booming in Mongolia, but you need to be careful about what you buy as some of it is illegal. Make sure the shop you buy it from can produce a certificate of authenticity.

Amarbayasgalant Antique (Map pp70-1; ☎ 310 000; Juulchin Gudamj 37/31; ☺ 9am-7pm) A quality shop for the serious buyer, it sells enormous sutras, traditional headdress, Buddhist statues and other rare items. Some of the items are creations of Zanabazar and not for sale. Great for browsing.

Other shops offering a good selection:

Eternal Art Antique Shop (Map pp70-1; ☎ 369 704; Sükhbaataryn Gudamj 1) One of the premier antique shops in the city. Credit cards are accepted.

Nomads Culture Antique Shop (Map pp70-1; ☎ 333 939; Juulchin Gudamj 35; ☺ 10am-7pm) Smaller shop opposite Amarbayasgalant.

Musical Instruments

Traditional musical instruments make perfect gifts for friends who are musically inclined. The *morin khuur* (horse-head fiddle) is particularly nice as a piece of decorative art (and Mongolians consider it good luck to have one in the home). **Argasun** (Map pp70-1; ☎ 336 565; Partizan Gudamj 48; ☺ 10am-6pm) is a *morin khuur* workshop near Aeroflot. Other instruments are available

at the **Egshiglen Magnai National Musical Instrument Shop** (Map pp70-1; ☎ 328 419; Sükhbaataryn Gudamj), on the east side of the Museum of Natural History. *Morin khuur* range from T100,000 to T450,000, and there are also *yattag* (zithers) and two-stringed Chinese fiddles.

Cashmere

The major cashmere and wool factories are Goyo (Mongolian-American joint venture), Gobi Cashmere (government-owned) and Buyan (owned by the prominent politician Jargalsaikhan). Excellent products can be purchased at the **Gobi Cashmere shop** (Map pp70-1; ☎ 326 867; Peace Ave; ☺ 11am-7pm Mon-Sat) opposite the Russian embassy. The State Department Store has cashmere on the 2nd and 5th floors. Tserendorjiin Gudamj, between the State Circus and the State Department Store, has around a dozen fashion shops.

Fine Art

Contemporary Mongolian artwork can be purchased at a small number of galleries around town. For more information see the section on art galleries (p73).

Crafts & Souvenirs

Souvenir shops are found absolutely everywhere in Ulaanbaatar – just toss a stone in the air and chances are you'll hit one. You can pick up cheap and authentic gifts such as landscape paintings, wool slippers, Mongolian jackets and felt dolls. There is also a lot of kitsch, such as Chinggis Khaan T-shirts and key chains. On the streets you will undoubtedly encounter amateur artists selling watercolours for under US$1.

The biggest souvenir outlet is on the 5th floor of the State Department Store. You'll also spot shops inside gers mounted on carts, notably outside the Bayangol Hotel and National Museum of Mongolian History.

Felt carpets produced by a women's co-operative in Khovd are sold at Sacher's Café (see p89).

The best contemporary artwork in the country is on sale in the **Red Ger Art Gallery** (Map pp70-1; ☎ 319 015) inside the Zanabazar Museum of Fine Arts (p69); it's open during museum hours.

Other shops to try include the following:

Möngön Zaviya (Map pp70-1; Peace Ave; ☺ 10.30am-8.30pm Mon-Fri, 11am-7.30pm Sat & Sun) Great for picking up silver cups, belt buckles and jewellery.

Souvenir House (Map pp70-1; ☎ 320 398; cnr Peace Ave & Khaddorjiin Gudamj) One of the largest souvenir shops in town.

Tsagaan Alt Wool Shop (Map pp70-1; ☎ 318 591; Tserendorjiin Gudamj) This nonprofit store, which sends money directly back to the craftspeople, has all manner of wool products, including toys, clothes and artwork. It's Christian-run, in case you were wondering about those Jesus Christ felt tapestries.

Market

Naran Tuul market (Наран Туул Зах; off Map p64; 9am-7pm Wed-Mon), east of the centre, is also known as the Black Market (Khar Zakh), but it's not the sort of place where you go to change money illegally and smuggle goods – though this certainly happens.

The market is huge, one of the biggest in Asia and in summer up to 60,000 people a day squeeze inside. There's a T50 entrance fee. You can buy cheap gear for a camping trip, among other things, but the real reason to visit is to marvel at this enormous emporium.

An undercover area has a decent selection of clothes, such as bags, leather boots and fake North Face jackets. This is also one of the cheapest places to get traditional Mongolian clothes such as a *del* (T35,000) and jacket (T30,000). Towards the back of the market you'll find saddles, riding tack and all the ingredients needed to build your own ger. The back area is also where you'll find antique and coin dealers, but they don't issue any official documentation (unlike the antique shops in town), making it illegal to export. New items, such as the snuff bottles (made in China anyway), can be purchased without worry.

The market is notorious for pickpockets and bag slashers so don't bring anything you don't want to lose. Don't carry anything on your back, and strap your money belt to your body. If you feel a group of men blocking your way from the front, chances are their friends are probing your pockets from behind.

A taxi to the market should cost about T1000 from the centre of town. Minibuses come here from Peace Ave (look for the sign '3ax'). To walk from the Square will take about 45 minutes. Try to avoid Saturday and Sunday afternoons, when the crowds can be horrendous.

Photography

There are several places to purchase cameras and camera equipment. The best are the **Canon Showroom** (Map pp70-1; ☎ 8811 7444; Peace Ave) and the **Mon Nip Camera Shop** (Map pp70-1; ☎ 315 838; Peace Ave 30). Photo-developing studios are everywhere, including the State Department Store; we like the **Fuji Film** (Map pp70-1; ☎ 328 554; M-100 Bldg, Juulchin Gudamj; 9am-9pm Mon-Fri, 10am-8pm Sat & Sun), northwest of Sükhbaatar Sq.

Electronics

Techie travellers will find joy at **Computerland** (Map pp70-1; Peace Ave; 10am-7pm Mon-Sat) a three-storey building crammed with dozens of private dealers selling everything from flash drives to the latest laptops. It is located behind the Canon Showroom (left), which also has a computer shop.

Shopping Centres

Known as *ikh delguur* or 'big shop', the **State Department Store** (Их Дэлгүүр; Map pp70-1; ☎ 319 292; Peace Ave 44; 9am-10pm Mon-Sat, 10am-10pm Sun) is virtually a tourist attraction in itself, with the best products from around the city squeezed into one building.

The 1st floor has a supermarket at the back. The 2nd floor has outlets for clothing, cashmere and leather goods. The 3rd floor has electronics, a Mobicom shop, CDs, books, sports equipment, camping and fishing gear. The 5th floor has a great collection of souvenirs, traditional clothing, maps and books about Mongolia.

Foreign-exchange counters are found on the 1st, 2nd, 3rd and 5th floors, with only cash changed. The store also sells phone and internet cards.

If you are based on the east side of town, the **Sky Shopping Centre** (Map p64; ☎ 319 090; 10.30am-9pm) may be more convenient than the State Department Store and offers similar goods and services. It's behind the Chinggis Khaan Hotel.

GETTING THERE & AWAY
Air

Chinggis Khaan International Airport is 18km southwest of the city. You can change money at a branch of the T&D Bank. There's also a post office and internet access for T50 per minute. A tourist booth opens when planes arrive.

Mongolia has three domestic carriers: MIAT, AeroMongolia and EZ Nis. The former two both have international connections with Ulaanbaatar. Note that on domestic routes

THE NAADAM

Mongolia's penchant for war games comes to a head each summer on the vast grasslands, where competitors show off their skills in wrestling, archery and horse racing. The annual Naadam Festival is the much anticipated culmination of these events, and a colourful spectacle enjoyed by locals and tourists alike.

Every village and city has a naadam; most (including the one in Ulaanbaatar) are held on 11 and 12 July, coinciding with Independence Day. Some rural naadams are held a few days before or after this date so some planning is required if you want to see one.

For travellers, rural naadams provide the opportunity to see genuine traditions and events not tarted up for the sake of tourism. You'll get closer to the action and may even be asked to make up the numbers during the wrestling tournament!

The Ulaanbaatar Naadam, by comparison, has all the trappings of a tourist holiday, with cheesy carnival events and souvenir salesmen outside the stadium. The horse racing is also quite far from the city and because the city swells with foreign tourists at this time, you can feel like a sheep being herded around with them. The main benefit of Ulaanbaatar Naadam is that the city takes on a very relaxed mood, and there are plenty of associated concerts and theatre events. While we recommend seeing a *sum*-level naadam, many tourists will do the festival in UB. If this includes you, keep reading.

Day one of the Ulaanbaatar Naadam starts at about 9.30am when an honour guard marches into the Parliament (Government) House to collect the nine yak-tail banners that will be brought to the stadium. Usually they exit the Parliament House from the backside.

The opening ceremony, which starts at about 11am at the **Naadam Stadium** (Map p64), includes an impressive march of monks and athletes, plus song and dance routines. By comparison, almost nothing happens at the closing ceremony. The winning wrestler is awarded, the ceremonial yak banners are marched away, and everyone goes home. It is held at about 7pm on the second day, but the exact time depends on when the wrestling finishes.

with MIAT and Aero Mongolia you can carry 15kg but EZ Nis allows 20kg. You'll pay around T1500 per kilogram over the limit. For details of international flights to Ulaanbaatar, see p266. Flight days always change so check updated schedules. The airlines accept credit cards for international and domestic flights. If paying cash, foreigners are supposed to use US dollars only.

Aero Mongolia (Map pp70-1; ☎ 283 029; www.aero mongolia.mn; MPRP Bldg; ☺ 9am-6pm Mon-Fri, 10am-2pm Sat, 11am-3pm Sun) is inside the Mongolian People's Revolutionary Party (MPRP) headquarters of the Square, next to the Ulaanbaatar Hotel.

Blue Sky Aviation (Map pp70-1; ☎ 312 085; www .blueskyaviation.mn; Peace Ave) has one nine-seat Cessna 208 aeroplane available for charter flights. The office is in the same building as Seven Summits, opposite the post office.

EZ Nis (Map pp70-1; ☎ 313 689; www.eznis.com; 8 Zovkhis Bldg; ☺ 9am-7pm Mon-Fri, 10am-4pm Sat) is the newest airline in the country and has an office is on Seoul St.

The head office of **MIAT** (Map pp70-1; ☎ 322 118, 1881; www.miat.com; ☺ 9am-6pm Mon-Sat, 9am-3pm Sun) is on Baga Toiruu west, near the Trade &

Development Bank. It is the cheapest airline in Mongolia.

Foreign airline offices include the following:

Aeroflot (Map pp70-1; ☎ 320 720; www.aeroflot .ru; Seoul St 15; ☺ 9am-6pm Mon-Fri, 10am-3pm Sat) US dollars and credit cards are accepted.

Air China (Map p64; ☎ 328 838, 452 548; www.fly -airchina.com; Ikh Toiruu Bldg 47; ☺ 9am-1pm & 2-5pm Mon-Fri, 10am-4pm Sat, 9am-noon Sun) Located on Big Ring Rd in the northeast of town.

Korean Air (Map pp70-1; ☎ 326 643, fax 320 602; www.koreanair.com; 2nd fl, Chinggis Khaan Hotel; ☺ 9am-5pm Mon-Fri) Payment in US dollars and tögrög.

United Airlines (Map pp70-1; ☎ 323 232; www.united .com, info@airtrans.mn; Air Trans office, Sükhbaataryn Gudamj 1; ☺ 9am-6pm Mon-Fri, 10am-4pm Sat) Handy for booking flights out of Seoul and Beijing.

Bus

Two stations handle most bus traffic. The eastern depot, **Bayanzürkh Avto Vaksal** (off Map p64; ☎ 463 386), is 6km east of Sükhbaatar Sq. The station has daily buses to Choibalsan (T15,800, 13 hours), Baruun-Urt (T13,800, 11 hours), Öndörkhaan (T7500, five hours) and

Archery is held in an open **archery stadium** (Map p64) next to the main stadium but the horse racing is held about 40km west of the city on an open plain called Hui Doloon Khutag. Buses and minivans go there from the Naadam Stadium for around T1000 (vehicles also depart from the Dragon bus stand). Otherwise, most guesthouses organise transport for around US$8 (also inquire at Chez Bernard, p90) or you could just hail a cab and pay the local rate.

A unique way to experience Naadam is to camp out at the horse race area, which will give you some insight into the rigorous lives of the trainers. A good day to visit is 13 July when a mini-naadam is held for the benefit of trainers who missed the archery and wrestling events. You could even ride your own horse to the racing grounds. **Steppe Riders** (www.stepperiders.com) does four-day trips from its base near Bogd Khan Uul.

A recent addition to the Naadam programme is anklebone shooting. This entails flicking a sheep anklebone at a small target (also made from anklebones) about 3m away. The competition is held in the **Anklebone Shooting Area** (Map p64) near the archery stadium.

Admission to the stadium (except for the two ceremonies), and to the archery and horse racing are free, but you'll definitely need a ticket for the opening ceremony and possibly the last round or two of the wrestling and closing ceremony. Ticket costs vary per section; the north side of the stadium (which is protected from the sun and rain by an overhang) is more expensive with tickets going for US$25 or more. This section is also less crowded and everyone will get a seat. These tickets are distributed via the tour operators and hotels.

There is no ticket window for general seating but you can buy a ticket from scalpers who hang around the stadium. The original price will be printed on the ticket (the cheapest sections go for T2000); you can expect to pay three or four times this for the service charge. Guesthouse owners normally help their guests buy tickets.

The general seating sections are always oversold so unless you get in early you'll end up sitting in the aisle or standing by the gate. The bandstand on the west end of the stadium offers some shade.

To find out what is going on during the festival, look for the events programme in the two English-language newspapers.

Dalanzadgad (T13,300, 12 hours), all leaving between 7.30am and 8am.

The western bus station, called the **Dragon (Luu) Avto Vaksal** (Dragon bus stand; off Map p64; ☎ 634 02), is on Peace Ave, 7km west of Sükhbaatar Sq. The station has a daily bus to Tsetserleg (T10,500, 11 hours), Arvaikheer (T9000, 10 hours) and Dundgov (T7100, six hours), all departing at 8am. A bus to Kharkhorin (T10,000, eight hours) leaves at 9am. Two buses travel to Erdenet (T8000, seven hours) at noon and 7pm, while four buses go to Darkhan (T4500, four hours) at 9am, 10am, 3pm and 4pm. On Monday Wednesday and Friday a bus travels to Bulgan (T7900, eight hours) at 8am.

A third station is located at **Teeveriin Tovchoo** (Map pp70-1; Undsen Khuulin Gudamj), the old bus station, about a 10- to 15-minute walk from the centre. It has a bus to Mörön (T20,000) departing at noon on Monday, Wednesday and Friday. Buy tickets in the New Mind building behind the station or call ☎ 9925 048 for info.

Bus tickets can be purchased two days prior to travel. Tickets purchased on the same day of travel may carry a higher price.

Hitching

Hitching is a necessary form of transport in the countryside, but is less certain and more difficult to organise out of Ulaanbaatar. Most Mongolians get out of the capital city by bus, minibus, train or shared jeep/taxi, and then hitch a ride on a truck for further trips around the countryside, where there is far less public transport. Unless you can arrange a ride at a guesthouse, you should do the same.

Minivan & Jeep

Minivans and buses heading for destinations in the north and west (but not east) leave from the **Dragon (Luu) Avto Vaksal** (Dragon bus stand; off Map p64; ☎ 634 902) on Peace Ave, 7km west of Sükhbaatar Sq. Minivans for all destinations use the Naran Tuul market. For the Gobi, the Mandalgov-bound minivans use the Dragon bus stand while vans for Ömnögov usually use Naran Tuul.

Overall, the Dragon bus stand is better for the casual traveller (riders at Naran Tuul are often traders with lots of bulky luggage to deal with). Naran Tuul, however chaotic, has many more vehicles leaving throughout the day.

Local bus 26, trolleybus 2 and some minivans (ask the tout) link Dragon bus stand with Sükhbaatar Sq. Van 13 goes to the Naran Tuul market.

Most departures from the bus stands are between 8am and 9am. If taking a long trip, get to the station by 7am to sort out what's going where. Almost all services are in Russian vans or jeeps. For local destinations you might find a Korean compact car or even a regular bus.

Both bus stands are essentially a bunch of vans sitting in a lot with their destinations posted in the dashboard (in Cyrillic). Tell the drivers where you want to go and you'll be directed to the correct van. Some vehicles may be ready to go but others might not be leaving for another day.

Don't expect to leave straight away, even if the van is already bursting with people and cargo. There are no fixed schedules and the drivers depart when they see fit. Try to find out exactly what time the driver is leaving and if it's not going immediately you could ask the driver to save your seat and you can return later.

For more information try calling the minivan companies at ☎ 321 730, 634 902 or 9525 3146.

Dragon bus stand and Naran Tuul both serve towns in Töv aimag. For Nalaikh (T700) and Baganuur (T3000) use Naran Tuul. For Zuunmod (T1000) and Eej Khad (T8000 return) use Dragon bus stand. These minivans go every hour or so.

MOUNTAIN BIKING NEAR ULAANBAATAR

The best short bike ride from Ulaanbaatar goes from Zaisan to the Observatory. From the city centre, travel south to the Zaisan Memorial. (Try to avoid going over congested Peace Bridge by taking Olympiin Örgön Chölöö over the railway tracks.) From Zaisan, continue in an easterly direction. The road follows the southern bank of the Tuul River for 11km until you reach the road to the Observatory. Follow the switchbacks uphill to the Observatory. From the Observatory you can descend briefly through the forest to the left (as you are looking downhill), pick up the trail in the next valley, and return to Ulaanbaatar on the same road. It's a two- to three-hour return trip.

Both stands also have jeeps and vans for hire at around T400 per kilometre. Budget travellers could try to deal directly with a driver for a multiday trip, as you would do in the countryside, although it's usually safer to go through a trusted travel agent or guesthouse.

The following list gives average prices for a seat in a minivan or jeep to selected locations. You'll also find vehicles to smaller villages, for example, vehicles from Naran Tuul direct to Dadal (T20,000) in northern Khentii.

Destination	Cost
Altai (Алтай)	T35,000
Arvaikheer (Арвайхээр)	T13,000
Baruun-Urt (Баруун-Урт)	T18,000
Bayankhongor (Баянхонгор)	T20,000
Bulgan (Булган)	T10,000
Choibalsan (Чойбалсан)	T20,000
Dalanzadgad (Даланзадгад)	T24,000
Darkhan (Дархан)	T8000
Kharkhorin (Хархорин)	T10,000
Khovd (Ховд)	T50,000
Mandalgov (Мандалговь)	T12,000
Mörön (Мөрөн)	T25,000
Öndörkhaan (Өндөрхаан)	T12,000
Tsetserleg (Цэцэрлэг)	T15,000
Ulaangom (Улаангом)	T50,000
Uliastai (Улиастай)	T30,000

Taxi

Taxis (shared or private) can only travel along paved roads, so they are only useful for trips around Töv aimag, to the towns along the main road to Russia (Darkhan, Erdenet and Sükhbaatar) and to the tourist site of Kharkhorin.

The cost of hiring a taxi to these places should be around T400 per kilometre. The taxi drivers may want more for waiting if you are, for example, visiting Mandshir Khiid, or because they may be returning with an empty vehicle if dropping you off somewhere remote. This is not unreasonable, but it *is* negotiable.

To avoid any argument about the final charge make sure that you and the driver have firstly agreed on the cost per kilometre, and have discussed any extra charges. Then write down the number shown on the odometer speedometer before you start.

Train

The train station (Map p64) has an information office, a left-luggage office, a phone office, a hotel and a restaurant.

DOMESTIC TRAIN TIMETABLE

Destination	Train No	Frequency	Departure	Duration (hr)	Fare (hard/soft seat)
Choir	284	Fri, Sun	5.40pm	6	T2000/5300
Darkhan	271	daily	10.30am	8	T2600/6400
Darkhan	211 (fast)	daily	3.50pm	5	T2600/6400
Erdenet	273	daily	7pm	11	T3600/9000
Sainshand	285	daily	10.15am	10	T6200/9500
Sükhbaatar	263	daily	7.35pm	7¾	T3500/8400
Sükhbaatar	271	daily	10.30am	7¾	T3500/8400
Zamyn-Üüd	276	daily	4.30pm	15½	T5100/12,800
Zamyn-Üüd	34 (fast)	Mon, Wed, Fri	8.05pm	12	-/T20,000

From Ulaanbaatar, daily trains travel to northern Mongolia and on to Russia, via Darkhan and Sükhbaatar, and southeast to China, via Choir, Sainshand and Zamyn-Üüd. There are also lines between Ulaanbaatar and the coal-mining towns of Erdenet and Baganuur.

Note that when buying a ticket you must show identification, either a passport or a driving licence will do (a student ID won't work).

DOMESTIC

The **domestic railway ticket office** (Map p64; ☎ 24137; ◷ 8am-12.30pm & 2.30-9pm) is located in the modern-looking building on the east side of the train station. Unfortunately, no-one inside speaks anything except Mongolian or Russian. Boards inside the office show departure times (in Cyrillic) and ticket prices for hard seats and soft seats. There's also a full timetable at the information desk on the station platform. See also the boxed text (above).

Tickets can be booked up to a month in advance for an extra T450, which is not a bad idea if you have definite plans and want a soft seat during peak times (mainly July to August). If you speak Mongolian, there is an **inquiries number** (☎ 24194).

INTERNATIONAL

The yellow International Railway Ticketing Office (Map p64) is about 200m northwest of the train station. Inside the office, specific rooms sell tickets to Irkutsk and Moscow in Russia, and to Beijing, Ereen and Hohhot in China. The easiest place to book a ticket is in the **foreigners booking office** (☎ 24133, inquiries 944 868; Room 212; ◷ 8am-8pm Mon-Fri). It's upstairs and staff here speak some English. On weekends you can use the downstairs booking desk.

GETTING AROUND
To/From the Airport

From the city to the airport, bus 11 (T200) stops at the Ard Kino on Baga Toiruu and opposite the Bayangol Hotel. On its way to the airport bus 22 stops near Liberty Sq and Ikh Toiruu, near the Cartography Co Map Shop. Coming to the city from the airport, it turns right on Peace Ave and then left up the east end of Baga Toiruu. To find the bus stop near the airport, head out of the terminal, walk north for a few hundred metres and look for a group of locals mingling around a tin shelter.

If you have a lot of gear, or don't know your way around, it's worth paying extra for a taxi. Make sure that you pay the standard rate, at the time of writing T300 per kilometre, which works out around US$5 one way to Sükhbaatar Sq.

Bicycle

Mongolian drivers are downright dangerous so riding a bike around town can be hazardous to your health. There are no bike lanes and you should never expect to have right of way. Seven Summits (p93) rents mountain bikes for US$16 per day. Korean-made bikes are sold opposite the State Department Store, they cost around US$100 and are a good investment if you plan to cycle for a week or more. They can probably be re-sold when you're done with it.

Bus & Minivans

Local public transport is reliable and departures are frequent, but buses can get crowded. Conductors collect fares (at the time of writing T200 for a bus or T150 for a trolleybus for any trip around Ulaanbaatar, including to the airport) and usually have change. Pickpockets and bag slashers occasionally

ULAANBAATAR

ply their trade on crowded routes. Seal up all pockets, hold your bag on your chest and be careful when boarding.

Minivans (T200) run along a similar route to the buses. Most will run the length of Peace Ave, often turning back at the Naran Tuul market or the train station. They stop at the bus stops or you can flag one down. Van 13 goes to the Naran Tuul market. The fixed routes posted in the windows are incomprehensible to most passengers. The best way to handle these vehicles is to tell the conductor where you're headed and wait for a positive response.

For short trips it's just as cheap to take a taxi, especially if there is more than one of you. Some useful buses and trolleybuses:

Destination	Bus No	Trolleybus No
Airport	11, 22	-
Dragon bus stand	2	26
Nalaikh	33	-
Naran Tuul market	32	-
Peace Ave (east)	1, 13, 20, 21, 23	2, 4, 5, 6
Peace Ave (west)	4, 21, 22, 23	2, 5, 26
Train station	6, 20	4
Winter Palace	3, 19	-
Yarmag	8	-
Zaisan Memorial	7	-

All destinations will be in Cyrillic; the route number is next to the destination sign on the front of the trolleybus or bus. The route is often marked on the side of the bus.

Car

Sixt Mongolia (Map pp70-1; ☎ 310 075; www.sixt.mn; Bodi Tower 101, Sükhbaatar Sq 3; ☼ 9am-6pm Mon-Fri), which has a second office on Undsen Khuulin Gudamj, hires out Toyota Landcruisers for US$125 per day and Scodas for US$54 per day with the driver. Prices decrease if you rent for multiple days. If that still sounds like too much, you could hire a taxi by the day (most hotels can organise this), and pay the usual rate of T300 per kilometre. Driving your own car is wrought with pitfalls. A simple fender bender, whether or not it was your fault, can land you in jail with a steep fine to pay. If you rent, check the insurance policy carefully.

Drive Mongolia (☎ 312 277, 9911 8257; www.drive mongolia.com) offers driving tours of Mongolia, allowing you to drive the car with a backup support vehicle.

Taxi

In Ulaanbaatar, there are official and unofficial taxis; in fact, just about every vehicle is a potential taxi. All charge a standard T300 per kilometre, though you'll need to check the current rate as this will increase regularly. Don't agree to a set daily price because you will always pay more than if you pay the standard rate per kilometre. Nowadays, all taxis and even some private cars have meters.

Taxi drivers will definitely try to take advantage of you if you are new to the city and don't know your way around. The more confident you appear the better chance you have of getting a fair deal. Know generally where you are going before you get in the cab so you don't get 'taken for a ride'. Always remember to have the driver reset the odometer to zero and agree on per kilometre rate before setting off.

Getting a taxi is just a matter of standing by the side of a main street and holding your arm out in the street with your fingers down. Alternatively, you can find them at designated taxi stands near the Zanabazar Museum of Fine Arts, outside the train station, in Liberty Sq and near the State Department Store. After dark, women should generally avoid using a private car, and stick to an official taxi.

The most visible official taxi company is **City Taxi** (☎ 300 000), which runs a fleet of modern, yellow Hyundai Accents.

The **Safe Taxi Company** (☎ 9979 8185; www .safetaxi.mn) is a British-Australian run venture established to provide safe and reliable transport around the city and to nearby sites such as Terelj and Mandshir Khiid. Airport transfers are also planned. There will be no cash transactions with the driver: flat-fee fares are paid for at hotels and restaurants around the city. You get a chit with the destination printed on it that you show to the driver. Expats and Mongolians can buy a pre-paid account and summon a taxi by text message.

Central Mongolia

Roll out of Ulaanbaatar in a Russian jeep and you'll only need to put a hill or two between yourself and the city before the vast steppes of cental Mongolia begin to unfold before your eyes. Verdant swaths of empty landscapes are sprinkled with tiny gers stretching to the horizon while magical light plays through clouds and across the valleys.

But central Mongolia offers more than steppes. Landscapes are broken by the forested hillsides of the Khan Khentii range, meandering rivers such as the Tuul and lunar-like lava fields spilling across central Arkhangai. The silhouette of a lone horseman on a hill or camels caravanning in the distance completes every perfect day.

The rivers and back trails of Gorkhi-Terelj National Park beckon the outdoor enthusiast. At Khustain National Park you can break out the binoculars and spot the reintroduced *takhi* horse. Alternatively, set out from Ulaanbaatar on foot, climb the holy Bogdkhan Uul to the south of the city, and camp out by Mandshir Khiid. Travelling by horse is another great way to get around the region. Travellers with more time on their hands can spend weeks exploring the ancient sites and remote areas of the mighty Khangai and its surrounding plains.

Central Mongolia's aimags (provinces), Töv, Arkhangai and Övörkhangai, are the most visited areas in the countryside. The roads and transport are far better here than in the rest of Mongolia, and there is plenty to see, including ancient monasteries, gorgeous lakes and many national parks. The people, mostly comprising the Khalkh majority, are accustomed to foreigners, and you can expect somewhat better services than in other parts of the country.

HIGHLIGHTS

- Saddle up and go on a horse trek to the beautiful but remote **Naiman Nuur Nature Reserve** (p119)

- Pedal your way over the hills and through the valleys of **Gorkhi-Terelj National Park** (p104) on a mountain bike and cap the experience with a night at a ger camp

- Focus your camera lens on the magnificent *takhi* (wild horse) at **Khustain National Park** (p115), where the wild horse roams free once again

- Hike into the forests to the splendid **Tövkhön Khiid** (p124), the site of religious leader and artist Zanabazar's workshop and meditation centre

- Camp by the striking **Terkhiin Tsagaan Nuur** (p130), a volcanic lake offering great fishing and lovely sunsets

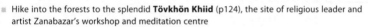

- POPULATION: 289,100
- AREA: 199,000 SQ KM

CENTRAL MONGOLIA

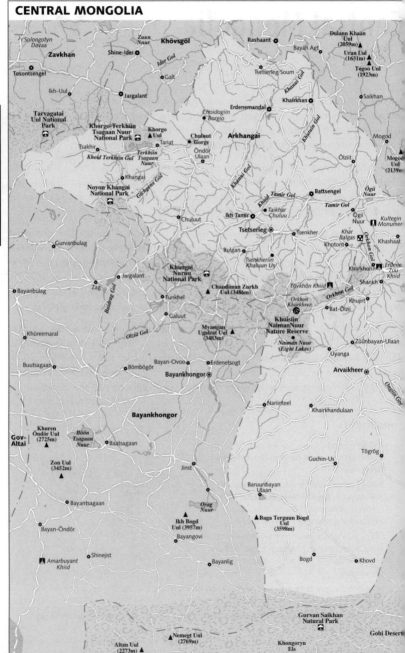

CENTRAL MONGOLIA

History

The many deer and 'animal art' stele found in the valleys of Arkhangai aimag are evidence of tribal existence here around 1300 BC, but the region really came into its own in the 3rd century BC, when the nomadic Xiongnu set up a power base in the Orkhon valley. Various 'empires' rose and fell in the Xiongnu's wake, including the Ruan-Ruan, the Tujue and the Uighurs, who built their capital at Khar Balgas in 715 AD. These Turkic-speaking peoples held sway over vast portions of Inner Asia and harassed the Chinese (whose attempts to defend the Great Wall were never really successful). They had their own alphabet and left several carved steles that describe their heroes and exploits. The most famous is the Kul-Teginii Monument (p129), located relatively close to Khar Balgas.

Chinggis Khaan and his merry men were only the latest in a string of political and military powers to use the Orkhon valley as a base. Chinggis never spent much time here, using it mainly as a supply centre for his armies, but his son Ögedei built the walls around Karakorum (near present-day Kharkhorin) in 1235, and invited emissaries from around the empire to visit his court.

Centuries after the fall of the Mongol empire it was religion, rather than warriors, that put the spotlight back on central Mongolia. Erdene Zuu Khiid (Buddhist monastery) was built from the remains of Karakorum and, with Manchu and Tibetan influence, Buddhism pushed the native shaman faith to the fringe of society.

The first eight Bogd Gegeens ruled from central Mongolia, and built up the most important religious centres, including Urga (now Ulaanbaatar), which shifted location along the Tuul Gol (river) for more than 250 years, until settling at its present site in the mid-18th century.

Climate

The central aimags lie in a transitional zone, with southern portions nudging into the Gobi and northern areas covered in Siberian taiga (larch and pine forests), with steppe inbetween. Winter daytime temperatures of −30°C to −15°C are typical, lasting from late November to early February. March and April suffer from strong, dry winds and changeable weather. July and August are good times to travel as the wet weather finally turns the steppe into a photogenic shade of green. Summer temperatures reach from 24°C to 30°C. October will bring cool evenings and snow flurries before the onset of winter.

National Parks & Nature Reserves

Gorkhi-Terelj National Park (293,200 hectares) A playground for Ulaanbaatarites. The park contains numerous ger camps and two golf courses. It's more pristine north of the Terelj Gol.

Khangai Nuruu (888,455 hectares) Encompasses most of the Khangai mountain range, protecting crucial watershed and a variety of animals including ibex and argali sheep.

Khögnö Khan Uul Nature Reserve (46,900 hectares) This nature reserve protects wolf and fox that inhabit the desert-steppe area.

Khorgo-Terkhiin Tsagaan Nuur National Park (77,26 hectares) Protected area for migratory birds as well as fish. The park includes lakes, cinder cones and volcanic flows.

Khustain National Park (50,620 hectares) Important rehabilitation site for *takhi* horses. Also contains gazelle, marmot and wolf among other creatures.

Getting There & Away

A paved highway, running from Ulaanbaatar to Kharkhorin, is traversed by share jeeps, minivans and buses that depart daily from the Dragon and Naran Tuul bus stand in Ulaanbaatar.

If coming from western Mongolia to UB, the route through Arkhangai is more interesting than the dull journey via Bayankhongor – the main access point is via the town of Tosontsengel in Zavkhan.

If you are travelling in the Gobi and heading towards northern Mongolia, go to Bayankhongor and pick up the scenic 210km road over the mountains to Tsetserleg. Hitchhikers might find a ride on a logging truck heading north but the chances are slim. You'll save a lot of time by hiring your own vehicle.

Getting Around

Töv aimag has a network of good unpaved and paved roads, so you can easily use public transport to make day or overnight trips from the capital.

For the other aimags, share jeeps will travel from the nearest provincial centre to other destinations, but off the main paved road traffic throughout these regions is light. In Övörkhangai, public transport will get you to Erdene Zuu Khiid, Khujirt and Arvaikheer, but if you want to visit Tövkhön

Khiid or Orkhon Khürkhree you'll need your own transport. Horse is the best way to reach Naiman Nuur. In Arkhangai, the main road is one of the few routes in Mongolia where hitchhikers can easily get to a few places of interest, including Taikhar Chuluu and Terkhiin Tsagaan Nuur.

A jeep is fine for getting around, but travelling by horse grants the best access via the river valleys and into the mountains.

TÖV ТӨВ

pop 88,500 / area 81,000 sq km

Sitting atop the pine-clad, boulder-strewn slopes of the Khan Khentii range, it's hard to believe that Ulaanbaatar with its one million citizens lies just a mountain range or two away. The proximity of Töv to the capital has by no means spoiled its pristine landscape, allowing for easy access to the great outdoors.

Töv has some restored monasteries including the pretty Mandshir Khiid in Bogdkhan Uul National Park. It also has a few oddball sights; you can visit the excessively large Chinggis Khaan statue near Nalaikh, lunch at a mock-up 13th-century Mongol war camp and sleep in the bizarrely named Dresden Ger Camp.

A large portion of the aimag is made up of the Gorkhi-Terelj, Khan Khentii and Bogdkhan Uul National Parks, which mostly occupy the northern part of the aimag. The southern half of Töv is bland desert steppe and most travellers pass through quickly on their way to Dundgov aimag.

Although Töv lies close to industrial Ulaanbaatar, its economy remains almost exclusively agricultural. This way of life has come under threat as poorer nomads are giving up and moving to the city; between 2004 and 2007 the population of Töv decreased by more than 20%.

ZUUNMOD ЗУУНМОД

☎ 01272 / pop 14,300 / elev 1529m

In great contrast to the big city on the other side of the mountain, Zuunmod is a peanut-sized place that typifies the provincial capitals of Mongolia. There is little reason to linger in the capital of Töv but you'll probably pass through the town on the way to Mandshir Khiid or Bogdkhan Uul National Park. Phone calls can be made from the Telecom Office, which also has an **internet café** (☎ 22044; per person T600; ☺ 8am-9pm Mon-Fri).

Sights

The chief attraction in Zuunmod is the **Central Province Museum** (☎ 23619; admission T1000; ☺ 9am-1pm & 2-6pm), opposite the southeast corner of the park – look for the sign in English. There are exhibits on local history and a section of stuffed animals including an enormous moose. It also has some interesting black-and-white photos of Mandshir Khiid, including the once-regular *tsam* (lama dances, performed by monks wearing masks during religious ceremonies).

CENTRAL MONGOLIA

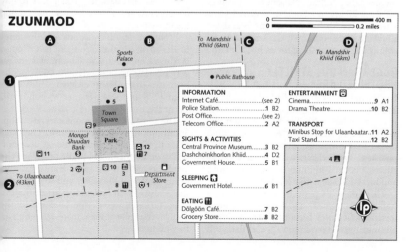

ZUUNMOD

0 _____ 400 m
0 _____ 0.2 miles

To Mandshir Khiid (6km)

To Mandshir Khiid (6km)

Sports Palace

Public Bathhouse

Town Square

Mongol Shuudan Bank

Park

Department Store

To Ulaanbaatar (43km)

INFORMATION
Internet Café..............................(see 2)
Police Station.............................**1** B2
Post Office................................(see 2)
Telecom Office...........................**2** A2

SIGHTS & ACTIVITIES
Central Province Museum........**3** B2
Dashchoinkhorlon Khiid...........**4** D2
Government House....................**5** B1

SLEEPING
Government Hotel......................**6** B1

EATING
Dölgöön Café............................**7** B2
Grocery Store............................**8** B2

ENTERTAINMENT
Cinema......................................**9** A1
Drama Theatre..........................**10** B2

TRANSPORT
Minibus Stop for Ulaanbaatar..**11** A2
Taxi Stand.................................**12** B2

Not in the same league as Mandshir Khiid but worth a brief visit is **Dashchoinkhorlon Khiid** (Дашчойнхорлон Хийд), a 700m walk directly east of the department store and across the creek. If you ask the monks, you can go inside the temple. Ceremonies start at around 11am on most days.

Sleeping & Eating

You can camp anywhere near town, although Mandshir Khiid is a better option than Zuunmod.

The large and refurbished rooms of **Government Hotel** (☎ 22184; s/d T10,000/15,000) are just about all that's on offer in Zuunmod. There's a bar and restaurant downstairs.

Offering an eclectic range of European, Mongolian, Chinese and Korean dishes, **Dölgöön Café** (☎ 9930 8344; ✆ 10am-10pm Mon-Sat) should have something to suit your tastes. There's a grocery store opposite the police station.

Getting There & Away

Minivans run through the pretty countryside (on a paved road) between Zuunmod and Ulaanbaatar (T1000, one hour, hourly) between 7am and 8pm, from Ulaanbaatar's old bus stand (Teeveriin Tovchoo). The bus stop in Zuunmod is just a short walk west of the main street.

A chartered taxi from Ulaanbaatar will cost between US$10 and US$13 one way. Taxis can be hired in Zuunmod from the taxi stand on the east side of the park. The fare should be the standard rate paid in Ulaanbaatar (around T300 per kilometre). Some drivers may want a waiting fee for hanging around Mandshir Khiid if you are going up there. This is reasonable as you may be there for an hour or two.

BOGDKHAN UUL STRICTLY PROTECTED AREA БОГДХАН УУЛ

Legend has it that Bogdkhan Uul (Map p107; 2122m) is the world's oldest nature preserve. It was founded in 1778 and for the next 150 years it was guarded by 2000 club-wielding lamas that protected the mountain from poachers. Lawbreakers were hauled away in chains, beaten within an inch of their lives, and locked inside coffin-like jail cells.

These days it's perfectly safe and legal to walk on the mountain and you can enjoy some terrific **hiking** and **horse-riding** trails. From Ulaanbaatar the mountain appears dark and menacing but, once you're on top, the forest and rocky outcrops are a beautiful sight.

For information on hiking to the mai peak from Zaisan Memorial (Map p107) o Mandshir, or combining the two in an over night hike from Mandshir to Ulaanbaata see opposite. For details on renting a horse see p108.

Entrance to the park costs T3000.

Sights
MANDSHIR KHIID МАНДШИР ХИЙД
elev 1645m

For the 350 monks who once called this plac home, the gorgeous setting around this **monas tery** (Map p107; ☎ 22764; GPS: N47° 45.520′, E106° 59.675 ✆ 9am-sunset) must have been a daily inspi ration. Like most monasteries in Mongoli Mandshir Khiid was destroyed in 1937 b Stalin's thugs, but was partially restored in th 1990s. Just 6km northeast of Zuunmod an 46km by road from Ulaanbaatar, the monas tery is a perfect half-day trip from the capita or can be used as a starting point for hikes int the Strictly Protected Area.

The main temple has been restored an converted into a museum, but the other build ings in the area remain in ruins. The mon astery and museum are not as impressive a those in Ulaanbaatar – it is the beautiful fores setting that makes a visit worthwhile.

As you enter from the main road from Zuunmod you'll be required to pay an ad mission fee of T5000 per person, which cov ers the T2000 museum entrance fee and th T3000 national park fee. You'll have to bu both tickets even if you don't plan on enterin the museum.

From the gate it's a couple of kilometre to the main area, where there is a shop, lacklustre museum, a restaurant and severa gers offering accommodation. Look for th huge two-tonne **bronze cauldron**, which date from 1726 and was designed to boil up 1 sheep at a time.

The remains of the monastery are abou 800m uphill from the museum. The care taker lives in the compound next door an will open up the main building for you. Th **monastery museum** has *tsam* masks, exhibit on the layout of Mandshir and some photo that show what it looked like before Stalin' thugs turned it into rubble. Look out for th controversial **Ganlin Horn**, made from huma thigh bones.

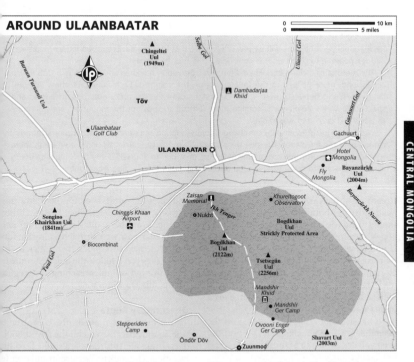

AROUND ULAANBAATAR

If you have time, it's worth climbing up the ocks behind the main temple, where there re some 18th-century Buddhist **rock paintings**. The views from the top are even more beautiul, and you'll find yourself in the midst of a ovely pine forest.

Activities

HIKING

There are several trails but the best hiking oute goes right over the top from Ulaanbaatar o Mandshir Khiid. Wherever you decide to go you'll be required to pay a national park ee of T3000. You can do this at the gate to he Bogdkhan Uul Strictly Protected Area or t Mandshir Khiid.

The highest point on the range is Tsetseegün Uul (2256m) although going here is not the quickest way over the top. The most direct oute follows a path west of Tsetseegün.

There are numerous approaches to the ummit, some easier than others; most go p one way and descend by another route. A popular option is to hike from Mandshir Khiid to Ulaanbaatar, either to the Zaisan Memorial (around a seven-hour walk) or the

Observatory (six hours). You'll need to get an early start or camp overnight in the park.

The trip is only really sensible from the beginning of June to the end of September. During the rest of the year, no matter how pleasant the weather is in the morning, sudden thunderstorms and icy winds can come out of nowhere (although this happens occasionally in summer as well). It's important to take a compass and know how to use it, as it's easy to get lost in the forest. Carry all the water you will need, plus extra food. Yellow paint on the trees marks the trail, but it can be hard to spot.

Some scrambling over fields of granite boulders is necessary, and the chance of slipping and injuring yourself should not be taken lightly. It would be wise to inform a friend or guesthouse owner in Ulaanbaatar of your itinerary and the time of your expected return.

Mandshir Khiid to Ulaanbaatar Route

This approach to Tsetseegün from the south side is the easiest route by far. As you face the monastery, cut over to your right (east) until you get to the stream. Just follow the

---

FOUR HOLY PEAKS

Recreational peak baggers will be pleased to note that Ulaanbaatar is surrounded by mountains and it's possible to climb what is considered the 'four holy peaks'.

The mountains include Bogdkhan, Chingeltei, Songino Khairkhan and Bayanzürkh Uuls which correspond, more or less, to the four points on the compass. Each mountain offers different landscapes, but between them you'll experience pine forests, rocky outcrops, meadows and spectacular views. Wildlife is becoming more difficult to spot but the mountains are still home to a few red deer, ibex and sable.

Weather on all the mountains can change rapidly in spring and summer, with occasional thunder, cloudbursts and even snow. Despite their proximity to the capital, locals don't often climb them so once you're on top you'll probably have the mountain to yourself. If you can't manage doing all four but want to try one, have a go at the biggest and best – Bogdkhan Uul.

---

stream until it nearly disappears and then head north. About three hours' walking should bring you out over a ridge into a broad boggy meadow, which you'll have to cross. If you've walked straight to the north, the twin rocky outcrops of the summit should be right in front of you. When you start to see Ulaanbaatar in the distance, you're on the highest ridge and close to the two large *ovoo* (a shamanistic pyramid-shaped collection of stones as an offering to the gods) on the **summit** (GPS: N47° 48.506', E107° 00.165'). From the *ovoo* you can return to Mandshir or descend to Ulaanbaatar.

A second route from the monastery begins from the left (west) side of the temples, passing a stupa on the way up to the ridge. This route, marked with yellow tags, is faster but you'll miss the *ovoo* on Tsetseegün.

Coming down from Tsetseegün the quickest way is to head due north, towards the Observatory and descend to the valley where you'll cross the train tracks. The road is close by and you can catch a taxi to town for around T3500. A longer route takes you to the Zaisan Memorial, on the southern fringe of the city. Be careful not to drop down too soon or you'll end up at Ikh Tenger, one valley short of Zaisan. Ikh Tenger is where the president lives with machine gun–wielding guards, who will be none too pleased if you drop by unannounced. If you see a flimsy barbed wire fence you are in Ikh Tenger; to get out, just continue west along the fence and over the next ridge.

Zaisan Route

It is more of an uphill battle to Tsetseegün if you start from the Zaisan Memorial. From the memorial, head up the road past the ger camp and enter the forest. Look for the yellow trail markers, which veer left when you've reached the top. From here, the slope levels off and becomes an easy walk through a pleasant forest for the next two hours. If you stick to the yellow tags you'll follow the quickest route to Mandshir but will miss reaching Tsetseegün. All up, this is a 15km walk.

Observatory Route

This is the easiest route on the Ulaanbaatar side, mainly because you hit the fewest boulders. However, this route is also the least interesting. The walk to Tsetseegün and over to Mandshir takes about six hours.

The problem is that getting to the Observatory ('Khureltogoot' in Mongolian) is difficult. You could catch a bus to Nalaikh and get out at the toll gate, then walk the last 6km up the hill. Otherwise, you'll have to take a taxi.

HORSE RIDING

In summer, some of the ger camps around Mandshir Khiid rent out horses. Horses are also available from **Stepperiders Camp** (☎ 9983993, 9665 9596; www.stepperiders.com; GPS: N 47° 43.649' E106° 47.418'), just off the main Ulaanbaatar-Zuunmod road. Stepperiders is run by Minde a recommended local horse guide who can give lessons, instructions and support to independent travellers planning their own expedition. This is a perfect place to test ride a Mongolian horse before a longer trip. Rides are great value at US$35 to US$50 per day and include pick-up, drop-off, guides, horses, food and even entry fees to the national park. As this camp is something of a hang-out for dedicated horse riders, you may be able to find partners for a trip.

Sleeping

The area around the monastery is one of the best camping spots near Ulaanbaatar. You should get permission from the caretaker at the monastery if you are camping nearby, or just hike off into the woods.

In a lovely spot amid trees about 200m northeast of the monastery's car park, the convenient **Mandshir Ger Camp** (Map p107; ☎ 01272-22535, 9192 4464; 4-bed ger T35,000) has hot showers but Mongolian-style toilets. There's a restaurant in the grounds, but it may only be open if a tour group is staying there, so take some food. Horse rental here is US$5 per hour. Another good option is **Ovooni Enger Ger Camp** (Map p107; ☎ 9666 9964, 9930 9216; with/without meals US$28/15), 800m off the road to Mandshir (look for the sign just after entering the park gate).

Getting There & Away

The most accessible entrances to the park are reached via Zaisan Memorial, the Observatory and Mandshir.

The monastery is easy enough to visit in a day trip from Ulaanbaatar or Zuunmod (from where it's a 7km drive; a taxi plus waiting time costs T5000). If you are walking from the north of Zuunmod it's 6km; you can either walk along the main northern road after visiting Dashchoinkhorlon Khiid, or save some time by walking directly north from Zuunmod, eventually joining up with the main road.

Trekking to Mandshir by horse is a good idea, but Zuunmod is not set up for tourists and it will require some effort to track a horse down. You could ask around the ger suburbs of town, at Stepperiders (opposite), or make inquiries from one of the guesthouses, such as Idre's Guest House (p82), in Ulaanbaatar. At Mandshir itself, wranglers from the nearby ger camps rent horses for US$5 per hour.

SONGINO KHAIRKHAN UUL
СОНГИНО ХАЙРХАН УУЛ

This small mountain to the southwest of Ulaanbaatar has the unusual name of 'Onion Mountain', possibly because wild onions grow here. The mountain is close to the village of Biocombinat, about 5km west of the airport. From the village, cross the wooden bridge and follow the road as it veers left, past the **Songino Resort** (GPS: N47° 51.153′, E106° 40.488′), towards the mountain itself. The road from the airport to Biocombinat is fairly busy so flagging down a taxi or bus shouldn't be problem.

EEJ KHAD (MOTHER ROCK)
ЭЭЖ ХАД

Vanloads of pilgrims can be found venturing a rough 48km south of Zuunmod to the sacred **Mother Rock** (Map p102-3; Eej Khad; GPS: N47° 18.699′, E106° 58.583′). Mongolians often come here to seek solace and advice, and make offerings of vodka, milk and *khatag* (silk scarves). Pilgrims ask for three wishes to be granted, circle the rock three times and make three separate visits.

There are several sacred rocks nearby that are thought to generate good luck, including one called **Dog Rock**, which Mongolians rub their body against to cure ailments.

Minivans depart from Teeveriin Tovchoo (T6000 each way) at 9.30am. It's also possible to stop here on your way to the Gobi, but be prepared for some off-roading as the jeep trails south of here will quickly peter out.

There is nowhere to stay near Eej Khad. You can camp but, for a modicum of privacy, pitch your tent at least 500m from the rock (and crowds of pilgrims).

NALAIKH НАЛАЙХ

The poor village of Nalaikh, 35km southeast of the capital, is part of the Ulaanbaatar autonomous municipality because it once supplied

CENTRAL MONGOLIA

MOTHER ROCK

During communism, visiting the sacred Eej Khad (Mother Rock) was a political crime, as it showed respect for religion, which was basically banned at the time. Some people, however, still went in secret.

Sometime in the late 1970s the communists decided to do away with the 'feudal' site once and for all. Workers tried dynamite to blow it up, and a tractor to haul it away, both to no avail. The next day workers awoke to find their tractor burnt and destroyed. Soon after the incident the official who ordered Eej Khad's destruction died and his family members became ill. It is said that all the other members of the team suffered a string of bad luck. Most Mongolians can recite a similar tale of provocation and retribution at the holy rock.

the capital city with its coal. Coal is now primarily supplied by Baganuur, as Nalaikh's mine closed down 15 years ago. However, small-scale private excavations (legal and illegal, and sometimes with child labour) continue in the mines. There's little reason to visit except to see a **Kazakh community**; in the 1950s many Kazakhs from Bayan-Ölgii were 'persuaded' to work in Nalaikh's mine.

To find Nalaikh's **mosque**, face the bright-blue town hall, turn 180° and walk about 25 minutes over a small hill. It's very basic and has a blue tin roof. Hourly buses (T500) depart from Teeveriin Tovchoo, the first at 7.30am and the last at 7pm.

Around Nalaikh

Around 19km southeast of Nalaikh is an 8th-century Turkic **stele of Tonyukok** (GPS: N47° 41.661′, E107° 28.586′). The stele is covered in runic script and there are *balbals* (stone figures believed to be Turkic grave markers) and grave slabs nearby.

To get to the stele you'll need to have your own transport. From Nalaikh, take the main highway towards Baganuur and travel for 16km until you see a sign that says 'Tonyukok'. Turn right onto this track and travel another 10km to reach the stele. Just past the site, a huge hanger contains a few relics found around the site; you could ask the local watchman to let you inside, though there is little to see.

Halfway between Nalaikh and Erdene, you'll spot the rear end of an enormous metal horse topped with a statue of Chinggis Khaan (it looks slightly more dramatic if approached from the other direction). The privately built **Chinggis Khaan monument** (Map p112; ☎ 11-321 763, 9911 2846; www.genco-tour.mn; GPS: N47° 48.494′, E107° 31.860′; admission T1000) stands 40m high and has a lift (elevator) rising up its tail, from where there are steps to the horse's head. The complex includes a museum, ger camp and an elaborate replica of a 13th century Mongol war camp, complete with towers and catapults. It also has workshops displaying the production of traditional clothing, jewellery, bows, arrows and battle gear. Rodeos and mini-naadams (games) are sometimes available; check the website.

TERELJ AREA ТЭРЭЛЖ

Terelj *sum* (district), about 55km northeast of Ulaanbaatar, is a playground for urban-weary Ulaanbaatarites. At 1600m, the area is cool and the alpine scenery magnificent, and there are great opportunities for hiking, rock climbing, swimming (in icy cold water), rafting, horse riding and, for hard-core extreme-sports fanatics, skiing in the depths of winter.

Terelj was first developed for tourism in 1964 and 30 years later it became part of **Gorkhi-Terelj National Park**. A few of the tourist developments here are hard on the eyes and ears; some ger camps have concrete car parks, ugly electricity poles, TV antennae and discos at night, and locals overcharge for goods and services. But you can easily get away from all this if you want.

In late summer, the mosquitoes at Terelj can be appalling – at times, the worst in the country – so make sure you have insect repellent with you.

There is a T3000 entry fee to the park for each person, which you'll have to pay at the park entrance, 6km from the main road.

Terelj village (Map p112; GPS: N47° 59.193′, E107° 27.834′) is about 27km from the park entrance at the end of a paved road. It's in a nice location near the river but there's not much here apart from a few shops, a café and a ger camp.

Günjiin Süm Гγнжийн Сγм

Surrounded by magnificent forests and not far from a lovely river, the Baruun Bayan Gol, the Buddhist temple of **Günjiin Süm** (Map p112; elevation 1713m; GPS: N48° 11.010′, E107° 33.377′) was built in 1740 by Efu Dondovdorj to commemorate the death of his Manchurian wife, Amarlangui. Once part of a huge monastery containing about 70 sq metres of blue walls, five other temples and a tower, Günjiin Süm is one of very few Manchurian-influenced temples in Mongolia to survive over the centuries. Only the main temple, and some of the walls of the monastery, remain.

Unlike most other monasteries in Mongolia Günjiin Süm was not destroyed during the Stalinist purges, but simply fell into ruin from neglect, vandalism and theft.

The temple is not a must – there are many better and more accessible temples and monasteries in Ulaanbaatar and Töv – but more of an excuse for a great **overnight trek** on horse or foot, or as part of a longer trip in the national park.

Günjiin is about 30km (as the crow flies) north of the main area where most of the ger camps are situated in Terelj. With a guide you can hike directly over the mountains, or take the easier but longer route along the Baruun Bayan Gol to get there. You can reach it in a day on horseback, while hikers should allow two days each way for the journey.

Khan Khentii Strictly Protected Area

To the northeast, Gorkhi-Terelj National Park joins the Khan Khentii Strictly Protected Area (Khentii Nuruu; Map pp102–3), comprising more than 1.2 million hectares of the Töv, Selenge and Khentii aimags. The Khan Khentii park is almost completely uninhabited by humans, but it is home to endangered species of moose, brown bear and weasel to name but a few, and to more than 250 species of birds.

Activities

HIKING

If you have good maps, a compass and some experience (or a proper guide), hiking in the Terelj area is superb in summer, but be careful of the very fragile environment, and be prepared for mosquitoes and unpredictable weather.

For more sedate **walks** in the Terelj ger camp area, follow the main road and pick a side valley to stroll along at your leisure. From the main road, look out for two interesting rock formations: **Turtle Rock** (Melkhi Khad; Map p112; GPS: N47° 54.509', E107° 25.428'), in a side valley to the south of Terelj, which really looks like one at a certain angle; and the less dramatic **Old Man Reading a Book** (Map p112), which can be spotted on the left side of the road when travelling south from Terelj village. Head north 3km from Turtle Rock to reach the **Aryapala Initiation & Meditation Centre** (Map p112; GPS: N47° 56.121', E107° 25.643'; admission T2000) set on a spectacular rocky hillside.

Some suggested easier hikes are to Günjiin Süm or along the Terelj or Tuul Gols towards Khan Khentii. This is a great area for wildflowers, particularly rhododendron and edelweiss. Places of interest on more difficult, longer treks in Khan Khentii:

Altan-Ölgii Uul (2656m) The source of the Akhain Gol.
Khagiin Khar Nuur A 20m-deep glacial lake, about 30km up Tuul Gol from the ger camps at Terelj.
Yestii Hot Water Springs These springs reach up to 35°C, and are fed by the Yuroo and Yestii Gols. Yestii is about 18km north of Khagiin Khar Nuur.

HORSE RIDING

Travelling on a horse is the perfect way to see a lot of the park, including Günjiin Süm and the side valleys of Tuul Gol. To travel long distances, you will need to have experience, or a guide, and bring most of your own gear. Horses can be hired through any of the ger camps, but you'll pay high tourist prices (around US$35 to US$40 a day). A mob of horse boys hang around Turtle Rock offering horse riding at US$5 per hour, or somewhere between US$12 and US$20 for the day. Alternatively, approach one of the Mongolian families who live around the park and hire one of their horses, though they may not be much cheaper.

RAFTING

Tuul Gol, which starts in the park and flows to Ulaanbaatar and beyond, is one of the best places in the country for rafting. The best section of the river starts a few kilometres north of Terelj village, and wraps around the park until it reaches Gachuurt, near Ulaanbaatar. Nomadic Journeys (p81) runs rafting trips here for around US$45 per day (minimum four people). You can also get a raft from the Seven Summits (p93).

SKIING

Some of the ger camps that stay open in winter cater to cross-country skiers – the season lasts from November to February. There are no set trails, so just take your own gear and ask the locals for some good, safe areas to try.

GOLF

The **Chinggis Khaan Country Club** (Map p112; ☎ 9911 0707) is just off the road in Gorkhi valley. Green fee is T60,000, a caddy is T12,000 and club rental is T24,000. A second course is at the UB2 hotel.

Tours

Most foreign and local tour companies include a night or two in a tourist ger at Terelj in their tours. Several local agencies based in Ulaanbaatar, such as Nomadic Journeys and Nomads (p80), run some of the more interesting trips around Terelj.

Sleeping

CAMPING

Unless you hike out into the hills it's best to get permission to camp, either from the nearest ger or, for a fee, a ger camp. Pitch your tent away from the main road, don't use wood fires and take all of your rubbish out.

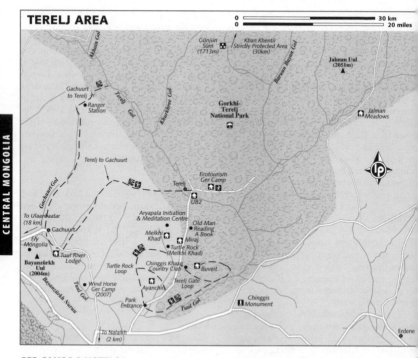

TERELJ AREA

CENTRAL MONGOLIA

GER CAMPS & HOTELS

During the peak season of July and August (and also at the more popular camps), it's not a bad idea to book ahead. Outside the normal tourist season (July to September), it's also a good idea to ring ahead to make sure the camp is open and serves food. A few places are open in winter, mostly for expats who want to ski.

If you are the only guests at a camp you may have to find staff to open up the restaurant, showers etc. The ger camps offer almost identical facilities and prices (about US$30 with three Western meals, or US$15 without).

Apart from the ger camps listed here, many individual families rent out a spare ger and/or hire horses, normally at cheaper rates than the ger camps. You'll have to ask around as none advertises.

Melkhi Khad (☎ 450 737, 9926 9670; 4-bed ger T20,000) This well-maintained camp has a cosy lodge. It's about 1km south of the Aryapala Meditation Centre. Don't confuse this with Domogt Melkhi Khad, the busy camp right next to Turtle Rock.

Ecotourism Ger Camp (☎ 9973 4710; bergroo@hot mail.com; GPS: N47° 58.702', E107° 29.837'; with/without meals US$16/6) For an offbeat experience, you could wade across Terelj Gol and hike to a pleasant ger camp run by a Dutchman named Bert. You'll need to get directions from the Terelj-Juulchin hotel (it's a 30-minute horse ride from here) or inquire about the place at Chez Bernard (p90) in UB. Bert sells homemade Dutch cheese and organises trips up to Günjiin Süm.

UB2 (☎ 9977 4125; ger bed T25,500, s/d T30,000/51,000 half-lux T35,000/52,500, lux T52,000/75,000) This large hotel complex and restaurant marks the end of the road, next to the village of Terelj. It also has a par-three golf course (green fees US$29 clubs US$15 and caddie US$10).

Miraj (☎ 325 188, 9919 3449; with meals US$30) Located 14km along the main road from the park entrance, Miraj is in a prime area for hiking. Horses cost US$5 per hour or US$10 per day, and hot showers are available. There are a couple of other camps up this valley.

Buveit (☎ 322 870, 9911 4913; ger bed US$35) About 13km along the main road from the park entrance, Buveit is in a beautiful secluded valley 3km east of the main road. It also has beds in a cabin for US$2 more than the gers, and you can get three meals for US$18

MOUNTAIN BIKING AROUND TERELJ

Gachuurt to Terelj Gol (North)

This challenging route combines mountain, forest and river scenery. To reach the trailhead from UB, go to Gachuurt and turn left when you get to the bridge. Follow the valley for about 19km to the end of the road where there is an obvious car park (you could get a taxi all the way). Ride up the valley that leads in a northwesterly direction. There is a ranger ger in the valley that marks the boundary of Gorkhi-Terelj National Park. Here you need to pay park fees. The steady climb up to the peak is about 2km, from where you descend into a valley that winds for 7km to Terelj Gol. Return the way you've come and then ride the 19km back to Gachuurt; it's downhill all the way. This route takes around five hours.

Terelj to Gachuurt (Central)

This rugged route goes from Terelj to Gachuurt, taking in two passes along the way. Get a ride all the way to the town of Terelj and then start riding on the road that heads west; it's about 2km to the next small settlement of gers. The trail continues west and starts heading into the wilderness, up a valley with a forest to your left. The ridge tops out at 1859m and descends to another valley. The trail climbs again, slightly to the right, to another 1859m ridge, from where you begin a long descent towards Gachuurt. At the end of the valley (it's about 15km) you'll reach Tuul Gol, which you follow back to Gachuurt town. All up it's a 30km ride and should take around five hours.

Turtle Rock Loop

This is a convenient route as it begins and ends at Turtle Rock in the Gorkhi valley. From Turtle Rock ride west down the slope until the road goes right into a ger camp (they built the camp over the trail). Go around the camp (or through it) and then it's a 30-minute climb to the top of the hill. From the top you get some great views of the rock formations in the next valley. The trail continues south past several ger camps and eventually leads back to the main road and back to Turtle Rock. This loop is 15km.

It's possible to do a longer loop: before turning left out of the valley (towards the main road), just veer right up a slope, and then down a long narrow valley (one valley west of the main road), eventually reaching Tuul Gol. At the end of the valley, turn left to return to Turtle Rock, or right to leave the park. From Turtle Rock to Tuul Gol its 14km. The full loop takes about four hours.

Terelj Gate Loop

This is a nice route for those who don't have their own car. Get a lift to the park entrance and start cycling east, up the valley that contains the Tuul Gol. After 30 to 40 minutes the trail turns left, leaving the valley and heading towards a ridge. It's a one-hour climb up to the top and then a gentle ride into Gorkhi valley and the ger camps. From here you head back to the park entrance to complete the three hour loop.

---

extra. Marked rock-climbing routes are nearby and the camp might be able to supply climbing gear. It's run by Tsolmon Travel agency (p81).

Ayanchin (☎ 319 211, 9911 2611; ger bed US$50, r US$75) This American-built camp has a Western-style lodge and modern (but ugly) shower and toilet block. At meal times (meals US$5 to US$11), enjoy a steak, pasta, sandwich or burger on the sunny deck. It's about 10km from the main entrance, marked with a big billboard.

Jalman Meadows (4-day package per person US$195) Nomadic Journeys runs this remote and low-impact ger camp in the upper Tuul valley, which makes a nice base if you are headed to Khagiin Khar Nuur, which is an eight-hour horse ride away. The camp has a library of books on Mongolia and a number of great activities, including mountain biking, yak carting, river boating and even portable saunas! You'll need to book well in advance for these trips. The price includes transfers to and from Ulaanbaatar.

Getting There & Away

BICYCLE

A mountain bike would be an excellent way of getting around some of the Terelj area if you could stand the 70km of uphill riding to get there and cope with the traffic in Ulaanbaatar along the way. The Seven Summits (p93) and Karakorum Expeditions (p81) in Ulaanbaatar both rent bikes.

BUS

The road from Ulaanbaatar to Terelj, which goes through part of the national park, is in pretty good nick. A bus departs at 4pm from Durvun Zam (Map pp70–1; corner of Peace Ave and Öndör Geegen Zanabazaryn Gudamj) and goes to the centre of the park, a few kilometres past the turn-off to Turtle Rock. The same bus comes back directly to UB. The cost is T1500 each way. If this doesn't pan out you'll have to hitch.

HITCHING

Hitching *out* of Ulaanbaatar can be difficult because vehicles going to Terelj could leave from anywhere. The cheapest way to hitch to Terelj is to take a minivan for Baganuur or Nalaikh and get off at the turn-off to Terelj, where you are far more likely to get a lift.

Hitching *back* to Ulaanbaatar from along the main road through Terelj is not difficult, as almost every vehicle is returning to the capital.

TAXI

A taxi from Ulaanbaatar is easy to organise; jeeps aren't necessary because the road is paved all the way. You should only pay the standard rate per kilometre, which works out at about US$25 one way, but the driver may understandably want more because his taxi may be empty for part of the return journey. You can also arrange with your taxi to pick you up later.

When there's enough demand shared taxis to Terelj sometimes leave from Naran Tuul market jeep station in Ulaanbaatar (off Map p64). This is more likely on summer Sundays when locals make a day trip to the area.

GACHUURT ГАЧУУРТ

Around 20km east of Ulaanbaatar, the town of Gachuurt offers the chance to quickly trade city traffic and bustle for riverside walks, horse riding, camping, fishing and rafting. The town is a rapidly growing suburb of the capital, popular with wealthy Mongolians who build gated villas on the hills surrounding the town. Despite the increased development, it remains an idyllic setting and a popular half-day trip from Ulaanbaatar.

Activities

Adrenaline junkies may want to spend an afternoon at the base camp of **Fly Mongolia** (Map p107; ☎ 9919 7933), a burgeoning adventure centre run by local aviation enthusiast Alex Amiya. Tandem paragliding (US$35) and ultralight aircraft tours (US$100) are two popular activities. With more time you can take a four-day paragliding lesson (US$180). Alex can teach in English, French, Russian or Mongolian. Note that spring is a dangerous time to paraglide in Mongolia because of the unpredictable winds. September is best for beginners. Fly Mongolia also has 4WD go-carts (per hour US$15). The camp is off the main Gachuurt road, 1km before Hotel Mongolia (look for the wooden sign by the road). Be warned that the place is pretty disorganised (even by Mongolian standards) and Alex may not be available when you get there.

Frenchman Côme Doerflinger runs adventure trips through his outfit **Xanadu** (☎ 9987 2912; www.mongolienomade.mn in French), based in Gachuurt. He mainly runs horse trips, and has French, Russian and English saddles. Côme also has kayaks and canoes that you can use to float down Tuul Gol, and mountain bikes which are great for excursions up Gachuurt's side valleys towards Terelj.

Sleeping & Eating

Gachuurt offers reasonable camping opportunities. About 2km before the town centre, near Tuul Gol, there are spots to pitch your tent. Just try to avoid the clusters of ger camps. For basic meals you could try the **Take Off Café** (☎ 9919 7933; meals T2000-3500; ⏱ 10am-6pm) at the Fly Mongolia base camp (Map p107).

Tuul River Lodge (Map p107; ☎ 9909 9365; www .tuulriverside.com; per person US$60-100) This upmarket option has en-suite gers that include bath and shower. Prices do not include meals but it does have a restaurant. It's about 10km past Gachuurt on the way to Terelj.

Hotel Mongolia (Map p107; ☎ 315 513; www.hotel -mongolia.com; ger s/d US$60/80, s/d US$80/120, ste US$125-250) This ger camp would impress even Kublai Khaan. Hotel Mongolia is the unmissable walled palace resembling ancient Karakorum,

WIND HORSE: ECOFRIENDLY GER CAMP

Many ger camps claim to be ecofriendly, but by constructing septic tanks near rivers and building permanent structures in the virgin landscape they are leaving an irremovable scar on the land. As you travel, look out for less-developed camps that utilise solar and wind power and other ecofriendly devices.

In the Gachuurt–Terelj area, a leader in sustainable practices is the Wind Horse Ger Camp, about 12km southeast of Gachuurt (Map p112; the position on the map is a guide only – the owner may move the camp at any time if he finds a better location). In true bush-camp tradition, Wind Horse has built no permanent structures; it has a dining ger, a shower ger (heated with driftwood from the river) and a bathroom tent with chemical toilets. Gers are scattered in the glen, giving each a sense of privacy. There are no wires, pipes or poured concrete whatsoever. Solar panels provide a limited energy source.

Despite the rustic setting, you can expect gourmet cuisine and quality wine. Horses with western saddles are available to ride and the camp can organise pack trips in the direction of Terelj.

A bed and three meals starts from US$60 per night (and can run up to US$400 depending on what sort of wine and food is ordered). Reservations are required at the camp as space is limited. Contact Hamid Sardar at mongolwindhorse@gmail.com.

a few kilometres short of Gachuurt. Luxurious rooms have private bath and shower and the price includes breakfast. The hotel includes a business centre, souvenir shops and a field behind the walls where mini-naadams are held according to tour-group bookings. Even if you don't stay here, it's worth visiting for the kitsch ambience and excellent Asian-style restaurant (meals T2500 to T3500), which serves a few delicacies such as horse stomach.

Getting There & Away

Buses pick up passengers every hour or so from the east end of Peace Ave in Ulaanbaatar, near the Jukov statue, a couple of kilometres east of the city centre, bound for Gachuurt (T500, 25 minutes). You can also easily get a taxi from UB (T6000).

CHINGELTEI UUL
ЧИНГЭЛТЭЙ УУЛ

To the north of Ulaanbaatar, Chingeltei Uul (Map p107; 1949m) has some pretty forests near the top. You can reach the base of the mountain by bus No 3, 16 or, best of all, 18 from Sambugiin Gudamj, near Liberty Sq, in Ulaanbaatar (T200). By taxi (T1500), you can go all the way up to a gate from where it's a 2km walk to the summit.

BAYANZÜRKH UUL
БАЯНЗУРХ УУЛ

This peak is in the Bayanzürkh Nuruu (Rich Heart Mountains; Map p112), to the east of Ulaanbaatar. There's a little forest at the top, and views from the summit (2004m) are great. You can reach the base of the mountains by taking the bus from Ulaanbaatar to Nalaikh and getting off before the women's prison ('*emegtei shorong*' in Mongolian; let the bus driver know to let you off here). Of the four holy mountains, this is the best for mountain biking.

KHANDGAIT ХАНДГАЙТ

About 40km north of Ulaanbaatar, **Khandgait** (Map pp102-3; GPS: N48° 07.066′, E106° 54.296′) is another lovely area of cow pastures, pine forests and wildflowers, surrounding the small village of the same name. Like Terelj, there are plenty of opportunities for hiking, rock climbing, and, in winter, ice-skating and cross-country skiing (it's possible to rent skis and sleds here in winter). If you're lucky, you might see some ice motorcycling at this time too. This is great countryside for camping. Just pick any site, preferably near a river, and enjoy, but be careful about wood fires and be sure to take your rubbish out.

Buses (T600) go here from Container (Bömbögör) Market in Ulaanbaatar at 7am, 11am, 1pm and 5pm. A taxi (jeeps aren't necessary) from UB is easiest, but, naturally, more expensive at around US$25 return, plus waiting time.

KHUSTAIN NATIONAL PARK
ХУСТАЙН НУРУУ

Also known as Khustain Nuruu (Birch Mountain Range), this park was established in 1993 and is about 100km southwest of

CENTRAL MONGOLIA

TAKHI – THE REINTRODUCTION OF A SPECIES

The year was 1969 and a herder in western Mongolia spotted a rare *takhi* (wild horse) in the distance. It was an extraordinary find as so few *takhi* were left in the wild. Alas, it was also the final sighting; with no new reports thereafter, scientists had to declare the species extinct in the wild – the result of poaching, overgrazing by livestock and human encroachment on their breeding grounds.

All was not lost for the *takhi*, however, as a dozen individual horses were known to exist in zoos outside Mongolia – their ancestors had been captured by game hunters in the early 20th century. A small group of conservationists dedicated themselves to breeding the animals with the hope that one day they could be reintroduced to Mongolia.

The conservationists did not fare so well with Mongolia's suspicious communist government, but when democracy arrived in the early 1990s they were welcomed with open arms. By that time the worldwide population was around 1500, scattered around zoos in Australia, Germany, Switzerland and the Netherlands.

Between 1992 and 2004 *takhi* were reintroduced into Mongolia at Khustain National Park, Takhiin Tal in Gov-Altai, and Khomiin Tal in Zavkhan. Today there are more than 200 *takhi* in Khustain, 80 in Takhiin Tal and 12 in Khomiin Tal. Given the political and logistical challenges to the project, their reintroduction is nothing short of miraculous, making it one of the best conservation stories of our times.

The *takhi*, also known as Przewalski's horse (named after the Polish explorer who first 'discovered' the horse in 1878), are now descended from the bloodline of three stallions, so computerised records have been introduced to avoid inbreeding. They are the last remaining wild horse worldwide, the forerunner of the domestic horse, as depicted in cave paintings in France. They are not simply horses that have become feral, or wild, as found in the USA or Australia, but a genetically different species, boasting two extra chromosomes in their DNA make-up.

Within the parks, the laws of nature are allowed to run their course; an average of five foals are killed by wolves every year in Khustain. The park gets locals onside by hiring herders as rangers, offering cheap loans to others and offering employment at a cheese-making factory on the outskirts of the park.

For more info check out www.treemail.nl/takh.

Ulaanbaatar. The 50,620-hectare reserve protects Mongolia's wild horse, the *takhi*, and the reserve's steppe and forest-steppe environment. In addition to the *takhi*, there are populations of *maral* (Asiatic red deer), steppe gazelle, deer, boar, manul (small wild cat), wolf and lynx. A visit to the park has become a popular overnight excursion from Ulaanbaatar in recent years.

Entry to the park is a one-off fee of US$5 (free for locals). It's worth spending at least one night in the park, as you are most likely to see *takhi* and other wildlife at dusk or dawn.

The park is run by the Hustai National Park Trust, which is supported by the Dutch government and the Mongolian Association for the Conservation of Nature and the Environment (Macne).

Orientation & Information

The information centre at the entrance to Khustain National Park has a ger with displays on the park and the *takhi*, a small souvenir shop and videos that include a documentary on Mongolian horses featuring Julia Roberts. Ten kilometres south into the park's core area is the former park headquarters. Another 13km or so west is Moilt camp.

Sights & Activities

In an effort to make the park self-financing, horse riding, hiking and jeep excursions are offered. Several **hiking** routes have been established, including a good hike that takes you from the visitors centre to Moilt camp (22km) in about five hours.

A fun horseback trek takes you to Turkic **stone monuments** (Map pp102-3; GPS: N47° 33.201', E105°50.991') southwest of the park and then on to Tuul Gol. Horse rental is US$12 per day. Contact the park for details.

With your own jeep you can drive to Moilt camp. Park regulations require you to take a park guide (free within the park) and stick only to existing tracks. Wildlife watching is best at dusk and at dawn. The *takhi* could be in any number of places, and park guides can direct your driver to the best spots.

The park runs a three-week volunteer program where you can help with research. See www.ecovolunteer.org for details.

A community-based tourism project at Khustain allows visitors to stay with nomad families, ride horses, learn felt-making and experience daily life in the countryside. See www.cbtn.mn for details.

Sleeping

Independent camping is not allowed inside the park so you have to camp outside the park boundary. The best place to go is the south side of the park by Tuul Gol.

There is a small **ger camp** (without meals per person US$15, tent US$5) at the entrance to the park (the payment for accommodation includes the park entrance). Rooms are available in the main building for US$20 per person. There are also cabins at **Moilt camp** (per person US$15). Meals are available at the camp (breakfast US$3, lunch US$8, dinner US$6)

To book accommodation in the park contact **Hustai National Park Trust** (☎ 011-245 087, 245 881; www.hustai.mn; Hustai Bldg, 2nd khoroo, Bayangol District) in Ulaanbaatar. It is about 2km west of the State Department Store, off Peace Ave.

Getting There & Away

To get to the park travel 100km west from Ulaanbaatar, along the road to Kharkhorin, where there is a signpost pointing you the 13km south to the park entrance. A Russian minivan departs on Friday from Khustain Nuruu at 4pm and returns from UB to the park at 7.30pm (from Minii Zakh, near UB Palace). On Sunday the van leaves the park at 3pm and returns from Ulaanbaatar at 5.30pm. The cost is US$10 one way and it's recommended to book ahead of time.

ÖVÖRKHANGAI
ӨВӨРХАНГАЙ

pop 110,200 / area 63,000 sq km
Övörkhangai contains one of Mongolia's top attractions, the Erdene Zuu monastery in Kharkhorin. This is Mongolia's oldest monastery and it has become a regular stop on most tour circuits. But while travellers flock to this site and then rush off to the points west, many miss some of the best parts of Övörkhangai, including the Naiman Nuur lake district and the spectacular Tövkhön Khiid. The southern part of the aimag, past Arvaikheer, is uninteresting desert steppe.

If travelling by rented jeep, it is easy to combine a visit to these sights with some other places that are clustered near the borders of Arkhangai, Bulgan and Töv aimags, including Khögnö Khan Uul Nature Reserve, the sand dunes of Mongol Els and Naiman Nuur. The paved road, which reaches Kharkhorin and the aimag capital of Arvaikheer, is also a definite attraction.

ARVAIKHEER АРВАЙХЭЭР
☎ 01322 / pop 23,400 / elev 1913m
A nondescript but friendly aimag capital, Arvaikheer is of little interest except as a place to eat and rest, refuel the jeep or arrange onward public transport. If you find yourself between rides, the museum is worth a look.

There is no need to go to Arvaikheer if you only want to visit Kharkhorin and northern Övörkhangai, as a paved road runs to Kharkhorin from Ulaanbaatar. The police station is southeast of the town square.

Information
Bathhouse (shower/sauna T1100/4000; ☯ 9am-10pm Tue-Sun)
Internet café (☎ 22193; per hr T600; ☯ 8.30am-12.30pm & 2-6pm Mon-Fri) In the Telecom office.
Khan Bank (☎ 22040; ☯ 9am-1pm & 2-4.30pm)
Telecom office (☎ 24098; ☯ 24hr) The post office is also here.

Sights
GANDAN MUNTSAGLAN KHIID
ГАНДАН МУНТСАГЛАН ХИЙД
This comparatively large monastery, about 900m north of the town square, contains a fine collection of *thangka* (scroll paintings), including one depicting the original monastery, which was destroyed in 1937. The current monastery was opened in 1991, and now has about 60 monks in residence. Visitors are welcome. To the left of the temple is a small shop selling religious items.

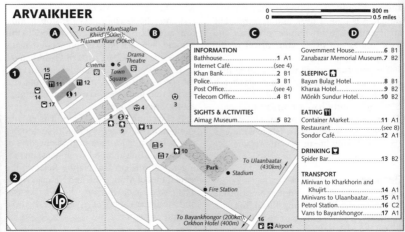

ARVAIKHEER

INFORMATION
Bathhouse	1 A1
Internet Café	(see 4)
Khan Bank	2 B1
Police	3 B1
Post Office	(see 4)
Telecom Office	4 B1

SIGHTS & ACTIVITIES
Aimag Museum	5 B2

Government House	6 B1
Zanabazar Memorial Museum	7 B2

SLEEPING
Bayan Bulag Hotel	8 B2
Kharaa Hotel	9 B2
Mönkh Sundur Hotel	10 B2

EATING
Container Market	11 A1
Restaurant	(see 8)
Sondor Café	12 A1

DRINKING
Spider Bar	13 B2

TRANSPORT
Minivan to Kharkhorin and Khujirt	14 A1
Minivans to Ulaanbaatar	15 A1
Petrol Station	16 C2
Vans to Bayankhongor	17 A1

MUSEUMS

Since Övörkhangai lies partly in the forested Khangai region and the Gobi Desert, the **Aimag Museum** (☎ 22075; admission T1500, photos T3500; ☼ 9am-12.30pm & 2-6pm Mon-Fri) boasts a better-than-average selection of stuffed mountain and desert animals. There are also some fossils and arrows, local artwork and leftovers from Karakorum.

Just around the corner is the **Zanabazar Memorial Museum** (admission T1500, photos T3500; ☼ 9am-12.30pm & 2-6pm Mon-Fri), which has a collection of religious artwork connected to the master sculptor (p40). Ask at the Aimag Museum for the key.

Sleeping

Like most aimag capitals, camping is a better option than the dreary hotels, but in Arvaikheer you'll have to walk a kilometre or so to find a quiet place to pitch your tent. It's best to head out to the area north of the monastery or drive 5km southeast to Ongiin Gol.

Bayan Bulag Hotel (☎ 23374; dm T3500, r with/without shower 6000/8000, half-lux/lux T12,000/15,000) This place has five clean, carpeted rooms. The half-lux and lux rooms have clean bathrooms with 24-hour hot water. The attached restaurant is one of the best places in town to eat.

Mönkh Sundur Hotel (☎ 9932 9677; r T8000) All the rooms are the same here, each with TV, toilet and washbasin. It has a restaurant with good food, beer and drinks, as well as a billiards room. It's in a compound behind the museum.

Kharaa Hotel (☎ 23655; d US$15, half-lux/lux US$20/25) This place has standard three-bed rooms with a shared bathroom. If the hotel isn't busy, solo travellers should be able to pay for just one bed; at other times you'll have to pay for at least two beds for privacy. Half-lux and lux rooms include bathroom and shower. Hot water comes on for a couple of hours in the morning and evening – check the times with reception. The place is clean and bright but overpriced so try for a discount.

Eating & Drinking

There are quite a few basic restaurants around town, including a good one in the Bayan Bulag Hotel. There are also *guanz* (canteens or cheap restaurants) and *tsainii gazar* (tea houses) near the container market. The bustling daily market also has yogurt, *airag* (fermented mare milk) after June and sheepskins, as well as the normal range of packaged foods.

Near the market is a popular *guanz* masquerading as a café, **Sondor Café** (dishes T800-1000; ☼ 8am-8pm). A gang of friendly, young locals run the popular **Spider Bar** (☎ 9939 5338; ☼ 10am-midnight), a great place for a few drinks after a long day on the road. In the late night it becomes a lively disco bar.

Getting There & Away

You can travel quickly along the 430km paved road between Ulaanbaatar and Arvaikheer. (There are plenty of *guanz* along the way.) The paved road finishes just west of Arvaikheer; from there it is about another 200km along the usual rough road to the next aimag capital of Bayankhongor. With a jeep, an experienced driver and lots of time you could venture south to Dalanzadgad, 377km away in Ömnögov aimag, either via Saikhan-Ovoo or (more adventurously) via Guchin Us, Khovd and Khongoryn Els.

AIR
MIAT flies between Ulaanbaatar and Arvaikheer twice weekly for US$66/117 one way/return, en route to/from Altai. The airport is less than 1km south of town.

HITCHING
The Ulaanbaatar–Arvaikheer road is one of the busiest in the country – at least one vehicle goes in both directions every minute. Hitching a ride on a truck or in a private car should be comparatively easy. Going further west along the main road to Bayankhongor won't be as easy, but it is possible (although it's a pretty uninteresting highway – the better route is through Arkhangai). In Arvaikheer, trucks hang around the market, so try there or at the petrol station on the main road.

JEEPS
If you want to hire a jeep to see the sights around northern Övörkhangai, it's better to catch a bus from Ulaanbaatar to Kharkhorin and hire a jeep there, rather than go to Arvaikheer. Jeep hire is around T40,000, not including petrol.

MINIVANS
Minivans and smaller microbuses run along the paved road between Arvaikheer and Ulaanbaatar daily (T13,000, seven hours). Look for them on the north side of the market. At least one car a day will travel north to Khujirt (T6000, two hours); as usual, when the driver says departure time is 'now' that means around 4pm. These vehicles leave from the west side of the market.

NAIMAN NUUR НАЙМАН НУУР
The area of Naiman Nuur (Eight Lakes), which was created by volcanic eruptions centuries ago, is now part of the 11,500-hectare **Khuisiin Naiman Nuur Nature Reserve**. The **lakes** (GPS: N46° 31.232′, E101° 50.705′) are about 35km southwest of Orkhon Khürkhree (waterfall), but the roads are often virtually impassable. Locals around the waterfall can rent horses for

the two-day trip to the lakes. It's also possible to get to the lakes from the Arvaikheer side by car, although only an experienced local driver could make it. Companies such as Nomads and Nomadic Expeditions (p81) run tours here, including horse-riding trips.

KHUJIRT ХУЖИРТ
After a lifetime on the steppes, the last thing any nomad needs is a holiday in the great outdoors. Fortunately, there is Khujirt, where local Mongolians can come and put on a pair of slippers and a bathrobe, enter a mud bath, dip into metal tubs filled with spring water and get some vitamin injections. This may not sound so inviting to foreign tourists but the **spa resort** (9am-6pm Mon-Sat) does make for an interesting stop if you are travelling though the Khujirt valley.

The 54km road between Kharkhorin and Khujirt is one of the best places in the country to see **falcons** and **hawks**, particularly the *sar* (moon) hawk. If you are ever likely to get a photo of one of these birds, this is the place.

Sleeping & Eating
Next to the spa resort, **Khujirt Tur** (9971 5262; per person T10,000) is the best choice in the area. The shower block has piping hot-water showers from the mineral springs. The Khujirt Tur ger camp serves meals for T4000. A cheaper *guanz* is in back of the resort.

Getting There & Away
Buses (T8500) run every Monday, Wednesday and Friday from UB's Dragon (Luu) Avto Vaksal bus stand. They return to Ulaanbaatar the following day, passing within 5km of Kharkhorin. Faster minivans also do the run daily for T10,000.

With the number of Mongolians using the Ulaanbaatar–Kharkhorin road to get to Khujirt in summer, it shouldn't be hard to hitch a ride between Kharkhorin and Khujirt.

SHANKH KHIID ШАНХ ХИЙД
Shankh Khiid, once known as the West Monastery, and Erdene Zuu are the only monasteries in the region to have survived the 1937 purge. Shankh was founded by the great Zanabazar in 1648 and is said to have once housed Chinggis Khaan's black military banner. At one time the monastery was home to more than 1500 monks. As elsewhere, the monastery was closed in 1937, temples were

burnt and many monks were shipped off to Siberia. Some of those that survived helped to reopen the place the early 1990s.

The **monastery** (GPS: N47° 03.079', E102° 57.236'; admission T1000, photos T1000) is exactly halfway along the main road between Kharkhorin and Khujirt, in the village of Shankh. If you have your own transport, it's a fine place to stop between both towns.

KHARKHORIN (KARAKORUM)
ХАРХОРИН (КАРАКОРУМ)
☎ 013258 / pop 8000 / elev 1913m

In the mid-13th century, Karakorum was a happening place. Chinggis Khaan established a supply base here and his son Ögedei ordered the construction of a proper capital, a decree that attracted traders, dignitaries and skilled workers from across Asia and even Europe.

The good times lasted around 40 years until Kublai moved the capital to Khanbalik (later called Beijing), a decision that still incites resentment among some Mongolians. Following the move to Beijing and the subsequent collapse of the Mongol empire, Karakorum was abandoned and then destroyed by vengeful Manchurian soldiers in 1388.

Whatever was left of Karakorum was used to help build Erdene Zuu Khiid in the 16th century, which itself was badly damaged during the Stalinist purges.

The charmless Soviet-built town of Kharkhorin (and its gigantic flour factory) was built a couple of kilometres away from Erdene Zuu. There is nothing of interest in the town and it's a big disappointment if you've come expecting the glories of Middle Ages, but a surge in tourism has improved local infrastructure. There are even plans to move the capital here and build a modern planned city (you'll see a billboard in town with the layout). Although this isn't expected to happen anytime soon, it doesn't hurt for a small town to dream.

Information
Kharkhorin has no information office, but the guides at Erdene Zuu (right) can answer most tourist-related questions.

Internet café (per hr T600; ☎ 8.30am-9.30pm Mon-Fri, 9am-7pm Sun) Located in the Telecom office.

Khan Bank (☎ 2124; ☎ 9am-5pm Mon-Fri) Can change US dollars, euros and travellers cheques.

Mongol Shuudan Bank (☎ 2723; ☎ 9am-5pm Mon-Fri) Gives cash against Visa debit cards. Inside the Telecom office.

Telecom office (☎ 2444; ☎ 24hr) The post office is also here.

Xac Bank (☎ 2648; ☎ 9.30am-4.30pm Mon-Fri) Changes money and gives cash advances on MasterCard.

Sights
ERDENE ZUU KHIID ЭРДЭНЭ ЗУУ ХИЙД
Founded in 1586 by Altai Khaan, Erdene Zuu (Hundred Treasures) was the first Buddhist monastery in Mongolia. It had between 60 and 100 temples, about 300 gers inside the walls and, at its peak, up to 1000 monks in residence.

The monastery went through periods of neglect and prosperity until finally the Stalinist purges of 1937 put it completely out of business. All but three of the temples in Erdene Zuu were destroyed and an unknown number of monks were either killed or shipped off to Siberia and never heard from again.

However, a surprising number of statues, *tsam* masks and *thangkas* were saved from the monastery at the time of the purges – possibly with the help of a few sympathetic military officers. The items were buried in nearby mountains, or stored in local homes (at great risk to the residents).

The monastery remained closed until 1965 when it was permitted to reopen as a museum, but not as a place of worship. It was only with the collapse of communism in 1990 that religious freedom was restored and the monastery became active again. Today, Erdene Zuu Khiid retains much of its former glory, and is considered by many to be the most important monastery in the country, though no doubt it's a shadow of what it once was.

Information
Entrance to the **monastery grounds** (☎ 9am-6pm summer, 10am-5pm winter) is free. If you want to see inside the temples, however, you'll have to go to the **ticket desk** (☎ 2285, 9926 8286) and souvenir shop on your left as you enter the grounds from the south and buy a ticket for US$3, which includes a guided tour of the site. Permission to take photos in the temples is an additional US$5 and video is US$10.

The monastery is an easy 2km walk from the centre of Kharkhorin.

Temples
The monastery is enclosed in an immense walled compound. Spaced evenly along each wall, about every 15m, are 108 stupas (108

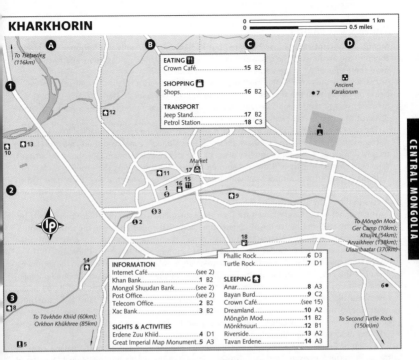

KHARKHORIN

CENTRAL MONGOLIA

EATING 🍴
Crown Café.................................15 B2

SHOPPING 🛍
Shops.......................................16 B2

TRANSPORT
Jeep Stand...............................17 B2
Petrol Station..........................18 C3

INFORMATION
Internet Café........................(see 2)
Khan Bank..................................1 B2
Mongol Shuudan Bank..........(see 2)
Post Office............................(see 2)
Telecom Office............................2 B2
Xac Bank....................................3 B2

SIGHTS & ACTIVITIES
Erdene Zuu Khiid.......................4 D1
Great Imperial Map Monument..5 A3
Phallic Rock...............................6 D3
Turtle Rock................................7 D1

SLEEPING 🛏
Anar..8 A3
Bayan Burd................................9 C2
Crown Café..........................(see 15)
Dreamland................................10 A2
Möngön Mod.............................11 B2
Mönkhsuuri...............................12 B1
Riverside..................................13 A2
Tavan Erdene...........................14 A3

To Tsetserleg (116km)

To Tövkhön Khiid (60km); Orkhon Khükhree (85km)

Market

Ancient Karakorum

To Möngön Mod Ger Camp (10km); Khujirt (54km); Arvaikheer (138km); Ulaanbaatar (370km)

To Second Turtle Rock (150m/m)

0   1 km
0   0.5 miles

---

is a sacred number to Buddhists). The three temples in the compound, which were not destroyed in the 1930s, are dedicated to the three stages of Buddha's life: childhood, adolescence and adulthood. See p37 for a brief description of some of the gods you will see in the monastery.

Dalai Lama Süm was built in 1675 to commemorate the visit by Abtai Khaan's son, Altan, to the Dalai Lama in Tibet. The room is bare save for a statue of Zanabazar and some fine 17th-century *thangkas* depicting the Dalai Lamas and various protector deities.

Inside the courtyard, **Baruun Zuu**, the temple to the west, built by Abtai Khaan and his son, is dedicated to the adult Buddha. Inside, on either side of Sakyamuni (the Historical Buddha), are statues of Sanjaa ('Dipamkara' in Sanskrit), the Past Buddha, to the left; and Maidar ('Maitreya' in Sanskrit), the Future Buddha, to the right. Other items on display include some golden 'wheels of eternity', *naimin takhel* (the eight auspicious symbols), figurines from the 17th and 18th centuries, and *balin* (wheat dough cakes, decorated with coloured medallions of goat or mutton fat),

made in 1965 and still well preserved. Look out for the inner circumambulation path leading off to the left, just by the entrance.

The main and central temple is called the **Zuu of Buddha**. The entrance is flanked by the gods Gonggor on the left and Bandal Lham (Palden Lhamo in Sanskrit) on the right. Inside, on either side of the statues of the child Buddha, are (to the right) Otoch Manal, the Medicine Buddha and (to the left) Holy Abida, the god of justice. The temple also contains statues of Niam and Dabaa, the sun and moon gods respectively, a few of the *tsam* masks that survived the purges, some carved, aggressive-looking guards from the 16th and 17th centuries, and some displays of the work of the revered sculptor and Buddhist, Zanabazar.

In the temple to the east, **Zuun Zuu**, there's a statue depicting the adolescent Buddha. The statue on the right is Tsongkhapa, who founded the Yellow Hat sect of Buddhism in Tibet. The figure on the left is Janraisig (Chenresig in Tibetan, Avalokitesvara in Sanskrit), the Bodhisattva of Compassion.

As you walk north you will pass the **Golden Prayer Stupa**, built in 1799. The locked temple

THE ANCIENT CAPITAL

Mongolia's ancient capital may be gone, but Karakorum is certainly not forgotten. By piecing together the accounts of the city written by visiting missionaries, ambassadors and travellers we have some idea of what the imperial capital once looked like.

Frankly, it wasn't much. The missionary William of Rubruck (1215–95) dismissed the city as being no bigger than the suburb of Saint Denis in Paris. Giovanni de Piano Carpine (1180–1252), an envoy sent to the Mongols in 1245 by Pope Innocent IV, described the city vaguely as 'at the distance of a year's walk' from Rome.

The city never had much time to expand; it was really only the active capital for 40 years before Kublai moved the capital to Khanbalik (Beijing). Few Mongols even lived there, most preferring to stay in their gers several kilometres away on the steppe. It was mainly inhabited by artisans, scholars, religious leaders and others captured by the Mongols during their foreign raids.

Its main feature was a brick wall with four gates that encircled the city. Each gate had its own market, selling grain in the east, goats in the west, oxen and wagons in the south and horses in the north.

The Mongol khaans were famed for their religious tolerance and split their time equally between all the religions, hence the 12 different religions that coexisted within the town. Mosques, Buddhist monasteries and Nestorian Christian churches competed for the Mongols' souls. Even powerful figures such as Ögedei's wife and Kublai's mother were Nestorian Christians.

The centrepiece of the city was the Tumen Amgalan, or Palace of Worldly Peace, in the southwest corner of the city. This 2500-sq-metre complex, built in 1235, was the palace of Ögedei Khaan. The two-storey palace had a vast reception hall for receiving ambassadors, and its 64 pillars resembled the nave of a church. The walls were painted, the green-tiled floor had underfloor heating, and the Chinese-style roof was covered in green and red tiles. Whenever he was at court, the khaan sat on a panther skin atop a great throne, to which stairs ascended from one side and descended from the other.

A team of German archaeologists recently uncovered the foundations of the palace, close to the stone turtle (opposite). You can also see a model of the palace in the National Museum of Mongolian History (p69) in Ulaanbaatar.

The most memorable aspect of the city was a fountain designed in 1253 by the French jeweller and sculptor Guillaume Bouchier (or Bouchee) of Paris, who had been captured by the Mongols in Hungary and brought back to embellish Karakorum. The fountain was in the shape of a huge silver tree, which simultaneously dispensed mare milk from silver lion heads, and wine, rice wine, *bal* (mead) and *airag* from four golden spouts shaped like snake heads. On top of the tree was an angel. On order a servant blew a pipe like a bugle that extended from the angel's mouth, giving the order for other servants to pump drinks out of the tree.

Rubruck disparagingly describes various pleasure domes and epic feasts (during one of which the Mongol guests guzzled 105 cartloads of alcohol). There were also quarters of artisans and traders, populated by a great mix of people brought back to Karakorum from all over Asia. So cosmopolitan was the city that both foreign and Mongol coins were legal tender.

next to this is said to be the first temple built at Erdene Zuu.

The large white temple at the far end is the Tibetan-style **Lavrin Süm**, where ceremonies are held every morning, usually starting at around 11am; the times vary so ask at the office. Visitors are welcome, but photographs during ceremonies are not.

Other Sights

Apart from the main temples, there are several other interesting things to see. The **gravestones** of Abtai Khaan (1554–88) and his grandson Tüshet Khaan Gombodorj (the father of Zanabazar) stand in front of the Dalai Lama Süm and are inscribed in Mongol, Tibetan and Arabic scripts. In the northeast of the monastery are the base stones of a gigantic ger (now called the **Square of Happiness and Prosperity**), set up in 1639 to commemorate Zanabazar's birthday. The ger was reported to be 15m high and 45m in diameter, with 35 concertina-style walls, and could seat 300 during the annual assemblies of the local khaans.

STONE TURTLES
Outside the monastery walls are two stone turtles (also called Turtle Rocks). Four of these sculptures once marked the boundaries of ancient Karakorum, acting as protectors of the city (turtles are considered symbols of eternity). The turtles originally had an inscribed stone stele mounted vertically on their back.

One is easy to find: just walk out of the northern gate of the monastery and follow the path northwest for about 300m. Often, an impromptu **souvenir market** is set up next to one stone turtle. You'll need a guide or directions to find the other one, which is on the hill south of the monastery, about 600m past the phallic rock.

ANCIENT KARAKORUM
Just beyond the stone turtle, stretching for about 1km south and east, is the site of ancient Karakorum. The foundations of Karakorum's buildings are all underground and little has been excavated, so you need lots of imagination when contemplating the grandness of it all. The plain was littered with bricks, ruined walls and pillars until the mid-16th century when everything was picked up and used to build the walls and temples of nearby Erdene Zuu. Next to the stone turtle you can see an area of raised earth surrounded by a wire fence. This was the alleged site of Ögedei Khaan's palace.

PHALLIC ROCK
Near Kharkhorin, a 60cm long stone penis attracts steady streams of curiosity-seekers. The 'phallic rock' (GPS: N47° 11.152′, E102° 51.235′), which points erotically to something interestingly called a 'vaginal slope', is hidden up a small valley, about 2km southeast of Erdene Zuu Khiid. A giant penis, painted onto a sign by the road, 'points' you in the right direction.

Legend has it that the rock was placed here in an attempt to stop frisky monks, filled with lust by the shapely slope, from fraternising with the local women.

GREAT IMPERIAL MAP MONUMENT
This large new **monument** (admission T500), built in 2004, is on a hill overlooking Kharkhorin to the southwest. The three sides honour various empires established on the Orkhon Gol, including the Hunnu period (300–200 BC), the Turkic period (AD 600–800) and the Mongol period (13th century). There are superb panoramic views from here.

Sleeping
CAMPING
The rash of ger camps have taken over the best camping spots, but if you head out towards the main cluster of camps west of town near the Orkhon Gol you should be a able to find somewhere to pitch a tent.

GER CAMPS
Kharkhorin is inundated with ger camps and the fierce competition keeps prices in check. Most camps are in a lovely valley 2km west of town.

Riverside (☎ 9975 3970; eastline@magicnet.mn; per person US$12) About 1km from the road, towards the river, this decent camp has clean gers and hot showers. It's hidden in the trees and popular with groups. The hostess speaks English.

Anar (☎ 9665 8101; per person US$15) This place is bigger and more commercialised than the others in the valley; it comes complete with Chinggis Khaan statues and a ger gift shop. Meals are also available (breakfast US$2, lunch US$7, dinner US$3). It's in a great location in the southwest corner of the valley, and offers plenty of walking and horse-riding opportunities.

Dreamland (☎ 9191 1931; 3-bed economy ger US$76, lux ger s/d US$55/82, s/d US$58/92 lux s/d US$100/174; 🖳) The nicest camp in Kharkhorin is owned and operated by a Mongolian sumo champion, and geared towards Japanese travellers. Dreamland consists of a log cabin–style lodge with immaculate rooms equipped with cable TV, fridge, balcony and little niceties like slippers and robes. Only the lux rooms come with attached shower and bath. It also has luxury gers, complete with air-con, carpets and comfy beds, or the option of standard gers. An internet offers free web access for guests. A beautiful Japanese-style sauna and bathhouse completes the picture. The restaurant is inside a huge ger and offers an excellent menu (dishes from T6000 to T12,000) designed by the California restaurant in Ulaanbaatar.

Möngön Möd (☎ 311 637, 99199134; www.intourtrade .mn; per person with 3 meals US$30) Located 11km from Kharkhorin on the road to Shankh Khiid, this place offers better-than-average services. Horse riding and tours are available for around US$50 a day for guide and driver. Don't confuse it with the hotel of the same name in Kharkhorin.

GUESTHOUSES & HOTELS

Mönkhsuuri (☎ 9937 4488, 2031; monkhsuuri_gh@
yahoo.com; GPS: N47° 12.125', E102° 48.718'; per person incl
breakfast & dinner US$5) This small, scruffy home-
stay is in the suburbs northwest of the market.
It consists of several gers in a *hashaa* (fenced
area), a pit toilet and a hot-water shower.
Mönkhsuuri is a friendly and helpful host;
she works as a guide at Erdene Zuu Khiid and
is most easily contacted there. Call ahead as
it's impossible to find on your own (unless
you have GPS).

Tavan Erdene (☎ 9919 4452; zandankhuu_d@yahoo
.com; GPS: N47° 11.334', E102° 48.461'; per person US$8)
This ger-guesthouse is a little cleaner and
nicer than Mönkhsuuri but more expensive. It has hot showers and clean flush
toilets. It's run by Zandankhuu, an English-
speaking guide at Erdene Zuu.

Crown Café (☎ 9924 2980; purevdashd@yahoo.com;
without meals T5000) Ger accommodation and hot
showers are available behind this restaurant.
The gers are OK but the yard is a mess and
they only have pit toilets.

Bayan Burd (☎ 2315, 9909 7372; dm US$6, half-lux/lux
US$9/11, shower/sauna T1500/2000) If you prefer a
midrange hotel rather than a ger, this is the
best choice. All rooms are clean and comfortable and the lux room with attached toilet is
good value. No rooms have hot water but you
can use the hot shower downstairs. The owner
is usually willing to bargain.

Möngön Mod (Silver Tree; ☎ 2777, 9989 3883; ger
T5000, d/tr T10,000/12,000) The building looks like
it's about to collapse but the rooms inside
aren't too bad. And most guests end up staying in one of the nicer gers outside. The hot-
water shower is fairly reliable. Don't confuse
this with the ger camp listed earlier.

Eating

All the ger camps serve meals, the best being
the Dreamland Camp, which has a branch of
Ulaanbaatar's California restaurant. **Crown Café**
(☎ 9924 2980; meals T2500-4000; ◷ 9am-11pm) has a
European-style menu that includes tasty items
such as fried chicken and tomato soup. Some
items, however, are pretty disappointing – the
Hungarian goulash is similar to regular old
Mongolian goulash. Service can also be very
slow and the staff are not very forthcoming.
On the plus side, it has homemade cookies
and other sweets.

Getting There & Away

Erdene Zuu and the nearby sights are a 2km
walk from town; otherwise ask around for a
lift (about T500).

AIR

There are no regularly scheduled flights here,
although EZ Nis sometimes does a charter
package deal that includes flights, hotels
and food.

HITCHING

Hitching along the main road between
Ulaanbaatar and Kharkhorin is fairly easy,
but remember that a lot of vehicles will be carrying tourists, so they may not want to pick up
a hitchhiker. Getting a lift between Arvaikheer
and Kharkhorin is less likely, but if you're
patient something will come along.

Hitchhiking between Kharkhorin and
Khujirt shouldn't be too much of a hassle;
many Mongolians take the Ulaanbaatar to
Kharkhorin road to reach the popular spa town
of Khujirt. In Kharkhorin, ask around the container market, or just stand by the road.

MINIVANS & JEEPS

Minivans run daily to Ulaanbaatar (T10,000,
eight hours) from the container market, leaving sometime after 8am, whenever they are
full. As the road is all but sealed, this is one of
the more bearable long-distance trips in the
countryside. There are far fewer vehicles going
to Khujirt (T2000) and Arvaikheer (T5000) –
maybe one or two per day if any at all.

A post office van runs every Wednesday
and Friday afternoon to Khujirt (T2000) and
Arvaikheer (T4500). Inquire at the post office
for details.

The road from Kharkhorin to Khujirt
(54km) is being upgraded. The aimag capital, Arvaikheer, is 138km to the southeast.
The 160km road between Kharkhorin and
Tsetserleg is likewise being upgraded.

WEST OF KHARKHORIN

Tövkhön Khiid Төвхөн Хийд

Hidden deep in the Khangai mountains, this
incredibly scenic **monastery** (GPS: N47° 00.772',
E102° 15.362') has become a major pilgrimage centre for Mongolians seeking spiritual
solace. Zanabazar founded the site in 1653
and lived, worked and meditated here for
30 years. The monastery was destroyed in

1937 but rebuilt with public funds in the early 1990s.

Situated at the top of Shireet Ulaan Uul, Zanabazar apparently liked the unusual formation of the peak; the rocky outcrop looks like an enormous throne. It was here that Zanabazar created many of his best artistic endeavours, some of which can be found now in the Zanabazar Museum of Fine Arts (p69) in Ulaanbaatar.

Several **pilgrimage sites** have grown up around the temple and hermits' caves, including one that is said to be Zanabazar's boot imprint. Locals will also instruct you to enter the rebirth cave although this is not recommended if you have a fear of heights (getting to the cave requires climbing up a steep precipice). The main temple closes after morning services (between 10am and 11am) and the complex shuts down by 7pm.

The temple is in **Khangai Nuruu National Park** (admission T3000) and best reached with your own vehicle. A good 4WD can drive the steep road up to the monastery in 20 minutes, but old Russian jeeps and vans can't make the trip so you'll have to walk (one hour) up the hill through the forest. From the car park it's 2.5km. The route is obvious and in summer locals offer horse rides (T1000) to the top. Swarms of flies will probably plague your ascent; wrap a T-shirt, bandana or towel around your head to keep them away. A small shop at the top sells bottled water and snacks.

It's not possible to camp at the monastery, but there are a couple of ger camps by the entrance to the national park. The **Tövkhön** (☎ 9191 3025; per person US$13) has hot showers and flush toilets. Nearby **Guruv Khangai** (☎ 9119 7254; 3-bed ger T15,000) is a cheaper option with basic facilities.

The monastery is around 60km from Kharkhorin. Just follow the Orkhon Gol southwest for around 50km and turn north, up a side valley. You can also get here from Khujirt.

Orkhon Khürkhree Орхон Хүрхрээ

From Tövkhön Khiid, you could continue onto this magnificent seasonal **waterfall** (GPS: N46° 47.234′, E101° 57.694′), also called Ulaan Tsutgalan (Улаан Цутгалан). A little way downstream from Orkhon Khürkhree, you can climb down to the bottom of the **gorge**; it's 22m deep and dotted with pine trees.

Despite heavy promotion by the tourist industry, the waterfall often disappoints visitors as it's dry for about 10 months of the year. Late July and August are the best times to see it. When it does run, the roads leading to it are often washed out, making transport here very difficult. Even in dry weather the road is pretty rough. Inquire about the status of the falls and the roads when you get to Kharkhorin or Khujirt.

In summer, a handful of nomad families open up a guest ger, charging T3000 per person. More formal ger camps in the area include **Möngön Khürkhree** (☎ 9910 3185, 9111 4444; www.bayangobi.com; per person without food US$8), which has hot shower and flush toilets.

If you have a rod and reel, you could try catching your dinner. Good spots for catching lenok trout can be found downstream from the waterfall.

EAST OF KHARKHORIN

There are several interesting places between Kharkhorin and Khustain National Park (p115) en route to/from Ulaanbaatar.

Khögnö Khan Uul Nature Reserve
Хөгнө Хан Уул

Although it's just off the main Ulaanbaatar–Kharkhorin highway, this nature reserve sees relatively few visitors. Its arid terrain of rocky semi-desert is good for short hikes and there are a few old temples to explore, both ruined and active. At the southern foot of the mountain are the ruins of **Övgön Khiid** (Өвгөн Хийд; GPS: N47° 25.561′, E103° 41.686′; admission T1000), built in 1660 and destroyed (and the monks massacred) by the armies of Zungar Galdan Bochigtu, a rival of Zanabazar's in 1640. About 10 monks reside here in the summer months. The head lama is a charming woman who professes soothsaying abilities.

The mountain is in Bulgan aimag but most easily accessed from the Ulaanbaatar–Arvaikheer road.

The ruins of the earlier **destroyed monastery** (GPS: N47° 26.267′, E103° 42.527′) are a lovely 45-minute (2km) walk along a well-defined path up the valley to the right. The surroundings belong to the 46,900-hectare **Khögnö Khan Nature Reserve** and you might spot ibex, wolves and many varieties of hawk. There are lots of **hiking** possibilities around here.

CENTRAL MONGOLIA

SLEEPING

Camping is excellent in the valley, though the only water comes from a hard-to-find well at the lower end of the valley. All of the following ger camps have horses for rent for about US$3 per hour.

Övgön Erdene Tour Camp (Monastery Ger Camp; with meals US$25) This well-built ger camp and wood lodge is a short walk from the temple. It is run by the monks at the Övgön Khiid.

Khögnö Khan (with/without meals US$30/15) Located 4km southwest of Övgön Khiid.

Bayangobi (with meals US$40) Some travellers have stayed for about US$15 without meals when the camp isn't busy. The camp can be reached by branching south for 6km off the main road, 3km west of the turn-off to Khögnö Khan Uul.

GETTING THERE & AWAY

To get to Khögnö Khan Uul from Kharkhorin by jeep, turn north off the main road, 80km east of Kharkhorin. The road passes several ger camps until, after 8km, you reach Khögnö Khan ger camp, where you turn right for the remaining 4km or so to the monastery ruins. There is a shortcut if you are coming from Ulaanbaatar (turn right after the Bichigt Khad ger camp).

There is no public transport to the monastery but you can take a Kharkhorin-, Khujirt- or Arvaikheer-bound minivan from Ulaanbaatar, get off at the turn-off on the main road (T5000) and then hitch (or more likely walk) the remaining 12km.

Mongol Els Монгол Элс

As you approach the border of Övörkhangai from Ulaanbaatar, one surprising sight that livens up a fairly boring stretch of road is the sand dunes of Mongol Els. If you don't have the time to visit the Gobi (where there are not a lot of sand dunes anyway), these are certainly worth wandering around.

ARKHANGAI
АРХАНГАЙ

pop 96,100 / area 55,000 sq km

Arkhangai is all about wild nature, nomads and downhome hospitality. The magic of this wild aimag reveals itself at every turn, from sunsets viewed from the top of volcanic craters to rushing streams where fish seem to leap onto your hook. It's also a great place for the classic 'Mongolian experience', with many opportunities to visit nomad camps, go horse riding and photograph the odd yak caravan plodding slowly along ancient trails.

Arkhangai lies mostly on the northern slope of the Khangai mountains, an undulating range with several peaks more than 3300m. The mountains are by no means impenetrable and it's possible to travel through the passes on horse and jeep trails to Bayankhongor aimag. In winter, nomads use the passes on traditional *otors* (treks) to find grazing land for their animals.

Travellers often hurry through the centre of Arkhangai on their way to Terkhiin Tsagaan Nuur. With a bike or horse, however, there are plenty of valleys and remote trails to explore both north and south of the main road. You barely need this book to find beautiful and interesting places; just head off into the hills and see what you can discover. Along the way you'll be invited into plenty of gers for cups of *airag* and hot tea to keep you full until you reach the next valley.

TSETSERLEG ЦЭЦЭРЛЭГ

☎ 01332 / pop 17,900 / elev 1691m

Nestled comfortably between rugged mountains, with tree-lined streets and a quaint temple overlooking the town, Tsetserleg gets our vote for Mongolia's most beautiful aimag capital.

Tsetserleg is a perfect place to break up your journey if you are combining a visit to Kharkhorin or Khujirt with a trip to Terkhiin Tsagaan Nuur or Khövsgöl Nuur. There are some decent restaurants and hotels, busy temples and a striking aimag museum. Nature lovers will appreciate the hiking opportunities and good camping spots. Tourist activities revolve around the Fairfield Café & Guesthouse, an attraction in its own right.

Information

Internet café (☎ 21110; per hr T440; ☯ 9am-9pm Mon-Fri, to 8pm Sat & Sun) In the Telecom office.

Mongol Shuudan Bank (☎ 22673) Changes cash and allows you to withdraw money from debit and credit cards.

Strictly Protected Areas office (☎ 21179; khangainuruu@yahoo.com; ☯ 9am-6pm) Has information on Arkhangai's national parks and can give advice on tourist sites, fishing licences and park fees.

Telecom office (☎ 21108; ☯ 24hr) The post office is also here.

Sights

The **Museum of Arkhangai Aimag** (☎ 22281; admission T2500, exterior/interior photos T2000/T5000; ⏱ 9am-6pm) is one of the best in the country. It's housed in the temple complex of **Zayain Gegeenii Süm**, which was first built in 1586 but expanded in 1679, when it housed five temples and up to 1000 monks. Miraculously, the monastery escaped the Stalinist purges because it was made into a museum.

The main hall concentrates on features of traditional Mongolian lifestyle, with exhibits of costumes, traditional tools, a ger, musical instruments, weaponry and saddles. The displays have some useful English captions. The second hall concentrates on religious icons. The other two rooms of the former main prayer hall are empty, while the last hall focuses on local artwork.

Further up the hill, the **Galdan Zuu Temple** has been renovated with donations given by the locals. It stands behind an impressive 7m statue of the Buddha. Behind the temple is a large, nearly vertical, rocky hill called Bulgan Uul, where there are some **Buddhist inscriptions**.

At street level the **Buyandelgerüülekh Khiid** (Буяндэлгэрүүлэх Хийд) is now the town's main functioning monastery. The temple has an atmospheric clutter of assorted religious artefacts, and religious services are held regularly, either in the main hall or in a ger next door.

In the north of town a trail leads to the pretty Gangin Gol, which offers great **hiking** potential. At the mouth of the valley is a ger camp and a pitiful **nature museum** of stuffed animals, which isn't worth the T1000 the caretaker will demand.

Sleeping

CAMPING

Gangin Gol has some great camping spots, though someone may come and collect a dubious 'fee' for camping in a 'nature reserve' (it's not). A few hundred metres past the ger camp is a grassy enclosure that's perfect for camping.

There are some nice spots a few kilometres south of town on the banks of the river.

GER CAMPS

Khavtgai Mod (☎ 9911 8262; without meals T3500) On a hillside a couple of kilometres out of town to the west, this camp has a good location in the forest and valley views. It's fine for a quick

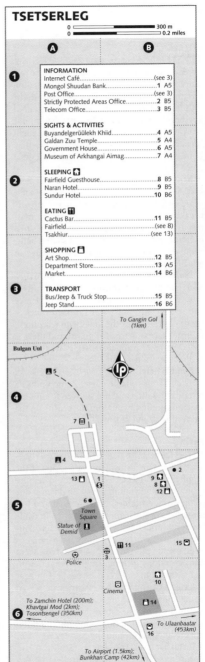

TSETSERLEG

0 — 300 m
0 — 0.2 miles

INFORMATION
Internet Café..............................(see 3)
Mongol Shuudan Bank.....................1 A5
Post Office................................(see 3)
Strictly Protected Areas Office..........2 B5
Telecom Office...........................3 B5

SIGHTS & ACTIVITIES
Buyandelgerüülekh Khiid..................4 A5
Galdan Zuu Temple........................5 A4
Government House.........................6 A5
Museum of Arkhangai Aimag................7 A4

SLEEPING 🛏
Fairfield Guesthouse.....................8 B5
Naran Hotel..............................9 B5
Sundur Hotel............................10 B6

EATING 🍴
Cactus Bar..............................11 B5
Fairfield...............................(see 8)
Tsakhiur................................(see 13)

SHOPPING 🛍
Art Shop...............................12 B5
Department Store.......................13 A5
Market.................................14 B6

TRANSPORT
Bus/Jeep & Truck Stop..................15 B5
Jeep Stand.............................16 B6

To Gangin Gol (1km)

Bulgan Uul

To Zamchin Hotel (200m);
Khavtgai Mod (2km);
Tosontsengel (350km)

Town Square

Statue of Demid

Police

Cinema

To Ulaanbaatar (453km)

To Airport (1.5km);
Bunkhan Camp (42km)

CENTRAL MONGOLIA

night's sleep but the facilities aren't great and there is no shower.

HOTELS

our pick **Fairfield Guesthouse** (☎ 21036, 9909 8612; per person incl breakfast T12,000) Attached to the restaurant of the same name, this nine-room guesthouse is a popular choice and one of the only hotels in the countryside where you need a reservation in summer. Nonattached rooms are clean and cosy and there is an excellent breakfast. The hotel is a travellers' hub with a book exchange and a popular café. It's a great place to pick up advice on regional travel.

Naran Hotel (☎ 9933 2900, 9908 9343; r per person T4000, half-lux/lux T8000/16,000) Although only a few years old, this seven-room hotel is already breaking down. Further complicating matters is the noisy Neptune Club in the same building. Standard rooms use a shared bathroom down the hall while lux rooms have an attached shower and bath.

Sundur Hotel (☎ 22359; r US$8, half-lux/lux US$15/20; 💻) The cheapest rooms here have only a toilet and no shower, but all others have nice bathrooms with hot water (at fixed times of the day only – check the times with reception). Internet access is free for guests and there is a decent restaurant downstairs that serves Mongolian food.

Zamchin Hotel (☎ 22274; d/tr US$8/12, half-lux/lux US$22/28; 💻) A reliable place, Zamchin has a restaurant, sauna and hot shower. Rooms are spacious but it's away from the centre, on the western road out of town.

Eating

our pick **Fairfield** (☎ 21026; meals T2000-6500; 9am-6pm Mon-Sat) This British-run café is one of the highlights of Tsetserleg and should feature prominently on your itinerary. Sit down at one of the wooden tables, order a meal and leaf through a copy of *Time* or the *Economist* while you wait. A full English breakfast (T6500) consists of bacon, sausage, eggs, toast and pancakes – a real treat in this part of the world. Lunch and dinner options include lasagne, burgers with Indian mutton, chilli con carne, beef in beer sauce and Cornish pasties. Pastries are served all day long and are great snacks to take with you on the road. The café is also a good place to ask about travel conditions and look for a ride if you are hitching around the country.

Cactus Bar (snacks T500-1000; 10am-10pm) Hot *khuushuur* (fried mutton pancakes) by day

and beer by night seems to be a standard course of events at the Cactus. It is opposite the Telecom office.

Tsakhiur (meals T1300; 11am-11pm) A little fancier than other places, this upmarket restaurant (it has tablecloths) is near the department store on the north end of town. It serves local favourites such as goulash and *puntutste khuurag* (clear or glass noodles).

Shopping

The **Art Shop** (☎ 9933 6851; 10am-7pm) sells Mongolian *dels* (traditional coats) and jackets, plus locally produced art and artefacts. It's next to the Fairfield Guesthouse. The Fairfield also has a fair-trade gift shop.

Everyday goods are best bought at the department store at the northern end of town.

The daily market *(khunsnii zakh)*, on the corner of the main road and the road to Ulaanbaatar, has enough products for a pre-trekking shopping trip.

Getting There & Away

There are no flights to Tsetserleg, so the only way here is by bus or shared vehicle.

BUS

A daily bus departs Tsetserleg at 8am for Ulaanbaatar (T10,500, 11 hours). Purchase the ticket at least one day ahead. Make inquiries at the Fairfield café.

HITCHING

All types of vehicles go to/from Tsetserleg and, generally, along the main road through Arkhangai. Wait on the main road into and out of town (heading east or west) and something will eventually stop.

MINIVAN & JEEP

Microbuses and minivans run between Tsetserleg and Ulaanbaatar (T15,000, 10 hours). In Tsetserleg, try the minivans at the jeep stand opposite the market. Drivers in Tsetserleg have developed a dual-pricing system so that tourists are charged twice as much as locals. Bargaining hard doesn't help much and you may have to pay their 'tourist prices'.

There are two routes between Tsetserleg and Ulaanbaatar – directly east via Ögii Nuur (453km) or along the longer but better road via Kharkhorin (493km). Tosontsengel is a mere 350km to the northwest.

If you are travelling from Tsetserleg to Mörön (for Khövsgöl Nuur), the quickest route is due north via Erdenemandal. However, if you've come this far (and have a couple of days to spare), it's worth heading a bit further west through central Arkhangai to Terkhiin Tsagaan Nuur, before heading north to Mörön via Jargalant.

TSENKHER HOT SPRINGS
ЦЭНХЭР ХАЛУУН РАШААН

Located 27km from Tsetserleg, these **hot springs** make for an easy detour from the main road. Three ger camps have been built around the springs; each pumps water into splash pools that cost around US$5 to enter. The pool at **Tsenkher Jiguur** (☎ 9914 5520; www.visit2mongolia.mn; GPS: N47° 19.241′, E101° 39.411′; ger US$16) is the cleanest and hottest of the bunch; it is lined with rocks (rather than concrete) and connected to a well-maintained bathhouse. There are separate pools for men and women. For directions from Tsetserleg ask at the Fairfield café.

ÖGII NUUR ӨГИЙ НУУР

On the road between Ulaanbaatar and Tsetserleg, near the border with Bulgan aimag, this **lake** (GPS: N47° 47.344′, E102° 45.828′) is a wonderful place for birdlife. Cranes and ducks, among other species, migrate to the area around late April. The lake is also renowned for its fishing (and the bugs by the shore!).

The lake and Khar Balgas ruins can only be reached from the direct road linking Tsetserleg with Ulaanbaatar. The lake makes a nice overnight stop with plenty of camping spots. A ger camp on the east shore serves meals.

If you are travelling west of Ögii Nuur you might want to carry onto the **Beaten Paths Ger Camp** (☎ 5033 1020, 5033 7376; rcshore@gail.com) in Battsengel *sum* (region). The camp was set up with the help of a local Peace Corps volunteer and offers horse riding among other activities. The camp is halfway between Ögii Nuur and Tsetserleg.

KHAR BALGAS ХАР БАЛГАС

The ruined citadel of Khar Balgas (Kara Balgasun in Turkic) is in Khotont *sum* on the banks of the Orkhon Gol. The city was founded in AD 751 as the capital of the Uighur Khaganate, which ruled Mongolia from 744 to 840.

There's not much to see except the outer walls (with gates in the north and south), a

Buddhist stupa and the ruler's **kagan** (castle), in the southwest corner. From the walls you can see the rows of stupas on either side of the walls and the remains of irrigated fields in the surrounding countryside. The city had an elaborate plumbing system, which brought water into the city from the nearby river.

The **ruins** (GPS: N47° 25.782′, E102° 39.490′) lie east of the road connecting Ögii Nuur and Khotont and aren't easy to get to. If you are travelling to/from the Kul-Teginii Monument, the best place to cross the river is 6km northeast of Khar Balgas; anywhere else and it's bog city.

KUL-TEGINII MONUMENT
КУЛ-ТЭГИНИЙ ХӨШӨӨ

When Chinggis Khaan decided to move his capital to Karakorum, he was well aware that the region had already been the capital to successive nomad empires. About 20km northeast of Khar Balgas lies the remainder of yet another of these pre-Mongol empires, the Turkic *khaganate* (pre-Mongol empire). All that's left of the *khaganate* is the 3m-high inscribed monument of Kul-Tegin (684–731), the *khagan* (ruler) of the ancient empire. The **monument** (GPS: N47° 33.837′, E102° 49.931′) was raised in AD 732 and is inscribed in Runic and Chinese script. You can see a copy of the stele in the entrance of the National Museum of Mongolian History in Ulaanbaatar (p69).

Just over 1km away is another **monument to Bilge Khagan** (AD 683–734), older brother of Kul-Tegin. Ten years after the death of Bilge, the Turkic *khaganate* was overrun by the Uighurs.

A Turkish-funded archaeological expedition, based out of a huge hanger near the site, is working on making reproductions of the monuments. If you don't see the monuments where they should be, ask the friendly caretaker to let you into the hanger.

The two monuments are 25km northwest of Khashaat in a region called Tsaidam, about 47km north of Kharkhorin, and are hard to find. Amateur historians who relish a challenge are best off packing a GPS into their jeep; otherwise ask at gers en route from either Khashaat or Ögii Nuur.

TAIKHAR CHULUU
ТАЙХАР ЧУЛУУ

The nondescript town of Ikh Tamir is 22km along the main road west of Tsetserleg. The reason to stop here is to inspect the enormous

CENTRAL MONGOLIA

RETREAT TO THE KHANGAI

Horse lovers, poets, writers, photographers, yogis, Buddhist practitioners or plain old refugees of commercialism are all welcome at the Bunkhan Camp, a lovely ger camp set deep in the Khangai mountains. The camp, 42km south of Tsetserleg, is operated by an American couple, anthropologist Carroll Dunham and photographer Thomas Kelly, and their Mongolian partners Gerlee and Toroo.

Workshops lasting two weeks include wilderness poetry, meditation, yoga and photography, with space for 10 to 12 people at a time. It's a great place to unwind, meet like-minded people and commune with nature. Horses are available and visitors can go on pack trips to nearby Blue Lake. The camp is kid-friendly, with plenty of options for fishing, archery and horse riding. Costs average out to US$150 per day for adults and US$80 per day for kids. For more information see www.wildearthjourneys.com or contact carrolldunham@yahoo.com.

Taikhar Chuluu rock formation. The rock is the subject of many local legends, the most common one being that a great *baatar* (hero), crushed a huge serpent here by hurling the rock on top of it. Locals claim there are some ancient Tibetan inscriptions on the rock, though you'll be lucky to spot them through 30 years of Mongolian graffiti. There is even an *ovoo* at the top.

You could camp anywhere along the Khoid Tamir Gol. **Taikhar Ger Camp** (☎ 9919 8512; per person US$12), next to the rock, has hot-water showers and flush toilets.

Taikhar Chuluu is about 2km north of Ikh Tamir along the river – you can see it from the main road.

KHORGO-TERKHIIN TSAGAAN NUUR NATIONAL PARK ХОРГО-ТЭРХИЙН ЦАГААН НУУР

Amid volcanic craters, pine-clad lava fields and the occasional herd of grazing yaks, the Great White Lake, as it's known in English, is the natural highlight of Arkhangai aimag. According to legend, the lake was formed when an elderly couple forgot to cap a well after fetching water. The valley flooded with water until a local hero shot a nearby mountain top with his arrow; the shorn top covered the well and became an island in the lake (Noriin Dund Tolgoi).

The freshwater **Terkhiin Tsagaan Nuur** is not as forested or as large as Khövsgöl Nuur, but it is closer to Ulaanbaatar, relatively undeveloped and just about perfect for camping (though there are a few flies in summer). The lake, birdlife and mountains are now protected within the 77,267-hectare Khorgo-Terkhiin Tsagaan Nuur National Park. The national park fee of T3000 applies.

The lake, which was formed by lava flows from a volcanic eruption many millennia ago, is excellent for **swimming**, though a bit cold in the morning – try the late afternoon, after the sun has warmed it. Hidden along the shore are stretches of sandy beach, perfect for lounging with a book or fishing line.

The **fishing** is great, though you should get a permit for around T3000 per day. There are several park rangers who sell permits but they can be hard to find; try asking at the park entrance by the bridge in **Tariat** (also known as Khorgo), or at the government building in Tariat.

One must-do excursion takes you to the top of **Khorgo Uul** volcano. A road leads 4km from Tariat village to the base of the volcano, from where it's a 10-minute walk up to the **cone** (GPS: N48° 11.187', E99° 51.259'). The volcano is in the park so you'll need to pay the park fee of T3000 if you haven't already.

There is also the option of exploring the lake by boat. A rowing boat and a motorboat cost around T5000 per hour to hire. Inquire at the Khorgo I ger camp.

Information
Tariat village has an **internet café** (per hr T600; ☽ 9am-9pm).

Festivals
If you've got a taste for yak cream or are keen on yak racing, plan a visit to Terkhiin Tsagaan Nuur in the second week of June, when **Tsolmon travel company** (☎ 011-322 870, 9929 5732) hosts its annual **Yak Festival** by the lake.

Sleeping
CAMPING
Except for a few annoying flies, Terkhiin Tsagaan Nuur is an excellent place for camp-

ng. There is good fishing, endless fresh water, and flat ground for pitching a tent. The western end of the lake, where it joins the Khoid Terkhiin Gol, is muddy. The best place to camp is the northern part, away from the ger camps. The area is cold year-round, and often windy, so a good sleeping bag is vital.

GER CAMPS

Several camps are built up along the shore of the lake, but they are all fairly spread out so it's not too crowded.

Tunga's Ger Camp (www.tungaguesthouse.com; GPS: N48° 09.318', E99° 45.206'; per person T6000) The only camp on the southern shore of the lake, this basic place is 12km west of Tariat. The price includes breakfast and hot shower; horse trips are also organised. It's run by local English teacher Tunga, who also has a guesthouse in Tariat.

Khorgo I (☎ 011-322 870, 9916 2847; GPS: N48° 12.246', E99° 50.834'; with/without meals US$30/14) In a lovely location in the Zurkh Gol Khundii (Heart River valley) by the northeast section of the lake, Khorgo I is run by Tsolmon Travel in Ulaanbaatar (p81). The camp has hot showers and there is excellent hiking nearby. To get there take the road north of Tariat into the park and take the branch to the right when you get near the volcano.

Tsagaan Nuur (☎ 9981 7465; GPS: N48° 10.621', E99° 48.691'; without meals US$10, meals T2500) This is the first camp on the north shore of the lake. Horses are T3000 per hour. The owners also rent fishing rods.

Further around the lake you'll see some 'ger hotels' that charge T4000 per person. There is also a shop nearby selling soft drinks, confectionary and fishing equipment.

Maikhan Tolgoi (☎ 9911 9730, 9908 9730; GPS: N48° 10.821', E99° 45.725'; without meals US$15) Set on a headland on the northern shore of the lake, this is perhaps the most attractive camp on the lake. It has flush toilets, hot showers and a cosy restaurant.

GUESTHOUSES

Tariat village, about 6km east of the lake, is the only town in the area. Accommodation is basic, with just one run-down hotel and a couple of guesthouses. **Tunga's Guesthouse** (☎ 9928 5710, 9983 6144; www.tungaguesthouse.com; GPS:

N48° 09.245', E99° 53.351'; per night T5000) is convenient if you want to do things like charge batteries and get your laundry done. Tunga speaks English. Guest gers are available behind the **Ma Bagsh** (☎ 9962 7615; per night US$5) restaurant.

Eating

All the camps around the lake provide reasonably priced meals. Self-caterers can stock up on supplies in either Tariat or the shops by the lake. In Tariat, you could try **Ma Bagsh** (☎ 9962 7615; meals T1500; ☺ 9am-midnight), a better-than-average restaurant serving mainly Mongolian meals. It's near the bridge.

Getting There & Away

Occasional minivans run to/from Ulaanbaatar and Tsetserleg. From anywhere else you are better off hitching.

From the lake to Tosontsengel (179km), the main road climbs over Solongotyn Davaa, a phenomenally beautiful area. You can see patches of permanent ice from the road. The road has been upgraded to an all-weather gravel road but is still rough in patches.

For the route to Mörön, see p162.

AROUND TERKHIIN TSAGAAN NUUR

There are a number of scenic areas in the environs of Terkhiin Tsagaan Nuur that are worth exploring on horseback. These include **Noyon Khangai National Park** (Ноён Хангай), a mountainous area rich in wildlife and **hot springs** (GPS: N47° 44.607', E99° 24.861') covered by wooden huts (the water is 33°C). By road it's a rough 78km from Tariat; the area is a national park so you may need to pay a T3000 entry fee, although there is rarely anyone around to collect the fees.

Around 60km northeast of Tariat village, **Choidogiin Borgio** (Чойдогийн Боргио), where the Chuluut and Ikh Jargalantiin Gols converge, is a fine **hiking**, **fishing** and **camping** area. The road here is even worse than the one to Noyon Khangai, which makes it a great destination by horse or bike but a lousy trip by car.

About 30km east of Tariat is the dramatic **Chuluut gorge**, which makes a pleasant picnic stop. Near the gorge, look out for a sacred tree, **Zuun Salaa Mod** (GPS: N48° 07.936', E100° 16.420'), draped with prayer scarves and debris.

CENTRAL MONGOLIA

Northern Mongolia

Log cabins, pine forests and monstrous fish do not conform to the classic image of Mongolia's desolate steppes. But strung along its northern border are three aimags (provinces) of such lush and serene vegetation that one might confuse them for bits of Switzerland. Selenge, Bulgan and Khövsgöl aimags actually have more in common with Siberia than Mongolia. Winters are long and cold, with snow staying on the ground until May. Summers bring wildflowers and the snowmelt fills up lakes and rivers, many of which flow north to Lake Baikal in Siberia. The area teems with elk, reindeer and bear, and the rivers and lakes brim with fish. Beautiful Khövsgöl Nuur, the major feature of the region, pokes Siberia in the belly.

Although the majority of the people are Khalkh, here are also Buriats and Turkic-speaking peoples, including the Tsaatan, the reindeer herders. Shamanism has long been the faith of choice in the forests and, after decades of persecution, it is being revived and encouraged.

The fragile environment is crucial to the economy and this area is a major battleground between environmentalists and business interests that want to log the forests and explore for minerals. Although ecotourism is making inroads, the concept of sustainable development is still relatively unknown. Old hunters lament that wildlife is now more difficult to spot.

If travelling by train to or from Russia, you'll pass through Selenge. Make a diversion and take in the wondrous Amarbayasgalant Khiid or horse trek by the shores of Khövsgöl Nuur. These are also attractions for domestic tourists; you may come across a vanload of urban Mongolians off to see the sights, stopping en route to taste the local *airag* (fermented mare milk) or pick berries in the forests.

HIGHLIGHTS

- Drop a fishing line into **Khövsgöl Nuur** (p152), and while away an afternoon by Mongolia's most spectacular alpine lake

- Ride a horse into the taiga (coniferous forest) around Tsagaannuur in the Darkhad Depression for a unique encounter with the indigenous **Tsaatan reindeer herders** (p160)

- Wander around the grounds of spectacular **Amarbayasgalant Khiid** (p140), the architectural highlight of the country

- Visit the bow-and-arrow-making workshop in **Dulaankhaan** (p137), one of the last of its kind in Mongolia

- Journey to **Chandman-Öndör** (p159), a little-visited region of fish-filled streams, hot springs, sacred caves and lush forests

Tsagaannuur ★
Khövsgöl ★ Nuur
★ Chandman-Öndör
Amarbayasgalant ★ Khiid   ★ Dulaankhaan

| ■ POPULATION: 448,600 | ■ AREA: 192,800 SQ KM |

History

For thousands of years northern Mongolia was the borderland between the Turkic-speaking tribes of Siberia and the great steppe confederations of the Huns, Uighurs and Mongols. Some of the Siberian tribes still survive in Mongolia, notably the Tsaatan people of northern Khövsgöl. Evidence of these steppe nomads is also found in Khövsgöl in the form of numerous burial mounds and deer stones.

Settled history really began in the 18th century under Manchu rule when thousands of monks poured into the area from Tibet and China to assist in the construction of monasteries. As the nomads were converted to Buddhism local shamans were purged and harassed into giving up traditional practices. The largest centre of religion, Amarbayasgalant Khiid, had more than 2000 lamas.

During communism, religious persecution boiled over into a 1932 rebellion that left thousands of monks and Mongolian soldiers dead. The fighting was particularly bloody in the north, where monks were reportedly stringing soldiers up in trees and skinning them alive. Later, the Russians improved their standing with the locals by developing a variety of industries. Darkhan and Selenge became important centres of agriculture, Bulgan became home to the Erdenet copper mine, and Khövsgöl developed a thriving industry of timber mills, fisheries and wool processing.

Climate

In the region around Khövsgöl aimag, the terrain is mainly taiga (subarctic coniferous forest) of Siberian larch and pine trees, where there's plenty of rain (often 600mm a year). Snowfall can exceed 2m in some regions during winter. After winter, the lakes and rivers remain frozen until May; travel can be hazardous at this time as trucks and jeeps can fall through the thin ice. Travelling in winter means faster drive times around the aimag as vehicles won't get bogged in the mud. July is warm and relatively dry, but this is also the time of the tourist crunch, leaving ger (traditional circular felt yurt) camps teeming. September, when the leaves change colour, is visually spectacular.

Getting There & Away

Selenge aimag is accessible by paved road or rail from Ulaanbaatar. A paved road now runs as far as Bulgan City. If your destination is Khövsgöl Nuur, the quickest way into the area is either on a flight from Ulaanbaatar to Mörön or by jeep via Bulgan. Main jeep tracks also run from Ulaangom and Tosontsengel in the west to Mörön, but tracks heading north from Tsetserleg in central Mongolia are more difficult to find. To travel between Selenge aimag and the east, you'll have to come back through Ulaanbaatar first, or go by horse.

Getting Around

Improvements to the roads to the Russian border, Erdenet and Bulgan make life a lot easier in terms of getting into the region. The fun starts as you travel further west, with the usual dirt roads and rocky terrain. Travellers who enjoy train travel can ride the rails as far as Erdenet and hire a vehicle from there. The horse is a popular form of transport in the mountains. While there is very little organised adventure travel, some tour companies offer mountain-biking trips in the region. A few crazies have even paddled kayaks down the Selenge Gol (Selenge River) to Sükhbaatar City!

SELENGE СЭЛЭНГЭ

pop 181,500 (incl Darkhan-Uul) / area 42,800 sq km
Mongolia's breadbasket, Selenge is a fertile landscape of rolling wheat fields, apple orchards and meandering rivers. Wide-scale agriculture has settled many nomads and nowadays wood cabins and lumbering trucks far outnumber gers and camel caravans.

The relatively well developed infrastructure of paved roads, cities and train lines means that Selenge sees a steady flow of through traffic, particularly from travellers heading to and from Russia. The main reasons to visit are the majestic but remote monastery, Amarbayasgalant Khiid, and some beautiful scenery.

Darkhan is the major population centre, although the city is actually part of its own tiny aimag, Darkhan-Uul. The aimag capital, Sükhbaatar, is comparatively small, but as a border town it remains a viable part of the local economy.

In the southeast, the open-pit coal mine at Sharyngol produces about two million tonnes of coal each year to provide electricity for the Erdenet mine in Bulgan aimag. Selenge's biggest revenue earner is the Canadian-owned

NORTHERN MONGOLIA

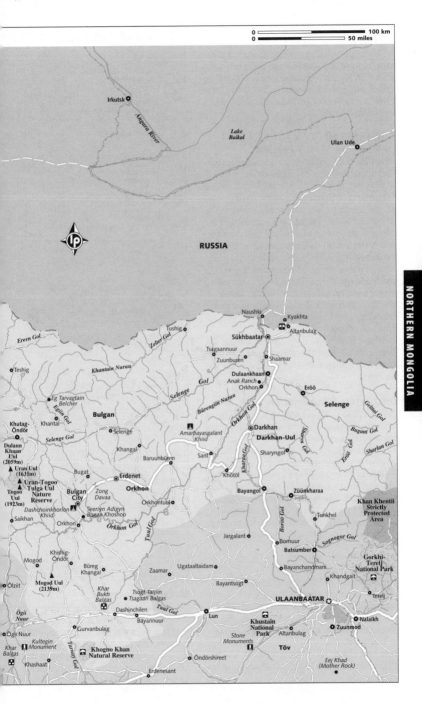

Boroo gold mine, which produces 5 tonnes of gold per year, netting US$65 million.

The mighty Selenge Gol starts in the mountains of western Mongolia and flows into Lake Baikal in Siberia, draining nearly 300,000 sq km of land in both countries. The other great river, the Orkhon Gol, meets the Selenge Gol near Sükhbaatar.

SÜKHBAATAR СУХБААТАР
☎ 01362 / pop 19,700 / elev 626m

With its hilly backdrop, riverside location and unhurried pace of life, Sükhbaatar makes a pleasant stopover for travellers heading into or out of Russia. The town was founded in the 1940s to facilitate trade between the USSR and Mongolia, and was named after the Mongolian general who helped usher in communism in 1921. Sükhbaatar himself spent time in nearby Altanbulag and Kyakhta where treaties were drawn up formalising Mongolia's independent status. There is little reason to stay, however, unless you want to break up the train journey to/from Russia, you prefer travelling on cheaper local trains or you are smuggling goods.

If you have time drop by the **Khutagt Ekh Datsan** temple near the town square. Unusual for a Mongolian monastery, its head lama is a woman.

Orientation & Information

Just north of the train station is the centre of town, where you'll find the main hotel, market and town square.

Private moneychangers appear at the station whenever a train arrives. If you are leaving Mongolia try to get rid of all your tögrög – they are worthless anywhere in Russia (including on the Trans-Mongolian Railway in Russia). The police station is to the south of town.

The daily market, behind the Selenge Hotel, is lively and friendly and, as a border town, well stocked.

Internet café (☎ 23901; per hr T400; ⏰ 24hr) Adjacent to the Telecom office.

Telecom office (☎ 22385; Tsagaan Eregiin Gudamj; ⏰ 24hr) The post office is also located here.

Trade & Development Bank (☎ 22407; ⏰ 9am-5pm Mon-Fri) Near the train station. Changes travellers cheques, US dollars and euros, and can give cash advances on Visa and MasterCard.

Zoos Bank (☎ 23110; ⏰ 8am-8pm Mon-Fri, 8am-3pm Sat) Near the Kharaa Hotel. Also gives cash advance on Visa and MasterCard.

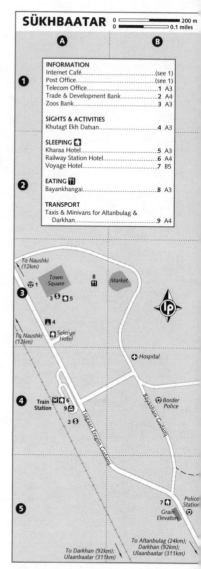

SÜKHBAATAR 0 — 200 m / 0 — 0.1 miles

INFORMATION	
Internet Café	(see 1)
Post Office	(see 1)
Telecom Office	1 A3
Trade & Development Bank	2 A4
Zoos Bank	3 A3

SIGHTS & ACTIVITIES	
Khutagt Ekh Datsan	4 A3

SLEEPING	
Kharaa Hotel	5 A3
Railway Station Hotel	6 A4
Voyage Hotel	7 B5

EATING	
Bayankhangai	8 A3

TRANSPORT	
Taxis & Minivans for Altanbulag & Darkhan	9 A4

To Naushki (12km)
Town Square
Market
To Naushki (12km)
Selenge Hotel
Hospital
Train Station
Border Police
Bayankhangai Gudamj
Tsagaan Eregiin Gudamj
Police Station
Grain Elevators
To Altanbulag (24km); Darkhan (92km); Ulaanbaatar (311km)
To Darkhan (92km); Ulaanbaatar (311km)

Sleeping & Eating

Selenge aimag is particularly pleasant for camping. At Sükhbaatar, the best place to try is across the train line and among the fields just west of town. Alternatively, there are great spots among the hills northeast of the market. Sükhbaatar's main hotel, the Selenge, was under renovation at the time of research.

NORTHERN MONGOLIA

Station Hotel (☎ 40371; per person T5000) Decent rooms are available at this wee hotel adjacent to the train station.

Kharaa Hotel (☎ 23876; tw/half-lux/lux T10,000/16,000/25,000) Close to the town square, this hotel has remodelled but unexciting rooms. Look for the 'Hotel Bar' sign.

Voyage Hotel (☎ 23839, 9949 5357; Tsagaan Eregiin gudamj; tw/lux T25,000/45,000) Newly built hotel in the south of the city with clean rooms and a reliable restaurant. Sauna available.

Bayankhangai (☎ 22106, 9949 8949; 🕙 9am-11pm) Between the market and Kharaa Hotel, Bayankhangai serves some tasty dishes including *moogtei khuurag* (mushroom and meat) and *sharsan takhia* (fried chicken).

Getting There & Away

HITCHING

Because of the regular transport along the main road between Ulaanbaatar and Sükhbaatar, you'll get a lift pretty easily along this road.

MINIVAN & TAXI

The road to Ulaanbaatar (311km) through Darkhan (92km) is well paved, so jeeps are not necessary. Because of the popularity and regularity of the train, there are relatively few share vehicles to Ulaanbaatar (T8000), but many to Darkhan (T5000, two hours) and Altanbulag (T1500, 20 minutes). These vehicles depart from outside the train station.

TRAIN

International trains going to/from Moscow, Irkutsk or Beijing stop at Sükhbaatar for two or more hours while customs and immigration are completed. This usually takes place late at night or very early in the morning. See p276 and p275 for more information about international trains.

Direct, local trains travel between Ulaanbaatar and Sükhbaatar (T3500/8400 for a hard/soft seat), with a stop at Darkhan. Train 271 departs Ulaanbaatar at 10.30am daily, arriving at 7.56pm. The same train departs for Ulaanbaatar the next morning at 6.10am. Returning to Ulaanbaatar, you could also opt for train 264, departing Sükhbaatar at 9.45pm.

The **train station** (☎ 40124; 🕙 8am-noon, 3-5pm & 8-10pm) sells local tickets and also tickets for Ulan Ude (T17,600), Irkutsk (T34,000)

and Moscow (T124,750), but you'll need a Russian visa.

ALTANBULAG АЛТАНБУЛАГ

Just 24km northeast of Sükhbaatar is Altanbulag, a small, peaceful border town opposite the Russian city of Khyakhta. Despite its location, the town sees few benefits of cross-border trade and many of the buildings have been abandoned, looted and left with only their skeletons intact. The only inspiring view is of **Khyakhta Cathedral**, right across the border in Russia. Unless you are crossing the border by road, or desperately want to see the aimag museum, there is no reason to visit Altanbulag.

Both Khyakhta in Russia and Altanbulag are of some historical importance to Mongolians. In 1915 representatives from Russia, China and Mongolia met in Khyakhta to sign a treaty granting Mongolia limited autonomy. At a meeting in Khyakhta in March 1921, the Mongolian People's Party was formed by Mongolian revolutionaries in exile, and the revolutionary hero Sükhbaatar was named minister of war.

Selenge's aimag museum is located here in Altanbulag. The **museum** (admission T2000; 🕙 10am-5pm Mon-Fri) contains lots of antiquated communist propaganda and exhibits dating back to Mongolia's independence movement of 1921; relics include some of Sükhbaatar's personal effects – his boots, gun and even his desk. The curator assured us that Sükhbaatar's office was housed in the small red building outside the museum.

Minivans run between Sükhbaatar and Altanbulag at various times during the day. If there is nothing going you could charter a taxi (T6000).

The border is located right at the edge of Altanbulag. You cannot cross by foot so you'll need to try and hitch a ride with a local or take any public transport available. The border is open between 8am to 5pm and you can expect delays of several hours. From Kyakhta there are daily buses to Novoselenginsk.

DULAANKHAAN ДУЛААНХААН

Forty-seven kilometres south of Sükhbaatar, this tiny village is worth a stop if you have your own vehicle. Dulaankhaan is home to a **bow and arrow workshop** (☎ 9913 1491, 9926 7291; www.hornbow.mn), one of only three in Mongolia. Bows and arrows are made from ibex and reindeer horn, bamboo and even fish guts. Only 30 to 40 sets are crafted every year because they take about four months to complete. Each set sells for about T180,000. In the village, look for the two-storey wood building, next to the red-and-blue monument. Ask for Boldbaatar.

The village is 6km west of the Sükhbaatar–Darkhan Hwy. Expect to pay about T15,000 for a taxi from Sükhbaatar. There is nowhere to stay in the village so carry on to Sükhbaatar or Darkhan, or camp nearby.

DARKHAN ДАРХАН
☎ 01372 / pop 73,500

With its vast acres of parkland, sporadic bursts of concrete and languorous street life, Darkhan is an unassuming blip on the Trans-Mongolian Railway. The Soviets created it in the 1960s as an industrial base for the north and for a while it worked as a model urban cooperative of factory workers, tractor drivers, coal miners and government officials. When the bottom fell out of the economy in 1990 everyone lost their jobs and the Russian advisors beat a hasty retreat to Moscow. The economy has since made small strides, thanks to grain production and some requisite coal mining at nearby Sharyngol. The city is not actually part of Selenge aimag, but an autonomous municipality, Darkhan-Uul.

Darkhan is not somewhere you would rush to see, but you may need to stay here while you arrange transport to Amarbayasgalant Khiid.

Orientation

Darkhan is spread out. The city is divided into an 'old town' near the train station and a 'new town' to the south. Near the central post office in the new town is Darkhan's pride and joy: a 16-storey building, one of the tallest in the country.

Information

Golomt Bank (☎ 23928; ☼ 9am-1pm & 2-5pm) It is 200m west of the taxi stand.
Library Internet (☎ 23205, 9940 9812; per hr T500; ☼ 10am-8pm Mon-Fri, 10am-6pm Sat & Sun) Located inside the Cultural Palace.
Telecom office (☎ 23275; ☼ 24hr) ATM and post office are also located here.
Trade & Development Bank (☎ 33713; ☼ 9am-3pm & 4-5.30pm Mon-Fri) Changes cash, travellers cheques and gives advances on Visa and MasterCard.

Zoos Bank (☎ 24173; ☼ 8am-10pm Mon-Fri) Opposit the Telecom office.

Sights

KHARAAGIIN KHIID ХАРААГИЙН ХИЙД
Probably the most interesting sight i Darkhan is this monastery. Housed in pretty log cabin in the old town, it has host of protector deities and a tree encase in blue *khatag* (silk scarves). Until 1989 th building served as an elementary school.

MUSEUM OF DARKHAN-UUL
This **museum** (☎ 27910; admission T1000; ☼ 9am 1pm & 2-7pm) contains a well-laid-out collec tion of archaeological findings, traditiona clothing, religious artefacts and a few obliga tory stuffed animals. Its most valued piec is the original painting of Lenin meetin Sükhbaatar, a classic work of myth-makin painted by B Tsultem in 1953. The museum is upstairs in a building on the norther side of the shopping square, across from th minibus and taxi stand.

MORIN KHUUR STATUE & SEATED BUDDHA
These two new monuments are across th road from each other, near the roundabou between the new and old towns. Both ar congregating points for locals who hang ou here at sunset.

Sleeping

CAMPING
Despite the size of Darkhan, it isn't hard t get away from the town and find a nearb secluded spot. Southwest of the train statio are some empty fields – but get away fron the drunks who hang around the station. Th fields to the north of the Darkhan Hotel ar also good.

HOTELS & GUESTHOUSES
our pick **Jammin Toast Guesthouse** (☎ 9996 3154 davruss2000@yahoo.com; dm US$5; ☼ May-Sep; ☐ Scotsman Dave Russell offers dorm beds in comfortable setting with a Scottish-Mongolia theme. It's a great place to overnight i Darkhan and Dave can provide logistical tip for getting around the area. It's located next t the Kiwi Hotel; look for the sign on the 4th floor balcony, or call for directions.

Darkhan Hotel (☎ 20001; s/d T6000/10,000, T12,000-16,000) This Soviet-era monster ha

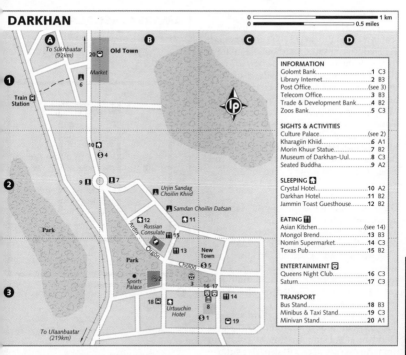

DARKHAN

To Sükhbaatar
(92km)

Old Town

Market

Train Station

To Ulaanbaatar
(219km)

Urjin Sandag
Choilin Khiid

Samdan Choilin Datsan

Russian
Consulate

New
Town

Park

Park

Sports
Palace

Urtuuchin
Hotel

INFORMATION
Golomt Bank...........................1 C3
Library Internet.......................2 B3
Post Office.........................(see 3)
Telecom Office.......................3 B3
Trade & Development Bank.........4 B2
Zoos Bank.............................5 C3

SIGHTS & ACTIVITIES
Culture Palace....................(see 2)
Kharagiin Khiid......................6 A1
Morin Khuur Statue.................7 B2
Museum of Darkhan-Uul...........8 C3
Seated Buddha......................9 A2

SLEEPING
Crystal Hotel.......................10 A2
Darkhan Hotel......................11 B2
Jammin Toast Guesthouse.......12 B2

EATING
Asian Kitchen.....................(see 14)
Mongol Brend.....................13 B3
Nomin Supermarket.............14 C3
Texas Pub..........................15 B2

ENTERTAINMENT
Queens Night Club................16 C3
Saturn..............................17 C3

TRANSPORT
Bus Stand..........................18 B3
Minibus & Taxi Stand.............19 C3
Minivan Stand.....................20 A1

NORTHERN MONGOLIA

scruffy old standard rooms and slightly better lux rooms, all with attached bathroom and hot water. It has a restaurant, a sauna (T1000) and a billiards room (T7000). It's located on the north side of the new town, opposite the Scorpion nightclub.

Crystal Hotel (☎ 36966; s/d T8000/10,000, s/d half-lux 12,000/15,000, lux 25,000) Stuck halfway between the new and old towns, this has modern amenities and nice bathrooms. Note that the standard rooms share a bathroom.

The train station has a **hotel** (☎ 42263; r T5000, lux T6000) on the top floor.

Eating
Asian Kitchen (Nomin Supermarket; ☻ 9am-9pm) Fast-food place reminiscent of Ulaanbaatar's Berlin restaurant. It's run by a Malaysian and serves up good, non-Mongolian curries.

Texas Pub (☎ 27961; ☻ 11am-midnight) Roy Rogers could not have designed a better restaurant. This Texan-themed joint, just south of the Darkhan Hotel in the new town, has an English-language menu with Hungarian goulash, steaks, salads and pasta plus Chinggis beer on tap.

Mongol Brend (☎ 27681, 9939 9181; ☻ 11am-midnight) A life-size photo of Miss Darkhan welcomes you to this brew pub on the main drag. Steaks and pasta are available and by evening the basement turns into a nightclub and karaoke bar.

If you are self-catering, the best place to shop is the Nomin Supermarket, southeast of the central park in the new town.

Entertainment
Locals bust out their moves at the **Queens Night Club** (☻ 6pm-midnight) in the centre of the new town. Saturn, next to Queens, is another club that has seen some refurbishment.

Getting There & Away
BUS
Two buses per day depart at 11am and 4pm for Ulaanbaatar (T4500, four hours). They leave from the lot west of the Urtuuchin Hotel.

MINIVAN, TAXI & JEEP
Constant demand ensures that shared taxis (T8000) and minivans (T6000) regularly do the four-hour run to Ulaanbaatar. Vehicles

depart from a bus stand just west of the Urtuuchin Hotel, where you can also get a seat in a van to Erdenet (T7000, three hours). For Sükhbaatar (T5000, two hours), vans leave from outside the market in the new town.

Darkhan enjoys the privilege of having a paved road to Ulaanbaatar (219km), Sükhbaatar (92km) and Erdenet (180km). Many *guanz* (canteens or cheap restaurants) along the way sell *airag* and basic meals.

For Amarbayasgalant Khiid you'll have to hire your own jeep or taxi at the bus stand near the Kharaa Hotel. A round-trip should cost around T50,000 but you'll need to bargain.

TRAIN

Darkhan is the only train junction in Mongolia: all northern trains to/from Ulaanbaatar, and all trains to/from Erdenet, stop here. The **domestic ticket office** (☎ 42301; 🕓 7.30-9.30am, 2.30-6.30pm & 10.30pm-4.30am) at Darkhan train station is at windows 1 and 2. Window 3 is reserved for international tickets. Hard-seat carriages are always crowded so consider taking a soft seat.

Travelling to Ulaanbaatar (hard/soft seat T2600/6400), a daytime train (272) leaves Darkhan at 8.33am, arriving in UB about 4pm. An overnighter (264) departs Darkhan at 12.05am, arriving at 6am. Other trains leave in the middle of the night.

The daily five-hour trip between Darkhan and Erdenet (hard/soft seat T2100/5300) goes through some lovely countryside, but you'll miss it as the train leaves Darkhan at 2.50am.

The daily Ulaanbaatar–Sükhbaatar train (271) leaves Darkhan for Sükhbaatar at 5.50pm (hard/soft seat T1200/2400, two hours), or at an ungodly 2am. See p276 and p272 for details about international trains that stop at Darkhan.

Getting Around

Darkhan is spread out, so you will probably have to take a taxi or hop in a minivan (T200) that connects the new and old towns.

AMARBAYASGALANT KHIID
АМАРБАЯСГАЛАНТ ХИЙД

The star attraction of Selenge aimag, this monastery is considered to be one of the top three Buddhist institutions in Mongolia (along with Erdene Zuu in Kharkhorin and Gandan in Ulaanbaatar) and the country's most intact architectural complex. It is well

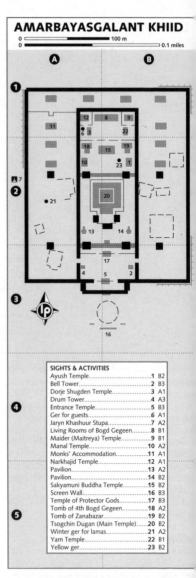

AMARBAYASGALANT KHIID

SIGHTS & ACTIVITIES	
Ayush Temple	1 B2
Bell Tower	2 B3
Dorje Shugden Temple	3 A1
Drum Tower	4 A3
Entrance Temple	5 B3
Ger for guests	6 A1
Jaryn Khashuur Stupa	7 A2
Living Rooms of Bogd Gegeen	8 B1
Maider (Maitreya) Temple	9 B1
Manal Temple	10 A2
Monks' Accommodation	11 A1
Narkhajid Temple	12 A1
Pavilion	13 A2
Pavilion	14 B2
Sakyamuni Buddha Temple	15 B2
Screen Wall	16 B3
Temple of Protector Gods	17 B3
Tomb of 4th Bogd Gegeen	18 A2
Tomb of Zanabazar	19 B2
Tsogchin Dugan (Main Temple)	20 B2
Winter ger for lamas	21 A2
Yam Temple	22 B1
Yellow ger	23 B2

worth visiting on the way to/from Khövsgö Nuur, or other areas in northern or west ern Mongolia. Otherwise, you are better of incorporating the monastery into a three or four-day countryside trip to take in th surrounding scenery.

Amarbayasgalant Khiid (www.amarbayasgalant.org GPS: N49° 28.648', E105° 05.122') was originally buil etween 1727 and 1737 by the Manchu emperor Yongzheng, and dedicated to the great Mongolian Buddhist and sculptor Zanabazar see boxed text, p142), whose mummified body vas moved here in 1779. The monastery is in the Manchu style, down to the inscriptions, symmetrical layout and imperial colour scheme.

The communists moseyed in around 1937, but 'only' destroyed 10 out of the 37 temples nd statues, possibly because of sympathetic nd procrastinating local military commanders. The monastery was extensively restored between 1975 and 1990 with the help of Unesco. These days about 30 monks live in he monastery, compared with more than 2000 n 1936.

The temples in the monastery are normally losed, so you'll have to ask the monks to find he keys and open them up if you want to see ny statues or *thangka* (scroll paintings). There re around nine temples open to tourists.

To the west of the complex you'll find eight ew stupas and a meditation centre (you can ee it from Amarbayasgalant). It takes about wo hours to hike there.

The main hall has a life-size statue of inpoche Gurdava, a lama from Inner Mongolia who lived in Tibet and Nepal before returning to Mongolia in 1992 and raising much of the money for the temple's restoration. It's normally possible to climb up to the poof for fine views of the valley.

To help with the restoration work, foreigners are charged an entry fee of T3000. eremonies are usually held twice a day at am and 4pm.

Travellers have raved about the scenery of he mountain range Bürengiin Nuruu, north f Amarbayasgalant.

estivals
he most interesting time to make the sojourn • Amarbayasgalant Khiid is 9 to 11 August, hen the **Gongoriin Bombani Hural** (prayer ceremony) is held. As part of the rituals the locals ke up to the eight white stupas. Festival-goers sually camp in the fields near the monastery – ke a Buddhist version of Woodstock.

leeping
here are excellent camping spots all around marbayasgalant Khiid.

Amarbayasgalant Meditation Centre (☎ 011-2 529; per person US$10) Located 300m west of e monastery, this camp has flush toilets,

hot showers, a restaurant and free meditation classes. It is operated by the monks of Amarbayasgalant so any money you spend here goes towards the continued preservation of the temples.

Great Selenge (☎ 011-451 743; www.nomadic-empire tour.mn; GPS: N49° 26.688', E105° 05.141'; ger with 3 meals US$26) Located 3.5km south of the monastery, this modern ger camp has clean flush toilets and hot showers. It's run by Baigal Tour.

Getting There & Away
HITCHING
The monastery is not on the way to anywhere but a couple of cars a day come here in summer so you may be able to bum a lift. The cheapest and best way from Ulaanbaatar is to catch a train to Darkhan, take a shared jeep to Khötöl, hitch (which is easy) from there to the turn-off, then hitch another ride (much more difficult) to the monastery.

JEEP
From Ulaanbaatar, travel north to the T-intersection for Erdenet (just short of Darkhan). Take the Erdenet road for 90km and then turn right onto a dirt track; look for the red sign (GPS: N49° 12.809', E104° 59.128') that says 'Amarbayasgalant 35km'. Altogether, the journey to/from Ulaanbaatar takes around six hours. If you don't have your own car you could charter one from Darkhan for T50,000.

BULGAN БУЛГАН

pop 143,600 (incl Orkhon) / area 49,000 sq km

Bulgan's lack of major tourist sights has kept it off the beaten track. Most visitors to northern Mongolia charge through the aimag en route to more prolific sights such as Khövsgöl Nuur and Amarbayasgalant Khiid, but travellers with a bit of time on their hands can find some interesting, rarely visited sights in Bulgan, as well as some beautiful scenery that makes for nice cycle touring.

The aimag is rich in natural resources; it's home to the Erdenet copper mine, one of the largest of its kind anywhere, as well as agricultural areas and a small-scale timber industry. The ethnic groups comprise Khalkh, Buriat and Russian people.

A small mountain range, the Bürengiin Nuruu, bisects the aimag, and though it only reaches a maximum altitude of 2058m, it provides plenty of lush habitat for wild animals and livestock. A few adventurous travellers have seen this spectacular landscape while floating down the broad Selenge Gol on a raft, although to do such a trip you'd need to be completely self-sufficient. In the south of the aimag are two unique historical sights, Tsogt Taijiin Tsagaan Balgas and Khar Bukh Balgas, which are both geographically more in line with sights found in central Mongolia.

This section includes the small aimag of Orkhon, which contains the city of Erdenet. This aimag was formed in 1994 after being previously run as a federal municipality under the capital, Ulaanbaatar.

ERDENET ЭРДЭНЭТ
☎ 01352 / pop 73,450

In the autonomous municipality of Orkhon, and not technically part of Bulgan aimag, Erdenet is a little slice of Russia in Mongolia. The reason for Erdenet's existence is the copper mine, which employs about 8000 people and is the lifeblood of the city.

Erdenet, Mongolia's second-largest city, is modern (built in 1974) and comparatively wealthy, so the facilities are the best outsi< of Ulaanbaatar. Up to one-third of the pop lation of Erdenet was Russian during con munist times, though now only about 10(Russians still work as technical advisers the mine. You'll hear plenty of Russian o the streets and will find restaurant men featuring *peroshki* (meat-filled fried pastr rather than *buuz* (steamed mutton dump lings). These days, you are just as likely bump into a pair of clean-cut Mormons, wh have set up a large base here.

With good road and rail connections, it likely that you'll eventually find yourse passing through Erdenet. Such a feat was le likely under communism – back then, th USSR preferred to keep the city a secret an on most old maps Erdenet was deliberate marked incorrectly.

Orientation

Erdenet is a sprawling city, though every thing you will need is along the main stree Sükhbaatar Gudamj. The train station is i conveniently located more than 9km east (the centre.

ZANABAZAR: THE MICHELANGELO OF THE STEPPES

The life of the great Zanabazar, artist, statesman and Living Buddha, was not without controversy. One day, while in his workshop, a group of aristocrats arrived to chastise him for living with an 18-year-old girl, which went against his monastic vows. Zanabazar's female disciple, the so-called Girl Prince, who was deeply offended by the men, appeared from the workshop holding a lump of molten bronze in her bare hands. She proceeded to fashion the hot metal into a beautiful sculpture before their eyes, an act that had them begging for forgiveness.

Although some of Zanabazar's life seems pulled from the pages of a fairy tale, he was in fact a real man, and today is considered one of the greatest Renaissance artists in all of Asia. He was born in 1635 and at the tender age of three was deemed to be a possible *gegeen* (saint), so when he turned 14 he was sent to Tibet to study Buddhism under the Dalai Lama. He was also proclaimed the reincarnation of the Jonangpa line of Tibetan Buddhism and became the first Bogd Gegeen (reincarnated Buddhist leader of Mongolia). He is also known in Mongolia as Öndür Gegeen.

When he returned from his studies in Tibet, the artist-lama kick-started a Mongolian artistic renaissance and become Mongolia's greatest sculptor. In his spare time he reputedly invented the *soyombo,* the national symbol of Mongolia, and reformed the Mongolian script. Zanabazar was also a political figure and his struggle with the Zungar leader Galdan led to Mongolia's submission to the Manchus in 1691.

Zanabazar died in Beijing in 1723. His body was taken to Urga (modern Ulaanbaatar) and later entombed in a stupa in Amarbayasgalant Khiid. You will see many of Zanabazar's creations in monasteries and museums in Mongolia, and there is a fine collection of his art (particularly his Tara and Dhyani Buddha statues) in the Zanabazar Museum of Fine Arts in Ulaanbaatar. You can recognise images of Zanabazar by his bald, round head, the *dorje* (thunderbolt symbol) he holds in his right hand and the bell in his left hand.

For more on Zanabazar, look for the *Guidebook to Locales Connected with the Life of Zanabazar,* by Don Croner.

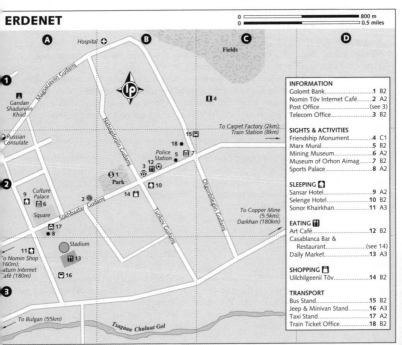

ERDENET

INFORMATION	
Golomt Bank	1 B2
Nomin Töv Internet Café	2 A2
Post Office	(see 3)
Telecom Office	3 B2

SIGHTS & ACTIVITIES	
Friendship Monument	4 C1
Marx Mural	5 B2
Mining Museum	6 A2
Museum of Orhon Aimag	7 B2
Sports Palace	8 A2

SLEEPING	
Sansar Hotel	9 A2
Selenge Hotel	10 B2
Sonor Khairkhan	11 A3

EATING	
Art Café	12 B2
Casablanca Bar & Restaurant	(see 14)
Daily Market	13 A3

SHOPPING	
Uilchilgeenii Töv	14 B2

TRANSPORT	
Bus Stand	15 B2
Jeep & Minivan Stand	16 A3
Taxi Stand	17 B2
Train Ticket Office	18 B2

NORTHERN MONGOLIA

nformation

olomt Bank (☎ 25200; ☻ 8am-7.30pm Mon-Fri,
am-5.30pm Sat & Sun) Changes US dollars and euros and
ives cash against Visa and MasterCard.

omin Töv Internet Café (☎ 20922; per hr T400;
☻ 10am-10pm) Small internet café on the main road.

aturn Internet Café (☎ 9911 8277; Sükhbaatar
udamj; per hr T500; ☻ 9am-midnight) Has 40 computers.

elecom office (☎ 27427; cnr Sükhbaatar Gudamj &
atsagorjiin Gudamj; ☻ 24hr) ATM and post office are also
cated here.

ights
OPPER MINE

he **open-cut mine** (www.emc.erdnet.mn), easily
een to the north of the city, is one of the
0-largest copper mines in the world. It is
lso a tremendous burden on the country's
nfrastructure and consumes nearly 50% of
longolia's electricity.

Open-cut mining is more damaging
o the environment but infinitely safer
han digging mine shafts below the sur-
ace. Since this particular mountain is al-
ost solid copper and molybdenum ore,
is is the only practical way to reach it.

Despite the destruction of the mountain,
the long-term environmental effects aren't
as bad as the gold mines in nearby Zaamar,
where rivers are being polluted.

The mine accounts for around 40% of
Mongolia's hard-currency earnings, producing some 25 million tonnes of copper/
molybdenum ore per annum. Thanks to sky-
rocketing copper prices the mine is now prof-
itable and it earns between US$150 million
and US$200 million in profit annually. Nearly
all the copper is sent to China and some bits of
it may be inside your mobile phone.

The mine is worth a visit if you've never
visited one like this before. You'll need to
show your passport to the guard at the gate.
No-one seems to mind if you look around
on your own, but it would be wise to check
in at the administration building, up the hill
from the guard station, on the left. A taxi to
the mine and back from the town centre costs
about T4000, including waiting time.

FRIENDSHIP MONUMENT

This communist monument, about 200m
northeast of the Selenge Hotel, is worth a

NORTHERN MONGOLIA

DOWN ON THE RANCH

Anak Ranch (☎ 011-316 181, 9909 9762; www.anakranch.com) is a working ranch where guests can get their hands dirty doing farm work. You can milk cows, herd the sheep, make cheese and lasso a half-wild horse or two. There is also plenty of time to relax, enjoy a barbecue, hike and fish. Prices are US$39 all-inclusive and a portion of the proceeds goes to improving conditions at Ulaanbaatar's dungeonlike Gants-Hudag prison. The ranch is close to the town of Orkhon, which you can easily access by train from Ulaanbaatar; there are daily trains in both directions (from Ulaanbaatar, trains depart at 7.35pm). If you contact the ranch ahead of time someone will meet you at the station with horses.

---

quick look. On the way from the town centre you pass a fine **Marx mural** and a picture of **Lenin** bolted to the wall. A little further to the east, the **ovoo** (a shamanistic collection of stones, wood or other offerings) is impressive if you haven't seen too many before. The hills north of the monument and south of the stadium are great for short hikes.

MINING MUSEUM
This Soviet-built **museum** (☎ 9935 0888; admission T1000; ◷ 8am-6pm Wed-Sun) belongs to the copper-mining company, Erdenet Concern. It's on the 2nd floor of the Culture Palace on the town square, and is worth a look.

MUSEUM OF ORKHON AIMAG
Opened in 1983 and hidden in a concrete complex on the right side of the Marx mural, this small **museum** (admission T1000; ◷ 9am-1pm & 2-6pm) includes a few oddities including a model of the copper mine (you can see it in 'day' or 'night') and a model of a modern ger with a TV inside. Look out for the two-headed calf, which hopefully is no indication of what the mine is doing to the local water supply.

Activities
If you have some time to kill, check out the **Sports Palace** (☎ 73436; Sükhbaatar Gudamj; ◷ 8am-9pm). You can take a hot shower (T1000) or sauna (T2000 per hour), watch some wrestling or go ice-skating in winter at the stadium at the back. There's an indoor pool (T2000), open weekdays only, but the staff may make life difficult by insisting on a medical examination before they let you swim.

Sleeping
CAMPING
Although the city is comparatively large, it is still possible to camp near Erdenet. The

best places to try are north of the Friendship Monument, or south of the stadium, over the other side of Tsagaan Chuluut Gol and among the pretty foothills.

HOTELS
Erdenet has a reasonable selection of hotels but no guesthouse or ger camp.

Selenge Hotel (☎ 27359; r T6000-20,000, half-lux T24,000, lux T30,000) This classic Soviet-style hotel has large, clean rooms with private bath-rooms. Renovations in some rooms include fresh wallpaper, carpeting and beds, although a few cheaper, unrenovated rooms have the same old lumpy beds and musty furnishing. It's on the main road.

Sonor Khairkhan (☎ 28120; d T3,000, half-lux T20,000, lux T28,000) Budget travellers after good value should head for this place – it has attractive, clean rooms, an excellent hot-water supply, phone, TV and the price includes breakfast in the room served promptly at 7.30am. It's near the daily market.

Sansar Hotel (☎ 27927; r T15,000, half-lux T36,000, lux T40,000) This new hotel is the best in town with clean rooms and modern bathrooms. It also sports one of the best restaurants around. It's on the street running northwest of the main square.

Eating
The restaurant in the Sansar Hotel offers a better-than-average selection of dishes, including stir-fried mushrooms with lamb (T3000), fried chicken (T4000) or, for the adventurous, horse meat (T2600).

Art Café (☎ 27316; ◷ 10am-midnight) A progressive café and bar on the main road with very orange interior, couches and modern art on the walls. A big-screen TV is tuned to local news. Food consists of standard Mongolian meat-and-potato dishes and a few Russian soups and salads.

Casablanca Bar & Restaurant (☎ 28546; ☾ 9am-
midnight) Various Russian and Mongolian dishes
and beers are served to customers sitting in
huge leather couches. Try the *azu,* a fried
meat and veggie dish inspired by Chinese
cooking. It's located in the department store
Uilchilgeenii Töv).

The daily market behind the Sports Palace is
surprisingly small and scrappy, though there's
a decent selection of (nonrefrigerated) dairy
products here. Most locals buy their food from
the shops along the main drag.

Shopping

Carpet Factory (☎ 20111; ☾ 8-11am & 1-5pm) If a
couple of tonnes of copper is a bit inconvenient to carry around, a carpet would make a
fine souvenir. The city's carpet factory produces more than a million square metres every
year using machinery from the former East
Germany. The factory is open year-round but
production is low in summer (June to August)
when supplies of wool are scarce. If you ask
the guard it may be possible to take a tour of
the entire operation. The factory is just off
the main road to the train station, about 2km
from the Friendship Monument.

Nomin Shop (☎ 21735; ☾ 9am-9pm) You can also
buy carpets and rugs here, about 500m west of
the Sports Palace. A huge Chinggis Khaan wall
carpet costs from T90,000 and smaller, towel-
ized carpets are around T5000 to T20,000.

For general goods (electronics, food and
clothing) the best place to shop is Uilchilgeenii
Töv (Үйлчилгээний Төв), the department
store opposite the Telecom office.

Getting There & Away

Travellers often bypass Erdenet and go straight
from Ulaanbaatar to Mörön via Bulgan. If you
have the time, and want a little luxury, take
the sleeper train from Ulaanbaatar to Erdenet
and catch a shared vehicle to Mörön; these
wait at the taxi stand outside the Sports Palace.
Don't make the mistake of first going to Bulgan
and then trying to hitch to Mörön. There are
comparatively few cars heading to Mörön
from Bulgan.

BUS, MINIVAN & JEEP

Two daily buses depart from Erdenet's bus
stand to Ulaanbaatar's Dragon bus stand
(T8000, seven hours, 371km) at noon and
2pm. Going the other way they depart Dragon
at the same times.

For shared vehicles to Mörön (T20,000, 10
hours), Bulgan (T3500, one hour), Tsetserleg
(T20,000, seven hours) and Uliastai (T40,000,
20 hours), the best place to look is at the market *(zakh).* The best place to look for a vehicle
to Ulaanbaatar is outside the Sports Palace.

The roads from Erdenet to Darkhan
(180km) and to Bulgan City (55km) are
both paved.

TRAIN

Train 273 departs Ulaanbaatar for Erdenet
at 7pm, arriving 11 hours later. It costs
T3600/9000 for a hard seat/soft-seat sleeper.
The sleeper is definitely worth the extra tögrög: the hard-seat carriages are packed to the
roof. The train returns to Ulaanbaatar from
Erdenet at the same time (7pm). In summer a
weekend train to/from Ulaanbaatar is added,
though the schedule is a little unreliable, so
check for times at the station.

To Darkhan (5½ hours), the train
costs T2100/5300 for a hard/soft seat. For
Sükhbaatar in Selenge aimag, change trains
in Darkhan.

You can buy tickets at the train station,
but it's better to queue on the day of, or before, departure at the **train ticket office** (☎ 22505;
☾ 9am-1pm & 2.30-6.30pm) in the northeast end
of town. Look for the small train sign on the
side of an apartment block, opposite the local
bus stand.

Buses meet arriving trains, but the stam-
pede of passengers quickly fills these to over-
flowing. It's best to get off the train as soon as
you can and find a taxi (about T4000) before
the crush starts.

It is more sedate going by bus *to* the train
station. Buses (T300), cars (T500 per person)
and taxis (T5000) leave from the local bus
stand, opposite the train ticket office.

BULGAN CITY БУЛГАН
☎ 01342 / pop 11,000 / elev 1208m

Bulgan is one of Mongolia's prettiest aimag
capitals. There is a grassy pine-clad park in
the middle of town and a lazy main street
where you are just as likely to see a horseman
as you are a passing vehicle. With Erdenet so
close by, the town has never had a chance
to develop much – there are only a couple
of small hotels and restaurants and very few
jeeps. As a quiet backwater it's not a bad place
to spend a night if you are travelling between
Mörön and Ulaanbaatar.

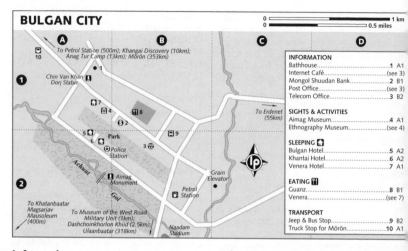

BULGAN CITY

Information

Bathhouse (admission T400; ⏰ 9am-6pm Thu-Mon)
Behind the pink government building.

Internet café (☎ 24024; per hr T690; ⏰ 9am-6pm
Mon-Fri) In the same building as Telecom.

Mongol Shuudan Bank (☎ 22169) Exchanges US
dollars and will give a cash advance on Visa.

Telecom office (☎ 24117; ⏰ 24hr) In the middle of
the main drag, about 150m southeast of the jeep stand.
The post office is also located here.

Sights

MUSEUMS

The **Aimag Museum** (☎ 22589; admission T1000;
⏰ 9am-6pm), on the main street, has some information on obscure sights in the aimag; a
display on J Gurragchaa, Mongolia's first man
in space; and some interesting old photos.

Next door, the **Ethnography Museum** (Ugsaatny
Muzei; admission T1000; ⏰ 9am-6pm) has a few interesting exhibits, such as ancient surgical
instruments, *airag* churners and saddles.

DASHCHOINKHORLON KHIID
ДАШЧОЙНХОРЛОН ХИЙД

Like most monasteries in Mongolia, this one
(built in 1992) replaced the original monastery, Bangiin Khuree, which was destroyed
in 1937. About 1000 monks lived and worshipped at Bangiin Khuree before they were
arrested and, presumably, executed. The remains of several stupas from the old monastery complex can be seen nearby.

The modern **monastery** (GPS: N48° 47.821′, E103°
30.687′) contains statues of Tsongkhapa and

Sakyamuni, and features a painting of the ol
monastery layout. About 30 monks now resid
there. The monastery is about 2.5km south
west of Bulgan City and is hidden behin
some hills. The run-down pavilion next to th
temple, called Divajin, was built in 1876.

KHATANBAATAR MAGSARJAV
MAUSOLEUM ХАТАНБААТАР
МАГСАРЖАВЫН БУНХАН

Located 1km southwest of the Bulgan Hote
across the stream and at the top of a hill, thi
curious blue building looks like a concret
ger but is actually a mausoleum in the shap
of a hat. It allegedly contains the remains o
Khatanbaatar Magsarjav, a key figure in th
1911 Revolution, who helped to liberate th
city of Khovd from Chinese rule. There ar
some murals of battle scenes inside, but t
see them you'll need to get the keys from th
caretaker. Ask at the Aimag Museum.

MUSEUM OF THE WEST ROAD MILITARY
UNIT БАРУУН ЗАМЫН ТУСГАЙ АНГИЙН
ШТАФ

The West Road Military Unit was a key forc
in freeing Mongolia from White Russian rul
in 1921. Its history is described in this smal
museum (☎ 9996 3472; admission T1000; ⏰ 9am-6pm
2.5km south of Bulgan. The building itsel
dates from 1668 and was used as a shop unt
being transformed into a military post in 1921
Choibalsan and Khatanbaatar Magsarjav bot
stayed here during Mongolia's military cam
paigns of the early 20th century.

Sleeping

CAMPING

The best place to pitch your tent is over the southern side of the river, the Achuut Gol; go past the market and find a discreet spot. If you have your own transport, consider camping a few kilometres north of town, along the road to Mörön.

GER CAMPS

Changai Discovery (☎ 9979 8810, 8876 6894; GPS: 48° 50.608′, E103° 25.427′; with/without food US$30/15) Located 10km north of Bulgan, this pretty ger camp is nestled below some forested hills. The camp includes about 20 gers and some A-frame huts. Horse riding is available (US$10). About 3km further up the valley is run-down Anag Tur camp.

HOTELS

Bulgan Hotel (☎ 22811; per person T3500-9000) This charmingly run-down Soviet hotel is in a peaceful location overlooking the park. With its decaying moose head on the wall and a

Ping-Pong table upstairs it has more character than most places in the countryside. The standard rooms are depressing but the lux rooms include cable TV and hot-water shower – good value for T9000.

ourpick Khantai Hotel (☎ 22964; s/d T7000/14,000) This small B&B offers six spotless double rooms, one with a gorgeous balcony overlooking the park. The bathroom and shower are both downstairs and there is 24-hour hot water. The friendly owner sometimes has breakfast available for an extra cost; she can offer eggs, bread and rice milk. Sometimes, in late summer, she adds blueberries and cream to the menu.

Venera Hotel (☎ 9960 4099, 9908 0944; r T10,000) Rooms here are clean and new but the size of a walk-in closet. On the main road.

Eating

The restaurant scene in Bulgan is pretty dire. There are a few hole-in-the-wall *guanz* on the main street, and in the daytime the hotels can usually scrape something together.

NOMADS TO NINJAS

Miners indulging in Mongolia's great new gold rush are turning verdant plains and pure rivers inside out in search of buried fortunes. But for once, it's not just the megacorporations from Ulaanbaatar who are to blame, it's the Ninjas.

When severe winters at the beginning of the millennium wiped out entire herds and family fortunes, many impoverished nomads turned to illegal gold mining in Bulgan, Töv and Selenge aimags. The green, shell-like buckets strapped to their backs, coupled with their covert, night-time operations, earned them the moniker 'Teenage Mutant Ninja Turtles' or Ninjas for short.

The Ninjas, who often pan what larger mining operations dredge from the flooded plains, attracted interest from businesspeople who sold them food and supplies. Soon 'Ninja ger (yurt) boomtowns' developed, each with ger-butchers, ger-shops, ger-karaoke bars, ger-sega parlours and ger-goldsmiths. Police have tried, often vainly, to break up the settlements, but the Ninjas return in larger numbers.

The Ninjas, who number more than 100,000, pose a serious threat to the environment and themselves. Unlike the licensed mining companies, they don't clean up after themselves; their work sites are often littered with discarded batteries and open pits. Mercury and cyanide, used to separate gold from the rock, add more problems. Health workers report that miners who use these methods have levels of mercury in their urine that are five to six times the safe limit.

Ninjas account for an incredible US$140 million in gold exports (although official bank figures say US$40 million). They receive US$500 per troy ounce, completely illegal and untaxed. Most Ninjas earn US$16 to US$24 per day. This kind of money, 10 times that of other rural salaries, has attracted more than out-of-work nomads. They've been joined by pensioners, redundant farm workers and poorly paid civil servants. Students who come in summer are able to finance their entire university education.

But this is dangerous business – a couple dozen Ninjas are buried alive in mine shafts each year. Recognising that the Ninjas won't go away, the government has considered ways to legalise their activities, protect their health and clean up their mess, if for no other reason than to tax their cache, which is mostly smuggled to China.

Venera (☎ 9908 0944; meals T1500-2500; ⏰ 10am-midnight) The nicest restaurant in Bulgan is in the hotel of the same name. It serves up decent Mongolian dishes, although promises of Korean meals are empty.

Getting There & Away

At the time of research there were no flights to Bulgan and there is little prospect these will resume in the near future.

HITCHING

As most tourist traffic between Ulaanbaatar and Mörön goes via Erdenet, there is not too much traffic going through Bulgan, but if you ask around the jeep stand or the petrol station, 500m northwest of town, something will turn up.

BUS, MINIVAN & JEEP

A bus departs Bulgan for Ulaanbaatar (T7900, eight hours) on Tuesday, Thursday and Saturday. When there is demand, minivans and jeeps go between Bulgan and Ulaanbaatar (T10,000, eight hours), but most people take a minivan to Erdenet (T3500, one hour, 55km) and then take the overnight train.

Vehicles to Mörön (or anywhere else) are very rare as these tend to leave from Erdenet. Usually on Monday a postal truck goes to Khutag-Öndör (T8000, four hours), but check details as the day is subject to change. Jeeps hang around the Önö Mandal Bar, northeast of the post office. You could charter one for about T400 to T500 per kilometre.

There are two routes between Ulaanbaatar and Bulgan City; the rougher but more direct southern route (318km) via Dashinchilen, or the paved northern route (467km) via Darkhan and Erdenet. If you want to visit Amarbayasgalant Khiid, the northern route is the way to go.

Bulgan City is 248km from Darkhan and 353km from Mörön.

AROUND BULGAN

There are a couple of obscure historical monuments around Bulgan. About 20km south of Bulgan, just north of Orkhon village, are seven standing deer stones, so called because the stones are carved with reindeer and other animals. The stones, known as **Seeriyn Adigyn Bugan Khoshoo** (GPS: N48° 38.537′, E103° 32.735′), mark what are thought to be Neolithic grave sites.

About 60km west of Bulgan City is the extinct volcano of **Uran Uul** (GPS: N48° 59.855′, E102° 44.003′) and nearby Togoo Uul, part of the 1600-hectare Uran-Togoo Tulga Uul Nature Reserve. It's a decent place to camp if you are headed to/from Khövsgöl aimag.

DASHINCHILEN ДАШИНЧИЛЭН

There are a couple of minor monuments in Dashinchilen *sum* (district), in the south of the aimag, which might be of interest if you are travelling between Ulaanbaatar and Tsetserleg, via Ögii Nuur.

On the western side of the Tuul Gol, about 35km northeast of Dashinchilen, are the impressive ruins of **Tsogt Taijiin Tsagaan Balgas** (GPS: N48° 01.422′, E104° 21.091′), a 17th-century fort that was the home of the mother of Prince Tsogt, a 17th-century poet who fought against Chinese rule. There is a **stone stele** nearby. The ruins are hard to find without a GPS so ask in Dashinchilen and keep asking at gers en route.

About 12km west of the *sum* capital, the ruined **Khar Bukh Balgas** (Khar Bakhin Fortress; GPS: N47° 53.198′, E103° 53.513′) is worth exploring and easy to reach as it's just a few kilometres north of the main road. The fortress inhabited by the Kitan from 917 to 1120, is sometimes known as Kitan Balgas. A small **museum** nearby is unlocked by a caretaker when visitors arrive.

KHÖVSGÖL ХӨВСГӨЛ

pop 123,500 / area 101,000 sq km

Tourist brochures tout it as the Switzerland of Mongolia, and this is no idle boast Khövsgöl is a land of thick forests, rushing rivers, sparkling lakes and rugged mountains. It's Mongolia's most beautiful aimag and seemingly every river bend or lake cove offers new and wonderful surprises. It does rain a lot during summer, but this only adds to the scenery: rainbows hang over meadows dotted with white gers and grazing horses and yaks.

While the Khalkh dominate the south there are also scattered populations of Buriat, Uriankhai, Khotgoid and Darkhad people. The Tsaatan, who live in the taiga in the far north of the aimag, herd reindeer and live in tepees resembling those of Native Americans. The north is a stronghold of sha

---

THE REINDEER HERDERS

Not far from Khövsgöl Nuur live the Tsaatan (literally 'Reindeer People'). Their entire existence is based around their herds of reindeer, which provide milk, skins for clothes, antlers for carving and medicine, transport and, occasionally, meat.

The Tsaatan are part of the Tuvan ethnic group, which inhabits the Tuvan Republic of Russia. There are only about 300 Tsaatan in total, spread over 100,000 sq km of northern Mongolian taiga landscape. They are truly nomadic, often moving their small encampments *(ail)* every two or three weeks, looking for special types of grass and lichen loved by the reindeer (of which there around 700 in total). The Tsaatan do not use gers, but prefer *orts,* similar to Native American tepees, traditionally made from birch bark, but now from store-bought canvas. The Tsaatan are strong practitioners of shamanism.

Visiting the Tsaatan is difficult and exhausting. The climate is exceedingly harsh, the area is prone to insects, the terrain is rough and mountainous, and it's easy to get lost without a good local guide. Plan to be self-sufficient with a quality sleeping bag, food and waterproof tents.

Irresponsible tourism, research and evangelical activities have put the Tsaatan culture and their reindeer at risk. Tourist dollars have already lured Tsaatan members down to Khövsgöl Nuur, an inhospitable elevation for their sensitive reindeer (see boxed text, p155). Others have been subjected to bible-thumping sessions and Tarzan films shown by Korean missionaries. It's estimated that 80% of their food comes as handouts from NGOs and tourists, which has made them considerably reliant on outsiders. If you are intent on making the trip, read up about permits (p160).

---

manism and you may be fortunate enough to see a shaman ceremony.

The main geographic feature of the province, as well as its major tourist destination, is enormous Khövsgöl Nuur. Most travellers fail to explore areas beyond the lake and this is a shame; the rest of the aimag has much to offer. The Darkhad valley, Chandman-Öndör and the south all make fine destinations, with plenty of opportunities for fishing, hiking and cycle touring. Note that if you want to fish anywhere but Khövsgöl Nuur you will need a permit from the Ministry of Nature in Ulaanbaatar. As these can be hard to get, consider hooking up with a licensed and responsible tour operator, a list of which can be found on p58.

MÖRÖN МӨРӨН
☎ 01382 / pop 36,100 / elev 1283m

For such a beautiful province, Khövsgöl has a rather disappointing capital. Mörön (pronounced 'mu-roon') sprawls over the north bank of the Delgermörön Gol, a treeless landscape that serves its purpose as an administrative centre. The town has few sights and most travellers only use the place to break up a journey to and from regions to the north.

Information

Border Guard office (☎ 24136, 24662; ⏲ 9am-6pm Mon-Fri) Might be able to issue permits for border towns such as Tsagaannuur, although it prefers that this be done in Ulaanbaatar. Located opposite the Ider restaurant.

Exchange Centre (☎ 9938 8858; Peace St; ⏲ 9am-6pm Mon-Fri) Located upstairs of the Khadgalamjiin Bank, it will change US dollars and euros.

Internet café (☎ 24706; per hr T700; ⏲ 9am-11pm Mon-Fri, 10am-5pm Sat & Sun) Attached to the Telecom office.

Mongol Shuudan Bank (☎ 22616) About 200m east of the Telecom office, this bank changes money and gives cash advances on Visa.

Orgil Bathhouse (☎ 22018; per person T1500; ⏲ 8am-midnight) On the east side of the market, this is the newest bathhouse in town.

Telecom office (☎ 21034; ⏲ 24hr) Opposite the town square. The post office is also located here.

Tourist Information Centre (☎ 9938 7009; hovsgul _info@yahoo.com; Centre St; ⏲ 9am-6pm Mon-Fri) Supplies maps and books for the region and can give some basic tips on transport and accommodation. A tourist kiosk (☎ 9938 9564) at the airport opens when a plane arrives.

Sights
MUSEUM

Given the variety of wildlife in the aimag, stuffed animals are, not surprisingly, the main feature of the **museum** (☎ 9938 6815; admission T2000; ⏲ 9am-6pm Mon-Fri). There's a large tusk from a woolly mammoth, but you won't see one of those in the flesh – they haven't inhabited this region for more than 40,000

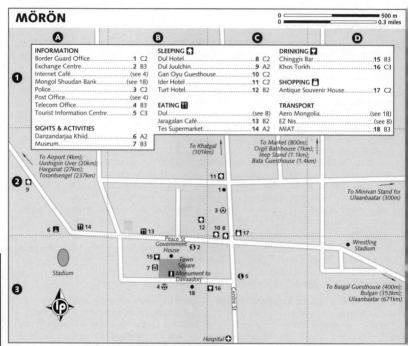

MÖRÖN

| 0 | 500 m |
| 0 | 0.3 miles |

INFORMATION
Border Guard Office...................1 C2
Exchange Centre.........................2 B3
Internet Café..........................(see 4)
Mongol Shuudan Bank............(see 18)
Police..3 C2
Post Office...............................(see 4)
Telecom Office..........................4 B3
Tourist Information Centre.........5 C3

SIGHTS & ACTIVITIES
Danzandarjaa Khiid.....................6 A2
Museum......................................7 B3

SLEEPING 🏠
Dul Hotel...................................8 C2
Dul Juulchin..............................9 A2
Gan Oyu Guesthouse................10 C2
Ider Hotel................................11 C2
Turt Hotel................................12 B2

EATING 🍴
Dul...(see 8)
Jaragalan Café..........................13 B2
Tes Supermarket......................14 A2

DRINKING 🍷
Chinggis Bar............................15 B3
Khos Torkh..............................16 C3

SHOPPING 🛍
Antique Souvenir House...........17 C2

TRANSPORT
Aero Mongolia.......................(see 18)
EZ Nis....................................(see 8)
MIAT.......................................18 B3

To Khatgal
(101km)

To Market (800m);
Orgil Bathhouse (1km);
Jeep Stand (1.1km);
Bata Guesthouse (1.4km)

To Airport (4km);
Uushigiin Uver (20km);
Harganat (27km);
Tosontsengel (237km)

To Minivan Stand for
Ulaanbaatar (300m)

Peace St
Government
House

Town
Square

Monument to
Davaadorj

Stadium

Wrestling
Stadium

To Baigal Guesthouse (400m);
Bulgan (353km);
Ulaanbaatar (671km)

Centre St

Hospital

NORTHERN MONGOLIA

---

years. Photographic exhibits of the Tsaatan people are also intriguing. The museum is housed inside the local Drama Theatre on the town square.

DANZANDARJAA KHIID
ДАНЗАНДАРЖАА ХИЙД

The history of this monastery is unclear, but the original (Möröngiin Khuree) was built around 1890 and was home to 2000 monks. It was rebuilt and reopened in June 1990, and now has 40 monks of all ages. It's a charming place, designed in the shape of a concrete ger, and contains a great collection of *thangka*.

The monastery is just back from the main road, on the way to the airport. Visitors are always welcome.

Tours

The guesthouses listed below can help to arrange transport out of Mörön. Local English-speaking guide **Saraa** (☎ 9938 5577; saraa_m3@ yahoo.com) can also help with logistics and travel in the area.

Sleeping
CAMPING

The best camping spots are by the river, the Delgermörön Gol. Twenty-seven kilometres east of Mörön, on the road to Bulgan City, a tiny, unmapped and unnamed lake offers good camping. If you are heading west, there are great spots on the river past Burentogtokh.

GER CAMPS

Dul Juulchin (☎ 22206; GPS: N49° 38.483', E100° 08.618'; s/d US$15/20, ger US$20) Good value for money, this extension of the Dul empire has clean and simple rooms in the lodge or comfortable gers. The toilets and showers are both clean.

Harganat (☎ 9938 7022; www.besudtour.com; GPS: N49° 38.521', E99° 50.030'; with/without meals US$30/15) Perched on a ridge over Delger-Mörön valley this attractive camp has hot showers and excellent French and Italian food. Even if you're not staying it's a nice place for lunch after visiting the deer stones at Uushigiin Uver. In summer, swans swim in the river below but the real time to visit is mid-September when more than 100 swans make their home here. It is 7km past Uushigiin Uver.

GUESTHOUSES

Bata Guesthouse (☎ 9138 7080; bata_guesthouse@ yahoo.com; GPS: N49° 39.053', E100° 10.018'; per person incl breakfast T4000) This *hashaa* guesthouse (basically a fenced-in yard) is a 20-minute walk from the centre, 400m past the market. Turn right at the water pump house and walk for another 150m; it's on the left. Look out for the 'Bata Guesthouse' sign. Locals know the address as '5-8-4'. The owner, Bata, speaks English and can help arrange transport around the aimag. Laundry service and hot showers are available.

Baigal Guesthouse (☎ 9938 8408; baigal_999@chin ggis.com; GPS: N49°38.176', E100° 10.798'; per person T4000, hot shower T1000) A similar option to the Bata, about 800m past the wrestling stadium. The price includes a breakfast of toast, bread, jam and eggs (Baigal raises chickens so you can be sure the eggs are fresh).

Gan Oyu Guesthouse (☎ 22349, 9938 9438; ganoyu _n@yahoo.com; Peace St; dm incl breakfast US$5; 🖳) This guesthouse is the best value in town, with a spotless dorm room and hot-water shower. It is on the 2nd floor of an apartment block next to the Dul Hotel. For a cheaper option, ask about its off-site ger camp, with beds for T3500. Laundry service available.

HOTELS

Turt Hotel (☎ 9905 8239; per person T6000) The Turt is an older hotel and pretty run-down but the management does keep it reasonably clean. It's far better than the Delger Möron, the dumpy hotel next door.

Ider Hotel (☎ 29612, 9938 2890; r T20,000, lux T35,000) This place is clean and all rooms have an attached bathroom, but it's a little disorganised and not as good value as the Dul. Located a block north of the Dul.

Dul Hotel (☎ 22206; s/d US$15/20, s/d half-lux US$20/25, lux US$30-45) The name of the place is a little self-defeating but in fact this is the best hotel in town. All rooms have been renovated and come with a modern bathroom, IDD phone and cable TV. The standard rooms have no hot water so a half-lux is a good option. It has an excellent restaurant downstairs. It is located 100m northeast of the square.

Eating & Drinking

Jaragalan Café (☎ 24409; meals T1300; 🕑 9am-8pm Mon-Sat) The streetside patio at this Mongolian restaurant is worth visiting on a warm day. It's just northwest of the square.

our pick Dul (☎ 22206; mains T2500-3500; 🕑 9am-midnight) Located in the hotel of the same name, the Dul is hardly descriptive of what this place has to offer. If the staff can get your order correct (a long shot at best) you can enjoy excellent pizza, roast beef, a taco salad or a Chinese dish. Round off your meal with an outstanding cinnamon roll or apple pie. Vegetarians should find a soup or salad to their liking. All these delights are enjoyed on comfy sofas in a clean, bright atmosphere.

Khos Torkh (☎ 24016; 🕑 10am-7pm) Easily spotted, this local watering hole features two giant beer barrels outside its entrance. The local drink of choice is Kvas, a brew made from fermented rye bread. The alcohol content is so low (1%) that you'd need to drink a few gallons of the stuff to feel any of its effects.

Chinggis Bar (☎ 24016; 🕑 10am-midnight) Depending on your perspective, the outer-space theme here seems totally surreal or completely appropriate for northern Mongolia. Chinese and Mongolian food served by day, beer by night.

Tes Supermarket (🕑 10am-8pm) Located on the main road, this is one of several shopping markets.

Shopping

Antique Souvenir House (☎ 9976 8837; 🕑 9am-9pm) Sells maps, books, antiques and locally produced handicrafts. On the main road.

Getting There & Away

AIR

MIAT (Mongolian Airlines; ☎ 9638 0002) is located in the Mongol Shuudan Bank building. Another office opens at the airport when planes arrive. MIAT runs direct flights between Ulaanbaatar and Möron for US$90/157 one way/return. **Aero Mongolia** (☎ 22478, 9997 7705), located in the same building, flies here for US$109/194 one way/return. **EZ Nis** (☎ 21199, 9904 9930) charges US$120/216 one way/return; its office is in the Dul Hotel. Between the three of these airlines there should be at least one flight a day.

Möron occasionally serves as a refuelling stop for flights headed further west, so you could theoretically combine a trip to the west with Khövsgöl Nuur. Check MIAT for details. Buy your ticket as early as possible.

Möron airport is about 5km from the centre of town. You will have to take a jeep or taxi there (T2500), or you can hop on the crowded bus.

NORTHERN MONGOLIA

BUS

A direct bus departs Mörön for Ulaanbaatar (T20,000) on Tuesday, Thursday and Saturday at 2pm. It leaves from the minivan stand. Going the other way, it departs from Ulaanbaatar's Teeveriin Tovchoo on Monday, Wednesday and Friday.

HITCHING

The Ulaanbaatar–Erdenet–Mörön road is fairly busy, so hitching a ride shouldn't be a problem. But be warned: the trip by truck between Ulaanbaatar and Mörön is a tough 27 or more nonstop hours (expect to pay at least T10,000 for a lift). Some travellers do it one way for the 'experience' – and then gratefully fly back. It's best to fly here from Ulaanbaatar as it's easier to get a seat. It's also easier to hitch *to* UB rather than *from* it, as all traffic tends to funnel back to the capital.

MINIVAN & JEEP

Minivans run between Ulaanbaatar and Mörön daily (T25,000, 17 hours, 671km). You can cut down on the time spent bumping around in a van by taking the sleeper train between UB and Erdenet.

Minibuses and jeeps leave most afternoons to Khatgal (T7000, two hours). There are occasional jeeps to Erdenet (T20,000, 10 hours) and Darkhan (T24,000, 13 hours, 601km).

Transport to Ulaanbaatar, Erdenet and Darkhan leaves from the southern side of the market. Transport to Khatgal and elsewhere leaves from north of the market.

From the city of Mörön it is 273km to Tosontsengel in Zavkhan aimag and 353km to Bulgan City.

UUSHIGIIN UVER
УУШИГИЙН ӨВӨР

A Bronze Age site, **Uushigiin Uver** (GPS: N49° 39.316', E99° 55.708'; admission T3000) contains 14 upright carved deer stones, plus sacrificial altars *(keregsuur)*. This remarkable collection is located 20km west of Mörön, and about 1km north of the Delgermörön Gol. The area is enclosed by a fence and small placards describe the stones. The most unique, stone 14, is topped with the head of a woman; there are only a handful of such deer stones in Mongolia. The carved stones are dated to around 2500 to 4000 years old, and the nearby mountain range contains around 1400 burial tombs. A caretaker living near the area can

show you around and provide commentary. Despite the uniqueness of the site, an ugly ger camp built nearby detracts from its allure.

KHÖVSGÖL NUUR NATIONAL PARK
ХӨВСГӨЛ НУУР

Known as the Blue Pearl of Mongolia, Khövsgöl Nuur is an extraordinary lake that stretches 136km deep into the Siberian taiga. The lake and mountains that surround it form the basis for this popular national park, a major destination for both Mongolian and international tourists.

In surface area, this is the second-largest lake (2760 sq km) in Mongolia, surpassed in size only by Uvs Nuur, a shallow, salty lake in the western part of the country. But Khövsgöl Nuur (sometimes transliterated as Hövsgöl or Hovsgol) is Mongolia's deepest lake (up to 262m deep) as well as the world's 14th-largest source of fresh water – it contains between 1% and 2% of the world's fresh water (that's 380,700 billion litres!). Geologically speaking, Khövsgöl is the younger sibling (by 23 million years) of Siberia's Lake Baikal, 195km to the northeast, and was formed by the same tectonic forces.

The lake is full of fish, such as lenok and sturgeon, and the area is home to argali sheep, ibex, bear, sable, moose and a few near-sighted wolverines. It also has more than 200 species of bird, including the Baikal teal, bar-headed goose (*kheeriin galuu* in Mongolian), black stork and Altai snowcock.

The region hosts three separate, unique peoples: Darkhad, Buriat and Tsaatan (aka

---

DEER STONES

Found across Mongolia, deer stones are ancient burial markers that date from the Bronze Age. The ancient steppe tribes believed that after death a soul departed this world and ascended to the sky on the backs of deer. The deer carved onto the stones are representational of this act. Many deer stones are also carved with a belt, from which hang various tools including axes and spears. These accessories would be required for successfully navigating the afterlife. Of the 700 deer stones known to exist worldwide, 500 are located in Mongolia. The best collection of deer stones is at Uushigiin Uver (see left).

Dukha). Shamanism, rather than Buddhism, is the religion of choice in these parts.

The lake water is still clean but a rise in livestock using the area for winter pasture has led to some pollution of the shore and feeder rivers, so you are better off purifying your water.

Khövsgöl Nuur is a pristine but increasingly heavily visited part of Mongolia. Please read boxed texts p54 and p60 for suggestions on how you can minimise your impact on this beautiful region.

Climate

Spring is a pleasant time to visit as it rains less and the flowers and birdlife are at their best. However, it will still be very cold, with snow on the ground and ice on the lake (some ice usually remains until early June).

The summer is a little more crowded (not so crowded that it would spoil your trip), but it can still be cold, and it often rains. The meadows around the lake are sprinkled with beautiful wildflowers during this time. Autumn is another pleasant time to visit, when the leaves are changing colour.

Winter is amazingly cold, though blue skies are the norm. Khövsgöl Nuur freezes to a depth of 120cm, allowing passenger trucks to cross the length of the lake in winter. Oil trucks once made this journey in vast numbers but this practice was stopped in 1990 when it was determined that they were polluting the water. About 40 trucks have fallen through the ice over the years.

Information

Discovery Initiatives produces a useful booklet on the park entitled *Lake Hovsgol National Park: A Visitors Guide*, which you can get in Ulaanbaatar and, maybe, in the national park office.

Information Centre (Мэдээллийн Төв; ⊗ 9am-8pm) Located near the MS Guesthouse in Khatgal. It has some interesting, museum-style displays on the lake but the staff speaks only Mongolian and has little practical information on touring the area. The caretaker (with the keys) can be found in a ger around the back.

Telecom office (☎ 01382-26513/36; ⊗ 8am-11pm) The post office is also located here; there're plans for an internet café but the only guaranteed place to check your email is back in Mörön.

Permits

On the main road, 12km before Khatgal, you'll be required to pay an entrance fee at a gate to

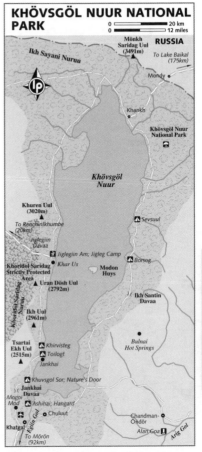

KHÖVSGÖL NUUR NATIONAL PARK

0 —— 20 km
0 —— 12 miles

Ikh Sayani Nuruu

Mönkh Saridag Uul (3491m) ▲

RUSSIA

To Lake Baikal (175km)

Mondy

Khankh

Khövsgöl Nuur National Park

Khövsgöl Nuur

Khuren Uul (3020m)

To Renchinlkhumbe (20km)

Jiglegiin Davaa

Khoridol-Saridag Strictly Protected Area

Jiglegiin Am; Jileg Camp

Khar Us

Uran Dösh Uul (2792m)

Modon Huys

Ikh Uul (2961m)

Tsartai Ekh Uul (2515m)

Khirvisteg

Toilogt

Jankhai

Khuvsgol Sor; Nature's Door

Jankhai Davaa

Mogoi Mod

Ashihai; Hangard

Chuluut

Khatgal

To Mörön (92km)

Sevsuul

Börsog

Ikh Santin Davaa

Bulnai Hot Springs

Chandman-Öndör

Alan Goa

Arig Gol

Egiin Gol

NORTHERN MONGOLIA

the national park. The cost is T3000/300 per person for foreigners/Mongolians. If there's no-one there you can buy permits at the information centre or from the ranger, who patrols the lakeside on horseback. With your permit you should receive a useful visitors' pamphlet explaining the permits and how to limit your impact on the lake. Hang onto the ticket as you may be asked to show it more than once.

Sights

KHATGAL ХАТГАЛ

As the southern gateway to Khövsgöl Nuur, Khatgal is the largest town on the lake. With some of the best budget accommodation in Mongolia, it is a good launching pad for the

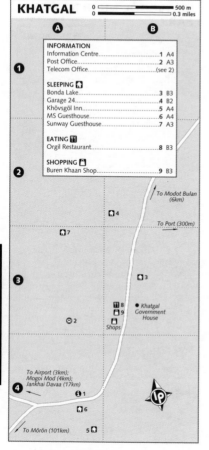

KHATGAL

INFORMATION
Information Centre...............................1 A4
Post Office...2 A3
Telecom Office................................(see 2)

SLEEPING
Bonda Lake..3 B3
Garage 24..4 B2
Khövsgöl Inn.......................................5 A4
MS Guesthouse....................................6 A4
Sunway Guesthouse............................7 A3

EATING
Orgil Restaurant..................................8 B3

SHOPPING
Buren Khaan Shop...............................9 B3

To Modot Bulan (6km)
To Port (300m)
Khatgal Government House
Shops
To Airport (3km); Mogoi Mod (4km); Jankhai Davaa (17km)
To Mörön (101km)

lake and most people spend at least a day here preparing for, or relaxing after, a trip. The town is actually on the arm of the lake that funnels into the Egiin Gol, so you don't get much of an idea of the lake's size from here.

Khatgal used to be a busy depot for trucks headed to and from Russia, but the town's economy is now based mainly on tourism.

There are easy walks up the lakeshore or, for an easier view of the lake, just climb the hill immediately north of Nature's Door camp (p158). You can also check out the **Mogoi Mod** (Snake Tree; GPS: N50° 27.080', E100° 07.274'), located 4km from town, past the airport, towards Jankhai Davaa (Jankhai Pass). This tree, which curves into a unique spiral, is honoured with *hadak* (ritual scarves).

WESTERN SHORE
From Khatgal, a reasonable road first heads southwest before swinging northeast across several dry riverbeds and over the pass Jankhai Davaa, 17km from Khatgal, where you receive your first magical glimpse of the lake. The road continues past the gorgeous headlands of **Jankhai**, once a Russian scientist station, and **Toilogt** (GPS: N50° 39.266', E100° 14.961') pronounced 'toy-logt' but routinely mispronounced 'toilet' by most travellers, where there is a rash of ger camps. The road then gradually deteriorates.

About 30km north of Toilogt is **Khar Us** (GPS: N50° 56.132', E100° 14.835'), a series of springs surrounded by meadows of beautiful wildflowers. In June locals flock here to eat the bailius fish for its medicinal properties (these fish are smoked and served with wild green onions, or sometimes boiled). This makes a great destination to reach on horseback – three days from Khatgal.

A jeep can travel about 10km past Toilogt, after which the trail becomes overgrown and is best managed on horseback for the trip up to **Jiglegiin Am** (GPS: N51° 00.406', E100° 16.003'), almost exactly halfway up the western shore. From Jiglegiin Am you could take the western trail to Renchinlkhumbe, on the way to Tsagaannuur. For that trip see p156.

EASTERN SHORE
The eastern shore is less mountainous than the west, but offers spectacular views across Khövsgöl Nuur. There is wildlife, golden fields of grass and plenty of fishing holes. It gets far fewer visitors than the western shore, making it a great destination for travellers seeking an off-the-beaten-path experience. The main drawback to this side of the lake is the appalling road that heads up to Khankh, possibly the worst stretch of road we encountered in 15,000km of overland travel! Expect mud, rocks, roots and the odd collapsed bridge.

From Khatgal, head for the bridge over the Egiin Gol, where you may need to ask directions. The trail meanders over some hills and continues past an interesting *ovoo* at the pass **Ikh Santin Davaa** (GPS: N50° 52.622', E100° 41.185') to a gorgeous spot called **Borsog** (GPS: N50° 59.677', E100° 42.983'), six hours by jeep and 103km from Khatgal.

If your spine hasn't suffered permanent damage by now, you could carry on further to a couple of gers known as **Sevsuul**. The road

---

BIZNESS TSAATAN

Some Tsaatan (Reindeer People) have discovered the fine art of capitalism and have moved to Khövsgöl Nuur to be nearer to their source of income – tourists. Their tepees are easy to spot on the lake shore, where they appear each summer, ready for photo opportunities (US$5) or the chance to flog antler carvings.

Members of their own community know them as 'Bizness Tsaatan', or sometimes 'Bizness Shaman' as they occasionally put on a shaman dance in broad daylight (another US$5). While this may sound like an innocent way of extracting money from tourist pockets, the presence of the Tsaatan on the shores of Khövsgöl Nuur has had detrimental effects on their reindeer. The lichen upon which the reindeer feed does not grow at lake elevation, causing illness and sometimes death. Each year the Bizness Tsaatan families return to the taiga to buy more reindeer from other Tsaatan families, knowing that they endanger these creatures when they travel to the lake.

The authorities have tried for years to move them out of the park, but business has been too good to keep them away. Tourists might consider refusing their services to dissuade them from returning. Also worth missing is the 'Reindeer Festival', a contrived midsummer event organised by local tourist companies who don't necessarily have the reindeer's best interests in mind.

If you want to visit a Tsaatan family, you'll need to visit their camps outside Tsagaannuur (see p162).

---

actually improves a little here, then hugs the lake and is usually passable all the way to Khankh. Surprisingly, a few sand dunes dot the landscape.

From Khatgal, allow at least 12 hours by jeep to travel the 200km or so to **Khankh** (Turt), a former depot for oil tankers headed to and from Siberia. Khankh is more Buriat and Russian than Mongolian, because it is closer to its northern neighbour than to Ulaanbaatar.

Remember that if you reach Khankh, you will have to come *all* the way back along the same bone-crunching, eastern road: there is no way any vehicle can get from Khankh to Jiglegiin Am, halfway up the western shore. At the moment going all the way around the lake is only possible by boat or horse. There have long been plans to open the border crossing into Russia at Khankh – check for updates at the border office in Ulaanbaatar or in Mörön.

Activities

FISHING

If you love fishing, then you'll get excited about Khövsgöl Nuur. If you don't have fishing gear already, you can buy some at the shops in Khatgal (Buren Khaan shop has the best selection).

Around a dozen species of fish inhabit the lake, including salmon, (bony) sturgeon, grayling and lenok. A fishing permit costs T10,000 and is valid for three days or 10 fish, whichever comes first. You can get them from the park rangers, Khatgal's Government House or MS Guesthouse. Fishing is not allowed between 15 April and 15 June. The fine for fishing illegally is US$40.

HIKING

This is one of the best ways to see the lake and the mountains surrounding it. You will need to be self-sufficient, although there are a few gers in the area from which to buy some meat or dairy products. The trails around the lake are easy to follow, or just hug the shoreline as much as you can.

Of the mountains in the southwestern region, the most accessible is Tsartai Ekh Uul (2515m), immediately west of Jankhai, where the hiking is excellent. Also try the numerous other mountains in the mountain range of Khoridol Saridag Nuruu, such as Khuren Uul (3020m), not far north of the trail to Renchinlkhumbe; Ikh Uul (2961m), a little northwest of Toilogt; and the extinct volcano of Uran Dösh Uul (2792m).

Longer treks are possible around the Ikh Sayani Nuruu range, which has many peaks over 3000m. It is right on the border of Russia, so be careful not to accidentally cross it or you may get shot at by border guards.

Both Garage 24 and MS Guesthouse (p157) in Khatgal have trained some local hiking guides in first aid, route finding and low-impact hiking and have scouted out some good treks in the surrounding mountains. Contact them for route ideas and/or guides.

NORTHERN MONGOLIA

TREKKING FROM KHÖVSGÖL TO DARKHAD

One of the most adventurous treks in Mongolia, done by either horse or foot, begins in Khatgal, goes up the western shore of the lake and over the Jiglegiin Davaa (Jiglegiin Pass) to Renchinlkhumbe.

From Khatgal to Jiglegiin Am, about halfway up the western shore of Khövsgöl Nuur, will take five days (four hours' riding each day). You start to feel the isolation after Ongolog Gol (the end of the jeep road), from where it's a 10-hour journey to Khar Us. There are endless camping spots along this route.

From Khar Us it's just three hours to Jiglegiin Am where you can find accommodation in a cabin (T2000) and get a cooked meal (T1000) – it's best to have exact change. The jeep trail that heads up to Jiglegiin Davaa (2500m) is very muddy even after a long dry spell – this is where a pair of Russian NBC overboots will come in handy. Expect to get to the pass in around three hours.

From the pass it's a gentle walk down to the Arsayn Gol, which you'll need to cross at least twice. There are also some side streams to cross. These crossings are usually OK but if it's been raining hard you can be stuck for hours or even days. In dry spells the river can disappear completely so you need to fill up with water whenever possible.

After a seven-hour walk from the pass you should be at Ooliin Gol (25km west of Jiglegiin Am) where there are some camping spots. It's then another seven hours to Renchinlkhumbe. When you reach the broad expanse of the Darkhad, make a beeline south for the town.

The final three hours of the trek are often marred by horrific swarms of flies and mosquitoes – a sanity-saving measure is to wrap your head with a towel or T-shirt. The bugs seem to disappear when you've reached the village.

From Renchinlkhumbe it's another two-day trek to Tsagaannuur, from where you can organise a trip to the Tsaatan camps. Alternatively, you could return to Khatgal via the old Russian logging route that runs through the mountains. If you have no intention of going to Tsagaannuur you could skip Renchinlkhumbe too and take a shortcut back to Khatgal. This involves following the Arsayn Gol around 35km upstream, eventually picking up the logging route.

This route involves moderate trekking in good weather. However, the area is prone to heavy rain and flash flooding that can stop you in your tracks. Hikers and horse riders are frequently made to wait on river banks (sometimes for several days) until water levels drop low enough for them to cross. Bring wet-weather gear, warm clothes and preferably a guide to get you across. If you don't have a guide, at least bring a good map, such as the *Lake Khövsgöl National Park Satellite Map* (Conservation Ink). Contact MS Guesthouse in Khatgal for further details on this trek.

HORSE RIDING

The only place to organise a horse trek around the lake is in Khatgal. The three main guesthouses can arrange everything within 24 hours. Prices are negotiable but reasonable at about T7000 per horse per day, and about T10,000 to T15,000 per day for a guide. Ger camps along the lake can organise horse rentals for day trips.

A guide is recommended for horse-riding trips in the region and, in fact, park regulations stipulate that foreigners should have one local guide for every four tourists. Guides will expect you to provide food while on the trail.

A complete circuit of the lake on horseback will take from 10 to 15 days. A return trip by horse from Khatgal to Tsagaannuur, and a visit to the Tsaatan, will take 15 to 20 days. An interesting two-week trip could take you east of the lake to Chandman-Öndör and Dayan Derkhiin Agui, a sacred cave. A trip to the Bulnai hot springs would take eight to nine days. You'll definitely need a guide.

Shorter trips include one to Toilogt, through the mountainous Khoridol Saridag Nuruu Strictly Protected Area, or up to Khar Us and back in five or six days.

KAYAKING & BOATING

Travelling by kayak allows you to see the lake without the strain of driving along the appalling roads. The lake is full of glorious little coves, perfect for camping and fishing, and you could even check out **Modon Huys**, an island almost exactly in the middle of the lake. Nomadic Expeditions (p81) runs kayaking trips in the region. Garage 24 (opposite) can rent kayaks for T25,000 per day.

Garage 24 has a Zodiac boat and can run travellers up to its camp and beyond to the island and the northern reaches of the lake. MS Guesthouse also has a motor boat. Ask about the two-day boat trip to Jiglegiin Am (T300,000 for up to six people, including meals).

Several large boats remain moored at the Khatgal docks. They *very* occasionally take passengers up to Khankh but these days they will only move when chartered, which will cost an arm and a leg. If you do charter a boat to Khankh, you'll still have to share it with a boatload of nonpaying passengers who have been waiting for some tourist or trader to fork out the money.

Festivals & Events

If for some strange reason you've come to northern Mongolia in winter, it is worth checking out the **Khatgal Ice Festival**, held on 28 February. The event includes cross-country skiing, ice-skating and horse-sledding competitions. Khatgal's **naadam** (traditional sports festival) is held on 11 July.

In late June or early July, the **Sunrise to Sunset Ultra-marathon** is held further up the lakeshore. Mongolian and international runners compete in 42km or 100km divisions; for more info, check the website: www.ultramongolia.org/.

Sleeping

KHATGAL

If you have a tent and are hanging around for a lift to the lake or to Mörön, you can camp in the forests along the shores of the Egiin Gol, either in town or in the beautiful valleys further south.

Bonda Lake (☎ 9996 3994; bond_lake@yahoo.com; camping T2000, r T3000, ger T4000) This new addition to Khatgal is located on the main road heading north, just past the shops. It has four-bed gers and one ger with a double bed. You can also stay in the lodge but these rooms are a bit boxy. The hot showers work well and the English-speaking owner has kayaks for rent. Ask for Bayara.

MS Guesthouse (☎ 9979 6030; lake_hovsgol@yahoo .com; bed per person T5000, camping T3000) This guesthouse (designed like a camp), in the extreme south of town, is the first collection of gers you see when you arrive in town. Perhaps the most congenial of ger camps around Khatgal; the staff makes visitors feel at home, with communal meals and activities. Owner Ganbaa is

very knowledgeable about hiking and horse-trekking routes in the area. The camp has hot showers, clean pit toilets and a lodge where you can order meals (T1200). Prices include breakfast. This place is open all year, and may be your only option in winter.

Garage 24 (☎ 011-323 957, 9911 8652; www .4thworldadventure.com; dm T5000, camping T3000) This environmentally conscious backpacker hangout is built from a reclaimed Soviet-era truck garage. The cosy lodge, warmed by a fireplace, feels like an old English country home. It has bunk beds and a dining area where you can get the best food in northern Mongolia. Mountain bikes, kayaks, horses and camping gear are rented out to suit your needs (note that some kit may be at the Jankhai camp). The staff is friendly but little English is spoken. Garage 24 is in the north of town, at the base of the hill, not far from the storage drums of the petrol station.

Khövsgöl Inn (☎ 9911 5929, 9838 9687; klm@boojum .com; dm T5000, ger T10,000) A welcome addition to Khatgal, this place offers quality accommodation at competitive rates. Beds are available in gers or dorms and there is a nice lodge with a cosy fireplace. It's affiliated with the Saridag Inn at Renchinlkhumbe and the Jigleg Camp on the lake so you can get info here if you are headed that way. It's between MS Guesthouse and the Egiin Gol.

Sunway (☎ 9975 3824; horsetrek_khuvsgul@yahoo .com; per person US$5) This camp is smaller and less communal than others, although some travellers may prefer it that way. The hot shower is powered by an inventive foot pump. It's on the northwestern part of town below the hills. It serves meals (T1500).

MODOT BULAN

This area extends due north of Khatgal, up the Egiin Gol mouth for about 6km. Most people miss it because the road up the coast bypasses this section. If you are exploring the lake by foot you can walk here and continue up the shore (which is blissfully ger-camp free for another 7km).

Hangard (☎ 011-311 333, www.ashihai.mn; with/ without meals US$30/15) Just past Ashihai, the Hangard camp is a large camp that caters to tour groups. It has a couple of boats and does yak cart trips.

Ashihai (☎ 011-315 459, 9968 5185; www.fly2mongolia .mn; with/without meals US$40/20) This camp nearly qualifies as a work of art. Beautifully decorated gers are embroidered with traditional patterns and the interior contains exquisitely carved furniture. Gers are elevated onto wood platforms and offer lake views. The camp has a fine location on spit of land overlooking the lake and the bay.

WESTERN & EASTERN SHORES
Camping

Khövsgöl Nuur offers excellent camping opportunities. There is endless fresh water, plenty of fish, and the hiking is outstanding. On the down side, it often rains in summer and you'll need to hike a bit to get past the rash of ger camps.

There are designated camp sites, marked by yellow signs with a triangle. There are camp sites near the Nature's Door camp, just past Jankhai camp, and two in the bay between Jankhai and Toilogt. These seem to be aimed primarily at Mongolian tourists and groups.

Away from these areas you can pretty much pitch your tent anywhere you want, though try to stay 100m from other gers. You should never camp, wash or build fires within 50m of the shore.

The best camping spots on the western shoreline are anywhere between Jankhai and Ongolog Nuur, 10km north of Toilogt. If you have your own jeep, and want to experience one of the worst roads in Mongolia, the best spot to camp on the eastern shoreline is at Borsog.

Ger Camps

There are several ger camps in stunning locations on the western shore (but only one or two on the east). Nearly all have electricity, running water, flush toilets and showers, though many are dangerously near the shoreline and have little environmental regard for the lake. Most places will offer a lower price if you bring and cook your own food. The majority open only in mid-June.

Several families also accept guests in a guest ger. They are not registered with the park and they don't advertise, but if you ask around you can probably find a family who will let you stay for a couple of US dollars. Note that none of these will have the above-mentioned facilities.

The main group of camps start where the road meets the lake, after descending from Jankhai Davaa. The following are listed south to north:

Khuvsgol Sor (☎ 011-300 150; with/without meals US$30/15) This is the first camp after the pass (Jankhai Davaa). Unlike many others on this part of the lake, this one is hidden in the trees and off the main road, providing some sense of isolation. Quality cabins and bathrooms available.

Nature's Door (☎ 9926 0919; ger without meals T15,000) This popular backpacker hangout has plush cabins, a lodge and excellent Western food options. Most people stay in the gers but for around US$30, the flashy cabins are also an option. Camping (US$3) allows you access to the hot-water showers. The staff speaks English although many travellers report frosty dealings with the management. If booking transport and trips here, do check the prices carefully, and compare with those offered by other operators where possible. Nature's Door is associated with Garage 24 in Khatgal; it's about 5km past Jankhai Davaa.

ourpick Toilogt (☎ 011-460 368; www.hovsgol travel.com; with/without meals US$35/18) Run by the Hovsgol Travel Company, this excellent camp is 5km north of Jankhai, and off the main road to the right. It is situated by a peaceful and lovely lake immediately adjacent to Khövsgöl Nuur. Facilities here are of high standard and the camp offers bikes, boats and horses for hire. Concerts are occasionally organised for guests. The camp has a boat that can transfer you here from Khatgal but you'll need to give advance notice to the Ulaanbaatar office.

Khirvesteg (☎ 9938 8955; with/without meals T25,000/5000) One of the last camps on the western shore, Khirvesteg is 42km north of Khatgal.

Jigleg Camp (dm T2000) Serves as a handy pit stop for trekkers on their way to Renchinlkhumbe (it's right at the Jigleg trail head). The camp is 90km north of Khatgal. Book through Khövsgöl Inn in Khatgal.

KHANKH

Northern Gate Ger Guesthouse (NGGH; per person T10,000) Operated by the people from MS Guesthouse in Khatgal (see p157). To find the guesthouse, walk over the bridge at the northern end of Khankh near the northernmost of the two jetties, turn right and follow the track up the steep hill where you will see the compound.

The **Last Frontier** (GPS: N51° 30.566', E100° 39.296'; per person with meals US$40) ger camp is another option in Khankh.

Eating

There are a few basic shops in Khatgal selling things such as beer, soft drinks, chocolate bars and a limited selection of vegetables. If possible, stock up in Mörön or Ulaanbaatar. The following places are all in Khatgal.

Orgil Restaurant (meals T900; ☺ 9am-9pm) Amid the row of downtown shops and *guanz*. Has an English-language menu that includes cream soup, goulash and vegetable *khuushuur* (fried pancake).

Garage 24 (p157) has a Western-oriented menu that will come as a welcome break after a few days of hard trekking in the wilderness. The English breakfast (T6000) includes bacon, toast, beans and sausage. Lunch and dinner menu items include shepherd's pie (T4800) and pizza (T5500). Give some advance warning as preparations take around an hour.

MS Guesthouse (p157) is another nice place to eat and will occasionally prepare *khorkhog* and authentic Mongolian barbecue for guests and visitors.

Getting There & Away

AIR

In summer MIAT has direct flights from Ulaanbaatar to Khatgal (via Mörön) four days a week; the cost is US$101/192 one way/return. Flights are cut back in the off season, but extra flights might be added for the July peak season. Schedules are continually in flux so check with MIAT in Ulaanbaatar. There are no longer any flights to Khankh.

HITCHING

For lifts from Mörön, hang around the market or the petrol station – and keep asking. Once in Khatgal, most trucks will stop in front of the post office.

From Khatgal, hitching a ride to Jankhai or Toilogt shouldn't be difficult in the summer, but you'll probably end up paying a fair bit for a lift anyway. Ask the guests at the camps for a lift. You should be self-sufficient with camping gear and food.

Hitching around the eastern shore is much more difficult and you could wait for days for a lift to come along.

JEEP

Minivans and jeeps regularly make the trip between Mörön and Khatgal (three hours) for T7000 per person or T70,000 for the jeep.

Inquire at the stand at the northern end of the market in Mörön.

Transport also meets the Ulaanbaatar flight at Mörön airport to take passengers directly to Khatgal. Some jeep owners will try to charge foreigners up to US$50 for the run; local drivers with the 'ХθА' license plate are likely to be fairer. Contact Bata Guesthouse (p151) in Mörön for transport to Khatgal.

A chartered jeep should not cost more than the normal T450 per kilometre. There are plenty of jeeps in Mörön but few in Khatgal, where it is best to ask at the guesthouses. Khatgal is 101km from Mörön over a raised gravel road.

CHANDMAN-ÖNDÖR
ЧАНДМАНЬ-ӨНДӨР

Nestled between pine-clad mountains and consisting almost entirely of log cabins, the village of Chandman-Öndör comes straight out of the pages of a Brothers Grimm fairy tale. The surrounding area is one of wide meadows, alpine forests and wildflowers, making it a good exploratory trip for hardy travellers.

The town **museum** (admission T500) shows off local history. More interesting is the **Alan Goa Museum** (admission T500), housed inside the ger-shaped log cabin. Alan Goa was an ancestor of Chinggis Khaan and revered locally.

Every three years a large **naadam** is held here to honour Alan Goa. The naadam attracts Mongols from Inner Mongolia, Kalmyks, Tuvans and Buriats as well as a host of Khalkh Mongols. The next instalment is in August 2009.

The only place to stay in town is **Alan Goa Töv** (☎ 01382-26535, 9577 6963; per person T5000), a fenced-off grassy area in the centre of town where some gers are set up in summer. Ask for Oyunchimeg or Enkhtuvshin, the local couple that manages the place.

Oyunchimeg can play the *shanz*, a sort of python-skin banjo, and will give lessons for a small fee.

Around 11km from town on the road to Mörön is a painted **statue of Alan Goa** (GPS: N50° 24.994', E100° 58.548'). About 5km west of the statue on the main road to Tsagaan-Uur is a **deer stone**.

Shared jeeps going to Chandman-Öndör (T11,000) occasionally leave from the northern side of the market in Mörön. From Khatgal you need your own jeep. The 85km ride is very rough and takes five to six hours.

NORTHERN MONGOLIA

It's muddy in places and the chances of getting bogged are pretty good (the worst bit is in a valley around 48km out of Khatgal). Don't attempt it after a heavy rain.

In the rainy season, the best way here is by horse; the trek from Khatgal takes four to five days. The route is spectacular, the lone drawback being swarms of flies in the boggy areas on the second day of the trek.

AROUND CHANDMAN-ÖNDÖR

Chandman-Öndör is the jumping-off point for several sites, including the **Bulnai hot springs** (Булнайн Рашаан; per person T5000), about 60km northwest of town. This Soviet-era resort has wood cabins over the springs, some of which reach 48°C.

Heading east of Chandman-Öndör, the road follows the Arig Gol. After 41km you'll pass a row of 13 **shamanic tepees** (GPS: N50° 30.727', E101° 17.478') made from sticks. These represent the 12 years according to the Asian calendar, plus one central **ovoo**. After another 13km you'll spot a **sacred tree** honoured with blue silk scarves. The town of **Tsagaan-Uur**, reached after another 5km, has shops and *guanz*. The bridge east of town washed away in 2006 and the river crossing now is a bit dicey. About 15km east of Tsagaan-Uur you'll spot another large wood **ovoo**.

Around 38km past Tsagaan-Uur (and 97km past Chandman-Öndör) is the **Dayan Derkh Monastery** (GPS: N50° 26.804', E101° 53.328'), set on a beautiful bend of the Uur Gol. The log cabin temple, rebuilt in 2006 over the remains of an older monastery, is home to seven lamas. Another 15km east of the temple is the **Dayan Derkhiin Agui** (Даян Дэрхийн Агуй), a cave considered holy by local Buddhists and shamanists. According to legend, the monastery was founded after the famed shaman Dayan Derkh turned to stone rather than be captured by Chinggis Khaan, whose wife the shaman had stolen. In winter you could reach the cave by vehicle, in summer the only way is by horse (a six-hour return journey). Herders in the area may be able to rent you a horse for T5000. In theory you need a border permit for Tsagaan-Uur and Dayan Derkhiin Agui, although there is rarely anyone around to check.

The road from Dayan Derkh Monastery to **Erdenebulgan** requires two difficult river crossings. A tractor might be available to haul you across (ask at the monastery), but you'll need to pay around T50,000 for this service (the crossings are 20km apart so the tractor needs to follow you).

About 26km downstream from the monastery is the confluence of the Eg and Uur Gols. Head west at the Eg and after about 35km you'll reach the town of Erdenebulgan, which offers basic food and lodging.

Alternatively, continue down the Eg-Uur Gol, a rough and remote journey into northern Bulgan aimag.

In the northeast of the aimag, the area around the Khökh, Arig and Kheven Gols is particularly good for **camping** and **hiking** enthusiasts.

DARKHAD DEPRESSION
ДАРХАДЫН ХӨНДИЙ

About 50km west of Khövsgöl Nuur, behind a wall of mountains, sits a harsh but mystical landscape of prairie, forest, and 300-odd lakes scattered over a wide plain called the Darkhad Depression. The depression is roughly the same size as Khövsgöl Nuur and was also originally formed as a glacial lake.

The difficulty in reaching the region ensures the unique Tsaatan people, who are among the inhabitants of the valleys (see p149), are able to continue their traditional lifestyle – but tourism is rapidly making an impact. Darkhad is one of Mongolia's strongest centres of shamanism.

This is one of the best-watered regions in Mongolia and the lakes are full of white carp and trout. Salmon and huge taimen can also be found in the region.

One definite drawback to visiting the region is the insects that invade the area in summer. Be warned: these little critters have insatiable appetites for foreign skin and will ruin your trip if you are not fully prepared with mosquito nets and repellent.

Permits

To visit Tsagaannuur (and probably Renchinlkhumbe) you will need a border permit, available in Ulaanbaatar. If you didn't get one in Ulaanbaatar you could try to get one in Mörön, although many travellers have been turned away so you're taking your chances. In either case, it's strongly advised that you register in Mörön. Border permits are free and are processed in one to three working days. Delays are common so apply as early as possible. You'll need a map of where you

THE NINTH JEBTZUN DAMBA

It's somewhat ironic that while Mongolia enjoys freedom of religion, its spiritual leader is not allowed to visit the country. The 76-year-old ninth Jebtzun Damba ('Bogd Khan' in Mongolian), who in 1999 was officially recognised as the chief Buddhist monk, currently makes his home in Dharamsala, India.

The debate regarding the status of the Jebtzun Damba has its roots back in 1924. When the eighth Jebtzun Damba died, the newly formed communist government refused to recognise any future 'reincarnations', ensuring their control over Mongolian Buddhism. Even after restrictions were lifted in 1990 the Mongolian government kept its distance from the ninth Jebtzun Damba, who was formally identified by the Dalai Lama in 1991.

The ninth Jebtzun Damba was born in Tibet in 1932 and was accepted as the ninth reincarnation at the age of four. To protect him from Stalin's thugs his identity was kept a secret and he later escaped anonymously to India.

In 1999, at the age of 67, he turned up in Ulaanbaatar, unannounced, having received a tourist visa in Moscow. (One can only imagine the customs form: 'Occupation: Reincarnation of Tibetan deity Vajrapani'!)

It seems all too coincidental that his visit coincided with that of then Chinese president Jiang Zemin, but whether or not the visit was orchestrated from Dharamsala remains pure speculation.

The Jebtzun Damba stayed in Mongolia for 60 days, visiting monasteries in both Ulaanbaatar and the countryside. Although mobbed by adoring fans wherever he went, he was pressured to leave after overstaying his visa.

The Jebtzun Damba still teaches Buddhism in Dharamsala and has among his students several Mongolian monks and nuns. He still hopes to return to Mongolia one day although current restrictions prevent him from doing so. For more information on Mongolia's exiled spiritual leader, see www.jetsundhampa.com.

intend to travel, passport copies and ideally a letter of support from a Mongolian organisation of some sort. In a pinch, guesthouses can arrange the permit in Khatgal through their Mörön contacts.

Additional permits are not needed to visit the Tsaatan camps, but an informal control system is in place to monitor visitors heading in and out of the area. One measure asks visitors to submit their name and travel dates to Tsaatan representatives in Ulaanbaatar. You can do this by emailing reindeer@hovsgol .org. The representative will inform you of the best travel dates and provide travel tips. Please respect the Tsaatan by dropping an email; you'll get a better welcome for it.

Once you reach Tsagaannuur, you are also encouraged to visit the Tsaatan Community & Visitors Center (p162).

Renchinlkhumbe Рэнчинлхүмбэ

Renchinlkhumbe is 42km west of the Jiglegiin Am trailhead on Khövsgöl Nuur, an adventurous two-day journey on foot or horseback. Most travellers heading further into the taiga will rest here for at least one night.

A nice time to visit the town is in mid-June when it hosts the **Blue Valley Awards Festival**, a great time to see traditional horse games and singing competitions.

Renchinlkhumbe hosts an excellent local **naadam** (July 11) complete with 'barrel racing' (horse racing around barrels) and mounted archery events, along with the usual wrestling, horse racing and standing archery.

The local ger camp, **Saridag Inn** (GPS: N51° 06.852′, E099° 40.135′; camping/r/ger T3000/4000/T5000) is run by Khövsgöl Lodge Company. Its hot-water showers and sit-down toilets are legendary. Prices are per person.

Tsagaannuur Цагааннуур

About 40km beyond Renchinlkhumbe is Tsagaannuur, the last stop before the Tsaatan encampments in the taiga.

Tsagaannuur's mid-June **Reindeer Festival** is now becoming an annual event. It includes reindeer polo, reindeer racing, arts and crafts, and a big bonfire. However, bringing the reindeer down to this elevation is definitely not good for their health, and the festival has become somewhat controversial within the community.

INFORMATION

The village is home to the **Tsaatan Community & Visitors Center** (TCVC; http://itgel.org/visitors_center .htm), which provides background info on the Tsaatan and important tips on travel in the area. The TCVC can organise guides, horses and other logistics for trips to the taiga; it's operated by the Tsaatan community with support from the **Itgel Foundation** (www.itgel.org).

It's a good idea to contact the TCVC well ahead of your visit (at least one week) as it can take a few days to organise guides and horses. Call or email the **Itgel office** (☎ 9972 2667; info@itgel.org) in Ulaanbaatar if you plan on using TCVC services. Otherwise, send an email to reindeer@hovsgol.org; you'll receive an auto-reply filled with useful tips on travel in the region.

A **bathhouse** (T1000) is located south of the taiga hotel and post office, next to the lake.

SLEEPING & EATING

The TCVC offers guesthouse accommodation at its new facility in Tsagaannuur. You can also stay with Ganbaa, a local who runs a **guesthouse** (incl breakfast T5000) and restaurant; it's located just north of the post office. A tent and your own food will also suffice.

Around Tsagaannuur

The Tsaatan live in two groups, known as the east *(zuun)* and west *(baruun)* taiga (this is a little confusing as the west taiga is actually south of the east taiga). From Tsagaannuur, it can take four to 12 hours to reach the west taiga by horse (the camps move but are usually closer in the early summer). The UN Development Programme has dropped several **tepee hotels** (per person T5000) in both taigas; these are operated by the Tsaatan themselves. The east taiga is 10km north of the Shishged Gol, which is crossed by ferry. The west taiga has more rugged beauty while the east taiga is easier to visit for travellers without much time.

Once you are in the taiga, you'll need your own tent, camping supplies and 100% DEET to keep the bugs at bay. The TCVC offers meal kits that you can bring to the taiga to be cooked by the Tsaatan families. Once you've left Tsagaannuur, figure on spending around US$30 a day for horses, guides, accommodation and meals.

Plenty of tour operators offer trips to the taiga. A specialist in the area is Dino de Toffol, whose Italian company **Lupo World Trekking**

(www.world-trekking.com) brings small groups into the area and contributes some of the profits back into the community.

Getting There & Away

AIR

There are no flights to Tsagaannuur, save the odd charter flight. Staff from foreign embassies and development agencies in Ulaanbaatar sometimes take a helicopter directly to the Tsaatan encampments and land like some flying saucer from outer space.

HITCHING

Traffic between Mörön and Tsagaannuur is extremely sparse, but if you have your own tent and food, and don't mind waiting for a day or two, something may come along during summer – or it may not.

HORSE

There is really only one way to get to the taiga: by horse. Horses can be hired in Tsagaannuur, otherwise you can take them from Khatgal. A return trip from Khatgal to Tsagaannuur, with a visit to the Tsaatan, will take from 15 to 20 days. You could go from Khatgal to Tsagaannuur on an easy trail in about five days (bypassing Jiglegiin Am), but you would miss Khövsgöl Nuur.

JEEP

By chartered jeep, you can get to Tsagaannuur from Mörön (but rarely from Khatgal) in a bone-crunching 12 to 20 hours, depending on the state of the road. A seat should cost around T20,000, but you'll have to negotiate hard and long for a reasonable price. There are no scheduled public shared jeeps to Tsagaannuur; hiring one would cost around T50,000.

MÖRÖN TO TERKHIIN TSAGAAN NUUR

A popular route out of Khövsgöl is south to Terkhiin Tsagaan Nuur in Arkhangai aimag. This is also an excellent road for cyclists. About 97km southwest of the aimag capital is **Zuun Nuur** (GPS: N49° 03.727′, E99° 31.096′), a large lake and the scenic highlight of the region. There is good camping in the region and in summer many nomadic families live here. An interesting headland jutting into the lake ends with a dramatic stick *ovoo*. The lake is 13km north of Shine-Ider village.

Around 30km south of Shine-Ider, right on the main road, is an area of **standing stones**

and graves (GPS: N48° 45.808′, E99° 23.084′). A further 8km brings you to a scenic pass and the historic **Gelenkhuugiin Suvraga** (GPS: N48° 41.182′, E99° 22.650′), an old stupa built in 1890 by local hero Khainzan Gelenkhuu (1870–1937), who leapt off a 200m cliff with a set of sheepskin wings and flew as if he were some kind of Icarus-incarnate. From the pass it's an easy 19km to Jargalant.

Jargalant is a pretty town near the confluence of the Ider and Khonjil Gols. The *sum* is perhaps most famous as being homeland of a herder named Öndöör Gongor (Tall Gongor) who was 2.63m in height (you can see pictures of him in the local museum).

The **museum** (admission T500; ☾ 8am-7pm) in Jargalant contains old photos, stuffed animals and religious objects. Two of the rooms are not lit so bring a torch (flashlight). It's run by a local elder named Shagdarsuren who will proudly show off some of his wood craft and demonstrate the use of hand-powered drills and other tools. The other attraction in town is **Jargalantiin Dugan** (also called Dashbijeliin Süm), an old monastery that dates back to 1890. It's run-down and boarded up but you could still have a look around.

Jargalant has three basic but clean hotels, each offering rooms for around T5000. The most established is the Deed Khonkh Hotel, which also contains the local bar (open 9am to midnight). More upscale is the **Jargal Jiguur** (☎ 011-450 093; admin@ajnewtour.mn; GPS: N48° 33.615′, E99° 22.061′; with/without meals US$42/16, shower US$2), a ger camp 3km east of town (meals are US$6 to US$8). The highlight of the camp is a mineral spring pool (you can see the natural pool across the river, just follow the pipes).

About 6km east of town are several burial mounds, including one with a tree growing from it. It's another 70km to the shores of Terkhiin Tsagaan Nuur.

NORTHERN MONGOLIA

Eastern Mongolia

Eastern Mongolia is where heaven and earth fuse into one part – a blank slate of blue sky colliding with an equally empty sea of yellow grass. The occasional wooden shack or ger reminds you that humans do inhabit this enormous landscape, but for the most part it's an unspoilt amphitheatre of bounding gazelle, scurrying marmots and jeep tracks that squiggle endlessly into the distance.

Biologists fawn over the region, touting it as one of the world's last great unharmed grassland ecosystems – imagine the scenery from *Dances with Wolves*. Yet, Mongolian politicians have their own vision of Manifest Destiny and threaten the region with ill-planned urban-development schemes. Get there before the grassland disappears.

Besides the grasslands, the major feature of the region is the Khan Khentii mountains. This was the homeland of Temujin, the embattled boy who grew up to become Chinggis Khaan. A number of sites recall his legacy – the highlight being Dadal, a storybook village of log cabins that claims to be the birthplace of the great khaan. In the southeast of the region, Dariganga remains an inspiring getaway. This volcanic area is filled with craters, lava tubes, ancient stone figures and legendary stories about horse bandits that harassed the Chinese.

Most travellers write off the east because it's not on the way to anywhere and lacks the sex appeal of the Gobi. This is a shame as it's one of the most beautiful areas of the country and relatively easy to get around by jeep. Yet it's something of a blessing for those travellers who want to leave the tourist buses behind and experience an almost untouched landscape.

HIGHLIGHTS

- Get on the Chinggis Khaan trail by working your way from his coronation site at **Khökh Nuur** (p171) to his childhood stomping grounds in **Dadal** (p173)

- Hire some sturdy horses and set off on an expedition to holy **Burkhan Khalduun** (p172), the hill sacred to Chinggis Khaan as described in *The Secret History of the Mongols*

- Climb the sacred **Shiliin Bogd Uul** (p183) to restore your soul and then tour the area around **Dariganga** (p182), rich in cultural relics and eerie landscapes

- Travel across the empty steppes to the war memorials at **Khalkhiin Gol** (Khalkhiin River; p179) and then spot wildlife, including moose and huge herds of gazelle, at nearby **Nömrög Strictly Protected Area** (p174)

- POPULATION: 195,100
- AREA: 287,500 SQ KM

History

he Tamtsagbulag Neolithic site in Dornod, ctive more than 4000 years ago, is proof that griculture predated nomadic pastoralism on ne eastern steppes. But it was the Kitan, a Manchurian tribal confederation, who made ne first big impression on the region, building orts and farming communities in the 10th cen-ary, including Kherlen Bar Khot in Dornod.

Another Manchu tribe, the Jurchen, de-osed the Kitan in the early 12th century, enamed itself the Jin, and returned eastern Mongolia to its warring ways. It wasn't until Chinggis Khaan united the fractured clans in 206 that peace took over.

It was from Avarga (modern Delgerkhaan) hat Chinggis launched expeditions south to-vards China. When the capital was moved o Karakorum in 1220 the region withdrew nto obscurity. It wasn't until 1939 that east-rn Mongolia was again in the headlines, this ime as a battlefield between Japanese and oviet forces. Heavy losses forced the Japanese nilitary machine south, but the Khalkh Gol egion is still littered with battle scars from he brief campaign.

The discovery of zinc and oil in the region n the 1990s brought the promise of develop-nent. Uranium is also found in the north-ast. However, resources have so far proven elatively small and whatever profits have een made have so far failed to stimulate the ocal economy.

Climate

Eastern Mongolia's climate and landscape has nore in common with northeastern China han it does with Central Asia. Temperature xtremes are less severe and winds less vio-ent than in the west. While the Khan Khentii nountains get a lot of rain in the summer, per-year precipitation on the steppes is around 250mm. Winter daytime temperatures fall to ninus 20°C but skies are usually blue.

Getting There & Away

A paved road between Ulaanbaatar and Öndörkhaan is nearly complete, allowing or a relatively hassle-free entry into the re-gion. Decent dirt roads connect other areas, although the far north can get boggy after heavy rains.

Vehicles for Öndörkhaan depart from Ulaanbaatar's Naran Tuul jeep station. You can also get a ride with vehicles from Ulaanbaatar that go through Öndörkhaan on their way to Baruun-Urt and Choibalsan. Another route into the region is through northern Khentii – daily minivans from Naran Tuul travel to Dadal via Ömnödelger and Binder. During the rainy season this trip can take more than 25 hours.

With your own vehicle, it's possible to drive to eastern Mongolia from the Gobi. You could even enter from Russia at the Ereentsav–Solovyevsk border crossing in Dornod aimag. If you are in Selenge aimag, the only direct way into Khentii is on foot or horseback; jeep travellers will need to go via Ulaanbaatar.

Getting Around

Public transport can get you to some places of interest, including Dadal and Dariganga. But if you want to maximise your time and see what the region really has to offer you'll need your own vehicle, either hired from Ulaanbaatar or from one of the aimag capitals. Make sure your guide and driver have some experience in the region, as this will make navigation easier (a GPS is a handy alternative). The best way to explore northern Khentii, including the Khan Khentii Strictly Protected Area, is on horse-back – both Batshireet and Dadal are great places to launch an expedition. The train that connects Choibalsan and Chuluunkhoroot is something of an adventure, but not that useful for serious exploration – you're better off with your own vehicle in the region.

KHENTII ХЭНТИЙ

pop 68,100 / area 82,000 sq km

Khentii is Chinggis Khaan territory. The great man grew up here, established his em-pire on its grasslands and, from Delgerkhaan, launched his military machine to the heart of Asia. As a nomad empire the khaans left few physical reminders of their existence, but with a jeep, a copy of *The Secret History of the Mongols* and a GPS unit you could launch your own expedition to scour the land for clues to their past. So far researchers have identified more than 50 historical sites relat-ing to Chinggis Khaan's life.

The aimag is named for the Khentii Nuruu (Khentii Mountain Range), which covers the northwestern corner of the aimag and is part of the giant 1.2-million-hectare Khan Khentii Strictly Protected Area (most of which is in

lonelyplanet.com

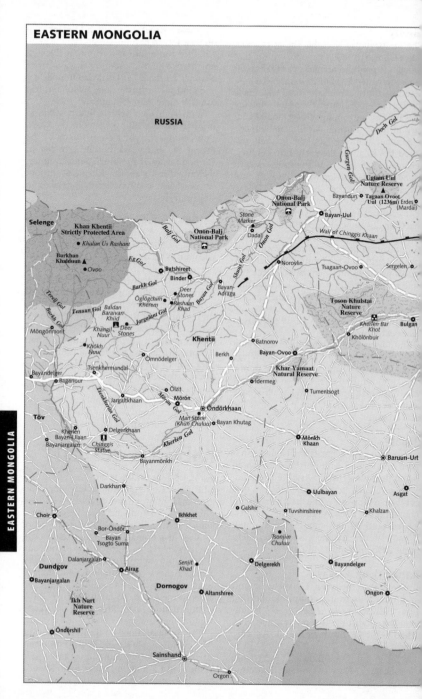

EASTERN MONGOLIA

RUSSIA

Doch Gol

Gurgen Gol

**Uglain Uul
Nature Reserve**

Bayandun ● ● Tagaan Ovoot
Uul (1236m) Erdes
(Mardai)

Selenge

**Khan Khentii
Strictly Protected Area**

● *Khalun Us Rashant*

**Burkhan
Khalduun** ▲
● *Ovoo*

Balj Gol

Eg Gol

Batshireet ●
Binder ●

Barkh Gol

*Öglögchiin
Kherem*

● *Deer
Stones*

● *Rashaan
Khad*

**Onon-Balj
National Park**

*Stone
Marker*

Dadal
●

**Onon-Balj
National Park**

Bayan-
Adraga

Bayan Gol

Shuus Gol

Onon Gol

**Onon-Balj
National Park**

● Norovlin

● **Bayan-Uul**

Wall of Chinggis Khaan

Tsagaan-Ovoo ●

Sergelen ●

**Toson Khulstai
Nature
Reserve**

*Kherlen Bar
Khot*

● **Bulgan**

Terelj Gol

Bychk Gol

Tenuun Gol

**Baldan
Baraivan
Khiid**

*Khangil
Nuur*

*Deer
Stones*

Jargalant Gol

Khentii

Khölönbuir
●

● Möngönmorit

● *Khökh
Nuur*

Tsenkhermandal ●

Ömnödelger ●

● Batnorov

Berkh ●

Bayan-Ovoo ●

**Khar Yamaat
Natural Reserve**

Töv

● Bayandelger

● Baganuur

Tsenkherlen Gol

Jargaltkhaan ●

Mörön Gol

Ölzit ●

Mörön ●

● **Öndörkhaan**

● Idermeg

● Tümentsogt

Kherlen ●
Bayan-Ulaan ●

● Bayanjargalan

*Chinggis
Statue*

Delgerkhaan

*Man Stone
(Khün Chuluu)* ● Bayan Khutag

Kherlen Gol

● **Mönkh
Khaan**

◉ **Baruun-Urt**

Bayanmönkh ●

Darkhan ●

● Uulbayan

Asgat
●

Choir ●

Bor-Öndör ●

Bayan
Tsogto Suma

● Ikhkhet

● Galshir

● Tuvshinshiree

Khalzan
●

Dundgov

Dalanjargalan ●

● **Airag**

*Senjit
Khad*

● Delgerekh

● **Bayandelger**

● Bayanjargalan

Dornogov

● Altanshiree

*Tsonjin
Chuluu*

Ongon ●

**Ikh Nart
Nature
Reserve**

● Öndörshil

Sainshand ◉

Orgon ●

EASTERN MONGOLIA

the adjoining Töv aimag). Although none of the peaks is over 2000m, these mountains are well watered and heavily forested. The thickets provide a home for wildlife and you stand a good chance at seeing deer and elk. Marmots are ubiquitous. The lush scenery, however, can make jeep travel arduous business – vehicles get bogged and in some areas the best way forward is on the back of a horse.

National Parks

Khan Khentii Strictly Protected Area (1.2 million hectares) Mostly in Töv aimag, the strictly protected area includes the northwest corner of Khentii, protecting taiga, steppe and the sacred mountain Burkhan Khalduun.

Onon-Balj National Park (415,752 hectares) Protects taiga and steppe along the Mongolia–Russia border. It's divided into two parts; part A is west of Dadal and Part B covers the area to the northeast.

ÖNDÖRKHAAN ӨНДӨРХААН

☎ 01562 / pop 15,200 / elev 1027m

With tree-lined streets, a growing number of Chinggis Khaan monuments and a small collection of well-preserved 18th-century buildings, Öndörkhaan (High King) is eastern Mongolia's most intriguing aimag capital. The surrounding area is barren steppe, but the Kherlen Gol flows through the southern part of Öndörkhaan, providing a fishing hole for locals and riverside campsites for tourists. Most of the residents live in wooden buildings, so gers are relatively few.

Öndörkhaan is a useful pit stop on the way to the sights in Dornod or Sükhbaatar, but you don't need to come here if you're exploring northern Khentii. The most interesting route to Dadal is not from the aimag capital but along the back roads from Tsenkhermandal.

Information

Internet café (☎ 23695; per hr T680; ☒ 9am-10pm Mon-Fri, 11am-5pm Sat & Sun) In the Telecom office.

Mongol Shuudan Bank (☎ 23091) Changes dollars and offers cash advances on Visa. Located one building west of the Telecom office.

Telecom office (☎ 22125; ☒ 24hr) On the eastern end of the main road; the post office is also located here.

Sights

The **Ethnography Museum** (☎ 22187; admission T1000, photos T1000; ☒ 9am-1pm & 2-6pm Tue-Sat), next to the City Hall, is housed inside the 18th-century home of the Tsetseg Khaan, a

Mongolian prince who governed most of eastern Mongolia during the Manchu reign. On building holds a portrait of the last Tsetse Khaan, painted in 1923. Other buildings contain ethnic costumes, Mongolian toys and some religious artefacts, such as statues and *thangka* (scroll paintings). On the museum grounds is a ceremonial ger with delicate carved wood furnishing and ornaments. It usually locked but you could ask the watch man to let you have a look inside.

The small **Aimag Museum** (☎ 23834; admissio T1000; ☒ 9am-1pm & 2-6pm Tue-Sat), north of th park, contains a mastodon tusk, a protocera ops skull, some Chinggis Khaan–era armou and the usual array of stuffed animals, inclu ing a saluting bear.

Shadavdarjaliin Khiid, in the western pa of town near the Sports Palace, is a livel place with a dozen or so monks. The origin monastery in this area was built in 1660 an housed the first Buddhist philosophy scho in Mongolia. At its peak, the monastery wa home to more than 1000 monks. In the sprin of 1938, the Stalinist purge reached Khent and the monks were all arrested. The build ings remained standing until the 1950s, whe they were torn down.

A well-preserved Turkic-era **balbal** (GPS: N4 16.722′, E110° 36.098′) is 7km west of Öndörkhaar past the airport. The squat-figured statu covered in blue silk *hadak* (ritual scarves has a disproportionately large head with pro nounced eyebrows and deep-set eyes. His lon hair is curled behind his ears, an unusual fea ture for this type of statue. Locals refer to th statue as 'Gelen', a religious title.

With Öndörkhaan being the capital c Chinggis Khaan's old stomping ground: local authorities have put much effort i recent years towards elevating the conquer or's cult status. Look out for a **bronze statue c Chinggis** seated on his horse; it's just outsid the Ethnography Museum. The statue wa commissioned as part of the celebrations t mark 800 years of statehood, in 2006. Nearby opposite Government House, is a **stone statu of Chinggis**.

The omnipresence of the great khaan i complete with **Chinggis Khaan garden**, at th west end of Central Park. The site feature a monument engraved with the image of ar approaching Mongol horde. It also contain a list of the Mongol khaans with the date that they ruled.

Sleeping

CAMPING

If you want to camp, head south past the wrestling stadium, and walk along the Kherlen Gol to the west until you've found a quiet spot.

HOTELS

Jargalan Hotel (☎ 23722, 9666 8694; dm T5000, half-lux T15,000, lux T20,000) Once a government guest-house, this place limps along as a hotel. Rooms are falling apart and hot water comes in a ther-mos; some have a TV, although it shows just one channel. If the hotel is empty the manager is open to bargaining. The entrance is around the back of Government House.

Khuvchin Jonon (☎ 23845, 9956 2222; r per per-son T10,000, half-lux per person T15,000, lux per person T25,000) About 350m north of Government House, this newly constructed hotel of-fers 17 comfortable rooms, and is the best Öndörkhaan has to offer. It's clean and the staff runs a tight ship. Standard rooms have a shared bathroom but other rooms have private bathroom and shower. Breakfast is included in the price and laundry services are available.

Erdes Hotel (☎ 23007; dm US$10, half-lux per person US$18, lux US$25) This overpriced Soviet dino-saur with its grumpy staff might be your only option, as hotel rooms are scarce in Öndörkhaan. The standard rooms are pretty dishevelled and use a shared bathroom so you might want to splash out on a half-lux room. It's on the main road, 150m west of the Telecom office.

Eating & Drinking

Nunga Café (☎ 9905 3505; Temujiidiin Gudamj; meals T1000-2000; ☯ 9am-7pm Mon-Sat) Smart and col-ourful, this friendly café is a popular busi-ness lunch spot. Despite the modern look of the place, the menu is a little bland, offer-ing the usual Mongolian meat-based dishes, soups and salads. But the owner speaks English and might be able to accommodate special requests.

Tiger Café (☎ 9956 9191; meals T1500-2000; ☯ 9am-9pm) Owned by the former Khentii governor, this café is one of the better places in town. Meals are served in sizzling iron dishes shaped like a cow, although promises of fried fish on the menu are unfounded. It's on the 2nd floor of a distinctive green build-ing on the main street.

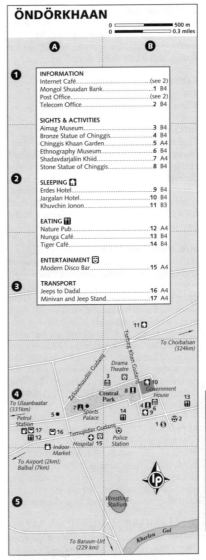

ÖNDÖRKHAAN

INFORMATION
Internet Café.............................(see 2)
Mongol Shuudan Bank.....................1 B4
Post Office.................................(see 2)
Telecom Office..........................2 B4

SIGHTS & ACTIVITIES
Aimag Museum...........................3 B4
Bronze Statue of Chinggis.............4 B4
Chinggis Khaan Garden................5 A4
Ethnography Museum...................6 B4
Shadavdarjaliin Khiid..................7 A4
Stone Statue of Chinggis..............8 B4

SLEEPING
Erdes Hotel...............................9 B4
Jargalan Hotel..........................10 B4
Khuvchin Jonon........................11 B3

EATING
Nature Pub..............................12 A4
Nunga Café..............................13 B4
Tiger Café...............................14 B4

ENTERTAINMENT
Modern Disco Bar......................15 A4

TRANSPORT
Jeeps to Dadal..........................16 A4
Minivan and Jeep Stand...............17 A4

Nature Pub (☎ 9909 3701; Temujiidiin Gudamj; meals T2500-3800; ☯ noon-midnight) Chinggis Khaan would feel quite at home downing pints in this rustic restaurant and pub. The red exterior leads into a dimly lit hall decorated with stretched goat skins, wolf traps and compound bows. The kitchen is probably the best in town, offering up a variety of dishes from pork steaks to fish.

Entertainment

Modern Disco Bar (Temujiidiin Gudamj; ☼ 9am-midnight)
By day it's a musty little café and by night
a dark drinking den with a scratchy sound
system and sticky dance floor.

Getting There & Away

AIR

There are no flights to Öndörkhaan.

HITCHING

Öndörkhaan is the gateway for eastern
Mongolia, so all vehicles heading to Dornod
aimag and Sükhbaatar aimag will come
through here. Getting a lift to Ulaanbaatar,
Choibalsan and Baruun-Urt is comparatively easy. Rather than waiting on the road
for a lift, it's better to ask the drivers at the
jeep stands.

BUS, MINIVAN & JEEP

Daily buses journeying between Ulaanbaatar
and Choibalsan or Baruun-Urt make a pit
stop in Öndörkhaan. Seats are limited and
there is really no way to book in advance, but
when the buses roll through you could check
to see if space is available.

Daily jeeps and minivans go between
Ulaanbaatar and Öndörkhaan (T12,000, five
hours, 331km), most of which is paved. The
jeep stand, which is about 450m west of the
park, also has vehicles to Choibalsan (T12,000,
eight hours, 324km) and Baruun-Urt (T8000,
five hours, 229km).

Postal trucks run to Dadal (T8820) on
Monday and Thursday, to Delgerkhaan
(T4410) on Friday, to Binder (T6170) on
Tuesday and to Batshireet (T6600) on
Wednesday; they usually leave in the early
morning. You could hire your own jeep at the
stand, but many private cars also seem to hang
around on the main street, near the market.

DELGERKHAAN ДЭЛГЭРХААН

Despite the historical significance of the area,
there's little to actually see in Delgerkhaan,
the *sum* (region) capital. Veering off the
Ulaanbaatar–Öndörkhaan paved road makes
it even less attractive these days, but if you
have a special interest in Chinggis Khaan then
coming makes sense.

Locals, and some historians, claim that
Avarga, not Karakorum, was the first capital
of the Mongol empire. The ancient tent-city
was located on a 20km-wide plain, Khödöö

Aral (Countryside Island), so named because the area is encircled by the Kherler
and Tsenkheriin Gols.

Sights

The main monument in the area is the **Chinggis
Statue** (GPS: N47° 06.157', E109° 09.356'), 13km south of
Delgerkhaan village. It was built in 1990 under
the sponsorship of Unesco, to commemorate
the 750th anniversary of the writing of *The
Secret History of the Mongols*. The symbols
on the side of the statue are the brands used
by about 300 different clans in the area for
marking their livestock.

One kilometre east of the statue is the **Avarga
Toson Mineral Spring**, from which Ögedei Khaan
drank and was cured of a serious stomach
ailment. The spring is covered by an *ovoo*
(a shamanistic collection of stones), but you
can fill your water bottles at a pump house
near the site.

Japanese researchers claim that foundations
of buildings from **Avarga** are located under
ground, between the statue and the spring.
So far little has been uncovered. It's unlikely
that there would be much to find anyway, as
the capital of Chinggis Khaan was made up
mainly of felt gers.

Sleeping

CAMPING

You can camp anywhere near the lake, though
it would help to have your own transport.

GER CAMPS

Avarga Resort (per person/half-lux/lux T5800/9000/11,500)
This is the place to come if you have a burning
desire to join Mongolian families on holiday.
The rather run-down resort offers hot-water
bathrooms or you could bury yourself in
mud on the shores of the lake. The two small
lakes behind the resort are said to contain
curative properties. The resort is 4km west
of Delgerkhaan.

Khödöö Aral (☎ 011-57 855, 9915 8698; per person with/without food US$24/10) Run by Ikh Zasag
University, it's not a particularly attractive ger
camp, but it does have hot showers. It's 7km
west of the Avarga Resort.

Getting There & Around

Delgerkhaan is close to the regional centres of
Öndörkhaan (124km) and Baganuur (95km).
If you are hitching, cars from Ulaanbaatar
turn off the main road at the bridge over the

Kherlen Gol, 16km south of Baganuur. The only public transport here is the Friday postal truck from Öndörkhaan (T4400). You *might* be able to hire a jeep or motorbike to see the local sights around Delgerkhaan.

KHÖKH NUUR ХӨХ НУУР

According to *The Secret History of the Mongols*, it was at **Khökh Nuur** (Blue Lake; GPS: N48° 01.150′, E108° 56.450′) that Temujin first proclaimed himself a khaan of the Mongol tribe. It's a great place for a coronation site; a beautiful lake at the foot of what is called Heart-Shaped Mountain.

The lake is about 35km northwest of Tsenkhermandal (which is just north of the Ulaanbaatar–Öndörkhaan road). As you approach the lake a caretaker from the nearby ger camp demands a fee of T1000, claiming it's a protected area (it's not). The only other drawback is the flies that invade the place in midsummer.

You'll need your own transport and a driver who knows where it is. Someone from nearby Tsenkhermandal might take you there by jeep or motorcycle. The area is sometimes labelled Khar Zurkhen (Black Heart) on maps, which refers to a mountain behind the lake.

The **Khökh Nuur Ger Camp** (☎ 9911 2825; per person US$25) has popped up right by the lake; it's the only place to stay in the area although you can camp pretty much anywhere (campers can use the hot shower for T3500). The camp has added some wood statues of the Mongol khaans, each with a barely legible plaque describing their deeds.

A further 49km away is the larger lake of Khangil Nuur (GPS: N48° 08.619′, E109° 22.132′).

BALDAN BARAIVAN KHIID БАЛДАН БАРАЙВАН ХИЙД

This **monastery** (GPS: N48° 11.910′, E109° 25.840′; admission T2000) in Ömnödelger *sum* was first built in 1700. At its peak it was one of the three largest monasteries in Mongolia and home to 5000 lamas. It was destroyed by communist thugs in the 1930s and by fire in the 1970s. Now only ruins remain, but impressive ruins they are. Near the monastery is the Eej (Mother) Cave, which acts a purifying place for anyone who passes through it.

The US-based **Cultural Restoration Tourism Project** (CRTP; www.crtp.net) made attempts to restore the monastery in the early 2000s (the wood posts in the temple are their work). Progress was halted in 2005 when local au-

thorities seized the site in an attempt to establish a private ger camp. CRTP was sadly run out of town but no such camp was ever built and neglect has left the fragile monastery in danger of further rot. A *manach* (watchman) will ask for T2000 to visit the site; paying this fee would debilitate future efforts to re-establish ecotourism in the area. You can take pictures from afar or explore the nearby hills on foot.

The road to the monastery heads north from Khangil Nuur and goes straight over the hills, it is about 9km. A flatter but more circuitous route goes northeast from Khangil Nuur. The area is perfect for camping but the closest place to stay is the **Bayangol Ger Camp** (☎ 011-451 016, 9918 3067; GPS: N46° 09.621′, E105° 45.590′; with/without food US$30/15), 15km to the west.

About 17km past the monastery, on the way to Binder, are two **deer stones** (GPS: N48° 11.916′, E109° 35.712′).

ÖGLÖGCHIIN KHEREM ӨГЛӨГЧИЙН ХЭРЭМ

Literally 'Almsgivers Wall', but also known as 'Chinggis Khaan's Castle' or 'Red Rock', this 3.2km-long **stone wall** (GPS: N48° 24.443′, E110° 11.812′), believed to date from the 8th century, stretches around a rocky slope in Binder *sum*. It was once thought to be a defensive work or a game preserve, but recent archaeological digs by a Mongolian-American research team have identified at least 60 ancient graves within the walls, indicating that it may have been a royal cemetery. As you walk inside the grounds you may see small red signs, marking the location of graves excavated in 2002. The nearby wooden cabins used by the researchers now lie dormant. The site is 8km west of the road to Binder.

Close to the turn-off to Öglögchiin Kherem is **Rashaan Khad** (GPS: N48° 22.766′, E110° 17.950′), a huge rock with 20 different types of (barely discernable) script carved upon it. About 2km past the turn-off towards Binder are more **deer stones** (GPS: N48° 25.098′, E110° 17.825′).

BINDER & BATSHIREET БИНДЭР & БАТШИРЭЭТ

At the confluence of the Khurkh and Onon Gols, the village of Binder is a good place to rest on your way to or from Dadal. There are a couple of cafés, a **ger camp** (with food US$20) 7km from the village and a small **Chinggis Khaan monument** 2km east of the village. If you are

THE GREAT TABOO

For the Mongols, disposing of a corpse has always been tricky business. According to steppe tradition, a person was left exposed to the elements to be consumed by wild animals. In some cases a person would be buried but the grave left unmarked to thwart grave robbers, who would not only steal possessions but also disturb the remains, thus destroying the soul of the deceased.

Thus when Chinggis Khaan died in 1227 his inner circle went to extraordinary lengths to ensure secrecy of his grave. According to lore, a burial guard slew everyone en route to the grave. Then, at the grave site, thousands of horses were raced over the tomb to conceal its location. (Another theory states that a river was temporarily diverted and Chinggis was buried in the riverbed.) The burial guard was then killed by 800 soldiers who themselves were massacred upon their return to the capital. Still today, the Mongols consider disturbing the grave of Chinggis to be 'The Great Taboo', an act that would invite natural calamity.

Flying in the face of local beliefs, various expeditions, often with Japanese and American assistance and technology, have attempted to locate the grave. The attraction is obvious – the tomb may contain millions, if not billions of dollars worth of gold, silver, precious stones and other priceless religious artefacts (as well as many women, men and horses who were buried alive with the khaan). But with so few clues, the teams are left to search for the proverbial needle in the haystack. The chances of digging in the right spot seem infinitely remote.

A Japanese team spent three years probing Khödöö Aral (near modern Delgerkhaan) before giving up, none the wiser. The Americans, working mainly at Öglögchiin Kherem near Binder, were forced to end their search in 2003 after a storm of protest by a retired politician native to the area.

Neither team achieved any earth-shattering results. On the contrary, the search only seemed to fuel local resentment of foreign archaeologists, not to mention waste millions of dollars that could otherwise have been spent on regional development. With these failures, the search has cooled for the moment, giving Chinggis Khaan's soul a chance to momentarily rest in peace.

travelling onto Dadal you'll need to cross the Onon Gol, just north of town. When the river is high locals will offer to tow you across for T7000 with a tractor.

Batshireet, 45km northwest, is worth the detour for some excellent camping, fishing and horse-riding opportunities. From this small Buriat community of 3000 souls you can follow the Eg Gol to the Onon and trek back to Binder. More challenging trails lead west towards the Khan Khentii Strictly Protected Area and Burkhan Khalduun.

The town has a couple of basic hotels, including **Altan Endert** (per person T10,000) located near the Telecom office. It can arrange horses for T5000 per day. There is fine camping in Batshireet; the best spots are 7km north of town on the Onon Gol. Camping is also allowed behind the Protected Areas office. The information officer, Tsetsegmaa, can also arrange horses for a pack trip. She has accommodation in her home for T3000 per night.

Because it's near Russia, you'll need a permit for Batshireet from the Border Protection Office in Ulaanbaatar. Expect a visit from the police, who will want to see

your permit, original passport and trekking route. If you've come without a permit you can probably buy one for T2000 at the police office.

BURKHAN KHALDUUN
БУРХАН ХАЛДУУН

This remote mountain, known as God's Hill in the Khan Khentii Strictly Protected Area is one of the sites mooted as the burial place of Chinggis Khaan. More than 800 burial sites have been found in the region, though the main tomb is yet to be found. Whether or not Chinggis was buried here, *The Secret History of the Mongols* does describe how the khaan hid here as a young man and later returned to give praise to the mountain and give thanks for his successes.

Because of its auspicious connections Mongolians climb the mountain, which is topped with many **ovoo** (GPS: N48° 45.430', E109° 00.300'), to gain strength and good luck. The hill itself is in a very remote location. To get there you'll need to head to Möngönmorit in Töv, and then travel north along the Kherlen Gol.

Around 22km due north of Burkhan Khalduun (as the falcon flies) is **Khalun Us Rashant** (Hot Springs; GPS: N48° 57.206', E109° 00.217'). The site has more than a dozen hot springs, a collection of log bathhouses and a small Buddhist temple (built in honour of Zanabazar who frequented the site). You can also reach the area by horse from Batshireet (it's possible to drive there in winter when the ground freezes).

DADAL ДАДАЛ

As written in *The Secret History of the Mongols,* it is now generally accepted that the great Chinggis was born at the junction of the Onon and Balj Gols (though his date of birth is still subject to great conjecture). The assumed spot is in Dadal *sum,* near the town of the same name.

Dadal is a gorgeous area of lakes, rivers, forests and log huts (very few people live in gers), reminiscent of Siberia, which is only 25km to the north. Even if you are not a Chinggisphile, there is no shortage of scenery to admire and hike around in. It wouldn't be hard to stay here a few days (which may be necessary anyway unless you have rented a jeep). The downside is that it often rains here in summer.

The 415,752-hectare **Onon-Balj National Park**, extending north from the village towards Russia, offers enticing camping spots, fishing holes and chances for spotting wildlife. Buy your national park ticket (T3000) in the Government House.

Information

Dadal is in a sensitive border area so it would be wise to register with the police (T2000). If you are heading any further out of town, it would also be a good idea to register with the border guards, on the western side of Dadal. Don't expect anyone to speak English. At the time of writing there were plans to build a tourist information centre in town.

Sights

About 3.5km north of Dadal village is a collection of hills known as **Deluun Boldog**. On top of one of the hills is a **stone marker** (GPS: N49° 03.158', E111° 38.590'), built in 1990 to commemorate the 750th anniversary of the writing of *The Secret History of the Mongols*. The inscription says that Chinggis Khaan was born here in 1162. Some historians may not be entirely convinced about the exact date or location of

his birth, but it's a great place to come into the world: the scenery and hiking around the valleys and forests are superb.

There's a more impressive **Chinggis Khaan Statue** in the Gurvan Nuur camp, built in 1962 to commemorate the 800th anniversary of Chinggis' birth. The monument was built at the height of the communist era and after it was complete the president purged the folks who built it. Somehow the monument itself was allowed to stand.

About 2.2km west of Deluun Boldog is the **Khajuu Bulag** (GPS: N49° 02.767', E111° 36.865') mineral water springs, where the great man once drank. Take your water bottles and fill them to the brim because this is the freshest (flowing) spring water you will ever taste. You could also hike up into the hills behind town, where there is a large **ovoo**.

For an offbeat adventure, you could drop by the home of **Zundoi Davag**, an old hunter who has built a private museum filled with the animals he has trapped over the years. Zundoi will be happy to show you his trophies and regale you with hunting stories, if you can find him. He will also let you practise shooting his bow and arrow. His camp moves with the seasons but a local should be able to take you there on horseback.

Activities

There are several **hiking** and **horse-riding** routes out of Dadal. Locals recommend the 30km hike to the junction of the Onon and Balj Gols, or the 45km trek further along the Onon Gol to the gorge at the confluence of the Onon and Agats Gols. You'll need to inform the border patrol of your itinerary and it would be wise to take a guide. Ask at the ger camps or track down Dorjsuren, who runs the guesthouse (p174).

There is good **fishing** in the area but permits are almost impossible to get unless you have gone through a licensed tour operator. Some locals get away with fishing illegally but if you get caught there could be hell to pay.

Sleeping
CAMPING

This is perfect camping country, so if you have your own tent and food supplies there is no need to stay in a hotel or ger camp. Just find a secluded spot away from the village and set up camp.

GER CAMPS & RESORTS

Khongor's Ger Camp (per person T5000) Next to the Naadam Stadium, this new place has basic accommodation and meals.

Chinggisiin Gurvan Nuur (Three Lakes; GPS: N49° 02.005′, E111° 39.267′; per person T10,000, hot shower T1000) This resort has a nice location on the shore of a lake about 2km from Dadal village. Meals are T1500. There are no gers. A good hiking trail starts from the back of the camp.

Onon (bed & 3 meals around US$30) Between Gurvan Nuur and the village, by the monastery, is this ger camp, which opens in summer when there is demand, which isn't often.

GUESTHOUSES

our pick **Guesthouse** (GPS: N49° 01.280′, E111° 38.562′; per person about T6000) Dorjsuren, a retired maths teacher, runs a hostel next to his home. The classic Buriat-style lodge includes a toilet and hot-water shower block (a shower costs T1000). There's a cast-iron stove for cooking and Dorjsuren can hunt down bread, eggs, milk, cream and vegetables. It is a 10-minute walk southeast of the centre, across the river, but there is no sign, so ask for directions from the Telecom office. Dorjsuren can arrange a variety of activities in the area.

Eating

Dadal has a few *guanz* (canteens/restaurants) that serve up hot soup and goulash, the best of which is probably **Buren Khaan Tsainy Gazar** (meals T1000-2000).

Getting There & Away

JEEP

One minivan or jeep a day usually goes to Ulaanbaatar (T22,000, 515km). The journey takes anywhere from 12 hours up to 35 hours after heavy rains.

A postal truck travels from Öndörkhaan (T8820) every Monday and Thursday morning at around 8.30am. Most traffic from Öndörkhaan takes the road via Norovlin. There are few vehicles for hire in Dadal, but if you ask around the shops something should be available. Expect to pay T450 per kilometre.

For travel from Dadal to Öndörkhaan or Dornod (but not Binder) you'll need to cross the Onon Gol at a lone bridge crossing (GPS: N48° 50.403′, E111° 38.746′). Dadal is 254km north by northeast of Öndörkhaan and 301km northwest of Choibalsan.

DORNOD ДОРНОД

pop 74,600 / area 123,500 sq km

One of Mongolia's most stunning landscapes, Dornod is pure steppe, with pancake-flat grasslands in all directions. There are few roads, towns or fences, making this an important ecological zone and habitat for white-tailed gazelle, which can outrun even the best jeep driver.

Dornod, which means 'east', has a number of worthy attractions, geared for both historians and ecotourists. These include Buir Nuur and Khalkhiin Gol, both the scenes of fierce fighting against the Japanese; Khökh Nuur, the lowest point in the country; and some lovely nature reserves. If you've already visited other more popular areas of Mongolia, Dornod offers scope for some challenging, offbeat exploration.

The northern *sums* of Bayan-Uul, Bayandun and Dashbalbar are home to the Buriats, who still practise shamanism. If you ask around you may be able to meet a shaman or, if you are lucky, watch a shamanist ceremony in these areas.

National Parks

Thankfully, the authorities have been convinced that the area's fragile environment and the endangered fauna and flora need to be conserved. Dornod aimag is currently the base of a multimillion-dollar environmental-protection project. This massive project involves researching everything from forest fires to field mice in an attempt to protect one of the world's last undisturbed grasslands. The Strictly Protected Areas (SPA) of the aimag include the following:

Dornod Mongol (570,374 hectares) Holds one of the last great plain ecosystems on earth, protecting seas of feather-grass steppe and 70% of Mongolia's white-tailed gazelle, which roam in herds of up to 20,000.

Mongol Daguur (103,016 hectares) The reserve is divided into a northern 'A' and southern 'B' section. Mongol Daguur A is hill steppe and wetland bordering on Russia's Tarij Nuur and Daurski Reserve, protecting endemic species such as the Daurian hedgehog; Mongol Daguur B, along the Ulz Gol, protects the *tsen togoruu* (white-naped crane) and other endangered birds. The area is part of a one-million-hectare international reserve, linking the Siberian taiga with the inner-Asian steppe.

Nömrög (311,205 hectares) An unpopulated area, which contains rare species of moose, crane, otter and bear. Ecologically distinct from the rest of Mongolia, the area takes in the transition zone from the eastern Monglian steppe to the mountains and forest of Manchuria.

Toson Khulstai (469,928 hectares) Protects large herds of white-tailed gazelle; easy detour if travelling between Khentii and Dornod.

The aimag also has several nature reserves, including Ugtam Uul (46,160 hectares) and Yakh Nuur (251,388 hectares).

CHOIBALSAN ЧОЙБАЛСАН
☎ 01582 / pop 39,800 / elev 747m

Lying on the banks of the Kherlen Gol, 324km downstream from Öndörkhaan, is Choibalsan, Mongolia's easternmost capital and the regional centre for trade and industry. The city has a better-than-average selection of hotels, plenty of shops and one of Mongolia's busiest markets. It's fractured in two parts, a half-abandoned district to the west and a more functional eastern section, where most of the action takes place.

Centuries ago, the city was a trading centre and part of a caravan route across Central Asia. It grew into a town in the 19th century and was called Bayan Tumen.

In 1941 it was named after the Stalinist stooge Khorloogiin Choibalsan, an honour bequeathed while the dictator was still in power. It's now a major economic centre for eastern Mongolia.

Orientation

Although the city is spread out along a narrow 5km corridor north of the Kherlen Gol, most of the facilities needed by visitors are near the Kherlen hotel. The market is 1.5km east of the main square. The train station is about 5.5km past the market.

Information

Eastern Mongolia Strictly Protected Areas Office
(☎ 23373, 9986 3888; fax 22217; ⏱ 9am-5pm Mon-Fri) Next to the Tovan hotel, this office can supply information on visiting protected areas in both Dornod and Sükhbaatar aimags. It can also arrange permits and sell tickets to protected areas and nature reserves.

Golomt Bank (☎ 22702) Gives cash advances against Visa and MasterCard. Next to Khishig Supermarket.

Internet Centre (☎ 21530; per hr T500; ⏱ 8am-10pm Mon-Fri, 10am-6pm Sat & Sun) Next to the Telecom office.

Library Internet Café (per hr T500; ⏱ 10am-6pm)

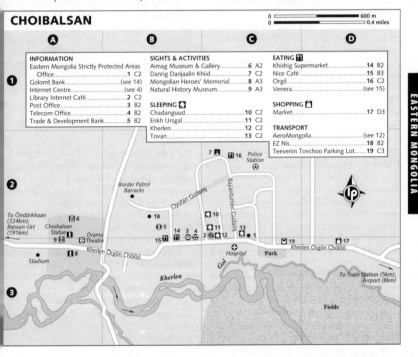

CHOIBALSAN

	0	600 m
	0	0.4 miles

INFORMATION
Eastern Mongolia Strictly Protected Areas
  Office...........................1 C2
Golomt Bank..........................(see 4)
Internet Centre......................(see 4)
Library Internet Café................2 B2
Post Office..........................3 B2
Telecom Office.......................4 B2
Trade & Development Bank.............5 B2

SIGHTS & ACTIVITIES
Aimag Museum & Gallery..............6 A2
Danrig Danjaalin Khiid..............7 C2
Mongolian Heroes' Memorial..........8 A3
Natural History Museum..............9 A3

SLEEPING 🛏
Chadanguud..........................10 C2
Enkh Ursgal.........................11 C2
Kherlen.............................12 C2
Tovan...............................13 C2

EATING 🍴
Khishig Supermarket.................14 B2
Nice Café...........................15 B3
Orgil...............................16 C2
Venera..............................(see 15)

SHOPPING 🛍
Market..............................17 D3

TRANSPORT
AeroMongolia........................(see 12)
EZ Nis..............................18 B2
Teeveriin Tovchoo Parking Lot.......19 C3

Police Station

Border Patrol Barracks

Oyutan Gudamj

Bayantumen Gudamj

To Öndörkhaan (324km); Baruun-Urt (191km)

Choibalsan Statue

Drama Theatre

Stadium

Kherlen Örgön Chölöö

Kherlen Örgön Chölöö

Hospital   Park

Kherlen

Gol

To Train Station (5km); Airport (8km)

Fields

EASTERN MONGOLIA

One building east of the Telecom office, the public library has good internet connection.

Post office (Kherlen Örgön Chölöö) Next door to the Telecom office.

Telecom office (☎ 21861; Kherlen Örgön Chölöö; ⊗ 24hr)

Trade & Development Bank (T&D Bank; ☎ 23009; ⊗ 9am-1pm & 2-4.30pm Mon-Fri) Gives cash advances against Visa and MasterCard. About 350m northwest of the Telecom office.

Sights

MUSEUMS & MEMORIALS

The **Aimag Museum & Gallery** (☎ 21940; admission T1000; ⊗ 10am-5pm Mon-Fri), in the former Government House in the old part of town, is one of the best of its kind outside of Ulaanbaatar. It contains some interesting paintings, fascinating old photos, some Choibalsan memorabilia and a giant bowl, made in 1861, which is large enough to boil mutton for 500 people (the mind boggles, the stomach churns). The aimag map marks the location of some ruined monasteries.

The **Natural History Museum** (⊗ 10am-7pm Mon-Fri), on the western side of the square, houses a collection of stuffed wildlife from around the aimag, plus exhibits on geology and flora. It's free if you've already paid for the Aimag Museum.

Choibalsan's **Mongolian Heroes' Memorial**, in the western town square, is one of the more dramatic pieces of Stalinist architecture in Mongolia. It is a large arch with a soldier on horseback charging towards the enemy. A Soviet tank next to the monument adds a quaint reminder of who really was boss.

DANRIG DANJAALIN KHIID

ДАНРИГ ДАНЖААЛИН ХИЙД
According to the chief monk, this monastery was built around 1840 and was once very active. It contained three northern temples and four southern temples, but less than half the 800 monks could be accommodated at one time, so most had to pray outside. It was closed in 1937.

The monastery reopened in 1990 and has two small temples where about 15 monks worship. The monks are particularly friendly; we were warmly welcomed and allowed to watch a ceremony. The monastery is about 400m behind the Kherlen hotel.

Sleeping

CAMPING

The best place to camp is anywhere south c the main street; walk for a few hundred metre and you will be sharing some great spots alon the Kherlen Gol with a few curious cows.

HOTELS

Kherlen (☎ 29058, 5058 1250; Kherlen Örgön Chölö per person r T7500, half-lux T25,000, lux T31,000) Thi friendly hotel, next to the library, has reno vated rooms with toilet and some with shower A common hot shower (T800) is available fo visitors in the standard rooms. A sauna is a additional T2500.

Enkh Ursgal (☎ 21666; s/d T8000/12,000, half-lu s/d T12,000/18,000, lux s/d T20,000/28,000) Rooms a this new hotel are small but well maintained Only the lux rooms have a shower. It's behind the library.

Tovan (☎ 21551; Kherlen Örgön Chölöö; half-lux s/ T10,000/15,000, lux s/d T21,000/30,000) Rooms ar large, reasonably clean and come with at tached toilet. The lux room, with shower, als includes breakfast.

ourpick **Chadanguud** (☎ 22355; r T17,000, half-lu T24,000, lux T30,000; 🖳) Choibalsan's newest hote 250m north of the library, is also its best. I has clean rooms with cable TV (including BBC news), reliable internet and 24-hou hot water. It also does laundry for T1000 pe kilogram. As a social hub, the place does ge busy, with lots of people using the billiard hall downstairs. The complimentary breakfas is fairly lamentable.

Eating

Nice Café (☎ 9958 7677; ⊗ 10am-midnight Mon-Sa Pleasant atmosphere, and pretty good gou lash and *khuurag* (fried meat chunks) mak a popular stand-by in Choibalsan. A few step west of the Khishig Supermarket.

Venera (☎ 9951 9309; ⊗ 10am-midnight) Next t the Nice Café, Venera has similar meals, an some Chinese dishes.

Orgil (☎ 21199) Decent Chinese restauran with a bona fide Chinese chef. It's in th northern part of town, near the monastery.

Self-caterers can shop for groceries a the **Khishig Supermarket** (⊗ 9am-10pm Mon-Fri noon-7pm Sat), next to the post office. Both the Tovan and the Kherlen hotels have decen restaurants.

EASTERN MONGOLIA

Shopping
Choibalsan's proximity to China means that its **market** (9am-7pm) is better stocked compared with other aimag capitals. It has lots of fresh fruit and vegetables, as well as an interesting shop selling ger furniture, saddles, Mongolian hats and boots. The back of the market plays host to gambling stalls where locals play cards, dominoes and *shagai* (a dice game using anklebones).

Getting There & Away
AIR
AeroMongolia (☎ 9958 8735) has an office in the Kherlen hotel building. It flies here from Ulaanbaatar three days a week (US$119/212 one way/return). **EZ Nis** (☎ 21177, 9904 9934) is in a building near the Trade & Development Bank. It also flies here three days a week (US$131/236 one way/return). The airport is about 10km east of the centre; buses, jeeps and minivans sometimes go there.

BUS, MINIVAN & JEEP
A daily bus departs for Ulaanbaatar (T15,800, 13 hours) at 8am from the market. Going the other way it leaves Ulaanbaatar's Bayanzürkh bus station at the same time.

Minivans and jeeps run along the good road between Ulaanbaatar and Choibalsan daily (T20,000, 655km), departing Ulaanbaatar from the Naran Tuul jeep station. Minivans depart Choibalsan in the morning from the Teeveriin Tovchoo parking lot at the eastern end of town. Daily vans and the odd jeep to Öndörkhaan (T10,000, 324km), Baruun-Urt (T10,000, 191km) and, less frequently, nearby *sums* such as Bayandun (T8000) leave from the same lot or from the market. You can charter a jeep for T450 per kilometre.

Postal minivans travel to Khalkhiin Gol (T10,500, Wednesday), Dashbalbar (T6500, Monday), Bayandun (T6300, Tuesday) and Bayan Uul (T7200, Wednesday).

The roads in the northern part of Dornod are often buried under mud in late summer, but roads to the other eastern aimag capitals are OK. The border crossing into Russia from Chuluunkhoroot was opened to foreigners in 2004, although so far it sees little traffic; see p178 for more information.

HITCHING
Choibalsan is a large city by Mongolian standards, so hitching a ride on a truck or any other vehicle in or out of the city should not be difficult. Hang around the market and keep asking.

TRAIN
A direct rail line from Choibalsan to Russia was built in 1939 to facilitate the joint Soviet–Mongolian war effort against Japan. It still functions, albeit only twice weekly. As a foreigner, you can go as far as Chuluunkhoroot on the Mongolian side of the border (no permit is apparently required), but the train no longer carries passengers across the border and only travels to Russia to pick up fuel.

The train leaves Choibalsan at 4pm every Monday and Thursday and takes seven hours. The return trip leaves Chuluunkhoroot at 8.30pm on Tuesday and Friday. These times will almost certainly change and you may be told that the train takes only cargo. Call for more info at the **station** (☎ 21502). Tickets cost T2000 for hard seat (the only class).

The train moves very slowly but this remains one of the most unique experiences you can have in Mongolia. Take food and plenty of water as the carriage can get stiflingly hot during the day.

The train station is about 7km northeast of the centre. You can reach the station by bus, but go early, because close to departure time the buses make a sardine tin look spacious.

KHERLEN BAR KHOT
ХЭРЛЭН БАР ХОТ
These small-scale **ruins** (GPS: N48° 03.287′, E113° 21.865′) and 10m-high tower from a 12th-century city were once part of the ancient state of Kitan. You can see a picture of the tower in the Aimag Museum & Gallery in Choibalsan (opposite).

Kherlen Bar Khot is about 90km west of Choibalsan, on the main road between Choibalsan and Öndörkhaan. It is worth a look if you have your own vehicle.

WALL OF CHINGGIS KHAAN
ЧИНГИСИЙН ХЭРЭМ
Stretching over 600km from Khentii aimag to China, and through all of Dornod, are the ruins of the Wall of Chinggis Khaan. This is not promoted by Mongolian tourist authorities because it was not built, or used, by Chinggis Khaan, but almost certainly created by the Manchu to limit frequent raids from rampaging Mongolian hordes.

EASTERN MONGOLIA

GAZELLE

A highlight of eastern Mongolia, as you bounce along in your jeep, is the sight of thousands of Mongolian gazelle darting across the steppes. When pre-eminent biologist George Schaller first visited in 1989 he proclaimed the immense herds to be one of the world's greatest wildlife spectacles.

Sadly, indiscriminate poaching for subsistence and bush-meat sale has reduced their numbers by as much as 50% in the past 10 years and it's harder to find such large herds these days, but they do exist. It's believed that up to 200,000 of these creatures are illegally shot every year, about 20% of their entire population. Gazelle are especially prized by Chinese and Mongolians for their meat, skins and horns: in China each one fetches from Y70 to Y100 (US$8.50 to US$12). There is a growing foreign souvenir market for gazelle-leg horse-whips (US$15) – please do not purchase these.

Habitat loss to overgrazing, road construction and the erection of barriers further puts their numbers at risk. Mining is another threat: oil exploration in southern Dornod has brought large-scale infrastructure and thousands of workers into a once-uninhabited region.

The New York–based **Wildlife Conservation Society** (www.wcs.org) has been researching the migration habits and ecological needs of these animals for nearly a decade and these findings have been provided to the Mongolian government. Specialists remain hopeful that the government will endorse conservation plans and efforts to reverse the decline can begin.

You will need a guide and jeep to find what little remains from the ravages of vandals and time, though it's doubtful whether it's worth the effort. Locals know it as the Chingissiin Zam, or Chinggis' Rd, which gives some indication of just how worn down the wall has become. The best place to start looking is about two-thirds of the way along the northern road from Choibalsan to the Russian border, near the village of Gurvanzagal.

UGTAM UUL УГТАМ УУЛ

Ugtam mountain (1236m) is part of the Ugtam Uul Nature Reserve (46,160 hectares), which also includes the nearby Tsagaan Ovoot Uul (1236m) and the ruins of some monasteries, one of which has recently reopened. The park is situated along the Ulz Gol in the northwest of the aimag, about 35km from the village of Bayandun.

KHÖKH NUUR ХӨХ НУУР

The lowest point in Mongolia is Khökh Nuur, a medium-sized freshwater lake at an altitude of 560m. Other than the thrill of standing in the lowest part of the country, there isn't much to keep you here, though the lake has a subtle beauty and you could combine it with an exploration of the Wall of Chinggis Khaan. The lake is also an important migration point for birds and you can spot many waders and shore birds here.

Khökh Nuur is visible from the railway line; you can get off the train at a stop near the lake, and then reboard the train the next day in the afternoon.

CHULUUNKHOROOT
ЧУЛУУНХОРООТ

The small village of Chuluunkhoroot (Stone Corral) is right at the border crossing with Russia. There is no accommodation but it does have a few shops. Locals with motorbikes can ride you out to **Mongol Daguur B**, a protected area along the Ulz Gol and important habitant for wader birds. The protected area has a couple of **eco-gers** (per night T5000), guest gers run by local families. The train ride here from Choibalsan is definitely one of the most unique transport experiences in Mongolia.

The actual border, just 3km away, is called Ereentsav. The Russian side of the border is called Solovyevsk. Locals ship cargo across the border on the train, but it's also possible to drive or walk across. If you have a Russian visa, this makes for an interesting crossing; you can hitch a ride to Borzya, a small Russian city on the Trans-Manchurian rail route, and then continue by road or rail to Chita and Ulaan Ude. Expect a serious passport check at the border as it's rarely used and you'll draw lots of attention.

BUIR NUUR БУЙР НУУР

This vast lake in eastern Mongolia is well known for the large stocks of fish. Amur Carp is the main species of fish in the lake, although it also contains taimen, grayling and lenok, among others. Most of the fish end up on the plates of Chinese restaurants as the northern shore is actually in China. The 40km lake has a maximum depth of 50m and is especially popular with mosquitoes so bring lots of repellent or you'll need a blood transfusion!

The lake is also great for bird-watching. Head for the northeast area around the Khalkhiin Gol delta.

Halfway between the lake and Choibalsan, a local family has erected an **Eco-ger** (per person T5000) for passing tourists. The family that runs the place can provide meals. The turn-off to the ger is marked with a sign.

The only way to Buir Nuur is by chartered jeep from Choibalsan, 285km away over a flat dirt road, which occasionally gets flooded.

SANGIIN DALAI NUUR САНГИЙН ДАЛАЙ НУУР

This saltwater **lake** (GPS: N46° 56.430', E116° 52.535'), in the southern part of the aimag, has a productive freshwater spring at one end. The 10 or so families that live in the area harvest salt from the lake using traditional methods.

From the lake you can travel another 29km southwest to **Vangiin Tsagaan Uul** (GPS: N46° 41.490', 117° 00.436'). From the top of the hill you are 400m above one of the flattest and most remote places on the planet, which makes for great views in the early morning or evening. East of the hill you'll encounter vegetated sand dunes that provide a home for wolves, gazelle, roe deer and the occasional herd of wild boar.

About 50km due east of Sangiin Dalai Nuur is the Tamtsag Basin oil field. From here you could hook up with the oil transport road that heads toward Erdenetsagaan in Sükhbaatar aimag.

KHALKHIIN GOL ХАЛХЫН ГОЛ

The banks of the Khalkhiin Gol, in the far eastern part of Dornod, are of particular interest to war historians because of the battles against the Japanese in 1939. The region is about a nine-hour drive east of Choibalsan.

Numerous **war memorials** are found in the area. The memorials are real socialist masterpieces, built to honour the Russian and Mongolian soldiers who died here. The monuments are easy to find as they are all along the road from Khalkhiin Gol to Sümber. The **Yakolevchudiin Tank Khoshuu** (Monument for Yakolev Tank Brigade; GPS: N47° 48.810', E113° 32.850') is located 23km northwest of Sümber. The largest memorial is the 10m-high **Yalaltiin Khoshuu**, located just outside Sümber town.

A **museum** (admission T1000) in Sümber (marked on some maps as Khalkhgol) offers some explanations (in Mongolian) about the history of the battles. The friendly caretaker will show you around the museum and probably issue you a commemorative pin to mark your visit. There is no electricity so bring a torch to see the exhibits. A small **hotel** (per person T5000) in Sümber, about 200m from the museum, has a pit toilet and electricity powered by a generator.

Another interesting site in the region is **Ikh Burkhant** (GPS: N48° 03.287', E113° 21.865'), where there is a huge image of **Janraisag** ('Avalokitesvara' in Sanskrit) carved into the hillside. The carving was commissioned in 1864 by local regent Bat Ochiriin Togtokhtooriin, or Tovan (*van* means 'lord') and was reconstructed between 1995 and 1997. The carving is right on the roadside, about 32km northwest of Sümber.

Going the other direction, it's another 70km or so to the spectacular but remote **Nömrög Strictly Protected Area**. The protected area only receives a handful of visitors each year, but those that go are rewarded with virgin fields and pine forests untouched by livestock or humans. The **border post** (GPS: N46° 59.019', E119° 21.522') at Nömrög is as far as you can go by vehicle. The border guards can rent you horses at inflated prices (around T15,000 per day) for further explorations of the SPA. A border guard must accompany you in the SPA.

Khalkhiin Gol is about 325km from Choibalsan. If you ask around the market in Choibalsan a shared van (T14,000) may eventually turn up bound for Sümber, but from here you'd still need to hire a vehicle to visit the sights. While this may be a cheap way to go if you are alone, it's better to hire your own vehicle and split the cost between travellers.

Permits

Khalkhiin Gol is near the Chinese border and a military base and there are three military checks en route from Choibalsan. You'll need a border permit issued from Ulaanbaatar to get through them.

EASTERN MONGOLIA

It is possible that you'll need two permits: your border permit and a second one issued at the checkpoints on the way to Khalkhiin Gol (which shouldn't cost more than T1000).

The permit given at Sümber (for Nömrög) may be fake (ie some guards there sell fake permits and keep the money for themselves). If you have a border permit from the border office in Ulaanbaatar (which should be free) you could probably get past the border guards at Sümber, without risking having to buy a phoney permit.

SÜKHBAATAR
СУХБААТАР

pop 52,400 / area 82,000 sq km

Sükhbaatar is a flat aimag wedged between the Gobi Desert and the pure steppes of Dornod. It contains elements of both – shifting sand dunes and barren rock feature prominently in the southwest while the east offers knee-high grass that provides important habitat for huge herds of gazelle.

The area is of some geologic importance as the southern *sum* of Dariganga contains some 200 extinct volcanoes; this is the most interesting part of the aimag, a legendary region of horse thieves, holy mountains and ancient stone statues. A highlight is watching a glorious sunrise from sacred Shiliin Bogd Uul.

Sükhbaatar is well off the tourist track but can be incorporated into a greater tour of eastern Mongolia. Because it receives so few visitors you feel like you have the aimag to yourself.

National Parks

Ganga Nuur Nature Reserve (28,000 hectares) Protects dunes and the Ganga Nuur, an important habitat for migrating swans.

Lkhachinvandad Uul Nature Reserve (58,500 hectares) On the border with China, this steppe area has plenty of gazelle and elk. It's reached via Erdenetsagaan.

BARUUN-URT БАРУУН-УРТ

☎ 01512 / pop 11,500 / elev 981m

Sükhbaatar's desolation is nowhere more evident than in its capital, Baruun-Urt, a scruffy, one-horse town in the middle of absolutely nowhere. The city is poor but some locals have found employment at a nearby Chinese-invested zinc mine, or at the coal mine 7km to the northwest.

One surreal image you can get in Baruun-Urt occurs in the cold season when it's possible to walk out into the empty, barren frozen steppe and feel as if you've landed on the moon. The ground underneath your feet, however, contains high levels of sulphur which has seeped into the local water supply – you are better off buying bottled water or filtering the tap water.

Information

Government House (Square) Ask for the latest information about permits to border areas here.

Internet café (☎ 21029; per hr T440; ◷ 8am-9pm Mon-Fri, 10am-6pm Sat) Inside the Telecom office.

Khan Bank (☎ 22268; ◷ 8am-6pm Mon-Fri, 9am-5pm Sat & Sun) Changes US dollars and gives cash against Visa and MasterCard. Located between the main square and the Sharga Hotel.

Mongol Shuudan Bank (☎ 21034; ◷ 8am-noon & 1-5pm Mon-Fri) Opposite the Sharga Hotel, this bank also changes US dollars.

Telecom office (☎ 21030; ◷ 24hr) The post office is also located here. It's on the south side of the main square.

Sights
MUSEUM

Baruun-Urt's surprisingly good **museum** (☎ 21486; admission T500; ◷ 8.30am-4.30pm) has a fine collection of costumes representing the three ethnic groups that inhabit the region: the Khalkh (the majority), the Dariganga (30,000 live in the south of Sükhbaatar aimag) and the Uzemchin (about 2000 live in Dornod aimag and Sükhbaatar aimag). Look out for the brass-studded Uzemchin wrestling jacket.

There are also beautiful examples of products from Dariganga's renowned silversmith and blacksmiths (often these are on loan to museums elsewhere in the world), some stuffed gazelle, a map showing the locations of the 'man' and 'woman' *balbals* (stone figures believed to be Turkic grave markers) in the aimag, and some Sükhbaatar memorabilia.

From the square, walk 400m south and turn right. The museum is located just past the drama theatre.

ERDENEMANDAL KHIID
ЭРДЭНЭМАНДАЛ ХИЙД

According to the monks, this monastery was originally built in 1830, about 20km from the

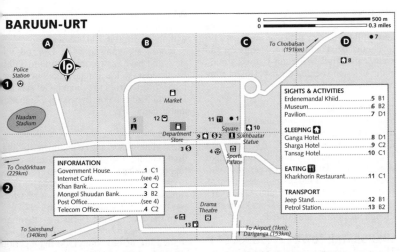

resent site. At the height of its splendour, here were seven temples and 1000 monks in esidence, but the Stalinist purges of 1938 had he same result as elsewhere. The new mon-.stery, surrounded by 108 distinctive stupas, s about 400m west of the square.

PAVILION

n the evenings, locals walk up to this lookout o survey the town and socialise. It features a tatue of Hoeloun and young Temujin (the uture Chinggis Khaan and his mother).

Sleeping

CAMPING

Baruun-Urt is the only aimag capital where amping is not a good idea. The town is in the middle of dusty plains and there is no river nearby. The only passable option is by a creek n the northeast of town.

HOTELS

Baruun-Urt is short on hotels and they tend o fill up if a mining crew rolls through town; ou may want to call one of the following to eserve a room.

Ganga Hotel (☎ 21212, 9979 4213; r/lux T8000/16,000) A ramshackle building with scruffy rooms hat have a shared bathroom. The lux room ias a private bathroom but no shower. The nanager is hardly ever around, but the *jijuur* watchman) will let you into the rooms and :ollect payment. It's in a blue building about a l 0-minute walk northeast of the centre.

Sharga Hotel (☎ 21101; r/lux T10,000/30,000) Next to the town square, this old hotel of commu-nist yore has passable standard rooms and better deluxe rooms with sitting room, TV and private bathroom. Hot water comes and goes as it pleases.

Tansag Hotel (☎ 22444; half-lux s/d T20,000/25,000, lux s/d T30,000/35,000) Easily the best in town, the Tansag has six rooms in a new build-ing on the east side of the main square. It has fairly reliable hot water and the price includes breakfast.

Eating

There will be no surprises with the mutton-heavy menu at the Tansag Hotel, but it's still the best in town. Otherwise, the *guanz* in the Government House doles up regulation gou-lash with aplomb.

Kharkhorin Restaurant (dishes T600-800; ☺ 9am-11pm) If you've already eaten at the Tansag, and for some reason you're still in Baruun-Urt, try this restaurant near the main square. The pictures of Mongolian pop stars, presumably those who stopped by and played here, add a little bit of character to the place.

Getting There & Away
AIR

EZ Nis has flights to and from Ulaanbaatar every Thursday for US$120/216 one way/return. The local **office** (☎ 21421) is at the air-port, 1km south of town.

HITCHING

This is difficult because few vehicles come here. Still, with some patience you'll get a lift to Choibalsan, Öndörkhaan, Dariganga and even Zamyn-Üüd. In Baruun-Urt, ask around at the jeep stand behind the department store or the petrol station.

JEEP & MINIVAN

Shared jeeps and minivans leave Ulaanbaatar daily (T18,000, 560km) from the Naran Tuul jeep station. From Baruun-Urt, vehicles wait at a small jeep stand behind the department store. The jeep stand also has occasional vehicles to Dariganga (T7000), Choibalsan (T9000, 191km) and Öndörkhaan (T7000, 229km). It's possible to hire a vehicle (T400 per kilometre) though the options are limited.

SÜKHBAATAR TOWN СҮХБААТАР

This small *sum* centre is 48km east of Baruun-Urt. It's not worth a trip in its own right but if you are passing through on your way to Dornod, there is an excellent **museum** dedicated to Damdin Sükhbaatar. Exhibits include printing-press implements used by Sükhbaatar during his days as a typesetter in an Ulaanbaatar printing house. To get inside, you'll need to ask Mr Batjargal, a music teacher at the nearby elementary school, for the keys.

DARIGANGA ДАРЬГАНГА

The vast grasslands of Dariganga are speckled with volcanic craters, small lakes and sand dunes, the sum of which makes the area one of the most scenic in eastern Mongolia. Before communism this area was a haven of aristocracy and its grasslands were the royal grazing grounds of horses belonging to the emperor in Beijing. Silversmiths and blacksmiths made their homes here, providing local women with stunning jewellery that now features prominently in the national museum in Ulaanbaatar. Dariganga's best days are now behind it, but it's still worth the effort of getting down here. With a jeep and a good driver you can set off from town to explore the lakes, volcanoes, caves, sand dunes and ancient stones nearby. The sacred mountain of Shiliin Bogd Uul is also not too far away.

Information

Although they are not usually checked, permits are required for Dariganga and Shiliin Bogd. Permits are available from the border office in Ulaanbaatar. The fine for travelling without a permit is T40,000 per head.

If you are coming from Dornod you shouldn't have any trouble getting to Shiliin Bogd and on to Dariganga; this allows you to travel directly from the Khalkh Gol area and Dornod Mongol SPA, bypassing Choibalsan and Baruun-Urt.

Sights

The skyline of Dariganga is dominated by **Altan Ovoo** (Golden Ovoo), a wide former crater topped by a **stupa**, which only men are allowed to visit. The stupa was built in 1990 on top of the ruins of the original Bat Tsagaan stupa, which was built in 1820 and destroyed in 1937.

In the area around Dariganga, there are dozens of broken *balbals* – mostly dating back to the 13th- or 14th-century Mongol period although some are earlier. According to tradition, you should place an offering of food in the cup held in the statue's left hand. There are also three *balbals,* known as the **king, the queen and the prince** (GPS: N45° 18.540′, E113° 51.224′) on the northern edge of town, near some hay sheds. In the village itself, you can visit the welcoming **Ovoon Khiid** (Овоон Хийд), which was built in 1990 and is served by a handful of monks.

There are six lakes in the vicinity of Dariganga; all are part of the Ganga Nuur Nature Reserve. The three main lakes Kholboo Nuur, Tsagaan Nuur and Ganga Nuur, are good for swimming, though a bit muddy.

The magnificent **Ganga Nuur** (Ганга Нуур GPS: N45° 15.994′, E113° 59.874′) is about 13km south east of Dariganga. From the end of September until mid-October, the lake is home to thousands of migrating swans. Along the shore in a fenced compound, is delicious and safe spring water. Entry to the lake is T1000 per person and T500 per car (but you can park your car by the gate and walk).

The sand dunes in the region are known as **Moltsog Els** (Молцог Элс) and stretch for 20km, coming to within walking distance of Dariganga.

Sleeping & Eating

Dariganga has three ger camps, about 1.5km south of the village. There is little to differentiate the Dagshin Amaralt, the Zigistei Nuur and the Ovor Khurem ger camps, which all have

MILLENNIUM ROAD

Mongolia's road network, little more than a series of dirt tracks that squiggle haphazardly across the plains, is taking a great leap forward. The Millennium Road project, launched by the Mongolian government in 2000, envisions a paved road running the length of the country, from Dornod to Bayan-Ölgii, plus several north–south roads, including one alongside the Trans-Mongolia Railway.

Defenders of the controversial project compare it to America's interstate system of the 1950s or Germany's autobahn, and claim boosts in trade and tourism. Builders point out that one road will reduce land degradation as drivers will end the practice of creating multiple tracks across the steppe. But a cash deficit has slowed progress and political opponents say it's called the Millennium Road because it will take 1000 years to build.

Around 25% of the 2640km road has already been constructed, mostly with loans from international lenders and far-flung countries such as Kuwait, whose royal family imports Mongolian falcons en masse.

Some economists discredit the road as a waste of time and money, saying it goes from nowhere to nowhere. (The current proposal seeks to end the road on a remote plain near Khalkh Gol, hundreds of kilometres from the nearest urban area.) They argue that the money would be better spent on building roads and infrastructure in sprawling Ulaanbaatar.

There is some credibility in the dissent, particularly in Dornod aimag, where plans show the road east of Choibalsan cutting into important gazelle migration routes and heading towards an oil field at Tamsagbulag.

Mining companies, oil men, cashmere traders, marmot-skin smugglers and gazelle poachers (both Chinese and Mongolian) may enjoy the benefits of the proposed route, but biologists would prefer to keep this pristine wilderness, and the gazelle migration route, untouched. An alternative route direct to Choibalsan, favoured by conservationists, is generally ignored by developers seeking cash benefits from the oil trade.

The situation remains murky; in 2007 the governor of Dornod agreed to extend the road towards the oil fields and Khalkh Gol. Public protest has spurred few results. Conservationists are hoping a deal can be arranged to shift the road towards Choibalsan but no-one is holding their breath.

Special-interest groups, conservationists, politicians and economists (not to mention local herders, traders and border-guard generals) remain locked in battle over the Millennium Road's eastern terminus. If the project proceeds in its current ill-planned manner, it could be a knockout punch for the majestic gazelle, a species already threatened by hunting and poaching.

EASTERN MONGOLIA

abins (no gers, actually) and basic facilities ɔr about T4000 per person. If prodded, the ꞓaretakers of these camps can provide meals. ᴎone of the camps has a shower or phone, but ̄ou can get both of these in the village.

There is nothing stopping you camping ꞁnywhere you want as long as you stay away ꞁrom the ger camps. If you have a vehicle, ꞓamp on the shores of Ganga Nuur.

Dariganga has a few basic shops on the ꞁnain road, alongside two or three *tsainii gazar* tea houses/cafés.

Ɡetting There & Away

Ɔccasional shared jeeps (T7000; four hours) ꞁonnect Dariganga with Baruun-Urt. A postal ꞏruck runs every Thursday from Baruun-Urt; ꞏsk the post office for timings.

One or two jeeps and even motorbikes are available for charter in Dariganga. Travellers report being able to hire horses through one of the ger camps.

SHILIIN BOGD UUL
ШИЛИЙН БОГД УУЛ

At 1778m, **Shiliin Bogd Uul** (GPS: N45° 28.350′, E114° 35.349′), about 70km east of Dariganga, is the highest peak in Sükhbaatar aimag. The extinct volcano is sacred to many Mongolians: the spirit of any man (and man only!) who climbs it, especially at sunrise, will be revived. The region is stunning, isolated and close to the Chinese border – so be careful.

A jeep can drive about halfway up the mountain, and then it's a short, but blustery, walk to the top. There are plenty of *ovoos* and awesome views of craters all around. About 3km to the south, the fire break that squiggles into the distance is the border with China. If you are camping, Shiliin Bogd offers one of the greatest sunrises in a country full of great sunrises.

On the road between Dariganga and Shiliin Bogd, 8km past Ganga Nuur, look out for the new statue of **Toroi-Bandi** (GPS: N45° 17.308', E114° 04.466'), the Robin Hood of Mongolia, who had a habit of stealing the horses of the local Manchurian rulers, then eluding them by hiding near Shiliin Bogd Uul. The statue, dedicated in 1999, pointedly faces China.

The only two roads to Shiliin Bogd start from Erdenetsagaan (70km) and Dariganga (70km). It's better to go to Dariganga first, where you are more likely to find a jeep for rent or a lift.

AROUND SHILIIN BOGD UUL

Assuming that you have a jeep to get to Shiliin Bogd Uul in the first place, you can make a good loop from Dariganga, to take in Ganga Nuur on the way to Shiliin Bogd Uul, and Taliin Agui and Khurgiin Khundii on the way back to Dariganga.

Taliin Agui (Талын Агуй; GPS: N45° 35.405', E114° 30.051'), 15km northwest of the mountain, is one of the largest caves in Mongolia. If the ice covering the entrance has melted (it's normally covered until August) you can squeeze through the narrow entrance. The large, icy cavern has three chambers to explore (the back wall looks like a dead end but you can squeeze under the overhang). You'll need a torch (flashlight) to see anything, and be careful on the slippery floor.

In summer, a basic **ger camp** (beds T2000, meals T1500) pops up near the cave.

Khurgiin Khundii (Хургийн Хөндий; GPS: N45° 33.165', E114° 13.970'), a pretty valley 40km west of Shiliin Bogd Uul, once contained seven stone statues that date back to the 13th or 14th century (only three statues can be found today). Although there are various legends to describe the origins of the stones, the most prominent recalls a certain khaan who, on a hunting trip, drove a herd of gazelle over a cliff, killing hundreds of them. Angered by this senseless slaughter, the sky god (Tenger) struck down the king's family members with disease and natural calamity. The statues in Khurgiin Khundii were erected in memory of the king and his family, and as a reminder for people to respect nature. Because the valley is considered to be haunted by the ghosts of the royal family, herders do not put their gers here. You will have to rely on your driver to find the statues and to locate **Bichigtiin Khavtsa** (Бичигтийн хавцал), a pretty canyon about 2km away.

LKHACHINVANDAD UUL NATURE RESERVE
ЛХАЧИНВАНДАД УУЛ

If you are visiting Shiliin Bogd by jeep, you may wish to carry on east for another 120km to the 58,500-hectare Lkhachinvandad Uul Nature Reserve, on the border with China. This reserve contains Lkhachinvandad Uul (1233m) and is full of gazelle and elk. You'll need a border permit to visit the area and it's wise to register with the police in the nearest town, Erdenetsagaan. While in the town, you could have a look at the old temple Eguzer Khutagtiin Khuree (Егүзэр Хутагтын Хүрээ), a two-storey building that managed to survive the communist purge.

EASTERN MONGOLIA

MISSION: MONGOLIA

Refugees of consumerism, 21st-century nomads and anyone with a passion for getting back to nature will appreciate what this mystical county has to offer. The capital, Ulaanbaatar, is a hotbed of liberal ideas and progressive attitudes, but elsewhere travellers find traditional Mongolian culture still very much alive.

Pitching a tent near a nomad camp, riding across unfenced landscapes on horseback and drinking *airag* (fermented mare milk) at Naadam will supply you with travel stories for years to come. Dive in wholeheartedly – any amount of adventure is possible in the 'Land of the Blue Sky'.

Activities

For the most part, adventuring in Mongolia comes without safety nets, slogans or hype. But with a bit of planning, thrill seekers can patch together their own excursions, including horse treks, cycle tours and rock climbing. A nascent group of adventure tour operators can help with the logistics, especially for fly-fishing enthusiasts or bird-watchers. In winter, you could even try your hand at cross-country skiing and dog sledding!

① Horse Sledding
If you can handle the cold, horse sledding at Khatgal Ice Festival (p157) is great fun! Gutsy travellers could hire a sledge for a self-guided tour up the shore of Khövsgöl Nuur.

② Eagle-hunting
Bayan-Ölgii is home to proud Kazakh eagle-hunters (p229). In winter you can mount up with these men and watch their trained birds swoop on unsuspecting wolves and foxes – not for the faint of heart.

③ Camping
Mongolia is the world's largest campground; load up your jeep and pitch your tent wherever you please. Altai Tavan Bogd National Park (p229) and Khövsgöl Nuur National Park (p152) offer some truly scenic vistas.

④ Dog Sledding
Mushing your way across the steppes on a dog sled (p252) is one of many new adventure options. Go for an easy day trip around Terelj or an epic, multiday journey across Khövsgöl Nuur.

Culture

The best part of Mongolia is its centuries-old customs and culture. Traditional crafts and artwork decorate the interior of gers, nomads still move camp each season and horses remain a major form of transport. Art, theatre, music and dance are best seen in Ulaanbaatar, but you'll experience the culture everywhere. In gers you can help spin wool or make dumplings, and even on long-distance bus rides you'll be serenaded by passengers singing folk tunes (iPod be damned!).

① Handicrafts

The Kazakhs of Bayan-Ölgii are renowned for their handicrafts. You can buy carpets and tapestries from locals and artisan workshops in the aimag capital, Ölgii (p226).

② Buddhism

Long suppressed by the communists, Buddhism is making a strong comeback with monasteries popping up in towns across the country. The biggest is Gandan Khiid (p73) in Ulaanbaatar.

③ Theatre

The timeless tradition of *tsam*-mask dancing comes complete with fearful demons, crashing cymbals and horns loud enough to wake the gods. See it in summer at the Choijin Lama Temple Museum (p75) in UB.

④ History

Cosmonauts and commissars have been replaced by cab drivers and capitalists in Ulaanbaatar, but a reminder of communist times (and the best views of the city) can be found at the Soviet-built Zaisan Memorial (p78).

⑤ Food & Drink

Dairy products feature prominently on any Mongolian summer menu (p43). Sample the hard and soft cheeses, yogurt, cream and curds, and go easy on the *airag* (fermented mare milk).

Landscapes

With its limited infrastructure and small population, Mongolia's environment remains in its natural state. The Gobi is spectacularly barren, with only a few distant mountains breaking a flat horizon. The more fertile north is lined with fields of wildflowers and fast-flowing rivers, while the 'Wild West' has big mountains, glaciers and lakes galore. The rarely visited east is perhaps the most enchanting – an endless sea of yellow grass inhabited mainly by huge herds of bounding gazelle.

❶ Zavkhan

The valleys in Zavkhan (p242) seem to go on forever. This little-visited aimag is great for horse trekking and self-guided exploration.

❷ Uvs

Hardy travellers journey to Uvs (p237) for its wild scenery, big mountains, desert lakes and ancient traditions. Large *ovoos* (holy stone piles) are found at the high passes and there are plenty of raised tombs and ancient honorary statues.

❸ Khentii

Northern Khentii (p165) is known for its lakes, meandering rivers and rolling grasslands. Pack a copy of *Mongoliin Nuuts Tovchoo* (The Secret History of the Mongols) and follow in the footsteps of Chinggis Khaan.

❹ The Gobi

The Gobi (p193) is not all sand dunes and wasteland – it contains surprisingly diverse landscapes, with mountains, cliffs and grassy plains (after a good rain). Bactrian camels are often spotted loping into the distance.

❺ Trans-Mongolian Railway

The Trans-Mongolian Railway (p272) crosses vast sections of the Gobi as it passes between Ulaanbaatar and Beijing. Riding the rails is a leisurely way to experience the haunting beauty of the desert, while saving your spine from the rough jeep trails.

❻ Bayan-Ölgii

The rumpled folds of the Mongol Altai Nuruu lift the peaks of Bayan-Ölgii (p222) to more than 4300m. Interspersed between them are lakes, undulating steppe, stony desert and permanent glaciers.

Naadam Festival

What do you get when you bring together 300-pound wrestlers in battle boots, archers who sing to their arrows and 20km-long horse races? Naadam! Mongolia's summer sports spectacular (p96) can resemble a training ground for Chinggis Khaan's mounted soldiers, and you'll quickly fill up your memory card with all the photo ops. Note that the biggest Naadams are by no means the best; find a village Naadam where you can get close to the action and have a more intimate experience with the locals.

❶ Wrestling

A game of skill as much as strength, two wrestlers size each other up on the wrestling pitch. The first to fall to the ground loses and there are no bonus points for style or fashion statements.

❷ Horse Racing

A young jockey nurses a soft drink. The sugar boost will be sorely needed during an exhausting horse race that can last two hours or more.

❸ Archery

Archers come in all shapes and sizes; men, women and also children compete in this 'manly sport'. Here a young boy takes aim on his target.

The Gobi

Be prepared to have some illusions shattered. The notion of the Gobi Desert as a wasteland of uninhabited sand dunes seems to have been developed solely in the minds of a few folklorists and Hollywood scriptwriters. While it *is* a fairly bleak part of the world, the Gobi is also enormously diverse, with various sprinklings of ice-filled canyons, John Ford–esque rock formations, and verdant oases. By comparison, sand dunes appear in short supply – they cover just 3% of the Gobi.

As you may expect, a trip to the Gobi is no cakewalk. Between the summer heat, winter cold, sandstorms, poor infrastructure and lack of water, this is one of the harshest landscapes on the planet. One Mildred Cable, an Englishwoman who passed through in the 1920s, noted: 'Only a fool crosses the Gobi without misgivings'.

Somehow, the Mongols have made a home of it, with scattered nomad camps still dotting the plains, ramshackle villages and the occasional ruined monastery to indicate long-disappeared settlements. A close look on the ground reveals a more ancient past as the Gobi supports a wealth of fossils, first made known to the world by American naturalist Roy Chapman Andrews, who visited in the early 20th century.

These days the lure of the Gobi extends mainly to minerals, specifically the Oyu Tolgoi gold and copper deposit, one of the largest of its kind anywhere. The Gobi aimags (provinces) of Bayankhongor, Dornogov, Dundgov, Gov-Altai and Ömnögov also support small-scale goat and camel herding and, increasingly, tourism – foreign travellers come here to spot wildlife, hunt for fossils, hike the canyons or just enjoy the terrific emptiness of it all.

HIGHLIGHTS

- Make a pilgrimage to **Khamaryn Khiid** and **Shambhala** (p202), once home to the legendary poet-monk Danzan Ravjaa

- Go fossil hunting at **Bayanzag** (p208), the remarkable 'flaming cliffs' that house rich deposits of dinosaur bones and fossilised eggs

- Scramble up and slide down the dunes at **Khongoryn Els** (p209), perfect for camel riding

- Step into the amazing **Yolyn Am** (p208), a canyon covered in ice for most of the year

- Stretch your legs with a Ger to Ger walk and rock-climbing adventure in the eerie **Ikh Gazryn Chuluu** (p198)

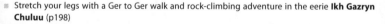

★ Ikh Gazryn Chuluu
Bayanzag ★
Khongoryn Els ★ ★ Khamaryn Khiid and Shambhala
★ Yolyn Am

THE GOBI

POPULATION: 309,021 | ■ AREA: 612,000 SQ KM

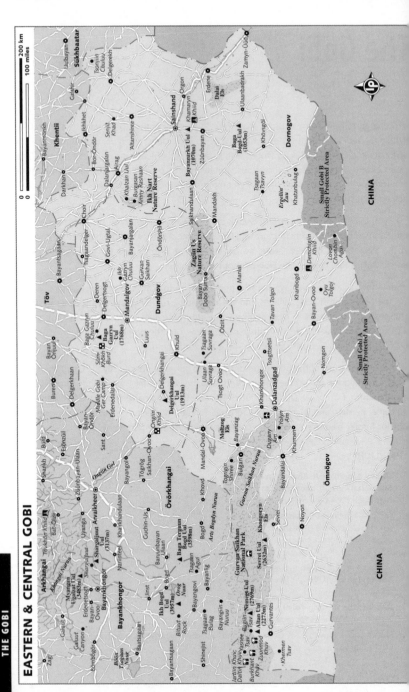

limate

While daytime temperatures in summer can ange from pleasant to stifling hot, nights re almost always cold, so take a sleeping ag. Dust storms can rock the region at any me but are especially common in April and lay. The tourist season lasts longer here than orthern areas; even October is not too late) see the sights. By December the desert will e blanketed with snow and daily maximum mperatures will fall to -15°C.

etting There & Away

here is plenty of public and private trans-ort heading from Ulaanbaatar to all the Gobi mag capitals, so it's easy enough to reach landgov, Sainshand, Dalanzadgad Altai and ayankhongor. You can fly to the latter three. you are travelling on local trains in China, s possible to enter Mongolia at Dornogov mag, although catching a jeep further west next to impossible; it's best to have a tour perator in Ulaanbaatar send a jeep down to eet you when you get off the train.

etting Around

obi infrastructure is almost nonexistent, ut the lack of roads does not prevent vehi-es from getting around. On the contrary, e rock-hard jeep trails are the best in the ountry and along main routes it's possible r jeeps to reach speeds of 100km/h. But reakdowns in the Gobi can be deadly.

Travel in this region is serious business and ou shouldn't think of setting off without a liable jeep and driver, plenty of water and pplies, and a good sense of direction. A map d a GPS unit would not go astray if your river is inexperienced. Hitchhiking is not commended, though we have mentioned stances in this chapter when it might be ssible. Otherwise, there are few vehicles ssing and hitchhiking (or a breakdown) n leave you stranded for days.

DUNDGOV
ДУНДГОВЬ

p 49,406 / area 78,000 sq km

undgov (Middle Gobi) is something of a isnomer. The aimag would be best described orth Gobi' as this area is the northernmost tent of the Gobi Desert. Lying just a few

hours drive south of Ulaanbaatar, it's also one of the most convenient Gobi regions to explore and is fast becoming a tourist destination.

Dundgov's allure lies in its mysterious rock formations, which appear mainly at two loca-tions: Baga Gazryn Chuluu and Ikh Gazryn Chuluu. At both you'll find large granite pin-nacles and winding canyons that make for great hiking and climbing. The water that manages to collect in these areas can support some wild-life, including argali sheep and ibex.

Dundgov is now home to a couple of trek-king routes for the Ger to Ger programme, one of which includes rock climbing. The project is boosting ecotourism in the region and this has spawned better hotels, restaurants and facilities. Besides trekking and the rock pinnacles, it's definitely worth visiting the ruined monastery Ongiin Khiid and the still-intact monastery at Erdenedalai.

National Parks

Ikh Gazryn Chuluu Nature Reserve (60,000 hectares) Extraordinary rock formations, argali sheep and ibex.
Zagiin Us Nature Reserve (273,606 hectares) Pro-tected mountain-Gobi area, saxaul trees, salt marshes and black-tailed gazelle.

MANDALGOV МАНДАЛГОВЬ
☎ 01592 / pop 13,820 / elev 1427m

Mandalgov came into existence in 1942 and originally consisted of just 40 gers. Today, it's a sleepy town that offers the usual amenities for an aimag capital: a hotel, a monastery, a museum and a few shops. It also has a useful Ger to Ger information office. A walk to the top of Mandalin Khar Ovoo, just north of the town centre, affords sweeping views of the bleak terrain. There is more to see in western Dundgov, but Mandalgov is a useful stop-off on the way to Dalanzadgad in Ömnögov.

Information

Ger to Ger office (☎ 9969 7456; zaanaa_999@chingiss .com; 2nd fl, Gandalai Supermarket, Buyan Emekhiin Gudamj; ☺ 9am-6pm) Assists with vehicle hire, bus tickets and general info, and is a contact point for Ger to Ger routes. Ask for Ganbaatar or Nara.
Internet café (per hr T460; ☺ 9am-6pm Mon-Fri) Located in the Telecom office.
Khan Bank (☎ 23881; ☺ 9am-noon & 1-6pm Mon-Fri) Can change US dollars and give a cash advance on Visa or MasterCard.
Telecom office (☎ 21212; ☺ 24hr) The post office is also located here.

THE GOBI

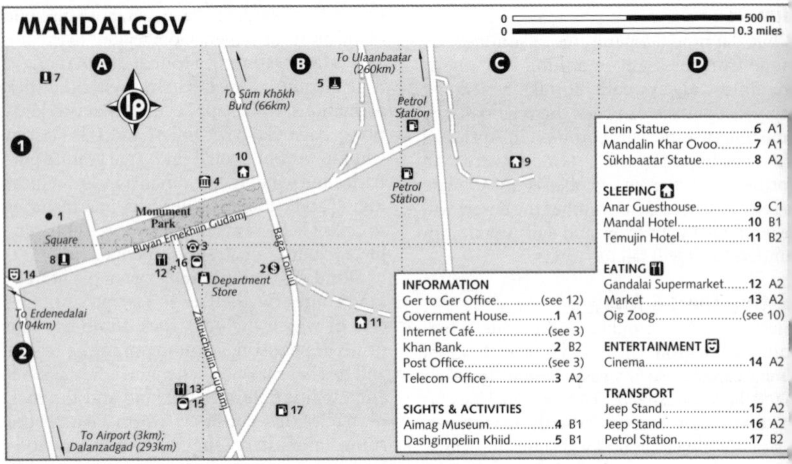
MANDALGOV
0 500 m
0 0.3 miles
To Ulaanbaatar (260km)
To Sūm Khōkh Burd (66km)
Petrol Station
Petrol Station
Monument Park
Square
Buyan Emekhiin Gudamj
Baga Toiruu
Department Store
Zaluuchidiin Gudamj
To Erdenedalai (104km)
To Airport (3km); Dalanzadgad (293km)
INFORMATION
Ger to Ger Office.............(see 12)
Government House.............1 A1
Internet Café.....................(see 3)
Khan Bank..........................2 B2
Post Office.........................(see 3)
Telecom Office....................3 A2
SIGHTS & ACTIVITIES
Aimag Museum....................4 B1
Dashgimpeliin Khiid.............5 B1
Lenin Statue........................6 A1
Mandalin Khar Ovoo..........7 A1
Sükhbaatar Statue...............8 A2
SLEEPING
Anar Guesthouse.................9 C1
Mandal Hotel.....................10 B1
Temujin Hotel....................11 B2
EATING
Gandalai Supermarket.......12 A2
Market..............................13 A2
Oig Zoog.........................(see 10)
ENTERTAINMENT
Cinema..............................14 A2
TRANSPORT
Jeep Stand.........................15 A2
Jeep Stand.........................16 A2
Petrol Station.....................17 B2

Sights

AIMAG MUSEUM

The renovated **Aimag Museum** (☎ 23690; Buyan Emekhiin Gudamj; admission T1000; ⏲ 9am-6pm) is divided into two main sections: a natural history section and a more interesting ethnography and history section. There's also a collection of priceless *thangka* (scroll paintings), old flintlock rifles, bronze arrowheads, silver snuffboxes, pipes, and chess sets carved out of ivory.

DASHGIMPELIIN KHIID

ДАШГИМПЭЛИЙН ХИЙД

In 1936 there were 53 temples in Dundgov; a year later, nearly all were reduced to ashes and rubble by the Mongolian KGB. In 1991 Dashgimpeliin Khiid was opened to serve the people of Mandalgov. The monastery is now served by 30 monks and services are held most mornings from 10am. It's 300m northeast of the Mandal Hotel.

MONUMENT PARK

Communism has been preserved in this small park, which contains statues of Sükhbaatar, Yuri Gagarin (first man in space), a pair of happy workers, various livestock and a Soviet–Mongolian friendship monument, among others.

Sleeping

Like other Gobi aimag capitals, Mandalgov has no great camping spots; the city has no river and is flat and dusty. Perhaps walk north of town and find somewhere past Mandali Khar Ovoo or the monastery.

Anar Guesthouse (☎ 9963 9767; nangaa_j999@yahc .com; per person US$4) The best option for independent travellers, Anar is a comfortable ge guesthouse, owned by the people who run th Ger to Ger office. It's just off the road to UB, i a fenced compound. There are no showers.

Mandal Hotel (☎ 22100; Buyan Emekhiin Gudam s/d T5000/10,000, lux s/d T7000/14,000) A slightly rur down hotel that offers good-value rooms th are regularly clean and fairly comfortable. H showers are available.

Temujin Hotel (☎ 23973; Baga Toiruu; dm/d/l T5000/12,000/25,000) Offers the best facilities i town, including rooms with shower and to let. It's in a white brick building, south of th main drag, a bit off Baga Toiruu.

Eating

Self-caterers can pick up food items at th local **market** or **Gandalai Supermarket** (Buy Emekhiin Gudamj) on the main street.

Oig Zoog (☎ 9996 1122; Mandal Hotel, Buy Emekhiin Gudamj; dishes T1100-1500; ⏲ 9.30am-10p Mon-Sat) Disco beats, black lights and a so cialist mural provide the backdrop for th funky '80s-style café. Serves Mongolia food and some vegetable dishes. It's in th Mandal Hotel.

Getting There & Away

HITCHING

Getting to Ulaanbaatar or Dalanzadgad c a truck or other type of vehicle won't ta

oo long if you are prepared to ask around
t the market and wait awhile.

EEP & MINIVAN

Daily share jeeps to Ulaanbaatar (T12,000, six
hours, 260km) and Choir (T8000, four hours,
187km) leave when full from the jeep stand
outside the Telecom office. You're unlikely to
nd a share jeep to Dalanzadgad (T12,000, six
hours, 293km), but Dalanzadgad-bound jeeps
oming from Ulaanbaatar might be able to
queeze you in. Wait for these at the petrol
ation in the south of town. The jeep stand
utside the market is another place to look.

AGA GAZRYN CHULUU
АГА ГАЗРЫН ЧУЛУУ

his granite rock formation in the middle
f the dusty plains sheltered Zanabazar dur-
ng conflicts between the Khalkh and Oirat
Mongols. Later it was home to two 19th-
entury monks who left **rock drawings** in the
rea. The rocks are worshipped by locals who
ometimes make pilgrimages here. Naturally,
here is a legend that Chinggis Khaan grazed
is horses here.

Five kilometres away, the highest peak in
he area, **Baga Gazryn Uul** (1768m), will take
bout an hour to climb. The mountain also
ontains a **cave** with an underground lake.
he **mineral water springs** and trees in the re-
on make it a great spot to camp, and there
re plenty of rocky hills topped by *ovoo* (sa-
ed pyramid-shaped collections of stone and
ood) to explore.

The **Bayan Bulag ger camp** (☎ 9825 0010; www
ayanbulag.mn; GPS: N 46°13.827′, E 106°04.192′; with/with-
t meals US$30/15) is one of the Gobi's more at-
active ger camps and offers good food and
ot showers. Guides (free) from the camp
an show you sights in the area, including
partially restored monastery and camel-
ekking routes. It also has a greenhouse grow-
g delicious tomatoes and cucumbers.

Baga Gazryn Chuluu is about 60km north
r northwest of Mandalgov, and about 21km
st of Süm Khökh Burd.

ÜM KHÖKH BURD
УМ ХӨХ БҮРД

he temple **Süm Khökh Burd** (GPS: N 46°09.621′, E
5°45.590′), which sits on an island in the mid-
e of a tiny lake, was built in the 10th century.
emarkably, the temple was built from rocks
at can only be found more than 300km

away. It was abandoned and in ruins a few
centuries after being built.

Three hundred years ago a **palace** was built
here, and 150 years later the writer Danzan
Ravjaa (p201) built a stage on top of the ruins.
Enough of the temple and palace remain to
give you some idea of what a magnificent
place it once must have been.

The lake itself, **Sangiin Dalai Nuur**, only encir-
cles the palace after heavy rains; at other times
you can slog through the mud to the palace.
There is good **bird-watching** here: various species of eagle, goose and swan come to this
spring-fed lake in summer and autumn.

The **Süm Khökh Burd Ger Camp** (☎ 9911 4684; per
person with meals US$26) is an old socialist place that
has seen some recent renovations. Otherwise,
you can pitch your tent anywhere.

The temple is located 72km northeast of
Erdenedalai, 65km northwest of Mandalgov
and 21km west of Baga Gazryn Chuluu. There
is no hope of getting here on public transport
or by hitching.

ERDENEDALAI ЭРДЭНЭДАЛАЙ

This sometime camel-herding community in
the middle of nowhere (114km northwest of
Mandalgov) is known for the **Gimpil Darjaalan
Khiid** (admission T1000), an old monastery that
somehow survived Stalin's purges. The monastery was built in the late-18th century to
commemorate the first ever visit to Mongolia
by a Dalai Lama. It was once used by some
500 monks.

The monastery was reopened in 1990 and
the current Dalai Lama visited in 1992. If no-
one is there, wait a few minutes and some boys
will materialise with the keys and admission
tickets. The spacious temple has a central
statue of Tsongkhapa (founder of the 'Yellow
Hat' sect of Buddhism), some large parasols
and some huge drums. Photos are permitted
outside the temple but not inside.

Middle Gobi Camp (☎ 9912 8783, 011-367 316;
with/without meals US$35/18) About 25km north of
Erdenedalai, it's not a bad place to spend the
night if you are headed in this direction.

Although the village is small, it is on a major
jeep trail, so a few vehicles come through here
every day.

ONGIIN KHIID ОНГИЙН ХИЙД

This small mountainous area along the Ongiin
Gol in the western *sum* of Saikhan-Ovoo
makes a pleasant place to break a trip between

THE GOBI

southern Gobi and either Ulaanbaatar or Arvaikheer. The bend in the river marks the remains of two ruined monasteries, the **Barlim Khiid** on the north bank, and the **Khutagt Khiid** on the south. Together the complex is known as **Ongiin Khiid** (GPS: N 45°20.367', E 104°00.306'; admission US$1, photos US$2, video US$5). A contingent of 13 monks has set up shop amid the ruins, completing a new temple in 2004. The ger in front of the temple is a **'museum'** (admission US$1) that houses some unimpressive artefacts found at the site. Despite it being illegal, locals may try to sell you some artefacts or dinosaur eggs.

There are plenty of places to camp along the forested riverside and there are five ger camps in the vicinity.

Great Gobi Ger Camp (☎ 011-329 350; 9191 6184; www.trip2mongolia.com/gobi_camp.htm; with/without meals US$33/12) is a friendly place with English-speaking staff. Amenities include a sauna, basketball court (!) and camel riding (per hour/day US$3/10). It is located next to the monastery.

In the town of Saikhan-Ovoo, a good option is the new **Zambagiin Tal Guesthouse** (☎ 9929 1892; per person US$10) which has a café and ger accommodation and is a jumping off point for Ger to Ger trekking. It's in the centre of town – look for the 'Ger to Ger' sign on the roof.

There is no public transport to Ongiin Khiid.

IKH GAZRYN CHULUU
ИХ ГАЗРЫН ЧУЛУУ

Caves, canyons and some excellent rock-climbing routes are a few of the reasons travellers head out to this remote Gobi area, 70km east of Mandalgov in Gurvan Saikhan *sum*. The area is the site of a Ger to Ger trekking route, which combines travel by camel, horse and on foot. Rock climbers with their own gear will find routes set in the boulders. In late June, the area hosts the **Roaring Hooves Music Festival** (www.roaringhooves.com), with participants coming from around the world.

You can overnight at the comfortable **Töv Borjigan ger camp** (☎ 9825 9985; tuv_borjigin@yahoo .com; GPS: N 45°45.664', E 107°15.977'; with/without meals US$20/10). The people who run it can show you caves in the area.

ULAAN SUVRAGA
УЛААН СУВРАГА

In the southernmost *sum* of Ölziit is Ulaan Suvraga, an area that might be described as a 'badlands' or a 'painted desert'. The eeri eroded landscape was at one time beneat the sea, and is rich in marine fossils ar clamshells. There are also numerous **ancie rock paintings** in the region. About 20km ea of Ulaan Suvraga is the equally stunnin **Tsagaan Suvraga**, an area of 30m-high wh limestone formations.

The best place to stay in the area is th **Tsagaan Suvraga ger camp** (☎ 9929 8155; ts_suvraga yahoo.com; GPS: N 44°34.405', E 105°48.542'; with me US$30), 8km east of Tsagaan Suvraga.

DORNOGOV
ДОРНОГОВЬ

pop 54,000 / area 111,000 sq km

Dornogov (East Gobi) is the first place vi ited by many overlanders, as the trainlir from Beijing to Ulaanbaatar runs straight u its gut. The landscape seen from the tra window is one of flat, arid emptiness and tl occasional station where locals shuffle abo on the platform. The railway supports loc trade while the rest of the economy lies c the back of copper mining and small-sca oil extraction.

Most travellers stop here with the pu pose of visiting Khamaryn Khiid, the mo astery established by the poet-monk Danza Ravjaa. The once-deserted monastery h become an important spiritual centre an pilgrimage point for Mongolians and fo eigners interested in Buddhism. Anoth reason to come down this way is to trav by local train, getting a quick and easy loc at the Gobi before heading into China.

National Parks

Dornogov's national parks are little visite but make for some good off-the-beate path travel destinations. **Ergeliin Zuu** (90,9 hectares), in the south of the province, a small protected area that has interestir rock formations and palaeontology sit that include 30-million-year-old mamm lian fossils. **Ikh Nart Nature Reserve** (67,00 hectares), only a four-hour drive fro Ulaanbaatar, is home to hundreds of ibe (mountain goat), black vulture and oth wildlife. The natural springs near Khalza Uul (Bald Mountain) are considered a loc health remedy. Burgasan Amny Rashaa is another mineral spring a few kilometre

---

ILLEGAL BUUZ *Michael Kohn*

'Sorry, no more *buuz*' said the woman on the train platform. She was the 10th person we had asked in futility.

'But we're starving,' we whined, 'we've been on the train all day and haven't eaten'.

The *buuz* seller lifted the lid off her red thermos to prove that she had indeed sold out of steamed mutton dumplings. But the look on our faces must have been pitiful. Shifting her eyes back and forth, she grabbed our shirt sleeves and led us to the end of the platform.

'Here,' she whispered, pointing to a sealed container held tightly by a granny in a green scarf, '*buuz*'. The granny slowly lifted the lid to show us a mountain of steaming hot dumplings.

'*Khoyor zuun tögrög*.'

It was twice the normal going rate for *buuz*, but we were desperate. Feeling as though we were buying some type of rare, illegal *buuz*, we peeked over our shoulder to make sure no-one was looking, and slipped the granny a wad of bills. Cloak-and-dagger-style she sealed up the *buuz* in a plastic bag, wrapped the package in newspaper and quickly handed over the goods.

As the train whistle blew into the dry Gobi night we hopped back into the cabin, satisfied with our purchase but still completely baffled at the secrecy of what would become known as 'Operation: Buuz'.

---

outh of Khalzan Uul. Nomadic Journeys (p80) has a ger camp here.

AINSHAND САЙНШАНД
☎ 01522 / pop 19,540 / elev 938m

Compared with other Gobi towns, the capital of Dornogov is reasonably well-equipped with facilities and shops, owing mainly to its location on the railway line and proximity to the Chinese border.

Sainshand (Good Pond) is divided into two parts: a cluster around the train station, and the more developed city centre 2km to the east. A leafy park at the centre of town offers cool respite from the Gobi heat; it's surrounded by the standard collection of banks, hotels, restaurants and museums. There are few jeeps for hire for trips to the desert; overland trips generally begin in Dalanzadgad in Ömnögov aimag. Recently the city has seen growing attention from Buddhist pilgrims, who use it as a jumping off point for nearby Khamaryn Khiid (p202).

Information
Luggage storage is available for a small fee at the Aimag Museum.

Internet café (☎ 22289; per hr T500; ☉ 24hr) In the telecom office.

Telecom office (☎ 22112; ☉ 24hr) The post office is also located here.

Trade & Development Bank (☎ 22298; ☉ 9am-8pm Mon-Fri) Changes US-dollar travellers cheques and gives cash advances on MasterCard and Visa. The Mongol Post Bank is in the same building.

Sights
AIMAG MUSEUM
The well-appointed **Aimag Museum** (☎ 22657; admission T1000; ☉ 9am-1pm & 2-6pm) houses plenty of stuffed Gobi animals, and a collection of sea shells and marine fossils (Dornogov was once beneath the sea). There is also an impressive skeleton of a Protoceratops and a dinosaur egg. Upstairs, look out for the wooden breastplate used by a Mongol soldier of the imperial fighting days. Lighting here is poor so bring a torch (flashlight).

MUSEUM OF DANZAN RAVJAA
Noyon Khutagt Danzan Ravjaa (1803–56), a well-known Mongolian writer, composer, painter and medic, was born about 100km southwest of Sainshand. The **museum** (☎ 23221; www.danzanravjaa.org; admission T1000, photos T5000; ☉ 9am-1pm & 2-6pm) has a collection of gifts presented to Danzan Ravjaa by Chinese and Tibetan leaders, costumes used in his plays, Buddhist statues presented to him by the 10th Dalai Lama, and some of Ravjaa's paintings. He was also very interested in traditional medicine, so the museum also has a collection of herbs.

In the centre of the museum is a statue of Danzan Ravjaa looming in the darkness. Note the small glass jar in front of the statue, which contains Danzan Ravjaa's bones; the poet's mummified body was burned along with his monastery in the 1930s.

Plans are afoot to move the museum to a new facility in the park.

THE GOBI

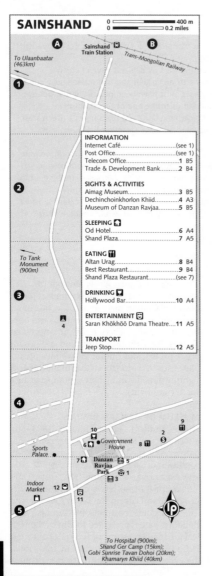

SAINSHAND

To Ulaanbaatar (463km)

Sainshand Train Station

Trans-Mongolian Railway

To Tank Monument (900m)

Sports Palace

Government House

Danzan Ravjaa Park

Indoor Market

To Hospital (900m);
Shand Ger Camp (15km);
Gobi Sunrise Tavan Dohoi (20km);
Khamaryn Khiid (40km)

0 — 400 m
0 — 0.2 miles

INFORMATION
Internet Café....................................(see 1)
Post Office...(see 1)
Telecom Office..1 B5
Trade & Development Bank.............2 B4

SIGHTS & ACTIVITIES
Aimag Museum..3 B5
Dechinchoinkhorlon Khiid.................4 A3
Museum of Danzan Ravjaa.................5 B5

SLEEPING
Od Hotel...6 A4
Shand Plaza...7 A5

EATING
Altan Urag..8 B4
Best Restaurant.......................................9 B4
Shand Plaza Restaurant.....................(see 7)

DRINKING
Hollywood Bar.....................................10 A4

ENTERTAINMENT
Saran Khökhöö Drama Theatre....11 A5

TRANSPORT
Jeep Stop...12 A5

DECHINCHOINKHORLIN KHIID
ДЭЧИНЧОЙНХОРЛИН ХИЙД

This **monastery** (🕐 10am-5pm Mon-Fri), which opened in 1991, is in a large walled compound at the northern end of the central district. There is an active temple and, although visitors are welcome, photographs are not allowed inside. The 25 monks are very friendly. The

THE GOBI

best views are from the **tank monument** locate behind the monastery.

Sleeping
CAMPING
Sainshand, like most aimag capitals in th Gobi, does not offer anywhere decent to pitc a tent. The best place to head for is the clif north of the monastery.

GER CAMPS
Gobi Sunrise Tavan Dohoi (☎ 9911 3820, 9909 015 gobisunrise@yahoo.com; GPS: N 44°45.418′, E 110°11.23€ with/without meals US$25/10) A well-run ger camp, has a restaurant, flush toilets and clean show ers with hot water. To arrange transport to th camp, which is about 20km south of Sainshan on the road to Khamaryn Khiid (p202), as Altangerel, the curator at the Danzan Ravja museum (p199).

Shand Ger Camp (☎ 9925 7883; with/without mea US$30/15) Located 15km south of Sainshan€ this camp is more expensive but not as nic as Gobi Sunrise. Arrange transport throug the Shand Plaza.

HOTELS
Shand Plaza (☎ 9914 8352, 23509; d/tr/half-lux/l€ T20,000/18,000/35,000/65,000) This reasonably com fortable hotel has a variety of rooms with T and clean bathroom. The triple room has n shower but the basement has a shared showe (T800) and sauna (T5000) that can be use even if you aren't staying here. The hotel als has a restaurant, disco, billiard room an local branch of the Anod Bank where yo can receive a money transfer.

Od Hotel (Star Hotel; ☎ 23245; dm T4500-5500) the west wing of the Government House, has a hot-water shower room and bland dor rooms. Enter the hotel from the north side.

At the time of research a seven-store hotel was being built in Sainshand, close the park.

Drinking & Eating
Altan Urag (dishes T1000-2500; 🕐 9am-11pm) Behind supermarket and just past the Danzan Ravja museum on the left, this place serves authen tic, if somewhat oily Chinese meals. One dis is big enough for two people.

Shand Plaza Restaurant (☎ 9952 2417; Shan Plaza Hotel; dishes T1500-2500; 🕐 9am-9pm) Th restaurant shows a little bit of local prid with the colourful décor resembling the in

DANZAN RAVJAA: POET, PLAYWRIGHT & SOCIAL CRITIC

Danzan Ravjaa was a hot-headed rebellious monk, a writer and popular leader of Mongolia's Red Hat Buddhists. He was recognised as a child prodigy by local people (he began composing and singing his own songs at the age of four) and was proclaimed the Fifth Gobi Lord in 1809. The Manchus had executed the Fourth Gobi Lord and forbade another and it was only by the narrowest of chances that the Manchu court allowed the young Gobi king to live.

Danzan Ravjaa's fame as a writer, artist and social critic spread far and wide. He received foreign students at his monastery and travelled to foreign countries, taking his acting troupe with him to study drama.

Ravjaa was also an expert at martial arts, Tantric studies, yoga and traditional medicine. He spent months in solitude writing, either in caves or in his ger. It is said that he so hated being disturbed that he built himself a ger with no door. He had a lousy temper that was often exacerbated by protracted bouts of drinking.

Many tall tales exist about Danzan Ravjaa and a little prodding will have locals spinning yarns about their beloved Gobi saint. It is said that Ravjaa could fly to Tibet in an instant to gather medicine, disappear into thin air and turn water into whisky (an important feat in Mongolia). Displaying his powers to the local people, he once peed off the roof of his temple and 'magically' made the urine fly into the air before it hit the ground.

Danzan Ravjaa's mysterious death came either at the hands of the rival Yellow Hat Buddhist sect or a jealous queen who failed to gain his love. His legacy remains strong and locals can still sing the songs he wrote and can recite his poetry. There are hopes to one day rebuilding his theatre at Khamaryn Khiid to again perform his famous play, *Life Story of the Moon Cuckoo*.

For more information on Danzan Ravjaa, pick up a copy of his biography *Lama of the Gobi* (Maitri Books, 2006), written by the author of this guidebook.

rior of a ger. The menu has your standard-sue Mongolian dishes and a couple of European meals.

Best Restaurant (☎ 9925 5579; dishes T1800-00; ⏰ 10am-11pm; ✸) A local favourite, this ace doles out excellent Mongolian dishes, e recommend the *bainshte shöl* (dumpng soup). It's in the 2nd floor of a brown rick building.

ntertainment

aran Khöökhöö Drama Theatre (☎ 22796) amed after the famous play by local hero anzan Ravjaa, who would be proud that is Sainshand theatre group is considered e best outside of Ulaanbaatar. The thea-e's in the centre of town on the west side f the park. Unfortunately, performances e sporadic.

Hollywood Bar (⏰ 2pm-midnight) For a cold beer y this dim watering hole located behind the overnment House.

etting There & Away

ecause at least one train links Sainshand ith Ulaanbaatar every day, there are no ights or scheduled bus services to or om Sainshand.

HITCHING

For the same reasons that jeeps are scarce, hitching is also hard. You will get a lift to Zamyn-Üüd or to Ulaanbaatar, but the train is quicker, more comfortable and cheap.

JEEP

Share jeeps park themselves at a stop south of the Sports Palace. These head out to the various villages in Dornogov, but it's nearly impossible to find a ride going to the neighbouring aimags. If you ask around you *might* be able to find someone to drive you to Khanbogd or Manlai *sums* in Ömnögov, from where you could find transport to Dalanzadgad, but the cost for such a trip could be from US$150 to US$200 (they would expect you to pay the return fare as the jeep would have to go back empty). Sainshand is 463km southeast of Ulaanbaatar, and 218km northwest of Zamyn-Üüd.

TRAIN

Local train 285 from Ulaanbaatar via Choir (daily), departs at 10.15am and arrives at 8pm. It returns to Ulaanbaatar from Sainshand at 9.05pm, arriving 8am. A second option is local train 276 to Zamyn-Üüd, which leaves

THE GOBI

Ulaanbaatar at 4.30pm, arriving at Sainshand at the inconvenient time of about 2am. The return train departs Sainshand at 11.03pm and arrives in Ulaanbaatar at 9.45am. There may be other departure times (and the aforementioned may change) so check when you book your ticket, or call the station in Sainshand: ☎ 52307. Tickets from Ulaanbaatar cost T6200/9500 for hard/soft sleeper. If you book your ticket more than a day ahead there is a T450 fee. Trains get crowded in both directions so book as far in advance as possible.

The Trans-Mongolian Railway and the trains between Ulaanbaatar and Ereen (just over the Chinese border) and Hohhot (in Inner Mongolia) stop at Sainshand, but you cannot use these services just to get to Sainshand unless you buy a ticket all the way to China. You must take the local daily train.

Getting *on* the Trans-Mongolian at Sainshand for China is fraught with complications unless you have bought your Ulaanbaatar–Beijing/Hohhot ticket beforehand in UB and arranged for someone to tell the train steward at Ulaanbaatar Station not to sell your seat. In Beijing, you can only buy a Beijing–Ulaanbaatar ticket, but you can get off at Sainshand.

SOUTH OF SAINSHAND
Khamaryn Khiid Хамарын Хийд
This reconstructed **monastery** (GPS: N 44°36.038′, E 110°16.650′), an hour's drive south of Sainshand, has grown up around the cult of Danzan Ravjaa (p201), whom many locals believe to have been a living god. His image is sewn into a carpet that hangs in the main hall. The original monastery and three-storey theatre, built by Danzan Ravjaa in 1821, was destroyed in the 1930s. Water from the spring nearby (surrounded by a concrete building) is said to hold curative properties.

From the monastery, a path leads for 3km to a bell tower which you must strike three times to announce your arrival at the 'energy centre,' known as **Shambhala**. In 1853, Danzan Ravjaa told the local people that he would die in three years but they could forever come to this place and speak to his spirit. Indeed, he died three years later and the site was marked by an ovoo. Shambhala is now surrounded by 108 new stupas ('108' being a sacred number in Buddhism). Note that major festivities are held here on 10 September.

RITUALS AT SHAMBHALA

There are several rituals to adhere to when you enter the Shambhala site. Do them in the following order:

- Write a bad thought on a piece of paper and burn it in the rocks to the left.

- Write down a wish, read it, throw some vodka in the air and drop some rice in the stone circles on the ground (representing the past, present and future).

- Take a white pebble from the ground, place it on the pile of other white pebbles and announce your family name.

- Take off your shoes and lay down on the ground, absorbing the energy of this sacred site.

- Circle the *ovoo* three times.

A watchman may be on hand to show you around.

A series of small **meditation caves** are located a short walk east of Shambhala. Here monks used to seal themselves inside the caves and meditate for 108 days.

Around 23km northwest of the monastery, **Bayanzürkh Uul** (elev 1070m; GPS: N 44°41.644′, E 110°02.707′) Legend tells that the mountain is home to the spirit of the third Noyon Khutagt (a predecessor of Danzan Ravjaa). The temple halfway up the mountain is as far as local women are allowed to go (although no-one seems to mind if foreign women go to the top). At the summit you are required to make three wishes and circle the peak along the well-worn path.

Altangerel, the curator of the Museum of Danzan Ravjaa in Sainshand (and the fifth generation in the hereditary line of Danzan Ravjaa's personal protectors, which extends from Danzan Ravjaa's assistant Balchinchoijoo) can help with accommodation. Contact him at the museum in Sainshand if you are thinking of heading to Khamaryn Khiid. The monastery has very basic facilities, but the Gobi Sunrise Tavan Dohoi ger camp (p200) is a 30-minute (20km) drive back towards Sainshand.

ZAMYN-ÜÜD ЗАМЫН-УУД
☎ 02524
The Trans-Mongolia railway line runs into China at this small, otherwise insignificant village in the Gobi Desert. If you are tra-

lling by local train between Mongolia and China you'll need to stop here and organise onward transport.

While Erlian booms with economic activity right across the border, little happens in Zamyn Üüd – there is no market and the roads are slowly being consumed by sand, blown in from the surrounding desert.

There are just enough transit travellers to keep some hotels and restaurants busy around the train station. Plans to build a casino in town could help, although after several years of talk nothing has happened yet.

nformation

The train station has banks, an ATM and money changers. Luggage storage is available for T250 per item.

elecom office (☎ 21112; ◷ 24hr) International calling available, and internet (per hour T470).

leeping

There are enough vehicles heading in and out of town that you probably won't have to spend the night, but in case you do, try the following.

Jintin (☎ 53289; dm/s/half-lux US$6/8/12) A cheap option located next to the train station.

Khaan Shonkhor Hotel (☎ 21608; half-lux/lux T16,000/20,000) Clean and modern hotel with restaurant serving better-than-average Mongol fare.

etting There & Away

The daily train (276) to Zamyn-Üüd, via Choir and Sainshand, leaves Ulaanbaatar every day at 4.30pm, arriving around 7.10am. Tickets cost T5100/12,800 for hard/soft sleeper. The train returns to Ulaanbaatar at 5.50pm, arriving the next morning at 9.45am. Tickets cost T2400/6500 to Sainshand and T3900/10,200 to Choir.

From UB you can also take the 34 express train, departing Monday, Wednesday and Friday at 8.05pm, arriving in Zamyn-Üüd at 7.55am for T20,000. It returns at 10pm on Tuesday, Thursday and Saturday. Contact the station in Zamyn-Üüd (☎ 53340, 53108) for more details.

To cross the border, most people take the frequent jeeps that run between the train stations of Zamyn-Üüd and Ereen (T12,000, km). The jeeps are generally quicker than the train. When the train arrives in Zamyn-Üüd there is a frantic rush for jeeps and

then a jockeying for position at the border. Keeping up with the crowd will get you to Ereen more quickly, so don't dally! See p269 for more information about crossing the border.

By jeep the price is the same if coming from Ereen. Jeeps assemble at the Ereen bus station and the market – ask the Mongolian drivers. There is a Y5 tax that you need to pay going either way (you can pay the driver in tögrög or US dollars and they will pay the tax for you).

The road border is open from 8am to 6pm daily except holidays. If it's closed for a holiday, a train will still run across the border.

If you are on a Trans-Mongolian train, or the service between Ulaanbaatar and Hohhot or Ereen, you will stop at Zamyn-Üüd for an hour or so while Mongolian customs and immigration officials do their stuff – usually in the middle of the night. See p272 for details.

NORTH OF SAINSHAND

Probably the best sight in Dornogov, **Senjit Khad** is a natural rock formation in the shape of an arch. It is about 95km northeast of Sainshand in Altanshiree *sum*.

The volcanic rock formation of **Tsonjiin Chuluu** looks rather like a set of hexagonal organ pipes. It's in the extreme northeast corner of Dornogov, in Delgerekh *sum*, about 160km along the northeast road from Sainshand.

Both sites can be visited only with your own vehicle en route between Dornogov aimag and eastern Mongolia.

CHOIR ЧОЙР

Choir, about halfway between Sainshand and Ulaanbaatar, was once home to a large **Russian air-force base** that was abandoned in 1992. The base is still there, although most of the buildings have been stripped to their core, leaving empty shells and wreckage everywhere. The base and landing strip, around 15km north of Choir near the village of Lun, are an eerie ghost town of old buildings and abandoned MiG fighters.

To promote rapid economic growth, Choir formally seceded from Dornogov (it is now an autonomous municipality called Gov-Sümber, with a population of 13,000) and was declared a Free Trade Zone. Nothing much was done to promote the area though, and it continues to languish in neglect.

THE GOBI

To get to Choir, train No 276 leaves Ulaanbaatar daily at 4.30pm and arrives at 9.23pm. Train No 284 departs at 5.40pm on Friday and Sunday, arriving at 11.33pm. Tickets cost T3000/6400 for a hard/soft seat. From Choir, the train departs for Ulaanbaatar at the unspeakable time of 3.48am. On Thursday, Saturday and Monday another train departs at 2.16am. On Monday at 8am a bus departs from the Bayanzürkh bus station in Ulaanbaatar for Choir (T5000, five hours). The road is newly paved.

ÖMNÖGOV ӨМНӨГОВЬ

pop 46,300 / area 165,000 sq km

Ömnögov (South Gobi) is the largest aimag in Mongolia, with a population density of only 0.3 people per square kilometre. It's not hard to see why humans prefer to live elsewhere: with an average annual precipitation of only 130mm a year, and summer temperatures reaching an average of 38°C, this is the driest, hottest and harshest region in the entire country.

Gurvan Saikhan Nuruu in the centre provides the main topographic relief in this pancake-flat region; the mountains make human habitation marginally possible by capturing snow in winter, which melts and feeds springs on the plains below, providing water for some livestock.

Ömnögov supports thousands of black-tailed gazelle, which you may see darting across the open plains. The aimag is also home to a quarter (around 80,000) of Mongolia's domesticated camels.

Tourism is an important business in the region and there are plenty of ger camps throughout the aimag. Far more important, however, is that the aimag passes out business cards printed with gold dust). The massive Oyu Tolgoi copper and gold deposit, located near the Chinese border in Khanbogd *sum,* is currently being developed by a Canadian mining company. When fully operational in a decade's time the mine could boost Mongolia's GDP by more than 30%.

National Parks

Gurvan Saikhan National Park (2,000,000 hectares) Wealth of sand dunes, canyons, dinosaur fossils and mountainous terrain. Desert wildlife includes argali sheep, ibex and snow leopard.

Small Gobi A Strictly Protected Area (1,839,176 hectares) On the border with China, includes dunes and saxaul forest. Last great bastion of the *khulan* (wild ass).

DALANZADGAD ДАЛАНЗАДГАД

☎ 01532 / pop 13,900 / elev 1465m

The capital of Ömnögov, Dalanzadgad is speck of civilisation in the desert, sitting i the shadow of Gurvan Saikhan Nuruu. As th capital of a mineral-rich aimag, there are som positive signs of development, including th construction of a massive new Governmen House. The town is also the main base fo explorations into the desert, although trave lers facilities are still a little basic.

Information

Bathhouse (admission T1000; 🕙 10am-8pm) One stre north of the Strictly Protected Areas office.

Internet café (per hr T690; 🕙 9am-10pm Mon-Fri, 10am-10pm Sat & Sun) In the Telecom office.

Khan Bank (☎ 22216; 🕙 9am-1pm & 2-4pm Mon-Fr 9am-1pm Sat) Changes dollars and can give a cash advan against Visa or MasterCard.

Strictly Protected Areas office (☎ 23973; gtzgobi@ magicnet.mn) In the southwest of town, this office mostl deals in bureaucratic affairs. For information, you are bett off at the information ger at the gate to Gurvan Saikhan National Park.

Telecom office (☎ 24110; 🕙 24hr) A one-minute ca to the US or Europe costs T772.

Sights
SOUTH GOBI MUSEUM

Surprisingly, this **museum** (☎ 23871; admissi T2000, photos T5000, video T10,000; 🕙 9am-6pm Mon-F has little on dinosaurs – just a leg, an ar and a few eggs. (All of the best exhibits are Ulaanbaatar or in other museums around th world.) There are a few nice paintings, a hug stuffed vulture and a display of scroll pain ings and other Buddhist items. The museu is on the main street, on the other side of th park from the pink Drama Theatre.

Sleeping
CAMPING

Like other Gobi aimag capitals, there no river or any decent place to camp

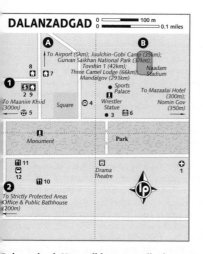

Dalanzadgad. You will have to walk 1km or 2km in any direction from town, and pitch your tent somewhere secluded.

GER CAMPS

There are more than 20 ger camps between Dalanzadgad and Khongoryn Els. A GPS unit will make your search easier if you are looking for a particular camp.

Mazaalai Hotel (☎ 22076, 23040; per person T5000) This small ger camp is on the eastern end of Dalanzadgad near the Nomin Gov store.

Tovshin 1 (☎ /fax 322 728, 9911 4811; GPS: N 43°45.841′, 104°02.838′; with/without meals US$30/15) Located 7km beyond Juulchin, this camp has good hot showers and toilets, and a decent restaurant and bar, but the location is uninteresting and the buildings are ugly.

Juulchin-Gobi Camp (☎ 26522; jgobi@magicnet mn; GPS: N 43°45.236′, E 104°07.578′; with/without meals US$40/22) This huge camp, 35km from town with an airstrip attached, is popular with organised tours. If you rock up with a tent it's possible to camp for US$5. It is about the same standard as the others, but the location isn't as good.

our pick Three Camel Lodge (in UB ☎ 011-330 998; www.threecamellodge.com; GPS: N 43°53.603′, E 103°44.435′; with/without meals US$70/35) A veritable oasis in the desert 66km northeast of Dalanzadgad, overlooking a great grassy plain and spectacular mountains, this place raises the bar for the Mongolian ger camp, with first-rate facilities and food. Run by Nomadic Expeditions, the cosy lodge offers nightly performances of folk singing and dancing. Asian/European meals are buffet-style and tasty. Lunch (US$12) is the main meal of the day (the dessert, a baked apple with raisins and custard cream, is reason enough to splurge). Visitors stay in luxurious gers that have easy access to a good-quality shared bathroom. It is a great way to break up a long journey. Even if you don't stay here, you could stop by for a drink on the terrace.

HOTEL

At the time of research the Dalanzadgad Hotel was undergoing extensive renovations and is expected to be one of the best hotels in town when it re-opens.

Tuvshin Hotel (☎ 22240; per person T5000) Looked after by a friendly granny, the Tuvshin has just two rooms in good condition. It's in the same building as the Khan Bank.

Gobi Gurvan Saikhan Hotel (☎ 23830; dm T6000, s/d with bathroom T10,000/20,000) This place is homely and bright. The double rooms have toilet and shower, although the latter just dribbles water.

Eating

Vegetarians could put together salad from the fresh veggies on sale in the **market** (Gobi vegetables are renowned in Mongolia for their sweet taste). Nearby, you'll also see women selling jars of lovely *tarag* (yogurt; T500) and packets of sugar.

Nomin Gov (☎ 24003; ⏰ 9am-11pm) If you need to stock up for an expedition, this is the

THE GOBI

DINOSAURS

In the early 1920s, newspapers brought news of the discovery of dinosaur eggs in the southern Gobi Desert by American adventurer Roy Chapman Andrews. Over a period of two years Andrews' team unearthed over 100 dinosaurs, including Protoceratops Andrewsi, which was named after the explorer. The find included several Velociraptors (Swift Robbers), subsequently made famous by *Jurassic Park*, and a parrot-beaked Oviraptor (Egg Robber). Most valuable in Andrews' mind was the discovery of the earliest known mammal skulls, 'possibly the most valuable seven days of work in the whole history of palaeontology to date'.

Subsequent expeditions have added to the picture of life in the Gobi during the late Cretaceous period 70 million years ago, the last phase of dinosaur dominance before mammals inherited the earth.

One of the most famous fossils unearthed so far is the 'Fighting Dinosaurs' fossil, discovered by a joint Polish–Mongolian team in 1971 and listed as a national treasure. The remarkable 80-million-year-old fossil is of a Protoceratops and Velociraptor locked in mortal combat. It is thought that this and other fossilised snapshots were entombed by a violent sand storm or by collapsing sand dunes. One poignant fossil is of an Oviraptor protecting its nest of eggs from the impending sands.

A picture of prehistoric Gobi has emerged of a land of swamps, marshes and lakes, with areas of sand studded with oases. The land was inhabited by a colourful cast of characters: huge duck-billed hadrosaurs; ankylosaurs, which were up to 25-feet tall, armour-plated and had club-like tails that acted like a giant mace; long-necked, lizard-hipped sauropods such as Nemegtosaurus, which may have grown to a weight of 90 tonnes; and the mighty Tarbosaurus (Alarming Reptile), a carbon copy of a Tyrannosaurus Rex, with a 1.2m-long skull packed with razor sharp teeth up to 15cm long.

---

best place. A smaller version of UB's State Department Store, the Nomin Gov is located at the eastern end of town.

Michid Restaurant & Bar (meals T1500) For a hot meal, try this restaurant located in the Gobi Gurvan Saikhan Hotel. It has some reasonable Mongolian food.

Gobi Restaurant (meals T1200-1800; ☼ 9am-11pm) A decent second choice if you've already been to the Michid. It's behind the market.

Getting There & Away

AIR

Both MIAT and EZ Nis airlines fly between Dalanzadgad and Ulaanbaatar. MIAT flights are US$78/134 one way/return and EZ Nis charges US$120/216 one way/return. During peak tourist season – July to mid-September – MIAT schedules extra daily flights between Ulaanbaatar and Juulchin-Gobi ger camp for the same price. Even if you have a ticket to Dalanzadgad, check that you are going to the city and not just the ger camp. The new airport is a designated 'international airport', but as yet has no international flights.

BUS

A daily bus travels between Dalanzadgad and Ulaanbaatar (T13,300, 12 hours, 553km). The bus leaves from the market in Dalanzadga around 8am (but expect delays).

HITCHING

Hitching around the Gobi Desert, includin to the attractions in Gurvan Saikhan Nation Park, is impractical and dangerous. Hitchin between aimag capitals and out to a few sur centres is possible but not easy. There won be anything of interest on the way so you still need to hire a jeep at some point to vis the attractions. Make sure you carry plent of water, food and a tent and sleeping bag fc the inevitable breakdowns.

JEEP

Daily vans run from Dalanzadgad to Ulaanbaata (T14,000); for details call ☎ 23708. The cheap est way to see the attractions in Gurvan Saikha National Park is to hang around for a fe days and ask other independent travellers share a jeep. Vans and jeeps can be hired i Dalanzadgad for T450 per km.

KHANBOGD ХАНБОГД

If you are travelling between Sainshand an Dalanzadgad, it's worth taking a slight detou to visit Khanbogd *sum*. Despite its apparen remoteness, the *sum* is set to enrich the who

Other weird and wonderful beasts that once roamed the southern Gobi include bone-headed pachycephalosaurs, which used their reinforced skulls as battering rams; the Embolotherium, with a periscope-style nose that allowed it to breathe while the rest of it was underwater; and Therizinosaurus (Scythe Lizard), a fierce carnivore with massive claws over 60cm long. Huge rhinos, over four times the size of an adult elephant and thought to be the largest land mammals ever to have lived, shared the land with tiny rodents, the forerunners of modern-day mammalian life.

With a bit of digging you may be able to find some dinosaur fossils in the southern Gobi, but please be aware that these fossils are very precious, and far more useful to palaeontologists. Locals may approach you at Bayanzag, the ger camps and even Dalanzadgad to buy dinosaur bones and eggs. Remember that it is *highly* illegal to export fossils from Mongolia.

Apart from the famous sites of Bayanzag and nearby Togrigiin Shiree, the richest sites of Bugiin Tsav, Ulaan Tsav, Nemegt Uul and Khermen Tsav are all in the remote west of Ömnögov aimag and impossible to reach without a jeep and dedicated driver (or a helicopter).

There are still plenty of fossils – in 2006 a team of palaeontologists from Mongolia and Montana unearthed 67 dinosaur skeletons in a single week! In 2007 a Canadian paleontologist reported finding large numbers of fossilised carnivores near Nemegt Uul. The proportion of carnivores is usually 5% but this site had closer to 50%. Sadly, he also described how poachers remove the skulls, hands and feet, scattering the other bones in their dirty work.

Today, the best places to come face to face with the dinosaurs of the Gobi are the Museum of Natural History in Ulaanbaatar and the American Museum of Natural History in New York, which also has a fine website (www.amnh.org). As for books, check out *Dinosaurs of the Flaming Cliffs* by American palaeontologist Michael Novacek.

---

of Mongolia, thanks to an enormous copper and gold deposit at Oyu Tolgoi, about 40km outhwest of the town centre.

The development of the mine is having profound effects on the town of Khanbogd, which has a new health clinic, shops and a renovated hotel (☎ 01535-12223; r T10,000). In order to facilitate all this change, plans are being set to expand the population; come back in 15 years and this dusty village of 1500 people could be home to as many as 30,000 folks working at the mine or in support businesses.

Unless you have a particular interest in copper mining, the main reason to come here it to visit **Demchigiin Khiid** (Дэмчигийн Хийдийн уйр; GPS: N 43°07.711′, E 107°07.668′) one of the monasteries built by the famed fifth Noyon Khutagt, Danzan Ravjaa (see p201). The monastery, about 20km from the town, was destroyed in 1937 but is undergoing a major renovation project funded by Ivanhoe Mines, the mining company exploiting Oyu Tolgoi). Gobi people consider the rocky area around the monastery to be an important energy centre for Buddhism, and as a result the place gets few pilgrims who come to meditate.

Serious explorers may want to carry on to **Lovon Chombin Agui** (Ловон Чомбын Агуй; GPS: 42°35.305′, E 107°49.529′), a 50m-long cave with numerous stalactites. The cave and adjacent monastery ruins are near the Chinese border so you'll definitely need a border permit from Ulaanbaatar (p66).

BULGAN БУЛГАН

There is little to see in this ramshackle village 95km northwest of Dalanzadgad, but you may end up here as it is located along the main tourist route between Bayanzag and places south.

By virtue of its central Gobi location, this small village is home to large-scale **Tsagaan Sar** (Lunar New Year) festivities, which take place in January or February. The two-day festival includes camel racing, camel polo and a camel beauty contest (unfortunately, good breath is not a key category). During the event, temporary ger camps pop up to house tourists.

The **Ankhsan Cooperative Guesthouse** (☎ 811 117, 811 134; treepool-06@yahoo.com; per person T3000-5000), run by a friendly local named Poli, is a great place to stay in the town. Food is available.

Nearby is **Ulaan Nuur** (Red Lake), the largest and just about the only lake in Ömnögov. It may not be there when you visit because it often dries out; it won't quench your thirst either – it is very salty.

THE GOBI

BAYANZAG БАЯНЗАГ

Bayanzag (Flaming Cliffs; GPS: N 44°08.311´, E 103°43.667´), which means 'rich in saxaul shrubs', is more commonly known as the 'Flaming Cliffs', penned by the palaeontologist Roy Chapman Andrews (see the boxed text, opposite). First excavated in 1922, it is renowned worldwide for the number of dinosaur bones and eggs found in the area, which you can see in the Museum of Natural History in Ulaanbaatar or, mostly, in other museums around the world.

Even if you are not a 'dinophile', the eerie beauty of the surrounding landscape is a good reason to visit. It's a classic desert of rock, red sands, scrub, sun and awesome emptiness. There's not much to do once you're here except explore the area or grab a cold drink from the souvenir sellers who hang out on the edge of the cliff.

Bayanzag Tourist Camp (☎ 5053 1005; info@mon goliagobi.com; GPS: N 44°10.466´, E 103°41.816´; with/without meals US$30/15), about 4km from the cliffs, is a reasonable choice in the area, notable for its giant tortoise-shaped restaurant. Camel rental here is T3000 per hour. You could camp near the *zag* (scrub) forest.

Bayanzag by road is about 100km northwest of Dalanzadgad and 18km northeast of Bulgan. It can be surprisingly hard to find so you really need to take a driver or guide who's been there before, or ask directions regularly from the few people who live in the area.

A further 22km northeast of Bayanzag is an area of sand dunes called **Moltzog Els**, which might be worth a visit if you're not planning to visit Khongoryn Els.

GURVAN SAIKHAN NATIONAL PARK ГУРВАН САЙХАН

With its iconic sand dunes, ice canyon, striped badlands and stunning mountain vistas this is understandably one of Mongolia's most popular national parks. Most travellers only see a fraction of it, sticking to the main sites. With more time it's possible to drive to the remote western area – an eerie landscape so lacking in life that you may feel as if you've landed on the moon.

Gurvan Saikhan (Three Beauties) is named after its three ridges (though there are four). Besides its spectacular natural beauty it contains more than 200 bird species, including the Mongolian desert finch, cinereous vulture, desert warbler and hou-

bara bustard. Spring brings further waves of migratory birds.

The park also has maybe 600 or more types of plants, a lot of which only bloom after (very infrequent) heavy rain. The sparse vegetation does manage to support numerous types of animals, such as the black-tailed gazelle, Kozlov's pygmy jerboa, wild ass and endangered species of wild camel, snow leopard, ibex and argali sheep.

Information

There is a national park entry fee of T3000 per person. You can pay the fee and get a permit at the park office in Dalanzadgad, at the entrance to Yolyn Am or from the ranger at Khongoryn Els. Keep your entry ticket as you may need to show it to rangers later in your trip.

Sights & Activities

YOLYN AM ЁЛЫН АМ

Yolyn Am (Vulture's Mouth) was originally established to conserve the birdlife in the region, but it's now more famous for its dramatic and very unusual scenery – it is a valley in the middle of the Gobi Desert, with metres-thick ice for most of the year.

The small **Nature Museum** (GPS: N 43°32.872, E 104°02.257´; admission US$1; ☉ 8am-9pm) at the gate on the main road to Yolyn Am has a collection of dinosaur eggs and bones, stuffed birds and a snow leopard. It also sells the excellent booklet *Gobi Gurvan Saikhan National Park*, by Bern Steinhauer Burkhart. More information in English on the park and its facilities can be found in an 'information ger', which also sells park entry tickets. There are several souvenir shops and a couple of places to stay, including **Tavan Erdene guesthouse** (☎ 9953 7058; per person US$3-5) which offers basic ger accommodation.

From the museum, the road continues for another 10km to a car park. From there, a pleasant 2km walk, following the stream, leads to an **ice-filled gorge** (GPS: N 43°29.332´, 104°04.000´) and one or two lonely souvenir salesmen. Locals also rent horses (T6000) and camels (T10,000) for the trip.

In winter, the ice is up to 10m high, and continues down the gorge for another 10km. The ice is not particularly accommodating for tourists, and usually disappears in the summer (June to September). It's possible to walk the length of the gorge – an experi-

ROY CHAPMAN ANDREWS

American adventurer Roy Chapman Andrews (1884-1960) had a restless spirit. 'I wanted to go everywhere', he wrote, 'I would have started on a day's notice for the North Pole or the South, to the jungle or the desert. It made not the slightest bit of difference to me'.

Born in Wisconsin, Andrews' itchy feet soon brought him to New York where he sought work at the Museum of Natural History; upon learning there were no job openings he offered his services as a janitor (eventually working his way up to Museum Director). Adventures in his youth included filming whales in the Atlantic, trapping snakes in the East Indies and hunting game in Yunnan. But he is best known for his explorations of the Gobi in the 1920s, where he found the first dinosaur eggs, jaws and skulls in Central Asia. Andrews' most famous expeditions were based at Bayanzag, which he famously renamed the 'Flaming Cliffs'.

According to his books and biographies, he was a real-life adventurer, who took the expeditions' ambushes, raids, bandits, rebellions and vipers in his stride (the camp killed 47 vipers in their tents one night). He was never one for understatement: as one expedition member said, 'the water that was up to our ankles was always up to Roy's neck'. In reality, one of the few times an expedition member was seriously injured was when Andrews accidentally shot himself in the leg with his own revolver.

Andrews worked for US intelligence during WWI and also explored Alaska, Borneo, Burma, Korea and China. He wrote such Boys' Own classics as *Whale Hunting with Gun and Camera* (1916), *Across Mongolian Plains* (1921), *On the Trail of Ancient Man* (1926) and *The New Conquest of Central Asia* (1932). Always kitted out in a felt hat, khakis and a gun by his side, Andrews is widely regarded as the model on which the Hollywood screen character Indiana Jones was based.

On his return to the US Andrews took the directorship of the American Museum of Natural History but was asked to resign in 1941 after a difficult tenure during the depression years. His death in California in 1960, at the age of 76, went almost unnoticed. For more information on RC Andrews, read *Dragon Hunter*, a biography by Charles Galenkamp.

---

enced driver could pick you up on the other side, about 8km east of the car park.

The surrounding hills offer plenty of opportunities for some fine, if somewhat strenuous, day **hikes**. If you are lucky you might spot ibex or argali sheep along the steep valley ridges. Yolyn Am is in the Zuun Saikhan Nuruu, 46km west of Dalanzadgad.

About 1km before the museum is a second ice valley called **Mukhar Shiveert**; visitors may be required to pay T3000 to visit the site (on top of the T3000 you already paid to enter the park).

If you are headed from Yolyn Am to Khongoryn Els, an adventurous and rough alternative route takes you through the **Dugany Am** (GPS: N 43°29.521′, E 103°51.586′), a spectacular and narrow gorge. The gorge is blocked with ice until July and can be impassable even after the ice has melted, so check road conditions with the park ranger's office at the park entrance.

KHONGORYN ELS ХОНГОРЫН ЭЛС

Khongoryn Els are some of the largest and most famous sand dunes in Mongolia. Also known as the Duut Mankhan (Singing Dunes), they are up to 300m high, 12km wide and about 100km long. The largest dunes are at the northwestern corner of the range. The views of the desert from the top are wonderful.

The sand dunes are also a popular place for organising camel rides; locals seem to appear from the woodwork when a jeep full of tourists arrives. To properly explore the area, you will need to stay the night in the desert before returning to Dalanzadgad. There are plenty of camping spots near the dunes (you'll need your own water) and a handful of ger camps.

Gobi Discovery (011-312 769; www.gobidiscovery .mn; GPS: N 43°46.495′, E 102°20.307′; with/without meals US$35/17) is a welcoming ger camp, about 2km north of the dunes. **Juulchin Gobi 2** (☎ 26522, 9914 8115; jgobi@magicnet.mn; with/without meals US$40/22) is about 6km past Gobi Discovery.

The dunes are about 180km from Dalanzadgad. There is no way to get there unless you charter a jeep or are part of a tour.

From Khongoryn Els it is possible to follow desert tracks 130km north to Bogd

THE GOBI

in Övörkhangai, or 215km northwest to Bayanlig in Bayankhongor. This is a remote and unforgiving area and you shouldn't undertake either trip without an experienced driver and full stocks of food, water and fuel.

BAYANKHONGOR
БАЯНХОНГОР

pop 82,200 / area 116,000 sq km

One of the most diverse aimags in the Gobi, this one has mountains in the north, deserts in the south, a handful of lakes and rivers, hot springs and a real oasis in the far south of the province.

Bayankhongor, which means 'rich chestnut' (named after the colour of the horses – or your skin after a couple of hours in the Gobi sun), is home to wild camels and asses and the extremely rare Gobi bear.

Most travellers bypass the aimag while travelling along the major southern Ulaanbaatar-Khovd road, but Bayankhongor does have some interesting, albeit remote, attractions. Some adventurous expeditionists have ridden horses from Bayankhongor over the Khangai Nuruu to Tsetserleg in Arkhangai. Other travellers have gone camel trekking between some of the remote towns in the south of the aimag.

Getting to these remote places is as much expedition as common travel, but if you are

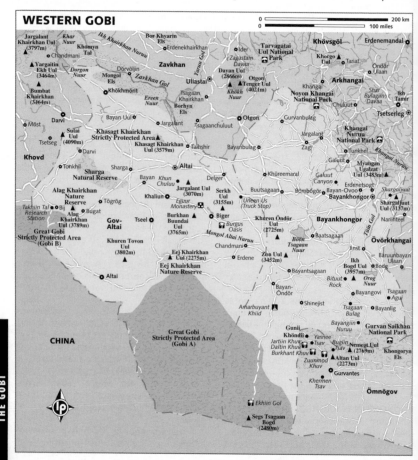

THE GOBI

well prepared the area offers some magical trips off the beaten track.

BAYANKHONGOR CITY
БАЯНХОНГОР
☎ 01442 / pop 23,800 / elev 1859m

The broad avenues, cantonment-style apartment blocks and parade ground in front of a monolithic Government House are straight out a Soviet planner's briefcase. There are also large patches of waste ground as if the builders gave up halfway through the project. Although the town itself is nothing special, the Khangai Nuruu, with several peaks of 3000m or more, is not too far away. You'll probably have to stay here if on a long haul to or from the west, to start explorations to more remote regions in the south, or to go on a day trip to the nearby springs at Shargaljuut (p212).

Information

Bathhouse (☎ 22652; per person T800, sauna T2000; ☼ 10am-10pm) Located 650m north of the Telecom office. The sauna needs to be booked ahead at least two hours.

Internet café (☎ 117; per hr T500; ☼ 9am-10pm) Next to the Telecom office.

Khan Bank (☎ 22981; ☼ 9am-1pm & 2-5pm Mon-Fri) Changes US dollars and gives cash advances on MasterCard.

Telecom office (☎ 24105; ☼ 24hr) The post office is also located here.

Sights

The skyline of the city is dominated by a **stupa** on a hill to the west of the square. If you are staying for a while, take a walk up there for views of the town and nearby countryside. A Peace Corps volunteer laid out a **frisbee golf course** in the town park, so if you have a disc ask some of the local kids to show you the first hole.

LAMYN GEGEENII GON GANDAN DEDLIN KHIID ЛАМЫН ГЭГЭЭНИЙ ГОН ГАНДАН ДЭДЛИН ХИЙД

The original monastery by this name was located 20km east of Bayankhongor city and was home to 10,000 monks, making it one of the biggest in the country. It was levelled by the communist government in 1937. The current monastery, built in 1991, is home to only 40 monks. The main temple is built in the shape of a ger, although it's actually made of brick. The main hall features a statue of Sakyamuni flanked by a green and white Tara. The monastery is on the main street, 700m north of the square.

MUSEUMS

Both museums are closed on weekends but can be opened upon special request.

The **Aimag Museum** (☎ 22339; admission T1500, photos T5000; ☼ 9am-1pm & 2-6pm Mon-Fri), inside the sports stadium in the park, is well laid out and worth a visit. There is a good display on Buddhist art, featuring two lovely statues of Tara, some fine old scroll paintings and *tsam* (lama dance) masks and costumes.

The **Natural History Museum** (T1500; ☼ 9am-1pm & 2-6pm Mon-Fri) across the street is filled with badly stuffed animals, a replica Tarbosaurus skeleton and some fossils, including a 130-million-year-old fossilised turtle.

Sleeping

The best place to camp is probably by the Tüin Gol, a few hundred metres east of the city.

Negdelchin Hotel (☎ 22278; d/tr/q/half-lux/lux T16,000/21,000/24,000/24,000/30,000) Located at the southern end of the main street, the 'Workers Hotel' is Bayankhongor's old Soviet-era stand-by. Some rooms have seen renovation, all have a toilet but only the lux rooms have a shower.

Khongor Hotel (☎ 22300, 9944 7337; tw/q/lux T14,000/20,000/30,000) Above a restaurant on the main road, this small hotel has clean, modern rooms with TV, fridge and toilet. There is a separate shower (T1000) and sauna (T5000). The staff are courteous and helpful.

Seoul Hotel (☎ 22754, 9944 0884; r T18,000, lux s/d T25,000/50,000) Newly built brick-fronted hotel in the centre of town near the Telecom office. The best rooms come with TV, fridge and hot shower while the more basic rooms have shared facilities. Locals say the restaurant is the best in town.

Eating

The hotels mentioned all have decent restaurants, with the Seoul Hotel offering the best quality meals, including some Western-style dishes. The Khongor also has some decent meals.

Uran Khairkhan (☎ 22062, 9944 8999; meals T1500-2000; ☼ 10am-7pm Mon-Fri) If the restaurants in the Seoul or Khongor hotels are closed this place *may* be able to rustle something up for you.

There are a few *guanz* nearby, including one just south of the Telecom office. Look for the sign: Зоогийн Газар.

THE GOBI

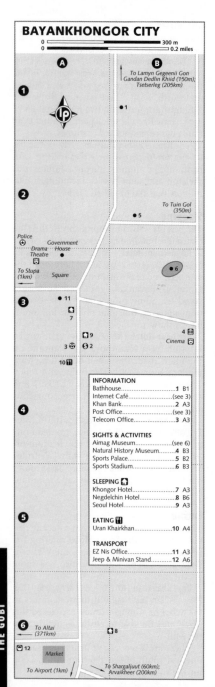

BAYANKHONGOR CITY

INFORMATION	
Bathhouse	1 B1
Internet Café	(see 3)
Khan Bank	2 A3
Post Office	(see 3)
Telecom Office	3 A3

SIGHTS & ACTIVITIES	
Aimag Museum	(see 6)
Natural History Museum	4 B3
Sports Palace	5 B2
Sports Stadium	6 B3

SLEEPING	
Khongor Hotel	7 A3
Negdelchin Hotel	8 B6
Seoul Hotel	9 A3

EATING	
Uran Khairkhan	10 A4

TRANSPORT	
EZ Nis Office	11 A3
Jeep & Minivan Stand	12 A6

Getting There & Away

AIR

On Tuesday, Thursday and Saturday, EZ Nis flies between Ulaanbaatar and Bayankhongor for US$120/216 one way/return. The airport is about 1km south of the city. The local **EZ Nis office** (☎ 24444, 9904 9933) is located on the south side of the square.

HITCHING

Bayankhongor city is on the main southern road between Ulaanbaatar and Khovd (city). A lot of vehicles going in either direction stop here, so getting a ride to Altai or Arvaikheer shouldn't be too difficult. South of Bayankhongor, or to Shargaljuut, you will have far less success. Ask around at the market, which doubles as a bus and truck station.

JEEP & MINIVAN

As a central point in southern Mongolia, Bayankhongor is well connected by bus, or better still by minivan to Ulaanbaatar (T20,000, 14 hours, 630km). Minivans leave daily and go via Arvaikheer. They stop at the market in Bayankhongor, about 300m south of the market square.

If you ask around at the market you should be able to find a minivan or jeep headed to west Altai (T20,000, 10 hours, 400km) or even Khovd (T30,000, 24 hours).

GALUUT CANYON ГАЛУУТ

This 25m-deep **canyon** is worth a visit if, for some bizarre reason, you are in the region. The canyon is only about 1m wide in places. It is 20km southwest of Galuut *sum* centre, which is about 85km northwest of Bayankhongor town.

SHARGALJUUT ШАРГАЛЖУУТ

The major attraction in Bayankhongor aimag is the 300 or so hot- and cold-water springs at **Shargaljuut** (GPS: N 46°19.940′, E 101°13.624′). About 70km northeast of Bayankhongor city, the springs are one of the few natural attractions in the Gobi region that are easily accessible from an aimag capital.

The springs and bathhouses cover the banks of the river between the peaks of Myangan Ugalzat Uul (3483m) and Shargaljuut Uul (3137m). The hot water, which can reach 50°C, is supposed to cure a wide range of complaints and many Mongolians come

THE GOBI

SPRINGS & BATHHOUSES

After driving around the hot and dusty Gobi for a few days, there is nothing better than washing away the accumulated dirt at either a city bathhouse or one of the springs in the area. Doing so almost feels like losing a layer of skin as the Gobi dust can stick like a layer of film to your body.

The public bathhouses are far from luxurious but they do the trick. Upon entering you pay for your visit at a little kiosk where you can also buy soap, shampoo and other beauty products. You'll be directed to the shower which has a small changing room. Flickering light bulbs, mildew, rusty pipes and generally poor maintenance make for a prison-like experience, but your body will thank you for it. There is no time limit but bear in mind the Gobi's limited water resources! Many bathhouses also have a small lobby and barbershop.

Springs like the ones at Shargaljuut (or elsewhere in Mongolia) are also basic. Usually, the spring water is piped into a small wood hut that contains an old bathtub. Use the wooden stopper to block the hole in the bottom and let the tub fill with water. The wood huts are small but there is enough room to change. When you're finished, just unplug the tub. Some springs are modernising and now have hot pools, the best of which are at Tsenkher (p129) in Arkhangai aimag.

---

for treatment at the **sanatorium** (🕙 9am-6pm Mon-Sat Apr-Dec).

Foreign guests can stay at the **ger camp & hotel** (☎ 26503; ger/half-lux/lux US$30/30/50) at the sanatorium, but should try to reserve in advance by calling the manager, Mr Tumendemberel.

A number of small **guesthouses** also offer beds for T3500 to T8000. The best is a small ger camp on the west side of the river before the main complex; ask for Dr Burnee who is a mine of information on the area.

Alternatively, you can camp further upstream next to the river on the little-used road to Tsetserleg.

Occasional share jeeps or minivans leave Bayankhongor's market for Shargaljuut (T3000, two hours, 70km). Chartering a minivan costs around T30,000 return. Alternatively, try Bayankhongor's airport on Tuesday and Saturday, when a minivan bound for the springs meets incoming passengers from Ulaanbaatar. In summer a local named Batbayar (☎ 9975 1276) also makes runs up to the springs for T20,000 one way.

From the springs it's possible to take a short cut through the mountains to Tsetserleg in Arkhangai if you have your own vehicle. It's a lovely route but gets muddy so ask about conditions before setting off.

BAYANGOVI БАЯНГОВЬ

The small town of Bayangovi is about 250km south of Bayankhongor (by road) in a beautiful valley dominated by Ikh Bogd Uul (3957m). While there is nothing of special interest in Bayangovi itself, the surrounding countryside

offers some intriguing desert sites, which can be visited on a one- or two-day excursion with the aid of a jeep and a local guide.

Gobi Camels (☎ 011-310 455; bed per person US$25) is an overpriced ger camp 6km northwest of town. It has hot showers and satellite TV but usually no food so bring your own if you want to stay. The other alternative is the unmarked and very basic **hotel** (per person T5000) within a compound on the southern edge of the town 'square'. It is usually deserted so you'll have to ask around the shops for the keyholder, Ms Dolumsuren.

The best way to get to Bayangovi and its surrounding attractions is in your own rented transport, either from Bayankhongor or as part of a longer trip. Failing this, shared minivans or jeeps occasionally run to Bayangovi from outside the central market at Bayankhongor. To get back to Bayankhongor ask at the post office or petrol station, and wait.

Once you get to Bayangovi your only option to see the surrounding sites is to hire a jeep from Gobi Camels camp.

AROUND BAYANGOVI

With a jeep and local guide it is possible to drive to the top of Ikh Bogd, to the north of Bayangovi, for stupendous views (nomads are sometimes camped up here in summer). Orog Nuur, featured on some maps and just north of Ikh Bogd, occasionally dries up thanks to over-use of its source river, the Tüin Gol.

About 90km east of Bayangovi lies **Tsagaan Agui** (GPS: N 44°42.604', E 101°10.187'). Situated in a narrow gorge, the cave once housed Stone

Age people 700,000 years ago. It features a crystal-lined inner chamber. Entrance to the cave costs T1000 (including a local guide), which is paid at the nearby ger.

Also near Bayangovi are several intriguing rock inscription sites. At **Tsagaan Bulag** (GPS: N 44°35.156', E 100°20.733'), 18km south, a white rock outcrop has the faint imprint of a strange helmeted figure, which locals believe was created by aliens. The area is also home to many herds of camel, attracted to the springs at the base of the outcrop.

Other noteworthy sites which you could add on to make a full day trip from Bayangovi include the vertical walls of the 4km-long **Gunii Khöndii** gorge, about 70km southwest of Bayangovi, and the beautiful **Bituut rock**, northwest of Bayangovi on the southern flank of Ikh Bogd, formed after an earthquake in 1957.

Further afield at **Bayangiin Nuruu** (GPS: N 44°17.218', E 100°31.329'), 90km south of Bayangovi, is a canyon with well-preserved rock engravings and petroglyphs dating from 3000 BC. The engravings depict hunting and agricultural scenes in a surprisingly futuristic style.

Travelling further south the landscape slowly descends into the Gobi Desert proper, along the border with Ömnögov aimag. Just over the border are numerous oases, among them **Jartiin Khuv**, **Daltin Khuv**, **Burkhant Khuv** and **Zuunmod Khuv**. Look out for wild ass, wild camel, black-tailed gazelle, antelope and *zam* lizard, which inhabit the area.

This region is rich in fossil sites. **Bugiin Tsav** (GPS: N 43°52.869', E 100°01.639') is a large series of rift valleys running parallel to the Altan Uul mountain range. A number of dinosaur fossils found here are now housed in the Museum of Natural History in Ulaanbaatar (p69). The other fossil site is at **Yasnee Tsav**, an eroded hilly region with some impressive buttes. Local guides claim they can point out authentic fossils at this site.

Continuing south will lead to the other famous fossil site of **Khermen Tsav** (GPS: N 43°28.006', E 99°49.976'), arguably the most spectacular canyons in the Gobi. The trip here from Bayangovi is a good seven to eight hours. From here one could continue east into the Gobi towards Gurvantes, Noyon and Bayandalai, but be warned that this section of road is notoriously treacherous. Don't go without plenty of water and well-equipped 4WD vehicles.

All of the sites mentioned above are very difficult to find without a good local guide. Bodio, the manager of the Gobi Camels ger camp (see p213), can organise local guides for US$15 per day (though few speak English so you really need your own translator). He also hires out jeeps for T450 per kilometre, which includes driver, petrol and local guide, and can arrange horse and camel tours for US$5 per person per day, plus US$5 per day for a guide.

BÖÖN TSAGAAN NUUR
БӨӨН ЦАГААН НУУР

This large **saltwater lake** (GPS: N 45°37.114', E 99°15.350') at the end of Baidrag Gol is popular with birdlife, especially relic gull, whooper swan and goose. It is possible to sleep in the abandoned cabins by the lake. A caretaker at the nearby ger will unlock one for T1000. The lake is about 130km southwest of Bayankhongor city, and 18km west of Baatsagaan.

AMARBUYANT KHIID
АМАРБУЯНТ ХИЙД

Located 47km west of Shinejist, this ruined **monastery** (GPS: N 44°37.745', E 98°42.214') once housed around 1000 monks until its destruction in 1937 by Stalin's thugs. Its claim to fame is that the 13th Dalai Lama, while travelling from Lhasa to Urga in 1904, stayed here for 10 days. The extensive ruins today include temples, buildings and walls and the main temple has been partially restored. Locals can also show you a small *ovoo* built by the Dalai Lama; out of respect no rocks were ever added to the *ovoo*.

EKHIIN GOL
ЭХИЙН ГОЛ

This fertile **oasis** (GPS: N 43°14.898', E 90°00.295') located deep in the southern Gobi produces a tremendous amount of fruit and vegetables. This is probably the only place in Mongolia where, upon entering a ger, travellers are served tomato juice rather than tea. Until the 1920s, Chinese farmers tilled this soil and grew opium, an era that ended when a psychopathic lama-turned-bandit named Dambijantsan came by here and slaughtered them all, down to the last man. Ekhiin Gol is a good place to start or end a camel trek from Shinejist.

CAMELS

They are known as the ships of the desert. The Mongolian Bactrian camel, a two-humped ornery beast with a shaggy wool coat, can still be seen hauling goods and people across the Gobi, as they have done for centuries.

Your first encounter with a camel may be a daunting experience: they bark and spit and smell like a thousand sweaty armpits. Sitting atop one you may be reminded of the unruly tontons from *Star Wars: The Empire Strikes Back*. But, excusing its lack of graces, the camel is a versatile and low-maintenance creature: it can last a week without water and a month without food; it can carry a lot of gear (up to 250kg – equal to 10 full backpacks); and it provides wool (on average 5kg per year), milk (up to 600L a year) and is a good source of (somewhat gamey) meat. The camel also produces 250kg of dung a year, and you can never have too much camel crap.

Monitoring the hump is an important part of camel maintenance. A firm and tall hump is a sign of good health, while a droopy hump means the camel is in need of food and water. If a thirsty camel hasn't drunk for some time it can suck up 200L of water in a single day. Most camels are tame, but male camels go crazy during the mating season in January and February – definitely a time to avoid approaching one.

Of the 260,000 camels in Mongolia, two-thirds can be found in the five aimags that stretch across the Gobi – 80,000 in Ömnögov alone. They are related to the rare wild camel known as the *khavtgai*. The current number of *khavtgai* is considerably lower than it was just 40 years ago, largely because they have been poached for their meat. In an attempt to stop the decline in numbers, several national parks in the Gobi have been established to protect the 300 or so remaining wild *khavtgai*.

GOV-ALTAI
ГОВЬ-АЛТАЙ

pop 64,000 / area 142,000 sq km

Mongolia's second-largest aimag is named after the Gobi Desert and Mongol Altai Nuruu, a mountain range that virtually bisects the aimag to create a stark, rocky landscape. There is a certain beauty in this combination, but there is considerable heartbreak too. Gov-Altai is one of the least suitable areas for raising livestock, and therefore one of the most hostile to human habitation.

Somehow a few Gobi bears, wild camels, ibex and even snow leopards survive, protected in several remote national parks. Most of the population live in the northeastern corner, where melting snow from Khangai Nuruu feeds small rivers, creating vital water supplies.

Mountaineers and adventurous hikers with a lot of time on their hands might want to bag an Altai peak. Opportunities include Khuren Tovon Uul (3802m) in Altai *sum*, Burkhan Buuddai Uul (3765m) in Biger *sum*, or the permanently snowcapped peak of Sutai Uul (4090m), the highest peak in Gov-Altai located right on the border with Khovd aimag. Most climbers approach Sutai Uul from the Khovd side.

National Parks

The beauty of Gov-Altai's diverse and sparsely populated mountain and desert environment has led to the designation of a large portion of the aimag as national park:

Alag Khairkhan Nature Reserve (36,400 hectares) Protected Altai habitat with rare plants, snow leopard, argali and ibex.

Eej Khairkhan Nature Reserve (22,475 hectares) About 150km directly south of Altai, the reserve was created to protect the general environment.

Great Gobi Strictly Protected Area Divided into 'Gobi A' (Southern Altai Gobi) and 'Gobi B' (Dzungarian Gobi). Gobi A is over 4.4 million hectares in the southern part of the aimag; Gobi B is 881,000 hectares in the southwest of Gov-Altai and neighbouring Khovd. Together, the area is the fourth-largest biosphere reserve in the world and protects wild ass, Gobi bear, wild Bactrian camel and jerboa, among other endangered animals.

Khasagt Khairkhan Strictly Protected Area (27,448 hectares) The area protects endangered argali sheep and the Mongol Altai mountain environment.

Sharga Nature Reserve Like the Mankhan Nature Reserve in Khovd aimag, it helps to preserve highly endangered species of antelope.

Takhiin Tal (150,000 hectares) On the border of the northern section of Gobi B (Dzungarian Gobi). *Takhi* (the

THE GOBI

Mongolian wild horse) have been reintroduced into the wild here since 1996 through the Research Station. Experts hope they will survive and flourish in this remote area of the Gobi.

ALTAI АЛТАЙ
☎ 01482 / pop 19,100 / elev 2181m

Nestled between the mountains of Khasagt Khairkhan Uul (3579m) and Jargalant Uul (3070m), the aimag capital is a pleasant tree-lined place, with friendly locals. It's a poor city but as it's a long way to anywhere else you'll definitely need to stop for a short while to refuel and plot your course to the next aimag or the national parks to the south.

Information

Internet café (per hr T700; ⏲ 11am-7pm Mon-Sat) Inside the Telecom office. If you ask the Telecom operator you could get internet access after regular working hours.

Khan Bank (☎ 23773; ⏲ 9am-1pm & 2-6pm Mon-Fri) Changes cash, does cash advances against MasterCard and, if you are persistent, travellers cheques.

Mobinet Internet Café (per hr T600; ⏲ 11am-9pm)

Telecom office (☎ 24117; ⏲ 24hr) The post office is also here.

Sights

The **Aimag Museum** (☎ 24213; admission T1500; ⏲ 9am-1pm & 2-6pm Mon-Fri) includes some excellent bronze statues, scroll paintings, some genuine Mongol army chain mail, and an interesting shaman costume and drum. Look out for the 200kg statue of Buddha, which was hidden in a cave during the purges and recovered in 1965. There may be no electricity so bring a torch (flashlight) to see the exhibits.

If you are headed south on the road to Biger, check out this *khun chuluu* (GPS: N 46°15.830′, E 96°16.484′), or *balbal*, said to date back to the 13th century (possibly earlier).

Sleeping

CAMPING

The road from Altai towards Khovd city goes through a surprisingly lush plain for about 10km. If you have a tent and your own vehicle, head out here. Another great patch of ground, which you will have to share with a few cows, is only a 20-minute walk northwest of town.

GER CAMPS

Zaiver ger camp (☎ 9948 4333; per person T10,000, meals T3000) This ger camp is 16km from Altai. The staff will pick you up from town if you call ahead. It's pretty basic – no shower and Mongolian-style toilets.

Juulchin Altai ger camp (☎ 9119 4946; juulchin -altai@yahoo.com; GPS: N 46°21.764′, E 96°12.978′; with/without meals US$30/20) Located 4km west of town, this ger camp offers hot showers, clean gers and western-style toilets. Ask for Chinzorig or Baazar.

HOTELS

Tulga Altai (☎ 23747; dm/d/lux T10,000/16,800/25,000) This newish hotel is located in a two-storey white building near the market. Hot showers

---

SAVING THE SNOW LEOPARD

The mountains of Gov-Altai are home to the beautiful and elusive *irbis* (snow leopard). Up to 50kg in weight, and about 1m long (the tail is an extra 70cm), snow leopards can easily kill an ibex three times its size. They remain solitary except during the brief mating season.

An estimated 7500 snow leopards live in an area of 1.5 million sq km across China, Pakistan, Afghanistan, India, Nepal and Mongolia (where 1000 to 1500 live). The principal threats are poaching, habitat loss and wild-prey loss. Declining numbers of argali sheep and ibex have forced snow leopards to kill livestock, which has brought them into conflict with local herders.

It is hoped that the establishment of several national parks, education programmes and local income-generation projects can help save the snow leopard. Otherwise, the few pelts on display in local museums and the odd ger camp will be all that is left of this beautiful creature.

Irbis (www.irbis-enterprises.com) is a local organisation that protects snow leopards in Mongolia by providing alternative sources of income to herders in snow-leopard habitat. The company sells and markets locally made handicrafts, such as felt mats and camel and cashmere goods, with proceeds going jointly to producers and a conservation fund.

If you would like more information about the protection of the snow leopard, contact the **International Snow Leopard Trust** (in the USA ☎ 206-632-2421; www.snowleopard.org). In Ulaanbaatar contact **Mr Munkh-Tsog** (☎ 011-329 632; isltmon@magicnet.mn).

are available and some rooms have attached bath. It also has a decent restaurant.

Altai Hotel (☎ 24134; tw/tr T10,000/20,000, half-lux/ lux T12,000/28,000) This unexciting relic from the Soviet past, smack in the centre of town and close to the drama theatre, has long been a stand-by for Altai visitors. Staff are friendly enough, and all rooms come with toilets, but only the half-lux and lux rooms have a shower (cold water only).

Eating

The **market** is reasonably-well stocked with foodstuffs (and warm clothing).

Both the Altai and Tulga Altai hotels have restaurants serving Mongolian favourites such as *buuz* (steamed meat dumplings) and goulash for around T1500. The Tulga Altai is the better option.

Sutai (☎ 23567; meals T900-3000; ☽ 8am-10pm) If you've been jonesing for a goulash or bowl 'o mutton come down to the Sutai to get your fill of luke-warm Mongolian food. The restaurant includes an attached billiards hall and karaoke bar and also offers basic accommodation for around T7000.

Gaav (☎ 23004; meals T1000-1500; ☽ 10am-11pm Mon-Fri, 11am-10pm Sun) Clean, good-value restaurant located just north of the square serving soups, salads, goulash and *tsuivan* (steamed flour slices with meat). One of the waitresses can speak some English.

Getting There & Away

AIR

MIAT flies from Ulaanbaatar to Altai and back once a week for US$132/232 one way/return. The airport and **reservation office** (☎ 23544, 9948 9665) are 2km northwest of the centre.

HITCHING

There is some traffic along the main road towards Khovd and Bayankhongor, but you may have to wait a few hours for something suitable. Very few vehicles travel between Altai and Uliastai; you will probably have to wait for something to arrive from Uliastai first. Almost no vehicles venture into the south of Gov-Altai.

MINIVAN & JEEP

Altai is a stop on the road to Khovd from UB and you'll find minivans departing every morning from Ulaanbaatar's Dragon

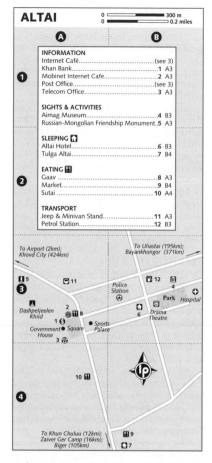

and Naran Tuul stations (T35,000, 25 hours, 1000km).

Altai is not somewhere you should expect to find any reliable jeeps for hire. You are more likely to have success in Uliastai and Khovd city. Shared minivans for Ulaanbaatar and Khovd leave from the roadside near the monastery.

The best place to ask around for a share jeep is at the southern entrance to the market. Expect to pay around T15,000 to T20,000 for a ride to Khovd or Bayankhongor.

BIGER

If you're travelling between Bayankhongor and Gov-Altai you'll likely pass through this small village, which has a few sights in the environs.

Around 13km northeast of Biger is the run-down **Shimt-els Sanatorium** (GPS: N 45°43.782′, E 97°19.979′), where locals bury themselves in sand and drink camel milk in hopes of curing kidney ailments and high blood pressure. You can stay here in **cabins** (per person T4500) that resemble WWII POW bunkhouses but expect no privacy.

Burgus (GPS: N 45°38.362′, E 97°24.480′), an attractive desert oasis, is located around 20km southwest of Biger. The oasis is famed for its production of wines and champagnes, as well as fruit and vegetables. You may be able to buy some of the wine in the *sum* centre.

Another worthwhile sight is the ruins of **Eguur Monastery** located 17km northwest of Biger, on the road to/from Altai. About a dozen destroyed buildings and foundations are scattered around this once active monastery.

EEJ KHAIRKHAN UUL
ЭЭЖ ХАЙРХАН УУЛ
Near the base of the Eej Khairkhan Uul (2275m), just north of 'Gobi A' National Park, you could camp at some delightful **rock pools** and explore the nearby **caves**. You will need a guide to show you around. Almost no suitable drinking water is available in the area, so take your own.

An A-frame hut is sometimes available for rent near the rock pools, but you should always bring your own camping equipment.

About 30 minutes' walk west of the hut are some spectacular ancient **rock paintings** of ibex, horsemen and archers.

The mountain is about 150km south of Altai, and is part of the Eej Khairkhan Nature Reserve.

SUTAI UUL СУТАЙ УУЛ
A locally revered mountain, Sutai Uul (4090m) is a relatively easy climb that offers good views of the surrounding Gobi. You can drive to the base of the mountain from Tonkhil in Gov-Altai or Tsetseg village in Khovd. From the base it's a two hour walk to the top, where you'll find permanent snow cover.

GREAT GOBI STRICTLY PROTECTED AREA
ГОВИИН ИХ ДАРХАН ГАЗАР
For both parts of the park you will need a very reliable vehicle and an experienced driver, and you must be completely self-sufficient with supplies of food, water and camping gear. A ranger will probably track you down and collect park entry fees (T3000 per person).

Gobi A (Southern Altai Gobi) ГОВЬ 'А'
The majority of this 4.4-million-hectare national park lies in the southern Gov-Altai. Established more than 25 years ago, the area has been nominated as an International Biosphere Reserve by the UN.

The park is remote and very difficult to reach, which is bad news for visitors but excellent news for the fragile flora and fauna.

There are a few mountains more than 1200m and several springs and oases, which only an experienced guide will find. To explore the park, start at Biger, turn southwest on the trail to Tsogt, and head south on any jeep trail you can find.

Gobi B (Dzungarian Gobi) ГОВЬ 'В'
Although the majority of this 881,000-hectare park lies in neighbouring Khovd aimag, most travellers enter from the Gov-Altai side, where a **research station** (GPS: N 45°32.197′, E 93°39.055′) has been set up to protect the reintroduced *takhi* (Przewalski's horse). Most of the *takhi* now run free, although a few still live in enclosures near the research station, which is about 15km southwest of Bij village. For more on *takhi*, see the boxed text, p116.

The scientists based here can provide information on tour options and the best places to camp. Besides *takhi*, you stand a good chance of seeing argali sheep, ibex and wild ass. The park also protects wild Bactrian camel and the elusive Gobi bear.

Western Mongolia

With its raw deserts, glacier-wrapped mountains, shimmering salt lakes and hardy culture of nomads, falconry and cattle rustling, western Mongolia is a timeless place that fulfils many romantic notions of the classic 'Central Asia'.

Squeezed between Russia, Kazakhstan, China and the Mongol heartland, this region has been a historical transition zone of endless cultures, the legacy of which is a patchwork of peoples including ethnic Kazakhs, Dorvods, Khotons, Myangads and Khalkh Mongols.

The Mongol Altai Nuruu forms the backbone of the region, a rugged mountain range that creates a natural border with both Russia and China. It contains many challenging and popular peaks for mountain climbers, some over 4000m, and is the source of fast-flowing rivers, most of which empty into desert lakes and saltpans.

The region's wild landscape and unique mix of cultures is known among adventure travellers and a small tourist infrastructure has been created to support them. Bayan-Ölgii leads the pack with its own clique of tour operators and drivers prepared to shuttle visitors to the mountains. But while aimag capitals are tepidly entering the 21st century, most of the region remains stuck in another age – infrastructure is poor and old-style communist thinking is the norm among local officials.

Despite the hardships, western Mongolia's attractions, both natural and cultural, are well worth the effort. With time and flexibility, the region may well be the highlight of your trip.

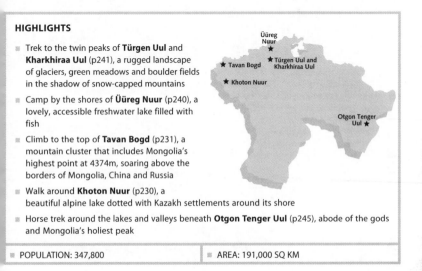

HIGHLIGHTS

- Trek to the twin peaks of **Türgen Uul** and **Kharkhiraa Uul** (p241), a rugged landscape of glaciers, green meadows and boulder fields in the shadow of snow-capped mountains

- Camp by the shores of **Üüreg Nuur** (p240), a lovely, accessible freshwater lake filled with fish

- Climb to the top of **Tavan Bogd** (p231), a mountain cluster that includes Mongolia's highest point at 4374m, soaring above the borders of Mongolia, China and Russia

- Walk around **Khoton Nuur** (p230), a beautiful alpine lake dotted with Kazakh settlements around its shore

- Horse trek around the lakes and valleys beneath **Otgon Tenger Uul** (p245), abode of the gods and Mongolia's holiest peak

Üüreg Nuur ★

★ Tavan Bogd   ★ Türgen Uul and Kharkhiraa Uul

★ Khoton Nuur

Otgon Tenger Uul ★

▪ POPULATION: 347,800	▪ AREA: 191,000 SQ KM

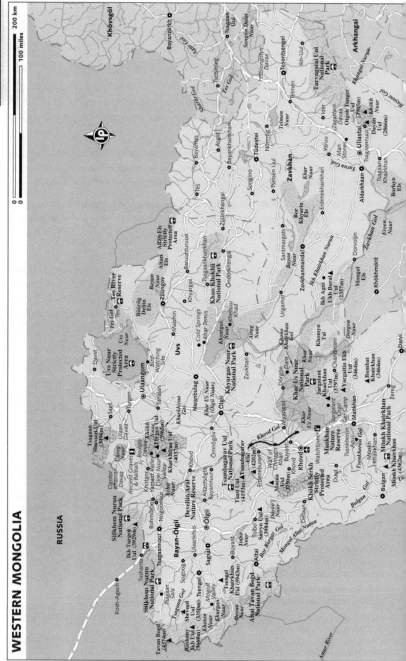

WESTERN MONGOLIA

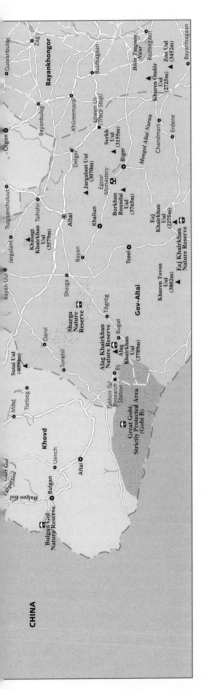

History

The Mongol Altai Nuruu (commonly referred to as the 'Altai Mountains') once stood as the easternmost territory inhabited by the Scythians, a vast empire of nomadic pastoralists who dominated Central Asia from around 700 BC to AD 300 – some of their tombs and rock carvings have been located in Mongolia and neighbouring Tuva.

Prior to Mongol domination in the 13th century, western Mongolia was a stronghold of the Oirads, a warrior tribe that initially resisted the expansionary tactics of Chinggis Khaan, but later submitted. Following the collapse of the Mongol empire, the Oirads reasserted their domination over the area and expanded to the Volga. These pioneers became known as Kalmyks and still inhabit the Caspian shores of Russia.

Manchu military outposts were created in Khovd city and Uliastai during the Qing dynasty. Both capitulated soon after the fall of the Manchu empire in 1911. The fighting was particularly bloody in Khovd, where a mystic Kalmyk named Dambijantsan (also known as Ja Lama) gathered an army of 5000 Oirads and Mongols, razed the fortress to the ground and skinned the Chinese soldiers inside.

Under Ulaanbaatar rule, western Mongolia was called Chandmandi until it was broken up into three aimags (provinces) in 1931. One of the three, Bayan-Ölgii, was designated as a homeland for ethnic Kazakhs living in the region.

Climate

Weather can be extremely temperamental in the Altai mountains. Brief snowstorms are common even in summer. These don't last long; usually within an hour the sun will be out again, but have a jacket ready. Summer is surprisingly cool in the Altai Mountains and you'll need a reliable, sub-zero rated sleeping bag and tent. The low-lying lakes and rivers of western Mongolia also attract some appalling packs of mosquitoes; arm yourself with serious bug repellent.

Language

In some parts of western Mongolia, especially Bayan-Ölgii, Kazakh is the dominant language. Other dialects are also spoken;

WESTERN MONGOLIA

ICE WARRIOR OF THE ALTAI

In 2006, archaeologists in the Mongol Altai made headlines whey they uncovered a 2500-year-old mummy believed to have been a Scythian warrior. The scientists noted that the mummy, well-preserved in the permafrost, had blonde hair and sported tattoos. He was believed to be a chieftain of some importance, between 30 and 40 years old. Clothed in a fur coat, he was entombed with two horses, saddles and weapons. Some of these treasures have been displayed in Ulaanbaatar's National History Museum while the mummy was packed off to Berlin for research.

---

the 1500 Tuvans in Tsengel *sum* (district; the administrative unit below an aimag) in Bayan-Ölgii have their own language. With the exception of small Kazakh children, most people will understand some Mongolian and possibly Russian.

Getting There & Away

Transport between western Mongolia and Ulaanbaatar is mainly by plane – so flights are often very full. Transport by land from Ulaanbaatar is a rough and tedious six days. The northern route via Arkhangai has several points of interest, but most share vehicles travel along the mind-numbingly dull southern route via Bayankhongor and Altai cities to Khovd city. The one-hour trip by air is well worth the money.

Though not a main traveller route yet, it is possible to enter or leave Mongolia at the Tsagaannuur border crossing (Bayan-Ölgii). With a bit of planning (you'll need a Russian visa; see p263) it's possible to tour the area and exit to Russia without hightailing it back to the capital. It may also be possible to fly between Khovd city and Urumqi in China; check with Air China for details.

Note that western Mongolia is in a different time zone from the rest of the country – one hour behind.

Getting Around

Hiring a jeep is relatively easy in any of the three western aimag capitals, and all three cities are linked by decent roads. You'll waste a lot of time if hitchhiking in the area; trucks will be most likely headed for the nearest border post and jeeps will be packed full of people. Your best chance of finding a lift is to ask for a share jeep at the markets, or hire your own jeep at a cost of around T450 per kilometre. If sharing a jeep with locals you'll save the anguish of waiting for additional passengers by asking the driver to pick you up at your hotel when he is ready. If you are determined to hitch, bring water, food, a tent and plenty of patience. Travelling by mountain bike or horse is great if you have the time.

BAYAN-ÖLGII
БАЯН-ӨЛГИЙ

pop 95,220 / area 46,000 sq km

Travelling to Mongolia's westernmost province gives one the distinct feeling of reaching the end of the road, if not the end of the earth. High, dry, rugged and raw, the isolated, oddly shaped province follows the arc of the Mongol Altai Nuruu as it rolls out of Central Asia towards the barren wastes of the Dzungarian Basin.

Many peaks in the province are more than 4000m and permanently covered with glaciers and snow, while the valleys have a few green pastures that support about two million livestock, as well as bear, fox and wolf. These valleys are dotted with small communities of nomadic families enjoying the short summer from mid-June to late August, as well as some beautiful alpine lakes.

Ethnic groups who call Bayan-Ölgii home include the Kazakh, Khalkh, Dorvod, Uriankhai, Tuva and Khoshuud. Unlike the rest of Mongolia, which is dominated by the Khalkh Mongols, about 90% of Bayan-Ölgii's population are Kazakh, almost all of them Muslim. The remaining 10% are mostly small minority groups.

The Kazakhs who live here hold little allegiance to Ulaanbaatar and increasingly find business, cultural and educational contacts in Russia, China and Kazakhstan. More than 10,000 people left for Kazakhstan in the 1990s, though some have returned.

The aimag has a rich collection of archaeological sites, with many *balbals* (Turkic stone figures believed to be grave makers), *bugan chuluu* (deer stones), *kurgans* (burial mounds) and a remarkable collection of 10,000 petroglyphs near the Russian border at Tsagaan Sala (also known as Baga

Digor). If you are particularly interested in these remote and obscure sites, contact the Mongol Altai Nuruu Special Protected Areas Administration (Manspaa) in Ölgii (see p224).

National Parks

Most parks come under the jurisdiction of Manspaa.

Altai Tavan Bogd National Park (636,161 hectares) Takes in Tavan Bogd, which includes Mongolia's highest mountain, and the stunning lakes of Khoton, Khurgan and Bayan. Fauna includes argali sheep, ibex, maral (Asiatic red deer), stone marten, deer, elk, Altai snowcock and eagle.

Develiin Aral Nature Reserve (10,300 hectares) A remarkable habitat around Develiin Island in the Usan Khooloi and Khovd rivers. It is home to pheasant, boar and beaver.

Khökh Serkh Strictly Protected Area (65,920 hectares) A mountainous area on the border with Khovd, which protects argali sheep and ibex.

Siilkhem Nuruu National Park (140,080 hectares) This park has two sections, one around Ikh Türgen Uul, the other further west.

Tsambagarav Uul National Park (110,960 hectares) Protects glaciers and the snow-leopard habitat; borders on Khovd.

ÖLGII ӨЛГИЙ

☎ 01422 / pop 27,800 / elev 1710m

Ölgii city is a windblown frontier town that will appeal to anyone who dreams of the Wild West. It's a squat, concrete affair, meandering along the Khovd Gol and surrounded by ger districts and rocky escarpments. Thunderclouds brew in the mountains above town, making for some dramatic climatic changes throughout the day and brilliant light shows in the late afternoon.

The town is predominantly Kazakh, and you'll soon start feeling it has more in common with Muslim-influenced Central

---

KAZAKHS

Ask anyone in Kazakhstan the best place to find genuine Kazakh culture and they will most likely to point to that small plot of land not in their own country but in western Mongolia. Bayan-Ölgii, thanks to its isolation for most of the 20th century, is considered by many to be the last bastion of traditional Kazakh language, sport and culture.

Kazakhs first migrated to this side of the Altai in the 1840s to graze their sheep on the high mountain pastures during summer. They then returned to Kazakhstan or Xinjiang for the winter. After the Mongolian Revolution in 1921, a permanent border was drawn by agreement between China, the USSR and Mongolia.

The word 'Kazakh' is said to mean 'free warrior' or 'steppe roamer'. Kazakhs trace their roots to the 15th century, when rebellious kinsmen of an Uzbek khan (king or chief) broke away, and settled in present-day Kazakhstan.

Traditional costume for Kazakh women is a long dress with stand-up collar, or a brightly decorated velvet waistcoat with heavy jewellery. Older married women often wear a white head-scarf. The men still wear baggy shirts and trousers, vests, long black cloaks and a skullcap or a *loovuuz* (fox-fur hat).

In many gers you'll be serenaded by women and men (and often children) who play the *dombra*, a two-stringed lute. Kazakh gers (traditional circular felt yurts) are taller, wider and more richly decorated than the Mongolian version. *Tush* (wall hangings) and *koshma* (felt carpets), decorated with stylised animal motifs, are common. *Chiy* (traditional reed screens) are becoming less common.

Kazakhs adhere rather loosely to Sunni Islam, but religion is not a major force. This is because of their distance from the centre of Islam, their nomadic lifestyle and the suppression of Islam during the communist era. Islam is making a comeback in Bayan-Ölgii, thanks to the lifting of restrictions against religion, aid packages from other Muslim countries, the construction of mosques and the annual hajj (pilgrimage) to Mecca. Islamic law has always sat lightly with the many Kazakhs, however, who enjoy a bottle of vodka as much as the next Mongolian. The main Kazakh holiday is the pre-Islamic spring festival of Navrus, celebrated on 21 March.

Kazakhs speak a Turkic language with 42 Cyrillic letters, similar to Russian and a little different from Mongolian. The Mongolian government is trying to placate the Kazakh minority and stop them returning to Kazakhstan, by encouraging the Kazakh language in schools in Bayan-Ölgii.

WESTERN MONGOLIA

Asia than Buddhist Mongolia: there are signs in Arabic and Kazakh Cyrillic, and the market, which is called a bazaar rather than the Mongolian *zakh*, sells the odd shashlik (kebab) and is stocked with goods from Kazakhstan.

A friendly local population makes the place a welcome break on a long road journey and the logical place to launch an expedition into the Altai mountains. It's not the most beautiful city around, but give it a day or two and Ölgii really starts to grow on you. There are reliable tour operators based here, surprisingly good restaurants and some excellent handicraft cooperatives selling high-quality carpets and wall hangings.

Information
Bathhouse (☎ 22442; per person T1000; 9am-10pm) Hot-water showers, sauna and barbershops. *Monsha* is 'hot water' in the local Kazakh dialect.
Immigration, Naturalization & Foreign Citizens office (INFC; ☎ 22195, 9942 8283; Government House; 9am-noon & 1-5pm Mon-Fri) Can register your passport if you have just arrived from Russia. In a pinch they can give a visa extension, which basically involves sending your passport to Ulaanbaatar.
Jarag Internet Café (☎ 23732; per hr T600; 9am-10pm) Good computers and a decent connection. One of the girls that hangs around here speaks Hebrew and likes to chat up the Israeli tourists. The Telecom office also has an internet café, but its connection is slower.
Khadgalamj Bank (☎ 22978; 8am-noon & 1-4.30pm Mon-Fri) Changes US dollars and euros. Gives cash advances against Visa. Private moneychangers can also be found in the market.
Mongol Altai Nuruu Protected Areas Administration office (Manspaa; ☎ 22111, 9942 9696; manspaa@mongo.net; 9am-noon & 1-5pm Mon-Fri, weekends by calling mobile) The office doubles as an information centre, with informed English-speaking staff plus photos, maps and reading material. The office can help with your border permit, sell national park tickets, provide itineraries for your trip and recommend drivers and guides.
Mongol Shuudan Bank (☎ 22462; 8am-noon & 1-3pm Mon-Fri, 10am-2pm Sat) Changes money and offers cash advances against Visa.
Telecom office (☎ 24117; 24hr) The post office is also located here.

Sights
The **Aimag Museum** (admission T3000; 9am-noon & 1-5pm Mon-Fri, 10am-5pm Sat) gives an excellent overview of Kazakh culture and the geography of Bayan-Ölgii. The 2nd floor is devoted to

history, and the 3rd floor has some interestin ethnographic displays.

Ölgii's **mosque** and madrasah (Islamic plac of learning) is worth a quick look, especiall on Friday at lunchtime when weekly praye are held, though you may not be allowe inside. The mosque holds the offices of th Islamic Centre of Mongolia. Its unusual angl is due to its orientation to Mecca.

Courses
Mr Cheryazdan (☎ 23358, 9942 5202) A music in structor at the Teachers College, gives *dombr* (two-stringed lute) lessons for a negotiate fee. The college is east of downtown, nea the Khovd Gol.

Ms Zoya (☎ 9942 3575) A local teacher wh can provide Kazakh language lessons. Fee are negotiable.

Tours
When booking a tour with one of the fol lowing outfits, try to get the owner to serv as your guide. If the owner is too busy yo may get stuck with inexperienced guide and drivers.
Bayan-Auul Tour (☎ 9942 9935; ba-tours@chinggis .com) Offers trips to all areas of Bayan-Ölgii. There is no office; contact Bolatbek by email or phone.
Blue Wolf Travel (☎ 22772, 9665 2637, 9911 0303; www.bluewolftravel.com) Offers a variety of trips includin winter eagle-hunting tours. The Ölgii office is about 400m south of the ochre-coloured Kazakh National Theatre.
Kazakh Tour (☎ 9942 2006; dosjan@yahoo.com) Friendly guide and owner Dosjan Khabyl has tailor-made trips throughout Bayan-Ölgii and leads trekking tours around Tavan Bogd. He speaks English, Mongolian, Russian and Kazakh, and gets good reviews from travellers. The Ölgii office is next to Pamukkale restaurant.

Sleeping
CAMPING
If you want to camp, walk east of the squar to Khovd Gol and then head southeast, awa from the market and ger suburbs.

GER CAMPS
our pick **Blue Wolf** (☎ 9911 0303, 9665 2637; www .bluewolftravel.com; per person T5000;) Offers gers flush toilets and a hot-shower block in a se cure walled compound. It's located behind th Blue Wolf café and tour office. It also has ger camp at Sagsai, charging US$27 per nigh including meals.

ÖLGII

Eagle Tour (9942 2100; eagle_tour@mongol.net; with/without meals US$30/15) Located 6km out of Ölgii in the direction of Sagsai, Eagle Tour has [g]ers, flush toilets and hot showers.

KTS (9942 2006; dosjan@yahoo.com) This camp [w]as just getting underway at the time of re[s]earch, contact them for details. It's affiliated [w]ith Kazakh Tour.

[H]OTELS
[H]otels in Ölgii want to keep your passport [f]or the duration of your stay. It is much bet[t]er to give a photocopy of your passport – [t]here is less to worry about if you forget to [p]ick it up when checking out.

Duman (9942 8174; s/d/half-lux T5000/10,000/[1]2,000, lux T15,000-17,000) This place has good-[l]ooking rooms and the reasonably priced lux [o]ptions have TV, comfy beds and 24-hour [h]ot-water showers. The only problem is the [n]oisy disco downstairs.

Bastau Hotel (23629; s/d/tr T5000/7000/10,500, [h]alf-lux s/d/tr T10,000/12,000/15,000, lux s/d T14,000/18,000) [T]his welcoming hotel has a variety of rooms [i]ncluding a handy three-bed dorm with two

couches and a TV. The lux room includes a cosy living room and attached bathroom. Other rooms use a share bathroom with luke-warm shower.

Tavan Bogd Hotel (23046, 9942 8877; dm/s/d US$4/6/12, half-lux s/d US$10/20, lux s/d US$12/24) This is the oldest hotel in town, a communist relic that has seen gradual renovations over the years, including a new restaurant. It is a little better than the Bastau Hotel, as the 2nd-floor rooms come with attached bathroom.

Eating

If you give some advance warning, one of the following restaurants should be able to prepare *besbarmak* (literally 'five fingers'), a traditional Kazakh dish of meat-and-pasta squares. Note that the Kazakh phrase for vegetarian is *'Min ate jimmi min'*.

Toganai Shaykhana (11am-7pm) Opposite the Bastau Hotel, this tiny café serves excellent *buuz* (steamed mutton dumplings; T70) and greasy *khuushuur* (fried mutton pancakes; T150) served with a delicious *khaluun nogoo* (chilli sauce).

FESTIVALS & EVENTS IN BAYAN-ÖLGII

Bayan-Ölgii has several festivals that are worth planning your trip around.

The biggest and best is the annual **Eagle Festival** (admission US$20), held on the first Sunday and Monday in October in Ölgii city. This is a good time to shop for arts and crafts and watch eagle-hunting competitions (though animal lovers may find it somewhat cruel as live foxes and wolves are used as bait). Contact Nomadic Expeditions (p81) for details. A smaller Eagle Festival is held two days earlier in Sagsai *sum*; contact Blue Wolf Travel (p224).

On 28 July a **Horse Festival** (admission US$30) is held between the two lakes in Tavan Bogd National Park. You'll see horse races, *kokpar* (tug of war with a goat) and *kyz kul* (kiss the girl). Blue Wolf Tours is also the contact point for this one.

The spring festival and family event of **Navrus** is held on 22 March. Family visits and feasting are common. During this festival you may see traditional games and contests, including one that sees men attempting to lift an ox off the ground. In another game, horse riders attempt to pluck a coin from the ground while in full gallop. You can see this in most Kazakh villages.

Tsengel Khairkhan (meals T1000-2000; 11am-7pm) Mongol-run restaurant with reasonable local fare and salads to accommodate vegetarians.

Blue Wolf (9911 0303; dishes T1500-2500; 9am-10pm) Run by the folks at Blue Wolf Tours, this café is in a bright room, its walls decorated with dramatic photos of eagle-hunters and the Altai Mountains. The menu includes delights such as American breakfast (eggs, sausage and bread) and Kazakh breakfast (sausage and apple). Vegetarians will appreciate some of the salads. The taco salad isn't particularly Mexican but does taste good. Kazakh crafts are also sold here.

our pick Pamukkale (9909 4593; meals T2500-7500; 10.30am-10.30pm 15 Jun-15 Sep, 9.30am-9.30pm rest of the year) A welcome addition to the local restaurant scene, Pamukkale is a Turkish-run outfit that serves authentic kebabs and Turkish soups. Unfortunately the doner plate is never available (the locals don't like it) but you may be able to score a tasty chicken dish. The Turkish desserts are also excellent but portions are miniscule so you may need to order a few to satisfy your sweet tooth.

Drinking & Entertainment

Nur Danesca (23720; admission T300; 6pm-1am) Popular with the local teen set, this modern disco club is behind the mosque. (The over-18 crowd tends to patronise the disco in the Duman Hotel.)

For a beer in a quieter atmosphere, try the **Aulum Sayajim beer garden** (23983, 9942 9094; admission T100; noon-11pm), near the police station. The walled compound contains several cabanas and a tent. On Fridays, the beer is covered with towels so as not to offend th local Muslim population, but they will st sneak you a bottle. The gers nearby are actu ally for rent, but would you really want sleep in a beer garden?

Shopping

The **market** (10am-5pm) has a decent sele tion of food supplies imported from Russ and China. Traditional Kazakh skullcaps an jackets can also be found amid the chaos. Ho and why the shopkeepers have 'Boots' plast bags is a mystery to us. There's a small charg to get into the enclosed part of the mark where all the food is. A more convenient plac to pick up food and supplies is the **Sunkh Supermarket** (9am-7pm), just west of the Tava Bogd Hotel.

CRAFTS & SOUVENIRS

If you are on the hunt for Kazakh wall hang ings and felt rugs, check out the gift shop the Aimag Museum. It has antiques and ne items including fox fur hats (US$70), wa hangings (US$70) and felt mats (US$40).

Altai Craft (9941 8119, 9142 2279; www.alt craft.com; 1pm-5pm) This project employs 4 women to create traditional Kazakh hand crafts. You can visit the workshop, watch ho the products are made and even take a fre one-hour lesson in chain-stitch embroider Items available include chalk bags, yoga mat bike bags, cushion covers and wall hanging A book exchange is also available. The work shop is behind the market and a little hard t find so you may want to call ahead.

Art Shop Burkit (9942 9906; narbek2001@yaho .com; 10am-7pm) Local craftsman Narbe

Khasim is a silversmith by trade but has recently entered the eagle-hunting accessory market, producing gauntlets, eagle hoods, belts and leather goods. He speaks English and is also a two-time tae kwon do national champion (of Kazakhstan) – one of Ölgii's more interesting characters.

Otau Cooperative (☎ 9942 9787; ◷ 9am-9pm) Sells Kazakh handbags (T6000 to T10,000), felt hats (T10,000 to T15,000) hats (T7000) and other handicrafts made by around 30 local women. It's next to the Bastau Hotel.

Getting There & Away

AIR
AeroMongolia and MIAT (Mongolian Airlines) share the Ulaanbaatar–Ölgii route. Schedules are erratic so you'll need to call and find out who is flying. There are currently two flights a week. AeroMongolia charges US$200/353 one way/return while MIAT charges US$161/281 one way/return. The four-hour flight provides breathtaking views of glacier-wrapped peaks as you approach Ölgii.

Both **AeroMongolia** (☎ 9942 5081) and **MIAT** (☎ 9942 8161) share an office in the Mongol Shuudan Bank, next to the post office. A smaller office opens at the airport on the mornings when a flight arrives.

The airport is 6km north of the centre, on the opposite side of the river. There is no bus, but it's usually possible to hitch a ride in a truck or on the back of a motorcycle.

To Kazakhstan
Twice a week, Trans Ölgii flies between Almaty and Ölgii via Üst Kamenogorsk in eastern Kazakhstan. This flight (US$112 to Üst Kamenogorsk or US$259 to Almaty, plus T5500 tax) is a little unreliable and you can only buy a ticket in Ölgii, which means there is no guarantee you'll get on the next flight. If you want to buy a ticket in advance, inquire with tour operators in Ölgii. The **ticket agent** (☎ 9942 8161, 318 000) is in the Government House. You may also want to inquire about the latest details with tour operators in Almaty and Üst Kamenogorsk (see Lonely Planet's *Central Asia* for details).

If at all possible, don't try to change the date of your ticket, as this always leads to ticketing problems and your new ticket may be invalid. Flights are always crowded and you may be asked to pay a dubious health tax (just ignore it). Customs for this flight are done in Almaty.

HITCHING
A few vehicles, most of which are petrol tankers, travel the road between Ölgii and Khovd city. The Ölgii–Ulaangom road is not as busy because most vehicles head east towards Ulaanbaatar and use the southern road via Khovd city. Most vehicles travelling between Ölgii and Ulaangom bypass Tsagaannuur and take the short cut via Achit Nuur.

A lot of Russian trucks hang around the market, waiting for cargo to take to Russia via Tsagaannuur. There is also quite a lot of traffic, with jeeps being driven from Russia and sold locally.

MINIVAN & JEEP
Public share jeeps to Khovd city (T11,000, six to seven hours, 211km), Ulaangom (T10,000, 10 hours, 300km) and Tsengel *sum* (T8000, three hours, 75km) leave from Ölgii market. Drivers may try to charge foreigners double here, so check to see what others are paying.

For Ulaanbaatar (T60,000, 60 hours, 1636km), vans assemble at the road next to the museum.

Many travellers looking to hire a private jeep for trips around the aimag turn to local travel agents. Be careful about who you hire as some local tour operators are quite satisfied with sending out poor-quality vehicles. **Kazakh Tour** (see p224) has a good reputation for hiring out jeeps. Another decent driver in Ölgii is named Bekbolat (beku800@yahoo.com).

Hiring a random driver at the Ölgii market is not a good idea – these drivers are not accountable to anyone and are known to change prices and itineraries midtrip; it's simply not worth trying to save a few tögrögs. The Manspaa office will have a list of recommended drivers who are more familiar with tourists' needs.

To/From Russia
There is no public transport across the Tsagaannuur–Tashanta border; however, trade across the border is brisk so if you ask around the market in Ölgii you should be able to negotiate a ride all the way to the Russian town of Kosh-Agach (68km from the border). There isn't much point in getting a ride just to Tsagaannuur as most cars drive right past

on their way to the border. It also doesn't help to get a ride just to the border as the no-man's land is several kilometres wide.

It's a similar scenario going the other way; you are best off getting a ride all the way to Ölgii from Kosh-Agach as there is nothing at the border itself. Kazakh and Mongol traders at the market in Kosh-Agach are your best hope for a ride.

TSAMBAGARAV UUL NATIONAL PARK
ЦАМБАГАРАВ УУЛ

The permanently snow-capped **Tsambagarav Uul** straddles the border between Khovd and Bayan-Ölgii aimags and is accessible from either side. Despite its altitude of 4208m, the summit is relatively accessible and easy to climb compared with Tavan Bogd, but you'll need crampons and ropes. A neighbouring peak, **Tsast Uul**, is slightly shorter at 4193m and also good for climbing.

The southern side of the mountain (near the main Khovd–Ölgii road) contains the **Namarjin valley**, where there are outstanding views of Tsambagarav. From here you can head west and then south to rejoin the main Khovd–Ölgii road, via several **Kazakh settlements** and a beautiful **turquoise lake**.

An alternative route from the Khovd side leads from the town of **Erdeneburen** (where you can see a deer stone dating back to the pre-Mongol era) and up the mountainside to the Bayangol Valley. The valley itself is nothing special but there are fine views southeast to Khar Us Nuur and you might be able to rent a horse for the hour-long ride to the Kazakh-populated **Marra valley**.

The Bayan-Ölgii (northern) side of the mountain is even more impressive. To reach the massif, a steep pass runs between Tavan Belchiriin Uul and Tsast Uul. Between the mountains is a 7m-high **waterfall** (GPS: N 48°44.741', E 090°42.378') that flows down a narrow gorge. A couple of kilometres to the east of the waterfall is a **glacier** and small glacial lake. Serious mountaineers can hike up the glacier to the peak.

From the glacier, the road dips through some spectacular **rocky gorges** before finally tumbling down to **Bayan Nuur**, a small, slightly salty lake.

The best time to visit the massif is late June to late August, when it's populated by Kazakh nomad camps. You can rent horses from the nomads to explore the area.

Outside of these months it's a cold, empty and forbidding place.

From Bayan Nuur, a desert road travel east through a Martian landscape of red boulders and rocky mountains. Near the town of Bayannuur and close to the Khovd Gol is an interesting white-stone **balbal** (Turkic stone statue; GPS: N 48°50.533', E 091°16.525').

To explore the area, you'll definitely need a driver who knows the region well. Contact one of the tour operators in Ölgii (p224) or Marka's Ger Camp in Khovd (p234) to arrange a trip. The area lies in a national park zone so expect standard park entry fees to apply.

TOLBO NUUR ТОЛБО НУУР

Tolbo Nuur (GPS: N 48°35.320', E 090°04.536') is about 50km south of Ölgii, on the main road between Ölgii and Khovd city, so it's an easy day trip or stopover. The freshwater lake is high (2080m), expansive and eerie but the shoreline is treeless and there are a few mosquitoes (camp away from the marshy shoreline). There are a few gers around the lake and the water is clean enough for swimming if you don't mind icy temperatures.

A major battle was fought here between the Bolsheviks and White Russians, with the local Mongolian general, Khasbaatar, siding with the Bolsheviks. The Bolsheviks won and there are a couple of memorial plaques by the lake.

TOLBO TO BULGAN

The southern road through the spine of the Mongol Altai Nuruu, one of the most remote roads in the country, is the back door into Khovd aimag. From Tolbo sum centre, which has an interesting mosque, it's an easy detour to Döröö Nuur and nearby **Sairyn Uul**, an increasingly popular place for horse trekking.

The next *sum* south of Tolbo is **Deluun** famed for its eagle-hunters and the starting point for a horse trek through the **Khök Serkh Strictly Protected Area** to Khovd city. Further south, the road winds through the spectacular canyon lands of Bulgan *sum* on the western flank of 4362m Mönkh Khairkhan Uul. From here it's a very rough six-hour drive through the **Bulgan Gol gorge**, which is navigable by kayak at the end of June if you can stand the mosquitoes and happen to have a kayak. Other navigable

EAGLE-HUNTERS

While travelling around Bayan-Ölgii, you may come across Kazakh eagle-hunters. If you ask gently, the Kazakhs may proudly show you their birds, though actual hunting only takes place in winter.

Eagle-hunting is a Kazakh tradition dating back about 2000 years (Marco Polo mentions it in his *Travels*). Female eagles are almost always used as they are one-third heavier than the males and far more aggressive. Young birds around two years' old are caught in nearby valleys and then 'broken' by being tied to a wooden block so that they fall when they try to fly away. After two days they are exhausted and ready for training, which involves being kept on a pole called a *tugir*, and catching small animal skins or lures called *shirga*. The eagles are trained to hunt marmots, small foxes and wolves (eagles have vision eight times more acute than humans), and release them to the hunter, who clubs the prey to death. Part of the meat is given to the eagles as a reward.

Tools of the trade include the *tomaga* (hood), *bialai* (gloves) and *khundag* (blanket to keep the bird warm). If well trained, a bird can live and hunt for about 30 years. Most hunters train several birds in their lifetime. When a bird dies, it is buried in the ground as if it were part of the family.

The most likely places to find a Kazakh eagle-hunter are in the mountain region of Tsast Uul between Khovd and Bayan-Ölgii, and the Deluun, Tsengel and Bayannuur regions of Bayan-Ölgii. For an up-close-and-personal look at the sport, try the Eagle Festival (p226).

ivers in the area include the Gurt and Türgen rivers.

Confusingly, the road comes out of the gorge at Bulgan *sum* in Khovd aimag. The mosquito-infested Mongolian–Chinese border post sees many petrol tankers but is closed to foreign travellers.

A locally run **ger camp** (bed with meals US$25) in Bulgan can organise horse trips in the area; contact **Jagaa** (jagaa3538ube@yahoo.com).

SOGOOG СОГООГ

This miniscule village (pop 1200), a 1½-hour drive northwest from Ölgii (or 20-minute drive past Ulaankhus), is a good place to stop en route to Tavan Bogd. The village recently opened a **handicraft cooperative** and a **kindergarten**, both of which are open to visitors. The cooperative welcomes volunteer English teachers, who are given free lodging for a few days or weeks. While in town you can learn to make yak yogurt, comb cashmere from goats or learn Kazakh embroidery.

At the cooperative you can get fresh coffee, espresso and pancakes, and if you give advance notice the locals can bake cookies and apple tart! 'Advance notice' is two or three days and the village has no phone so you'll need to contact **Barb** (☎ 9979 6838; barbmongolia@yahoo.com), the English-speaking contact who can forward information to the village. Once in town, ask for Kakila or Baatarjav.

For transport to Sogoog you can ask around the market in Ölgii or hire your own vehicle at a cost of T450 per kilometre. Another option is to contact a local named **Amaka** (☎ 9942 5205) who has contacts with Sogoog drivers.

ALTAI TAVAN BOGD NATIONAL PARK
АЛТАЙ ТАВАН БОГД

This beautiful park stretches south from Tavan Bogd and includes the **stunning lakes** of Khoton Nuur and Khurgan Nuur (and the less interesting Dayan Nuur). It's a remote area divided from China by a high wall of snow-capped peaks and known to local Kazakhs as the Syrgali region.

The three lakes are the source of the Khovd Gol, which eventually flows into Khar Us Nuur in Khovd aimag. It's possible to make **rafting trips** down river from Khoton Nuur. No agencies offer rafting trips at present, but you could check with the Protected Areas office.

Tsengel, Mongolia's westernmost town, is the jumping-off point for the southern part of the park. It occupies a nice setting amid the mountains and there is good camping away from town, by the river. There are a couple of *guanz* (canteens or cheap restaurants) and a small market, but no hotel. Hiring a jeep could be difficult; you are better off bringing one from Ölgii. The Tavan Bogd area is best reached via Ulaankhus (see p231).

Permits

Park entry fees are the standard T3000 per person. Fishing permits cost T500 per day, but fishing is not permitted between 15 May and 15 July (there is a US$50 fine). The main entry to the park is by the bridge over the Khovd Gol, south of Tsengel. You can pay for permits there, or at the Manspaa office in Ölgii (p224) or from rangers around the lake. It's best to get one from the office in Ölgii if you can as rangers in the park can be hard to find. If you go into the park without a permit the border police will give you trouble.

You definitely need a border permit as well. It's best to get one in Ulaanbaatar but, failing that, try the **Border Patrol office** (Khiliin Tserenk Alb; ☎ 22341; ☗ 8-11am & 2-5pm Mon-Fri) in Ölgii, located a couple of kilometres from the centre. The permit will be checked by the border guards at Dayan Nuur, Tavan Bogd base camp, Aral Tolgoi (western end of Khoton Nuur) and Syrgal (the point where Khoton Nuur meets Khurgan Nuur). If you don't have a permit you will be fined about US$100 and given 72 hours to leave the area. The soldiers have nothing to do with the national park and cannot be negotiated with. Note that your guide and driver will need their Mongolian passports.

At the time of research border permits were free, but this may change. Processing the permit takes between 10 minutes and an hour. You must bring your original passport (no photocopies accepted) and be prepared to describe your itinerary. Also note that you cannot get a border permit on your own; you need to be with a guide or local affiliate.

Sights

There are many archaeological sites in the region. Mogoit Valley (Snake Valley) contains a moustachioed **balbal** (GPS: N 48°44.099', E 88°38.930') and a Kazakh cemetery with an interesting beehive-shaped mausoleum about 2km to the north. Yet another **balbal** (GPS: N 48°39.506', E 88°37.863') can be found south of Mogoit Valley, on the way to Khurgan Nuur. More interesting Kazakh cemeteries and ancient burial mounds are easily spotted from the road. Closer to Tavan Bogd, Sheveed Uul (3350m) contains some fascinating **petroglyphs** (GPS: N 49°06.238', E 88°14.918') depicting wild animals and hunting scenes. Keep your eyes peeled (and binoculars ready) for ibex which inhabit the mountain above.

The best **petroglyphs** in the area, if not al of Central Asia, can be found at Tsagaar Sala (aka Baga Oigor), on the route betweer Ulaankhus and Tavan Bogd. The drawings more than 10,000 of them, are scattered ove a 15km area; you'll need a guide to find th best ones.

THE LAKE REGION

This is one of the most beautiful regions i the park, with the scenery growing more spec tacular the further west you travel. The are is best explored on foot or horseback. Kazakl families living around Khoton Nuur in sum mer can rent horses.

The shoreline of **Khurgan Nuur** is dry an exposed. Few people travel along its south ern shore but if you are going this way ther is a stupa-like construction and severa burial sites. Nearby is a **balbal** (GPS: N 48°32.006 E 88°28.549').

The northern shore along **Khoton Nuur** ha excellent camping spots, especially aroun **Ulaan Tolgoi** (Red Head), the spit of land tha juts majestically into the lake. The norther tip of the lake is marked by **Aral Tolgoi** (Islan Head), a unique hill surrounded by verdan pastureland and rocky escarpments. A bor der station at the northern end of the lake wi check to see if your border permit is in orde

Coming around the southern shore o Khoton Nuur, you can camp in secluded cove or explore the valleys that lead towards China There are some difficult river crossings on your way back to Syrgal.

About 25km northwest of Khoton Nuu you can also visit Rashany Ikh Uul, an are of 35 **hot springs** (GPS: N48°55.655', E88°14.288'). Th springs (which are really just luke-warm) are facilitated by **Aksu Rashan Suvlal** (☎ 9942 2979; pe person with breakfast US$10), a small ger camp run b a local entrepreneur. The springs are aroun 33°C to 36°C and cost US$5 to enter.

Northwest of Khoton Nuur the mountain close in and there's some fine **hiking** possibili ties. For experienced backcountry walkers, i is even possible to travel up river for 90kn all the way to Tavan Bogd. It is a five-da walk and you'll need to be completely self sufficient. Be prepared for border-permi checks en route. It's usually not possible t cross until early July because of deep snow on the highest pass (Dakilbay Davaa).

Note that Khar Tsalaagiin Gol is in a re stricted border area and should be avoided

make sure you are walking up the next valley, **Tsagaan Us Gol Valley** (good maps are essential).

TAVAN BOGD ТАВАН БОГД

Tavan Bogd (Five Saints) is a soaring cluster of mountains that straddles the border between Mongolia, Russia and China. The highest peak in the range, **Khuiten Uul** (Cold Peak; 4374m), is the tallest mountain in Mongolia and is of interest to professional climbers. It's fairly dangerous to climb: you need to be with an experienced group, properly equipped with ice axes, crampons and ropes; don't even consider attempting it solo. The best time to climb is August and September, after the worst of the summer rains.

Besides Khuiten, the range includes Naran (Sun), Ölgii (Land), Bürged (Eagle) and Nairamdal (Friendship) *uuls*. In 2006 the president of Mongolia climbed Khuiten and renamed it Ikh Mongol; however, noone seems to use this name and it's not included on new maps, so for now we'll stick with Khuiten.

Even if you are not a climber, it's worth trekking up to the Khuiten Uul **base camp** (elev 3092m; GPS: N 49°09.036', E 87°56.528'), where you can get stunning views of all the peaks as well as the 12km-long **Potanii glacier**, which tumbles out of the range. It's possible to walk onto the glacier but be careful of deep snows and crevasses. If you're not too exhausted already, head to the top of **Malchin Peak**. The three-hour walk is rewarded with views of Russia and the surrounding mountains.

Note that there are two trails to the base camp. One starts from the end of the road in Tsagaan Gol Valley. From here it's a 14km trek to the base camp. The trailhead has a ranger station and a place to camp. Across the river are some gers occupied by an extended family of Tuvans. They can rent horses (T5000) and one of the younger family members can guide you up to the base camp (for around T4000). From here, the shortest route is via the Tarmid Pass. It takes about three hours by horse or four to five hours on foot. To return from the base camp, follow the Tsagaan Gol back to the trailhead. The route is a little longer but offers better views.

The other trail to base camp begins in the Sogoog Gol valley (north of Tsagaan Gol); from here it's 17km to the base camp. This trailhead also has a ranger station. You will need border permits to visit the mountain and will have to pay national park fees.

Sleeping & Eating

There is no official accommodation in the park (the aforementioned Aksu Rashan Suvlal has no permit to operate and may be shut down by the time you arrive), so you'll need to camp and be completely self-sufficient. The best camping spots are around the lakes. Dayan Nuur has some nasty mosquitoes but the other two lakes are largely bug free. The lakes teem with fish. Tavan Bogd also has camping spots but it's always cold here. At **Syrgal** (GPS: N 48°36.004', E 88°26.672'), between the lakes, there are a couple of very basic shops selling sweets, vodka, water and little else.

Getting There & Away

The main road from Tsengel leads 38km south to the bridge over the Khovd Gol (there's a T400 toll) and then continues 33km to the junction of Khoton and Khurgan *nuurs*, where there is a bridge across the wide water channel between the two lakes.

A more scenic route takes you from Sagsai over a pass and up the beautiful Khargantin Gol valley, past Tsengel Khairkhan Uul and Khar Nuur, and then down to Dayan Nuur. A good option would be to enter the park this way and exit via the main road. It's possible to drive from Dayan Nuur to Buyant by jeep, but you'll need an experienced driver who knows the way.

Getting to Tavan Bogd can be tricky. On the map the shortest route looks to be via Tsengel and up the Tsagaan Gol. From Tsengel, head across the river and travel 110km to the end of the road. There is no bridge across the Khovd Gol, however, so after heavy rain it's difficult to cross. The alternative route from Khovd is via Ulaankhus and up the Sogoog Gol. You can continue strait to Tavan Bogd but it's more interesting to go over Hagiin Davaa (Hagiin Pass) which leads to Tsagaan Gol. From Ölgii city to the end of the road is 190km.

KHOVD ХОВД

pop 92,400 / area 76,000 sq km

Khovd aimag has long been a centre for trade, business and administration in western Mongolia, a status that began during the Qing dynasty when the Manchus built a military garrison here. The aimag still does robust trade with China through the border at Bulgan and its Agricultural University is the largest of its kind outside Ulaanbaatar. The province is set to become a major producer of energy, once the hydro-electric power plant on the Chono-Khairaikh Gol is complete.

Besides its developing economy, Khovd is notable for being one of the most heterogeneous aimags in Mongolia, with a Khalkh majority and minorities of Khoton, Kazakh, Uriankhai, Zakhchin, Myangad, Oold and Torguud peoples. Its terrain is equally varied, with large salt lakes, fast-flowing rivers and the Mongol Altai Nuruu almost bisecting the aimag.

Khovd is a character-filled place; you could spend a day with Kazakh carpet makers in Khovd city, learn throat singing from the old masters in Chandmani or hang out with an emanation of the Green Tara in Dörgön. If you have a little time to spend in the area, there are also good ecotourism opportunities around Khar Us Nuur and fantastic hiking opportunities around Tsambagarav Uul (4202m; see p228), on the border with Bayan-Ölgii.

National Parks

Bulgan Gol Nature Reserve (1840 hectares) On the southwestern border with China, it was established to help preserve *minj* (beavers), sable and stone marten. A border permit is required.

Great Gobi Strictly Protected Area (also known as 'Gobi B') Created to protect *khulan* (wild ass), gazelle, jerboas and *takhi* (wild horses).

Khar Us Nuur National Park (850,272 hectares) Protects the breeding grounds for antelope and rare species of migratory pelican, falcon and bustard.

Khökh Serkh Strictly Protected Area (65,920 hectares) On the northwestern border with Bayan-Ölgii, it helps protect argali sheep, ibex and snow leopard.

Mankhan Nature Reserve (30,000 hectares) Directly southeast of Khovd city, it preserves an endangered species of antelope.

Mönkh Khairkhan National Park Established in 2006, this protects an important habitat for ibex and argali sheep.

KHOVD CITY ХОВД
☎ 01432 / pop 31,000 / elev 1406m

Khovd city is a pleasant tree-lined place developed by the Manchus during their 200-year rule in Outer Mongolia. Somewhat more developed than other cities in western Mongolia, it boasts an Agricultural University and some

food processing and textiles manufacturing. It also has the region's busiest airport, one reason why so many tourists end up here.

The town offers a few sights to keep you busy for a day and some pleasant ger camps outside town. Shops are well stocked and there are plenty of jeeps, making this a good place to launch a trip to the Altai Mountains or the lakes region. Khovd city also boasts a significant population of Kazakhs – some local Kazakh women have set up a felt-making craft cooperative that is worth visiting.

Information
Bathhouse (☎ 23690; shower/sauna T900/3500; ⏰ 9am-10pm) Just north of the market.
Internet café (☎ 22472; per hr T460; ⏰ 8am-10pm Mon-Fri) Inside the Telecom office.
Internet Kafé (per hr T400; ⏰ 10am-10pm) Open on weekends as well.
Khar Us Nuur National Park office (☎ /fax 22539; kharus2006@chinggis.com; ⏰ 8am-5pm Mon-Fri) Opposite the Telecom office, this office gives information on, and permits for, nearby Khar Us Nuur National Park.
Mongol Shuudan Bank (☎ 24004; ⏰ 8am-5pm Mon-Fri, 10am-2pm Sat) Gives cash advances against MasterCard.
Telecom office (☎ 22471; ⏰ 24hr) The post office is also located here.
XAC Bank (☎ 22669; ⏰ 8am-4pm Mon-Fri) Changes money and gives cash advances on travellers cheques.
Zoos Bank (☎ 24004; ⏰ 8am-5pm Mon-Fri, 10am-2pm Sat) Changes dollars but not travellers cheques. Gives cash advances against MasterCard.

Sights
MUSEUM
The **museum** (☎ 9943 4502; admission T2000; ⏰ 8am-noon & 1-5pm Mon-Fri) is located on a corner near the police station and has the usual collection of stuffed wildlife, plus some excellent ethnic costumes, Buddhist and Kazakh art and a snow-leopard pelt tacked up on the wall. One of the more interesting exhibits is the re-creation of the cave paintings at Tsenkheriin Agui (p236), which is actually better than the original. There are also several examples of the many deer stones scattered around the aimag, plus a model of the original Manchurian fortress.

SANGIIN KHEREM (MANCHU RUINS)
САНГИЙН ХЭРЭМ
At the northern end of the city are some crumbling walls built around 1762 by the Manchu (Qing dynasty) warlords who once

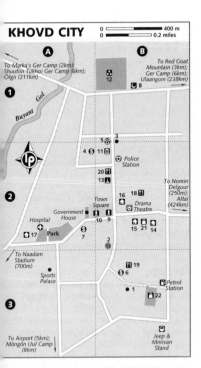

KHOVD CITY

0   400 m
0   0.2 miles

To Marka's Ger Camp (2km);
Shuutiin Tokhoi Ger Camp (6km);
Ölgii (211km)

To Red Goat
Mountain (3km);
Ger Camp (6km);
Ulaangom (238km)

Buyant Gol

Police
Station

To Nomin
Delgüür
(250m);
Altai
(424km)

Town
Square

Drama
Theatre

Government
House

Hospital

Park

To Naadam
Stadium
(700m)

Sports
Palace

Petrol
Station

To Airport (5km);
Möngön Uul Camp
(8km)

Jeep &
Minivan
Stand

conquered and brutally governed Mongolia. The 40,000-sq-metre walled compound once contained several temples, a Chinese graveyard and the homes of the Manchu rulers, though there's little left to see. Three enormous gates provided access. At one time there was a moat (2m deep and 3m wide) around the 4m-high walls, but this has been completely filled in. The 1500-man Chinese garrison was destroyed after a 10-day siege and two-day battle in August 1912. The one legacy of Manchurian rule that has remained is the 200-year-old trees that line the streets of Khovd city.

While you are around this part of town, the nearby mosque **Akhmet Ali Mejit**, constructed in 2000, is worth a look. Friday services are held at 2.30pm.

TÜREEMEL AMARJUULAGAI KHIID
ТҮРЭЭМЭЛ АМАРЖУУЛАГАЙ ХИЙД
The original Shar Süm (Yellow Temple) was built outside of Khovd in the 1770s but was completely destroyed during the Stalinist purge of 1937. The **monastery** (admission T2000; ☺ 9am-5pm) was recently relocated to the centre

of the city (in the former billiards club) but it's not all that active.

TOWN SQUARE
Two statues in the town square honour local heroes. One of them, **Aldanjavyn Ayush** (1859–1939), was a local revolutionary hero who agitated against the Manchus to lower taxation and was made head of Tsetseg *sum* after the 1921 revolution. The other statue (close to the Government House) is of **Galdan Boshigt** (1644–97), ruler of the Zuungar Mongols. Although only a blip on the pages of history, Galdan Boshigt's military victories in Central Asia gave him brief rule over the Silk Road cities Samarkand and Bukhara.

Sleeping
CAMPING
There are fine camping spots along the Buyant Gol; head out of the town towards Ölgii, turn right (downstream) at the river, and pitch your tent anywhere. It can get buggy here in late summer so make sure you have adequate insect repellent.

WESTERN MONGOLIA

GER CAMPS

our pick **Shuutiin Tokhoi** (☎ 9943 8200; bayar huub@yahoo.com; GPS: N 48°02.960′, E 091°40.253′; per person T10,000) About 6km from town, this basic camp is run by a local school teacher named Bayarkhuu (locals know the place as Bayarkhuu camp). It has a gorgeous location along the Buyant Gol, at the foot of sheer cliffs that make for good rock climbing. You can buy meals for T2000. It's just past a half-abandoned chicken farm.

Marka's Ger Camp (☎ 9943 8849; markasl2002@yahoo .com; GPS: N 48°01.360′, E 091°37.685′; per person T10,000) Just 2km from town, next to the Buyant Gol, this is a reasonable place to stay if you don't have your own transport. It includes two Kazakh gers and meals are available. Contact Marka at the Khovd Handicraft Cooperative.

Möngön Uul (☎ 9943 7770; mungun_uul@yahoo .com; GPS: N 47°56.425′, E 091°34.803′; per person T13,000) Slightly better setup than the other two camps, but the location is dry and exposed. It's 3km southwest of the airport.

HOTELS

Agricultural University Dorms (☎ 22178; dm T5000) Clean and bright basic rooms, run by the local university. Bathrooms are detached.

Khovd Hotel (☎ 23063; s/d T3000/6000, half-lux s/d T6000/12,000, lux s/d T8000/16,000) Scruffy, communist-era hotel near the Drama Theatre.

Buyant Hotel (☎ 23860; dm T5000, half-lux T15,000-18,000, lux T25,000) Though nothing extravagant, this is the best hotel in town. The lux room has a huge living room with fridge and TV plus hot-water shower. The half-lux rooms include toilet and cold-water shower. If you are considering a dorm, bear in mind that the bathroom is two floors below.

Myangan Ugalzit Hotel (☎ 22086; s/d T8000/16,000, half-lux s/d T10,000/20,000, lux T18,000/36,000) A government-run hotel on the edge of town. It's well maintained and has spacious rooms but it can be hard to get in here unless you've booked ahead.

Eating

Naran Restaurant (☎ 9143 5555; meals T1300-1900; 🕙 9am-10pm) Somewhat upscale atmosphere for a basic Mongolian eatery. The fish looks like a progressive menu item although they never seem to have it.

Tsomorlig Kafé (☎ 9943 9765; meals T1500-2000; 🕙 9am-9pm) Sizzling platters of meat are served in this hole-in-the-wall café on the

main street. Ask for the house specialty, *on dogtei hurag* (fried eggs and meat).

Ikh Mongol (☎ 22388; meals T1500-2500; 🕙 9am-midnight) Mongolian-themed restaurant that goes all out with traditional leather art and wolf pelts on the walls. The menu, however, is mainly Chinese dishes with a few Mongolian stand-bys. In the late evening it's mainly a beer bar.

SELF-CATERING

The daily **market**, south of the town centre, is large, lively and well stocked. Khovd aimag is justifiably famous for its miniature watermelons (normally best in late summer) which are available at the market.

Probably the easiest place to shop is the **Nomin Delguur** (🕙 10am-7pm), a big and modern supermarket on the eastern side of town.

Shopping

The **Khovd Handicraft Cooperative** (☎ 9943 8849) made up of 12 local women, produces and sells handmade felt carpets and wall hangings. You can meet the women in their homes and purchase their work, or you can buy it from a shop next to the Buyant Hotel. A 1.2m x 2m carpet will cost around US$70. Some customers claim that having product shipped abroad can be unreliable – if you are buying, take the carpet with you.

Getting There & Away

AIR

At least one plane a day travels the Khovd–Ulaanbaatar route. MIAT flies for US$161/282 one way/return, AeroMongolia flies for US$183/324 and EZ Nis flies for US$201/362.

Khovd to Ulaanbaatar flights (and vice versa) are popular, so it is vital to buy tickets well in advance. If you have a return ticket from Ulaanbaatar, reconfirm it as soon as you arrive. The **EZ Nis office** (☎ 22880) is in the same building as XAC Bank. **AeroMongolia** (☎ 9982 1265) is at the Mongol Shuudar Bank. **MIAT** (☎ 9943 4130, 22414) can be found at the airport. The airport is 5km south of the city.

At the time of research Air China had plans to start a route between Khovd and Urumqi in Xinjiang (China). If the route opens up you'll need to have a valid Chinese visa to make the journey.

THE GREEN TARA OF KHOVD

In Dörgön *sum*, two hours drive from Khovd city, an elderly woman is performing miracles. Megjin, 60, has spent the past several years clearing out a demon-infested charnel ground near the shores of Khar Us Nuur. The once-barren ground has been planted with more than 3500 trees and shrubs; several Buddhist temples have also been erected here.

Megjin, clearly no ordinary granny, is in fact a certifiable Green Tara (Buddha of enlightened activity) recognised as such when she was seven. The threat of persecution by local communists kept her identity under wraps but locals still took her title seriously. It is said that her mother's pregnancy lasted three years and local doctors had wrongly assumed that the woman was carrying an enormous tumour in her belly. In 2006 Megjin was officially recognised as a Tara by the Mongolian government and was given an enthronement ceremony in Ulaanbaatar.

Megjin's Buddhist park overlooks Kar Us Nuur and is surrounded by a landscape of green, red, black and white rocks. As Megjin explains, the place is connected to Khamaryn Khiid (see p202) through an underground geomantic line.

HITCHING

Hitching to anywhere from Khovd is a hassle and not recommended. Your time will be spent more wisely slugging it out on a share Furgon (Russian-made minivan) or jeep. If you do hitch, the easiest destination is probably Ölgii and you might get a lift from other tourists. Although it's the main highway to Ulaanbaatar, hitching to Altai (in Gov-Altai aimag) isn't easy and you may end up stranded halfway in **Darvi** (Дарви). Darvi has a **motel** (per person T1000), but you'll need to wait by the petrol station should the rare vehicle pass through. Cars do pass this way, but they are usually too full to take an extra passenger.

MINIVAN & JEEP

Furgons wait at the market. You should be able to get a ride somewhere within a day, or maybe two. Approximate fares are T20,000 to Altai (15 hours, 424km), T35,000 to Bayankhongor (28 hours, 795km) and T50,000 to Ulaanbaatar (50 hours, 1425km).

At least one Furgon per day will travel to Ulaanbaatar. As usual, these vans leave around four to eight hours after the suggested departure time; ask the driver to pick you up at your hotel when he is ready. Bear in mind that the ride to Ulaanbaatar is 45 to 50 nonstop hours of driving, during which time you'll be allotted less than half a seat (think 23 people in a 10-seat van) and, unlike the northern road, there is almost nothing to see on the southern route. Flying back to Ulaanbaatar saves both time and sanity.

There's less traffic headed to Ölgii (T11,000, six to seven hours, 238km) and less still to Ulaangom (T12,000, seven to eight

hours, 238km) but, again, something should come up.

Jeeps cost around T450 per kilometre, including petrol. Ask around at the market. The road from Khovd city to Ölgii is pretty good; to Altai it is rough and boring in patches; and to Ulaangom the road is often marred by broken bridges and flooded rivers after heavy rain.

KHAR US NUUR NATIONAL PARK
ХАР УС НУУР

About 40km to the east of Khovd city is Khar Us Nuur (Dark Water Lake), the second-largest freshwater lake (15,800 sq km) in Mongolia – but with an average depth of only 4m. Khovd Gol flows into this lake, creating a giant marsh delta. Khar Us Nuur is the perfect habitat for wild ducks, geese, wood grouse, partridges and seagulls, including rare relict gulls and herring gulls – and by late summer a billion or two of everyone's friend, the common mosquito. The best time to see the birdlife is in May and late August.

As at Uvs Nuur (p239), bird-watchers may be a little disappointed: the lake is huge, difficult to reach because of the marshes and locals know very little, if anything, about the birdlife. The best idea would be to go with one of the national park workers and head for the delta where the Khovd Gol enters the lake. You'll need several litres of drinking water and mosquito repellent.

The easiest place to see the lake is from the main Khovd–Altai road at the southern tip of the lake, where a metal **watchtower** (GPS: N 47°50.541′, E 092°01.541′) has been set up to view the nearby reed islands.

STEPPE ASIDE TUVANS, THERE'S A NEW VOICE IN TOWN

Thanks to good PR in Tuva, everyone has heard of the Tuvan throat singers. Less known is that Mongolia also has its own contingent of throat singers who you'll surely hear at concerts staged in Ulaanbaatar.

Known as *khöömii*, throat singing allows the human voice to produce a whole harmonic range from deep in the larynx, throat, stomach and palate, and has the remarkable effect of producing two notes and melodies simultaneously: one a low growl, the other an ethereal whistling.

Throat singing is traditionally centred on western Mongolia (particularly Chandmani in Khovd) and the neighbouring republic of Tuva (Russia). It's rare to hear a concert out in the countryside, but if you prod some locals someone might strike up a tune.

Several recordings of throat singing are available abroad, though most are from Tuva. Some singers, including the well-known Aldyn Dashka, have blended throat singing with rock'n'roll beats. Mongolian singer Dangaa Khosbayar is backed by a range of instruments including the sitar and didgeridoo. Most *khöömii* singers are male although a few female singers are breaking onto the scene; look for recordings by Alimaa or Undarmaa.

To check out some throat singing try the CDs *Choomej: Throat Singing From the Center of Asia* (Tuvinian Singers) and *Deep in the Heart of Tuva: Cowboy Music from the Wild East.*

For more information on throat singing, and to learn how to do it, see www.khoomei.com.

The outflow from Khar Us Nuur goes into a short river called Chono Khairkhan, which flows into another freshwater lake, **Khar Nuur** (Black Lake), home to some migratory pelicans. See this area while you can: construction of a hydropower dam on the Chono Khairkhan is nearly complete. When finished, the dam will inundate canyons and huge tracts of grassland, and almost certainly kill off rare aquatic life.

The southern end of Khar Nuur flows into **Dörgön Nuur**, which is a large alkaline lake good for swimming. The eastern side of Dörgön Nuur is an area of bone-dry desert and extensive sand dunes. West of the lake, on the road to Chandmani, you have a better-than-average chance of spotting saiga antelopes.

Just to the south, and between the Khar and Khar Us lakes, are the twin peaks of **Jargalant Khairkhan Uul** (3796m) and **Yargaitin Ekh Uul** (3464m). You can see the massif as you drive to Ölgii from Altai in Gov-Altai aimag. With the help of a guide you'll find numerous springs in these mountains. The canyons also hide a 22m high waterfall.

If you are driving in a loop through the park, the village of **Chandmani** makes a logical place to camp. There are good camp sites, a few shops and, for once, no mosquitoes. Chandmani is also renowned as a centre for *khöömii* singers and Westerners sometimes come here for informal study from the old masters. Well-known local singers include Tserendavaa, Tsenee and Davaajav.

Accommodation in the area includes **Jargalant Orgil** (☎ 9943 8800; tseveenravdand@ yahoo.com; per person T15,000), a new ger camp between Khar Us Nuur and Jargalant Khairkhan Uul.

TSENKHERIIN AGUI
ЦЭНХЭРИЙН АГУЙ

The **Tsenkheriin Agui** (GPS: N 47°20.828′, E 091°57.225′, is located in an attractive setting next to a stream in Mankhan *sum*, 100km southeast of Khovd city. Until just a few years ago the walls of these caves were strewn with dozens of 15,000-year-old wall paintings. Vandals have wrecked all but a couple of the drawings and only an experienced local could find the best examples. The museum in Khovd city (see p232) has a re-creation of how the cave paintings looked before their senseless destruction.

MÖNKH KHAIRKHAN NATIONAL PARK
МӨНХ ХАЙРХАН УУЛ

At 4362m, Mönkh Khairkhan Uul is the second-highest mountain in Mongolia. You can walk up the peak if you approach from the northern side. There is plenty of snow and ice on top, so you'll need crampons, an ice axe and rope, but the climb is not technically difficult. A jeep trail runs to the base from Mankhan. The peak is known locally as Tavan Khumit. This is also Khovd's newest national park and visitors are charged the standard T3000.

UVS УВС

pop 81,200 / area 69,000 sq km

After travelling around this aimag for a while you may start to wonder why they named it Uvs (Grass) as most of the region is classified as high desert. Really the main feature of this diverse aimag is its lakes, which come in all shapes, sizes and levels of salinity. The biggest, Uvs Nuur, is more like an inland sea, while smaller lakes such as Khökh Nuur make excellent hiking destinations. Together the lakes and the surrounding deserts make up the Ikh Nuuruudin Khotgor: a 39,000-sq-km Great Lakes Depression that includes bits of neighbouring Khovd and Zavkhan aimags.

However, the main attraction of Uvs has to be the twin peaks of Kharkhiraa (4037m) and Türgen (3965m) *uuls*. From these mountains spill permanent glaciers, fast-flowing rivers and verdant plateaus. This is also one of Mongolia's most seismically active regions. In 1905 an earthquake measuring greater than eight on the Richter scale ripped through the province and left a distinct fault line in the eastern part of the aimag.

Uvs aimag was originally named Dorvod after the main ethnic group that inhabited the area. The Dorvod people, who still represent just under half of the population of Uvs, speak their own dialect. Other minority ethnic groups include the Bayad, Khoton and Khalkh.

National Parks

The Great Lakes Depression is a globally important wetland area for migratory birds and is a Unesco World Biosphere Reserve. Many other parks have been established in the aimag and, together with parks in Russia, Tuva, China and Kazakhstan, form a Central Asian arc of protected areas.

Khan Khökhii National Park (220,550 hectares) An important ecological indicator and home to musk deer, elk, red deer and wolf.

Khyargas Nuur National Park (332,800 hectares) An area of springs and rocky outcrops that harbours abundant waterfowl.

Tes River Reserve (712,545 hectares) The newest conservation area in Uvs protects waterfowl, beaver and fish.

Uvs Nuur Strictly Protected Area (712,545 hectares) Consists of four separate areas: Uvs Nuur, Türgen Uul, Tsagaan Shuvuut Uul and Altan Els. Contains everything from desert sand dunes to snowfields, marsh to mountain forest. Snow leopard, wolf, fox, deer and ibex are among

the animals protected. Part of the Man and the Biosphere Unesco programme, and the Ramsar Wetland Convention.

ULAANGOM УЛААНГОМ

☎ 01452 / pop 22,900 / elev 939m

Ulaangom (Red Sand) is a charmless city stuck in the middle of the desert. Still, it's not a bad place to hang around while planning a trip around western Mongolia: it has a bustling market, well-stocked shops and a worthwhile museum.

Information

Border Patrol office (Khiliin Tserenk Alban) Opposite the market, ask about a border permit here.

Eco Ger (Airport) This small tourist-information ger has details on good horse trekking and hiking areas. It opens when an aeroplane arrives from Ulaanbaatar.

Gurvan Gan Internet Café (☎ 9945 6810; per hr T400; ☼ 9am-11pm) Near the main square.

Internet café (☎ 23370; per hr T500; ☼ 8am-5pm Mon-Sat) At the Telecom office.

Mongol Shuudan Bank (☎ 24022; Marshal Tsedenbal Gudamj; ☼ 8am-5pm Mon-Fri, 9am-2pm Sat) Does cash advances on Visa.

Strictly Protected Areas office (☎ 22271; delhii novuvsnuur_mn@yahoo.com; ☼ 9am-5pm Mon-Fri) Located at the western end of the main road, this office provides information on, and permits to, the protected areas in the aimag.

Telecom office (☎ 107; ☼ 24hr) The post office is also here.

XAC Bank (☼ 8am-5pm Mon-Fri, 9am-3pm Sat-Sun) Changes money and gives cash advances on Visa and MasterCard.

Zoos Bank (☎ 23899; ☼ 8am-5pm) Next door to XAC Bank. Changes money and gives cash advances on MasterCard.

Sights

The comprehensive **Aimag Museum** (☎ 24720; admission T2000; ☼ 9am-5pm Mon-Sat) has the usual stuff plus a section on the 16th-century Oirad leader Amarsanaa (the chain-mail jacket is supposedly his). There's a newly built wing dedicated solely to the reign of one-time dictator Yu Tsedenbal (who was born in Uvs), featuring photos of the man with other commie leaders like Fidel Castro and Ho Chi Minh.

Dechinravjaalin Khiid, on the eastern end of town near the airport, was originally founded on this spot in 1738. It contained seven temples and 2000 monks; an artist's rendition hangs inside the office of the head monk. The place was pulverised in 1937 thanks to Stalin,

WESTERN MONGOLIA

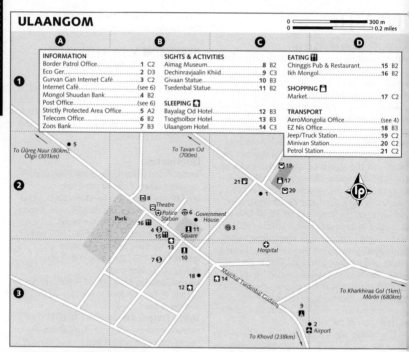

ULAANGOM

INFORMATION			SIGHTS & ACTIVITIES			EATING 🍴		
Border Patrol Office	1	C2	Aimag Museum	8	B2	Chinggis Pub & Restaurant	15	B2
Eco Ger	2	D3	Dechinravjaalin Khiid	9	C3	Ikh Mongol	16	B2
Gurvan Gan Internet Café	3	C2	Givaan Statue	10	B3			
Internet Café	(see 6)		Tsedenbal Statue	11	B2	SHOPPING 🛍️		
Mongol Shuudan Bank	4	B2				Market	17	C2
Post Office	(see 6)		SLEEPING 🛏️					
Strictly Protected Area Office	5	A2	Bayalag Od Hotel	12	B3	TRANSPORT		
Telecom Office	6	B2	Tsogtsolbor Hotel	13	B3	AeroMongolia Office	(see 4)	
Zoos Bank	7	B3	Ulaangom Hotel	14	C3	EZ Nis Office	18	B3
						Jeep/Truck Station	19	C2
						Minivan Station	20	C2
						Petrol Station	21	C2

and its current incarnation consists of a concrete ger and about 20 welcoming monks.

The **bronze statue** in front of Government House is of Yumjaagiin Tsedenbal, who ruled Mongolia for about 40 years until 1983, and was born near Ulaangom. Opposite the town square, another **statue** honours Givaan, a local hero who was killed in 1948 during clashes with Chinese troops.

Sleeping
CAMPING

The only place to camp nearby is along Gumbukh Gol, which you cross as you come from Ölgii. Walk about 300m northwest of the town square to find a spot. If you have your own vehicle, camping is far better along the Kharkhiraa Gol or anywhere south of the city on the road to Khovd.

HOTELS

Ulaangom Hotel (☎ 9969 5251; per person T10,000) This centrally located hotel has a few rooms that share a bathroom, but there is no shower.

Tsogtsolbor Hotel (☎ 24614; Marshal Tsedenbal Gudamj 15; s/d T9000/17,000, half-lux s/d T11,000/20,000,

lux s/d T16,000/22,000) The lux rooms here come with TV and twin beds while the ordinary rooms have king-size beds but no TV. As usual, plumbing is haphazard at best. The hotel does have a swanky little bar and night-club that draws some late night crowds.

Tavan Od (☎ 23409, 9945 9418; d/q/lux T15,000/20,000/25,000) This 10-room hotel on the north edge of town offers basic but clean rooms at reasonable rates. It has a shop, hot water and sauna. It also has a restaurant but the meat they served us tasted like the cow had died of old age.

Bayalag Od Hotel (☎ 22445, 9984 3261; s/d US$10/20, lux US$25-35) Located in an unexciting brick heap, lux rooms have their own bathroom with TV. The management informs us that hot water is available on Monday, Tuesday and Saturday – but even those days are a bit of a gamble.

Eating

For some really cheap *khuushuur* (mutton pancakes) or *buuz* (steamed dumplings), if you're not fussy about hygiene, try the train-car *guanz* outside the **market**.

Ikh Mongol (☎ 9983 9292; Marshal Tsedenbal Gudamj 29; meals 1500-2500; ☷ 8am-10pm) Reputedly the best place in town, Ikh Mongol has a diverse menu with Mongolian and Chinese dishes. Seating is in big red booths and the walls are designed like the interior of a ger. It's owned by a local kingpin who runs a similar restaurant in Khovd city.

Qinggis Pub & Restaurant (☎ 9945 2688; Marshal Tsedenbal Gudamj 27; meals T2000-3000) A couple of doors down from Ikh Mongol is the Qinggis Pub, another restaurant that goes beyond goulash (try one of their soups or a steak). Guns and daggers mounted on the wall add a touch of the Wild West.

Getting There & Away

AIR
EZ Nis and AeroMongolia share the Ulaanbaatar–Ulaangom route; check the schedules to find out when each flies. **EZ Nis** (☎ 25252, 9904 9939) charges US$199/359 one way/ return. Its office is near the Bayalag Od Hotel. **AeroMongolia** (☎ 9945 9551) charges US$144/252 one way/return and its office is in the Mongol Shuudan Bank building. The airport is a dirt field just 1km from the town centre.

HITCHING
Getting to and from Ulaangom is fairly difficult and you'll need time and patience on your side. For points east most vehicles head to and from Tosontsengel (Zavkhan), the halfway point to Ulaanbaatar. Very few vehicles go to or from Mörön (Khövsgöl).

An occasional vehicle travels to or from Ölgii (Bayan–Ölgii). From Ulaangom to Khovd city, hitching is even harder. In Ulaangom, ask around the modern and busy petrol station near the market, and at the market itself.

JEEP & MINIVAN
A few public share jeeps leave for Ölgii (T10,000, 10 hours, 300km) and Khovd (T12,000, seven to eight hours, 238km) when full. Ask around the jeep/truck station by the market.

Share minivans to Ulaanbaatar (via Tosontsengel and Tsetserleg; T50,000, about 48 hours, 1336km) wait by the road near the market (a different place from the jeep/truck stand).

It's very difficult to find a van going to Mörön (T30,000, about 25 hours, 680km); ask around the market and, if there is nothing

available, consider riding a UB-bound minivan as far as Tariat (T25,000, 26 hours, 700km) and then attempt to bum a lift to Mörön from other backpackers at Terkhiin Tsagaan Nuur.

You'll need to bargain hard for any vehicle as local drivers tend to overcharge foreigners. A recommended local driver with fair prices is Erdenejav (☎ 9945 5799), who speaks no English.

The Khovd city–Ulaangom road sometimes suffers from flooded rivers and collapsed bridges after heavy rain.

UVS NUUR УВС НУУР
Uvs Nuur is a gigantic inland sea in the middle of the desert. The lake's surface occupies 3423 sq km, making it Mongolia's largest lake, though it's very shallow at an average depth of 12m. (Still, legend has it that the lake is bottomless.)

Uvs Nuur is five times saltier than the ocean and devoid of edible fish. It has no outlet, so a lot of the shoreline is quasi-wetland. This environment, plus the clouds of mosquitoes, make Uvs Nuur tourist unfriendly. With the exception of serious **ornithologists**, most visitors will better appreciate the prettier, smaller and more accessible freshwater Üüreg Nuur.

Ornithologists have documented more than 200 bird species around Uvs Nuur, including crane, spoonbill, goose and eagle, as well as gulls that fly thousands of kilometres from the southern coast of China to spend a brief summer in Mongolia.

Only the most determined birdwatchers spend much time around the lake. Uvs Nuur is huge and public transport around it nonexistent; trails often turn into marsh and sand; only park officials know anything about the birdlife; and you may not be there at the right time anyway. Real enthusiasts should venture to the northeastern delta around **Tes**. Note that Tes is a border area and you'll need a border permit from the border office in Ulaangom (see p237). Contact the Uvs Nuur Strictly Protected Areas office in Ulaangom (see p237) for a list of visiting species and ideas on how to spot them.

Forget about hitching to the lake, you'd almost certainly be dumped in a marshy wasteland. The only way to come to grips with this beast of a lake is in your own hired vehicle. Because of the marshes, you'll need to park 1km or so from the shore and walk to the lake.

If you are travelling between Ulaangom and Mörön you can get decent views from the road (about 1km from the shore) and maybe persuade your driver to veer off for a closer look.

BAYAN NUUR БАЯН НУУР

Close to Uvs Nuur and certainly more welcoming, Bayan Nuur is a pretty lake amid sand dunes. From Züüngov *sum* you can reach its shore in about 20 minutes by car. These are allegedly the world's northernmost sand dunes.

ULAANGOM TO ÖLGII

This route between the two aimag capitals can be done in two days by jeep or a pleasant four days by bicycle. The journey begins with a 40km tarmac road heading northwest out of Ulaangom. Just past Türgen village the road becomes a jeep trail and heads up to **Ulaan Davaa** (Red Pass; elev 1972m), notable for its enormous *ovoo*.

From the pass there are two routes. One heads due south and then southeast to Khökh Nuur (opposite). The other leads west to lovely Üüreg Nuur (right), which is a good area for camping.

From Üüreg Nuur, cargo trucks take a less-rugged (but longer) route (301km) via **Bohmörön village** (where you can check out the 8th-century Turkic *balbal*). If you end up in Bohmörön with no onward transport, it's possible to walk 9km to Nogoonuur *sum* in Bayan-Ölgii province, from where you can get a ride to Ölgii city. The difficulty here is crossing the wide river, the Boh Mörön; you'll definitely need a guide and pack horse to get you across.

Light vehicles (jeeps and vans) bypass Bohmörön and take the short cut (254km) over the steep **Bairam Davaa** (Bairam Pass), past the desolate coal-mining village of Khotgor. Long-distance cyclists take note: this is the only place to pick up supplies between Ulaangom and Ölgii. Most maps show no road via Bairam Davaa but, rest assured, you can make it with a halfway decent vehicle or bike.

From Khotgor you could opt for a detour into the **Yamaat Valley**, which leads to Türgen Uul (opposite). Otherwise, continue south for 60km to the **Achit Nuur** bridge. From here it's another 75km to Ölgii. The road passes the surprisingly lush riverside forests of the

Develiin Aral Nature Reserve, a 16km stretch along the fast-flowing Khovd Gol.

Üüreg Nuur Үүрэг Нуур

Large and beautiful **Üüreg Nuur** (GPS: N 50°05.236', E 091°04.587'), at an elevation of 1425m, is surrounded by stunning 3000m-plus peaks, including Tsagaan Shuvuut Uul (3496m), which are part of the Uvs Nuur Strictly Protected Area. The freshwater Üüreg Nuur has some unidentified minerals and is designated as 'saltwater' on some maps, so it's best to boil or purify all water from the lake. There is a freshwater well on the southeastern edge of the lake near some deserted buildings.

The lake is great for swimming (albeit a little chilly) and locals say there are plenty of fish. One added attraction is that it's one of the few bug-free lakes in the region. Camping is the only sleeping option.

One definite attraction of the lake is its accessibility: it's just a little off the main road between Ulaangom and Ölgii. You could hitch a ride there fairly easily.

Tourist facilities in the area are limited to **OT Tour Camp** (☎ 9913 7772, 9919 1761; www.ottour.com), located 25km southeast of the lake. The camp has a restaurant, modern toilet, hot water and horse-riding tours.

SOUTH OF ÜÜREG NUUR

If you are travelling from the lake over Bairam Davaa (in the direction of Achit Nuur) look out for several **ancient graves and balbals** (GPS: N 50°00.484', E 091°02.932') by the road, a few kilometres south of Üüreg Nuur. The *balbals* (anthropomorphic statues) represent either local heroes or, possibly, enemies killed in battle. They date from around the 8th century. Another set of **graves and balbals** (GPS: N 50°00.220', E 091°02.713') is a further 550m south. The circular piles of stones in the area are *kurgans* (burial mounds).

On the south side of Bairam Davaa, the road passes more *kurgans* and standing stones (thin, stone pillars used as grave markers). The most impressive, 7km north of Khotgor, include two **mounds** (GPS: N 49°54.910', E 090°54.527') surrounded by concentric circles and radiating spokes. Around the eastern mound you can see tiny stone circles forming a great arc around the mound. There are two carved **deer stones** nearby.

Khotgor is a rough-and-ready coal-mining town inhabited by Kazakhs and Mongols.

WHICH KHARKHIRAA?

Near Ulaangom there are several areas known as Kharkhiraa. The main places of interest for travellers are Kharkhiraa Gol (river) and Kharkhiraa Uul (mountain), both described below. A third Kharkhiraa is a run-down Soviet-era holiday resort, located in a valley called, you guessed it, Kharkhiraa. The valley is gorgeous but very steep, which makes for difficult hiking. The holiday resort does a lot to ruin the charm of the area and the local caretaker will attempt to charge you T5000 per person for camping. If you are heading into the mountains for a multi-day adventure, the best access remains the Kharkhiraa Gol. There is plenty of scope for confusion so make sure you, your guide and driver know where you are going!

There are a few shops and a barely function-ing *guanz* near the petrol pump.

KHARKHIRAA UUL & TÜRGEN UUL ХАРХИРАА УУЛ & ТҮРГЭН УУЛ

The twin peaks of Kharkhiraa Uul (4037m) and Türgen Uul (3965m), which dominate the western part of the aimag, are curiously almost equidistant between Achit, Üüreg and Uvs *nuurs*. As vital sources of the Uvs Nuur, the mountains are part of the Uvs Nuur Strictly Protected Area. In summer, the area has some excellent hiking opportunities and the chance to meet Khoton nomads who graze their flocks in the area. Khoton people are famed throughout Mongolia as shamans.

Getting There & Away

The mountains can be approached from dif-ferent directions. Most hikers walk from east to west, from Tarialan to Khotgor. In Tarialan you can organise pack camels and a guide.

Tarialan is 31km south of Ulaangom. From here follow the Kharkhiraa Gol into the moun-tains; you'll need to cross the river up to nine times as you go up the valley. Three days and 50km later you'll cross over the Kharkhiraa Davaa (2974m), which is accessible on foot but difficult going for pack camels.

From the pass you descend into the pretty Olon Nuur Valley, a marshy area of lakes and meadows. Turn north to walk over Yamaat Davaa (2947m) into Yamaat Valley, an area inhabited by snow leopards. In summer a ger camp is sometimes open in this valley. At the end of the valley you can easily reach the town of Khotgor.

It's 50km from Kharkhiraa Davaa to Khotgor, so you should plan six days for the entire route. Mongolia Expeditions (p81) and Off the Map Tours (p270) both run walking trips through this area.

If you start in Khotgor, it's possible to drive into Olon Nuur valley, but it's pretty boggy here so stick to existing jeep tracks.

A third route leads from Khökh Nuur (see below).

KHÖKH NUUR ХӨХ НУУР

This pretty alpine **lake** (elev 6322; GPS: N 49°50.413', E 91°41.141') is surrounded by mountains and makes a great destination on foot or horse. The area is inhabited by many ethnic Dorvod nomads.

On foot or horse you could get there from Tarialan; the trip is about 15km up Davaan Uliastai (one valley north of the Kharkhiraa Gol).

It's possible for a car to reach the lake in a very roundabout manner and only an experienced driver could do it. The road route involves driv-ing up Ulaan Davaa (from Ulaangom), sweep-ing around the mountains close to Üüreg Nuur, and then heading southeast. The trip is around 120km; travelling this distance really only makes sense if you are doing the trip as part of a tour to Üüreg Nuur and Türgen Uul.

Trekkers can continue from the lake for 25km to the glacier-wrapped Türgen Uul. The walk takes about two days through a harsh landscape of prairie, mountains, glaciers and rivers, but the topography is wide open so it's fairly easy to navigate. There are good **camping spots** (GPS: N 49°42.485', E 91°29.525') along the Türgen Gol, near the northern base of Türgen Uul.

KHAR US NUUR ХАР УС НУУР

To confuse things a little, another freshwater lake in the region is called Khar Us Nuur, but it is sometimes referred to as Ölgii Nuur. You can swim and fish in Ölgii Nuur, and it makes a logical camping spot if travelling between Ulaangom and Khovd city. The lake is 102km south of Ulaangom.

WESTERN MONGOLIA

ACHIT NUUR АЧИТ НУУР

The largest freshwater lake in Uvs, Achit Nuur is on the border of Uvs and Bayan-Ölgii aimags, and is an easy detour between Ulaangom and Ölgii. It offers stunning sunsets and sunrises and good fishing.

The lake is home to flocks of geese, eagles and other **birdlife**. One drawback is the absolute plethora of mosquitoes during the summer. Some camping spots are better than others for mozzies, so look around. Locals claim they are almost bearable by October.

The small Kazakh encampment on the southeastern edge has a *guanz*.

A **bridge** (GPS: N 49°25.446', E 90°39.677') just south of the lake allows for relatively steady traffic between Ulaangom and Ölgii. You can hitch a ride or charter a jeep to the lake from either city without too much trouble.

KHYARGAS NUUR NATIONAL PARK ХЯРГАС НУУР

Khyargas Nuur, a salt lake amid desert and scrub grass, provides an attractive summer home for birds but sees little tourist traffic. Some travellers visit the lake when travelling between Uvs and Zavkhan aimags.

On the northwestern side of Khyargas Nuur, there is a **cold spring** (GPS: N 49°20.153', E 093°09.355') that dribbles out of the mountain – locals say drinking some has health benefits. Near the spring is **Khar Temis** (☎ 9945 6796; r T5000, half-lux T10,000), an old Soviet holiday camp that has seen some renovations. It has lake views and a sandy beach.

The main attraction of the lake, and possibly the weirdest sight in western Mongolia, is **Khetsuu Khad**, an enormous rock sticking out of the water that attracts migratory cormorant birds. The birds arrive in April and hatch their young in large nests built on the rock. When the chicks hatch, their squawking is constant and deafening. The aura created by the white cliffs and shrill birds makes you feel as if you've arrived at the ocean. By October the cormorants are off again, migrating back to their breeding grounds in southern China.

The water around the rock is a bit slimy and the beach is rocky, so the swimming isn't so great here. This habitat, however, is ideal for fish and you'll spot plenty swimming idly in the shallow waters. There are no laws against fishing although given the sensitivity of this unique ecosystem, it's probably best to leave them alone, tempting though they may be.

Adding to the surreal nature of the place is the **Khetsuu Khad Ger Camp** (☎ 11-310 158; 991 6966; GPS: N 49°01.968', E 093°28.783'; with/without meal US$33/15) set down here in the middle of absolutely nowhere. It has hot showers, flush toilets, a restaurant (meals T5000 to T6000) and lonely staff.

The last 15km of the road to Khetsuu Khad are very sandy and it's easy to get stuck – don't attempt it without a reliable 4WD vehicle and confident driver. The drive is easier in July and August when rains harden the sand. (The rain also stirs up waves on the lake, which can make for spectacular viewing.)

A national park fee of T3000 applies around the lake, though you'd be lucky (or unlucky) to find a ranger to pay it to.

South of Khyargas Nuur but still in the national park is the freshwater lake **Airag Nuur** (GPS: N 48°57.126', E 093°22.011'), at the end of the mighty Zavkhan Gol. Despite the name, the lake is not full of fermented mare milk, but it does have about 10 breeding pairs of migratory **Dalmatian pelican**. There were about 400 pelican in the 1960s, but the numbers are tragically decreasing because poachers kill them for their beaks, which are used to make a traditional implement for cleaning horses called a *khusuur* (currycomb), which you may see in use at the Naadam Festival.

ZAVKHAN ЗАВХАН

pop 79,000 / area 82,000 sq km

Zavkhan aimag occupies a transitional zone between the well-watered Khangai mountain range of central Mongolia and the harsh Great Lakes Depression of western Mongolia. In between the two regions, Zavkhan has its own micro-climates and varied terrain that ranges from snowy peaks to steppe to lake surrounded by sand dunes.

The aimag is in an awkward location and very few travellers are likely to pass through much or any of Zavkhan. This is a pity because the scenery is some of the most dramatic and varied in the country; one minute you are travelling through lush valleys and hills and then a few kilometres further you are in desert reminiscent of *Lawrence of Arabia*.

The highlight of the aimag is Otgon Tenger Uul, a 4021m hulk at the western edge of the Khangai. The mountain is considered holy and a new law prohibits anyone from climbing it, although you could do some fine horse treks around the mountain. If you are looking for an interesting route to western Mongolia, try driving from Uliastai across the desert to Khar Nuur or Khyargas Nuur.

ULIASTAI УЛИАСТАЙ

☎ 01462 / pop 19,100 / elev 1760m

Along with Khovd, Uliastai is one of Mongolia's oldest cities, founded by the Manchus during their reign in Mongolia. The old garrison is long gone but the town has retained a pleasant, antiquated feel, with a tree-lined main street and rows of one-storey shops and restaurants. Rivers flowing nearby and a lush valley surrounded by mountains complete the picture, making this an enjoyable place to stay while you consider the direction of your next plunge.

History

Manchurian generals established a military garrison here in 1733 to keep one eye on the Khalkh Mongols to the east and the other on the unruly Oirad Mongols who lived west of the Khangai mountains. The fortress (the remains of which are visible 3km northeast of town) contained up to 3500 soldiers and was surrounded by an inevitable Chinese trading quarter called Maimaicheng. Chinese farmers tilled the lands along the Bogdiin Gol and, as Russian ethnologist Alexei Pozdneev noted during his 1890 visit, a large contingent of local women were on hand to 'serve' the soldiers.

The fort was emptied in 1911 with the disintegration of the Manchu dynasty, but Chinese troops made an attempt to retake the fort four years later, only to be booted out once and for all in March 1921, following the taking of Urga (Ulaanbaatar) by White Russian forces. One of the few traces left visible of the Manchu era is the shackles and torture devices used by the Manchus, now on display in the History Museum.

Orientation

The town is divided into two main districts: west of the Chigistei Gol is the central area with hotels, restaurants and other life-support systems; across the bridge on the eastern bank is the industrial area, which you are

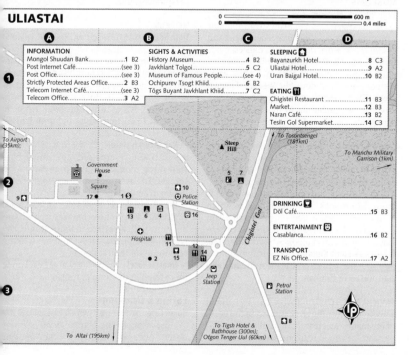

ULIASTAI

0 — 600 m
0 — 0.4 miles

INFORMATION	
Mongol Shuudan Bank	1 B2
Post Internet Café	(see 3)
Post Office	(see 3)
Strictly Protected Areas Office	2 B3
Telecom Internet Café	(see 3)
Telecom Office	3 A2

SIGHTS & ACTIVITIES	
History Museum	4 B2
Javkhlant Tolgoi	5 C2
Museum of Famous People	(see 4)
Ochipurev Tsogt Khiid	6 B2
Tögs Buyant Javkhlant Khiid	7 C2

SLEEPING	
Bayanzurkh Hotel	8 C3
Uliastai Hotel	9 A2
Uran Baigal Hotel	10 B2

EATING	
Chigistei Restaurant	11 B3
Market	12 B3
Naran Café	13 B2
Tesiin Gol Supermarket	14 C3

DRINKING	
Döl Café	15 B3

ENTERTAINMENT	
Casablanca	16 B2

TRANSPORT	
EZ Nis Office	17 A2

unlikely to visit. The airport is 35km west of Uliastai, close to the town of Aldarkhaan.

Information

Mongol Shuudan Bank (☎ 23686) Gives cash advances on Visa and MasterCard.

Post Internet Café (☎ 9908 7824; per hr T600; ☒ 10am-9pm) In the entry to the post office.

Strictly Protected Areas office (☎ 22361, 9946 9477; ☒ 9am-1pm & 2-5pm) This office contains a small information room with brochures and pictures, though no English is spoken. The staff can also sell you entry tickets to Otgon Tenger Strictly Protected Area.

Telecom Internet Café (☎ 21120; per hr T600; ☒ 9am-10pm Mon-Fri, 11-5pm Sat-Sun) In the Telecom office.

Telecom office (☎ 24117; ☒ 24hr) The post office is also located here (but has a separate entrance).

Tigsh Bathhouse (☎ 9972 3976; shower T800) Located behind the Tigsh Hotel. Opening times are sporadic so call ahead.

Xac Bank (☎ 21315; ☒ 9am-5pm Mon-Fri, 10.30am-4pm Sat) Changes dollars and gives cash advances on MasterCard.

Sights
MUSEUMS

The **History Museum** (☎ 23097; admission T2000; ☒ 9am-6pm Mon-Fri), on the main street, contains a mammoth bone, some fine religious art and a *tsam* mask, worn during lama dances, made from coral. There is also a fine collection of photographs taken of Uliastai in the early 20th century. Next door, the **Museum of Famous People** (☒ 9am-6pm Mon-Fri) features well-known Zavkhanites, including Mongolia's first two democratically elected presidents, P Ochirbat and N Bagabandi. Admission is free if you already bought a ticket to the History Museum.

TÖGS BUYANT JAVKHLANT KHIID
ТӨГС БУЯНТ ЖАВХЛАНТ ХИЙД

This small, well-appointed monastery has around 20 monks. You are allowed to watch their ceremonies, which start at about 10am every day. The monastery is on the eastern side of Javkhlant Tolgoi. A second temple, **Ochirpurev Tsogt Khiid**, a Nyingmapa monastery with five lamas, is near the museums and signposted in English.

JAVKHLANT TOLGOI ЖАВХЛАНТ ТОЛГОЙ
This hilltop near the river and just to the north of the main street features a pavilion, nine stupas and the concrete likenesses of an elk, ibex and argali sheep. The views from the top are good. To the northeast, about 3km away, you can barely make out the remains of the old **Manchu military garrison** (GPS: N 47°44.922', E 96°52.198') It is possible to walk to the garrison in about 30 minutes, though there's not much to see and it is generally regarded by locals as a waste dump.

Courses

Mr. Enkhjargal is a professional music teacher at the local music college and can give lessons in *khöömii* (throat singing). He can be reached through the Chigistei restaurant.

Sleeping
CAMPING

Along the lush valley that hugs the Chigistei Gol for 15km from town, and parallel to the northern road to Tosontsengel, there are some gorgeous (though a little busy) camping spots. Just get off the bus, truck or jeep at somewhere you like.

APARTMENT

Tuya, the owner of the Chigistei Restaurant, rents out a four-bed apartment for T5000 per person per night.

HOTELS

Tigsh Hotel (☎ 9546 9208; ger/dm T5000/6000, half-lux s/d T14,000/28,000) A clean hotel with a handful of bright rooms. There is a large yard behind the hotel with trees, a bathhouse and an elaborate three-bed ger. The disinterested management *might* allow you to do your laundry in the bathhouse. It's a 15-minute walk from the centre of town in a white building labelled Зочид Вудал (Hotel).

Bayanzurkh Hotel (☎ 9946 9198, 9920 3988; per person T11,000) Overpriced apartment-hotel with three rooms and a kitchen but no hot shower. It's a 10-minute walk southeast of the town centre.

Uran Baigal Hotel (☎ 9914 0603; dm T8000, half-lux s/d 10,000/20,000) This hotel has reasonable rooms but none with an attached toilet. It is located north of the police station and has a decent restaurant on the 1st floor.

Uliastai Hotel (☎ 9191 9198) Large hotel under renovation at the time of research.

Eating & Drinking

Naran Café (☎ 9967 5485, 9984 2721; meals T1500-2000; ☒ 10am-midnight) The Naran serves up some decent plates of meat with either *ondogte* (egg), *chinjuurtei* (peppers) or *moogtei* (mushrooms). Vegetarians can order a plate of salads and rice (but the potato salad will invariably come with bits of ham). After 9pm it turns into a very dark disco.

Döl Café (☎ 9946 9174; meals T1500-2000; ⏲ noon-11.30pm Mon-Sat) One of the more progressive places in town, the Döl serves meals during the day and is a popular evening haunt for dancing and drinking.

Chigistei Restaurant (☎ 9946 0506; meals T2000; ⏲ 9am-midnight) Large restaurant with a retro-Soviet décor and Mongolian meals. The owner, Tuya, plans to expand the menu to include cheeseburgers(!) and Korean dishes, so it's worth checking out. Tuya speaks English and can help travellers find guides and horses for countryside trips.

Self-caterers can explore the busy **market** or try the **Tesiin Gol Supermarket** (⏲ 10am-6pm) near the roundabout.

Entertainment

Casablanca (☎ 9946 7039; ⏲ 10am-11.30pm) Everyone from kids to teens to grannies turns up here in the evenings to stretch their vocal cords along with the karaoke machine.

Getting There & Away

AIR
AeroMongolia (☎ 9983 4347) flies between Ulaanbaatar and Uliastai twice a week for US$158/280 one way/return. The airport is about 35km west of Uliastai; a taxi will cost about T9000.

HITCHING
The road between Uliastai and Tosontsengel is fairly busy, so hitching shouldn't be difficult, but because it rains a fair bit in summer, hanging around for a lift may not be pleasant. Hitching to anywhere else from Uliastai is really hard – Zavkhan's isolated location ensures that few vehicles come this way.

MINIVAN & JEEP
Several minivans and jeeps leave each day for Ulaanbaatar (T30,000, 26 hours, 984km) via Tosontsengel (T10,000, five to six hours, 181km) Tariat (for Terkhiin Tsagaan Nuur; T14,000, 10 to 11 hours, 399km) and Tsetserleg T18,000, 15 hours, 531km). You may need to bargain for these prices.

If you are lucky you might find a minivan or jeep headed north to Mörön (T15,000, 10

to 11 hours, 389km), but very little traffic heads south to Altai. Almost all traffic leaves from the **jeep station** between the river and the market. In the last week of August it is easy to get a ride to Khovd city (T30,000, 18 hours, 480km) when vans fill up with students headed back to university.

The road between Uliastai and Tosontsengel is unpaved, but pretty reasonable and easy to follow. The turn-off to Tosontsengel is 148km north of Uliastai and 33km west of Tosontsengel.

ZAGASTAIN DAVAA
ЗАГАСТАЙН ДАВАА

Forty-eight kilometres northeast of Uliastai on the Uliastai–Tosontsengel road is a spectacular mountain pass with the unusual name of **Zagastain Davaa** (Fish Pass; GPS: N 48°04.157', E 097°09.900'). At the top, there are fine views and a large *ovoo*. The weather is infamously changeable up here, with the possibility of snow, rain or wind at anytime. There is decent camping and hiking on the stretch of road between the pass and Uliastai. Look out for the two **balbals** and **burial mounds** (GPS: N 47°56.396', E 097°00.824') 20km south of the pass.

OTGON TENGER UUL STRICTLY PROTECTED AREA
ОТГОН ТЭНГЭР УУЛ

One of Mongolia's most sacred mountains, Otgon Tenger Uul (3905m) is the spiritual abode of the gods and an important place of pilgrimage for many Mongolians. The mountain, located about 60km east of Uliastai, is the highest peak in the Khangai Nuruu and is now part of the 95,510-hectare Otgon Tenger Strictly Protected Area. Normal park fees of T3000 per person apply; pay just past the children's camp, about 45km from Uliastai.

The mountain's sanctity means that climbing is prohibited – attempting to do so will incur the wrath of park rangers and the authorities in Uliastai. You'll need to be content with viewing Otgon Tenger from **Dayan Uul**, a 30-minute drive past the children's camp (passing pretty Tsagaannuur en route), where you'll also get views of lovely **Khökh Nuur** (GPS: N 47°37.447', E 97°20.546'). Taxi drivers will take you to Dayan Uul for petrol money plus T20,000.

A second route into the area is via the town of **Otgon**, 138km southeast of Uliastai, where a decent road heads up the Buyant Gol towards the southeastern flank of the mountain. The route from Uliastai to Otgon is littered with impressive pre-Mongol-era burial mounds.

Otgon Tenger is a great area for **horse trekking** and it's possible to encircle the mountain in a few days. Tuya at the Chigistei Restaurant (see p245) in Uliastai can put you in touch with horse wranglers.

TOSONTSENGEL ТОСОНЦЭНГЭЛ
☎ 014546 / elev 1716m

Occupying a pretty valley along the Ider Gol, with forested mountains on all sides, Tosontsengel is Zavkhan's second-biggest city and a transit hub for west-bound traffic. Tosontsengel once supported a booming timber trade and its many wood-fronted buildings, coupled with unpaved lanes and wandering horsemen, give it a Wild West atmosphere. Most people only stop long enough to see the truck-stop area of shops and restaurants; if you have some time to kill, walk 400m southwest to see the deserted town square.

The **Computeriin Sugalt Medeliin Töv** (☎ 1800; per hour T1200; ☒ 10am-9pm) offers internet access. It is 250m north of the main square, and 50m south of the main road.

Rashaant Hotel (☎ 9946 5000; per person T4000), on the eastern side of the square, has musty, crumbling rooms and basic facilities. The main road is piled up with truck-stop style cafés and canteens, none better than the other.

Cross-country cyclists will want to stock up on fruit and veggies in Tosontsengel. It has a great selection of food items, though you may need to ask around.

As a transit hub between eastern and western Mongolia there is plenty of traffic, and hitchhikers should find a ride to Uliastai (five hours, 181km), Tariat (five hours, 190km), Mörön (seven hours, 273km), or Ulaangom (15 hours, 533km). If you are coming from Uliastai or Ulaangom to Mörön you don't need to come to Tosontsengel at all; the turn off to Mörön is 33km to the west of the city.

TELMEN AREA ТЭЛМЭН
Around 65km west of Tosontsengel is the town of Telmen, which has a well-preserved **deer stone** in the centre of town. A collection of **burial mounds and deer stones** (GPS: N48°30.674', E97°27.169') can be seen a further 21km south of Telmen, on the main road to Uliastai.

Around 20km northwest of Telmen town is **Telmen Nuur**, a large salt lake home to migrating waterfowl (and swarming flies). It is on the main road from Tosontsengel to Ulaangom. You could **camp** (GPS: N48°48.889', E97°31.068') at the eastern end of the lake, but bring your own water.

WESTERN ZAVKHAN
If you are travelling overland from Uliastai to western Mongolia (or vice versa) there are a few places of interest to stop on the way.

Khar Nuur (Xap Hyyp), located in the sum of Erdenekhairkhan, is a pretty freshwater lake bordering on alpine and desert zones. Most of the lake is ringed by sand dunes making vehicle access difficult. West of Khar Nuur, **Bayar Nuur** (Баян Нуур) is another difficult-to-reach salt lake amid extraordinary scenery. Locals say the fishing is good here. The lake is easiest to reach after rain, when it becomes easier to drive over the sand dunes. If it hasn't rained it's easy to get stuck and stranded.

A more southerly route from Uliastai travels due west towards the **Ikh Khairkhan Nuruu** (Их Хайрхан), an area of cliffs that provide shelter for ibex and wolf. There are caves in the area, including **Ikh Agui** (Big Cave; GPS: 47°57.080', E 94°59.854'). Ikh Agui has a 150m deep tunnel but no stalactites. Make sure to have a torch (flashlight).

From Ikh Agui you could travel northwest to the village of **Urgamal** (which has a man stone 1km west of town) and then Airag Nuur in Uvs Aimag or head due west to **Khomyn Tal** (Хомын Тал), the newest rehabilitation area for *takhi* horses. Twelve *takhi* were sent here from France in 2004 to start a breeding program. Khomyn Tal is in the buffer zone of Khar Us Nuur National Park in Dorvoljin *sum*.

EREEN NUUR ЭРЭЭН НУУР
The beautiful Ereen Nuur is surrounded by rolling sand dunes, some of them high enough to resemble small mountains. It's technically in Gov-Altai Aimag but most travellers reach the lake via Uliastai, from where it's a six- to seven-hour drive. You need to cross the Zavkhan Gol near the lake if coming from Uliastai, but this is usually not a problem. From Altai it's a eight- to 10-hour drive but no river crossing is required. The lake can be visited as part of a trip to Ikh Agui (see above).

Directory

CONTENTS

ACCOMMODATION

Like most things about Mongolia, the accommodation situation in Ulaanbaatar is vastly different from what you will find anywhere outside of the capital city. In Ulaanbaatar, there is a wide range of accommodation, from dorm-style places for US$4 a night to suites in the Chinggis Khaan Hotel, which cost almost as much as Mongolia's gross domestic product. Outside the capital, hotel options are limited and generally poor in quality and services.

One unique option, particularly popular with organised tours, is to stay in tourist gers, which are like those used by nomads – except for the hot water, toilets, sheets and karaoke bars. Also seriously consider bringing your own tent and camping – it's free, and you really experience what Mongolia has to offer.

Payment for accommodation is usually made upon checkout, but some receptionists will ask for money upfront. Remember that most hotels in the countryside will charge you a 'foreigner price' (which is sometimes double the local rate).

If you negotiate a reasonable price with the management, try to pay immediately and get a receipt. Asking for a receipt can sometimes drop the price dramatically; in some cases the staff will charge you the 'foreigner price' but register you as a Mongolian (ie put the 'Mongolian price' down on paper and pocket the difference).

Hotel staff may ask to keep your passport as 'security'. This is not a good idea, for three reasons: staff often do not show up for work (so the person with your passport cannot be found when you want to depart); once staff have your passport, it leaves you open to possibly being asked to pay more for your room while a taxi waits for you outside; or you may simply forget to pick it up and be 300km away before you realise. An expired passport, student card or some other ID with your photo is a great alternative to leaving your real passport.

Security should be a consideration. Always keep your windows and door locked (where possible). Staff may enter your room while you're not around; take any valuables with you or at least keep them locked inside your luggage and don't leave cameras and money lying around your room. Most hotels have a safe where valuables can be kept.

Apartments
Apartment rental is really only an option in Ulaanbaatar; see p82 for details.

Camping
Mongolia is probably the greatest country in the world for camping. With 1.5 million sq km of unfenced and unowned land, spectacular scenery and freshwater lakes and rivers, it is just about perfect. The main problem is a lack of public transport to great camping sites,

PRACTICALITIES

■ The weekly English-language newspapers are the *Mongol Messenger* (www.mongolmessenger .mn) and the *UB Post* (http://ubpost.mongolnews.mn). Both have good articles, events listings and classified sections.

■ Major private dailies in Mongolian include *Ardiin Erkh* (People's Right), *Zunny Medee* (Century News), *Odriin Sonin* (Daily News) and *Önöödör* (Today).

■ BBC World Service has a nonstop service at 103.1FM. Local stations worth trying include Jag (107FM), Blue Sky (100.9FM) and Radio Ulaanbaatar (102.5FM). Voice of America news programmes are occasionally broadcast on 106.6FM.

■ Local TV stations don't start broadcasting until the afternoon and switch off around 11pm. All the stations have political allies: Channel 25 favours the Democrats, Channel 9 prefers the MPRP and the others go with whoever is in power.

■ Electric power is 220V, 50Hz. The sockets are designed to accommodate two round prongs in the Russian/European style.

■ Mongolia follows the metric system.

■ As in the USA, the ground floor is called the 1st floor, as opposed to the UK system, where the next floor above ground level is the 1st floor.

though there are some accessible sites near Ulaanbaatar, such as in Gachuurt, Khandgait and Terelj. Camping is also well worth considering given the poor choice of hotels and the expense of ger camps.

Local people (and even a few curious cows or horses) may come to investigate your camping spot, but you are very unlikely to encounter any hostility. Your jeep driver will have ideas about good places to stay, otherwise look for somewhere near water or in a pretty valley. If you're hitching, it is not hard to find somewhere to pitch your tent within walking distance of most aimag capitals and towns. You will need to bring your own tent and cooking equipment if you want to camp away from the main towns or avoid the local *guanz* (canteen).

To wash yourself, you'll probably need to use the local town's bathhouse. Many are listed under the Information entries in this book. Be aware, though, that the bathhouses won't be like what you'd expect to find in Turkey; in Mongolia they are simply for getting a hosedown.

Be mindful of your security. If drunks spot your tent, you could have a problem. If the owners (and their dog) give you permission, camping near a ger is a good idea for extra security; otherwise camp at least 300m from other gers. Mongolians have little or no idea of the Western concept of privacy, so be prepared for the locals to open your tent and look inside at any time – no invitation is needed.

You can often get boiled water, cooked food, uncooked meat and dairy product from nearby gers in exchange for other good or money, but always leave something and don't rely on nomads, who may have limited supplies of food, water and fuel. It is best to bring a portable petrol stove rather than use open fires, which are potentially dangerous use precious wood and may not be possible where wood is scarce.

A few extra tips:

■ Burn dried dung if you are being eaten alive by mosquitoes (you may then have to decide which is worse: mozzies or burning cow shit) and bring strong repellent with as much DEET as possible. Other anti-mosquito measures include wearing light-coloured clothing, avoiding perfumes or aftershave, impregnating clothes and mosquito nets with permethrin (nontoxic insect repellent), making sure your tent has an insect screen and camping away from still water or marshe (camping in hills or mountains is always better than low-lying areas).

■ Make sure your tent is waterproof before you leave home and always pitch it in anticipation of strong winds and rain.

■ Ensure your gear is warm enough for sub-zero temperatures, or you'll freeze Cheap and flimsy Chinese-made ten and sleeping bags bought in UB won't cut it, especially for camping in the mountains. Bring the best stuff you can get your hands on for an enjoyable trip.

■ Store your food carefully to protect it from creatures of the night.

■ Don't pitch your tent under trees (because of lightning) or on or near riverbeds (flash floods are not uncommon).

For more advice on camping responsibly in Mongolia, see p60.

Gers

For information of ger etiquette, see p33.

TOURIST GER CAMPS

Tourist ger camps are found all over Mongolia. They may seem touristy and are often surprisingly expensive but if you are going into the countryside, a night in a tourist ger is a great way to experience a Western-oriented, 'traditional Mongolian nomadic lifestyle' without the discomforts or awkwardness of staying in a private ger.

A tourist ger camp is a patch of ground with several (or sometimes dozens of) traditional gers, with separate buildings for toilets, hot showers and a ger-shaped restaurant/bar. Inside each ger, there are usually two to three beds, an ornate table, four tiny chairs and a wood stove that can be used for heating during the night – ask the staff to make it for you. The beds are really just smallish cots – if you are built like an NBA basketball player or a sumo wrestler, you'll need to make special arrangements.

Toilets are usually the sit-down types, though they may be (clean) pit toilets.

Prices for tourist camps often depend on the location. Where there is lots of competition, ie Lake Khövsgöl, Kharkhorin and Terkhiin Tsagaan Nuur, you can find basic camps for under T5000 per night. Better camps or camps in remote areas may charge US$20 to US$30 or more) per person per night, including meals. Activities such as horse or camel riding will cost extra. A surprising amount of the charge goes to the food bill, so you may be able to negotiate a discount of 50% to 65% by bringing your own food. This is pretty reasonable for a clean bed and a hot shower.

Meals are taken in a separate restaurant ger. With only a few exceptions, expect the usual Mongolian fare of meat, rice and pota-

toes. Most camps have a bar (and sometimes satellite TV and a blasted karaoke machine). There's often little to differentiate between ger camps; it's normally the location that adds the charm and makes your stay special.

If you plan to stay in a ger camp you may want to bring a torch for nocturnal visits to the toilets, candles to create more ambience than stark electric lights (though not all have electricity), towels (the ones provided are invariably smaller than a handkerchief), and toilet paper (they may run out).

Book ahead if possible. Not all ger camps have a phone so numbers in this book may be for the office in Ulaanbaatar, which will somehow get the message out that you are headed for the camp.

Except for a handful of ger camps in Terelj catering to expat skiers, most ger camps are only open from June to mid-September, although in the Gobi they open a month earlier and close a little later.

In a few touristy places, such as Terelj, Terkhiin Tsagaan Nuur and Khövsgöl Nuur, private families often have a guest ger and take in paying guests. In this case the advice of offering gifts as payment does not apply – this is a commercial transaction. These families are rarely registered with local authorities so they don't advertise, so you'll have to ask around (any ger that is set up next to a road is a good bet).

TRADITIONAL GERS

If you are particularly fortunate you may be invited to spend a night or two out on the steppes in a genuine ger, rather than a tourist ger camp. This is a wonderful chance to experience the 'real' Mongolia.

If you are invited to stay in a family ger, only in very rare cases will you be expected to pay for this accommodation. Leaving a gift is strongly recommended. While cash payment is usually OK as a gift, it's far better to provide worthwhile gifts for the whole family, including the women (who look after the guests). Cigarettes, vodka and candy are customary gifts, but with some creativity you can offer more useful items. Constructive presents include sewing kits, lighters, toothbrushes, toothpaste, duct tape, Mongolian-language books and newspapers, and hand-powered flashlights and radios. Children will enjoy colouring books, pens, paper and puzzles.

DIRECTORY

Your host may offer to cook for you; it is polite for you to offer to supply some food, such as biscuits, bread, fruit, salt, rice and pasta. Pack out any garbage or packaging leftover from these items. Mongolians love being photographed. If you take pictures of your host family, remember to take down their name and a mail them a copy (for address purposes, you'll need their name, *sum* and aimag).

If you stay longer than a night or two (unless you have been specifically asked to extend your visit), you will outstay your welcome and abuse Mongolian hospitality, making it less likely that others will be welcome in the future. (Never rely on families to take you in; always carry a tent as a backup.)

Guesthouses

Ulaanbaatar now has around 20 guesthouses firmly aimed at foreign backpackers. Most are in apartment blocks and have dorm beds for around US$4, cheap meals, a laundry service, internet connection and travel services. They are a great place to meet other travellers to share transportation costs, but can get pretty crowded before and during Naadam (11 and 12 July).

Outside Ulaanbaatar only Dalanzadgad in the Gobi and Khövsgöl Nuur in Khövsgöl have accommodation aimed at backpackers.

Hotels

Most *zochid budal* (hotels) in the countryside (and budget hotels in Ulaanbaatar) have three types of rooms: a *lux* (deluxe) room, which includes a separate sitting room, usually with TV and private bathroom; a *khagas lux* (half-deluxe), which is much the same only a little smaller but often much cheaper; and an *engiin* (simple) room, usually with a shared bathroom. Sometimes, *niitiin bair* (dorm-style) beds are also available. Invariably, hotel staff will initially show you their deluxe room (costing a minimum of T17,000) so ask to see the standard rooms if you're on a budget. Simple rooms cost around T6000 per person per night. Some rooms may cost extra if they come with TV; try the channels first as some pick up BBC while others only get Russian TV.

Budget hotels in Ulaanbaatar, lying on the fringe areas of the city, mainly cater to Mongolian truck drivers – guesthouses are a much better idea. If you plan to stay in budget hotels in the countryside you should bring sleeping bag. An inner sheet (the sort used inside sleeping bags) is also handy if the sheet are dirty. Blankets are always available, but are generally dirty or musty.

Midrange places are generally good but rather overpriced, charging US$40 to US$6 for a double. These rooms will be comfortable and clean and probably have satellite TV. Hot water and heating is standard for most buildings and hotels in Ulaanbaatar and air-conditioning is never needed. The staff in midrange and top-end places will speak English. A private room or apartment available through the guesthouses, may b a better idea.

The 'foreigner price' in this book may b quoted in US dollars (because the exchang rate fluctuates), but you should pay in tö grög because it is now the law.

In the countryside, most hotels are generally empty and falling apart, though facilities continue to improve and almost ever aimag capital will have one decent new place. Even at the best places you can expec dodgy plumbing, broken locks and electrical outages. The quality of hotels in the countryside is reason enough to take a tent and go camping.

As for service, it is generally poor, except for top-end places in Ulaanbaatar. You'll gain little by getting angry – just be businesslike and eventually you'll get what you want. If the staff haven't seen guests for long time (very possible in the countryside) they might have to search for some sheets, blankets, even a bed, washstand and water and then rouse a cook to light a fire to ge some food ready a few hours later.

If the hotel has no hot water (most likely outside UB) or no water at all, it's worth knowing that most aimag capitals have public bathhouse.

ACTIVITIES

Mongolia is all about getting out into the countryside; there are a host of active options for you to pursue. For details of overseas companies that organise activities, se p270; for companies based in Mongolia se p80. Some of the most popular activities such as cycling, hiking, rafting, fishing and of course, horse riding – can be found i our Mongolia Outdoors chapter (p55 Additional activities are listed following.

irding

1ongolia is rich in birdlife; for a comprehen-
ve look see http://birdsmongolia.blogspot
om. The best places to get out your binoculars
nd telephoto lens are the following areas:
anga Nuur (p182) Migratory swan.
har Us Nuur and Khar Nuur (p235) Goose, wood
ouse and relict gull, and migratory pelican.
hyargas Nuur and Airag Nuur (p242) Migratory
rmorant and pelican.
1ongol Daguur Special Protected Area (p174)
hite-napped crane and other waterfowl.
angiin Dalai Nuur (p197) Mongolian lark, eagle, goose
nd swan.
vs Nuur (p239) Spoonbill, crane and gull.

une Buggying

or a true outdoor adventure, consider trav-
ling across the Gobi in a souped-up dune
uggy. Trips are run by **Vast Gobi** (☎ 9908 2785;
ww.vastgobi.com), which has several homemade
wo-seat buggies equipped with CB radio and
;PS unit. Gobi trips cost US$190 to US$200
er day while a day trip in Töv aimag is
'S$150 (prices are per vehicle).

olf

lthough not the first sport that comes to mind
hen planning an adventure in Mongolia, golf-
1g is possible. The Chinggis Khaan Country
lub in Terelj (p111) is the best place to get in
round, although the UB Golf Club (p78) is a
heaper option. The more adventurous could
y playing natural golf across the steppes. Just
ack a five or three iron in your jeep, along with
few dozen golf balls, and golf wherever the
rass looks best. There are some perfect natural
airways in northern Khentii, eastern Zavkhan,
he Chandman-Öndör area in Khövsgöl, and
1 Övörkhangai, south of Khujirt.

You may now be wondering if it's possible
> golf *all* the way across Mongolia. As a mat-
er of fact, it is. In 2003 and 2004 an eccentric
.merican golfer named Andre golfed from
Choibalsan to Khovd city, designating 18 cit-
s and towns as 'holes'. Andre shot the round
1 12,170 strokes, but lost more than 500 golf
alls en route. You can read more about his
dventure at www.golfmongolia.com.

ce Skating

1 winter you won't have to worry about fall-
1g through the ice, as many lakes and riv-
rs freeze right down to the bottom. Many
1ongolians are keen ice skaters – at least
those who live near water, or in big cities with
rinks. The soccer stadium in Nairamdal Park
(p78) becomes an ice rink in winter but it is
not maintained so the ice gets pretty chewed
up. You can rent skates here but the quality
is terrible so if you're serious about this sport,
bring your own equipment. Long-distance
skating is possible on Lake Khövsgöl. A one-
week trip with support costs around US$1300,
contact Nomadic Journeys (p81).

Mountain Biking

Mongolian roads are made for strong mountain bikes and masochistic riders. There are
great biking trails in Terelj, see p113. You'll also
find good trails in Altai Tavan Bogd National
Park (p229) and all around Khövsgöl aimag
(p57). For more cycling tips see p55.

Mountaineering

Mongolia also offers spectacular opportunities for mountain climbing. In the western
aimags, there are dozens of glaciers, and 30
to 40 permanently snow-capped mountains.
You must have the necessary experience, be
fully equipped and hire local guides. The best
time to climb is July and August.

While you don't need permits from the
Ministry of Nature & Environment unless
the mountain is in a national park, you may
want to consult the **Mongol Altai Mountaineering
Club** (☎ 011-455 246; anji@mongol.net; PO Box 49-23,
Bayanzürkh, Ulaanbaatar). The club runs specially
designed mountain-climbing trips. The office is in room 405 of the Physical Training
Institute, opposite the Indian embassy.

The highest peaks (in ascending order):
Otgon Tenger Uul (3905m; p245) Mongolia's holiest
mountain, located in Zavkhan aimag. Its sanctity means
that climbing is strictly prohibited.
Türgen Uul (3965m; p241) One of the most easily
climbed with spectacular views; in Uvs.
Kharkhiraa Uul (4037m; p241) In Uvs; a great hiking area.
Sutai Uul (4090m; p218) On the border of Gov-Altai and
Khovd aimags.
Tsast Uul (4193m; p228) On the border of Bayan-Ölgii and
Khovd aimags. It's accessible and the camping here is great.
Tsambagarav Uul (4202m; p228) In Khovd; it is rela-
tively easy to climb with crampons and an ice axe.
Mönkh Khairkhan Uul (4362m; p236) On the border of
Bayan-Ölgii and Khovd aimags. You will need crampons, an
ice axe and ropes.
Tavan Bogd (4374m; p231) In Bayan-Ölgii, on the border
of Mongolia, China and Russia. This mountain cluster is full
of permanent and crevassed glaciers.

Rock Climbing

There are excellent opportunities for rock climbing in Mongolia, although the sport is still in its infancy with few established routes. For now the best place to climb is in Terelj, where routes have been established on a 35m-high rock near the Buveit ger camp (p112). Plans have been laid to keep climbing gear at the ger camp, where you can turn up and climb at a cost of US$40 to US$50 per day. With your own gear it's US$35. Climbing routes have also been established at Ikh Gazryn Chuluu (p198) in Dundgov; climbers will need to bring their own equipment.

Skiing

Despite the cold temperatures and rugged terrain, there are virtually no opportunities for downhill skiing in Mongolia. Cross-country skiing, on the other hand, is limitless, as long as you can stand the cold. Ger camps in Terelj (p112) that stay open year-round make a good base for cross-country skiing. However, the snow is usually better in Khandgait (p115). The best months for skiing are January and February, although be warned: the average temperature during these months hovers around a very chilly -25°C.

Offbeat Activities

Blokarting Mongolia is perfect for blokarting (aka land sailing), but as there is nothing set up you need to BYOB (bring your own blokart). See www.gobiblokartraid .com for details.

Dog sledding Organised by Wind of Mongolia (p82). Trips are held in Terelj (December to February) for US$60 to US$80 per day and Khövsgöl Nuur (March to April); cross-lake trips take eight days (all-inclusive US$2600).

Kite boarding There is nothing organised on this front so you need to bring all your own gear, but there is great boarding to be had on both Terkhiin Tsagaan Nuur and Lake Khövsgöl.

Polo Legend has it that Chinggis Khaan's troops used to play polo using their enemies' heads as the ball, but this practice seems to have died out long ago. Modern polo (sans severed heads) is occasionally played by local clubs. See www.ghengiskhanpolo.com for details.

BUSINESS HOURS

Government offices are usually open from 9am to 5pm Monday to Friday. Many banks stay open until 7pm and in Ulaanbaatar there are several offering 24-hour banking. Most private and state-run businesses open at about 10am and close sometime betwee 5pm and 8pm. Many open on Sundays.

In the countryside, banks, museums an other facilities may close for an hour at lunc sometime between noon and 2pm.

Outdoor markets are usually open fro 9am to 7pm daily (or sunset in winter), whi indoor markets open from 10am to 8pm.

Museums have reduced hours in wint and are normally closed an extra couple days a week.

For details on the opening hours of plac to eat, see p44.

CHILDREN

Children can be a great icebreaker and are good avenue for cultural exchange with t local people; however, travelling in Mongo is difficult for even a healthy adult. Long je rides over nonexistent roads are a sure route motion sickness and the endless steppe lan scape may leave your children comatose wi boredom. Mongolian food is difficult to stor ach no matter what your age. That said, childr often like the thrill of camping, for a night two at least. There are also lots of opportuniti to sit on yaks, horses and camels, and plenty opportunities to meet playmates when visiti gers. For a child-friendly experience, try the ve tame rides at Nairamdal Park (Children's Par p78) in Ulaanbaatar. Check out LP's *Travel w Children* for more general tips.

Practicalities

Items such as formula, baby food and na pies (diapers) are sold at the State Departme Store (Map pp70–1) and Sky Shopping Cent (Map p64) in Ulaanbaatar, but can be mo difficult to find in the countryside. Few ca in Mongolia even have working seat belts you can pretty much rule out finding a car se You'll have to bring your own if you have ve small children. When travelling in the cou tryside, deluxe hotel rooms normally con with an extra connecting room, which can ideal for children.

CLIMATE CHARTS

It is said that Mongolia can experience fo seasons in a single day. This seems especia true in spring when changeable weather cr ates snowstorms intermixed with bouts wind and sun. Bear in mind the wind-ch factor: a 10-knot wind can make 0°C fe like -5°C.

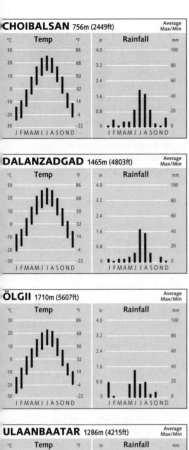

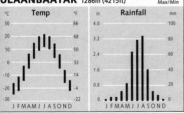

The four seasons are very distinct – winter lasts from November to February, spring from March to mid-May, summer from mid-May until late August, and autumn is during September and October. The cold weather in the far north can last a month or two longer than the Gobi areas. The highest rainfalls occur in the taiga areas (subarctic coniferous forests of Siberian larch and pine trees) along the northern border, especially Khentii and Khövsgöl. See p13 for advice about the best times to visit.

CUSTOMS

Customs officials want to keep out pornography, drugs and expensive imports that might be sold to Mongolians; they want to keep in old paintings, statues, fossils, works of art and mineral samples. Baggage searches of foreigners exiting Mongolia by air are sometimes rigorous, but are less so at border crossings by train to China or Russia, when most passengers are asleep.

When you enter Mongolia, you must fill out an English-language customs declaration form to declare any prohibited items, all precious stones and all 'dutiable goods'. You are also asked to list all monies in your possession. There is no need to be too accurate: this form is rarely checked on your way out. You should, nevertheless, keep all receipts when you change money at banks, though changing money with licensed moneychangers (who will not issue receipts) is legal.

The customs declaration is checked by the customs official and then returned to you. When you leave Mongolia, you will be asked to hand in the form – so keep it safe during your trip.

You can bring 1L of spirits, 2L of wine, 3L of beer, three bottles of perfume and 200 cigarettes into Mongolia duty-free.

If you are legally exporting any antiques, you must have a receipt and customs certificate from the place you bought them. Most reliable shops in Ulaanbaatar can provide this. If you don't get one of these you'll need to get one from the **Centre of Cultural Heritage** (☎ 011-312 735, 323 747) in the Cultural Palace in Ulaanbaatar. You'll need to fill in a form with your passport number, where the antique was purchased and two photos of the antique itself.

If you have anything that even *looks* old, it is a good idea to get a document to indicate that it is not an antique. That goes for Buddha images and statues as well.

During your trip you will probably be offered furs of rare animals, antique items such as snuffboxes, bits and pieces from Erdene Zuu Khiid, and even fossilised dinosaur bones and eggs. Please do not take up these offers. These items are precious to Mongolia's history and the fine for illegally exporting fossils is from US$100 to US$150, or five years in jail.

DIRECTORY

DANGERS & ANNOYANCES

Mongolia is a reasonably safe country in which to travel, but given the infrastructure of the country, state of the economy and other development problems, you are bound to run into hiccups along the way. With a bit of patience and planning, you should be able to handle just about anything.

Alcoholism

Alcoholism is a real problem but is far worse in the cities than in the countryside. Drunks are more annoying than dangerous, except when they are driving your vehicle. Drivers who work for tour companies have been disciplined to hold their alcohol on trips, but hitchhikers may encounter drunk drivers.

Drinking is pretty common on the trains, which is another reason to travel in coupé class or 'soft seat' (you can close your cabin door). If the offending drunk happens to be *in* your cabin, ask the attendant to move you to another cabin.

If camping, always make sure that you pitch your tent somewhere secluded, and that no drunks see you set up camp; otherwise, they will invariably visit you during the night.

Dogs

Stray dogs in the cities and domestic dogs around gers in the countryside can be vicious and possibly rabid. In the countryside, some dogs are so damn lazy that you wouldn't get a whimper if 100 lame cats hobbled past; others will almost head-butt your vehicle and chase it for 2km or 3km while drooling heavily. Before approaching any ger, especially in the countryside, make sure the dogs are friendly or under control and shout the phrase '*Nokhoi khor*', which roughly translates as 'Can I come in?' but literally means 'Hold the dog!'. Getting rabies shots is no fun; it's easier to just stay away from dogs, even if they appear friendly.

If you need to walk in the dark in the countryside, perhaps for a midnight trip to the toilet, locals have suggested that if you swing a torch in front of you it will stop any possible dog attack.

Scams

Professional scamming is not common; the main thing to be aware of is dodgy tour companies that don't deliver on their promises. We've had letters from readers who booked

tours where the promised accommodation food and service standards fell short of expectations. It might be good to get in writing exactly what is offered, and ask about compensation if things don't work out as planned. The riskiest tour companies are the ones operated by guesthouses and the ones that specialise in onward trips to Russia.

Theft

Petty theft is a fact of life in Ulaanbaatar and you need to stay vigilant of bag slashers and pick pockets, especially around Naadam time when muggers do brisk trade on all the starry-eyed tourists wandering about. In the countryside, keep an eye on your gear and don't leave valuables lying around your camp site if you wander off. Lock your kit inside your jeep or hotel whenever possible (drivers do a good job of watching your stuff). When horse trekking, be wary of Mongolians who seem to be following you; they may be after your valuables or even your horses, which are easily stolen while you sleep. For information on the dangers of theft in Ulaanbaatar, see p68.

Other Annoyances

Heating and hot-water shortages and electricity blackouts are common in aimag capitals. Some villages go for months without any utility services at all. Although official police have relaxed considerably since the arrival of democracy, some of the old KGB-inspired thinking still occurs among the police, especially in rural backwaters and border areas.

Quarantine sometimes affects travel in Mongolia. Foot-and-mouth disease, malignant anthrax and the plague pop up all the time and may prevent you from travelling to

rtain areas. Some regions that have been
t by foot-and-mouth require drivers to
econtaminate their cars when they enter
nd leave cities. This requires the spraying
f tyres (or the whole car) and can cost a
w thousand tögrög.

ISCOUNT CARDS

n ISIC student card will get a 25% dis-
ount on train tickets plus discounts with
me tour operators. Check the ISIC website
vww.isiccard.com) for updates.

MBASSIES & CONSULATES

ongolian Embassies & Consulates

ou'll find a full listing of Mongolia's embas-
es and consulates at www.mongolianconsul
e.com.au/mongolia/embassies.shtml.

mbassies & Consulates in Mongolia

few countries operate embassies in
laanbaatar, though for most nationali-
es the nearest embassies are in Beijing or
loscow. If your country has an embassy in
laanbaatar, it's a good idea to register with
if you're travelling into the remote coun-
yside, or in case you lose your passport.

Note that the German embassy also looks
ter the interests of Dutch, Belgian, Greek
nd Portuguese citizens. The British embassy
andles normal consular duties for most
ommonwealth countries.

For details on getting visas for China,
azakhstan and Russia, see p263.

ustria (Map pp70-1; ☎ 324 804; hk_at_ub@magicnet
n; Peace Ave 7)

anada (Map pp70-1; ☎ 328 285; fax 328 289;
nada@mongolnet.mn; Bodicom Tower, 7th fl, Sükhbaa-
ryn Gudamj)

hina (Map pp70-1; ☎ 320 955; fax 311 943; Zaluuchu-
yn Örgön Chölöö 5) The consular section is actually on
ga Toiruu.

enmark (Map pp70-1; ☎ 312 625; fax 312 175;
@mcs.mn; MCS Plaza, Seoul St)

ance (Map pp70-1; ☎ 324 519; www.ambafrance
nn.org in French; Peace Ave 3)

ermany (Map pp70-1; ☎ 323 325; fax 312 118;
rmanemb_ulanbator@mongol.net; Negdsen Undestnii
udamj 7)

apan (Map pp70-1; ☎ 320 777, 313 332; www.mn
mb-japan.go.jp; Olympiin Gudamj 6)

azakhstan (Map pp70-1; ☎ 312 240; kzemby@mbox
n; Apt 11, Diplomatic Services Corps Bldg 95)

ussia (Map pp70-1; ☎ 327 191, 312 851; fax 327 018;
ww.mongolia.mid.ru; Peace Ave A6)

South Korea (Map pp70-1; ☎ 321 548; fax 311 157;
www.mofat.go.kr; Olympiin Gudamj 10)

Spain (Map pp70-1; ☎ 329 856; fax 324 620; oyunit
gel@yahoo.com; Chamber of Commerce Bldg, Suite 602,
Sambugiin Örgön Chölöö 11)

Switzerland (Map pp70-1; ☎ 331 422; fax 331 420;
www.swissconsulate.mn; Diplomatic Services Bldg 95, 4-36)

UK (Map p64; ☎ 458 133; fax 458 036; britemb@
mongol.net; Peace Ave 30)

US (Map p64; ☎ 329 095; http://ulaanbaatar.usembassy
.gov; Ikh Toiruu 59/1)

FESTIVALS & EVENTS

With the exception of Naadam (p96), held
on 11 and 12 July, Mongolia has few genuine
festivals. The Maidar Ergekh festival, held at
a date according to the lunar calendar (usually August), is a religious festival that used
to draw thousands of monks and spectators
before it was banned in the 1920s by the communist government. Since being reinstated in
1990, the festival has been held in a different
monastery each year. It involves *tsam*-mask
dancing and the parading of a statue of the
future Buddha (Maitreya) around the monastery. Although small and unpublicised, it's
worth asking about, especially if you have an
interest in Buddhism.

Ikh Duichin, or Buddha's Birthday, is held
on 18 May and marked by *tsam* dancing in
Gandan Khiid in Ulaanbaatar and by special
services in most other monasteries.

In an effort to boost tourism, travel companies and tourist officials have launched a
series of festivals in countryside areas. Some
are fairly obscure, such as the Airag Festival in
Dundgov aimag, which is held in late August,
and the International Gobi Marathon, held
in September (www.gobimarathon.com).
Others are catching on with both locals and
foreigners. The Yak Festival (Arkhangai; early
August), the Eagle Festival (Bayan-Ölgii; early
October), the Camel Festival (Ömnögov; one
week after Tsagaan Sar) and the Sunrise to
Sunset 100km run (Khövsgöl Nuur; late
June) are worth checking out, especially if
you've missed Naadam. See the website of
the **Tourism Board** (www.mongoliatourism.gov.mn) for
upcoming events.

FOOD

See the Food & Drink chapter (p42) for details
on what is on offer, the type of eateries and
costs. For this book, expect main dishes to
cost T800 to T1500 in budget joints, T2000

DIRECTORY

to T5000 in midrange places and T6000 to T12,000 in most top-end restaurants.

GAY & LESBIAN TRAVELLERS

Mongolia is not a gay-friendly place and not a place to test local attitudes towards homosexuality. While homosexuality is not specifically prohibited, some laws could be interpreted to make it appear illegal. Harassment by police has been reported by the gay and lesbian community, thus it should come as no surprise to hear that Ulaanbaatar's small gay and lesbian community is not well-organised.

Meeting places come and go quickly, so you'll need to quietly tap into the scene and ask. As you never know what sort of reaction you'll get from a Mongolian, try making contacts through the web. Insight can be found at www .globalgayz.com/g-mongolia.html and travel info at www.geocities.com/gaytomongolia/.

HOLIDAYS

Mongolians do not get many holidays. Naadam Festival and Tsagaan Sar warrant three days off each, plus a day off for New Year's. Most tourist facilities remain open during holidays, but shops and offices will close down. The following holidays are observed:

Shin Jil (New Year's Day) 1 January
Constitution Day 13 January; the adoption of the 1992 constitution (generally a normal working day)
Tsagaan Sar (Lunar New Year) January/February; a three-day holiday celebrating the Mongolian New Year (for more information see p44)
Women's Day 8 March (generally a normal working day)
Mothers' & Children's Day 1 June; a great time to visit parks
Naadam Festival 11 &12 July; also known as National Day celebrations
Mongolian Republic Day 26 November (generally a normal working day)

INSURANCE

A policy covering loss, theft and medical expenses, plus compensation for delays in your travel arrangements, is essential for Mongolia. If items are lost or stolen you'll need to show your insurance company a police report. You may also need to prove damage or injury so take photos. All policies vary so check the fine print. For more on insurance, see p287.

INTERNET ACCESS

There are internet cafés on nearly every street in downtown Ulaanbaatar; most are identified with English-language signboards. Nearly a aimag capitals have an internet café in th central Telecom office, and some of the bi ger cities also have private internet cafés. handful of *sum* (district) centres also ha internet access. Expect to pay between T4(to T800 per hour at internet cafes, double triple that for hotel business centres.

Wi-fi (wireless) access is available some spots in Ulaanbaatar; see the boxe text, p65. If you are staying in an apartme or otherwise have access to a phone lin you can buy a pre-paid card that gives yc a dial-up connection. A 10-hour intern card costs T4000 and a 30-hour card cos T6000, but remember that you will als be charged a per-minute fee by the pho company while you are logged on, usual around T15 per minute. The cards ca be bought at exchange kiosks in the Sta Department Store.

There are three internet service provide (Magicnet, Bodicom or Micom), of whic **Magicnet** (Map pp70-1; ☎ 011-312 061; info@magicr .mn; National Information Technology Park, 2nd fl) is th largest. If you live in UB, you can sign u for an ADSL connection. The minimum fe is US$20 per month for a 128kbps conne tion (with a US$40 installation fee). **Ulusn** (Map pp70-1; ☎ 321 434; www.ulusnet.mn; Sambug Gudamj 18) offers internet via WiMax techno ogy, although for now it's prohibitively e: pensive (US$270 for the unit alone, US$1 activation fee, US$80 per month).

If you are going on a research proje in remote areas and need an internet co nection (and have a lot of spare cash lyir around), it's possible to set up a conne tion using Broadband Global Area Netwo (BGAN) technology. See www.inmars .com/Services/Land/BGAN. The system cos around US$2800 and the service is US$40 month plus US$6 per megabyte. Monsat (s p260) provides BGAN service. Of cours you'll also need to power your device, whic you can do with back-up computer batterie or a solar-powered charger; see Sierra Sola (www.sierrasolar.com).

LEGAL MATTERS

Foreigners' rights are generally respecte in Mongolia, although you may bump int the occasional bad cop or customs inspe tor who won't be satisfied unless they'v gotten a piece of what's inside your walle f caught, drug use will give you a peek into Mongolia's grim penitentiary system.

The most common offence committed by oreigners is straying too close to a border vithout a permit. Violators end up paying a ine and a few unlucky souls have been im-risoned for a few days. If you run into serious rouble, ask to contact your embassy.

Making life difficult is that police often lame the victim; don't expect any sympathy f you've been a victim of a crime or road ccident. You're more likely to be scolded bout how careless you've been, which can be demoralising. Overall, police are harmless, but unreliable when you really need one.

MAPS

Maps of Mongolia produced outside the ountry are routinely inaccurate and best voided. Maps can be ordered from www shopmongolia.com; otherwise, just wait until ou arrive in Ulaanbaatar.

Independent travellers should look out for he 1:1,500,000 Road Network Atlas (T15,000) roduced by MPM Agency. Another handy nap is the 1:2,000,000 Road Map of Mongolia T6000). It has the most accurate road layout nd town names and usefully marks the kilo-metres between all towns.

Also useful is the Tourist Map of Mongolia T6000), which marks a host of obscure histor-al, archaeological and natural sights, as well s ger camps. On the back it has detailed maps f the areas around Ulaanbaatar, Kharkhorin nd Khatgal. Similarly, the Tourist Map of 'laanbaatar (T6000) has a detailed 'around 'laanbaatar' map on the back. All these maps re updated almost yearly.

Explorers will want to check out the 500,000 series of topographic maps, which vers Mongolia in 37 maps. The cost of each ries between T5500 and T7000, but don't unt on all being available. The topographic aps are particularly useful if travelling by orse or foot or using a GPS unit, but they can t expensive. A cheaper alternative is a series f all 21 aimag maps (T25,000).

All these maps are available from the artography Co Map Shop in Ulaanbaatar 65). It also sells handy regional maps (T3500 ch) to the most popular tourist areas, includ-g Khövsgöl Nuur (1:200,000), Gobi Gurvan aikhan (1:200,000), Terelj (1:100,000) and e stretch of road between Ulaanbaatar and harkhorin (1:500,000).

Conservation Ink (www.conservationink) produces maps (US$8) using satellite images combined with useful information on culture, wildlife and tourist facilities. The national park series includes Altai Tavan Bogd, Khövsgöl Nuur, Gobi Gurvan Saikhan, Gorkhi-Terelj and Khustain Nuruu.

Chinggis Khaan junkies will want to check out the Chinggis Khaan Atlas, available around Ulaanbaatar for about T8000, which maps his every presumed movement in obsessive detail. The Welcome to the Land of Chinggis Haan tourist map is a more reasonable survey of Khentii aimag, with good historical detail.

In many Western countries, you can buy the ONC and TPC series of topographical maps published by the Defense Mapping Agency Aerospace Center in the USA. The maps are topographically detailed but dated and are not reliable for place names or road layout. Mongolia is covered by ONC (1:1,000,000) and TPC (1:500,000) maps E-7, E-8, F-7 and F-8. Order from www.omnimap.com.

MONEY

The Mongolian unit of currency is the tögrög (T), which comes in notes of T5, T10, T20, T50, T100, T500, T1000, T5000, T10,000 and T20,000. (T1 notes are basically souvenirs.) There are also T50 and T100 coins. The highest-value note is worth around US$17.

Banks and exchange offices in Ulaanbaatar will change money with relative efficiency. Banks in provincial centres are also fine; they change dollars and give cash advances against debit and credit cards. However, since they are so remote it's still a good idea to leave the

---

MONGOLIA'S CURRENCIES

Mongolia's various rulers have ensured a constant change of currencies. During Chinggis Khaan's time coins called sükh, made from gold and silver, were used as currency. During the Manchurian rule Chinese currency was used but Mongolian traders preferred to use Russian gold, British notes and goods such as tea, silk and furs.

In 1925, four years after independence from China, the tögrög was introduced. At that time, one tögrög was worth US$0.88 cents; by 1928, one tögrög was worth up to US$52! Currently, about 1170 tögrög are worth just US$1.

DIRECTORY

capital with enough cash to keep you going for a week or so.

When paying out large sums of money (to hotels, tour operators and sometimes airlines) its fine to use either US dollars or tögrögs. Other forms of currency aren't usually accepted, although the euro is probably second best. Cash offers the best exchange rates and you won't be paying any commission charge, but for security purposes you can also use debit cards (travellers cheques are going the way of the dinosaur).

Moneychangers who hang around the markets may or may not be legal. They offer the best rates for US dollars and are usually safe, but the risks are obvious. Remember to change all your tögrög when leaving the country as it's worthless elsewhere.

See the inside front cover for exchange rates at the time of publication and p14 for the costs of everyday items.

ATMs

The Trade and Development Bank has plonked down ATMs at a few key locations in Ulaanbaatar, Darkhan and Erdenet. These ATMs accept Visa and MasterCard and work most of the time, allowing you to withdraw up to T400,000 per day. Because most of the Golomt Bank branches are open 24 hours, they don't have ATMs (just give your card to the teller). Ordinary ATM cards issued from your bank at home probably won't work; try to get a 'debit' card linked to your bank account. It should be associated with a credit card company.

Credit Cards

You can't rely on plastic for everything, but credit cards are becoming more widely accepted in upmarket hotels, travel agencies and antique shops. Most of these, however, charge an additional 3% if you use a credit card. Banks can give cash advances off credit cards, often for no charge if you have Visa, but as much as 4% with MasterCard.

PHOTOGRAPHY & VIDEO

Mongolia's remote and beautiful landscapes make for some incredible photography, but it's this same remoteness that requires extra planning when taking pictures. As you may go several days in a row without seeing a shop, internet café or electrical outlet you'll need extra batteries and memory cards for your digital camera. These are best bought at hom or in Ulaanbaatar as electronic goods in aima centres can be hard to find. Once you reach a aimag capital you can go to an internet ca and burn your pictures to a CD or save the to a storage drive.

If you use film there are several place around Sükhbaatar Sq that will process pr film cheaply, but the quality may not great; it is generally best to wait until yo get home. Slide film is rare and expensiv so bring what you need and get it develope when you get home.

In summer, days are long, so the best tim to take photos is before 10am and betwee 6pm and 8pm, when Mongolia basks in go geous light. As bright, glaring sunshine is t norm, a polarising filter is essential. If you a jeep trip on an unsurfaced road, you ca expect plenty of dust, so keep the camera we sealed in a plastic bag.

For professional tips on how to take bett photos, check out LP's *Travel Photograph* by Richard I'Anson.

Photographing People

Always ask before taking a photograph. Kee in mind that monks and nomads are not ph tographic models, so if they do not want be photographed, their wishes should be r spected. Point a camera at an urban Mong on the street and chances are they will cov their face. Don't try sneaking around for a di ferent angle as this may lead to an argumer Markets are often a place where snap-hap foreigners are not welcome.

On the other hand, people in the countr side are often happy to pose for photograp if you ask first. If you have promised to ser them a copy, *please* do it, but explain that may take several months to reach them some nomads believe that all cameras a (instant) Polaroids. Several nomads al told us how devastated they were becau they had not received photos as promised foreigners. To simplify matters, bring blar envelopes and ask them to write their a dress on the outside. On the inside, ma a note to yourself about who they were case you forget.

When Mongolians pose for a portrait th instantly put on a face that looks like th are in mourning at Brezhnev's funeral. Yo may need to take this Soviet-style portrait order to get a more natural shot later. 'Car ke your photograph?' in Mongolian is *'Bi ny zurgiig avch bolokh uu?'*

estrictions

hotography is prohibited inside monasteries nd temples, although you may photograph uilding exteriors and monastery grounds. ou can sometimes obtain special permission ▸ take photographs for an extra fee.

In most museums throughout the coun-y you need to pay an (often outrageously igh) extra fee to use your still or video umera. It is best to have a look around first efore you decide whether to fork out the xtra tögrög.

Don't photograph potentially sensitive reas, especially border crossings and military stablishments.

OST

he postal service is reliable but can often be ery slow. Allow ·at least· a couple of weeks ▸r letters and postcards to arrive home from Iongolia. Foreign residents of Ulaanbaatar nd it much faster to give letters (and cash ▸ buy stamps) to other foreigners who ▸re departing.

You won't find letter boxes on the streets. n most cases, you will need to post your ▸tters from the post office. You can buy :amps in post offices (and top-end hotels) ▪ Ulaanbaatar and aimag capitals.

Postal rates are often relatively expensive, specially for parcels, for which there is only n 'airmail' rate – yet they often arrive months ▸ter (probably by sea). Normal-sized letters ▸st T700 and postcards cost T440 to all coun-ies. A 1kg airmail parcel to the UK will cost 14,000, or T18,000 to the USA.

The poste restante at the Central Post)ffice in Ulaanbaatar seems to work quite ·ell; bring along your passport as proof f identification. Don't even think about sing poste restante anywhere else in ne country.

Contact details for the more reliable cou-·er services, including DHL and FedEx, are)und on p67.

HOPPING

Iongolia has a number of unique items that ·re worth bringing home. Cashmere and ·ool products are usually at the top of the st; Gobi, Goyo and Buyan brands are all good quality. A cashmere sweater will cost around US$40 to US$60.

Antique shops are good for Buddhas, *thangkas* (scroll paintings) and marvellous silver jewellery. For any of these you could pay from a few dollars to several thousand. If you are a serious buyer, ask a local friend to help you shop for the best quality stuff and remember to pick up a certificate of authenticity for customs purposes.

The best place in the country for sil-ver jewellery is Möngön Zaviya (p94). Handmade felt carpets and wall hangings are a speciality from western Mongolia, and you can buy them directly from cooperatives in Khovd and Bayan-Ölgii.

Mongolian clothes such as *dels* (traditional coats), *hurrum* (jackets) and boots are nice to take home; these are available at the State Department Store and Naran Tuul Market. The market also has all the pieces needed for a ger. The problem, of course, is how to ship one home. Try asking Daka at **Happy Pioneer** (☎ 9909 7698; www.yurt-ger-yourte.com).

No matter how many times you're offered them, dinosaur bones and eggs are definitely not souvenirs (legal ones anyway). Please say 'no'.

SOLO TRAVELLERS

The high costs of jeep hire mean that solo budget travellers will need to hook up with others for countryside trips. This usually isn't too much of a problem in summer, when vanloads of backpackers depart daily from the guesthouses in Ulaanbaatar.

In Ulaanbaatar, single travellers on a budget will probably have to go for a dorm bed in a guesthouse, or find another single traveller to share the cost of a double room. Countryside hotels usually have a per bed option. Cycling, camping and hiking trips into the wilderness are safer in twos. If you do go off alone make sure to tell someone of your route and expected time of return.

Solo female travellers get around Ulaanbaatar without any problems. Travelling to the countryside alone can bring hassles from drunk or aggressive Mongolian men. This is not to say it can-not be done (many women do travel alone), but it can be just easier to go with a group or partner. See p264 for more information for solo women travellers.

DIRECTORY

TELEPHONE

It's easy to make international or domestic calls in Ulaanbaatar. Outside the main cities, making phone calls is a challenge. Aimag capitals are upgrading their systems but in the *sum* centres you'll run head on into WWII-era technology, complete with wind-up phones and operators languishing behind massive metal boards, busily plugging and unplugging wires and shouting *'bain uu?!'* (is anybody there?!) into the receiver. Fortunately, mobile phone technology is allowing many towns to leapfrog this old technology.

Ulaanbaatar landline phone numbers have six digits, while most countryside numbers have five. Every aimag has its own area code; we have listed them in this book under the aimag capital headings.

If you are calling out of Mongolia and using an IDD phone, just dial ☎ 00 and then your international country code. On non-IDD phones you can make direct long-distance calls by dialling the international operator (☎ 106), who may know enough English to make the right connection (but don't count on it).

The other options are making a call from a private international phone office (*Olon Ulsiin Yariin*), which are becoming common in Ulaanbaatar but not in other cities. These charge reasonable rates to call abroad: T50 per minute to the USA or T100 per minute to Europe. Calls from the central Telecom offices in any city will be more expensive, but not outrageous: T560 per minute to the USA and UK, T820 per minute to Australia. To make the call, you need to pay a deposit in advance (a minimum equivalent of three minutes). Computers are often set up with headsets and Skype (www.skype.com) software.

A couple of the top-end hotels have Home Country Direct dialling, where the push of a button gets you through to international operators in the USA, Japan and Singapore. You can then make a credit-card, charge-card or reverse-charge (collect) call.

Making a call *to* Mongolia is a lot easier, with one catch. Dial the international access code in your country (normally ☎ 00) and the Mongolian country code (☎ 976). Then, for a landline number dial the local code (minus the '0' for Ulaanbaatar, but include the '0' for all other areas) and then the number. Be aware, though, that there are different requirements for area codes if usin or phoning a mobile phone; see below.

In Ulaanbaatar, the domestic operator number is ☎ 1109.

Mobile & Satellite Phones

The three main companies are Mobicon Skytel and Unitel. The mobile-phone network is the standard GSM (Global System for Mobile communication). If you brin a GSM phone you can get a new SIM car installed in Mongolia. The process is sim ple – just go to a mobile-phone office (Mobicom office is located on the 3rd floor the State Department Store), sign up for basi service (around T15,000), and buy units a needed. Cards come in units of 10 (T2500), 3 (T6600), 50 (T10,250) and 100 (T19,000). It free to receive calls and text messaging charge are almost negligible. If you are abroad, an calling a mobile-phone number in Mongoli just dial the country code (☎ 976) without th area code. Note that you drop the '0' off th area code if dialling an Ulaanbaatar numbe *from* a mobile phone but you retain the '0' using other area codes.

Every aimag capital (and a few *sum* centre including Kharkhorin, Khujirt and Tariat) ha a mobile-phone service, and calls are fairl cheap, making this a good way to keep i touch with home.

New and used mobile phone shops are every where in UB and also in some rural cities. It a good idea to have a phone while travelling i the countryside as it allows you to commun cate with your tour operator should problem arise on your trip.

Note that if you have a GPRS phon (General Packet Radio Service) you can acces the internet with a normal SIM card.

If you are planning a serious mountainee ing or horse-trekking expedition, considerin bringing or renting a satellite phone, whic isn't too bulky and can be used anywher A local company, **Monsat** (Map pp70-1; ☎ 01 323 705, 9120 6050; www.monsat.mcs.mn; MCS Plaza, Seo St, Ulaanbaatar), rents 'sat' phones for US$5 t US$10 per day depending on the model. Cal are an additional US$1.65 per minute to th USA or Europe.

Phone Cards

If you have access to a private phone and nee to make international calls, the easiest optio is to buy an international phone card, sold i various outlets including the post office, State Department Store or mobile-phone shops. Instructions for the card are in Mongolian, but you can ask at the post office for English instructions. The Personal Identification Number (PIN) for these cards is the last four digits of the code on the card. Be careful where you scratch off the code, poachers can peek over your shoulder, steal the code and use it before you do (which has happened at the post office).

There are a variety of phone cards available, and you usually get what you pay for; the cheaper ones (such as Bodicom) have terrible sound quality and echo, but cost less than US$0.10 per minute.

TIME

Mongolia is divided into two time zones: the three western aimags of Bayan-Ölgii, Uvs and Khovd are one hour behind Ulaanbaatar and the rest of the country. Mongolia does not observe daylight-saving time, which means that the sun can rise at very early hours in summer.

The standard time in Ulaanbaatar is UTC/GMT plus eight hours. When it is noon in Ulaanbaatar, it is also noon in Beijing, Hong Kong, Singapore and Perth; 2pm in Sydney; 8pm the previous day in Los Angeles; 11pm the previous day in New York; and 4am in London. See the world time-zone map on p310–11. The 24-hour clock is used for plane and train schedules.

TOILETS

In most hotels in Ulaanbaatar, aimag capitals and in most ger camps, toilets are the sit-down European variety. In other hotels and some more remote ger camps, you will have to use pit toilets and hold your breath.

MARGASH & YOU

There is another form of 'Mongolian time': add two hours' waiting time to any appointments you make. Mongolians are notorious for being late, and this includes nearly everyone likely to be important to you, such as jeep drivers, your guide or the staff at a museum you want to visit. You could almost adjust your watch to compensate for the difference. The Mongolian version of 'mañana' (tomorrow) is *margash*.

In the countryside, where there may not be a bush or tree for hundreds of kilometres, modesty is not something to worry about – just do it where you want to, but away from gers. Also, try to avoid such places as *ovoos* (sacred cairns of stones), rivers and lakes (water sources for nomads) and marmot holes.

The plumbing is decrepit in many of the older hotels, and toilet paper can easily jam up the works. If there is a rubbish basket next to the toilet, this is where the waste paper should go. Most of the toilet paper in hotels resembles industrial-strength cardboard, or may be pages torn from Soviet-era history books or recently distributed bibles. To avoid paper cuts, stock up on softer brand toilet paper, available in the larger cities.

TOURIST INFORMATION

Handy tourist information desks are available at Ulaanbaatar's Central Post Office, Discovery Mongolia Information Centre, train station and airport. They all stock books, maps and brochures and have English-speaking staff. Outside UB, the only similar tourist desk is in Mörön. In Mandalgov, the Ger to Ger office acts as an information desk, and in Bayan-Ölgii, the Strictly Protected Areas office does the same.

TRAVELLERS WITH DISABILITIES

Mongolia is a difficult place for wheelchair travellers as most buildings and buses are not wheelchair accessible, and in addition there are rough roads and generally poor standards of accommodation. Still, travel to Ulaanbaatar and jeep trips to places such as Kharkhorin shouldn't cause too many insurmountable problems.

If any specialised travel agency might be interested in arranging trips to Mongolia, the best bet is the US company **Accessible Journeys** (☎ 800-846-4537; fax 610-521 6959; www.disabilitytravel .com) in Pennsylvania. At the very least, hire your own transport and guide through one of the Ulaanbaatar agencies (see p80). If you explain your disability, these agencies may be able to accommodate you.

The following organisations offer general travel advice for the disabled but provide no specific information on Mongolia.
Holiday Care Service (☎ 0845-124 9974; www .holidaycare.org.uk; The Hawkins Suite, Enham Place, Andover SP11 6JS, UK) British holiday and travel information service for disabled and older people.

DIRECTORY

Mobility International USA (☎ 541-343-1284; www .miusa.org; 132 E. Broadway, Suite 343, Eugene, OR 97401, USA) Organises international exchanges.

Nican (☎ 02-6241 1220; www.nican.com.au; Unit 5, 48 Brookes St, Mitchell, ACT 2911, Australia) Australian organisation which provides information on recreation, tourism, sports and the arts for disabled people.

SATH (Society for the Advancement of Travel for the Handicapped; ☎ 212-447-0027; www.sath.org) This US website contains tips on how to travel with diabetes, arthritis, visual and hearing impairments, and wheelchairs.

For general advice, bulletin boards and searchable databases try the following websites:

Access-able Travel Source (www.access-able.com) Provides access information for mature and disabled travellers.

New Mobility Magazine (www.newmobility.com) An excellent online resource for disability culture and lifestyle.

VISAS

Currently, a 30-day tourist visa is easily obtained at any Mongolian embassy consulate, consulate-general or honorary consuls.

To get a visa for longer than 30 days, you must be invited or sponsored by a Mongolian citizen, foreign resident (expat) or Mongolian company, or be part of an organised tour. It is therefore possible to get a 90-day visa for most nationalities; you just need to pay the inviting agency a fee of around US$30 (most guesthouses can do this).

If you cannot get to a Mongolian consulate, you can pick up a 30-day tourist visa on arrival at the airport in Ulaanbaatar or at the land borders of Zamyn-Üüd and Sükhbaatar. You'll need US$53 and two passport photos.

Israeli and Malaysian citizens can stay visa-free for up to 30 days and Hong Kong and Singaporean citizens can stay visa-free for up to 14 days.

US citizens can stay in Mongolia for up to 90 days without a visa. If you stay less than 30 days nothing needs to be done, other than having your passport stamped when you enter and leave the country.

All visitors who plan to stay *more* than 30 days must be registered within seven days of your arrival (see p264).

Mongolian honorary consuls can issue transit visas and nonextendable tourist visas but only for 14 days from the date of entry. However, these visas are for entry only; they cannot issue normal entry/exit visas, so you will have to spend some of your precious time in Ulaanbaatar arranging an exit visa (see opposite) from the **Office of Immigration Naturalization & Foreign Citizens** (INFC; Map pp70-1; ☎ 011-315 323; 🕑 9am-1pm & 2-5pm Mon-Fri), on the west side of Peace Bridge, opposite Naran Plaza. Note that on Wednesday it's only open in the afternoon.

To check current regulations, try the web site of the Mongolian embassy in Washington DC at www.mongolianembassy.us.

For information on getting visas to China, Kazakhstan or Russia from Mongolia, see opposite.

Tourist Visas

Standard tourist visas generally last 30 days from the date of entry and you must enter Mongolia within three months of issue. Tourist visas usually cost US$25 for a single entry/exit, though there may be a 'service fee'. Each embassy or consulate sets its own price. For single entry/exit visas you can expect to pay: A$65 in Sydney, UK£40 in London, C$80 in Ottawa and Y270 in Beijing.

Visas normally take several days, or even up to two weeks, to issue. If you want your visa quicker, possibly within 24 hours, you will have to pay an 'express fee', which is double the normal cost. If you want to stay longer than 30 days, tourist visas can be extended in Ulaanbaatar (see below).

Multiple-entry/exit tourist visas (which cost US$65 and are valid for six months after the date of issue) are usually only issued to foreign residents who do a lot of travel.

Transit Visas

These visas last 72 hours from the date of entry. This period will only allow you to get off the Trans-Mongolian train for a very short time before catching another train to Russia or China. A single-entry/exit transit visa costs US$15 (US$30 for express service), but cannot be extended. (As with the tourist visas, the fee varies by embassy.) You will need to show the train or plane ticket and a visa for the next country (Russia or China).

Visa Extensions

If you have a 30-day tourist visa you can extend it by another 30 days. For extensions, go to the INFC office (left). The only catch is that if you stay longer than 30 days you have to be registered at this office (see opposite).

VISAS FOR ONWARD TRAVEL

China

The consular section of the Chinese embassy in Ulaanbaatar is a good place to get a visa for China. It is open from 9.30am to noon Monday, Wednesday and Friday. Transit visas (single or double entry) last up to seven days from each date of entry. Single- and double-entry tourist visas are valid for 30 days from the date of each entry and you must enter China within 90 days of being issued the visa. Single-/double-entry tourist visas cost US$30/60 and take a week to issue. For three-day or same-day service, you'll have to fork out an extra US$50 or US$60. You must pay in US dollars. Visas for US citizens are US$100, regardless of type.

In the summer of 2007, travellers reported being able to get a visa on the spot at the border in Erlian. Only time will tell if this becomes standard practice so ask around or check lonelyplanet .com's Thorn Tree travel forum.

Kazakhstan

The Kazakhstan embassy is open from 10am to noon and 3pm to 5pm Monday to Friday. Single-entry, one-month visas cost US$65 and take five days to process (or pay double to get it the next day). A double-entry, three-month visa costs US$100. A multiple-entry visa valid for one year costs US$205.

Russia

Getting a visa is by no means a straightforward process, but is not impossible. The consular section is open for visas from 2pm to 3pm daily. Almost everyone ends up paying a different price for their visa; costs vary between US$25 and US$200 depending on your itinerary and nationality. You will need three photos, an invitation or sponsor, and possibly vouchers for hotels. You can get a visa for 21 days but not more than that. You will also need 'health insurance', which local agents can organise for about US$1 per day. A visa normally takes a couple of days to issue or, if 'urgent', it can be issued on the spot for double the normal cost. However, your tour agent will need around 10 days to get the vouchers, so start the process early. If you need vouchers the consular will give you directions to a travel agent (usually Legend Tours; see p67). For additional support, contact: http://waytorussia.net.

The INFC office is a branch of the main visa office of the **Ministry of External Relations** (Map p70-1; cnr Peace Ave & Olympiin Gudamj; 🕑 9.30am-noon Mon-Fri). You may be sent to the Ministry if your visa situation is complicated (ie you require a work permit). The entrance is around the back.

If you have already registered, you should apply for an extension about a week before your visa expires. It costs US$15 for the first seven days and a further US$2 per day for up to an additional 23 days (they may otherwise charge a flat T3000 per day). You will need a passport-sized photo and must pay a T5000 processing fee. It should take two or three days to process. If you can't wait you can leave the passport here, but must pick it up four days before the first 30 day visa expires. For an extra US$20 you can get one-day service.

Several guesthouses in Ulaanbaatar will take care of visa extensions (and registration) for a small fee. If you don't have a letter of support you can write your own (handwritten is OK); the letter should state the date of your arrival, the date of extension and the reason for travel.

Getting a visa extension outside of Ulaanbaatar is difficult, as they would need to send your passport back to Ulaanbaatar. In an extreme situation this might be possible at the INFC office in Ölgii.

Exit Visas

Transit and tourist visas are good for one entry and one exit (unless you have a double or multiple-entry/exit visa). If you are working in Mongolia, or if you obtained your visa at an honorary consul, you are usually issued a single-entry visa (valid for entry only). In this case, another visa is required to *leave* the country. These visas are available from the INFC office (see opposite). For most nationalities the exit visa costs around US$20 and for US citizens it is US$100 (plus an additional

DIRECTORY

US$3 processing fee). It is valid for 10 days, which means that you can stay 10 days after your normal visa has expired. The exit visa situation in particular applies to Israeli and US passport holders (who usually enter without visas). Israelis need an exit visa if they stay more than 30 days and Americans need one if they stay more than 90 days.

Registration

If you intend to stay in Mongolia for more than 30 days you must register with the police in Ulaanbaatar before the end of your first 30 days of being in the country. (US passport holders must register within the first seven days.)

Registration takes place at the INFC office. The process is free, but you have to pay T1200 for the one-page application. You'll need one passport-sized photo. Most guesthouses can rustle up an invitation to Mongolia for you if you require one.

As a formality, the registration also needs to be 'signed out', almost as if you were checking out of a hotel; however, the official you are dealing with will usually do this when you register so you won't have to come back. A specific date is not needed, just set the exit date as far out as possible and you can leave anytime before that date.

If you've arrived from Russia to western Mongolia, the INFC office in Ölgii (p224) can get you registered.

If you don't register, you are liable for a fine (theoretically from US$100 to US$300) when you leave the country.

Long-Term Stays

The only way to remain in Mongolia on a long-term basis (ie more than three months) is to get a work or study permit. The company or organisation you are working for should handle this for you, but if you are working independently you need to go it alone. In most cases, with a letter from your employer, you can get your stuff done at the INFC office. The staff may send you to the **Labour Registration Department** (Map pp70-1; ☎ 011-260 376, 260 363) in the Supreme Court building on Sambuugiin Örgön Chölöö. Independent researchers and students are usually registered through the Ministry of Enlightenment (in Mongolian 'Shinjileh Uhaan Bolovsroliin Yam'), in a building behind the Ulaanbaatar Hotel.

WOMEN TRAVELLERS

Mongolia doesn't present too many problem for foreign women travelling independently The majority of Mongolian men behave i a friendly and respectful manner, withou ulterior motives. However, you may com across an annoying drunk or the occasiona macho idiot. The phrase for 'Go away!' i 'Sasha be!'.

There are occasional incidents of sol female travellers reporting being harasse by their male guide. If your guide is male it is best to keep in touch with your tou agency in Ulaanbaatar, perhaps making con tingency plans with them if things go awr (have a mobile phone with a local SIM card) Better yet, take a female guide wheneve possible.

Tampons and pads are available i Ulaanbaatar and other main cities such a Darkhan and Erdenet, though these will be very hard to find the deeper you go into the countryside. Many women also find it usefu to wear long skirts while in the countryside so that they can relieve themselves in som semblance of privacy on the open steppes.

Although attitudes towards women are more conservative in the mostly Muslim Bayan-Ölgii aimag, you don't need tc cover up as you would in other areas of Central Asia.

WORK

Mongolia is certainly not somewhere you can just turn up and expect to get paid employment – the demand is not high even for teaching English. Also, if you do get work the pay will be poor (possibly the same as the locals) unless you can score a job with a development agency, but these agencies usually recruit their non-Mongolian staff in their home country, not from within Mongolia.

If you are keen to work in Mongolia and are qualified in teaching or health, contact the organisations listed opposite, network through the internet or check the English-language newspapers in Ulaanbaatar.

Permission to work is fairly easy to obtain if you have been hired locally. In most cases, your employer will take care of this for you. See also Long-Term Stays on left.

For any project you get involved with, ask the organisation to put you in touch with former volunteers or workers to get a better idea of what you may be in for.

.anguage Teaching

iome Mongolians want to forget Russian and earn a useful European language, particularly inglish, so there is a demand (albeit low) or teachers. Colleges and volunteer agencies re, however, on the lookout for qualified eachers who are willing to stay for a few erms (if not a few years), but not just for a veek or two. Contact the voluntary-service gencies in your home country or the ones isted below.

Informal, short-term work may be possible hrough smaller organisations, such as the nany private universities that have sprung p, or you may be able to do freelance tuoring for a while, but don't expect to make nuch money. In Ulaanbaatar try the **Mongolian nowledge University** (☎ 011-327 165; fax 011-358 54), the **Ikh Zasag University** (☎ 011-457 855), the **ternational School** (☎ 011-452 839; www.isumongolia du.mn), the **Turkish School** (☎ 9978 0173) or **Orchlon** ☎ 011-353 519; www.orchlon.mn).

Volunteer Work

ome organisations are anxious to receive help rom qualified people, particularly in educaion, health and IT development. Agencies are nore interested in committed people who are villing to stay two years or more, although hort-term projects are available. In most inances, you will be paid in local wages (or ossibly a little more). Besides the following,

a good starting reference is **Golden Gate Friends of Mongolia** (www.ggfom.org).

Asral (☎ 011-304 838; fax 011-304 898; www.asral mongolia.org; PO Box 467, Ulaanbaatar-23) Travellers can volunteer as English teachers at this Buddhist social centre or work on the project farm in Gachuurt.

Australian Volunteers Abroad (AVA; ☎ 03-9279 1788; fax 03-9419 4280; osb@osb.org.au; PO Box 350, Fitzroy Vic 3065) AVA has a handful of Australian volunteers in Mongolia.

Itgel Foundation (☎ 9972 2667; www.itgel.org) Organisation that assists the Tsaatan people in Khövsgöl. Various opportunities from IT support to veterinary assistance.

Khustain National Park (www.ecovolunteer.org) The park runs a three-week eco-volunteer programme where you can help with research.

Peace Corps (Enkh Tavnii Korpus; ☎ 011-311 520) The organisation is well represented throughout the country. Alternatively, contact your local Peace Corps office in the USA (☎ 1-800-424 858, 202-606 3970; fax 606 3110; www.peacecorps.gov).

UN Development Program (UNDP; ☎ 011-327 585; fax 011-326 221; PO Box 46/1009, Ulaanbaatar, Negdsen Undestnii Gudamj 12) The UNDP is always on the lookout for committed and hard-working volunteers but normally recruits abroad.

Voluntary Service Overseas (VSO; ☎ /fax 011-313 514; vsomongolia@magicnet.mn; PO Box 678, Ulaanbaatar) This British-run organisation is set up mainly for Brits. It prefers you to contact the organisation through its UK head office (☎ 020-8780 2266; fax 020-8780 1326; 317 Putney Bridge Rd, London SW15 2PN).

Transport

TRANSPORT *(side tab)*

GETTING THERE & AWAY

ENTERING THE COUNTRY

When entering Mongolia, by land or air, you should fill out straightforward immigration and customs forms. You shouldn't have to pay anything if your visa is in order (see p262 for visa information). You'll have to register if you plan to be in Mongolia for more than 30 days; see p264 for details. Registering in Ulaanbaatar is fairly straightforward, and it's also possible in Ölgii if you arrive in western Mongolia.

Flights, tours and rail tickets can be booked online at www.lonelyplanet.com/travel_services.

THINGS CHANGE...

The information in this chapter is particularly vulnerable to change. Check directly with the airline or a travel agent to make sure you understand how a fare (and ticket you may buy) works and be aware of the security requirements for international travel. Shop carefully. The details given in this chapter should be regarded as pointers and are not a substitute for your own careful, up-to-date research.

Passport

Make sure that your passport is valid for at least six more months from the date of arrival. If you lose your passport, your embassy in Ulaanbaatar can replace it, usually in one day. Before leaving Mongolia, check whether you'll need an exit visa from the Office of Immigration, Naturalization & Foreign Citizens (INFC; p262).

AIR

Airports & Airlines

Ulaanbaatar's **Chinggis Khaan airport** (☎ 198 011-983 005) is Mongolia's major international airport; the code is ULN. Because the runway was built on a slope, landings are one-shot deals for modern jets. There are constant rumours of a new international airport in Töv aimag, though nothing has been established formally.

The only other airport with international flights is Ölgii, which is connected to Almat (Kazakhstan).

Mongolia's national airline, MIAT, has brought its safety practices for international flights to near Western standards (domestic flights are a different story altogether). Online booking is available through its website. On international flights, MIAT allows 30kg of baggage for business travellers and 20kg for economy travellers.

Most people fly in from Beijing, Berlin or Moscow; there are additional nonstop flights from Osaka and Seoul. Current airline schedules also allow you to fly from Ulaanbaatar to Irkutsk, on Lake Baikal in Russia, and Hohhot (Khökh Khot), the capital of the autonomous region of Chinese Inner Mongolia.

In July and August, most flights are full, so book well in advance.

Airlines flying to and from Mongolia:
Aero Mongolia (airline code MNG; ☎ 9191 2903; www.aeromongolia.mn)
Aeroflot (airline code SU; ☎ 011-320 720; www.aeroflot.com)
Air China (airline code CA; ☎ 011-328 838; www.airchina.cn)
Korean Air (airline code KE; ☎ 011-326 643; www.koreanair.com)
MIAT (airline code OM; ☎ 011-322 118; http://miat.com

HANDY TIPS FOR AIR TRAVEL

Tip one: your luggage weight is determined by the airline with which you begin your journey, not any middle segment or final segment. So if you are flying from the US it doesn't matter that MIAT's baggage allowance is only 20kg or 30kg; you can bring as much as your original flight allows. (This applies if you check your baggage all the way through, but won't work if you have a long layover en route.)

Tip two: when changing planes in Beijing, your luggage will arrive on the carousel but you don't need to haul it back upstairs when you check in with MIAT/Air China. An attendant downstairs will collect onward baggage and send it to your next flight.

Tip three: if you have an onward ticket for Mongolia, you can stay in Beijing for 24 hours without a visa (despite what any Chinese embassy might tell you). Luggage storage is available at the airport if you need to spend the night in town.

Tickets

Full-time students and people aged under 26 years (under 30 in some countries) have access to better deals than other travellers. You have to show a document proving your date of birth or a valid International Student Identity Card (ISIC) when buying your ticket.

Most travel agencies will offer discounted tickets to Beijing and Moscow but not to Ulaanbaatar. In fact, unless you buy a through-ticket with Aeroflot or Air China you will find it hard to even book a Moscow–Ulaanbaatar or Beijing–Ulaanbaatar ticket from abroad. The solution is to buy e-tickets from MIAT's website.

Australia & New Zealand

Flights to Mongolia go via Seoul or Beijing. The cheapest return flights from Sydney to Ulaanbaatar, on Korean Air, go for about A$1990. Low-season return fares to Beijing from the east coast of Australia start at around A$1080. The lowest fares are offered by Vietnam Airlines. Useful travel agencies:

Flight Centre (☎ in Australia 133 133, in New Zealand 0800 243 544; www.flightcentre.com)

STA Travel (☎ in Australia 1300 733 035, in New Zealand 0800 474 400; www.statravel.com)

China

From Beijing there are daily flights on either Air China or MIAT. Between 15 April and 15 September MIAT flies to Beijing daily except Friday for US$191/341 one way/return. At other times flights are limited to Monday, Wednesday and Friday. Air China has six flights per week (three in winter) from Beijing for the same price. Air China's one-way flight is US$349 at the full fare, but an advance ticket (booked two or three weeks ahead) is US$192.

Note that you'll need a double-entry visa to return to China, or you'll have to buy one in Ulaanbaatar. Travellers without a Chinese visa have been refused boarding flights to Beijing. **MIAT** (☎ in Beijing 8610-6507 9297) has an office in Room 705 on the 7th floor of Sunjoy Mansion, opposite the Beijing International Club, just off Jianguomenwai Dajie.

Aero Mongolia flies to/from Hohhot in China on Monday and Thursday for US$180/280. It also flies to/from Tianjin on Monday, Wednesday and Thursday for a reasonable US$150/241; the ticket comes with a free bus transfer to Beijing.

Travel agencies include the following:

BTG Ticketing Co (☎ 8610-6515 8010; www.btgtravel .com)

China International Travel Service (CITS; ☎ 010-6512 0507; www.cits.net)

Continental Europe

Most Europeans generally fly to Mongolia from Moscow (see Russia, p268) or Berlin on either MIAT or Aeroflot. The fare to/from Berlin is US$601/929 one way/return on MIAT and US$886/971 on Aeroflot.

Fares to Beijing from Western Europe are similar to those from London (see UK, p268).

Some travel agencies to check out:

CTS Viaggi (☎ 06-462 0431; www.cts.it) Italian company that specialises in student and youth travel.

NBBS Reizen (☎ 0900 10 20 300; www.nbbs.nl in Dutch) Branches in most Dutch cities.

Nouvelles Frontiéres (☎ 0825 000 747; www .nouvelles-frontieres.fr in French) Many branches in Paris and throughout France.

STA Travel (☎ in Paris 01 43 59 23 69, in Frankfurt 069-430 1910; www.statravel.com) Branches across much of Europe.

TRANSPORT

Japan & Korea

In summer, MIAT flies to/from Tokyo on Monday, Wednesday and Saturday (US$471/706 one way/return), to/from Osaka on Friday (US$406/794), and to Seoul daily in summer for US$381/498. Korean Air flies daily to Seoul for US$379/493. For travel agencies try the following:

No 1 Travel (☎ 03-3205 6073; www.no1-travel.com)
STA Travel (☎ 03-5391 2922; www.statravel.co.jp)

Kazakhstan

Border junkies may be interested in this obscure route into Mongolia. Trans Ölgii flies from Almaty to Ölgii via Üst Kamenogorsk on Wednesday morning. One-way flights cost about US$300. For information on flying in the other direction, see p227. Remember that after arriving in Ölgii, you'll need to get your passport registered within seven days if you plan on staying in Mongolia for more than 30 days. The police in Ölgii can do this.

Russia

Aeroflot has four flights a week between Ulaanbaatar and Moscow (US$450/580 one way/return). MIAT flies to Moscow (US$361/587) on Tuesday and Sunday, continuing to Berlin and returning the same day. MIAT also flies to/from Irkutsk on Monday, Wednesday and Friday for US$117/200.

Aero Mongolia flies to Irkutsk on Tuesda and Friday (US$150/250).

UK & Ireland

To Beijing, low-season return fares from London start at £720 with Air China (flying direct). Aeroflot flies Ulaanbaatar to London on Friday for £563 one way, with a change of planes but no overnight stay or airport transfer required. The Saturday connection is not as convenient as it entails a night in Moscow at your own expense.

Agencies to try include:

Flight Centre (☎ 0870 499 0040; www.flightcentre .co.uk)
North-South Travel (☎ 01245 608 291; www.north southtravel.co.uk) North-South Travel donates part of its profits to projects in the developing world.
STA Travel (☎ 0870 163 0026; www.statravel.co.uk)
Trailfinders (☎ 0845 058 5858; www.trailfinders.com)

USA & Canada

The cheapest fares to Ulaanbaatar are from San Francisco, Los Angeles and New York on Korean Air, Air China, Northwest Airlines and United Airlines. From the US west/east coast, return fares start at US$1750/2000, unless you use the cheaper Air Bridge (see opposite). Bear in mind that ticket prices from the US can fluctuate wildly depending on the month and day of travel (sometimes

---

CLIMATE CHANGE & TRAVEL

Climate change is a serious threat to the ecosystems that humans rely upon, and air travel is the fastest-growing contributor to the problem. Lonely Planet regards travel, overall, as a global benefit, but believes we all have a responsibility to limit our personal impact on global warming.

Flying & climate change

Pretty much every form of motorised travel generates CO_2 (the main cause of human-induced climate change) but planes are far and away the worst offenders, not just because of the sheer distances they allow us to travel, but because they release greenhouse gases high into the atmosphere. The statistics are frightening: two people taking a return flight between Europe and the US will contribute as much to climate change as an average household's gas and electricity consumption over a whole year.

Carbon offset schemes

Climatecare.org and other websites use 'carbon calculators' that allow travellers to offset the level of greenhouse gases they are responsible for with financial contributions to sustainable travel schemes that reduce global warming – including projects in India, Honduras, Kazakhstan and Uganda.

Lonely Planet, together with Rough Guides and other concerned partners in the travel industry, support the carbon offset scheme run by climatecare.org. Lonely Planet offsets all of its staff and author travel. For more information check out our website: www.lonelyplanet.com.

y hundreds of dollars). Return high-season
ares between Toronto and Ulaanbaatar are
round C$2200.

Agencies include the following:

ir Bridge (☎ 1-303-757-1929; www.airbridgeusa.com)
ne US office for Ulaanbaatar-based AirTrans offers the
neapest tickets to Mongolia (return fares from US$1580
vest coast) to US$1730 (east coast). The company accepts
ayment by PayPal.

rbitz (☎ 888-656-4546; www.orbitz.com)

TA Travel (☎ 800-777-0112; www.statravel.com)
ffices in Boston, Chicago, Miami, New York, Philadelphia,
an Francisco and other major cities.

ravel CUTS (☎ 1-866-246-9762; www.travelcuts.com)
anada's national student travel agency, which has offices
all major cities.

AND

here are two main land border cross-
ngs open to foreigners: Ereen (Erenhot or
rlliàn in Chinese) and Zamyn-Üüd, on the
hinese–Mongolian border, and Naushki and
ükhbaatar, on the Russian–Mongolian bor-
er. It's possible to cross borders by minivan
r train, though the latter is the more com-
ion and convenient option. There are also
ther border crossings between Russia and
1ongolia; see p274.

hina

ORDER CROSSINGS

he only border open to foreigners is the one
etween Zamyn-Üüd and Ereen. It's open
aily but note that on holidays only the train
1ot the road) crossing will operate.

In 2007 travellers were reporting that it was
ossible to get a Chinese visa at the border,
ut until this becomes a regular thing it's best
• have a visa already in your passport. If you
re heading for Mongolia and need a visa,
1ere is a **Mongolian consulate** (☎ /fax 479-7539200;
eijian Binguan Er Lou, Bldg 206; ☻ 8.30am-noon Mon-Fri) a
)-minute walk past the main long-distance
us station in Ereen; a taxi will take you there
r Y3. The consulate can process a visa in
ne day for US$55.

If you are taking the direct train between
hina and Mongolia you will have up to three
ours to kill in Ereen. You can buy snacks
r the train at the market or one of the well-
ocked shops. Many of the shop signs are in
yrillic Mongolian for the benefit of the many
aders that come here. There are money-
angers and banks in and around the station.
you're going *to* China and still have tögrög,

change it here or you'll be keeping it as a souvenir. If you need to spend the night there are
some cheap and reliable hotels opposite the
train station.

Zamyn-Üüd, on the Mongolian side, is not
an interesting place, so you aren't missing
anything if the train stops in the middle of
the countryside (usually in the middle of the
night), and not at Zamyn-Üüd. Mongolian
customs and immigration officials take about
two hours to do their stuff.

Remember that if you are carrying on to
central China there is absolutely no need to go
to Beijing first. From Ereen you can travel on
to the rail junction at Datong and then catch
trains or buses to Pingyao, Xi'an and beyond.
Read Lonely Planet's *China* guide for details
on connections from Datong.

CAR & MOTORCYCLE

As long as your papers are in order there is
no trouble crossing the Chinese–Mongolian
border in your own car. Driving around
Mongolia is a lot easier compared with China,
where drivers require a guide and Chinese
driving permit.

MINIVAN

Minivans shuttle between the train stations
of Zamyn-Üüd, on Mongolia's southern border, and Ereen, the Chinese border town. For
details see p203.

TRAIN

Mongolia has trains to both Russia and China.
Getting a ticket in Ulaanbaatar can be very
difficult during the summer tourist season,
so you need to plan ahead.

The yellow International Railway Ticketing
Office (Map p64) is about 200m northwest
of the train station. Inside the office, specific
rooms sell tickets to Beijing, Irkutsk (Russia),
Moscow, and Ereen and Hohhot (both in
China), but as a foreigner you'll be directed
to a **foreigners' booking office** (☎ 24133, inquiries 243
848; Room 212; ☻ 8am-7pm). It's upstairs and staff
here speak some English. On weekends you
can use the downstairs booking desk. You'll
need your passport to buy a ticket. You can
book the ticket by phone for a T4500 booking
fee. If you cancel a ticket there is a minuscule
T1000 charge. There is no departure tax if
travelling on the train.

You can book a ticket for international
trains out of Ulaanbaatar up to one month

TRANSPORT

TRAVEL AGENCIES & ORGANISED TOURS

In this section we list reliable agencies outside Mongolia that can help with the logistics of travel in Mongolia, including visas, excursions or the whole shebang. These include travel agencies, adventure-tour operators and homestay agencies. The following can hook you up with tickets, individual itineraries or group packages. For Ulaanbaatar-based travel companies, see p80.

The largest travel company specialising in Mongolia is **Juulchin** (www.juulchin.com), the former state company that has gone private. Juulchin has offices in Beijing, Berlin, Tokyo, Seoul and New Jersey.

Asia

Monkey Business Shrine (☎ 8610-6591 6519; www.monkeyshrine.com; Room 201, Poachers Inn, 43 Beisanlitun Nan, Chao Yang District, 100027, Beijing)
Moonsky Star Ltd (☎ 852-2723 1376; www.monkeyshrine.com; Flat D, 11th fl, Liberty Mansion, 26E Jordan Rd, Yau Ma Tei, Kowloon, Hong Kong)
STA Travel Bangkok (☎ 02-236 0262; www.statravel.co.th); Hong Kong (☎ 852-2736 1618; www.statravel .com.hk); Japan (☎ 03-5391 2922; www.statravel.co.jp); Singapore (☎ 65-6737 7188; www.statravel.com.sg)

Australia

Intrepid Travel (☎ 03-9473 2626; www.intrepidtravel.com.au; 11 Spring St, Fitzroy, Victoria 3065)
Peregrine Adventures (☎ 03-9663 8611; www.peregrine.net.au; 258 Lonsdale St, Melbourne, Victoria 3000)

UK & Continental Europe

Discovery Initiatives (☎ 01285-643333; www.discoveryinitiatives.com; Travel House, 51 Castle St, Cirencester, GL7 1QD, UK) Runs environmentally friendly conservation trips to Khövsgöl, the Gobi and elsewhere, in cooperation with local scientists.
Equitour (☎ 061-303 3105; www.equitour.com; Herrenweg, 60 CH-4123 Allschwil, Switzerland) Specialises in horse-riding tours.
Exodus (☎ 020-8675 5550; www.exodus.co.uk; 9 Weir Rd, London SW12 0LT, UK)
In the Saddle (☎ 01299-272 997; www.inthesaddle.co.uk; Reaside, Neen Savage, Cleobury Mortimer, Shropshire DY14 8ES, UK) Runs horse-riding tours.
KE Adventure (☎ 017687-73966; www.keadventure.com; 32 Lake Rd, Keswick, Cumbria CA12 5DQ, UK) Organises mountain-biking tours and guided ascents of Tavan Bogd Uul.
Mongolei Reisen GmbH (☎ 3303-214 552; www.mongoliajourneys.com; Am Spargelfeld 3, 16540 Hohen Neuendorf, Berlin, Germany)
Off the Map Tours (☎ 0116-2402625; www.mongolia.co.uk; 20 The Meer, Fleckney, Leicester, LE8 8UN) A Mongolia specialist with motorbiking, mountain-biking, horse-riding and hiking trips.

USA & Canada

Boojum Expeditions (☎ 1-800-287-0125, 406-587-0125; www.boojum.com; 14543 Kelly Canyon Rd, Bozeman, MT 59715) Offers horse-riding, mountain-biking, fishing and trekking trips. In Ulaanbaatar, Boojum's local office is called Khövsgöl Lodge Company.
Geographic Expeditions (☎ 1-800-777-8183, 415-922-0448; www.geoex.com; 2nd fl, 1008 General Kennedy Ave, San Francisco, CA 94129) Horse-riding trips to Khentii and jeep trips combining western Mongolia and Tuva in western Siberia.
Hidden Trails (☎ 604-323-1141; www.hiddentrails.com; 659A Moberly Rd, Vancouver, BC V5Z 4B3) Horse-riding tours to Terelj and Darkhad Depression, in conjunction with Equitour.
Mir Corporation (☎ 1-800-424-7289; www.mircorp.com; Suite 210, 85 South Washington St, Seattle, WA 98104)
Nomadic Expeditions (☎ 1-800-998-6634, 609-860-9008; www.nomadicexpeditions.com; Suite 20A, 1095 Cranbury-South River Rd, Jamesburg, NJ 08831) One of the best Mongolia specialists, offering everything from palaeontology trips to eagle hunting and camel trekking. It also has an office in Ulaanbaatar.
Turtle Tours (☎ 888-299-1439; www.turtletours.com; PO Box 1147, Carefree, AZ 85377)
Steppes East (☎ 01285-880 980; www.steppeseast.co.uk; 51 Castle St, Cirencester, GL7 1QD, UK)

in advance, but for the Moscow–Beijing or Beijing–Moscow trains you will have to scramble for a ticket on the day before departure (although you could try asking two days in advance). If you have trouble booking a berth, ask your guesthouse manager or hotel reception desk for assistance.

A taxi between Sükhbaatar Sq and the train station costs about T900.

It's also possible to buy train tickets at the Discovery Mongolia Information Centre (see p67).

Refer to the boxed text on p275 for international train services.

Direct Trains

Most travellers catch the direct train between Beijing and Ulaanbaatar.

There are two direct trains a week each way between Beijing and Ulaanbaatar. One of these (3 and 4) is the Trans-Mongolian train, which runs between Beijing and Moscow. The other (23 and 24) is easier to get tickets for.

It is also possible to travel directly between Ulaanbaatar and Hohhot twice a week, allowing you to either bypass Beijing completely or catch a train or flight (US$80) on to Beijing from there.

Trains leave from **Beijing Train Station** (☎ 6563 8262/42). If your luggage weighs over 35kg, on the day before departure you'll have to take it to the Luggage Shipment Office, which is on the right-hand side of the station. The excess is charged at about US$11 per 10kg, with a maximum excess of 40kg allowed.

The best place to buy tickets in China is at the **China International Travel Service** (CITS; ☎ 010-6512 0507; www.cits.net; ✆ 8.30am–noon & 1.30-5pm) in the International Hotel, Jianguomenwai Dajie, Beijing. Tickets are also available at **BTG Travel & Tours** (☎ 010-6800 5588; Beijing Tourism Bldg, 28 Jianguomenwai Dajie), between the New Otani and Gloria Plaza hotels.

With CITS it is possible to book up to six months in advance for trains originating in Beijing if you send a deposit of Y100, and you can collect your ticket from one week to one day before departure. There is a Y150 cancellation fee.

CITS only sells tickets from Beijing to Moscow or Ulaanbaatar – no stopovers are allowed. Tickets to Ulaanbaatar cost Y657/1006 in hard/soft sleeper on the Saturday train and Y595/999 in hard/soft sleeper on the Wednesday train.

You can also buy train tickets privately; they will be more expensive than at CITS, but you may also be able to arrange a stopover and visas. In Beijing, **Monkey Business Shrine** (☎ 8610-6591 6519; fax 6591 6517; www.monkeyshrine. com) can put together all kinds of stopovers and homestay programs. The company has a lot of experience in booking international trains for independent travellers. In Hong Kong, it goes under the name **Moonsky Star Ltd** (☎ 852-2723 1376; fax 2723 6653).

Note that the Russian embassy in Beijing is only accepting visa applications from official residents of China. You are more likely to get a visa from the Russian consulate in Hong Kong.

The costs in tögrög for destinations in China from Ulaanbaatar are found in the following table.

Destination	2nd class (hard sleeper)	1st class (soft sleeper)	Deluxe* (coupé)
Beijing	66,350	101,800	113,700
Datong	55,150	76,450	88,250
Ereen	37,100	50,900	63,310
Hohhot	47,710	64,140	77,000

* Prices are for Chinese trains. Mongolian trains are about 15% to 20% cheaper for deluxe (coupé) class.

Local Trains

If you're on a tight budget it's possible to take local trains between UB and Beijing. This will save some money but involves more hassle and uncertainty and requires more time. During the summer season, from mid-June to mid-August, international train bookings are almost impossible to get, unless you have booked your seats weeks or months in advance. The local train may be your only option.

The first option is train 22 or 21, which runs between Ulaanbaatar and Ereen just inside China. This Mongolian train leaves Ulaanbaatar at 10.10pm on Thursday and Sunday and arrives in Ereen at about 10.25am the next morning, after completing immigration and customs formalities. In reverse, train 21 leaves Ereen on Tuesday and Friday evenings and arrives the next day. The schedules for this train change regularly.

The second option is to take local trains to Zamyn-Üüd in Mongolia (see p203) and then cross the border by minivan or jeep. From Ereen you can ply deeper into China by either train or bus.

TRANSPORT

TRANS-MONGOLIAN RAILWAY

Travelling from Russia or China to Mongolia directly on the Trans-Mongolian Railway line is arguably the most epic train journey you can make. The following gives general information on this travelling route.

The names of the rail lines can be a bit confusing. The Trans-Mongolian Railway goes from Beijing through Ulaanbaatar and onto a junction called Zaudinsky, near Ulan Ude in Russia, where it meets the Trans-Siberian line and continues on to Moscow. The Trans-Siberian Railway runs between Moscow and the eastern Siberian port of Nakhodka – this route does not go through either China or Mongolia. The Trans-Manchurian Railway crosses the Russia–China border at Zabaikalsk–Manzhouli, also completely bypassing Mongolia.

General Train Information

At the stations in Mongolia and Russia, there may be someone on the platform selling food; in the more entrepreneurial China, someone on the platform will have some delicious fruit and soft drinks for sale.

The restaurant cars on the Russian and Chinese trains have decent food and drinks on offer, for around US$2 to US$4. Staff on the Russian train to Moscow have a tendency to sell off all the food at stops in Siberia, so you may find food supplies have dwindled by the time you reach Novosibirsk.

Note that toilets are normally locked whenever you are in a station and for five minutes before and after. Showers are only available in the deluxe carriages. In 2nd and 1st class, there is a washroom and toilet at the end of each carriage – which always get progressively more filthy. It's a good idea to bring a large enamel mug (available in most Chinese railway stations) and use it as a scoop to pour water over yourself from the washbasin.

Generally you are allowed 35kg of luggage, but for foreigners this is rarely checked, except perhaps when departing Beijing. A lot of smuggling is done on this train, so never agree to carry anything across the border for anyone else.

The trains are reasonably safe but it's still a good idea to watch your bags closely. For added safety, lock your cabins from the inside and also make use of the security clip on the upper left-hand part of the door. The clip can be flipped open from the outside with a knife, but not if you stuff the hole with paper.

If you want to get off or on the Trans-Mongolian at Sükhbaatar, Darkhan (travelling from Russia) or Sainshand (from China), you will still have to pay the full Ulaanbaatar fare. If you are not actually getting *on* the train in Ulaanbaatar, you should arrange for someone in the capital to let the attendant know that you will be boarding the train at a later stop. This is to ensure that your seat is not taken.

Tickets list the departure times. Get to the station at least 20 minutes before *arrival* to allow enough time to find the platform and struggle on board, as the train only stops in Ulaanbaatar for about 30 minutes.

For detailed information on the Trans-Mongolian and Trans-Siberian trains, try Lonely Planet's *Trans-Siberian Railway*.

What to Bring

US dollars in small denominations are useful to buy meals and drinks on the train, and to exchange for the local currency, so you can buy things at the train stations. It's a good idea to buy some Russian roubles or Chinese yuan at the licensed moneychangers in Ulaanbaatar before you leave Mongolia.

Stock up on munchies such as biscuits, chocolate and fruit, and bring some bottled water or juice. A small samovar at the end of each carriage provides constant boiling water, a godsend for making tea and coffee, as well as instant packet meals of noodles or soup.

Other essential items include thongs (flip flops) or slippers, an enamel mug, a flannel, toilet paper, plenty of reading material and loose, comfortable long pants. Tracksuits are a must for blending in with the locals.

Classes

With a few exceptions, all international trains have two or three classes. The names and standards of the classes depend on whether it is a Mongolian, Russian or Chinese train.

On the Russian (and Mongolian) trains, most travellers travel in 2nd class – printed on tickets and timetables as '1/4' and known as 'hard sleeper', 'coupé' or *kupeynyy* in Russian. These are small, but perfectly comfortable, four-person compartments with four bunk-style beds and a fold-down table.

First class (printed as '2/4') is sometimes called a 'soft sleeper' or *myagkiy* in Russian. It has softer beds but hardly any more space than a Russian 2nd-class compartment and is not worth the considerably higher fare charged. On Chinese trains it is nonsmoking, which can be a godsend.

The real luxury (and expense) comes with Chinese deluxe class (printed as '1/2'): it involves roomy, wood-panelled two-berth compartments with a sofa, and a shower cubicle shared with the adjacent compartment. The deluxe class on Russian trains (slightly cheaper than the Chinese deluxe) has two bunks but is not much different in size from 2nd class and has no showers.

Customs & Immigration

There are major delays of three to six hours at both the China–Mongolia and Russia–Mongolia borders. Often trains cross the border during the middle of the night, when alert Mongolian and Russian officials maintain the upper hand. The whole process is not difficult or a hassle, just annoying because they keep interrupting your sleep.

Your passport will be taken for inspection and stamping. When it is returned, inspect it closely – sometimes they make errors such as cancelling your return visa for China. Foreigners generally sail through customs without having their bags opened, which is one reason people on the train may approach you and ask if you'll carry some of their luggage across the border – *this is not a good idea*.

During these stops, you can alight and wander around the station, which is just as well because the toilets on the train are locked during the inspection procedure.

Tickets

The international trains, especially the Trans-Mongolian Railway, are popular, so it's often hard to book this trip except during winter. Try to plan ahead and book as early as possible.

If you are in Ulaanbaatar and want to go to Irkutsk, Beijing or Moscow, avoid going on the Beijing–Moscow or Moscow–Beijing trains; use the other trains mentioned on p271 and p276, which *originate* in Ulaanbaatar. In Ulaanbaatar, you cannot buy tickets a few days in advance for the Beijing–Moscow or Moscow–Beijing trains, because staff in UB won't know how many people are already on the train. For these trains, you can only buy a ticket the day before departure, ie on Wednesday for trains from Ulaanbaatar to Moscow, and on Saturday for trains from Ulaanbaatar to Beijing. You will need to get to the ticket office early and get into the Mongolian scramble for tickets.

For details on buying tickets in Ulaanbaatar see p99.

Several agencies in Western countries can arrange tickets on the international trains, but their prices will be considerably higher than if you bought tickets from the point of departure. They often only make the effort if you also buy an organised tour from them.

Overseas branches of China International Travel Service (CITS) or China Travel Service (CTS) can often book train and plane tickets from Beijing to Ulaanbaatar. Also try the following places:

Gateway Travel (☎ 02-9745 3333; fax 02-9745 3237; www.russian-gateway.com.au) In Australia.
GW Travel Ltd (☎ 0161-928 9410; www.gwtravel.co.uk) In the UK.
Intourist (☎ 020-7538 8600; fax 020-7538 5967; www.intourist.com) In the UK.
Lernidee Reisen (☎ 030-786 0000; www.lernidee-reisen.de) German company.
Regent Holidays (☎ 0845-277 3317; www.regent-holidays.co.uk) In the UK.
The Russia Experience Ltd (☎ 020-8566 8846; www.trans-siberian.co.uk)
Sundowners (☎ 03-9672 5300; fax 03-9672 5311; www.sundowners.com.au) In Australia.
Trek Escapes (☎ 866-338 8735; www.trekescapes.com) In Canada.
White Nights International Tourism (☎ /fax 800-490-5008; 610 La Sierra Dr, Sacramento, CA 95864, USA)

TRANSPORT

From Beijing, the local train for Jining departs at 11.42am and takes about nine hours. A second train departs at 9.20pm and continues to Hohhot. The train from Jining to Érliàn (Ereen) departs around noon and takes six hours. (Alternatively, a 7am bus takes just four hours.) If you have to stay the night in Jining, there's a budget hotel on the right (south) side of the plaza as you walk out of the train station. Most transport between Ereen and the border takes place in the morning.

Russia

BORDER CROSSINGS

Most travellers go in and out of Russia at the Naushki–Sükhbaatar train border crossing. In addition, there are three road crossings: Tsagaannuur–Tashanta in Bayan-Ölgii aimag, Altanbulag–Kyakhta in Selenge and Ereentsav–Solovyevsk in Dornod. The crossings are open from 9am to noon and 2pm to 6pm daily except holidays.

There is hope that the Khankh–Mondy border in northern Khövsgöl will soon be opened; check the situation before heading out this way.

Both the road and rail crossings can be agonisingly slow, but at least on the road journe you can get out and stretch your legs. Trai travellers have been stranded for up to 1 hours on the Russian side, spending muc of this time locked inside the train cabin Procedures on the Ulaanbaatar–Moscow trai are faster than on the local trains.

We have received a number of complaint about scams and problems with customs o the Russian side of the border, so be read for anything.

One thing to be careful about is th Russian exit declaration form. The currenc you list on the form must match the cur rency you listed on the customs form yo received when you entered the country. the form shows that you are leaving wit more dollars or euros than you had whe you arrived, you will have to get off th train and change all the excess money int roubles. Further, if the entry form was no stamped when you arrived in Russia (or you never received one) it will be considere invalid, so have the form stamped even you have nothing to declare.

MONGOLIA OR BUST

In an age when getting from point A to point B has been simplified to the point of blandness, the Mongol Rally attempts to put a bit of spark back into the journey to Mongolia. According to rally rules, the London-to-Mongolia trip must be made in a vehicle that has an engine capacity of 1L or less. In other words, you have to travel 16,000km (10,000 miles) across some of the world's most hostile terrain in a piece of crap barely capable of a drive down to the corner shop.

The wacky idea of driving from London to Mongolia in a clapped-out banger was dreamt up by Englishman Thomas Morgan, whose own attempt to accomplish the feat failed miserably in 2003. Morgan had another go in 2004 and completed the trip, along with a few friends who were inspired by the utter lunacy of it all. Since then the Mongol Rally has become an annual rite of passage for English adventurers.

The journey begins by selecting a vehicle. Antique gutless wonders such as old Fiat Pandas and Ford Fiestas can be purchased for around 100 quid in England. Next, assemble your team – you can have as many people as you can squeeze into the damn thing. Then pay your dues: it's £387 to enter and then you must raise another £1000, which will go to a charity in Mongolia or another country en route (in 2007 the Mongol Rally raised over £200,000 in charity money). Finally, zoom out of London with 200 other likeminded drivers on 1 July.

The organisers give absolutely no advice on how to actually get to Mongolia; that you've got to figure out on your own. Teams have travelled as far north as the Arctic Circle and as far south as Afghanistan on their way across the Asian landmass. This is by no means a race – whether you arrive first or last, your only reward is a round of free beers at the finish line at Dave's Place (p91). Some teams make the trip in around five weeks, while others have taken as long as three months, stopping off at places en route.

The rally is organised by the grandly titled **League of Adventurists International** (http://mon golrally.theadventurists.com). If you want to sign up, contact the organisers early as there are only a limited number of spots available and these sell out a year in advance.

TRAINS TO/FROM MONGOLIA

Schedules change from one summer to another, and services reduce in winter, and can increase in summer. The durations below refer to the journey time to/from Ulaanbaatar.

Train	Train no	Day of departure	Departure time	Duration
China–Mongolia				
Beijing–Ulaanbaatar	23	Tue	7.40am*	30hr
Beijing–Ulaanbaatar–(Moscow)	3	Thu	1.50am	30hr
Hohhot–Ulaanbaatar	215	Sun, Wed	10.40pm	30hr
Mongolia–China				
Ulaanbaatar–Beijing	24	Thu	8.05am	30hr
(Moscow)–Ulaanbaatar–Beijing	4	Thu	8.05am	30hr
Ulaanbaatar–Hohhot	34	Mon, Fri	8.10pm	24hr
Mongolia–Russia				
Ulaanbaatar–Irkutsk	263	daily	7.35pm	36hr
Ulaanbaatar–Moscow	5	Tue, Fri	1.50pm	70hr
(Beijing)–Ulaanbaatar–Moscow	3	Thu	1.15pm	100hr
Russia–Mongolia				
Irkutsk–Ulaanbaatar	264	daily	7.10pm	36hr
Moscow–Ulaanbaatar	6	Wed, Thu	9pm	70hr
Moscow–Ulaanbaatar–(Beijing)	4	Sun	7.55pm	100hr

*Train 23 passes through Datong at approximately 2.15pm, Jining at 4.15pm, Ereen at 8.45pm and Zamyn-Üüd at 11.45pm.

To avoid these problems, either don't cross the border with foreign currency (roubles are OK) or be vigilant with that exit declaration form. Lying about not having foreign cash is one option, but you run the risk of being searched. Telling the border guard you plan to use a credit card may work.

Russian & Mongolian Border Towns

Customs and immigration between Naushki and Sükhbaatar can take at least four hours. You can have a look around Naushki, but there is little to see and the border crossing usually takes place in the middle of the night. Surprisingly, you may have difficulty finding anyone at the Naushki station to change money, so wait until Sükhbaatar or Ulaanbaatar, or somewhere else in Russia. (Get rid of your tögrög before you leave Mongolia, as almost no-one will want to touch them once you are inside Russia.)

The train may stop for one or two hours at, or near, the pleasant Mongolian border town of Sükhbaatar, but there is no need to look around. You may be able to buy some Russian roubles or Mongolian tögrög from a moneychanger at the train station, but the rate will be poor. If there aren't any moneychangers, you can use US dollars cash to get by until you change money elsewhere.

BUS

Bus is probably the fastest form of public transport between Mongolia and Russia. A daily bus operated by **Vostok Trans** (☎ 9666 5531) departs Ulaanbaatar bound for Ulan Ude. It departs at 7.30pm, and the journey takes 10 hours and costs T33,600. Buses leave from outside the Discovery Mongolia Information Centre (p67). An Ulan Ude bus departs at the same time for Ulaanbaatar, leaving from the Hotel Baikal in Ulan Ude. In Ulan Ude contact **Trio-Impex** (☎ 3012-217 277; trio-tour@mail.ru) or **Buryat-Intour** (☎ 3012-210 056; bintur@yandex.ru).

CAR & MOTORCYCLE

It's possible to drive between Russia and Mongolia at Tsagaannuur (Bayan-Ölgii), Altanbulag (Selenge) and Ereentsav (Dornod). However, these road crossings can be difficult and time consuming – up to six hours if traffic is backed up or if you have visa problems.

In order to speed things up, it may help to have a letter written by the Mongolian consular (or Russian consular if you are headed that way) when you get your visa. The letter should state that you are authorised to take a car or motorcycle across the border. A carnet (passport for your car) may be useful but is not necessary. US citizens may want to bring documentation stating that visas are not needed as proof to inexperienced border guards.

Foreigners are currently not allowed to 'walk' across the Kyakhta–Altanbulag border, but they are allowed to pass through in a car or even on a motorcycle, so you may have to pay someone to drive you across. Things continue to change so it's worth asking if you can walk across the border.

TRAIN

Besides the Trans-Mongolian Railway connecting Moscow and Beijing, there is a direct train twice a week connecting Ulaanbaatar and Moscow, which is easier to book from Ulaanbaatar. The epic trip takes four days.

If you are headed to Lake Baikal, there is a daily train between Ulaanbaatar and Irkutsk, which stops en route in Darkhan. These trains stop at every village, however, and train 263 travels past Lake Baikal at night, so if you are in a hurry or want to see the lake, take the Ulaanbaatar–Moscow (train 5) as far as Irkutsk. Note that departure and arrival times at Irkutsk are given in Moscow time, although Irkutsk is actually five hours ahead of Moscow.

This trip can be done more cheaply by travelling in stages on local trains (eg from Ulan Ude to Naushki, Naushki to Sükhbaatar, and Sükhbaatar to Ulaanbaatar), but this would

---

BOGIES

Don't be concerned if you get off at Ereen (on the Chinese side of the border) and the train disappears from the platform. About two hours are spent changing the bogies (wheel assemblies) because the Russians (and, therefore, the Mongolians) and the Chinese use different railway gauges. Train buffs may want to see the bogie-changing operation. Stay on the train after it disgorges passengers in Ereen. The train then pulls into a large shed about 1km from the station. Get off immediately before the staff lock the doors – they really don't want you in the train anyway. It's OK to walk around the shed and take photos, but don't get in anybody's way.

---

involve more hassles, especially as Russia visas are more difficult to arrange tha Chinese due to Russian officials wanting fu details of your itinerary.

In Moscow you can buy tickets at th building on Ulitsa Krasnoprudnaya next door to the Yaroslavl train statior from where the trains to Ulaanbaatar an Beijing leave.

Infinity Travel (☎ 095-234 6555; fax 095-234 655 www.infinity.ru) in Moscow is affiliated with th Traveller's Guesthouse and is one of the bet ter private sellers.

A reliable agency in Ulan Ude is **Burya Intour** (☎ 3012-210 056; bintur@yandex.ru; 12 Ranzhurc Sta, Ulan Ude 670000).

In Irkutsk, you can try **Irkutsk-Baika Intourist** (☎ 3952-290 161; Hotel Intourist, 14 Bulva Gagarina 44, Irkutsk 664025) or **Irkutsk Baikal Travel In** (☎ 3952-200 134; fax 3952-200 070; www.irkutsk-baika .com; 1a Cheremhovsky Lane, Irkutsk 664025).

Approximate costs (in tögrög) for majo destinations in Russia from Ulaanbaatar ar listed below. Exact costs depend on whethe the train is Russian, Chinese or Mongolian we have listed the most expensive.

Destination	2nd class (hard sleeper)	1st class (soft sleeper)	Deluxe (coupé)
Irkutsk	33,100	53,720	60,430
Krasnoyarsk	60,540	74,220	99,220
Moscow	101,420	139,510	160,880
Naushki	21,450	24,970	35,750
Novosibirsk	69,210	84,860	113,280
Omsk	77,020	94,370	126,220
Perm	94,220	114,400	152,130
Ulan Ude	28,630	43,060	n/a
Yekaterinburg	91,020	110,350	148,080

GETTING AROUND

Travelling around the countryside independ ently is the best way to see Mongolia an meet the people, but there are several matter you need to be aware of. Annual outbreaks o forest fires, the plague, foot-and-mouth an even cholera may affect your travel plans i there are quarantine restrictions.

Generally, shortages of petrol and spare parts are now uncommon, except in remote regions. Accidents are not uncommon. Try to avoid travelling at night, when unseer potholes, drunk drivers and wildlife car vreak havoc. Driving in the dark is also a reat way to get completely lost.

AIR

Mongolia, a vast, sparsely populated country with very little infrastructure, relies heavily on ir transport. It has 44 functioning airports, although only 12 of those have paved airstrips.

Almost all of the destinations are served directly from Ulaanbaatar, so flying from, ay, Dalanzadgad to Bayan-Ölgii is impossible without first returning to UB. A T2000 domestic departure tax is payable at the airport.

Airlines in Mongolia

MIAT (☎ 011-322 118; http://miat.com) is the state-owned airline that once flew to every corner of the country. A lack of functioning aeroplanes and increased competition has limited its service to only a handful of cities, namely Mörön, Arvaikheer, Altai, Khovd and Dalanzadgad.

MIAT is not known for its safety record, although it hasn't had a fatal crash since 1998. Its domestic planes may be old but the pilots are the most experienced in the business. MIAT's international service, on the other hand, has seen dramatic improvements in recent years. Its fleet includes an Airbus 310 and a Boeing 737.

Aero Mongolia (☎ 011-283 029; www.aeromongolia nn) began service in 2003 and now operates two Fokker aircraft. Routes change but in 2007 it flew domestic services to Ölgii, Donoi (Uliastai), Dalanzadgad, Mörön, Ulaangom, Choibalsan and Khovd. It is really stingy on baggage allowance, allowing only 15kg (including hand luggage); any kilogram over the limit costs T2500. It only accepts cash payments and the rate will be better if you pay in US dollars. Aero Mongolia also serves Hohhot and Tianjin in China, and Irkutsk in Russia.

EZ Nis (☎ 011-313 689; www.eznis.com) operates two Swedish-built Saab 340B propeller aeroplanes and has domestic flights to/from UB and Choibalsan, Baruun-Urt, Mörön, Ulaangom, Khovd, Bayankhongor and Dalanzadgad. More destinations are planned, so check the schedule. It's a slick and reliable operation, but more expensive than Aero Mongolia and MIAT.

Blue Sky Aviation (☎ 011-312 085; fax 011-322 857; www.bsamongolia.com) has a nine-seat Cessna that can be chartered for any part of the country.

Checking In

Get to the airport at least one hour before your flight. Even if you have a ticket, flight number and an allocated seat number, don't assume the plane won't be overbooked. There are usually no assigned seats so you'll have to do some scrambling once on board. Try to make certain your luggage has gone on the plane. If possible, carry your pack on as hand luggage to save time and the worry of losing your bag. However, make sure you don't have any sharp or blunt objects in your carry-on (including bike tools). Gas canisters are not allowed on any flight.

Costs

The foreigner price is often several times more than what Mongolians pay for tickets. Anyone can buy a ticket on your behalf, but you will always have to pay in US dollars (or by credit card in Ulaanbaatar). Tickets range from US$66 (to Arvaikheer) to US$183 for a four-hour, 1380km flight to the far west – pretty reasonable, considering the distances. Children aged between five and 16 years pay half; under fives fly free. If you've come on a student visa you can get 25% to 50% off the cost of the ticket.

Ask about baggage allowances when you buy your aeroplane ticket. EZ Nis allows you to carry 20kg without extra charges.

Reservations & Tickets

A domestic ticket reservation isn't worth diddly-squat until you have a ticket in your hand. In the countryside, buy your ticket as soon as you arrive.

You can buy a return ticket in Ulaanbaatar, but there is no computerised reservation system connecting the various airports around the country so you will have to reconfirm your reservation at the airport as soon as you arrive at your destination.

If you wish to fly in one direction and return by road in the other (for example to Mörön), it's best to fly from Ulaanbaatar, where you are more likely to get a ticket and a seat, and then return overland – otherwise you may wait days or more for a flight and ticket in Mörön.

Seats can be difficult to get in summer, especially in the July tourist peak and in late August as students return to college.

TRANSPORT

BICYCLE

For keen bikers with a sense of adventure, Mongolia offers an unparalleled cycling experience. The vast, open steppes make for rough travel but if properly equipped there is nothing stopping you from travelling pretty much anywhere (although a trip to the Gobi could only be done with vehicle support). For details on cycle touring, see p55.

BOAT

Although there are 397km of navigable waterways in Mongolia, rivers aren't used for transporting people or cargo. The biggest boat in the country is the *Sükhbaatar,* which very occasionally travels around Khövsgöl Nuur. There's also a customs boat that patrols the Selenge Gol on the border of Russia and Mongolia. Some ger camps at Khövsgöl Nuur also own small boats that can be chartered.

BUS

Private bus companies serve a handful of Mongolian cities, all connected to Ulaanbaatar. These include Baruun-Urt, Öndörkhaan, Dalanzadgad, Tsetserleg, Arvaikheer, Erdenet, Darkhan and Mörön. Most buses are old rust buckets, except the services to Darkhan and Erdenet, which use modern buses. The benefit of using buses is that they leave on time and drive straight to their destination, as opposed to private vans, which run on Mongolian time.

CAMEL & YAK

Intractable yaks and confrontational camels are recognised forms of transport in Mongolia. Camels, which can carry around 250kg, carry about one-third of all cargo around the Gobi Desert. Yaks are also a useful and environmentally friendly way of hauling heavy cargo.

At Ongiin Khiid and Khongoryn Els you can arrange a multiple-day camel trek. A few travel agencies include a ride on a camel or yak in their programme. Otherwise, you can always ask at a ger.

CAR & MOTORCYCLE

Travelling around Mongolia with your own car or motorcycle – without a driver – is not recommended. What look like main roads on the map are often little more than tyre tracks in the dirt, sand or mud, and there is hardly a signpost in the whole country. In Mongolia, roads connect nomads, most of whom by their

nature keep moving, so even the roads a seminomadic, shifting like restless river Remote tracks quickly turn into eight-lar dirt highways devoid of any traffic, makin navigation tricky – some drivers follow th telephone lines when there are any, or else as for directions at gers along the way. Town with food and water are few and far between and very few people in the countryside wi speak anything but Mongolian or, if you ar lucky, Russian.

To help you find your way around, us the GPS Coordinates Table (p284), whic contains many towns and villages, and som sights. The coordinates for a number of othe sights are included in the regional chapters.

There are a couple of car-rental agencie in Ulaanbaatar, but they require that you b driven by one of their drivers. **Drive Mongoli** (☎ 011-312 277, 9911 8257; www.drivemongolia.com is a tour operator that allows you to driv a hire vehicle, but you need to go with thei support vehicle or be accompanied by Mongolian driver. Their jeeps cost aroun US$50 per day.

If you want to buy a vehicle, you wi have to ask around, or check out the *tsar zakh* (car market) in the northeastern par of Ulaanbaatar. A new Ij Planeta – th Russian-made motorcycle you see all ove the countryside – sells for around US$900 A new Russian jeep costs around US$5000 In markets the sign *'zarna'* (Зарна) on a jee means 'for sale'.

Travellers can use an international drivin licence to drive any vehicle in Mongolia; expa residents need to apply for a local licence. I you buy a vehicle, inquire about registratio at the local police station.

Two types of Russian fuel are available: '93 is the best and the type used by Japanese jeeps but it's only generally available in Ulaanbaatar all Russian-made vehicles use '76', which is a that is available in the countryside. Petrol sta tions are marked by the initials 'ШТС', whic is Mongolian for station.

HITCHING

Hitching is never entirely safe in any countr in the world and we don't normally recom mend it. People who choose to hitch will b safer if they travel in pairs and let someon know where they are planning to go.

Mongolia is different, however. Because th country is so vast, public transport so limite

T R A N S P O R T

d the people so poor, hitching (usually on ucks) is a recognised – and, often, the only – rm of transport in the countryside. Hitching seldom free and often no different from just aiting for public transport to turn up. It is *ways* slow – after stopping at gers to drink, xing flat tyres, breaking down, running out f petrol and getting stuck in mud and rivers, truck can take 48 hours to cover 200km.

Hitching is not generally dangerous per onally, but it is still hazardous and often ex emely uncomfortable. Don't expect much affic in remote rural areas; you might see ne or two vehicles a day on many roads, and ometimes nobody at all for several days. In ue towns, ask at the market, where trucks in variably hang around, or at the bus/truck/jeep ation. The best place to wait is the petrol ation on the outskirts of town, where most ehicles stop before any journey.

If you rely on hitching entirely, though, you ill just travel from one dreary aimag town to nother. You still need to hire a jeep to see, for xample, the Gobi Desert, the mountains in hentii or some of the lakes in the far west.

Truck drivers will normally expect ome negotiable payment, which won't be nuch cheaper than a long-distance bus or hared jeep; figure on around T1500 per our travelled.

Bring a water- and dust-proof bag to ut your backpack in. The most important nings to bring, though, are an extremely arge amount of patience and time, and a high nreshold for discomfort. Carry camping gear or the inevitable breakdowns, or suffer along vith your travel mates.

ORSE

Horses have provided reliable transport for Mongolians for the past few thousand years. If t worked for the Mongol hordes, it can work or you. In recent decades though, many herd rs have acquired motorcycles, but most still se horses as their primary mode of transport. Mongolians rarely walk anywhere.

It's impossible to see everything by horse nless you have a lot of time, but it is the best vay to travel around some areas (see p59 for ome ideas). Most importantly, riding a horse elps you meet locals on a level footing and xperience the country as Mongolians have one for centuries.

If you are a serious rider, there are horses verywhere; with some luck, guidance and experience, you should be able to find a horse suited to your needs. Mongolians swap horses readily, so there's no need to be stuck with a horse you don't like, or which doesn't like you. The only exception is in April and May, when all animals are weak after the long winter and before fresh spring plants have made their way through the melting snows. The best time for riding is in the summer (June to September).

You can rent a horse and guide in most tourist areas for between US$6 and US$20 per day (the latter at ger camps). Most foreign (see p270) and local travel agencies also organise horse-riding trips.

One thing to bear in mind is that when mounting a horse (or camel), do so only from the left. The animals have been trained to accept human approach from the left, and may rear if approached the wrong way. The Mongolians use the phrase '*chu!*' to make their horses go. Somewhat telling about the obstinate nature of Mongolian horses is that there is no word for 'stop'. If you are considering a multiday horse trip, remember that horses attract all kinds of flies. Also, if you're not used to riding a horse, you're likely to get mighty stiff and sore.

A few foreigners cherish the idea of buying a horse and taking off around Mongolia. It's a fine adventure (if you can get a visa for long enough), but there are several pitfalls to be aware of. For some handy advice see the boxed text, p281.

Some final advice: watch and learn. Mongolians almost invented horsemanship. Also be prepared for at least one spill.

LOCAL TRANSPORT
Bus, Minibus & Trolley-bus
In Ulaanbaatar, regular and very crowded trolley-buses, buses and minibuses ply the main roads for around T200 a ride. Cities such as Darkhan and Erdenet have minibuses that shuttle from one end of town to the other, but you are unlikely to need them because most facilities are located centrally.

Taxi
Only in UB and a couple of the bigger cities is there taxi service, though in UB any vehicle on the street is a potential taxi – just flag down the driver and agree on a price. The rate at the time of writing was T300 per kilometre, but this will certainly increase.

MINIVAN & JEEP

Both minivans and jeeps are used for long-
and short-distance travel in the countryside.
They can be shared among strangers, which
is good for a group of people headed from
one aimag centre to another (or usually to/
from Ulaanbaatar). Alternatively, they can be
hired privately. In most cases, the grey, 11-seat
Furgon minivans are used for longer cross-
country trips that see a lot of traffic. Jeeps,
khaki-coloured or green, are found in more
remote areas such as *sum* (district) centres.
They are nicknamed *jaran yös* (shortened to
jaris), which means '69' – the number of the
original model. The large and comfortable
Toyota Landcruiser–style jeeps are owned by
wealthy Mongolians and never used for share
purposes (though some travel agencies might
have them for hire, but expect to pay at least
30% more than for a good Russian jeep).

On the terrible Mongolian roads, these
jeeps and minivans are an important form of
transport, and are mandatory when visiting
more remote attractions. They can typically
only travel between 30km/h and 50km/h. The
Gobi region generally has the best roads and
here you can average 60km/h.

Share Minivan & Jeep

Share jeeps and minivans are the most common form of public transport in Mongolia.
Private vehicles go from Ulaanbaatar to all
aimag capitals, major cities and tourist destinations. Less frequent and reliable services
operate between most aimag capitals, but very
few minivans go to the *sums*.

If you rely solely on share vehicles to
get around, you'll see surprisingly little of
Mongolia. Most vehicles drive between u▮
interesting cities with little to see on the wa▮
You'll still need to hire a car from the aim▮
or *sum* centres to see anything, and it's usual▮
easier to organise this from Ulaanbaatar.

For a long-distance trip bring snacks an▮
water; stops at a roadside *guanz* (canteen ▮
cheap restaurant) can be few and far betwee▮
You can expect at least one breakdown an▮
it would be a good idea to bring a slee▮
ing bag and warm clothes just in case yo▮
have to spend the night somewhere. Long
distance travel of over 10 hours is fiendish▮
uncomfortable. Most people who take a long
distance minivan to Mörön or Dalanzadga▮
end up flying back.

Minivan fares are reasonable, costing th▮
equivalent of US$12 to get to Dalanzadga▮
(21 hours) from Ulaanbaatar or US$15 t▮
Mörön (25 hours).

In the countryside, the post office operate▮
postal vans, which accept passengers. The▮
have fixed departure times, normally runnin▮
once a week between an aimag capital and
sum capital. The local post office should hav▮
a list of departure times and fares.

Hiring a Minivan or Jeep

The best way to see the countryside ▮
Mongolia independently is to hire your ow▮
minivan or jeep, which will come with a driv▮
and, for a little extra, a guide. If you share th▮
costs with others it doesn't work out to be to▮
expensive. With enough time, camping equip▮
ment, water and food, and a reliable jeep an▮
driver, you'll have the time of your life.

You can save money by using publi▮
transport to major regional gateways – tha▮

THE MINIVAN WAITING GAME

A real problem with share vehicles is that they are privately operated and won't leave until they
are packed tighter than a sardine tin. The waiting game sometimes has the effect of turning
your hair grey.

In the countryside, most vans just park at the local market and wait for passengers to turn
up, which means that if the van isn't already mostly full you'll be waiting around all day for the
seats to fill up, if they ever do.

The process can be agonising. Even after the 11-seat van has 20 or so passengers, the driver
will vanish for an hour or two for lunch, or to find more cargo, spare parts and petrol.

One solution is to ask the driver to pick you up at your hotel or the local internet café when
they are ready to go, which they usually agree to. This arrangement works out well and allows
you to do something productive (such as sleep or catch up on your emailing) while the other
passengers sweat it out at the market. The waiting time from Ulaanbaatar isn't as bad, but you
could still count on two hours or more.

BLAZING SADDLES *Joshua Handler*

If horses are of interest, Mongolia is the place to mount up. Riding from the time they can sit up straight, Mongolians have built their culture around the horse. They use it for work, transportation and nutrition. No, Mongolians don't eat horses; instead, they drink fermented mare milk during the summer months.

Creating a horseback adventure is certainly doable; it just takes patient perseverance. (Actually, these two words go well together regardless of your activity in Mongolia.)

Gear and horses are the two most important subjects to focus on. A saddle, bridle, halter and hobble can all be bought at the outdoor market in Ulaanbaatar. An English hybrid saddle can be bought for T55,000 to T65,000, packsaddles for half that.

Unless you have thighs of steel and have previously ridden in a Mongolian saddle, it is best to admire their beauty from afar. If you are long-legged, bring narrow stirrup leathers from home. To round out your appearance, buy a *del* (overcoat) or have one made for you. Most country folk wear them and they are great protection against wind, rain and snow, as well as for use as a blanket or ground cloth.

Once outfitted, locate a horse or two. You may buy or rent. Despite their vast numbers, horse prices are on the increase. A good horse may cost T300,000 and up. Herdsmen are loath to part with their well-mannered, quiet horses and may try to sell an oldie without much go. Make sure the horse walks at a comfortable pace, and load up a packhorse before buying. Also with packhorses, extra quiet is good.

Renting is a perfectly viable option if you are making a loop, because you will never recoup your investment when you sell back your horses. A fair price is T5000 to T10,000 per day; if you hire a guide, double that amount.

On Mongolia's steppe an open-door policy exists for locals and foreigners alike. If you are in desperate need of food and drink, or would simply like to say hello, you may approach a ger. Remember to call out prior to dismounting so the ferocious animal barking at you will be restrained. Break the language barrier with pictures of your family and hometown, and it is recommended that you offer the family a small gift, such as sweets or horse/car/motorcycle magazines.

It is not necessary to carry all your foodstuffs from the beginning if you will be passing towns along your journey. Topographic maps are best bought in UB; double-check that marked towns have a store, as some may no longer exist in this nomadic culture.

Rivers are a great source of water, however, the smaller ones are seasonal. Wells will be your other option, though these can also be dry. Ask around. Where there are animals and people, there is water.

Unless you speak Mongolian or Russian, communication will be difficult in the countryside. Lonely Planet's *Mongolian Phrasebook* will be invaluable. A majority of Mongolians are literate and will be able to read the words you are stumbling over.

When the trip ends and you say farewell to your horses, do as the Mongolians do and pluck some hairs from the mane and tail. Tie them around something to remind you of the freedom you felt in the Land of the Great Blue Sky.

For more information about travelling on horseback in Mongolia, see Joshua Handler's website:
www.stepintoyourselfexpeditions.com.

Mörön for Khövsgöl Nuur, Khovd for the est, Dalanzadgad for the south Gobi and hoibalsan for the far east. Then, from these aces, you will be able to rent a jeep fairly asily, though drivers outside Ulaanbaatar will ave little experience of dealing with tourists. ou may not find a local English-speaking uide, so bring one from Ulaanbaatar.

Don't expect to rent a jeep outside of an aimag capital. Villages do have jeeps, but they may not be available or running.

Note that when hiring a vehicle in the countryside to take you to another rural city you will have to pay for the return fare because the driver will have to go back with an empty van. This does not apply when travelling to

Ulaanbaatar as the driver can find passengers there. The upshot of this is that it will cost almost the same to hire a driver to take you from, for example, Ulaangom to Mörön as it would from Ulaangom to Ulaanbaatar.

In Ulaanbaatar, the best place to start looking for a driver and a guide is at the various guesthouses. These guesthouses will take a commission, but you'll get a driver and/or guide who understands the needs of a tourist. More importantly they know the tourist routes and can locate hard-to-find attractions such as caves, deer stones and ruined monasteries. Finding a driver from the jeep stand or market, and negotiating on your own, will be cheaper, but they will probably be in a hurry to get back home, which won't work well if you want to take it slow and see the sights.

On a long-distance trip, tour operators will have a per-day charge (usually US$50 to US$60) that will probably include petrol. This may be more if they throw in camping and cooking gear.

Vehicles that you hire on your own (from a market) usually charge US$35 per day without petrol. Russian jeeps have terrible fuel economy: you'll need 20L to travel around 100km. Petrol was around T900 per litre at the time of research. Some drivers may want to charge a per-kilometre rate; in the countryside this is around T450. Vehicle hire is more expensive the further you get from Ulaanbaatar.

It is vital that you and the driver agree to the terms and conditions – and the odometer reading – before you start. Ask about all possible 'extras' such as waiting time, food and accommodation. There are several private bridges and tolls around the countryside (each costing about T500), which are normally paid for by you. If you arrange for a jeep to pick you up, or drop you off, agree on a reduced price for the empty vehicle travelling one way.

Three can sit in the back seat of a Russian jeep, but it may be uncomfortable on long trips. Five or six people can ride in a minivan. If you also take a guide, rather than just driver, you can therefore take a maximum of three passengers in a jeep, though two would be more comfortable. There is usually ample room at the back of the jeep and minivan for backpacks, tents, water and so on.

TRIP PREPARATION

There are several other factors you should consider when embarking on a jeep or minivan tour of Mongolia. Before the trip explain your itinerary in detail to the driver and make sure they have a map and agree on the route. For long expeditions, also ensure your driver has jerry cans, for extra petrol and a water drum. A wide-mouthed plastic drum is also very useful for storing food, as boxes will rapidly disintegrate. Resealable bags are useful for opened bags of sugar, pasta and so on. Your backpacks will get filthy so it's a good idea to put them in a water- and dust-proof bag.

Drivers from tourist agencies will assume that you will feed them along the way. On a longer trip it's easiest for everyone to cook, eat and wash up together. If you don't want to do this, you will have to agree on a fee for the driver's food or buy them the food yourself. This shouldn't cost more than T4000 per day.

Experienced drivers will have their own Soviet-built petrol stove, though it's a good idea to bring your own stove as a backup and to boil water for tea while the other stove is cooking dinner. If you are cooking for a group you'll need a big cooking pot and a ladle. Everyone should bring their own penknife, cutlery, bowl and torch. Avoid drinking from the same water bottles as this spreads viruses around the group.

OTAM VANS

Mongolia's unreliable, slow and uncomfortable public transport system has led to the birth of **Open Tour Around Mongolia** (OTAM; Map p64; ☎ 7015 0159; www.otamecotours.com; Room 504, 5th fl, Alyska Bldg, Peace Ave), a private travel company that dispatches vans from Ulaanbaatar to make a loop tour of the countryside. With an OTAM ticket you can hop off wherever you like and get back on when the next OTAM van appears (usually two days later). The company has two separate routes that service the Gobi and northern Mongolia; each costs US$123. It also runs a western Mongolia tour (US$280) and a tour to sights near Ulaanbaatar, including Khustain National Park, Mandshir Khiid and Terelj (US$40).

TRANSPORT

TAKING A GPS

When you are travelling around the featureless plains of eastern Mongolia, the deserts of the Gobi or a tangle of confusing valleys in the west, a Global Positioning System (GPS) can be very useful in determining where exactly you are, as long as you have a reliable map on which to pinpoint your coordinates. We have given GPS coordinates for many hard-to-find places in this book, plus coordinates for *sum* (district) and aimag centres (to an accuracy of up to 1km from the town centre). Many places are listed in the table on p284.

A GPS won't help you every time, as you'll still need to know which road to take, even if you know the rough direction. Gobi and steppe areas are particularly tricky – except for the main routes there probably won't be any one road between places. Every few kilometres the track you're on will veer off in the wrong direction, requiring constant corrections and zigzagging.

It is always a good idea to ask about road conditions at gers along the way. Often a good-looking road will become impassable, running into a river, swamp or wall of mountains; herders can offer good info on the best route to take. If all else fails, you can always rely on Mongolian GPS (Ger Positioning System), which requires following the vague sweep of the ger owner's hand over the horizon, until you reach the next ger.

Shop as a group when you reach a city or own. If you are travelling with strangers, it's good idea to keep everyone happy by ro-ating seats so that everyone (including the uide) has a go in the front seat. Don't push e driver or guide too hard; allow them (and e vehicle) to stop and rest. However, regular nd lengthy stops for a chat and a smoke can dd time to the journey.

Lastly, if you are on a long trip, you'll find orale boosted by a trip to a bathhouse (hot ater!) in an aimag capital. Another morale ooster is the occasional meal in a decent *uanz*. If you are camping a lot then add in t least one night in a decent hotel to clean up nd sort out your stuff.

UIDES

o-one in the countryside speaks anything ther than Mongolian and Russian, so a uide-cum-translator is very handy, and al-ost mandatory. A guide will explain local aditions, help with any hassles with the po-ce, find accommodation, negotiate jeeps, xplain captions in museums and act as lin-uistic and cultural interpreter.

In Ulaanbaatar you can find guides through avel agencies, guesthouses or the bulletin oard at Chez Bernard (p90). In the country-de, there is nothing to do but ask – try the otels and schools. Guides are easier to find etween 15 June and 1 August, when schools nd universities are on summer break.

For getting around Ulaanbaatar, a non-rofessional guide or a student will cost a egotiable US$8 to US$15 per day. To take one around the countryside from the capital you will have to include expenses for travel, food and accommodation. In an aimag capital, a guide (if you can find one) costs about US$5 per day, plus any expenses. For a professional guide who is knowledgeable in a specific interest, such as bird-watching, and fluent in your language, the bidding starts at US$20 per day.

HAZARDS

Flat tyres are a time-honoured tradition. Insist that your driver bring a spare and a tyre-patch kit consisting of rubber patches, glue, extra tyre valves and a valve tool. Be sure the driver has a tyre pump, hydraulic jack and tyre irons. If the driver doesn't have a useable spare tyre, request that they buy one before leaving the city.

The quickest distance between two points is a straight line, and the only thing that could (but not always) put off a Mongolian jeep driver from taking a shortcut is a huge mountain range or raging river. If renting a jeep by the kilometre, you will welcome a shortcut, especially to shorten an uncomfortable trip. If you have an experienced driver, allow them to take shortcuts when they feel it is worthwhile, but don't insist on any – they are the expert. The downside of shortcuts is the possibility of breaking down on more isolated roads.

Serious mechanical breakdowns are a definite possibility. Should your vehicle break down irreparably in a rural area, you'll be faced with the task of trying to get back to civilisation either on foot (not recommended), by

TRANSPORT

GPS COORDINATES TABLE

The table shows latitude and longitude coordinates for various locations in Mongolia, in degrees, minutes and decimal minutes (DMM). To convert to degrees, minutes and seconds (DMS) format, multiply the number after the decimal point (including the decimal point) by 60. The result is your seconds, which can be rounded to the nearest whole number. The minutes is the number between the degree symbol and the decimal point. For example: 43°52.598′ DMM is equal to 43°52′36″ DMS.

CENTRAL MONGOLIA	Latitude (N)	Longitude (E)
Arvaikheer	46°15.941	102°46.724
Bat-Ölzii	46°49.028	102°13.989
Battsengel	47°48.157	101°59.040
Bayan-Öndör	46°30.018	104°05.996
Bayan Önjuul	46°52.859	105°56.571
Bayangol	45°48.505	103°26.811
Bayantsagaan	46°45.806	107°08.709
Bogd	44°39.971	102°08.777
Burenbayan Ulaan	45°10.276	101°25.989
Chuluut	47°32.830	100°13.166
Delgerkhan	46°37.097	104°33.051
Eej Khad (Mother Rock)	47°18.699	106°58.583
Erdenemandal	48°31.445	101°22.265
Erdenesant	47°19.071	104°28.937
Guchin Us	45°27.866	102°23.726
Gunjiin Süm	48°11.010	107°33.377
Ikh Tamir	47°35.221	101°12.413
Jargalant	48°43.716	100°45.120
Khandgait	48°07.066	106°54.296
Khangai	47°51.553	99°26.126
Kharkhorin	47°11.981	102°50.527
Khashant	47°27.034	103°09.708
Khotont	47°22.196	102°28.746
Khujirt	46°54.225	102°46.545
Khustain National Park	47°45.459	105°52.418
Mandshir Khiid	47°45.520	106°59.675
Möngönmorit	48°12.192	108°28.291
Naiman Nuur	46°31.232	101°50.705
Ögii Nuur (Lake)	47°47.344	102°45.828
Ögii Nuur	47°40.319	102°33.051
Ölziit	48°05.573	102°32.640
Ondor Ulaan	48°02.700	100°30.446
Orkhon Khürkhree	46°47.234	101°57.694
Övgön Khiid	47°25.561	103°41.686
Stele of Tonyukuk	47°41.661	107°28.586
Tariat	48°09.574	99°52.982
Terelj	47°59.193	107°27.834
Tögrög	45°32.482	102°59.657
Tövkhön Khiid	47°00.772	102°15.362
Tsakhir	49°06.426	99°08.574
Tsenkher	47°26.909	101°45.648
Tsetseguun Uul	47°48.506	107°00.165
Tsetserleg City	47°28.561	101°27.282
Tsetserleg Soum	48°53.095	101°14.305
Ulaanbaatar	47°55.056	106°55.007
Uyanga	46°27.431	102°16.731
Zaamar	48°11.843	104°46.629
Züünbayan-Ulaan	46°31.176	102°34.971
Zuunmod	47°42.357	106°56.861

EASTERN MONGOLIA	Latitude (N)	Longitude (E)
Asgat	46°21.724	113°34.536
Baldan Baraivan Khiid	48°11.910	109°25.840
Baruun-Urt	46°40.884	113°16.825
Batnorov	47°56.952	111°30.103
Batshireet	48°41.405	110°11.062
Bayan Tumen	48°03.076	114°22.252
Bayan Uul	49°07.550	112°42.809
Bayandun	49°15.276	113°21.565
Binder	48°36.967	110°36.400
Chinggis Statue	47°06.157	109°09.356
Choibalsan	48°04.147	114°31.404
Chuluunkhoroot	49°52.163	115°43.406
Dadal	49°01.291	111°37.598
Dashbalbar	49°32.794	114°24.720
Delgerkhaan	47°10.735	109°11.423
Erdenetsagaan	45°54.165	115°22.149
Galshar	46°13.324	110°50.606
Khalkhgol	47°59.565	118°05.760
Khalzan	46°10.019	112°57.119
Kherlen Bar Khot	48°03.287	113°21.865
Khökh Nuur (Blue Lake)	48°01.150	108°56.450
Matad	46°57.007	115°16.008
Mönkh Khaan	46°58.163	112°03.418
Norovlin	48°41.449	111°59.596
Öglöchiin Kherem	48°24.443	110°11.812
Ömnödelger	47°53.469	109°49.166
Öndörkhaan	47°19.071	110°39.775

	Latitude (N)	Longitude (E)
Ongon	45°21.509	113°08.297
Shilin Bogd	45°28.350	114°35.349
Sükhbaatar	46°46.285	113°52.646
Sümber	47°38.174	118°36.421
Tsagaan Ovoo	48°33.864	113°14.380
Tsenkhermandal	47°44.673	109°03.909
Uul Bayan	46°30.036	112°20.769

NORTHERN MONGOLIA	Latitude (N)	Longitude (E)
Altanbulag	50°19.225	106°29.392
Amarbayasgalant Khiid	49°28.648	105°05.122
Arbulag	49°54.949	99°26.537
Baruunburen	49°09.753	104°48.686
Bayangol	48°55.472	106°05.486
Borsog	50°59.677	100°42.983
Bugat	49°02.874	103°40.389
Bulgan City	48°48.722	103°32.213
Chandman-Öndör	50°28.436	106°56.378
Chuluut and Ider	49°10.415	100°40.335
Darkhan	49°29.232	105°56.480
Dashchoinkhorlon Khiid	48°47.821	103°30.687
Dashinchilen	47°51.179	104°02.891
Dulaankhaan	49°55.103	106°11.302
Erdenebulgan	50°06.880	101°35.589
Erdenet	49°01.855	104°03.316
Five Rivers	49°15.475	100°40.385
Gurvanbulag	47°44.499	103°30.103
Jiglegiin Am	51°00.406	100°16.003
Khangal	49°18.810	104°22.629
Khankh	51°30.070	100°41.382
Khar Bukh Balgas	47°53.198	103°53.513
Khatgal	50°26.517	100°09.599
Khishig-Öndör	48°17.678	103°27.086
Khötöl	49°05.486	105°34.903
Khutag-Öndör	49°22.990	102°41.417
Mogod	48°16.372	102°59.520
Mörön	49°38.143	100°09.321
Orkhon	49°08.621	105°24.891
Orkhontuul	48°49.202	104°49.920
Renchinkhumbe	51°06.504	99°40.234
Saikhan	48°39.448	102°37.851
Selenge	49°26.647	103°58.903
Shine-Ider	48°57.213	99°32.297
Sükhbaatar	50°14.196	106°11.911
Teshig	49°57.649	102°35.657
Toilogt	50°39.266	100°14.961
Tosontsengel	49°28.650	100°53.074
Tsagaan Uur	50°32.391	101°31.806
Tsagaannuur (Khövsgöl)	51°21.778	99°21.082
Tsagaannuur (Selenge)	50°05.835	105°25.989
Tsetserleg	49°31.959	97°40.311
Ulaan Uul	50°40.668	99°13.920
Uran Uul	48°59.855	102°44.003
Züünkharaa	48°51.466	106°27.154

THE GOBI	Latitude (N)	Longitude (E)
Altai City	46°22.388	96°15.164
Altai Soum	44°37.010	94°55.131
Altanshiree	45°32.046	110°27.017
Baatsagaan	45°33.266	99°26.188
Baga Gazryn Chuluu	46°13.827	106°04.192
Bayan Dalai	43°27.898	103°30.763
Bayan-Ovoo	42°58.607	106°06.994
Bayan-Uul	46°59.129	95°11.863
Bayanbulag	46°48.223	98°06.189
Bayangovi	44°44.017	100°23.476
Bayankhongor	46°11.637	100°43.115
Bayanlig	44°32.555	100°49.809
Bayanzag	44°08.311	103°43.667
Biger	45°42.583	97°10.354
Bömbogor	46°12.279	99°37.234
Böön Tsagaan Nuur	45°37.114	99°15.350
Bugat	45°33.440	94°20.511
Bulgan	44°05.312	103°32.297
Buutsagaan	46°10.411	98°41.637
Choir	45°47.994	108°18.462
Dalanzadgad	43°34.355	104°25.673
Delger	46°21.074	97°27.011
Delgerekh	45°48.157	111°12.823
Erdenedalai	46°00.418	104°56.996

	Latitude (N)	Longitude (E)
Erdentsogt	46°25.080	100°49.234
Galuut	46°42.061	100°07.131
Govi-Ugtal	46°01.916	107°30.377
Gurj Lamiin Khiid	43°29.030	103°50.930
Gurvantes	43°13.759	101°03.360
Jargalant	47°01.480	99°30.103
Khamaryn Khiid	44°36.038	110°16.650
Khanbogd	43°12.000	107°11.862
Khatanbulag	43°08.882	109°08.709
Khökhmorit	47°21.248	94°30.446
Khövsgöl	43°36.314	109°39.017
Khüreemaral	46°24.523	98°17.037
Mandakh	44°24.122	108°13.851
Mandal-Ovoo	44°39.100	104°02.880
Mandalgov	45°46.042	106°16.380
Manlai	44°04.441	106°51.703
Nomgon	42°50.160	105°08.983
Ondorshil	45°13.585	108°15.223
Ongiin Khiid	45°20.367	104°00.306
Orog Nuur	45°02.692	100°36.314
Saikhan-Ovoo	45°27.459	103°54.110
Sainshand	44°53.576	110°08.351
Sevrei	43°35.617	102°09.737
Shinejist	44°32.917	99°17.349
Süm Khökh Burd	46°09.621	105°45.590
Taishhir	46°42.671	96°29.623
Takhi Research Station	45°32.197	93°39.055
Tsagaan Agui	44°42.604	101°10.187
Tseel	45°33.266	95°51.723
Tsogt	46°37.333	96°37.166
Tsogt-Ovoo	44°24.906	105°19.406
Tsogttsetsii	43°43.541	105°35.040
Ulaanbadrakh	43°52.598	110°24.686
Yolyn Am	43°29.332	104°04.000
Zag	46°56.168	99°09.806
Zamyn-Üüd	43°42.967	111°54.651

WESTERN MONGOLIA	Latitude (N)	Longitude (E)
Altai	45°49.115	92°15.497
Altantsgets	49°02.700	100°26.057
Batuunturuun	49°38.578	94°23.177
Bulgan (Bayan-Ölgii)	46°55.559	91°04.594
Bulgan (Khovd)	46°05.486	91°32.571
Chandmani	43°39.100	92°48.411
Darvi	46°56.181	93°37.158
Deluun	47°51.553	90°44.160
Dörgon	48°19.768	92°37.303
Erdeneburen	48°30.131	91°26.811
Erdenkhairkhan	48°07.228	95°44.229
Khökh Nuur	47°37.207	97°20.546
Khovd (Uvs)	49°16.720	90°54.720
Khovd City	48°00.430	91°38.474
Mankhan	47°24.557	92°12.617
Möst	46°41.626	92°48.000
Naranbulag	49°23.164	92°34.286
Nogoonuur	49°36.923	90°13.577
Ölgii (Uvs)	49°01.306	92°00.411
Ölgii City	48°58.070	89°58.028
Öndörkhangai	49°15.849	94°51.154
Otgon	47°12.488	97°36.391
Sagsai	48°54.688	88°39.429
Telmen	48°38.197	97°09.900
Tes	49°39.013	95°49.029
Tolbo	48°24.557	90°16.457
Tolbo Nuur	48°35.320	90°04.536
Tosontsengel	48°45.286	98°05.992
Tsagaanchuluut	47°06.531	96°39.497
Tsagaankhairkhan	49°24.209	94°13.440
Tsagaannuur	49°31.437	89°46.697
Tsengel	48°57.213	89°09.257
Tsenkheriin Agui	47°20.828	91°57.225
Tüdevtei	48°59.390	96°32.229
Ulaangom	49°58.764	92°04.028
Ulaankhus	49°02.525	89°26.929
Uliastai	47°44.591	96°50.582
Urgamal	48°30.653	94°16.046
Üüreg Nuur	50°05.236	91°04.587
Zavkhan (Uvs)	48°49.463	93°06.103
Zavkhanmandal	48°19.071	95°06.789

tching, or by whatever means is available. he safest solution is to travel with a small oup using two jeeps (or bring a satellite 1one; see p260).

A warning: Russian jeeps easily overheat. here is no easy solution, but it helps to travel uring the early-morning or late-afternoon urs when temperatures are relatively low.

Most of Mongolia is grassland, desert and ountains. You might think that mountain riving would pose the worst problems, but rests cause the most trouble of all. This is cause the ground, even on a slope, is often springy alpine bog, holding huge amounts water in the decaying grasses, which are stantly compacted under tyres, reducing a ildflower meadow to slush.

Mongolian drivers have one of two reac- ons when they get bogged. Some will sit on eir haunches, have a smoke and then send ord to the nearest farm or town for a trac- r to come and tow the vehicle out. Other rivers will get out a shovel and start digging; u can help by gathering flat stones to place nder the wheels (drivers usually try to jack e tyres out of the mud).

TAXI

Mongolia claims to have about 49,250km of highway – of which only around 1900km is actually paved. Taxis are only useful along these paved roads, eg from Ulaanbaatar to Zuunmod, Terelj, Darkhan, Erdenet and pos- sibly Kharkhorin. But just as a Humvee is impractical on Hong Kong's backstreets, so is a Hyundai-style taxi on the unpaved steppes. The general appalling quality of roads around the countryside means that most travel is by jeep or Furgon minivan.

TRAIN

The 1810km of railway line is primarily made up of the Trans-Mongolian Railway, connect- ing China with Russia. (Both the domestic and international trains use this same line.) In addition, there are two spur lines: to the copper-mining centre of Erdenet (from Darkhan) and the coal-mining city of Baganuur (from Ulaanbaatar). Another train runs weekly from Choibalsan, the capital of Dornod aimag, to the Russian border.

From Ulaanbaatar, daily express trains travel north to Darkhan, and on to Sükhbaatar

TRANSPORT

ROAD DISTANCES (km)

	Altai (Gov-Altai aimag)	Arvaikheer	Baruun-Urt	Bayankhongor	Bulgan	Choibalsan	Dalanzadgad	Darkhan	Khovd	Mandalgov	Mörön (Khövsgöl aimag)	Ölgii	Öndörkhaan	Sainshand	Sükhbaatar	Tsetserleg	Ulaanbaatar	Ulaangom
Arvaikheer	571																	
Baruun-Urt	1561	990																
Bayankhongor	371	200	1190															
Bulgan	874	373	878	503														
Choibalsan	1656	1085	191	1285	973													
Dalanzadgad	948	377	856	577	725	1074												
Darkhan	1122	596	779	751	248	874	772											
Khovd	424	995	1985	795	1180	2080	1372	1519										
Mandalgov	879	308	613	508	578	741	293	479	1303									
Mörön (Khövsgöl aimag)	583	679	1231	627	353	1326	1056	601	853	913								
Ölgii	635	1206	2196	1006	1344	2291	1583	1582	211	1314	991							
Öndörkhaan	1332	761	229	961	649	324	710	550	1756	417	1002	1967						
Sainshand	1234	663	340	863	781	531	516	682	1658	355	1134	1869	302					
Sükhbaatar	1214	688	871	830	340	966	864	92	1612	571	693	1823	642	774				
Tsetserleg	502	266	1013	218	289	1108	643	537	438	500	413	1220	784	855	629			
Ulaanbaatar	1001	430	560	630	326	655	553	219	1425	260	671	1636	331	463	311	430		
Ulaangom	662	1188	1896	988	1033	991	1585	1281	238	1383	680	311	1667	1738	1373	883	1336	
Uliastai	218	659	1544	497	807	1639	1074	989	465	967	388	676	1315	1355	1147	531	984	529

or Erdenet. To the south, there are daily direct trains from Ulaanbaatar to Zamyn-Üüd, via Choir and Sainshand. There are also trains terminating at Choir twice a week. You can't use the Trans-Mongolian Railway for domestic transport.

When travelling in hard-seat class (see below), you will almost certainly have to fight to get a seat. If you're not travelling alone, one of you can scramble on board and find seats and the other can bring the luggage on board. Young boys and girls usually travel around the train selling bread and fizzy drinks. Otherwise, there is nothing to eat or drink on local trains.

Classes

There are usually three classes on domestic passenger trains: hard seat, hard sleeper and soft seat. In hard-seat class, the seats are actually padded bunks but there are no assigned bunks nor any limit to the amount of tickets sold, so the carriages are always crowded and dirty. A hard sleeper *(platzkartnuu)* looks just like the hard seat but everyone gets their own bunk and there is the option of getting a s of sheets and a blanket (T900). Upgrades a available to soft seat if you decide you ca stand the hard seats.

Soft seats are only a little bit softer, but t conditions are much better: the price diffe ence (usually at least double the price of t hard seat) is prohibitive for most Mongoliar The soft-seat carriages are divided into cor partments with four beds in each. You a given an assigned bed, and will be able sleep, assuming, of course, that your cor partment mates aren't rip-roaring drunk ar noisy. If you travel at night, clean sheets a provided for about T900, which is a wise i vestment since some of the quilts smell li mutton. Compared with hard-seat class, i the lap of luxury, and worth paying extra.

If you're travelling from Ulaanbaatar, it important to book a soft seat well in advance this can be done up to 10 days before depa ture. There may be a small booking fee. general, booking ahead is a good idea for a class, though there will always be hard-se tickets available.

Health

CONTENTS

Mongolia's dry, cold climate and sparse human habitation means there are few of the infectious diseases that plague tropical countries in Asia. The rough-and-tumble landscape and lifestyle, however, presents challenges of its own. Injuries sustained from falling off a horse are common in the summer season. In winter, the biggest threats are the flu and pneumonia, which spread like wildfire in November.

The biggest risk to your health in Mongolia may be the hospitals. The number of doctors is chronically low and the standard of medical training is patchy at best, and often very poor. If you do become seriously ill in Mongolia, your local embassy can provide details of Western doctors. Emergencies require evacuation to Seoul or Beijing. If in the countryside, make a beeline for Ulaanbaatar to have your ailment diagnosed.

The following advice is a general guide only; be sure to seek the advice of a doctor trained in travel medicine.

BEFORE YOU GO

Prevention is the key to staying healthy while abroad. A little planning before departure, particularly for pre-existing illnesses, will save trouble later. See your dentist before going on a long trip, carry a spare pair of contact lenses and glasses, and take your optical prescription with you. Bring medications in their original, clearly labelled containers. A signed and dated letter from your physician describing your medical conditions and medications, including generic names, is also a good idea. If carrying syringes or needles, be sure to have a physician's letter documenting their medical necessity.

Western medicine can be in short supply in Mongolia. Most medicine comes from China and Russia and the labels won't be in English, so bring whatever you think you might need from home. Take extra supplies of prescribed medicine and divide it into separate pieces of luggage; that way if one piece goes astray, you'll still have a back-up supply.

INSURANCE

If your health insurance does not cover you for medical expenses abroad, consider supplemental insurance. (Check the Lonely Planet website at www.lonelyplanet.com/travel_services for more information.)

While you may prefer a policy that pays hospital bills on the spot, rather than paying first and sending in documents later, in Mongolia the only place that might accept this is the SOS Medica clinic (see p66).

Declare any existing medical conditions to the insurance company; if your problem is pre-existing the company will not cover you if it is not declared. You may require extra cover for adventurous activities – make sure you are covered for a fall if you plan on riding a horse or a motorbike. If you are uninsured, emergency evacuation is expensive, with bills over US$100,000 not uncommon.

RECOMMENDED VACCINATIONS

The **World Health Organization** (WHO; www.who.int) recommends that all travellers be covered for diphtheria, tetanus, measles, mumps, rubella and polio, regardless of their destination. As most vaccines don't produce immunity until at least two weeks after they're given, visit a physician at least six weeks before departure. Specialised travel-medicine clinics are your best source of information; they stock vaccines and will be able to give specific

HEALTH

recommendations for you and your trip. This is especially important for children and pregnant women. Ask your doctor for an International Certificate of Vaccination (otherwise known as the yellow booklet) which will list all of the vaccinations yo have received, and take it with you.

INTERNET RESOURCES

There is a wealth of travel health advice o the internet. For further information, th Lonely Planet website at www.lonelyplane .com is a good place to start. The WHO publishes a superb book called International Travel & Health, which is revised annuall and is available online at no cost at www .who.int/ith. Another website of general in terest is MD Travel Health at www.mdtrave health.com, which provides complete trave health recommendations for every countr and is updated daily.

FURTHER READING

Lonely Planet's Healthy Travel Asia & Indi is a handy pocket size and packed wit useful information including pre-trip plan ning, emergency first aid, immunisation an disease information, and what to do if yo get sick on the road. Other recommende references include Traveller's Health by D Richard Dawood and Travelling Well by D Deborah Mills (www.travellingwell.com.au Lonely Planet's Travel with Children is usefu for families.

> ### MEDICAL KIT CHECK LIST
>
> Following is a list of items you should consider including in your medical kit – consult your pharmacist for brands available in your country.
>
> - Antibacterial cream (eg Muciprocin)
> - Antibiotics (prescription only) – for travel well 'off the beaten track' carry the prescription with you in case you need it refilled
> - Antifungal cream or powder (eg Clotrimazole) – for fungal skin infections and thrush
> - Antinausea medication (eg Prochlorperazine)
> - Antiseptic (such as povidone-iodine) – for cuts and grazes
> - Aspirin or paracetamol (acetaminophen in the USA) – for pain or fever
> - Bandages, Band-Aids (plasters) and other wound dressings
> - Calamine lotion, sting-relief spray or aloe vera – to ease irritation from sunburn and insect bites or stings
> - Cold and flu tablets, throat lozenges and nasal decongestant
> - Insect repellent (DEET-based)
> - Loperamide or diphenoxylate – 'blockers' for diarrhoea
> - Multivitamins – consider for long trips, when dietary vitamin intake may be inadequate
> - Rehydration mixture (eg Gastrolyte) – to prevent dehydration, which may occur during bouts of diarrhoea (particularly important when travelling with children)
> - Scissors, tweezers and a thermometer – note that mercury thermometers are prohibited by airlines
> - Sunscreen, lip balm and eye drops
> - Water purification tablets or iodine (iodine is not to be used by pregnant women or people with thyroid problems)

IN TRANSIT

DEEP VEIN THROMBOSIS (DVT)

Blood clots may form in the legs during plane flights, chiefly because of prolonge immobility. The longer the flight, the greate the risk. The chief symptom of DVT swelling or pain of the foot, ankle, or ca usually but not always on just one sid When a blood clot travels to the lungs, may cause chest pain and breathing difficu ties. Travellers with any of these symptom should immediately seek medical attentio

To prevent the development of DV on long flights you should walk regular about the cabin, contract the leg muscle while sitting, drink plenty of fluids an avoid alcohol.

JET LAG & MOTION SICKNESS

To avoid jet lag (common when crossin more than five time zones) try to drin plenty of nonalchoholic fluids and eat ligh

HEALTH

REQUIRED & RECOMMENDED VACCINATIONS

The WHO recommends the following vaccinations for travel to Mongolia:

Adult Diphtheria & Tetanus Single booster recommended if none in the previous 10 years. Side effects include sore arm and fever.

Hepatitis A Provides almost 100% protection for up to a year; a booster after 12 months provides at least another 20 years' protection. Mild side effects such as headache and sore arm occur with some people.

Hepatitis B Now considered routine for most travellers, it provides lifetime protection for 95% of people. Immunisation is given as three doses over six months, though a rapid schedule is also available, as is a combined vaccination for Hepatitis A. Side effects are mild and uncommon, usually headache and sore arm.

Measles, Mumps & Rubella (MMR) Two doses of MMR are recommended unless you have had the diseases. Occasionally a rash and flu-like illness can develop a week after receiving the vaccine. Many young adults need a booster.

Typhoid Recommended unless your trip is less than a week. The vaccine offers around 70% protection, lasts for two to three years and comes as a single dose. Tablets are also available, although the injection is usually recommended as it has fewer side effects. A sore arm and fever may occur.

Varicella If you haven't had chickenpox discuss this vaccination with your doctor.

The following are recommended for long-term travellers (more than one month) or those at special risk:

Influenza A single jab lasts one year and is recommended for those over 65 years of age or with underlying medical conditions such as heart or lung disease.

Japanese B Encephalitis Involves a series of three injections with a booster after two years. Recommended if spending more than one month in rural areas in the summer months.

Pneumonia A single injection with a booster after five years is recommended for all travellers over 65 years of age or with underlying medical conditions that compromise immunity, such as heart or lung disease, cancer or HIV.

Rabies Three injections are required. A booster after one year will then provide 10 years' protection. Side effects are rare – occasionally headache and sore arm.

Tuberculosis (TB) A complex issue. High-risk adult long-term travellers are usually recommended to have a TB skin test before and after travel, rather than a vaccination. Only one vaccine is given in a lifetime. Children under five spending more than three months in China and/or Mongolia should be vaccinated.

eals. Upon arrival, get exposure to natu-l sunlight and readjust your schedule (for eals, sleep etc) as soon as possible.

Antihistamines such as dimenhydrinate)ramamine) and meclizine (Antivert, onine) are usually the first choice for eating motion sickness. A herbal alterna-ve is ginger.

N MONGOLIA

VAILABILITY & COST OF HEALTH CARE

ealth care is readily available in Ulaan-aatar, but choose your hospital and doctor arefully. Ordinary Mongolians won't now the best place to go, but a reputable avel agency or top-end hotel might. The est advice will come from your embassy. onsultations cost around US$5, although)S Medica, a reliable clinic in Ulaanbaatar ith Western doctors, charges around $200. Iost basic drugs are available without a pre-scription. See p66 for more details. Health services in the countryside are abysmal or nonexistent. Taking very small children to the countryside is therefore risky. Female travellers will need to take pads and tampons with them on a trip as these won't be available outside the main cities.

INFECTIOUS DISEASES
Brucellosis

The UN Food & Agricultural Organization (FAO) reports that Mongolia is a high-risk area for brucellosis. This is a disease of cattle yaks, camels and sheep but it can also affect humans. The most likely way for humans to contract this disease is by drinking unboiled milk or eating home-made cheese. People with open cuts on their hands who handle freshly killed meat can also be infected.

In humans, brucellosis causes severe headaches, joint and muscle pains, fever and fatigue. There may be diarrhoea and, later, constipation. The onset of the symptoms

HEALTH

can occur from five days to several months after exposure, with the average time being two weeks.

Most patients recover in two or three weeks, but people can get chronic brucellosis, which recurs sporadically for months or years and can cause long-term health problems. Fatalities are rare but possible.

Brucellosis is a serious disease which requires blood tests to make the diagnosis. If you think you may have contracted the disease seek medical attention, preferably outside Mongolia.

Bubonic Plague

This disease (which wiped out one-third of Europe during the Middle Ages) makes an appearance in remote parts of Mongolia in late summer. Almost 90% of reported cases occur in August and September.

The disease (also known as the Black Plague) is normally carried by marmots, squirrels and rats and can be transmitted to humans by bites from fleas that make their home on the infected animals. It can also be passed from human to human by coughing. The symptoms are fever and enlarged lymph nodes. The untreated disease has a 60% death rate, but if you get to a doctor it can be quickly treated. The best drug is the antibiotic streptomycin, which must be injected intramuscularly, but it is not available in Mongolia. Tetracycline is another drug that may be used.

During an outbreak, travel to infected areas is prohibited, which can greatly affect overland travel. All trains, buses and cars travelling into Ulaanbaatar from infected areas are also thoroughly checked when an outbreak of the plague has been reported, and vehicles are sprayed with disinfectant.

Hepatitis

This is a general term for inflammation of the liver. It is a common disease worldwide. The symptoms are similar in all forms of the illness, and include fever, chills, headache, fatigue, aches and pains and feelings of weakness, followed by loss of appetite, nausea, vomiting, abdominal pain, dark urine, light-coloured faeces, jaundiced (yellow) skin and yellowing of the whites of the eyes. People who have hepatitis should avoid alcohol for some time after the illness, as the liver needs time to recover.

Hepatitis A is transmitted by contaminated food and drinking water. You should seek medical advice, but there is not much you can do apart from resting, drinking lots of fluids, eating lightly and avoiding fatty food. Hepatitis E is transmitted in the same way as hepatitis A; it can be particularly serious in pregnant women.

Hepatitis B is endemic in Mongolia. It is spread through contact with infected blood, blood products or body fluids. The symptoms of hepatitis B may be more severe than type A and the disease can lead to long-term problems such as chronic liver damage, liver cancer or long-term carrier state. Hepatitis C and D are spread in the same way as hepatitis B and can also lead to long-term complications.

There are vaccines against hepatitis A and B, but there are currently no vaccines against the other types of hepatitis.

Rabies

In the Mongolian countryside, family dogs are often vicious and can be rabid; it is their saliva that is infectious. Any bite, scratch or even a lick from an animal should be cleaned immediately and thoroughly. Scrub with soap and running water, and then apply alcohol or iodine solution. Medical help should be sought promptly to receive a course of injections to prevent the onset of the symptoms and death. The incubation period for rabies depends on where you're bitten. On the head, face or neck it's as little as 10 days, whereas on the legs it's 60 days.

Sexually Transmitted Diseases (STDs)

The most common STDs in Mongolia include herpes, syphilis, gonorrhoea and chlamydia. People carrying these diseases often have no signs of infection. Condoms will prevent gonorrhoea and chlamydia but not syphilis or herpes. If after any sexual encounter you develop any rash, lumps, discharge or pain when passing urine seek immediate medical attention. If you have been sexually active during your travels, have an STD check upon your return.

Tuberculosis (TB)

TB is a bacterial infection usually transmitted from person to person by coughing but which may be transmitted through consumption of unpasteurised milk. Milk that has been boiled is safe to drink, and the souring of milk

---

DRINKING WATER

- Bottled water is generally safe – check that the seal is intact at purchase.

- Tap water in Ulaanbaatar and other cities probably won't make you sick but because of antiquated plumbing the water may contain traces of metals which won't be good for your long-term health.

- Be cautious about drinking from streams and lakes as they are easily polluted by livestock. Water is usually OK if you can get it high up in the mountains, near the source. If in doubt, boil your water.

- The best chemical purifier is iodine. It should not be used by pregnant women or those with thyroid problems.

- Water filters should filter out viruses. Ensure your filter has a chemical barrier such as iodine and a small pore size (eg less than four microns).

...ake yogurt or cheese also kills the bacilli. ...ravellers are usually not at great risk as close ...ousehold contact with an infected person is ...ally required before the disease is passed ...n. You may need to have a TB test before you ...avel as this can help diagnose the disease ...ter if you become ill.

TRAVELLER'S DIARRHOEA

...o prevent diarrhoea, avoid tap water un-...ss it has been boiled, filtered or chemically ...isinfected (with iodine tablets), and steer ...ear of ice. Only eat fresh fruits or vegeta-...les if cooked or peeled, and be wary of dairy ...roducts that might contain unpasteurised ...ilk. Eat food that is hot through and avoid ...uffet-style meals.

If you develop diarrhoea, be sure to drink ...lenty of nonalcoholic fluids, preferably an ...ral rehydration solution (eg Dioralyte). A ...w loose stools don't require treatment, but ...you start having more than four or five ...day, you should start taking an antibiotic ...sually a quinolone drug) and an antidiar-...oeal agent (such as Loperamide). If diar-...oea is bloody, persists for more than 72 ...ours or is accompanied by fever, shaking, ...ills or severe abdominal pain you should ...ek medical attention.

Giardiasis is a parasite that is relatively ...ommon in travellers. Symptoms include ...ausea, bloating, excess gas, fatigue and in-...rmittent diarrhoea. 'Eggy' burps are often ...tributed solely to giardiasis, but may not be ...ecific to giardiasis. The parasite will eventu-...ly go away if left untreated, but this can take ...onths. The treatment of choice is tinidazole; ...etronidazole is a second option.

ENVIRONMENTAL HAZARDS
Altitude Sickness

Except in rare cases, only mountaineers will experience altitude sickness in Mongolia. Mild symptoms include headache, lethargy, dizziness, difficulty sleeping and loss of appetite. Treat mild symptoms by resting at the same altitude until recovery – usually a day or two. Paracetamol or aspirin can be taken for headaches. If symptoms persist or become worse, however, immediate descent is necessary; even 500m can help.

Heatstroke

This serious, occasionally fatal, condition can occur if the body's heat-regulating mechanism breaks down and the body temperature rises to dangerous levels. Long, continuous exposure to high temperatures and insufficient fluids can leave you vulnerable to heatstroke.

The symptoms are feeling unwell, not sweating very much (or at all) and a high body temperature. Where sweating has ceased, the skin becomes flushed and red. Victims can become confused, aggressive or delirious. Get victims out of the sun, remove their clothing and cover them with a wet sheet or towel and fan continually. Give fluids if they are conscious.

Hypothermia

In a country where temperatures can plummet to -40°C, cold is something you should take seriously. If you are trekking at high altitudes or simply taking a long bus trip across the country, particularly at night, be especially prepared. Even in the lowlands,

HEALTH

sudden winds from the north can send the temperature plummeting.

Hypothermia occurs when the body loses heat faster than it can produce it and the core temperature of the body falls. It is best to dress in layers; silk, wool and some of the new artificial fibres are all good insulting materials. A hat is important, as a lot of heat is lost through the head. A strong, waterproof outer layer is essential (and a 'space' blanket for emergencies if trekking). Carry basic supplies, including food containing simple sugars to generate heat quickly and fluid to drink.

Bites & Stings

Bee and wasp stings are usually painful rather than dangerous. Calamine lotion or sting-relief spray will give relief and ice packs will reduce the pain and swelling. However, people who are allergic to bees and wasps may suffer severe breathing difficulties and require urgent medical care.

Mongolia has four species of venomous snakes: the Halys viper *(agkistrodon halys)*, common European viper or adder *(vipera berus)*, Orsini's viper *(vipera ursine)* and the small *taphrometaphon lineolatum*. To minimise your chances of being bitten always wear boots, socks and long trousers where snakes may be present. Don't put your hand into holes and crevices, and be careful whe collecting firewood.

Bedbugs live in various places, but par ticularly in dirty mattresses and bedding evidenced by spots of blood on bedclothes c on the wall. Bedbugs leave itchy bites in nea rows. Calamine lotion or a sting-relief spra may help. All lice cause itching and discom fort. They make themselves at home in you hair, your clothing, or in your pubic hair. Yo catch lice through direct contact with infecte people or by sharing combs, clothing and th like. Powder or shampoo treatment will ki the lice and infected clothing should then b washed in very hot, soapy water and left i the sun to dry.

TRADITIONAL MEDICINE

Traditional medicine has made a comebac in Mongolia, after suppression during com munism. Medicine often involves the use c native herbs, ground-up rock or bone, an even the swallowing of prayers written on tin pieces of paper. Lamas are often employe to read prayers for the sick. Tradition medicine here is based on both Chinese an Tibetan practices. In Ulaanbaatar, there a traditional-medicine clinics at the Baku Rinpoche Süm (see p76).

Language

CONTENTS

Mongolian is a member of the Ural-Altaic family of languages, which includes Finnish, Hungarian, Turkish, Kazakh, Usbek and Korean. The traditional Mongolian script looks like Arabic turned 45 degrees, and is still used by the Mongolians living in China (Inner Mongolia, parts of Xinjiang, Qinhai, Liaoning and Jilin). In 1944 the Russian Cyrillic alphabet was adopted, with the two additional characters, ө and ү. It remains in use today in Mongolia and also in two autonomous republics of Russia: Buryatia and Kalmykia.

Mongolian also has a Romanised form, though the 35 Cyrillic characters give a better representation of Mongolian sounds than the 26 of the Roman alphabet. Partly a result of Russian influence, different Romanisation schemes have been used, and this has caused widespread confusion. A loose standard was adopted in 1987, so the capital city previously written as 'Ulan Bator' (transliterated Russian spelling), is now Ulaanbaatar.

Mongolian pronunciation is not easy. In the words of travel writer Tim Severin, the Mongolian language is '...like two cats coughing and spitting at each other until one finally throws up'. One particular word, which conveys agreement (rather like nodding one's head) is little more than a sharp, guttural intake of breath, as if you were having difficulty breathing.

It's important to give double vowels a long pronunciation, as getting it wrong can affect meaning. Syllables marked in italics in the following words and phrases represent word stress. If all vowels in a word are short, the first will take the stress and the rest will become 'neutral' (as the 'a' in 'ago'). In words with a long vowel, stress falls on that vowel and any short vowels in the word will become neutral. If there's more than one long vowel the stress will generally fall on the second-last syllable.

If you'd like a more comprehensive guide to the language, pick up a copy of Lonely Planet's *Mongolian Phrasebook*.

ACCOMMODATION

Can you recommend a good hotel?
Та сайн зочид буудал зааж өгнө үү?
ta *sain* zo·chid *buu*·dal zaaj ög·nö *üü*?

Can you show me on the map?
Та газрын зураг дээр зааж өгнө үү?
ta gaz·*ryn* zu·rag deer zaaj ög·nö *üü*?

Do you have any rooms available?
Танайд сул өрөө байна уу?
ta·*naid* sul ö·*röö* bai·na *uu*?

I'd like a single room.
Би нэг хүний өрөө авмаар байна.
bi neg khü·*nii* ö·*röö* av·*maar* bai·na

I'd like a double room.
Би хоёр хүний өрөө авмаар байна.
bi kho·yor khü·*nii* ö·*röö* av·*maar* bai·na

What's the price per night/week?
Энэ өрөө хоногт/долоо хоногт ямар үнэтэй вэ?
ene ö·*röö* kho·nogt/do·*loo* kho·nogt *ya*·mar ün·*tei* ve?

Can I see the room?
Би энэ өрөөг үзэх болох уу?
bi e·ne ö·*röög* ü·zej *bo*·lokh *uu*?

Are there any others?
Өөр өрөө байна уу?
öör ö·*röö* bai·na *uu*?

LANGUAGE

THE MONGOLIAN CYRILLIC ALPHABET

А а	a	as the 'u' in 'but'
Г г	g	as in 'get'
Ё ё	yo	as in 'yonder'
И и	i	as in 'tin'
Л л	l	as in 'lamp'
О о	o	as in 'hot'
Р р	r	as in 'rub'
У у	u	as in 'rude'
Х х	kh	as the 'ch' in Scottish *loch*
Ш ш	sh	as in 'shoe'
Ы ы	y	as the 'i' in 'ill'
Ю ю	yu	as the 'yo' in 'yoyo'
	yü	long, as the word 'you'
Б б	b	as in 'but'
Д д	d	as in 'dog'
Ж ж	j	as in 'jewel'
Й й	i	as in 'tin'
М м	m	as in 'mat'
Ө ө	ö	long, as the 'u' in 'fur'
С с	s	as in 'sun'
Ү ү	ü	long, as the 'o' in 'who'
Ц ц	ts	as in 'cats'
Щ щ	shch	as the 'shch' in 'fresh chips'
Ь ь		* 'soft sign' (see below)
Я я	ya	as in 'yard'
В в	v	as in 'van'
Е е	ye	as in 'yes'
	yö	as the 'yea' in 'yearn'
З з	z	as the 'ds' in 'suds'
К к	k	as in 'kit'
Н н	n	as in 'neat'
П п	p	as in 'pat'
Т т	t	as in 'tin'
Ф ф	f	as in 'five'
Ч ч	ch	as in 'chat'
Ъ ъ		* 'hard sign' (see below)
Э э	e	as in 'den'

* The letters ь and ъ never occur alone, but simply affect the pronunciation of the previous letter – ь makes the preceding sound soft (the consonant before it is pronounced as if there's a very short 'y' after it), while ъ makes the previous sound hard (it prevents it being pronounced as if there's a 'y' after it).

CONVERSATION & ESSENTIALS
Hello.
Сайн байна уу? sain bai·na *uu*?
(literally: How are you?)
Fine. How are you?
Сайн. Та сайн sain ta sain bai·na *uu*?
байна уу?

What's new?
Сонин сайхан *so*·nin *sai*·khan
юу байна? yu bai·na?
Nothing really.
Тайван сайхан. *tai*·van *sai*·khan
(literally: It's peaceful.)
Goodbye.
Баяртай. ba·yar·*tai*

Yes.	Тийм.	tiim
No.	Үгүй.	ü·*güi*
Thanks.	Баярлалаа.	ba·yar·la·*laa*
Excuse me.	Уучлаарай.	uuch·*laa*·rai

I'm sorry, what did you say?
Уучлаарай, та юу гэж хэлсэн, бэ?
uuch·*laa*·rai ta yu gej khel·sen *be*?
What's your name?
Таны нэрийг хэн гэдэг вэ?
ta·*ny* ne·riig khen ge·deg *ve*?
My name is ...
Миний нэрийг ... гэдэг.
mi·*nii* ne·riig ... ge·deg
What country are you from?
Та аль улсаас ирсэн бэ?
ta a·li ul·*saas* ir·sen *be*?
I'm from ...
Би ... улсаас ирсэн.
bi ... ul·saas *ir*·sen
How old are you?
Та хэдэн настай вэ?
ta *khe*·den nas·*tai* ve?
I'm ... years old.
Би ... настай.
bi ... nas·*tai*
Are you married?
Та гэр бүлтэй юу?
ta ger *bül*·tei *yü*?
No, I'm not.
Үгүй, би гэр бүлгүй.
ü·*güi* bi ger *bul*·güi
Yes, I'm married.
Тийм, би гэр бүлтэй.
tiim bi ger *bül*·tei
Do you have any children?
Та хүүхэдтэй юу?
ta *khüü*·hed·tei *yü*?
Can I take photographs?
Зураг авч болох уу?
zu·rag avch bo·lokh *uu*?
May I take your photograph?
Би таны зургийг авч болох уу?
bi ta·*ny* zur·*giig* avch bo·lokh *uu*?

The Herder's Domain

We'd like to see inside a herder's ger.

Бид малчны гэрт орж үзэх гэсэн юм.

bid malch-*ny* gert orj ü-zekh ge-sen yum

How long will it take to get there?

Тэнд хүрэхэд хир удах вэ?

tend *khü*-re-khed khir u-dakh *ve*?

Can we walk there?

Бид явган явж болох уу?

bid *yav*-gan yavj *bo*-lokh *uu*?

Please hold the dogs!

Нохой хогио!

nok-*hoi* kho-ri-o!

We'd like to drink some airag.

Бид айраг уух гэсэн юм.

bid *ai*-rag uukh ge-sen yum

If you're visiting a family, especially in the country, having agreed that everybody's fine, you should proceed to asking about family members and livestock and only then to more general matters:

How's your family?

Танай гэр бүлийнхэн сайн уу?

ta-*nai* ger bü-*liin*-hen sain *uu*?

I hope your animals are fattening up nicely.

Мал сүрэг тарган тавтай юу?

mal *sü*-reg *tar*-gan tav-*tai* yü?

Are you very busy?

Та ажил ихтэй байна уу?

ta a-jil ikh-tei bai-na *uu*?

I'm very busy.

Би тун завгүй байна.

bi tun *zav*-güi bai-na

cooking pot	тогоо	to-*goo*
powdowing box	араг	a-rag
door	хаалга	*khaal*-ga
felt material	эсгий	es-*gii*
felt roof cover	эсгий дээвэр	es-*gii* dee-ver
ger	гэр	ger
airag bag	хөхүүр	khö-*khüür*
smoke-hole cover in a ger	өрх	örkh
stove	зуух	zuukh
support post	багана	*ba*-ga-na
wooden frame for flue in a ger	тооно	*too*-no
wooden lattice of a ger	хана	kha-na
camel	тэмээ	te-*mee*
chicken	тахиа	*ta*-khia
cow	үнээ	ü-*nee*
donkey	илжиг	*il*-jig
enclosure	малын хашаа	*ma*-lyn kha-*shaa*
goat	ямаа	ya-*maa*
herding (literally: cattle breeding)	мал аж ахуй	mal aj ak-*hui*
horse	морь	*mo*-ri
pig	гахай	ga-*khai*
reindeer	цаа буга	tsaa bu-ga
sheep	хонь	*kho*-ni
summer camp	зуслан	*zus*-lan
yak	сарлаг	*sar*-lag

DIRECTIONS

How can I get to ...?

... руу би яаж очих вэ?

... *ruu* bi yaj o-chikh *ve*?

Is it far?

Хир хол вэ?

khir khol *ve*?

Do you have a (town) map?

Танайд (хотын) зураг байна уу?

ta-*naid* (kho-*tyn*) *zu*-rag bai-na *uu*?

What ... is this?

Энэ ямар ... вэ? e-ne *ya*-mar ... *ve*?

square

талбай — tal-*bai*

street

гудамж — *gu*-damj

suburb

дүүрэг — *düü*-reg

municipality

хотын захиргаа — kho-tyn za-khir-*gaa*

SIGNS

Орох Хаалга	Entrance
Гарах Хаалга	Exit
Орж үолохгүй	No Entry
Гарч үолохгүй	No Exit
Эмэгтэйчүүдийн	Ladies
Эрэгтэйчүүдийн	Gentlemen
Хүнгүй	Vacant
Захиалгатай	Reserved
Касс	Cashier
Лавлах	Information
Шуудан	Post
Такси	Taxi
Хаалттай	Closed
Анхаар	Caution
Засвартай	Under Repair
Тамхи Татахыг Хориглоно	No Smoking
Зураг Авахыг Хориглоно	No Photography

EMERGENCIES

| Help! | Туслаарай! | tus-*laa*-rai! |
| Stop! | Зогс! | zogs! |

Call ...!

| ... дуудаарай! | ... duu-*daa*-rai! |

an ambulance

түргэн тусламж   *tür*-gen *tus*-lamj

a doctor

эмч   emch

the police

цагдаа   tsag-*daa*

I'm ill.

Миний бие өвдөж байна.
mi-*nii* bi-ye *öv*-döj bai-na

Could you please take me to hospital?

Намайг эмнэлэгт хүргэж өгнө үү?
na-*maig* em-ne-legt *khür*-gej ög-nö *üü*?

Could you help me please?

Та надад туслана уу?
ta *na*-dad tsus-la-na *uu*?

I've lost my way.

Би төөрчихлөө.
bi töör-chikh-*löö*

I wish to contact my embassy.

Би элчин сайдын яамтайгаа холбоо
баримаар байна.
bi *el*-chin sai-diin *yaam*-tai-gaa khol-boo
ba-ri-*maar* bai-na

Where's the toilet?

Бие засах газар хаана байдаг вэ?
bi-ye za-sakh ga-zar khaa-na *bai*-dag ve?

north	хойд/умард	khoid/*u*-mard
south	урд/өмнө	urd/*öm*-nö
east	зүүн/дорно	züün/*dor*-no
west	баруун/өрнөд	ba-*ruun*/*ör*-nöd
behind/after	хойно/ард	khoi-no/ard
in front/before	өмнө/урд	*öm*-nö/urd
to the left	зүүн тийш	*züün* tiish
to the right	баруун тийш	ba-*ruun* tiish
straight ahead	чигээрээ	chi-*gee*-ree
	урагшаа	u-rag-*shaa*

LANGUAGE DIFFICULTIES

Do you speak English?

Та англиар ярьдаг уу?
ta an-*gliar* yair-dag *uu*?

Could you speak more slowly?

Та арай аажуухан ярина уу?
ta a-rai *aa*-juu-khan *ya*-ri-na *uu*?

Please point to the phrase in the book.

Та энэ хэллэгийг номон дээр зааж өгнө уу?
ta e-ne khel-le-*giig* no-mon *deer* zaaj ög-nö *uu*?

I understand.

Би ойлголоо.
bi *oil*-go-loo

I don't understand.

Би ойлгохгүй байна.
bi *oil*-gokh-güi bai-na

NUMBERS

0	тэг	teg
1	нэг	neg
2	хоёр	*kho*-yor
3	гурав	*gu*-rav
4	дөрөв	*dö*-röv
5	тав	tav
6	зургаа	zur-*gaa*
7	долоо	do-*loo*
8	найм	naim
9	ес	yös
10	арав	*ar*-av
11	арван нэг	*ar*-van neg
12	арван хоёр	*ar*-van *kho*-yor
13	арван гурав	*ar*-van *gu*-rav
14	арван дөрөв	*ar*-van *dö*-röv
15	арван тав	*ar*-van tav
16	арван зургаа	*ar*-van zur-*gaa*
17	арван долоо	*ar*-van do-*loo*
18	арван найм	*ar*-van naim
19	арван ес	*ar*-van yös
20	хорь	kho-*ri*
21	хорин нэг	*kho*-rin neg
22	хорин хоёр	*kho*-rin *kho*-yor
30	гуч	guch
40	дөч	döch
50	тавч	taiv
60	жар	jar
70	дал	dal
80	ная	naya
90	ер	yör
100	зуу	zuu
101	зуун нэг	zuun neg
1000	мянга	myang-ga
one million	сая	sa-*ya*

SHOPPING & SERVICES

Where's the nearest ...?

Ойрхон ... хаана байнаг вэ?
oir-khon ... khaa-na bai-dag *ve*?

bank

банк   bank

department store

их дэлгүүр   ikh del-*güür*

hotel

зочид буудал   zo-chid *buu*-dal

market

зах   zakh

post office

шуудан   *shuu·dan*

public bathhouse

нийтийн халуун   *nii·tiin kha·luun*

усны газар   *us·ny ga·zar*

When will it open/close?

Хэзээ (онгойх/хаах) вэ?

khe·zee on·(goikh/khaakh) ve?

I'd like to change some money.

Би мөнгө солих гэсэн юм.

bi *möng·*go so·likh *ge·sen yum*

I'd like to change some travellers cheques.

Би чек солих гэсэн юм.

bi chek so·likh *ge·sen yum*

What's the exchange rate?

Солих ханш хэд байна вэ?

*so·*likh khansh hed bai·na *ve?*

TRANSPORT

Where's the ... ?

.. хаана байдаг вэ?

*.. khaa·*na bai·dag *ve?*

train station

галт тэрэгний   *galt te·re·ge·nii*

буудал   *buud·al*

bus station/stop

автобусны буудал   av·*to*·bus·ny *buu·*dal

trolley-bus stop

троллейбусны   *trol·lei·*bus·ny

буудал   *buu·*dal

ticket office

тасалбаг түгээгүүр   ta·sal·bag tu·*gee·*güür

How much is it to go to ...?

... хүрэхэд ямар үнэтэй вэ?

*... hu·re·*hed ya·mar ü·ne·*tei ve?*

Can I walk there?

Тийшээ явган очиж болох уу?

*tii·*shee *yav·*gan o·chij *bo·*lokh *uu?*

What times does ... leave/arrive?

... хэдэн цагт явдаг/ирдэг вэ?

*... khe·*den tsagt yav·dag/ir·deg *ve?*

the bus

автобус   av·*to*·bus

the trolley-bus

троллейбус   trol·*lei*·bus

the train

галт тэрэг   galt *te*·reg

the plane

нисэх онгоц   *ni*·seh *on*·gots

Does this bus go to ...?

Энэ автобус ... руу явдаг уу?

e·ne av·*to*·bus ... ruu *yav·*dag *uu?*

Which bus goes to ...?

... руу ямар автобус явдаг вэ?

*... ruu ya·*mar av·*to*·bus yav·dag *ve?*

Can you tell me when we get to ...?

Бид хэзээ ... хүрэхийг хэлж өгнө үү?

bid khe·*zee* ... khu·re·*hiig* helj ög·nö *uu?*

I want to get off!

Би буумаар байна!

bi *buu·*maar bai·na!

Is this seat taken?

Энэ суудал хүнтэй юү?

e·ne *suu·*dal khün·tei yüü?

What's this station called?

Энэ ямар нэртэй буудал вэ?

e·ne ya·mar ner·tei *buu·*dal *ve?*

What's the next station??

Дараагийн буудал ямар нэртэй буудал вэ?

da·*raa·*giin *buu·*dal ya·mar ner·tei *buu·*dal *ve?*

LANGUAGE

Glossary

See p46 in the Food & Drink chapter for some useful words and phrases dealing with food and dining. See the Language chapter (p293) for other useful words and phrases.

agui – cave or grotto
aimag – a province/state within Mongolia
am – mouth, but often used as a term for canyon
aral – island
arkhi – the common word to describe home-made vodka
ashkhana – restaurant (Kazakh)

baatar – hero
bag – village; a subdivision of a *sum*
baga – little
balbal – stone figures believed to be Turkic grave markers; known as *khun chuluu* (man stones) in Mongolian
baruun – west
bayan – rich
bodhisattva – Tibetan-Buddhist term; applies to a being that has voluntarily chosen not to take the step to nirvana in order to save the souls of those on earth
Bogd Gegeen – the hereditary line of reincarnated Buddhist leaders of Mongolia, which started with Zanabazar; the third-holiest leader in the Tibetan Buddhist hierarchy; also known as *Jebtzun Damba*
Bogd Khaan (Holy King) – title given to the Eighth Bogd Gegeen (1869–1924)
bökh – wrestling
bugan chuluu (deer stones) – upright grave markers from the Bronze and Iron ages, on which are carved stylised images of deer
bulag – natural spring
Buriat – ethnic minority living along the northern frontier of Mongolia, mostly in Khentii and Dornod

chuluu – rock; rock formation

davaa – mountain pass
deer stones – see *bugan chuluu*
del/deel – the all-purpose, traditional coat or dress worn by men and women
delger – richness, plenty
delgüür – a shop
dombra – two-stringed lute (Kazakh)
dorje – thunderbolt symbol, used in Tibetan Buddhist ritual
dorno – east
dov – hill
dund – middle

els – sand; sand dunes
erdene – precious

Furgon – Russian-made 11-seater minivan

gegeen – saint; saintlike person
ger – traditional circular felt *yurt*
gol – river
gov – desert
guanz – canteen or cheap restaurant
gudamj – street

hard seat – the common term to describe the standard of the 2nd-class train carriage

ikh – big
ikh delgüür – department store
Inner Mongolia – a separate province within China
irbis – snow leopard

Jebtzun Damba – see *Bogd Gegeen*

Kazakh – ethnic minority, mostly living in western Mongolia
khaan – emperor; great *khan*
khad – rock
khagan – *khaan*; generally used for leaders during the Turkic (pre-Mongol) period
khaganate – Turkic (pre-Mongol) empire
khagas – half-size
Khalkh – the major ethnic group living in Mongolia
khan – king or chief
khar – black
khashaa – fenced-in *ger*, often found in suburbs
kherem – wall
khetsuu – difficult/hard
khiid – Buddhist monastery
khödöö – countryside
khoid – north
khöndii – valley
khoroo – district or subdistrict
khot – city
khulan – wild ass
khun chuluu (man stones) – see *balbal*
khuree – originally used to describe a 'camp', it is now also in usage as 'monastery'
khuriltai – nomadic congress during the Mongol era
khürkhree – waterfall
khutukhtu – reincarnated lama, or living god
kino – cinema

lama – Tibetan Buddhist monk or priest
Lamaism – an outdated term, and now properly known as Vajramana, or Tibetan Buddhism
Living Buddha – common term for reincarnations of Buddha; Buddhist spiritual leader in Mongolia (see *Bogd Gegeen*)
loovuuz – fox-fur hat

malchin – herder
man stones – see *balbal*
maral – Asiatic red deer
mod – tree
morin khuur – horse-head fiddle
mörön – another word for river, usually a wide river
MPRP – Mongolian People's Revolutionary Party

naadam – games; traditional festival with archery, horse racing and wrestling
nairamdal – friendship
nuruu – mountain range
nuur – lake

ömnö – south
ordon – palace
örgön chölöö – avenue
Outer Mongolia – northern Mongolia during Man-churian rule (the term is not currently used to describe Mongolia)
ovoo – a shamanistic collection of stones, wood or other offerings to the gods, usually found in high places

rashaan – mineral springs

shaykhana – tea house (Kazakh)
soft seat – the common term to describe the standard of the 1st-class train carriage
soyombo – the national symbol
stupa – a Buddhist religious monument composed of a solid hemisphere topped by a spire, containing relics of the Buddha; also known as a pagoda, or *suvrag* in Mongolian

sum – a district; the administrative unit below an *aimag*
süm – Buddhist temple
suvrag – see *stupa*

taiga – subarctic coniferous evergreen forests (Russian)
takhi – the Mongolian wild horse; also known as Przewalski's horse
tal – steppe
talbai – square
thangka – scroll painting; a rectangular Tibetan Buddhist painting on cloth, often seen in monasteries
tögrög – the unit of currency in Mongolia
töv – central
Tsagaan Sar – 'white moon' or 'white month'; a festival to celebrate the Mongolian New Year (start of the lunar year)
tsainii gazar – tea house/café
tsam – lama dances; performed by monks wearing masks during religious ceremonies
tsas – snow
tsuivan gazar – noodle stall
tuuts – kiosk selling imported foodstuffs

ulaan – red
urtyn duu – traditional singing style
us – water
uul – mountain
uurga – traditional wooden lasso used by nomads

yavakh – depart
yurt – the Russian word for *ger*

zakh – market
zochid budal – hotel
zud – a particularly bad winter, involving a huge loss of livestock
zun – summer
zuu – one hundred
züü – needle
zuun – century
züün – east

Behind the Scenes

THIS BOOK

This 5th edition of Mongolia was written by Michael Kohn, who also wrote the previous edition. Bradley Mayhew updated the 3rd edition, and Paul Greenway updated the 2nd edition. Jack Weatherford and Dulmaa Enkhchuluun wrote the History chapter for this guide. Josh Handler updated the boxed text 'Blazing Saddles', which appears in the Transport chapter. Jeff Williams assisted Michael with research in Bayankhongor and Gobi Altai. Jeff has lived in Mongolia for more than ten years and works as a guide for a tour company. Dundgov and Ömnögov were researched by Peter Weinig. Peter is an eight-year Mongolia veteran who runs an outdoor-gear shop. This guidebook was commissioned in Lonely Planet's Melbourne office, and produced by the following:

Commissioning Editors Marg Toohey, Tashi Wheeler, Holly Alexander
Coordinating Editor Erin Richards
Coordinating Cartographer Barbara Benson
Coordinating Layout Designer David Kemp
Managing Editors Katie Lynch, Geoff Howard
Managing Cartographer David Connolly
Managing Layout Designer Celia Wood
Assisting Editors Michelle Bennett, Adrienne Costanzo, Kate Evans, Justin Flynn

Cover Designer Nic Lehman
Colour Designer David Kemp
Indexer Erin Richards
Project Manager Fabrice Rocher
Language Content Coordinator Quentin Frayne

Thanks to Chris Lee Ack, Erin Corrigan, James Ellis, Emma Gilmour, Lisa Knights, Baigalmaa Kohn, Chris Love, Adam McCrow, Wayne Murphy, Naomi Parker, Adrian Persoglia

THANKS
MICHAEL KOHN

In LP's Melbourne office, special thanks to editors Marg, Tashi, Emma and Holly.

In Mongolia, special thanks to Guido Verboom for companionship on my restaurant tour of Ulaanbaatar and for keeping me up to date on all things political. Kudos to Toroo for all his superhuman efforts on procuring vehicles, permits and the like. Cheers to drivers Dorj, Ochiro and my man Erdenejav, our saviour in western Mongolia.

Big thanks to Peter Weinig and Jeff Williams, without their combined efforts the Gobi chapter would have been a blank.

Cheers to my travel partners in western Mongolia: Ziv Hagai, Eshed Gol, Moira Mains and Alona Shmuel.

THE LONELY PLANET STORY

Fresh from an epic journey across Europe, Asia and Australia in 1972, Tony and Maureen Wheeler sat at their kitchen table stapling together notes. The first Lonely Planet guidebook, *Across Asia on the Cheap,* was born.

Travellers snapped up the guides. Inspired by their success, the Wheelers began publishing books to Southeast Asia, India and beyond. Demand was prodigious, and the Wheelers expanded the business rapidly to keep up. Over the years, Lonely Planet extended its coverage to every country and into the virtual world via lonelyplanet.com and the Thorn Tree message board.

As Lonely Planet became a globally loved brand, Tony and Maureen received several offers for the company. But it wasn't until 2007 that they found a partner whom they trusted to remain true to the company's principles of travelling widely, treading lightly and giving sustainably. In October of that year, BBC Worldwide acquired a 75% share in the company, pledging to uphold Lonely Planet's commitment to independent travel, trustworthy advice and editorial independence.

Today, Lonely Planet has offices in Melbourne, London and Oakland, with over 500 staff members and 300 authors. Tony and Maureen are still actively involved with Lonely Planet. They're travelling more often than ever, and they're devoting their spare time to charitable projects. And the company is still driven by the philosophy of *Across Asia on the Cheap*: 'All you've got to do is decide to go and the hardest part is over. So go!'

In UB, thanks to: Hamid Sardar-Afkami, Annie Li, Gary Newton, Sylvia Hay, Brian White, Glenn Mullin, Ben Stubbs, Morgan Keay, Ron Zeidel, Luke Distelhorst, Kirk Olson, Kevin Price, Don Croner, Fergus Bootman, Douglas Love, Konchog Norbu, Barbara Leonard, Andy Parkinson, and the staff at VCS (Amanda Fine, Ann Winters, N Odonchimeg and S Bolortsetseg). More help came from Timur and Aldar, Rik and Tseren and Graham Taylor.

Back home, thanks to Baigalmaa for holding down the fort and for constant insight on all things Mongolia. *Bayarlalaa.*

OUR READERS

Many thanks to the travellers who used the last edition and wrote to us with helpful hints, useful advice and interesting anecdotes:

Leonore Ander, Mongolia Man Arrested, Lyndon Beharry, Jessica Bell, Frank Boase, Antje Boehmert, Lilian De Boer, Nasanjargal Byambadorj, Stephen Carroll, Luigi Cavaleri, Katie Church, Alex Cole, William Cox, Mike Dawson, Cyril Delafosse, Simone Dischler, Jessica Doran, Saba Dozio, Saba N Dozio, Jean Maurice Dupont, Catherine Eagles, Christoph Eidinger, Tal Ellenbogen, Terje A Falkvoll, Julia Fitzgerald, Teresa Fung, Lea M Goepfert, Hadar Goshen, Anke & Bela Gosse, Rosalind Hackett, Michael Hamel-Green, Grant Hannaford, Kent Harbison, George Harris, Haili Heaton, Catherine Heffernan, Mike Hoer, Tim Houldey, Frank Keim, David Kerkhoff, Ronny Kern, Lisa Kiernan, Harry Korendijk, Fredrik Larsen, Dan Leon, Susan Linthicum, Nicole Long, Jim Mackie, Ed Manning, Laure Marchand, Alan Mead, Claudia Meyer, Kuba Michalowicz, Marcus Micheaux, Alick Mighall, Pierre Monestie, Anna-Barbara Moser, Sambuu Munkhzaya, Amanda Musker, Masaki Nagai, Baigalmaa Nanjaa, Alexander Nicolas, Gwenda Nurse, Luis Carlos Pardo, Judith Perle, Hans Ragas, Eva Ramirez, Janne Retkin, Lars Ritterhoff, Annick Sallet-Versolatto, Orly Sapir, Kevin Shannon, Ward Stone, Virginia Sutton, Brooke Swafford, Joshua Tokita, Joanna Trawczyska, Aviv Tron, Ganzorig Tsogtoo, Gjermund Valand, Debbie Vercellino, Elke Wetzel, Robert Whiting, Philip Winkler, Erik Wright, Jonathan Wrobel, Andrew Young

SEND US YOUR FEEDBACK

We love to hear from travellers – your comments keep us on our toes and help make our books better. Our well-travelled team reads every word on what you loved or loathed about this book. Although we cannot reply individually to postal submissions, we always guarantee that your feedback goes straight to the appropriate authors, in time for the next edition. Each person who sends us information is thanked in the next edition – and the most useful submissions are rewarded with a free book.

To send us your updates – and find out about Lonely Planet events, newsletters and travel news – visit our award-winning website: **www.lonelyplanet.com/contact**.

Note: we may edit, reproduce and incorporate your comments in Lonely Planet products such as guidebooks, websites and digital products, so let us know if you don't want your comments reproduced or your name acknowledged. For a copy of our privacy policy visit www.lonelyplanet.com/privacy.

ACKNOWLEDGMENTS

Many thanks to the following for the use of their content:

Globe on title page ©Mountain High Maps 1993 Digital Wisdom, Inc.

Internal photographs: p187 (#3) by Michael Kohn; p186 (#1), p187 (#4) Andy Parkinson. All other photographs by Lonely Planet Images, and by Scott Darsney p190 (#2); Jerry Galea p185, p189 (#4&5), p191 (#3), p192 (#1); Paul Greenway p191 (#4); Richard I'Anson p188 (#2), p189 (#3), p191 (#5); Bradley Mayhew p190 (#1), p191 (#6) p192, (#2); Cathleen Naundorf p186 (#2), p188 (#1), p192 (#3).

All images are the copyright of the photographers unless otherwise indicated. Many of the images in this guide are available for licensing from Lonely Planet Images: www.lonelyplanetimages.com.

Index

INDEX

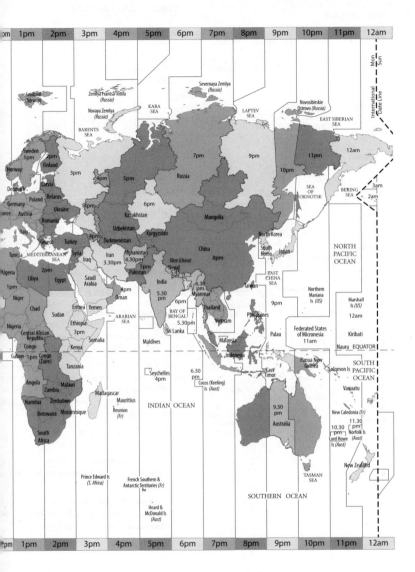

MAP LEGEND

ROUTES

Primary	Mall/Steps
Secondary	Walking Tour
Tertiary	Walking Trail
Lane	Walking Path
Unsealed Road	4WD Track

TRANSPORT

Rail

HYDROGRAPHY

River, Creek	Lake (Dry)
Intermittent River	Lake (Salt)
Swamp	Mudflats
Water	

BOUNDARIES

International	Ancient Wall
State, Provincial	Cliff

AREA FEATURES

Area of Interest	Market
Desert	Park
Building	Rocks
Forest	Sports
Land	Urban

POPULATION

○ CAPITAL (NATIONAL)	◉ CAPITAL (STATE)
● Large City	○ Town, Village

SYMBOLS

Sights/Activities
- Buddhist
- Cycling, Bicycle Path
- Islamic
- Monument
- Museum, Gallery
- Point of Interest
- Pool
- Ruin
- Trail Head

Eating
- Eating

Drinking
- Drinking

Entertainment
- Entertainment

Shopping
- Shopping

Sleeping
- Sleeping
- Camping

Transport
- Airport, Airfield
- Border Crossing
- Bus Station
- General Transport
- Petrol Station
- Taxi Rank

Information
- Bank, ATM
- Embassy/Consulate
- Hospital, Medical
- Information
- Internet Facilities
- Police Station
- Post Office, GPO
- Telephone
- Toilets

Geographic
- Lookout
- Mountain, Volcano
- National Park
- Oasis
- Pass, Canyon
- Shelter, Hut
- Waterfall

LONELY PLANET OFFICES

Australia

Head Office
Locked Bag 1, Footscray, Victoria 3011
☎ 03 8379 8000, fax 03 8379 8111
talk2us@lonelyplanet.com.au

USA

150 Linden St, Oakland, CA 94607
☎ 510 893 8555, toll free 800 275 8555
fax 510 893 8572
info@lonelyplanet.com

UK

2nd Floor, 186 City Road,
London ECV1 2NT
☎ 020 7106 2100, fax 020 7106 2101
go@lonelyplanet.co.uk

Published by Lonely Planet Publications Pty Ltd
ABN 36 005 607 983